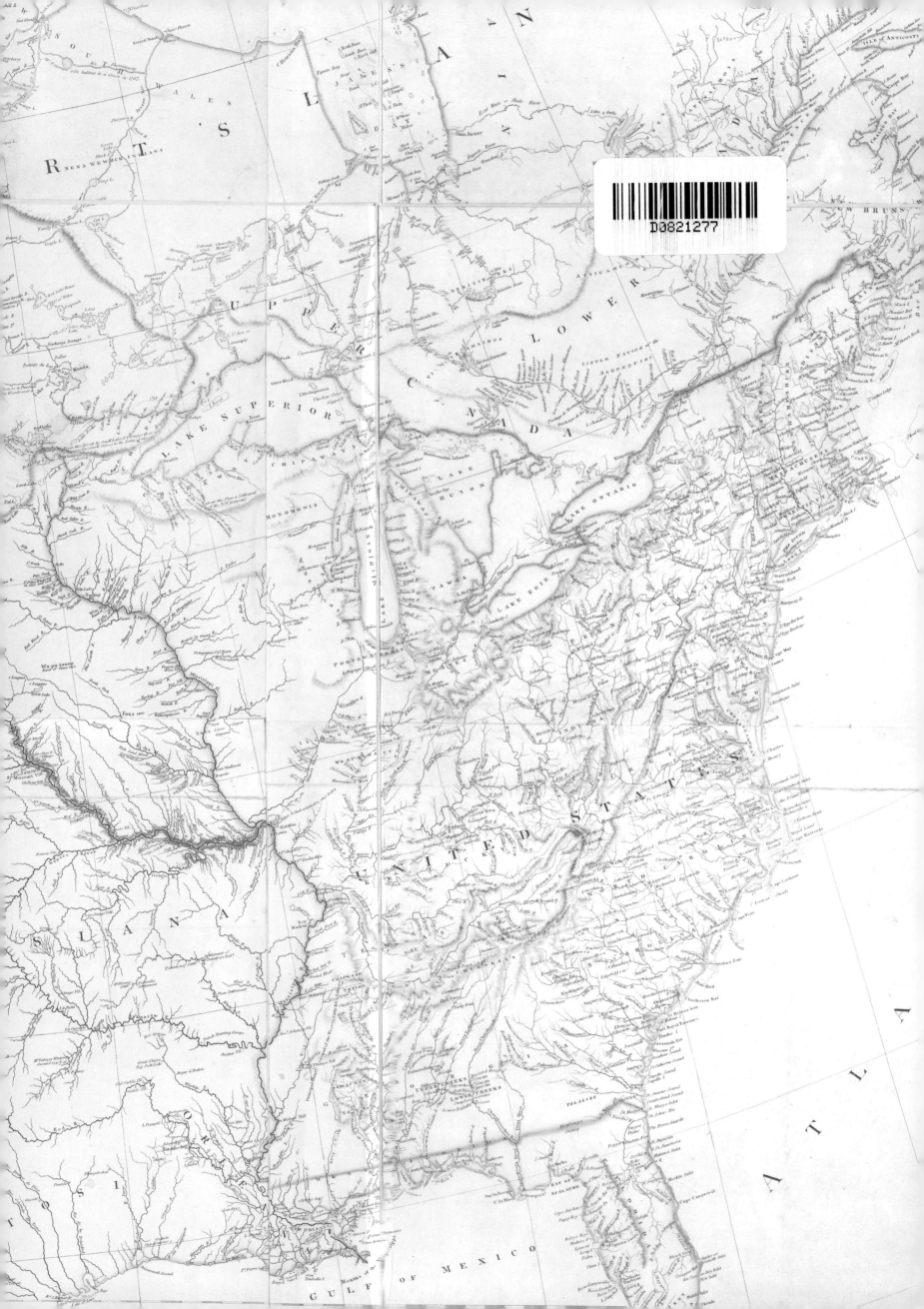

Historical Atlas
of the United States

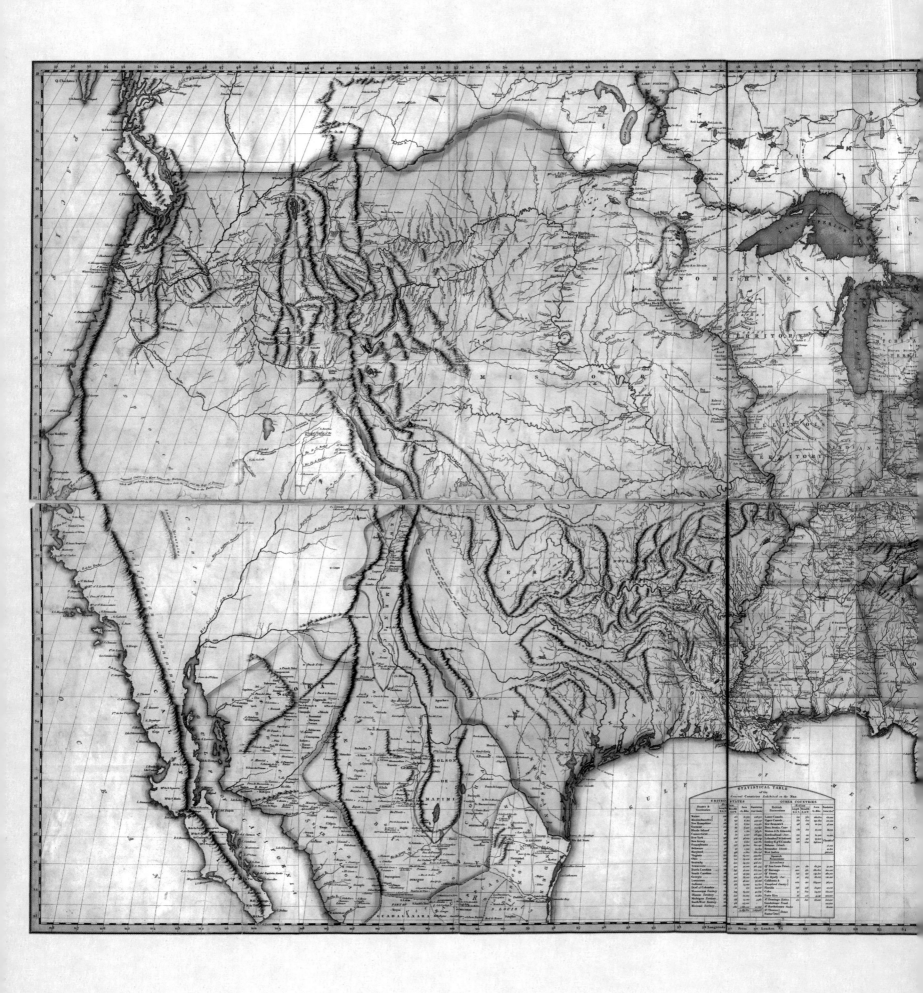

HISTORICAL ATLAS OF THE UNITED STATES

WITH ORIGINAL MAPS

DEREK HAYES

UNIVERSITY OF CALIFORNIA PRESS

BERKELEY · LOS ANGELES · LONDON

University of California Press, one of the most distinguished university presses in the United States, enriches lives around the world by advancing scholarship in the humanities, social sciences, and natural sciences. Its activities are supported by the UC Press Foundation and by philanthropic contributions from individuals and institutions. For more information, visit www.ucpress.edu.

University of California Press
Berkeley and Los Angeles, California

University of California Press, Ltd.
London, England

First published in 2006 by Douglas & McIntyre, Ltd.
2323 Quebec Street, Suite 201, Vancouver, BC, Canada V5T 4S7

Cataloging-in-Publication Data for this title is on file with the Library of Congress.

ISBN-13: 978-0-520-25036-9 (cloth : alk. paper) • ISBN-10: 0-520-25036-2 (cloth : alk. paper)

Manufactured in China by C&C Offset Printing Co., Ltd.

15 14 13 12 11 10 09 08 07
10 9 8 7 6 5 4 3 2 1

Printed on acid-free paper

Design and layout: Derek Hayes
Editing and copyediting: Naomi Pauls
Fact-checking: Angela Wheelock
Jacket design: Nicole Hayward

To contact the author:
www.derekhayes.ca / derek@derekhayes.ca

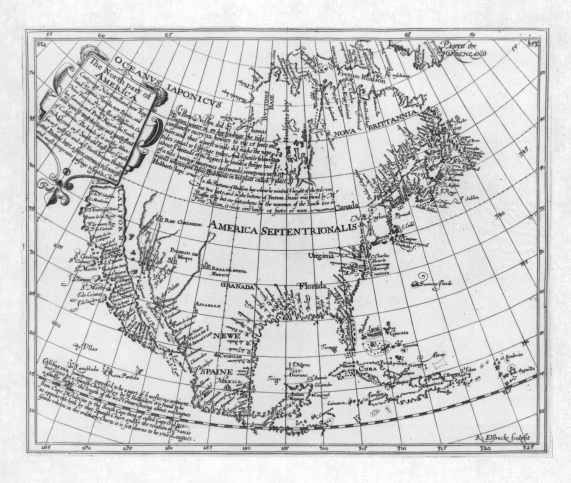

Acknowledgments

As is usual with a work such as this, many people have helped the author obtain map reproductions and information. The following have assisted in this way: John Anderson, Texas State Archives; Ken Sanders and Karen North of Ken Sanders Rare Books, Salt Lake City; Dorothy Sloan, Dorothy Sloan Rare Books, Austin, TX; Brian Leigh Dunnigan, Clements Library, University of Michigan; Patrick Morris and John Powell, Newberry Library, Chicago; Barbara J. Meiboom and Gijs Boink, Nationaal Archief (Netherlands); Steve Boulay; John Magill, the Historic New Orleans Collection; Katherine (Kit) Goodwin, University of Texas at Arlington; Edward Redmond, Library of Congress; Cynthia Luckie, Alabama Department of Archives and History; Marianne Martin, John D. Rockefeller, Jr. Library, Colonial Williamsburg Foundation; April Carlucci, British Library; David M. Reel, West Point Museum; Ann Morgan Dodge, John Hay Library, Brown University Library, Providence, RI; Kate Molan and Jessie Kratz, Center for Legislative Archives, NARA (U.S. National Archives), Washington. In particular I should like to thank David Rumsey for permission to use a considerable number of maps from his extensive collection. Finally, thanks to my ever vigilant editor, Naomi Pauls, and Scott McIntyre at Douglas & McIntyre.

MAP 1 (*half-title page*).
A beautiful 1670 map of North America by Dutch mapmaker Jan Jansson. The map is notable for its depiction of California as a large island (see page 104).

MAP 2 (*title page*).
American mapmaker John Melish published several editions of his important map of the United States; this is the 1816 edition. It shows the northern boundary of the country west of the Great Lakes as interpreted from an American point of view. The Convention of 1818 (see page 91) established the boundary between Lake of the Woods and the Rockies as the forty-ninth parallel, and this was continued to the Pacific—but excluding Vancouver Island—in 1846. The boundary of Spanish territory to the southwest is interpreted to be the Rio Grande, an assumption challenged by Spain and later Mexico and not settled until the independence of Texas following the Battle of San Jacinto in 1836 (see page 150).

MAP 3 (*left*).
This famous map by Englishman Henry Briggs, published in 1625, was one of the first to show California as an island, although it was primarily drawn to illustrate the discoveries of explorer Thomas Button on the west side of Hudson Bay. The shape of much of the West was speculative; the Northwest was hidden.

Right. The remains of the British fort at Crown Point, on Lake Champlain, in the strategic valley used by invading armies of several nations (see page 61). The fort was begun in 1759 but was never completely finished, and was abandoned after the British lost the War for Independence.

Contents

A New Visual History

The story of America's past has been told in many different ways, but never before in any comprehensive form from the unique geographical perspective allowed by the study of original maps. The present book is an attempt to redress that omission. One of the ways in which history can be brought to life is through the study of contemporary documents, and this book is a history principally illustrated with one such type of document, the map.

Historical maps can show, for instance, an explorer's ideas of what lay over the mountains ahead, his notions of what he had discovered, or his explanation of the land's potential for his sponsors back home; a general's assessment of a coming battle or a field assessment of what went wrong; a promoter's attempt to sell his project to settlers, perhaps enhancing the truth to encourage purchasers—often producing fine art in the process; or a surveyor's depiction of a railroad route or wagon trail,

a picture impossible to adequately communicate in mere words. In short, maps can convey the ideas of historical figures in a way that abets and complements their written record.

Maps here take priority over words, although the accompanying text tries to explain the stories behind the maps, how they were created, and what they show. Map captions are an integral and essential part of the book. Of course, the vast sweep of American history contained in so few pages cannot be other than an exercise in compression, and thus this book is best viewed as a complement to other written histories.

America was discovered by Europeans searching for a sea route to Asia, men who stayed in their New World when they found that the land offered different prizes, other benefits. The United States, wrested from the primary colonial power and born as a land of freedom, had to endure a vicious and debilitating Civil War before it was set on the path to lib-

MAP 4.

The seminal and unique wall map of the world produced by Martin Waldsee-müller and Matthias Ringmann in Lorraine in 1507. The map, together with gores for a globe that were printed from woodcuts at the same time, has been called "America's birth certificate," because it was the first document of any type to contain the word "America." (It is shown on South America.) The name was derived from Amerigo Vespucci, about whose voyages of exploration Waldseemül-ler and his associates had read. Vespucci seems to have been the first to espouse the idea that the western discoveries up to 1505 were a "New World," rather than the eastern shores of Asia, as had been assumed up to that time by Columbus, Cabot, and others. Waldseemüller and Ringmann were the first to show these ideas of a New World in map form. It was therefore not entirely inappropriate that Waldseemüller should choose to name the newly depicted lands after Amerigo. This map was the first printed map to show North and South America,

and the first of any kind the show them completely. It is an ongoing mystery as to where the delineations of the west coasts of both continents came from, since both were completely unknown to Europeans at this time. The map was discovered in 1901 by a Jesuit historian, Josef Fischer, in the library of Castle Wolfegg, in Baden-Württemberg, Germany, and was purchased in 2002 by the Library of Congress for a record-breaking $10 million. About one thousand of these maps were printed, but this is the only extant copy; it survived because it was made up of twelve smaller sheets bound into a portfolio assembled by the globe maker Johannes Schöner. The exact date of this map continues to be debated, as there are watermarks in the paper of pasted-on texts at either corner that have been dated to 1515. However, even the dating of the watermarks is itself uncertain. The map remains the only copy of the Waldseemüller and Ringmann work, which was certainly first published in 1507.

erty for all. Powered by a lust for land, settlers spread themselves westward across the continent, largely at the expense of America's native peoples, at least right up to the closing decade of the nineteenth century.

This book covers the more than five hundred years from conception to colonization and the Cold War; from 1492 to 9/11, if you will. It documents the discoveries and explorations, the intrigue and negotiations, the technology and the will that led the United States to become the world leader it is today. And wars, always wars: of conquest, colonial, revolutionary; Civil, Mexican, Indian; war for Empire, war for survival, and war against tyranny, the aggressive vigilance that has characterized America from its beginnings.

A few explanations are in order here. An attempt has been made to use respectful names while avoiding the excesses of political correctness. In particular the term "EuroAmericans" is used to refer to those of European origin who were then citizens or at least residents of the United States. Early visitors were, however, truly just "Europeans" and are referred to as such. The term "Indians" is used for Native Americans because for most of our history that is the only name by which they were known, and the name they called themselves. English versions of Indian names are used when they are familiar, with the transliteration added where possible. Thus, for example, Sioux chief Sitting Bull is also Tatanka Iyotake or Tatanka Yotanka. Sioux is itself the collective name for the Lakota, Nakota, and Dakota, and there were also subdivisions; Sitting Bull was the leader of the Teton Lakota.

A significant number of the original maps reproduced in this book are held in the Library of Congress. The Geography and Map Division of that institution has had for some time the most laudable policy of placing maps scanned digitally for use in books and for other purposes on their website in compressed form. Thus many of the maps shown here (for sources see the map catalog, page 258) can now be viewed online in detail, much enlarged from the printed versions. The way of the future has been applied to artifacts from the past.

MAP 5 (above).

This artistically produced map of the new United States of North America was published in 1793 by the British commercial mapmaker William Faden to illustrate a segment of the British Empire that was no more. The original Thirteen Colonies are demarcated from Georgia in the south to the Maine part of Massachusetts—Maine did not separate from Massachusetts until 1820. Although the boundary between the United States and Canada and the remaining British territory to the north was determined by the 1783 Treaty of Paris, which officially ended the war with Britain and recognized the United States of America as an independent and sovereign nation, in reality it was ill-defined (see page 90). Thus the boundary of Maine is strangely shaped; this situation would not be rectified until 1842 (see page 158). Vermont, admitted as a state in 1791, is shown, covering the territory that is now New Hampshire as well. Between the original Thirteen Colonies and the Mississippi is land previously proclaimed as Indian lands and now included in U.S. territory, including the new state of Kentucky, admitted in 1792. To the south is Florida, which would be ceded to the U.S. in 1819 (see page 138).

MAP 6 (right).

This patriotic map, published in 1832, fuses the American eagle—though it looks somewhat more like a pigeon—with a map of the United States. Under the eagle's wings is Missouri Territory. Also shown are the states of Missouri, admitted in 1821, Illinois (1818), Indiana (1816), and Louisiana (1812), the latter the first part of the huge 1803 Louisiana Purchase (see page 112) to become a state.

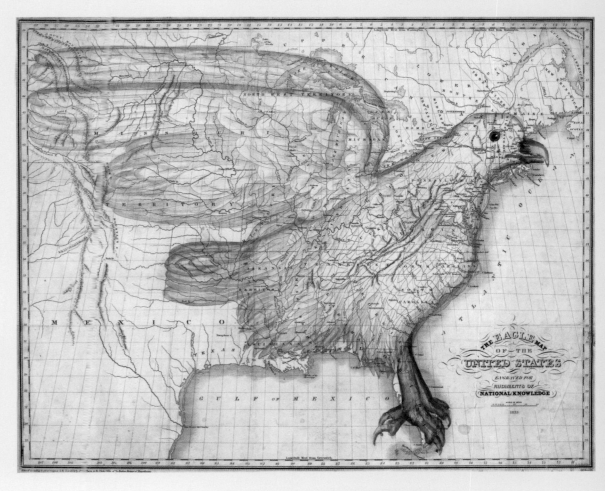

The First Peoples

A North American continent initially devoid of humans was populated by migrants from eastern Asia either via a land bridge across the Bering Strait or directly by sea perhaps as long as 30,000 years ago, although it took another 20,000 years or so for population increase and competition to spread the first Americans to all regions of the continent. But initial settlement may have been much earlier, for in 2003 scientists found what appear to be 40,000-year-old human footprints in volcanic ash near Puebla, close to Mexico City.

The pathway taken southwards was likely created by cyclical retreats in the Laurentide ice sheet that covered much of the North, leaving a gap just east of the Rocky Mountains. Some people, it is now believed, took a coastal route along the shores of the Pacific Northwest using small boats of wood and skins. The climate slowly improved as the Ice Age ended, and about 3,500 years ago it became much as it is today. With dispersion and adaptation to local conditions came the development of cultural and language differences, so that by the time the first Europeans arrived, perhaps six hundred autonomous native groups lived on the continent, speaking about 170 different languages, though derived from far fewer root stocks (MAP 9, *right*). Native population estimates at the time of contact vary considerably, but it seems that there were at least fourteen million people living in North America at the time of Columbus; a million of these lived in what would become the United States of America.

Whatever the exact numbers, it is clear that there was a tremendous diversity of peoples and corresponding complexities of societies, much of which is still unknown to modern historians (MAP 7, *left*). In many places, and particularly among Mexico's Mayans and Aztecs and Peru's Incas, true civilizations equal to or greater than those of Europe had arisen. Far from being a few savages, as most of the early Europeans thought, the original Americans formed an already established system of nations finely adapted to their land, and usually ready and able to defend it from interlopers, just as had been necessary before the arrival of Europeans. With contact, a clash of cultures would begin.

MAP 7 (*left, top*).
A map of Serpent Mound in south-central Ohio, surveyed in 1846. Once considered to be of Adena Indian cultural origin and thus built 1,900 to 2,800 years ago, the mound is now thought (from radiocarbon dating) to have been built by a Mississippian Indian culture known as Fort Ancient, whose members lived in this area between about 900 and 1600. Although surrounded by some burial sites, it is not itself a burial mound, and it is believed to have had some religious significance. Whatever it actually represents, it does show a highly developed level of culture long before Europeans arrived on the scene.

Top left. A Plains Indian is hunting buffalo in this classic 1870 painting by George Caitlin. Buffalo were a way of life to the Indian but seen as a nuisance by EuroAmericans.

Below. A model of an Iroquoian village showing longhouses made from saplings and bark.

MAP 8.
Drawn on an animal hide in 1641, this singular map shows the distribution of native groups in the area around the Great Lakes at about the time of contact. Called the Huron Map, it was likely drawn by a Jesuit missionary with information from a Huron person. Some of the names are French but most are Huron (Algonkin), notably those ending in "onon," the Huron word for "people." The largest area is that of the Iroquois. *Lac de Sainct Louis* is Lake Ontario, *Lac de Gens Du Chat* is Lake Erie, *La Mer Douce* is Lake Huron, and *Grand Lac* is Lake Superior. This map itself has a colorful history, being plundered from the Jesuits by the British when they captured the city of Québec in 1759.

Below and below, right. Photographer Edward S. Curtis traveled all over North America recording what was often a disappearing way of life, photographing native peoples in their cultural environments. He is particularly well known for his eloquent portraits, two of which are shown here: a Qahatika girl (*below*) and Brule Sioux Hollow Horn Bear (*below, right*). Both portraits were originally published in 1908.

MAP 9 (*above*).
This hand-colored map of the Indian tribes of North America was produced in 1836 by Albert Gallatin, who, as secretary of the treasury, was the person who found the money to fund the Louisiana Purchase in 1803; he also negotiated the Treaty of Ghent in 1814, which ended the War of 1812. Later in life he became interested in America's first peoples, and this map illustrated a magazine piece he wrote on the subject. Note that his information principally covers only the eastern half of the continent.

MAP 10 (*left*).
This map was produced by another famous American, John Wesley Powell, explorer of the Colorado River. The map was produced in 1890, when Powell was director of the U.S. Bureau of Ethnology, which he had pushed Congress to establish in 1879. Powell had a great respect for native peoples in an age when most EuroAmericans did not. The map shows the distribution of linguistic stocks, which have generally broader ranges than individual tribes, many of which might speak language derived from a common source. The Pacific coast has much smaller linguistic areas than the rest of the continent. This is due to the relative natural richness of the region, based mainly on the salmon, which permitted a multiplicity of cultures to develop.

Conceptions of a Continent

It was perhaps inevitable that Europeans would find America as the fifteenth century drew to a close. After the fall of Constantinople—today's Istanbul—to the Ottoman Turks in 1453, Europeans had sought alternative routes to the spices of the East. Spice was a critical requirement in the days when food could not be properly preserved or kept for long periods and typically tasted dreadful. In 1487–88 Portuguese explorer Bartolomeu Dias succeeded in rounding the southern tip of Africa, and by 1497 Vasco da Gama had reached India.

Scientific-minded people at this time knew that the world was round and realized that the East could be reached by sailing west. One, a Florentine physician named Paolo dal Pozzo Toscanelli, was in correspondence with an adventurous navigator, Christopher Columbus, as early as 1475. The account of the travels of Marco Polo, written at the end of the

thirteenth century, was enormously influential (even though modern scholars doubt that he actually reached China). Polo placed the eastern coastline of Asia about 30° farther east than it really was. Accumulating all the information he could find, Columbus concluded he could sail westwards to Cathay. He even calculated the distance, which just happened to be the same as the approximate distance across the Atlantic, so when his *Santa Maria, Niña,* and *Pinta* made a landfall in the Bahamas in October 1492, it was clear to him where he was—Asia. America was depicted as the eastern coast of Asia by a number of mapmakers, and the misconception lasted well into the sixteenth century, despite the fact that a map showing America as a separate continent had appeared by 1507 (Map 4, *page 6,* and Map 18, *overleaf*).

Columbus has become one of the most iconic explorers in American history, despite the fact that he never actually made it to the mainland. His importance is that he began the long process of European exploration and then colonization that was to transform the continent.

King Henry VII of England had been offered the chance to sponsor Columbus and turned it down. Now, faced with what was regarded as a highly successful voyage by Columbus under the auspices of the Spanish, Henry was not about to be outdone again, and when a Genoese navigator named Giovanni Caboto came knocking in 1496, he received his support for a new, more northern voyage. Caboto, who soon anglicized his name to John Cabot, sailed west from Bristol in 1497 (and may have also sailed the year before, but no absolute proof exists), reaching the coast of Newfoundland. Thinking, like Columbus, that he had reached the eastern shore of Asia, he set out again in 1498 with five ships—and was never heard from again.

It seems possible, even probable, that Cabot was the first European to cruise down the eastern coast of the United States, for information from his voyage appears to be incorporated into the first map of the North American continent, drawn by Juan de la Cosa about 1500 (Map 19, *overleaf*). La Cosa had been a pilot with Columbus and in 1499 was in the same capacity with the Spanish explorer Alonso de Hojeda (or Ojeda), who was known for his particularly murderous tendencies. Hojeda's explorations centered

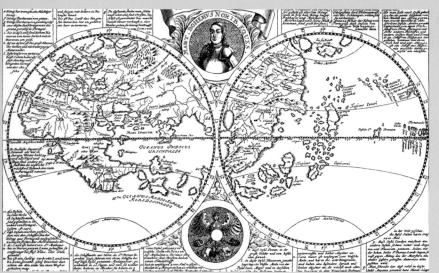

Map 11 (*left, top*).
The first archeologically proven European visitors to the North American continent were the Norse. At the beginning of the eleventh century a settlement was established at L'Anse aux Meadows, at the northern tip of Newfoundland's Northern Peninsula. It lasted only a few years, perhaps because of predations by native Beothuk. This map is one of several compiled in the early seventeenth century when the king of Denmark sent out expeditions to determine if any settlers of the Norse Greenland colonies had survived. The maps may therefore include later knowledge. Here, in a map by Jón Gudmonson drawn in 1640, the landmass at bottom left is *Terra florida* and its northern end *America pars*—part of America. Norse knowledge of America seems to have become lost to Europeans, and hence the journeys of Columbus and Cabot were made on the basis of their own information only.

Map 12 (*left*).
This world map is a 1730 transcription of a globe made by Martin Behaim in 1492, thought to have been finished while Columbus was at sea. It shows the world as Columbus believed it to be, without an American continent and with only Japan (*Cipangu Insula*) between Africa and Asia. Thus Columbus quite reasonably thought he had reached Cathay when he encountered land in the Caribbean on that fateful 12 October 1492. America—in the form of the island he called San Salvador—had been discovered. To him, it was truly a "new world."

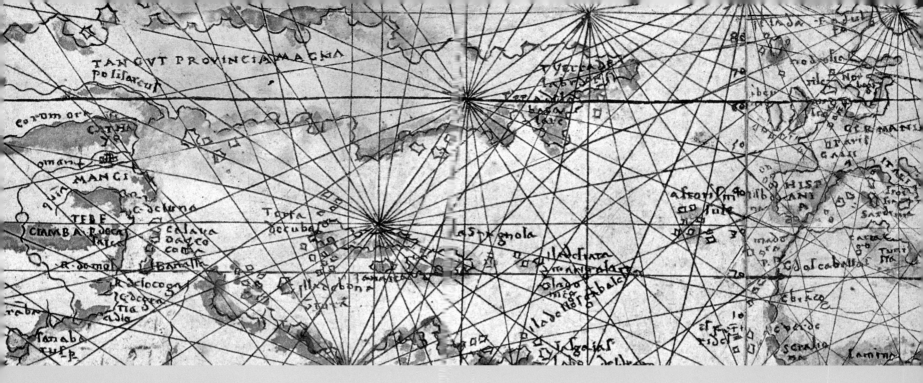

MAP 13 (*above*).
To mapmakers for several decades after John Cabot's rediscovery of Newfoundland in 1497, this was what the world west of Bristol looked like. The American landmass has been made to conform to expectations that it was in fact Asia by extending the Asian continent eastwards in a long peninsula to the approximate position of the northern shores of America. One of Columbus's first discoveries, Hispaniola, here *ile spagnola*, is preserved as an island in an east Asian sea. To its immediate west is *Terra de cuba*, Cuba. This map was drawn by Florentine mapmaker Francesco Rosselli in 1508.

MAP 14 (*left*).
Columbus's discovery of Hispaniola in 1492 is depicted in this highly stylized pictomap. *Insula hyspana* is Hispaniola.

MAP 15 (*below*).
A similar conception of North America as an eastward extension of Asia is shown in this "map of the known world" printed in 1507 or 1508 by Johann Ruysch in Rome. The northernmost peninsula of Asia is Greenland, with *Terra Nova* to its south likely Newfoundland. Immediately south is the Caribbean, with the islands of Hispaniola and Cuba. The area that is now the United States is somehow lost in between. Within twenty years Europeans would know that there was indeed land in this knowledge gap.

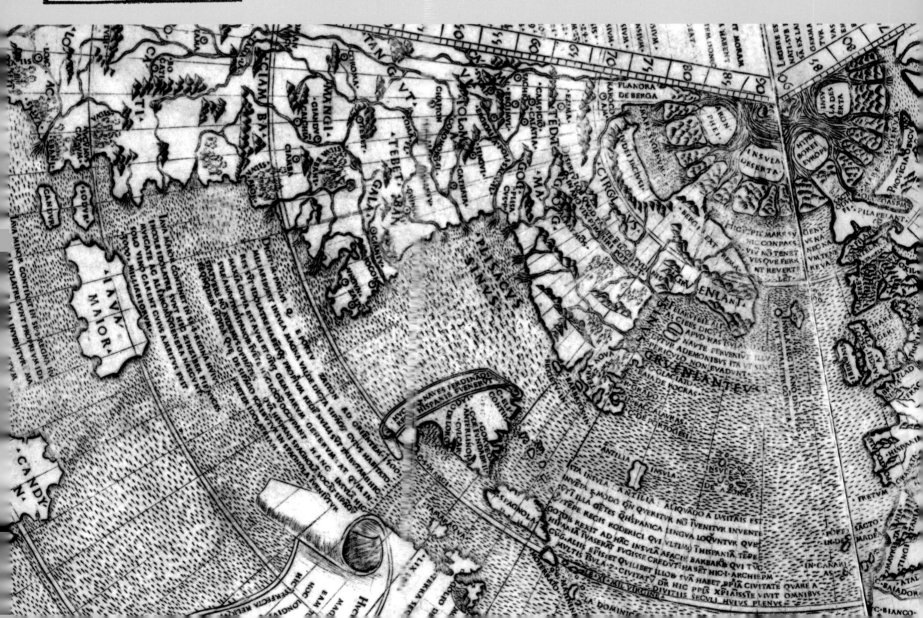

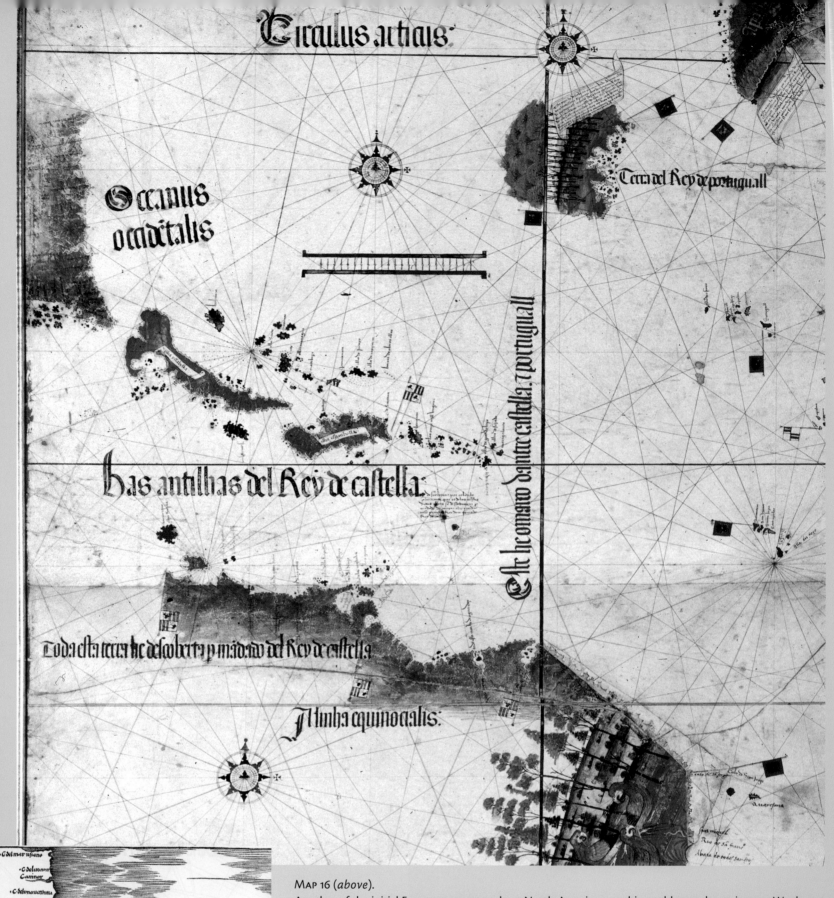

Circulus artitus.

Occanus occidctalis

Terra del Rey de portuguall

has antilhas del Rey de castella.

Toda esta terra he descoberta p mãdado del Rey de castella.

Alinha equinoctialis:

MAP 16 (*above*).

Another of the initial European maps to show North America was this world map drawn in 1502. We do not know the name of the map's creator, but the map is known as the "Cantino planisphere" after Alberto Cantino. He was the envoy of the Italian duke of Ferrara to the Portuguese court. The map was made in Lisbon and accompanied a letter outlining the results of the explorations of Portuguese explorer Gaspar Corte-Real to Newfoundland in 1500. The landmass in mid-ocean (top) is *Terra del Rey de portuguall* (Land of the king of Portugal), shown so far east so that it was east of the so-called Tordesillas line and thus in Portuguese territory. This line, also shown on the map, was an arbitary division of the world in 1493 between Portugal (the eastern part) and Spain (the western part); other nations were disregarded. In the Spanish world, Hispaniola and Cuba are again predominant, but what looks very much like the American mainland including Florida, running off the left-hand side of the map, is in fact an enigma, for the Spanish did not find Florida until 1513 (see page 14), and scholars have long argued over what the land shown on this map could represent.

MAP 17 (*left*).

The "phantom Florida" shown on the Cantino planisphere is even better shown on this map, a printed version. Here the unknown land is covered with detailed names, strongly suggesting knowledge of the American mainland. Yet nothing found in Spanish archives documents exploration of Florida until Ponce de León's expedition in 1513. Could some critical documents have become completely lost? Possibly the source of the information was unrecorded Portuguese voyages to America, kept secret because they were not supposed to be west of the Tordesillas line. We will likely never know.

on the coasts of Venezuela and Colombia, but it is thought Cabot sailed into the Caribbean and that Hojeda slaughtered him and all his men. The rationale for this hypothesis comes from a patent granted to Hojeda in June 1501, after his return to Spain. The document seems to state that the grant is in consideration "for the stopping of the English." The only English potentially in the region in 1499 were the men of Cabot's expedition.

La Cosa thus acquired Cabot's map, which would have been the first map of any part of the United States, and incorporated the information into his own map (MAP 18, *below*).

Seafaring Europe had found America. Its explorers soon learned to exploit the prevailing winds and currents to reach its new source of wealth quickly and reliably, and soon the main European powers were vigorously competing with one another for territory. This quest for wealth in some form, whether gold, spices, cod, or a fountain of youth, would ultimately colonize a continent, marginalizing its original peoples and creating new nations in the process.

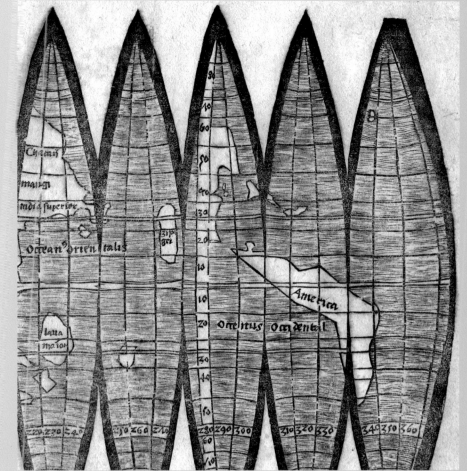

MAP 18 (*below*).
What is probably the earliest map of the North American continent was this map drawn on an animal skin by Spanish pilot Juan de la Cosa in 1500, although some authorities have suggested that the western part was drawn a few years later. It appears to incorporate information from the last voyage of John Cabot as well as Spanish information that La Cosa could have collected himself. The easternmost flag is likely Cabot's landfall, as it is on the same latitude as Bristol, in England, the port he sailed from. Latitude sailing was the most common means of navigation at the time because sailors could determine their latitude from the elevation of the sun but were not able to do more than guess at longitude. The orientation of this part of the coast, east-west, is inaccurate, but this may be explained by the fact that the magnetic declination of the east coast of America varied from that in Europe, a fact not allowed for until somewhat later. The Spanish discoveries of the islands of Hispaniola and Cuba are shown overscale, but the western end of the Caribbean had not yet been explored, for a hoped-for passage through Central America is covered by a St. Christopher icon. At this time Europeans knew more about South America than they did about North America, for initial discoveries of gold had ensured that resources were at first directed southwards.

MAP 19 (*above*).
Gores for a globe produced in 1507 by Martin Waldseemüller, the first representation (with MAP 4, *page 6*) of North and South America as continents separate from Asia. Like the world map, the gores also use the name "America" for the first time, on South America, after Amerigo Vespucci, an early Spanish explorer of that continent, and are thus, equally with MAP 4, "America's birth certificate." This map is in the collections of the James Ford Bell Library at the University of Minnesota. There are only three other copies in existence, including one sold at auction in June 2005 for just over $1 million. Some experts now believe this map may be a 1526 reprint, but this belief is based on watermark comparisons that are themselves not certain.

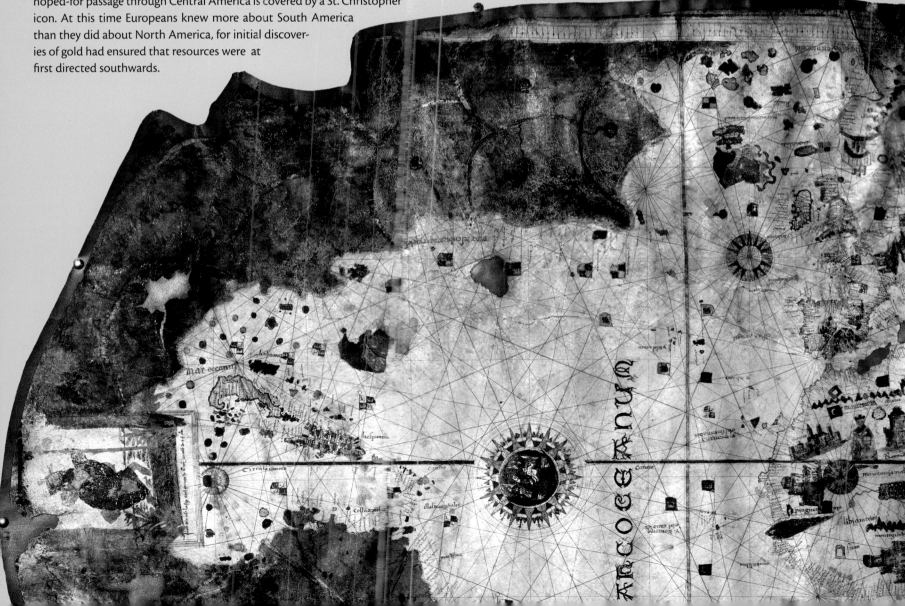

Cities of Gold, Cities of Mud

The early Spanish explorers of the Americas were really interested in one thing—gold. Naturally enough, most of the first explorers went where they expected to find it, and thus were more interested initially in Mexico than the region farther north. But later explorers did investigate the area that is now the United States, hoping for a repeat of the Mexican discoveries.

The discoverer of mainland America was motivated by gold, but also by another potentially valuable item—a fountain of youth. Juan Ponce de León was the governor of Puerto Rico. In 1513 he obtained a royal license to search for the island of Bimini, where the fountain was reputed to be found. Sailing northwards he found an unknown coast on 2 April, during the Spanish festival of Pasqua Florida. Thus he named his discovery Florida, a name that would be applied to most of the southern United States for a couple of centuries before it came to mean only the peninsula.

When Ponce de León tried to land he was driven off by native people. Realizing that more resources would be needed he sailed away, and it took him until 1521 to return, this time with two hundred and fifty men. A settlement was attempted in Tampa Bay but was unsuccessful due to native attacks, one of which killed Ponce de León.

In 1519 a rival Spanish governor, Francisco de Garay, of Jamaica, dispatched Alonzo Alvarez de Pineda to Florida. Pineda followed the coastline westwards and ended up almost circumnavigating the Gulf of Mexico. In the process he determined that there was no outlet to the Pacific at the western end of the gulf (MAP 22, *below, right*).

The Spanish were also interested in the possibility of a passage to the Pacific farther north. In 1524–25 Estévan Gomez, a Portuguese pilot in the service of Spain, who had sailed with Magellan, searched for a passage much farther north. He found the Gulf of St. Lawrence but did not penetrate west of Prince Edward Island due to ice. He then investigated Penobscot Bay in Maine, a large bay full of islands, but finding no passage, returned to Spain in August 1525.

MAP 20 (*above*).
Juan Ponce de León's portrait adorns this little map of the west coast of Florida showing his ships either at Tampa Bay or Charlotte Harbor. The illustration is from a 1728 Spanish history book.

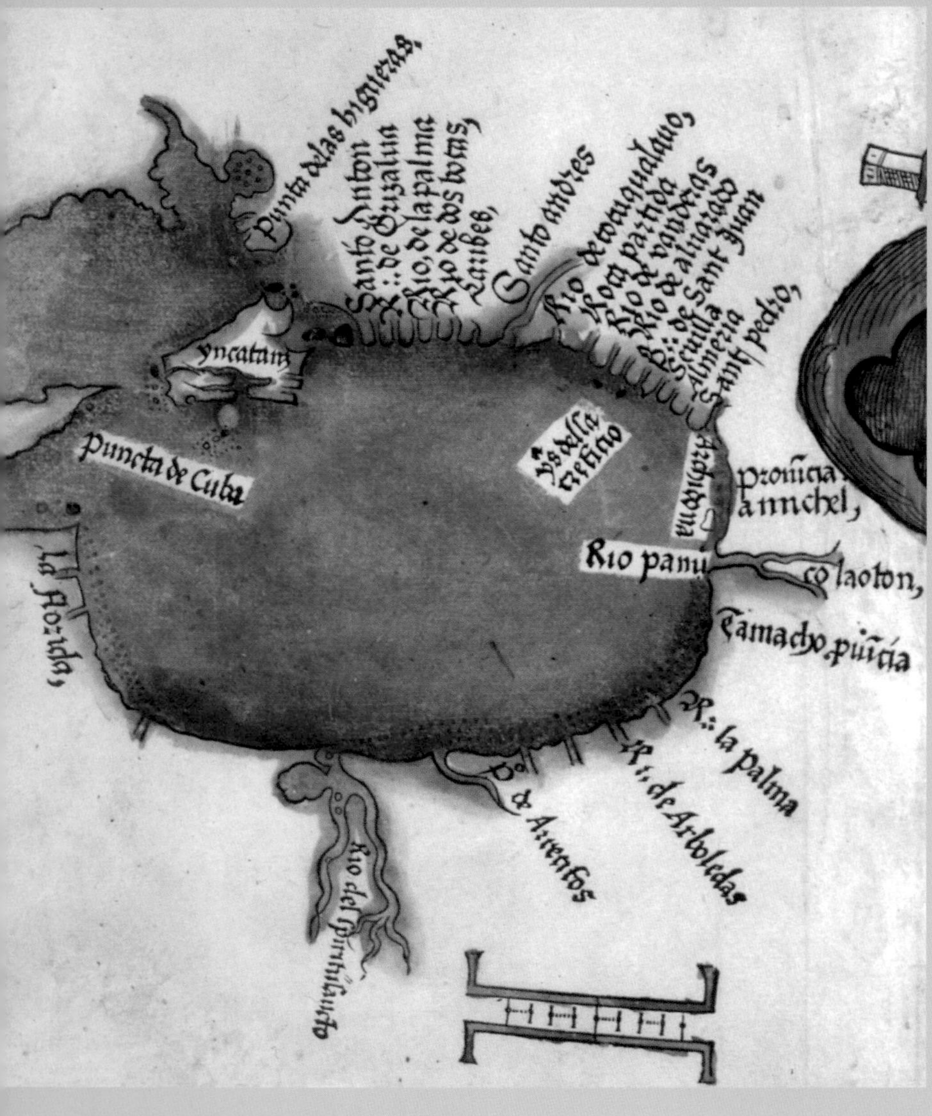

MAP 21 (*left*).
This is the first printed map of the Gulf of Mexico, published with a letter of Hernán Cortés in 1524. Note that south is at the top. A number of American rivers are shown, including the Rio Grande (*Rio panu*), but the *Rio del Spiritu Sancto* (at bottom) is probably the rivers flowing into Mobile Bay rather than the Mississippi.

MAP 22 (*below*).
With north now at the top, this map of the Gulf of Mexico by Alonzo Alvarez de Pineda was the first to conclusively show that there was no passage to the Pacific through Central America. Drawn in 1519, the map was attached to a royal grant of land to Jamaican governor Francisco de Garay two years later. It was Pineda who first demonstrated that Florida was a peninsula rather than an island.

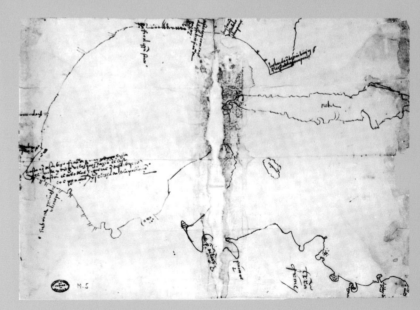

The first attempt at settlement on the mainland coast was made by a Hispaniola judge, Lucas Vásquez de Ayllón. Exploratory probes were made by captains Francisco Gordillo and Pedro de Quexos in 1521, and by Quexos alone in 1525, when he may have sailed as far as Chesapeake Bay. Then in June 1526 Ayllón sailed north, intending to found a colony. He took with him six hundred men, a few women, and some African slaves. This marked the first time slaves were transported to the American coast.

The site chosen, which Ayllón called San Miguel de Gualdape, was possibly on Winyah Bay in South Carolina, although its location is not known for sure. At any rate, it was low-lying and marshy and not suitable for a settlement. Within months colonists began to die, as did Ayllón himself in November 1526. The colony was in disarray, the slaves revolted and escaped, and the survivors—only 150 of them—limped back to Hispaniola.

A permanent Spanish presence on the U.S. mainland was established in 1565, when St. Augustine was founded as San Agustín on the east coast of the Florida peninsula by Pedro Menéndez de Avilés (see page 21). It was to become the oldest continuously occupied city in North America.

In April 1528 another attempt was made to find gold in Florida. Pánfilo de Narváez, who had been appointed governor of the huge territory now called Florida, landed on the west coast of the Florida peninsula with four hundred conquistadors, sending away his ships. It was a fatal mistake, for the Indians picked them off one by one. Moving north, only 242 of them were alive when they reached the Apalachicola River, near today's Tallahassee. Here they managed to construct some small boats, in which they floated westwards, heading for—they thought—Mexico, which had been subjugated by Hernán Cortés in 1519.

They passed the Mississippi, which allowed them to drink fresh water directly from the sea, then were driven ashore on the Texas coast. Narváez was drowned, and command—such as it was—passed to Alvar Núñez Cabeza de Vaca. For four years Cabeza de Vaca and four others lived as slaves in several Indian tribes that inhabited the area. In fall 1534 they escaped and fled north and west, keeping away from the coast, where they

MAP 23 (*above*).

The nephew of Amerigo Vespucci and pilot of the king of Spain, Juan Vespucci, drew a world map on vellum in 1526; this is the magnificently decorated American part of it. The gap in the east coast of the United States shows where Vespucci considered he did not have enough information to depict the shore—a creditable practice not followed by many mapmakers then or later. Marked with a Spanish flag is *trá nueva de ayllón*—the new land of Ayllón. The location of Ayllón's colony, long thought to have been on the South Carolina coast, is now considered by some to be on Sapelo Sound, in Georgia.

MAP 24 (*below*).

The Spanish royal cartographer Alonzo de Santa Cruz drew this map with quill and ink about 1544, based on reports from the survivors of the 1539–43 expedition of Hernando de Soto. It is the only contemporary map to illustrate De Soto's wanderings. Some of the rivers shown may actually be a confusion of native trails and rivers following a single route.

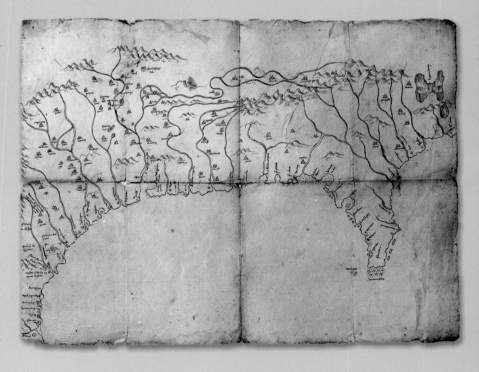

Map 25 (*above*).

This elaborately engraved map shows the North American coast as it was known to the Spanish by 1554, the date its author, Diego Gutiérrez, Spanish pilot major, died. It was published in 1562. The interior explorations of De Soto, however, are not shown. It does contain names bestowed by Ponce de León, Ayllón, and others. An allegorical Victoria rules the unknown interior, and a Neptune-like figure rides a chariot across the waves of the Atlantic.

expected to find hostile Indians. Aided by interior natives who considered them gods (one of their number was Estéban, a Moroccan, whose blackness was miraculous to those who had never seen such before), the survivors wandered toward the Gulf of California, where they were found by Spanish slave hunters in April 1536.

Back in Mexico City, Cabeza de Vaca regaled the viceroy with tales of great interior cities: stories gained from native sources, which in fact referred to large villages of mud huts. But cultural differences led the viceroy to interpret the information as meaning there was another Peru to the north, waiting to be looted. In his mind, large cities meant gold. A reconnaissance by Estéban reaped more stories, based on the Zuni pueblos.

These metamorphosed into a story of seven rich cities of gold—the Seven Cities of Cibola (Map 26, *below*).

In 1539 the brutal Hernando de Soto was commissioned by the king of Spain to find gold in the new Florida. He tried, on a massive scale, taking 720 men with him to Tampa Bay. Killing and maiming as he went, De Soto wandered widely over what is now the southern part of the United States, from South Carolina making the first European crossing of the Appalachians, killing 2,500 Choctaw Indians in Alabama, and making the first European crossing of the Mississippi, near Memphis. In 1542 De Soto died of a fever, and the survivors of his army, some 311 men, built boats and coasted down the Mississippi, eventually finding their way to a Spanish settlement at the western end of the Gulf of Mexico.

While De Soto was rampaging through the South, Antonio de Mendoza, the viceroy of New Spain, in February 1543 sent another army north to find—and loot—the cities of gold of Cabeza de Vaca's reports. He wanted to get there before De Soto. It was exploration on a grand scale. The governor of New Galicia (in northern New Spain), Francisco Vásquez de Coronado, led an army of 330 men together with 1,000 native allies. He covered a lot of ground, sending out smaller exploration parties from the main expedition. One of these, led by López de Cárdenas, found the Grand Canyon, becoming the first Europeans to see it. Another party went north and east to the edge of the Great Plains, capturing an Indian who described a city of gold called Quivira. Coronado immediately marched on Quivira, near today's Kansas City, finding only villages of mud and thatch, but no gold. He did, however, report huge buffalo herds in the area.

Sixty years later another Spanish explorer went searching for Quivira, which by then had become a fabled city of legend. Juan de Oñate led 400 men, 130 families, and 7,000 cattle north with the intention of founding a new Spanish colony. His explorations spanned seven years, 1601–08, ranging from Wichita, Kansas, to the Gulf of California. Oñate was recalled

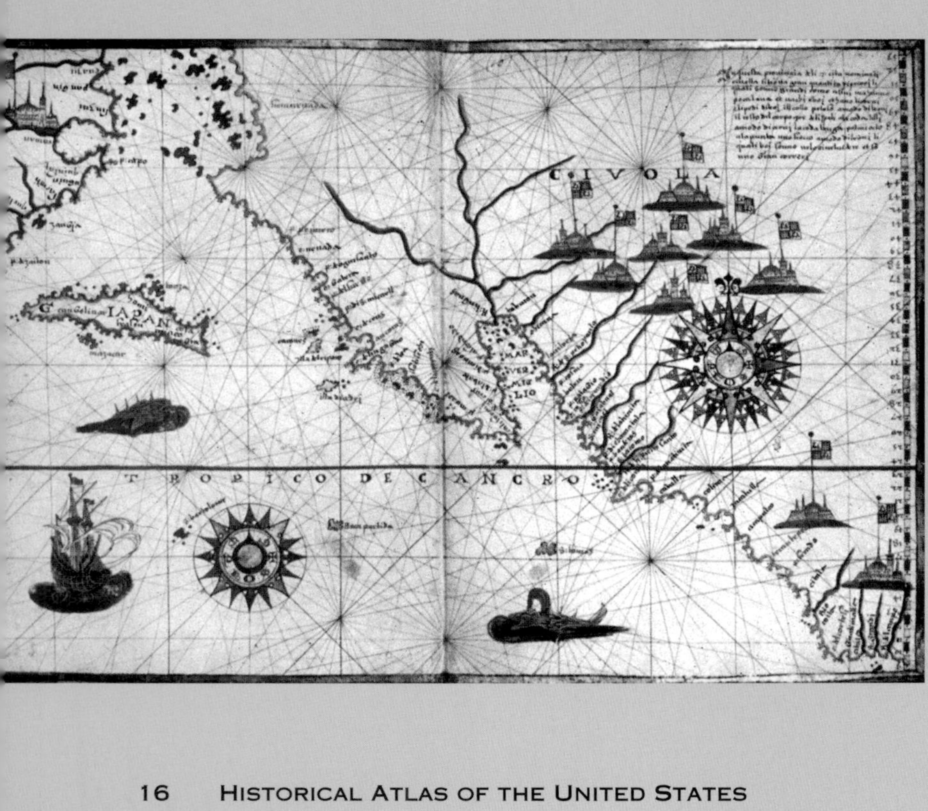

Map 26 (*left*).

The legendary Seven Cities of Cibola so long sought by Spanish explorers are depicted on this map with a golden border by Joan Martines, drawn in 1578. The Colorado River system is shown. Hernando de Alarcón ascended this river to its junction with the Gila River in 1540, while searching for Coronado to resupply him.

that year, but friars from his expedition established a mission at Santa Fe in 1610.

The Spanish also paid some attention to the west coast. Vasco Núñez de Balboa had crossed the Isthmus of Panama to the Pacific Ocean in 1513. In 1533 an expedition sent out by Hernán Cortés found the southern tip of Baja California, which was thought to be an island. Cortés himself led an expedition two years later, and the settlement of Santa Cruz (today's La Paz) was founded on the east coast of the peninsula as a base for a pearl industry in the Gulf of California.

In 1539 Cortés sent Francisco de Ulloa to search for sources of wealth. Ulloa first sailed to the head of the Gulf of California, and then, having established that Baja was not an island, traced the coast to about halfway up the peninsula on the Pacific shore. Another expedition, this one sent out to resupply Coronado, left the following year. Hernando de Alarcón entered the Colorado River at the head of the Gulf of California and dragged boats upriver for ninety miles before deciding that he was not going to find Coronado.

A more adventurous expedition was sent up the Pacific coast in 1542, to search for gold, of course, but also to investigate reports of a northern river or even a strait that might make communication with Spain easier. Or the coast might be followed all the way to China. This was the expedition of conquistador Juan Rodriguez Cabrillo, and it was he who first found the excellent harbor he called San Miguel—today's San Diego. To the north, winds and current necessitated sailing offshore, and thus Cabrillo did not see the harbors of either Monterey or San Francisco. He retreated to the Channel Islands of Los Angeles but died there during the winter. The expedition was taken over by Cabrillo's second-in-command, Bartolomé Ferrer (or Ferrelo), who sailed as far north as Cape Blanco in February 1543 before deciding that there was no practical strait.

No Spanish ships sailed north again until the turn of the next century. By then the galleon trade with the Philippines was well established, but there was a need to find harbors that could be used by the galleons on their route down the coast to New Spain after crossing the Pacific. A merchant involved in the trade, Sebastian Vizcaíno, sailed north in search of harbors in 1602. He refound Cabrillo's San Miguel, renaming it San Diego; the Spanish did not often give an explorer the maps of the previous ones, which led to a multiplicity of names in some cases. He also found the harbor at Monterey.

Vizcaíno mapped the coast of California in some detail (MAP 28, *above*). One of the ships in his fleet, commanded by Martín de Aguilar, became separated from the others in a storm and forced northwards, where a large river, which could have been the Columbia, was discovered. Aguilar named it the Rio Santa Iñez, and this "entrance of Martin Aguilar" shows up on many subsequent maps as a passage to a River of the West or a Sea of the West (see page 105).

Vizcaíno, instructed to follow any westward-trending coast toward Asia, stopped exploring once the coastline turned east, north of Cape Mendocino. This configuration of the coast was used for some time to justify the notion that California was an island (see MAP 199, *page 104*). No further voyages were made north for another 172 years, when the Spanish became concerned about possible Russian encroachment southwards from Alaska (see page 106).

MAP 27 (*above*).
Baja California and a red-colored Gulf of California are shown on this 1544 Spanish map.

MAP 28 (*left*).
A Spanish map of the west coast from Baja to Cape Mendocino from the voyage of Sebastian Vizcaíno in 1602, but not published for two hundred years. Some of the features found by Vizcaíno are named: the "good harbor" *P. buena de S. Diego*, first discovered by Cabrillo in 1542 but found again independently by Vizcaíno; and *Pto. de Monte Rey*, today's Monterey.

MAP 29 (*below*).
This Dutch map dated 1622 shows the extent of Spanish knowledge of the southern United States quite well. The legendary *Quivira* is located in California, and *La Florida* covers the entire South. The figures at top are explorers (from left): Balboa, in 1513 first to find the Pacific; Magellan, whose expedition from 1519–23 was the first to circumnavigate the globe; and Jacob Le Maire, Dutch discoverer of the southern tip of South America in 1616.

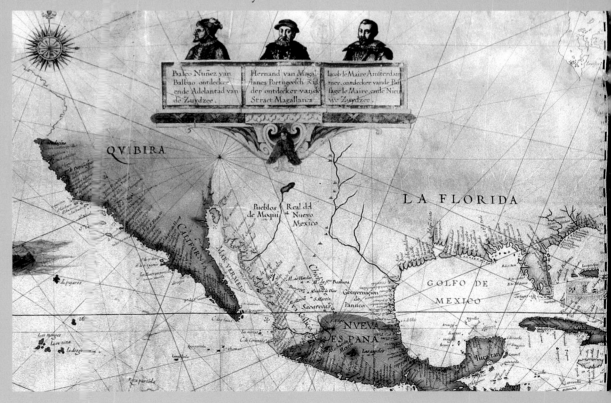

A French Claim to America

The French, who had been left out of the division of the world by the 1493 Treaty of Tordesillas, soon sought to rectify the situation. French interest in overseas ventures began with the accession to the throne of François I in 1515. His wife was duchess of Brittany, a province with a long seafaring tradition. French interest was soon directed at the apparent gap on the map between the Spanish activities in Florida and those of the English in Newfoundland. A search for lands of gold and a western passage to Cathay was to be directed at this gap.

The Spanish and the English had sent Italian navigators to search out new lands, and likewise the French turned to Giovanni Verrazano, a Florentine. François granted him a commission in 1523 to search for a strait, and Verrazano sailed the following year and made a landfall near Cape Fear, at about 34°N. After a short sail southwards in search of a harbor he turned northwards, not wishing to encroach on perceived Spanish territories. Near Cape Hatteras he looked over the sandbanks and spied the very strait he had been seeking. The North Carolina coast is twenty miles distant at this point, so it is quite possible Verrazano did not see that his strait was but the large and long lagoon that is Pamlico Sound. Perhaps he was simply too anxious to fulfill his commission from the king, or perhaps he chose to interpret what he saw as what he wanted to see; we shall never know. A vast "oriental sea" was added to his map (Map 30, below).

Verrazano could find no entrance to his newfound ocean and so continued northwards, surprisingly missing other potential straits such as Chesapeake Bay but finding the entrance to New York Harbor, today Verrazano Narrows. He anchored there on 17 April 1524.

Off the tip of Long Island Verrazano saw a small island which, he wrote, reminded him of Rhodes. He named it Luisa after the mother of King François, but his attribution was taken up by the first colonists: in 1637 Roger Williams gave the name to an island in nearby Narragansett Bay, and thus did Rhode Island later become the name of the state.

The voyage continued round Cape Cod and up the coast of New England to Cape Breton, where, since he was running low on provisions, Verrazano sailed back to France, arriving in Dieppe on 8 July. Although it had been but a short foray by the exploration standards of the day, it laid the foundations for French interest in America, not least of all because Verrazano reported not only his oriental sea but also that the northern lands were where gold was to be found, both claims as false as each other. One suspects he told the king what he knew he wanted to hear.

In 1533 King François negotiated a deal with the pope that let France into the club of world dividers. Henceforth the Tordesillas division was to apply only to land already discovered; any new discoveries by France would be French. This agreement, plus Verrazano's glowing reports, spurred the explorations of Jacques Cartier in 1534, 1535, and 1541, when he found the St. Lawrence and attempted but failed to found a colony, nevertheless establishing the French claim to Quebec, which ultimately led to a French empire in North America.

Cartier, of course, did not find the promised gold. The next French venture, then, proposed to take it from the Spanish instead. A base was to be founded in Florida near where the Spanish galleons plied northwards on the Gulf Stream, and from whence French ships could rob the galleons and then slip quickly away. This undertaking was also to provide a refuge for Huguenots, a religious group persecuted in France.

Map 30 (below).
In 1529 Giovanni Verrazano's brother Girolamo drew this map to illustrate the discoveries of his brother. A vast and widening ocean leads westward to Cathay from the shores of North Carolina, flanked by *Terra Incognita*. Just below the middle black flag is *Luisa*, the island that reminded Verrazano of Rhodes and eventually led to the naming of Rhode Island. Farther west, about halfway between the middle flag and the westernmost one, two small parallel lines mark what is thought to be Verrazano Narrows, the entrance to New York Harbor.

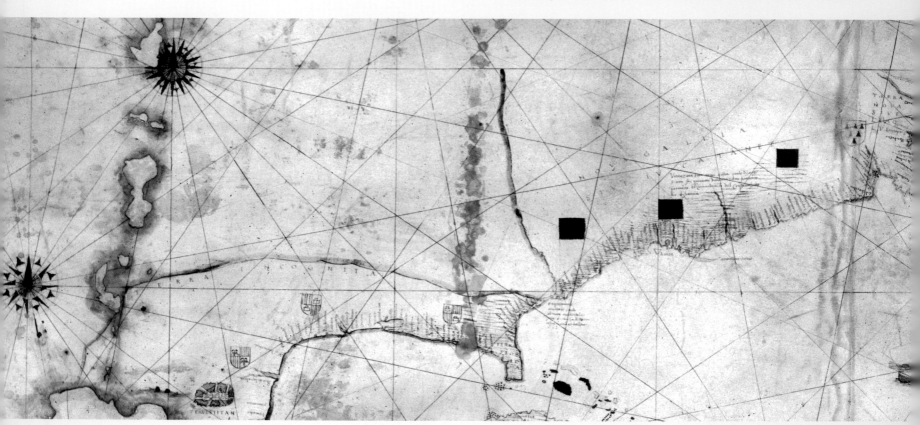

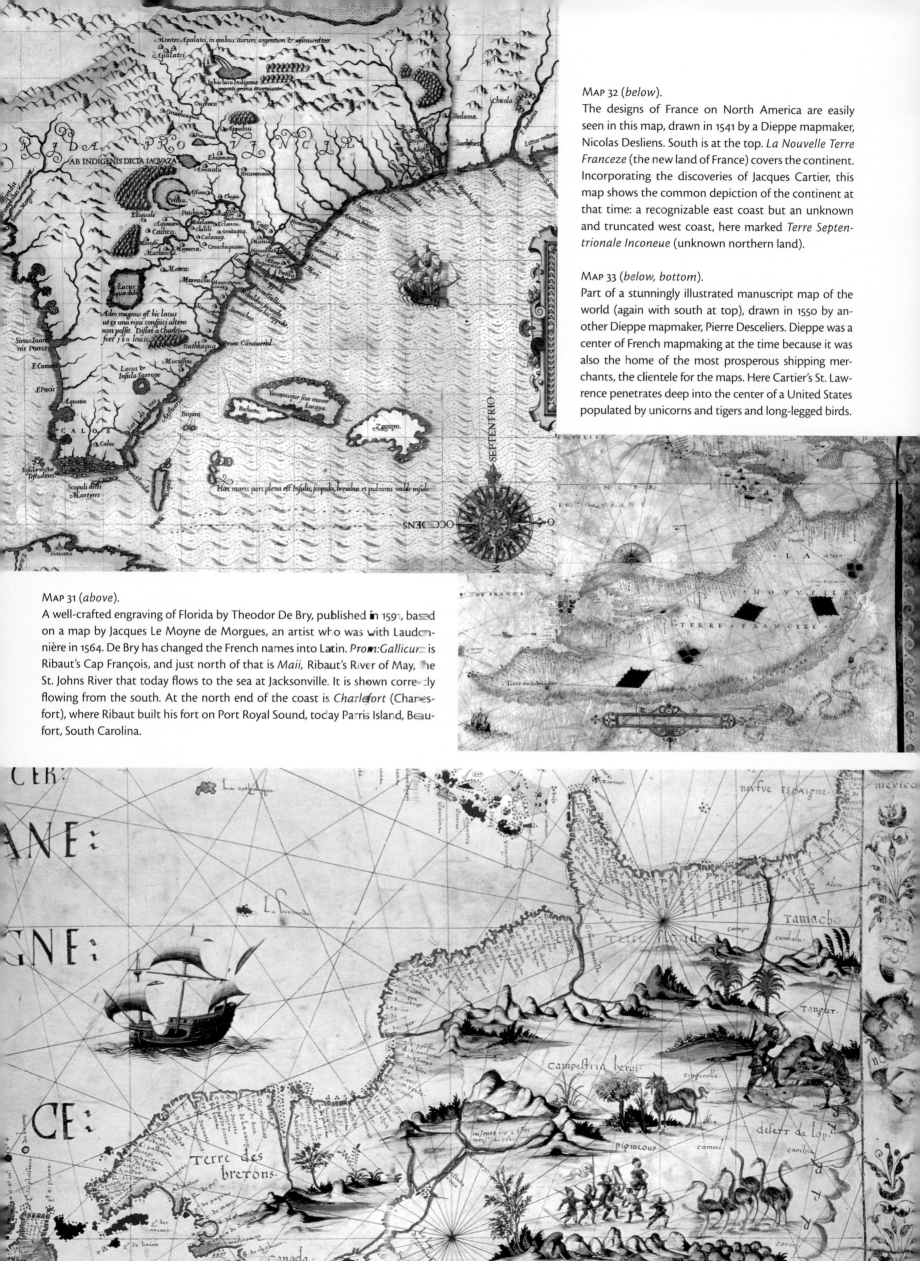

MAP 32 (below).
The designs of France on North America are easily seen in this map, drawn in 1541 by a Dieppe mapmaker, Nicolas Desliens. South is at the top. *La Nouvelle Terre Franceze* (the new land of France) covers the continent. Incorporating the discoveries of Jacques Cartier, this map shows the common depiction of the continent at that time: a recognizable east coast but an unknown and truncated west coast, here marked *Terre Septentrionale Inconeue* (unknown northern land).

MAP 33 (below, bottom).
Part of a stunningly illustrated manuscript map of the world (again with south at top), drawn in 1550 by another Dieppe mapmaker, Pierre Desceliers. Dieppe was a center of French mapmaking at the time because it was also the home of the most prosperous shipping merchants, the clientele for the maps. Here Cartier's St. Lawrence penetrates deep into the center of a United States populated by unicorns and tigers and long-legged birds.

MAP 31 (above).
A well-crafted engraving of Florida by Theodor De Bry, published in 1591, based on a map by Jacques Le Moyne de Morgues, an artist who was with Laudonnière in 1564. De Bry has changed the French names into Latin. *Prom:Gallicur* is Ribaut's Cap François, and just north of that is *Maii*, Ribaut's River of May, the St. Johns River that today flows to the sea at Jacksonville. It is shown correctly flowing from the south. At the north end of the coast is *Charlefort* (Charlesfort), where Ribaut built his fort on Port Royal Sound, today Parris Island, Beaufort, South Carolina.

It was organized by a Huguenot leader, Gaspard de Coligny, and was supported financially by the French royal family. Said to be one of the ablest seamen of his day, another Huguenot, Jean Ribaut, was placed in command of three ships and 150 men, sailing from Le Havre in February 1562. Soon after a landfall on the east coast of the Florida peninsula, Ribaut found the St. Johns River, at today's Jacksonville, naming it the River of May on account of the date—1 May. Sailing north, Ribaut came upon what he called "a country full of havens, rivers and islandes of such frutefullnes as cannot with tonge be expressed, and where in shorte tyme great and precyous commodyties might be founde." No matter where they searched, it seems early explorers were convinced that gold was just around the corner. Soon Ribaut found what he wanted: a hidden and defensible site. Here, on Parris Island, about thirty miles south of Savannah, Georgia, on an inlet he named Port Royal, Ribaut built Charlesfort.

Ribaut then returned to France for supplies, leaving behind thirty men at Charlesfort. Unfortunately for everyone concerned, when he reached France he found civil war had broken out against the Huguenots. He fought with his compatriots at Dieppe, but when it surrendered in early 1563 he fled to England, where the English, interested in his Floridian exploits, imprisoned him. This meant that the colonists he had left behind at Charlesfort were without supply. Eventually they built a boat and made for France, running out of food and resorting to cannibalism on the way.

A peace in France later in 1563 gave Coligny a chance to outfit another expedition. This time René Goulaine de Laudonnière, who had been with Ribaut on the first voyage, was in charge. Laudonnière's colonists built Fort Caroline in 1564 on the St. Johns River and made brief forays inland searching for the gold that they thought must exist there. The colony was soon in trouble, but was saved for a while by the

Map 34 (left, top).
Part of an English map of French Florida drawn by John White (see page 24). Near the southern end of this coast full of rivers is the *R. de May*, the St. Johns River, Ribaut's River of May, where Laudonnière built Fort Caroline. At the northern end of the coast is *Port Royal*, where Ribaut built Charlesfort.

Map 35 (left).
A Theodor De Bry pictomap engraving showing the French under Jean Ribaut sailing north along the coast of Florida toward Charlesfort in 1562. Some of the many rivers and islands are depicted in this fine illustration.

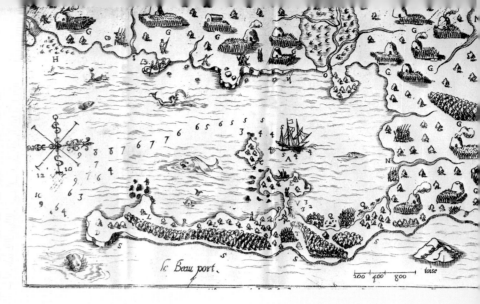

arrival of the temporarily friendly English buccaneer John Hawkins, who was on his way back to England from raiding in the Caribbean. Hawkins noted a strange habit of the Indians, who sucked the smoke of a herb burning in a cup, an early reference to tobacco.

Laudonnière's colony still did not prosper, but in August 1565, just before they intended to sail back to France, Ribaut arrived with seven ships and hundreds of new colonists. He had escaped from his English prison and been sent to take command once more. However, the Spanish had by this time learned of the French presence and, determined to oust them from what they saw as their domain, sent a new governor of Florida, Pedro Menéndez de Avilés, to find the French and destroy them. Ribaut's colonists were no match for Menéndez's army, and Ribaut's ships were caught in a hurricane, further adding to their distress. Ribaut was killed, but Laudonnière escaped back to France. French colonization of Florida was ended.

St. Augustine, founded by Menéndez in 1565, was itself ransacked twenty-one years later by an English fleet under Francis Drake (Map 45 page 25). Nonetheless, the settlement survived. In 1566 Menéndez sent Juan Pardo into the interior to, like the French, search for gold, and also find a route to Mexico. Pardo explored up the Savannah River valley and crossed the Appalachians to the Tennessee River valley before marching south to Alabama and back to St. Augustine. Although he heard reports of a mountain of diamonds he was, not surprisingly, unable to find it.

A later French expedition, much farther to the north, was much more prosaic, searching for furs and harbors rather than gold. Samuel de Champlain conducted a survey of the coasts of New England south from a base at Port Royal—today Annapolis Royal—in Nova Scotia in 1605 and 1606 and 1607. He was looking for a site for a fur trading post but in 1608

French commercial efforts were directed at a more promising site for this trade, up the St. Lawrence River. Here at Québec Champlain founded a settlement that was to endure to this day and form the imperial base for the French claim to most of the then known North American continent.

MAP 36 (above).
Samuel de Champlain made many maps of individual harbors along the coast of New England. This one is his *Le Beau Port*, today's Gloucester, Massachusetts. It was drawn in September 1606. His ship, a pinnace, is shown anchored at *A*.

MAP 37 (below).
Champlain made this excellent summary map of his explorations along the New England coast in 1605–07. At center top is *Pentagoet*, Penobscot Bay; at its head is *Norumbegut*, which as Norumbega was the early name for New England. Boston Harbor is at left, and the long promontory at the southern end of the map is the island of Monomoy, at the elbow of *Cap blanc*, Cape Cod, which is itself one of the less accurately shown features.

The First English Settlement

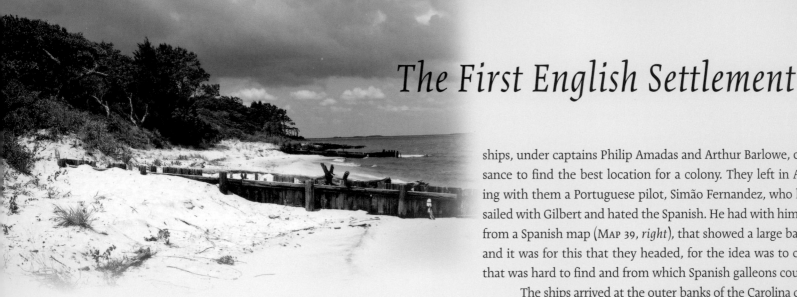

Above. A modern view of the beach in front of the fort at Roanoke Island, North Carolina, where Ralegh's colonists first landed.

The French were not the only ones who liked the idea of taking gold from the Spanish as an alternative to seeking it out themselves. Jean Ribaut had been forcibly co-opted as a pilot in 1565 by the English buccaneer Thomas Stukeley to lead him to the French colony in Florida, where he proposed to oust the French and take over the raiding of Spanish galleons himself. It was only Ribaut's escape that put an end to that venture.

In 1566 Humfrey Gilbert wrote a treatise on the importance for England of finding a Northwest Passage—a way through North America to the East—and of "planting" colonies to send wealth back to the mother country. Gilbert obtained a royal charter to set up a colony in Norumbega—New England—but, after being delayed by war in Ireland, Gilbert got only as far as Newfoundland in 1583. Sailing south his ships were wrecked in a storm, and he was drowned while trying to return to England. Gilbert's map, drawn for him by polymath John Dee, embodies his geographical ideas and is illustrated as Map 50, *page 29.*

The idea of "planting" an English colony in America was taken up by Gilbert's half-brother, Walter Ralegh (often spelled "Raleigh," although he never spelled it that way). Gilbert's younger brother Adrian sent mariner John Davis to find a Northwest Passage while Ralegh dispatched two ships, under captains Philip Amadas and Arthur Barlowe, on a reconnaissance to find the best location for a colony. They left in April 1584, taking with them a Portuguese pilot, Simão Fernandez, who had previously sailed with Gilbert and hated the Spanish. He had with him a map, copied from a Spanish map (Map 39, *right*), that showed a large bay with islands, and it was for this that they headed, for the idea was to create a colony that was hard to find and from which Spanish galleons could be raided.

The ships arrived at the outer banks of the Carolina coast on 13 July, at the latitude of the bay on Fernandez's map. With some difficulty a way was found between the outer islands into Pamlico Sound. Contact was made with the local Indians, led by a chief named Wingina, who proved friendly. Amadas and Barlowe spent three weeks exploring the region before returning to England—taking with them two Indian men, Manteo and Wanchese—with glowing reports of the suitability of the coast for a colony. Many animal skins and pearls were taken back to England. The lack of a good harbor, an essential requirement on a hurricane-prone coast, seems to have been overlooked in preference to a very hard-to-find location.

Meanwhile, Ralegh had been promoting the idea of an English colony in America in order to interest investors. He engaged chronicler Richard Hakluyt to write a propaganda piece called *A Discourse on Western Planting,* which was a big hit. Queen Elizabeth I invested her money and gave Ralegh use of one of her ships, the *Tiger.* She also knighted him and allowed him to name the new colony-to-be Virginia. A royal patent granted Ralegh all the lands between Cape Fear and Cape Henry (principally today's North Carolina).

A veritable fleet of seven ships and six hundred men was assembled and provisioned; in the swashbuckling ways of these times, one of the ships was a Dutch ship taken as a prize, and supplies came partly from piracy on other ships. To lead the expedition Ralegh chose Richard Grenville, a young but ruthless commander fresh from the Irish wars. With him went Fernandez as pilot, Thomas Cavendish as "high marshall," Amadas as "admiral of

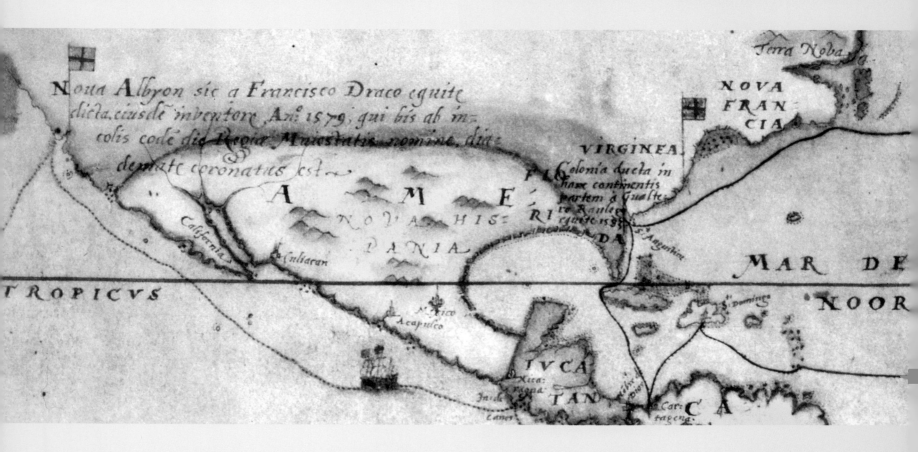

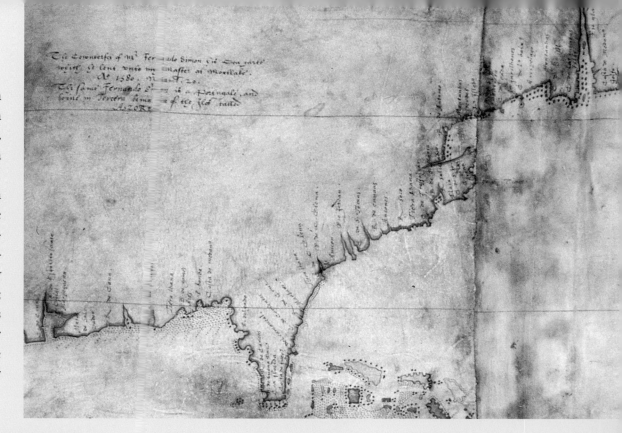

Virginia," a soldier, Ralph Lane, the artist John White, and Thomas Hariot, a mathematician employed in Ralegh's household, as scientist, naturalist, ethnographer, and mapmaker all in one. They sailed from England in April 1585.

After more diversions, raiding Spanish ships and losing one ship in a storm, Grenville arrived off the outer banks in June. Here the considerable planning that had gone into this colonization effort began to break down. The *Tiger* grounded and sank crossing into Pamlico Sound; although refloated, much of the ship's stores were ruined. Grenville recognized immediately the need for a proper harbor but none could be found. And relations with the once-friendly

MAP 39 (*right, top*).
This map, a copy by John Dee of pilot Simão Fernandez's map, itself a copy of a Spanish map, shows the large bay with islands that the English fleet headed for, a bay that is at the latitude of Roanoke Island. This map explains why the first English colony was at that location, even though it was not completely suitable for a settlement because of a lack of harbors and difficulties with crossing the outer sandbars.

MAP 40 (*right, center*).
Likely drawn by John White or Thomas Hariot in 1585, this is the first map of Virginia, in what is now North Carolina. North is at right. The offshore sandbanks are at bottom. The entrance through the banks is Wococon, with the notation *the port of saynt maris wher we arivid first*, for this is where they expected to find *Bahia de Santa Maria*, marked on **MAP 39** (*above*). Roanoke Island is at center right.

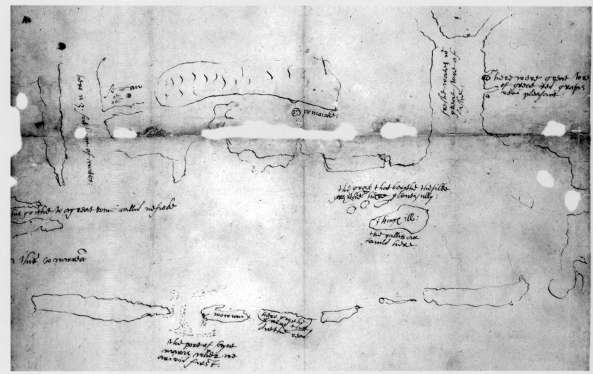

MAP 41 (*right, bottom*).
This detail of a pictomap engraved by Theodor De Bry shows the colonists approaching Roanoke Island. The treacherous navigation of the sandbanks is illustrated by the sinking vessels.

MAP 38 (*left*).
England's first engagement with America was in 1579, on the West Coast near San Francisco, at the time an essentially unknown and unmapped region. Buccaneer, adventurer, and navigator par excellence Francis Drake claimed the coast for England under the name New Albion—Latin for New England. Drake was on his voyage of circumnavigation between 1577 and 1580, and in 1579, having raided Spanish ports in South America and captured a Spanish galleon, he was running from his pursuers. At a place he called *Portus Nova Albion*, Drake landed to career and repair his ship. There have been endless arguments as to the location of this bay, but the most likely place is Drake's Harbor, on the south side of Point Reyes, just north of San Francisco. Drake stayed here for thirty-six days, going inland during that time in the company of coastal Miwok people and visiting several native villages. When he left New Albion Drake sailed some distance north, probably to about 48°N, though some claim he reached Alaska, perhaps in search of a western entrance to a Northwest Passage, which, had it existed, would have allowed him to return speedily to England. As it was he returned westwards across the Pacific, in the process becoming the first captain to sail with his ship round the world. (Magellan died en route, though his ship *Vittoria* completed the circumnavigation.)

This map is part of a world map known as the Drake Mellon map, now at Yale University. Drake's voyage up the West Coast in 1579 is shown, including his landing at New Albion and his indefinite northern probe. The map, which was drawn in 1587, also shows another Drake voyage, during which he attacked and sacked the Spanish city of St. Augustine (see **MAP 45**, *overleaf*) and visited Ralegh's colony at Roanoke in June 1586, taking all the colonists back to England. The unknown creator of this map has been careful to define the Spanish domains by confining them to the southern part of the United States and Mexico, thus likely deliberately giving the impression that the entire northern part of the continent was open for English colonization.

Indians took a distinct turn for the worse when the impetuous Grenville burned an entire village in retaliation for the theft of a silver cup.

A fort was built on Roanoke Island, but by August a decision was made that most would return to England to procure more supplies. Loaded with "a great amass of good things" to convince Ralegh and his investors of the wisdom of their venture, Grenville left, leaving Ralph Lane in charge at Roanoke. Grenville captured a straggler from the Spanish galleon fleet on the way home, showing the investors that the plan to set up the colony as a base for raiding Spanish treasure was working.

Lane spent much of his time ranging far and wide in search of a better location for the colony, "a good mine, or a passage to Southsea," and a route to Chesapeake Bay. He had to deal with now hostile Indians upset with the way they had been treated and the way Lane overpowered them with the use of firearms. The promised relief ship was late in arriving the next year but in the meantime a fleet led by Francis Drake arrived, fresh from the sacking of St. Augustine (MAP 45, *right, bottom*). Drake gave the colonists food, ammunition, and a small ship, a pinnace, for exploration, but all were destroyed in a storm. The colonists then accepted Drake's offer of a return to England. Just after they had departed the relief ship arrived but, finding the place deserted, did not stay. Grenville also arrived a little later, again finding no one. He, however, was determined to hold the colony and so left fifteen men as a token force while he returned to England once more for supplies. But those left behind perished on this now hostile shore.

The following year the undaunted Ralegh tried again, sending John White with three ships and 150 men, women, and children, including White's own daughter, Elenore Dare. They were to pick up the fifteen men left the year before and then establish a new colony, "the citie of Ralegh in Virginia," on Chesapeake Bay, which had been determined by this time to provide better potential sites, with harbors.

But they got no farther than Roanoke. White's colonists immediately began to feel pressure from the Indians, the result of Lane's violent approach to them the previous year. White was selected to return to England to obtain more support. The colonists reasoned that White would not abandon his daughter—who had just given birth to a daughter she named Virginia—and thus could be relied upon to return.

White did indeed try to return, but the threat of the Spanish Armada led Queen Elizabeth to forbid any ship to leave England, and despite the defeat of the Armada in 1588 it was not until 1590 that White was authorized to sail once more for Virginia. When he finally arrived back at Roanoke Island in August 1590, he found it deserted. One hundred and fourteen colonists had disappeared. The legend of the "lost colony" has lived on in

MAP 42 (*left*).
The first maps by John White were lost when a storm hit Drake's ships as they were being loaded in June 1586. This finished and quite accurate map was likely drawn in England in late 1586 or early 1587. The map shows the large amount of exploration that had been undertaken by the colonists in the short time they had been on America's shores. The island of Roanoke is colored pink.

folklore, but there seems little doubt the colonists were overwhelmed by Indian attacks.

It would be another century and another generation before England would once again aspire to an American colony, but the seeds had been sown. In 1588 Thomas Hariot published his *Brief and true report of Virginia,* which was an immense popular success, painting a picture of an idyllic and fertile land with a temperate climate. Despite what would prove to be a temporary English disenchantment with America, the potential of this new land was too great to ignore for long.

Map 43 (*above*).
An engraved version by Theodor De Bry of an original John White birc's-eye-view map of the Indian village of Secoton. The location of Secoton can be seen on Map 42 (*left*) on one of the mainland inlets near the bottom of the map.

Map 44 (*right, top*).
This part of a later map shows the location of the fort on Roanoke Island. The map is by John Collett and was published in 1770.

Right. The reconstructed fort on Roanoke Island as it is today.

Map 45 (*below*).
Drake attacking the Spanish city of San Agustin (St. Augustine), 28 May 1586, drawn by John White. The Spanish forces had deserted the fort, and Drake seized it, finding two thousand pounds of gold bullion. Drake burned the fort to the ground before leaving.

A New Kind of Englishman

Sixteen years after John White returned to England alone, charters were granted to two English companies to establish colonies in the New World. In 1606, driven once again by dreams of gold, investors invested and gentlemen volunteered. The Virginia Company was to create a "plant-ation" in the southern part of Virginia, while the Plymouth Company was to try its luck to the north.

In December 1606 three ships belonging to the Virginia Company set sail from London—the *Discovery*, the *Godspeed*, and the *Susan Constant*. On board were over a hundred men (but no women), mainly so-called gentlemen adventurers. Four months later they arrived at Chesapeake Bay, sailed up the James River, and established a little settlement at a place they named Jamestown, after their king.

It is a measure of the expectations of this group that soon after their arrival Captain John Smith, who was soon to emerge as the group's leader, was sent with Christopher Newport up the James River, "not to returne without a lumpe of gold," having seen the South Sea, or having found one of Ralegh's lost colonists. Needless to say, the pair returned empty-handed on all counts.

An inability to fend for themselves led to the death of sixty-six of the men over the ensuing winter, during which time Smith was reputedly captured by Powhatan, the local Indian chief, then saved by the intervention of his famous daughter Pocahontas. Only the willingness of others to chance their luck in such an uncertain place kept the colony alive, for the mortality rate continued to be horrific and the original company went bankrupt. Salvation arrived in the form of a different gold: to-bacco. The plant the Indians smoked was soon taken up by the colonists, and in 1612 John Rolfe discovered a way to cure tobacco so that it could be exported. Two years later the first shipment left for England, where its addictive properties led to instant sales; the fortunes of Virginia seemed assured.

In addition to this economic benefit, many English believed that the new American colony returned profits of a moral sort as well, providing a place of redemption for the lost souls of London, in reality a place where undesirables could be shipped to begin their lives anew. Virginia, preached the poet and clergyman John Donne, was breeding "a fine, new kind of Englishman."

In 1609 the Virginia charter had been amended to grant all the land to the Pacific, felt certain to lie just over the mountains, and for over a hundred years men searched to the west for the elusive ocean (see page 52).

Indian attacks continued to be a problem for the settlers until Rolfe married Pocahontas in 1614, despite the fact that he took her to England and she died soon after. After Powhatan's death in 1618, Indian assaults began again. The new chief, Opechancanough, led an attack on 22 March 1622 designed to wipe the English forever from his lands. Some three hundred and forty-seven colonists were massacred. Even in 1644, by which time there were really too many settlers to annihilate, the chief led another massacre. But this time he was captured and killed by one of his captors, finally ending any major threat from the Powhatan Confederacy.

To the north, the Plymouth Company made an unsuccessful attempt to settle on the coast of Maine, but it was the Puritan religious group popularly known as the Pilgrims that began continuous occupation in New England. They had arranged for passage to Virginia Company lands to the south, but on board their ship, the famous *Mayflower*, a decision was made to land instead in New England. And then a compact was signed by almost all, whereby they agreed to form themselves into "a civil body Politick," agreeing to "all due Submission and Obedience" to its "just and equal lawes." This was the beginning of the plantation covenant, subsequently used in some form

Map 46 (*left*).
The many adventures of the illustrious Captain John Smith are shown in this highly illustrated map from his 1624 book the *Generall History of Virginia, the Somer Iles, and New England*. The map of *Ould Virginia* refers to the lands of Sir Walter Ralegh's grant. The Somer Iles was the original name for Bermuda.

Top left. A model of the Jamestown Colony in 1607, on display at the Jamestown Historic Site.

by other colonies and considered the origin of the American tradition of government depending on the consent of the governed.

The Pilgrims began building their settlement on Christmas Day 1620 at Plymouth, across Cape Cod Bay from Provincetown, where they had made their landfall. Although the first to settle, they were not very successful because the colony was poorly located. It would finally be taken over in 1691 by the much more successful Massachusetts Bay Company, whose Puritan settlers arrived in New England in 1630 (see page 30).

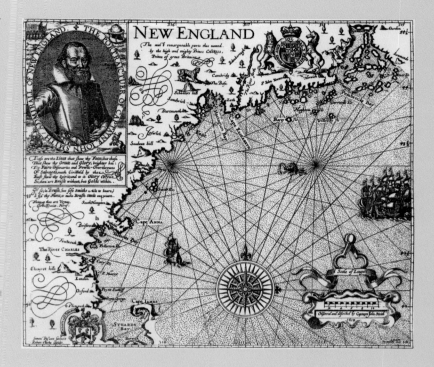

MAP 47 (*right*).
This map of New England is from Smith's *Generall History*. Smith explored the New England coast in 1614. The original grant of Virginia by James I in 1606 defined it as extending from 34° to 44°N, and it thus included much of New England. Cape James (at bottom) is Cape Cod. It seems to have been John Smith who coined the name New England for the region previously known as Norumbega. The new name was confirmed by King Charles I. Names were deliberately anglicized with the idea that they might encourage English colonization in these strange new lands.

MAP 48.
Captain John Smith's map of Virginia, drawn in 1611 and first published the following year in an explanatory booklet *A Map of Virginia, With a Description of the Country*; this copy is from his 1624 *Generall History of Virginia*. Small crosses are visible on many of the rivers, denoting the limits of Smith's own explorations. Everything beyond them is based on information from native sources. It was common for maps to combine known information with the speculative. The map was engraved by William Hole, who drew it from sketches provided by Smith.

A River Runs Through It

America was found by Europeans when they sought to sail westwards to Cathay and an unexpected continent inconveniently got in the way. Having accepted the reality of an intruding landmass, the next logical step was to try to find a way around it. Thus was born the quest for a Northwest Passage. But many still hoped that there might be a channel through the center of the continent, in temperate latitudes. Many of the early explorers thought they had found the eastern end of such a pathway. Giovanni Verrazano's channel was an entire sea, Jacques Cartier's a great river, the St. Lawrence. This was extended west not by him but by overzealous mapmakers seeking to please their monarchs by showing them in paper form what they wanted to believe. Somehow drawing a map made the feature more real.

Erroneous reports of a large interior lake in the southeast, rumors of the Great Lakes to the north and a northern passage, compounded with reports of Verrazano's sea and theories about where Jacques Cartier's St. Lawrence River went, induced mapmakers to produce a number of speculative maps that seem so outlandishly bizarre to us today. The ideas are long dead, but their maps live on to amuse us.

MAP 49 (*below*).
Drawn by Portuguese cartographer Diogo Homem in 1558, this striking map shows one early rather extreme conception of the North American continent. Cartier's St. Lawrence not only carves a broad path to the center of the United States but becomes one with a northern ocean called *Mare le paramàtiù* that takes up most of the continent. Entirely imaginary islands line its shores. America is *Terraæ florida*. The bight on the northeastern coast is the Bay of Fundy.

Map 50 (*above*).

Another beautifully eccentric map is *Humfray Gylbert knight his charte*, a polar projection drawn in 1583 by John Dee for English buccaneer, explorer, and adventurer Humfrey Gilbert, holder of a royal patent for the planting of an American colony before Ralegh. Here Verrazano's ocean *Mare de Verazana 1524* has been inventively reconciled with Cartier's St. Lawrence, which flows right through North America to the Gulf of California, the discovery of which by Hernán Cortés was known to the world by this time. A large lake sits in the interior of Florida independent of Verrazano's sea, and a clear Northwest Passage across the top of the continent allows easy sailing to the East. The fabled land of *Quivera* is shown on the coast of California.

Map 51 (*below*).

Michael Lok, English promoter of Martin Frobisher's voyages to the north, drew this map, which was published in Richard Hakluyt's *Divers Voyages* in 1582. Here Verrazano's ocean joins with the Northwest Passage. The map was apparently based on an "olde excellent mappe" that Verrazano gave to English king Henry VIII. To the north of California is *Anglorum 1580*, the first published record of Francis Drake's voyage to the Northwest Coast in 1579.

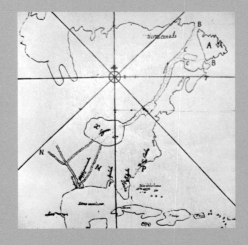

Map 52 (*right*).

A century later some of these ideas still lingered. This map was drawn in 1686 by Spanish pilot Martin de Echagaray for the Spanish authorities when they were searching for the French explorer René-Robert Cavelier, Sieur de La Salle. He had in 1682 descended the Mississippi to the Gulf of Mexico and in 1685 attempted to set up a French colony on the coast—well into territory Spain claimed as its own (see page 41). Here what is presumably a representation of the Great Lakes has both the St. Lawrence and the Mississippi flowing from it. Apart from a portage from several of the Great Lakes to the Mississippi system, the concept behind this map was not that wrong.

Colonial America

The migration that was to populate and change America forever really began in 1630 when Puritans, fleeing economic hardship and religious persecution in England, formed the Massachusetts Bay Company, which was granted a charter in 1629. Led by John Winthrop, the Puritans quickly established themselves in New England, founding many towns and imposing a strict code of conduct and religious interpretation on all.

Inevitably, those whose thought took them down different paths soon challenged the mainstream edicts. Preacher Roger Williams insisted—among other things—that title to land could come only from the Indians rather than from the king, a very radical thought for its day. He was expelled from Massachusetts in 1636 and made his way through the forest south, where he founded his own colony at Providence, Rhode Island.

Anne Hutchinson, banished from Massachusetts for independent thoughts that did not align with those of the church elders—and perhaps really for being an outspoken woman at a time when women were not supposed to think for themselves—purchased Aquidneck Island (Rhode Island) from the Narragansett Indians and founded Pocasset, a year later renamed Portsmouth, in 1638, establishing the first civil government in that region. Only a year later dissenting factions of these dissenters went to the other end of the island and founded Newport. Hutchinson's brother-in-law, John Wheelwright, exiled for the same reasons, fled to Exeter, New Hampshire. Although claimed by Massachusetts, New Hampshire became a separate royal province in 1679.

Preacher Thomas Hooker thought Massachusetts government too strict, and in 1635 he led followers to Connecticut, where his towns of Hartford, Wetherfield, and Windsor set up a government based on prop-

MAP 53 (left).
Drawn by or for early Dutch explorer Adriaen Block, this map, now in the Dutch national archives, was attached to a memorial dated October 1614 by Block and a group of merchants requesting a trade monopoly in *Nieu Nederlandt*. Block Island, Verrazano's Luisa (see page 18), is *Adrianociqra eland* at the eastern end of Long Island. Block was the first to show that Long Island was an island. His explorations followed those of Henry Hudson and were largely responsible for the creation of the Dutch colony of New Netherlands in 1624. On the Hudson River, *Fort van Nassouiben* is shown. It was established near Albany in 1614.

MAP 54 (below, left).
The coast from Chesapeake Bay to Maine, drawn in 1639 by Dutch mapmaker Joan Vingtboons. The English colonies of New England and Virginia are acknowledged, but between them, covering most of today's New Jersey, New York, and Connecticut, is the Dutch colony of *Niew Nederlandt*—New Netherlands. The large lake *Mere van der Irocoisin* shown in the interior of New England is a confusion caused by reports of Lake Champlain and the Champlain Valley, in reality much farther west.

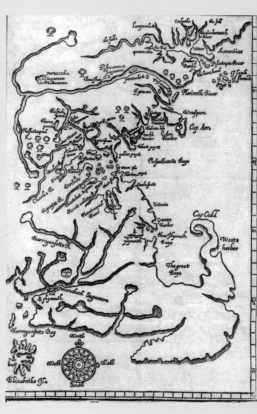

erty rather than religious qualifications. These "Fundamental Orders" are sometimes considered to be the first written constitution. Puritan scholar John Davenport, on the other hand, thought Massachusetts government too loose, leading followers to New Haven, Connecticut, and setting up a strict theocracy. This did not last beyond 1662, when a charter was issued for all Connecticut, but the various differences in opinion both major and minor had the effect of dispersing settlement.

The Indians of New England, the Pequots, Narragansetts, Wampanoags, and others, suffered from intertribal rivalries that made them unable to resist the English advance. In many cases they were on friendly terms with settlers, whose religious principles led them to purchase land rather than take it. But the Puritans kept trying to impose their will on the Indians. The clash of cultures reached a crescendo in 1675 when Wampanoag chief Metacom—popularly known as King Philip—led an attack on the town of Swansea. Puritan retaliation was swift. For a year New England was in turmoil. When it ended with the death of Metacom in the summer of 1676, thirteen towns

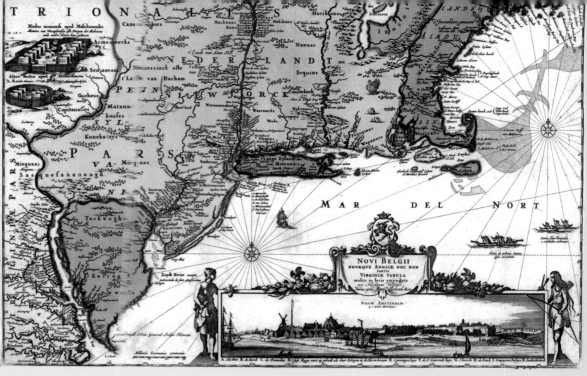

MAP 56 (*above*).
Dutch mapmaker Nicolas Visscher produced this detailed map of New Netherlands and New England about 1651, though it was published in 1685, after the demise of the Dutch colony. The map is famous for its view of Nieuw Amsterdam, now Manhattan, New York. It is one of the earliest views of the city.

MAP 55 (*below left, center*).
This was perhaps the first map of New England drawn by a resident. It was published in 1634 in *New Englands Prospect*, a book by William Wood. The map was titled *The South part of New-England, as it is Planted this yeare, 1634.*

MAP 57 (*below*).
On this 1677 map of New England, with north at right and the oversized Connecticut River at the top, many of the interior rivers are not only known but have settlements on them. *The White Hills* are the White Mountains, explored by Darby Field in 1642. The other oversized river is the Merrimack, shown flowing from an enlarged Lake Winnipesaukee. This map was the first to be drawn, engraved, and printed in America. It illustrated *Narrative of the troubles with the Indians in New England*, a book about the clashes between Puritans and Indians popularly known as King Philip's War.

MAP 58 (*below right*).
King Phillips Country is shown on this 1675 English map by John Seller. A year later King Philip—Wampanoag chief Metacom—would be dead.

had been burned, hundreds of isolated farms destroyed, and a thousand colonists killed. The Indians lost perhaps three times that number. Indian power would never recover, and expansion of settlement continued.

To the west, New York was until 1664 the purview of the Dutch. Their interest in the region had begun with the voyage of Henry Hudson in 1609 up the river that bears his name. Hudson was an Englishman but was contracted to the Dutch at the time. Searching for a Northwest Passage, he sailed up the Hudson River as far as Albany before coming to the realization that this was only a river, not a strait. On his return to England Hudson was arrested and charged with "voyaging to the detriment of his country." It was to England's detriment, for the Dutch were immediately interested in the possibilities of the region. The New Netherlands Company sent Adriaen Block to investigate. In 1613–14 he found Manhattan's East River, determined that Long Island was an island, and ascended the Connecticut River perhaps as far as Hartford; all this territory was claimed for Holland. His map is shown as MAP 53, *opposite*.

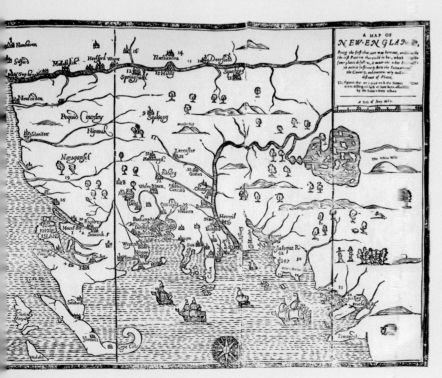

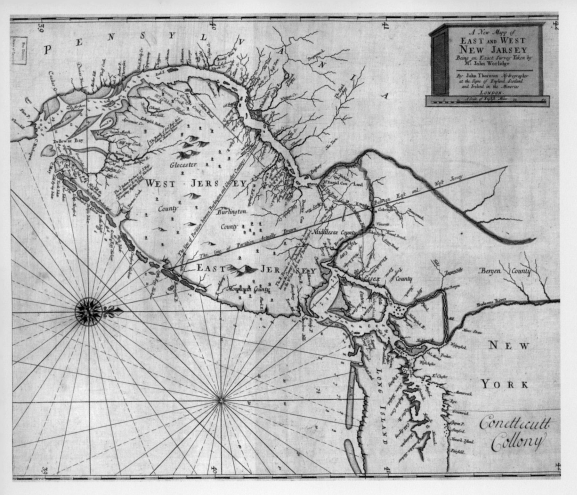

The Dutch West India Company settled colonists on Manhattan and throughout the Hudson Valley, even granting charters for some English towns. Nonetheless, the Dutch and the English came into conflict, and in 1664 a fleet under James, Duke of York, ousted the Dutch from their settlement of New Amsterdam; it was renamed New York. MAP 358, *page 173,* shows New Amsterdam at the time of its capture. The city and the colony returned briefly to Dutch control in 1673 but were given back to the English under the terms of a peace treaty the following year. With the accession of the Duke of York as James II in 1685, New York became a royal colony.

Part of the Duke of York's grant included what is now New Jersey; further disposition of this area to two competing proprietors, John Berkeley and George Carteret, led to the official creation of two Jerseys in 1676: West and East (MAP 59, *left*). In 1702 the two were united, but under the governorship of New York, and not until 1738 did New Jersey gain its own governor.

A charter for Maryland was issued by Charles I to George Calvert, the first baron Baltimore, in 1632. Calvert, a Catholic, but nonetheless a favorite of the king, had been interested in colonies as a refuge for those of his religion, since Catholics were persecuted in England at that time. In 1621 he had sent colonists to Newfoundland, but the barren shores, "furious Windes and Icy Mountaynes" had defeated

MAP 59 (above).
This 1706 *New Mapp of East and West Jarsey* was not really a new map at all, since the two Jerseys were amalgamated in 1702. The map has north at right; it was drawn by English mapmaker John Thornton from a survey by John Worlidge.

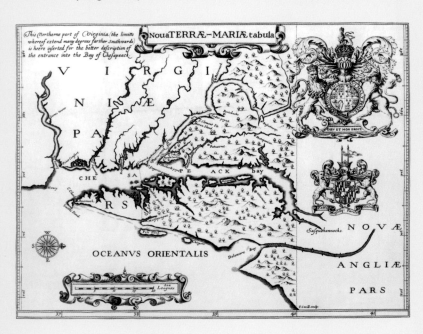

MAP 60 (left).
A map of Maryland published by Lord Baltimore in 1635. The northern limit of his grant had been set at 40°N, but on this map that parallel has been drawn too close to the head of Chesapeake Bay. A revised version (MAP 132, *page 66*) adjusted the boundary farther north by re-engraving a few more trees. This boundary was to become a constant source of friction between the Calverts and the Penns. A compromise boundary at 39°43′19″ was the famous line surveyed in 1763–68 by Charles Mason and Jeremiah Dixon (see page 66).

MAP 61 (left, below).
This delightful *Land-Skip [landscape] of the Province of Mary Land* was drawn by George Alsop and published in a 1666 book.

MAP 62 (right).
The first permanent European settlement in the Delaware Valley was that of New Sweden, shown here on a 1654 map. The New Sweden Company was formed in Sweden in 1637 to trade for furs and tobacco in America. Land along the Delaware River was purchased from the Indians in 1638 and Fort Christina founded at today's Wilmington. Perhaps half of the colony's settlers were actually Finns. The Dutch captured New Sweden in 1655, and the English took over after the fall of the New Netherlands in 1664. The area of settlement along the west bank of the Delaware was included in the grant to William Penn in 1681.

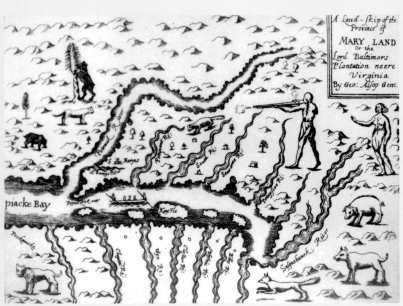

them. Instead he cast his eyes south to more favorable climes. Terra Maria (Mary Land) was named after the queen, Henrietta Maria, and the grant was taken up by the second baron Baltimore, Cecil Calvert, on his father's death. In March 1634 the first 150 settlers arrived on their ships the *Ark* and the *Dove*. They purchased land from the Indians and founded St. Mary's City on the southern tip of the peninsula, between the Patuxent and the Potomac rivers.

Although Calvert created a colony of religious tolerance, his charter was essentially feudal; settlers on the 6 million-acre grant owed allegiance directly to him. Religious tolerance—though for Christians only—was embedded in the Maryland Toleration Act, passed in 1649 by the colonial assembly. Yet the following year Puritans who had settled in Maryland overthrew the proprietorial government, burned churches, and outlawed both Catholics and Anglicans. It was not until 1658 that Calvert regained control, reaffirming the Toleration Act that year and *not* outlawing Puritanism. Neighboring Virginia went in the opposite direction, outlawing all religions except Anglicanism. Puritans streamed into Maryland, finding refuge on the banks of the Chesapeake at a place they called Providence, renamed Annapolis in 1708.

A later proprietorship was that of Pennsylvania. It was granted to a wealthy English Quaker, William Penn, in 1681 as a payoff from King Charles II for a large debt that he owed to Penn's father; the rights to Delaware were obtained from his friend James, Duke of York, a year later. Pennsylvania was both a utopian "holy experiment" and a commercial venture from which the potential for making money seemed endless.

Penn sent agents ahead to survey land, and in 1682 twenty-three ships arrived with Quaker colonists. He himself arrived in his colony late that year and stayed for two years. During that time he negotiated a series of land purchases with the Leni Lanape (Delaware) Indians that gave him much of the land along the north bank of the Delaware River, including the site of Philadelphia. The land was quickly divided into "Countyes, Townships and Lotts" (MAP 63, *below*). In keeping with his ideals, Penn envisaged a landscape full of country estates and his city, Philadelphia, as a "greene Countrye Towne," stretching across the peninsula between the Delaware and the Schuylkill rivers. It had a green belt, spacious squares, and broad avenues, and was for the time a fine example of a planned city (MAP 144, *page 72*). Having experienced the Great Plague and Great Fire of London in 1665 and 1666, Penn was determined to design a city that would be free from these two great fears of the seventeenth-century urban dweller.

MAP 63 (*below*).
This map of the "improved" (by which was meant settled by Europeans) part of Pennsylvania, about 1690, was created by Thomas Holme, William Penn's land agent and later colonial surveyor. It includes the plan for his "great towne" of Philadelphia. Other maps of colonial Philadelphia and the area surrounding it are shown on pages 72–73.

MAP 64 (*left*).
The English colonies in 1699, from the Carolinas north, shown on a map dedicated to the English king William.

MAP 65 (*below*).
Hermann Moll, a Dutch mapmaker working in England, published this *New and Exact Map of the Dominions of the King* in 1715. This is a 1731 edition. Detailed but not very up-to-date even when first published, it shows East and West Jersey separately. The Carolinas have been added as an inset map.

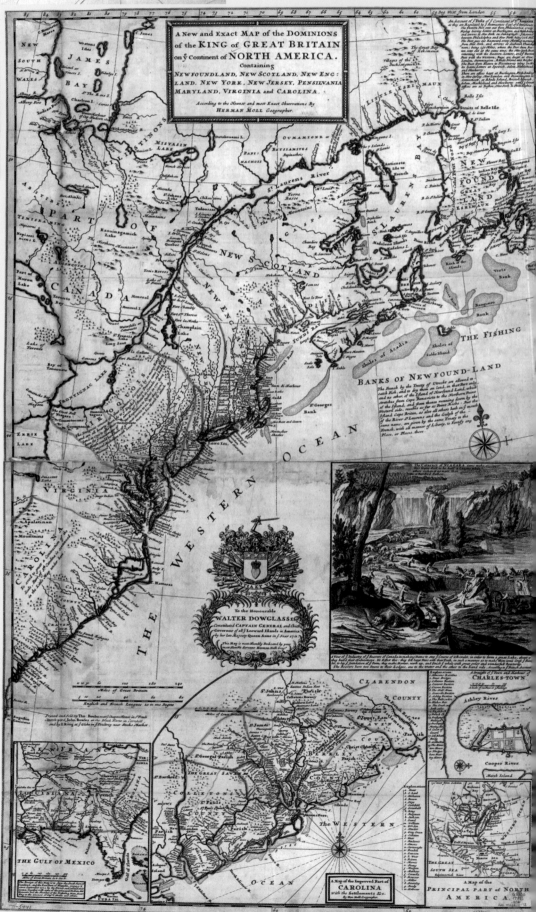

After 1718 the promise of religious freedom began to attract German and Scots-Irish settlers in increasing numbers, and the non-Quaker population grew. Initially, Pennsylvania suffered less from Indian attacks than most of the other colonies thanks in part to Penn's and later Quaker policy of negotiating with Indians as equals. The pacifism of the Quakers would not allow for retaliation against Indian raids in any case. Non-Quakers—and many frontier Quakers too—increasingly demanded protection from Indians that the Quakers in government were not prepared to give. This policy ultimately led, after war had been declared against the Shawnee and Delaware Indians in 1756, to the withdrawal of most Quakers from government, the so-called Quaker abdication.

The three "lower counties" along the Delaware, New Castle, Kent, and Sussex, were mainly populated with those of Swedish, Dutch, and Scots-Irish descent and were never really absorbed into the Quaker proprietorship. In 1704 the counties gained a separate legislature and in 1710 a separate executive council and became the colony of Delaware.

In Virginia, following the massacre of about five hundred colonists by Indians in 1644 (see page 26), an Indian-free area, the "Pale," was created, following a method used in Ireland. Tobacco planting grew quickly with the expansion of the market for the leaves. After all, the colony was the domain of the Virginia Company, a commercial operation intended for profit. By company decree settlements had to be at least ten miles part, the better to manage the tobacco plantations. This tended to restrict the development of cities. Beginning in the mid-seventeenth century slaves replaced indentured company servants as the labor force (see page 100).

In what some consider a forerunner of the American Revolution, in 1676 a recent immigrant,

Nathaniel Bacon, led an uprising against the governor, ostensibly protesting the lack of action against Indian uprisings on the frontier. It seems that Bacon intended to have Virginia secede from the English empire a hundred years before it actually did. But Bacon suddenly died of dysentery and his revolution died with him.

The Act of Union between England and Scotland in 1707 (creating now "British" instead of "English") allowed the immigration of Scottish merchants, who took business from the established English interests all along the Tidewater as well as in Virginia, and the population began to grow more rapidly.

A huge area stretching south from Virginia to Spanish Florida was granted as the Province of the Carolanas by Charles I to a favorite, his attorney general, Robert Heath. Heath did nothing with his grant and effectively lost it when the king lost his head in 1649. A second grant of much of this area, from Virginia south to 31°N, was made on the restoration of the monarchy in England in 1660. Charles II rewarded eight of his supporters in 1663 with the grant of Carolina, which was named in Latin form after his late father. The eight men became "lords proprietors."

A small English settlement had been established on Albemarle Sound in 1653, and another was begun on the Cape Fear River, but under the lords proprietors what was to become a significant city, Charles Town (after 1783 Charleston), was founded in 1670 (and moved to its present position in 1680) on a good harbor well positioned for trade with the West Indies (Map 66, *above, right*). The most active proprietor, Antony Ashley Cooper, first earl of Shaftesbury, drew the street plan for Charles Town. The small city became the center of social life in the colony, and most settlers lived in it or close by if they could.

Isolation and disagreements between the rest of the widely dispersed colonists led to a separation of the colony in 1712, creating North and South Carolina, and this division was formally ratified in 1729, when seven of the lords proprietors sold their shares back to the Crown.

MAP 66 (*above*).
The 1680 site of Charles Town (Charleston, South Carolina) on a map published in 1711 by Edward Crisp as part of *A Compleat Description of the Province of Carolina in 3 Parts*. (MAP 106, *page 53*, shows another part.) The Ashley and Cooper rivers are named after Antony Ashley Cooper, one of the eight lords proprietors.

MAP 67 (*below, left*).
A map showing the vast extent of the Carolina grant, drawn in 1671 by the philosopher John Locke, Cooper's secretary. Locke is reputed to have drawn up the constitution for Carolina, but it was never ratified.

MAP 68 (*below, right*).
The *Country of Carolina* in a 1682 map. North is to the right, and *Charles Town* is shown on the map's fold at center.

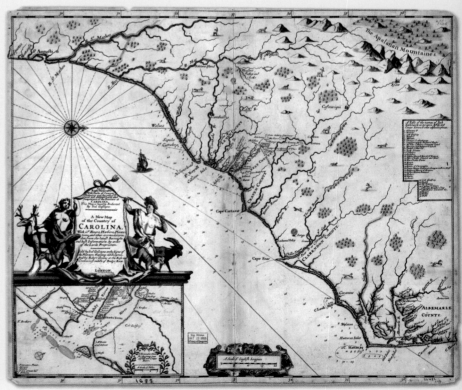

Georgia has belatedly been added to this 1733 map, carved out of what was South Carolina. The map is the index map to a large and famous multisheet wall map by Henry Popple, *Map of the British Empire in America*.

Map 70 (below).
James Oglethorpe's *Map of the County of Savannah*, drawn in 1734 and published in 1735 in Halle, Germany, where Oglethorpe hoped to recruit settlers. His plan for Savannah, the rectangular grid, is divided into several parts. The small block right beside the "H" of "SAVANNAH" is divided into six wards, each of which was to have forty house lots; four large "Trust" lots flanked an open square. Each household was also granted a five-acre garden lot (the second most dense grid on the map) and a forty-five-acre farm lot farther away (the medium-density grid on which is the letter "A" of "GEORGIA"), with yet larger blocks for later expansion.

At the beginning of the eighteenth century there were numerous conflicts between settlers and traders and the Indians of the region. In the north, on the Neuse River, New Bern (perhaps better known today as the birthplace of Pepsi-Cola) was founded in 1710 by German and Swiss immigrants. The local Tuscarora Indians attacked them in 1711, and this Tuscarora War lasted for two years before the Europeans gained control. Far to the south, the Yamassee War flared. Yamassee (Creek) Indians, supported by the French in Louisiana and the Spanish in Florida, began killing British traders and launched an attack on the town of Port Royal, whose inhabitants fled. Charles Town prepared its defenses. South Carolina was close to collapse and was saved only by the intervention of the Cherokee.

Something had to be done. As usual, the machinations of the British government were slow, but a decision was made to establish a buffer settlement south of South Carolina—a colony to be called the Province of Georgia, after King George II. The main idea was to create stability, but the colony's founders, John Percival and James Edward Oglethorpe, had other, humanitarian ideas. The colony, granted by the Crown as a trusteeship in 1732, was to become a "Utopia in the New World," an alternative abode for debtors, otherwise imprisoned in England, and a haven for Protestants from Catholic parts of Europe. Land between the Altamaha and the Savannah rivers was given to a group of trustees for twenty-one years, after which the colony would revert to the Crown. Land ownership was to be restricted to males to ensure that there was a potential force to oppose any Spanish incursions.

The first settlers landed at what was to become Savannah in February 1733. In keeping with his utopian ideas Oglethorpe laid out the city-to-be on a model plan (MAPS 70 and 71, *below*) and forbade slavery, hard liquor, and (interestingly) lawyers. He intended that his colony should produce silk and mandated the growing of two mulberry trees on each plot to feed silkworms. Also to be grown were cotton, indigo, olives, dates, rice, and other semitropical produce, but Oglethorpe made things more difficult for his farmers by refusing to modify his idealistic plans to take into account varying quality of the land.

On Saint Simons Island near the mouth of the Altamaha River, Oglethorpe in 1736 built Fort Frederica to protect the southern boundary of his colony. Considered at the time to be well into Spanish territory, the fort survived Spanish attacks in 1742 (during the so-called War of Jenkin's Ear) and by so doing firmly established a new boundary of British influence far to the south of where

Map 71 (below).
A bird's-eye map of Savannah *as it stood the 29th of March 1734*. This is nearer the reality than Oglethorpe's utopian plan in MAP 70. The beginnings of the urban wards are in a clearing hacked out of the forest. The garden lots and farm lots are nowhere to be seen. The open squares of the first four wards can be seen from the layout, though much is undeveloped at this point, a mere year after the city was begun.

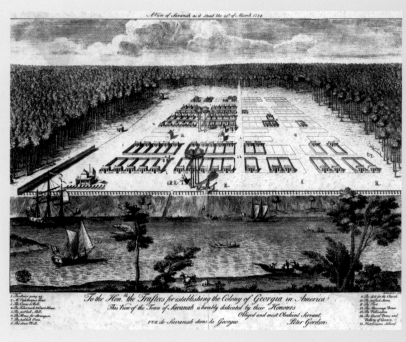

MAP 72 (*above*).
Many of the grants of colonies failed to specify a western boundary or gave the
Pacific Ocean as the boundary. This was initially due to a failure to understand
the real width of the continent and later acceptable as an incursion into French
claims. This is the first edition, published in 1755, of a famous map by Virgin-
ian mapmaker John Mitchell. It shows well the westward claims of many of the
colonies, completely disregarding any of the French claims to the Mississippi
Valley. A later edition of his map (MAP 172, *pages 90–91*) was used to negotiate
the first boundaries of the new United States.

it had been previously considered to be. MAP 137, *page 68*, a Spanish map
dated 1742, shows that the Spanish had accepted the fact of Georgia at
that time, for on it the southern boundary of Georgia is clearly indicated
as the new limit of British territory.

Only a few debtors actually came to Georgia. The colonists Oglethorpe attracted in the main did not share his high-minded views and
proceeded to act much like their Carolina neighbors to the north, soon
demanding the introduction of slavery. The ban on hard liquor was
lifted in 1742 and slavery was legalized in 1750—though the law against
the practice had been ignored for some years before that. A year later
all pretense of creating a utopia finally ceased, and the trustees surrendered their charter back to the Crown. All that the ex-trustees were able
to achieve was a guarantee that Georgia would not be swallowed up by
South Carolina. Georgia became much like the other southern colonies,
with an economy based on plantations and slavery, an economy and a
way of life that was eventually to lead the South to become so different
from the North that it would attempt to become a separate nation.

Georgia was not the last British American colony. Britain gained all
Florida from the Spanish by the Treaty of Paris in 1763, after the end of the

Seven Years' (French and Indian) War. The territory was exchanged for
Havana, which the British had captured in 1762. By a royal proclamation
of 7 October 1763 two new British provinces, East and West Florida, were
created.

But, of course, by this time the days of all British colonies in
America were limited. Like the rest of its colonies, the two Floridas were
lost to Britain after the American Revolution, but unlike the northern
ones, Florida was given back to Spain, and Spanish it would remain until
1819 (see page 138).

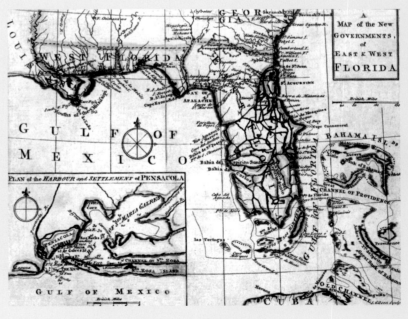

MAP 73.
East and West Florida, the fourteenth British American colony, is shown in this
1765 magazine map published to inform readers of Britain's new possession.

A French Empire in America

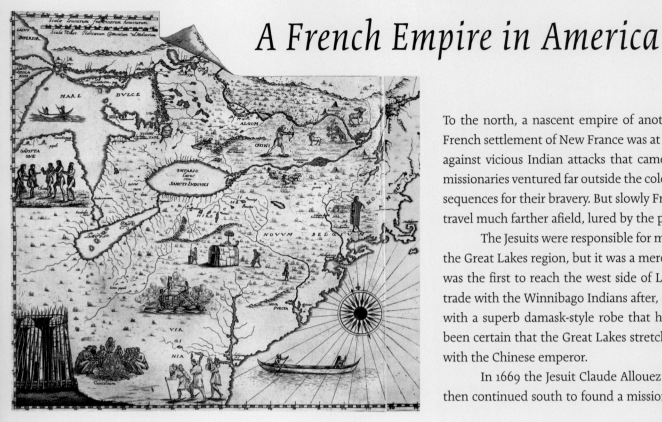

To the north, a nascent empire of another European power was stirring. The French settlement of New France was at first kept small and compact, to defend against vicious Indian attacks that came with daunting regularity. Only Jesuit missionaries ventured far outside the colony, and often suffered horrendous consequences for their bravery. But slowly French adventurers felt secure enough to travel much farther afield, lured by the promise of wealth from the fur trade.

The Jesuits were responsible for much of the first European knowledge of the Great Lakes region, but it was a merchant, Jean Nicollet de Belleborne, who was the first to reach the west side of Lake Michigan. In 1634 he established a trade with the Winnibago Indians after, so the story goes, first impressing them with a superb damask-style robe that he had taken with him because he had been certain that the Great Lakes stretched to China, and he expected to meet with the Chinese emperor.

In 1669 the Jesuit Claude Allouez followed Nicollet's route to Green Bay, then continued south to found a mission among the Fox Indians of Wisconsin.

MAP 74 (*above*).
The lands known to French Jesuit missionaries in 1657 are shown in this illustrated map by Father Francesco Giuseppe Bressani, who drew the map despite having only a few fingers, the result of horrific torture by the Iroquois he was so earnestly attempting to help. Of the Great Lakes, Lakes Ontario and Erie are well defined, Lake Huron less so, while Lakes Michigan and Superior are known only at their eastern ends. This map is one of the rarest printed maps of America, with only two copies known to exist.

MAP 75 (*left, inset*).
The first map of Lake Superior, drawn by Jesuits Claude Allouez and Claude Dablon in 1670 and published the following year. Lake Michigan is named *Lac des Ilinois* after the native group.

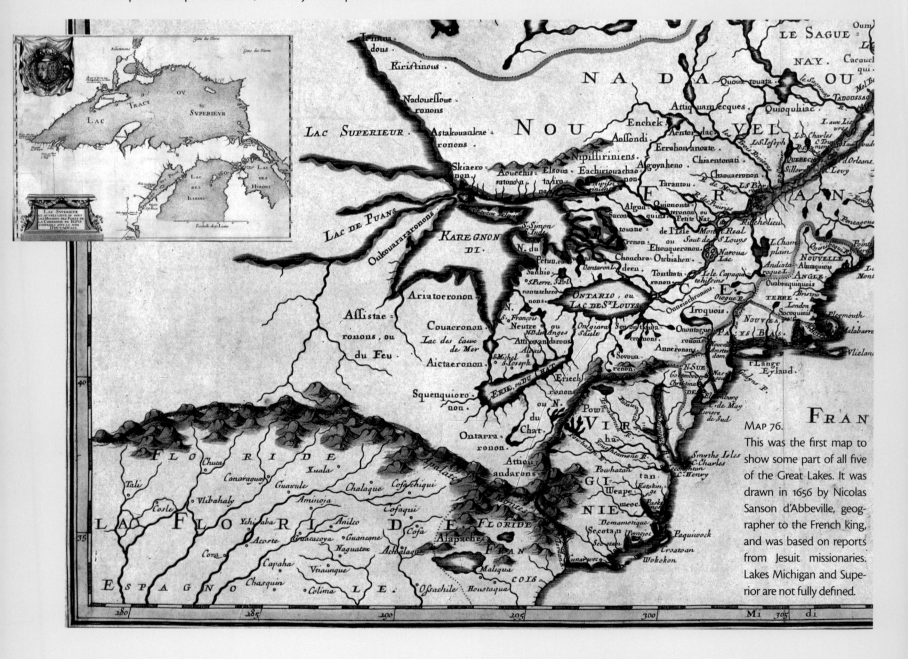

MAP 76.
This was the first map to show some part of all five of the Great Lakes. It was drawn in 1656 by Nicolas Sanson d'Abbeville, geographer to the French king, and was based on reports from Jesuit missionaries. Lakes Michigan and Superior are not fully defined.

It was here he learned that he was only six days away from a major river flowing south—the Mississippi. Allouez and another Jesuit, Claude Dablon, the following year became the first to explore Lake Superior and the first to draw a map of that lake (Map 75, *left, inset*).

The French authorities soon acted to—as was the custom of the day—claim these new-found territories, and the promise of more to come, for France. At Sault Ste. Marie on 4 June 1671 French government representative Simon-François Daumont de Saint-Lusson held a ceremony attended by Jesuits and emissaries from fourteen Indian tribes of the region. He formally claimed all the territory to the west, south, and north—much of America—for France. The French now considered they had a legitimacy to explore far and wide.

And explore they did. The first order of business was to check out the Indian reports of the great river flowing to the south. An official French government expedition was dispatched—though funded, as was the French custom, by private investors hoping to find new wealth. Louis Jolliet was accompanied by Jesuit Jacques Marquette—for heathen might need to be converted—and five voyageurs, whose main job would be to paddle.

They left Fort Michilimackinac, where Lake Huron and Lake Michigan meet, in May 1673. The route they took is shown on Marquette's map (Map 77, *right*), still preserved in Jesuit archives. Untroubled by tales of demons and monsters told to them by the natives, they entered Green Bay and ascended the Fox River, crossing a short portage to the Wisconsin River, which is part of the Mississippi River system. Canoeing now southwards, they reached a large silt-laden river flowing in from the west. This was called the Pekitanoui, or Muddy River—the Missouri. Here Jolliet reported that he had been to a village only five days' journey away from a tribe reported to trade with the natives of California.

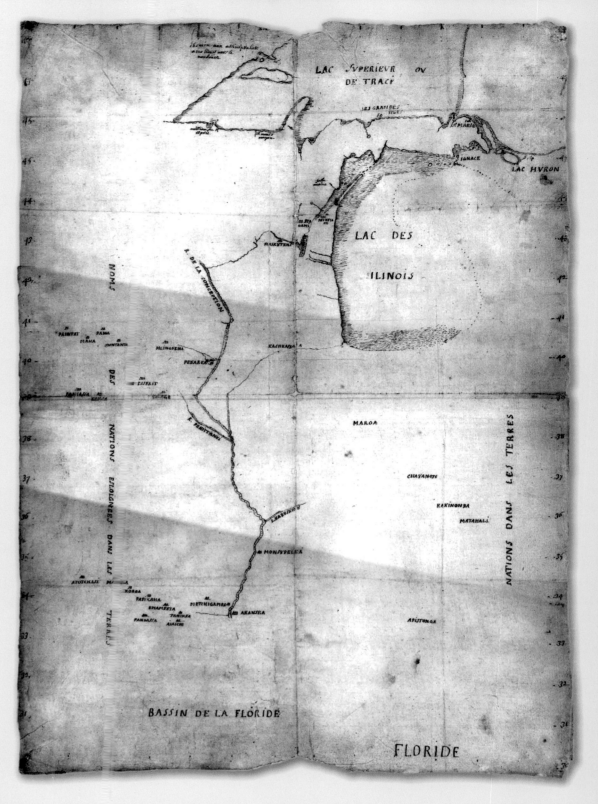

MAP 77 (*above*).
This is the map drawn by Father Jacques Marquette in 1673. It shows the route he and Louis Jolliet took from Lake Michigan (*Lac des Ilinois*) into Green Bay, up the Fox River, across to the Wisconsin River, and down the Mississippi as far as the Arkansas River. The Missouri is shown as *Pekittan8i*, the Ohio as *8ab8skig8*. The region to the south that they did not explore is labeled *Bassin de la Floride*.

Since Jolliet had started on his exploration expecting the Mississippi to empty into the Gulf of California (as the Colorado does), this information must have been of considerable interest to him.

After another one hundred and thirty miles he noted the Oua-bougkigou—the Ohio River—flowing in from the east. Farther south they went, but four hundred miles from the mouth of the Mississippi, at the approximate location of the Arkansas River, they stopped, feeling

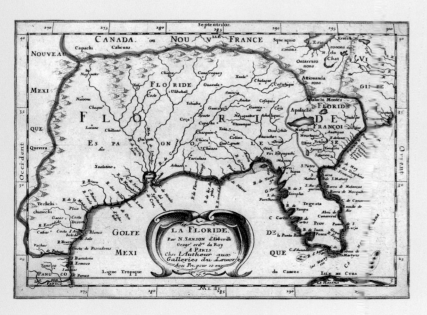

MAP 78 (*left*).
The Mississippi was not shown on this 1657 French map of *Floride* (Florida), the term applied here to the entire southern part of the United States. This was despite the fact that the mouth of the river had been seen by Spanish explorer Alvar Núñez Cabeza de Vaca in 1529 and the river crossed by Hernando de Soto in 1541 (see page 16).

Map 79 (*left*).
Louis Jolliet's map of his exploration of the Mississippi in 1673. He called it the Rivière Colbert after the French king Louis XIV's first minister, Jean-Baptiste Colbert. The assumed path of the river south of the Arkansas is shown by a dashed line, approximately correctly, unlike other efforts, such as those shown in Map 83, *overleaf*.

Map 80 (*below*).
The upper Mississippi, the Illinois, and the Ohio rivers are shown on this superb map drawn in 1685 and republished in 1688 by the Venetian Franciscan mapmaker Vincenzo Coronelli. *P. Coronelli* in the cartouche refers to Père (Father) Coronelli. As geographer to the French king, he received manuscript maps from explorers. The extent of *Nouvelle France* (New France) has been expanded thousands of miles west and south to encompass much of what is now the American Midwest.

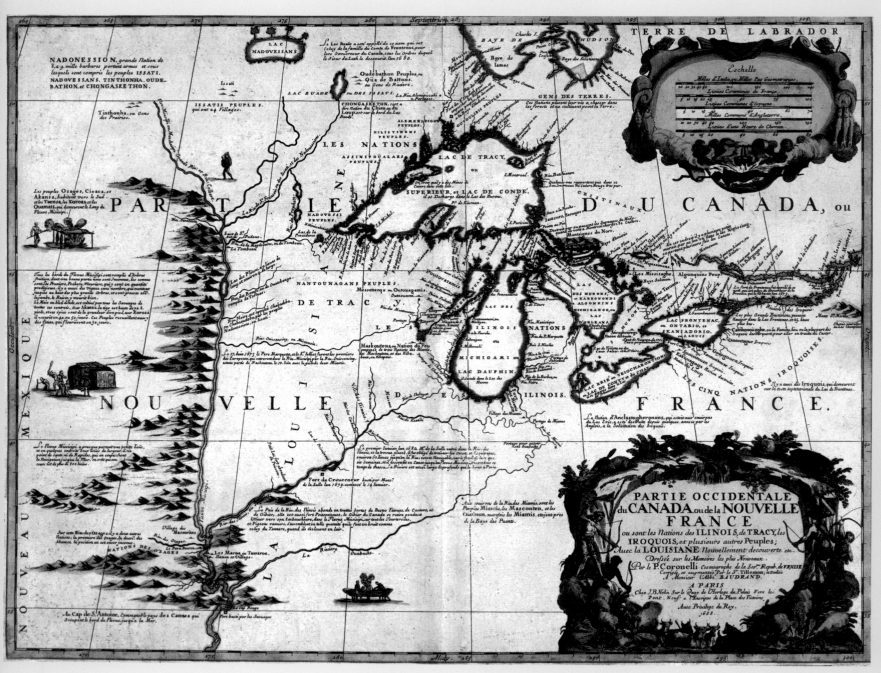

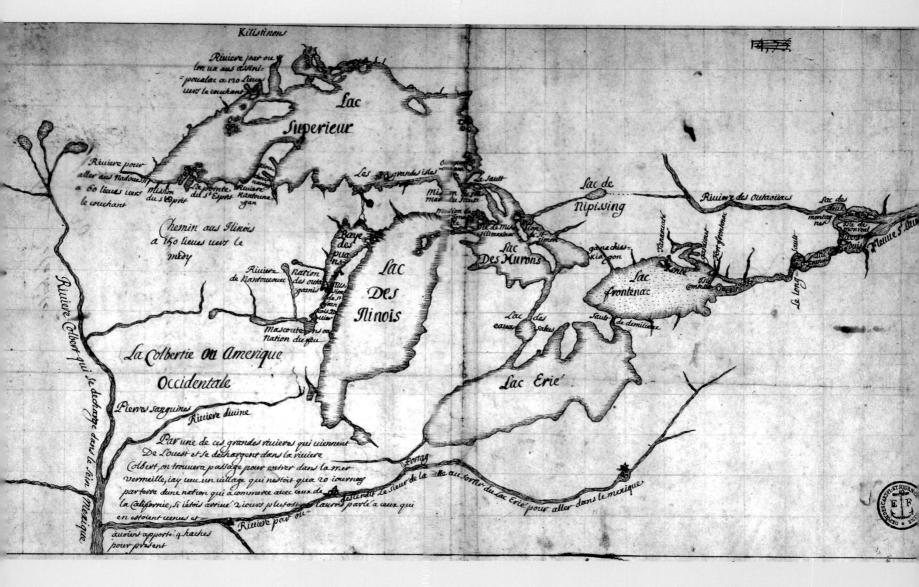

The map contains various handwritten French labels, including:

Killistinons
Lac Superieur
Riuiere pour aller aus Nadouessi a 60 lieues uers le couchant
Chemin aus Ilinois a 150 lieues uers le midy
Riuiere de Nantouessie
La Colbertie ou Amerique Occidentale
Pierres sanguines
Riuiere diuine
Riuiere Colbert qui se decharge dans le Sein Mexique
Baye des puans
Lac Des Ilinois
Les grandes isles
Lac de Nipissing
Riuiere des outaouacs
Lac Des Hurons
Lac frontenac
Lac Erie
Par une de ces grandes riuieres qui uiennent De L'ouest et se dechargent dans la riuiere Colbert, on trouuera passage pour entrer dans la mer uermeille...

Map 81.
This is a contemporary copy of one of Louis Jolliet's maps, the originals of which have been lost. Drawn about 1675, it shows the connections of the Great Lakes with the Mississippi River system. Jolliet's first route down the Wisconsin River and his return via the Illinois and the Chicago rivers is also shown. But this map is controversial for its depiction of another connection, from Lake Erie to the Wabash and the Maumee rivers to the Ohio. La Salle claimed to have discovered this as early as 1669, but recent research has shown this to be unlikely. It could have been the result of work by Sulphican missionaries François Dollier de Casson and René de Bréhant de Galineé, who were with La Salle in 1669, but a 1670 map by Bréhant de Galineé does not show it. The source remains a mystery, but there is no doubt that by the time this map was drawn the French knew of the route from Lake Erie to the Ohio. Jolliet has extrapolated the river west to join the Mississippi based on his own realization that the great river he had seen entering the Mississippi from the east must be none other than the Ohio.

that they were now deep within Spanish territory. Thus the maps Jolliet produced show the Mississippi only as far south as the Arkansas (MAP 79, left, top). Jolliet felt sure that the river emptied into the Gulf of Mexico rather than the Gulf of California.

On their return, Jolliet and Marquette found the Illinois River, which led to the Des Plaines River and the important portage to the Chicago River and Lake Michigan, a route that would become a viable link in future.

But the French government was none too keen on spreading its people far and wide across the continent, and it was only the lure of the wealth of the fur trade that led to the exploration of the rest of the Mississippi. In 1679, René-Robert Cavelier, Sieur de La Salle, was granted a monopoly of the French southwestern fur trade, and he established a fort on the St. Joseph River at the southern end of Lake Michigan. Aided by his lieutenants Henri de Tonti and Louis Hennepin, he found here another portage, this one to the Kanakee River, a tributary of the Illinois. The fur trade proved lucrative, and La Salle did not bother to travel farther south for some time. In 1680 he built Fort Crèvecoeur on the Illinois near present-day Peoria.

In 1681 La Salle finally was ready for a venture farther south. He left Montréal in August and reached the Mississippi by February 1682. By mid-March he had reached the Arkansas, now traveling quite fast with the spring current. La Salle arrived at the mouth of the Mississippi on 9 April 1682, explored the delta region, and ceremonially claimed the entire river basin for France, calling it Louisiane after King Louis and his queen, Anne. In English it became Louisiana.

La Salle returned to Fort Michilimackinac by September, a speedy transit made possible, despite being against the current, because of the lack of rapids. Traveling French explorers and fur traders normally had many rapids and waterfalls to portage around.

La Salle is known to have broken his compass during his voyage down the Mississippi. This may account for his initial maps, which show the river reaching the Gulf of Mexico hundreds of miles too far to the west (MAP 83, overleaf). What else to explain the vast gyration of the river to the west starting, interestingly but naturally enough, at just the point where Jolliet's exploration had halted?

In 1683 La Salle went back to France to gain support for the idea of establishing a colony at the mouth of the Mississippi. When this was approved, he interested investors and sailed back to the Gulf Coast in January 1685 with three hundred men in four ships. But, following his own map, he missed the Mississippi and sailed much farther west, ending up at Matagorda Bay, Texas. He soon realized that this was not the place he had visited two years before, but making the best of his situation, he built a fort he called Fort Saint-Louis. He then began a series of explorations both to the west and to the east to try to find the Mississippi. To the west he found the Rio Grande, which he ascended for three hundred miles. Overland to the northeast he found the Trinity River in eastern Texas. Trying again in 1687 La Salle was murdered by some of his men, presumably because they were fed up with his failures. But without La Salle, the rest of the men fared no better; most were massacred by Indians. Thus

MAP 82.

It's a kangaroo—no, it's a bird. North America takes on a fantastic shape in this interpretation drawn in 1678 by the hydrographer of New France, Jean-Baptiste-Louis Franquelin. Franquelin was the on-the-spot synthesizer of information from French explorers and fur traders, drawing manuscript maps that were then sent to France, where others made embellished published versions—and usually got the credit for them too. No such version of this map appears to have been made, however. Despite its obvious inaccuracies, the map was a reasonable depiction of French geographical knowledge at the time. The Mississippi, drawn from the reports of Jolliet and La Salle, flows into the Gulf of Mexico too far west, and the river rises too far north; indeed, the Mississippi would for many years be thought to have its source in what is now Canada; it would cause a myriad of problems when it came time to draw a boundary for the new United States (see page 91). A Pacific coast has been assumed not far from the Mississippi. The *Mer Vermeille* (Vermillion Sea) is the Gulf of California, where Jolliet thought he would end up. Note the dedication to French minister Colbert.

ended France's first attempt to establish a colony in their new domain of Louisiana.

The French were, perhaps understandably, slow to make another attempt to found a colony in Louisiana. In the meantime, the Spanish government became concerned that the French were encroaching on what they saw as Spanish territory. Some five overland expeditions and five naval expeditions were sent to find La Salle. In 1689 Fort Saint-Louis was found and burnt to the ground. Despite finding only a few children survivors, the searches continued. One of the naval expeditions, led by Andrés de Pez and López de Gamarra, rediscovered Pensacola Bay, which, like many features, had been known to the Spanish previously but overlooked due to excessive secrecy. In 1698 the Spanish built a fort in Pensacola Bay.

The French were finally prodded into action in 1698 by rumors of an English interest in the region. Indeed, the English in Carolina were at this time becoming interested in the lands to the west, having found the Indian trail around the southern Appalachians in 1685. And Carolina, in common with many of the English colonies, by its charters stretched right across the continent.

French naval hero Pierre Le Moyne d'Iberville was chosen to lead the expedition. He sailed in October 1698 with his brother, Jean-Baptiste

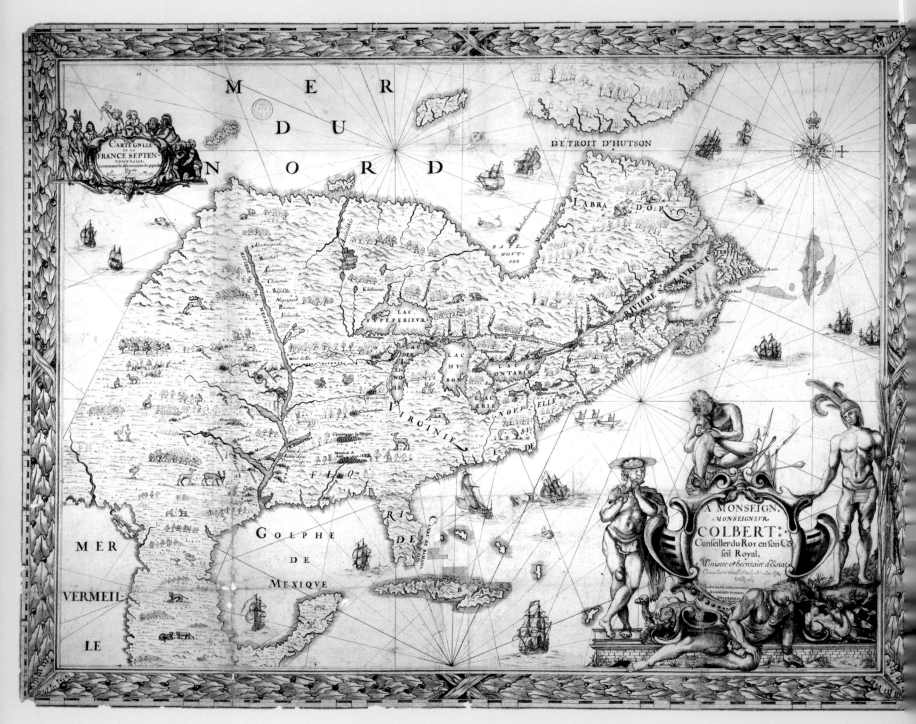

MAP 83.
La Salle's original maps have been ost, but this is a copy made by Jean-Bap ste-Louis Franquelin. It shows La Salle's grossly misplaced Mississippi flowing through Texas to the sea, a depiction perhaps the result of his broken compass. La Salle was misled by his own map, sailing to Matagorda Bay in 1685 in search of the river's mouth.

le Moyne de Bienville, four hundred men, and four ships. Like La Salle, he first had to find the Mississippi, but at least by this time French geographers had determined that it was in the center of the Gulf Coast. He first found Pensacola, where he was repulsed by the Spanish garrison, and then searched Mobile Bay. Then, on 2 March 1699, his boats located the North Pass entrance to the Mississippi. The delta area was explored, and D'Iberville established a base at Biloxi Bay before returning to France for reinforcements. When he returned in January 1700 he searched for an easier entrance to the Mississippi, for the river juts out fifty miles beyond the rest of the delta. Bienville, with the trader Louis Juchereau Saint-Denis, followed Indian advice and located a short portage to the river from Lake Pontchartrain. Here Bienville would found the city of New Orleans in 1718.

One day Bienville was shocked to suddenly encounter an English ship coming round a bend in the river. It had been sent by Daniel Coxe to investigate the country to which he had purchased an original 1629 land grant from the English king, the *Carolana* grant (see page 35). Although this was superseded by the *Carolina* grant of 1663—to eight "lords proprietors"—Coxe intended to test his rights. Bienville must have been quite the diplomat, for he managed to convince the ship's captain that the region was already claimed and in the possession of France.

Later in 1700 Bienville explored upriver, reaching as far as today's Oklahoma, while Saint-Denis explored the Red River and, the following year, the region between the Red and the Ouachita rivers. Later that year all this information was taken to France by D'Iberville, where the famous

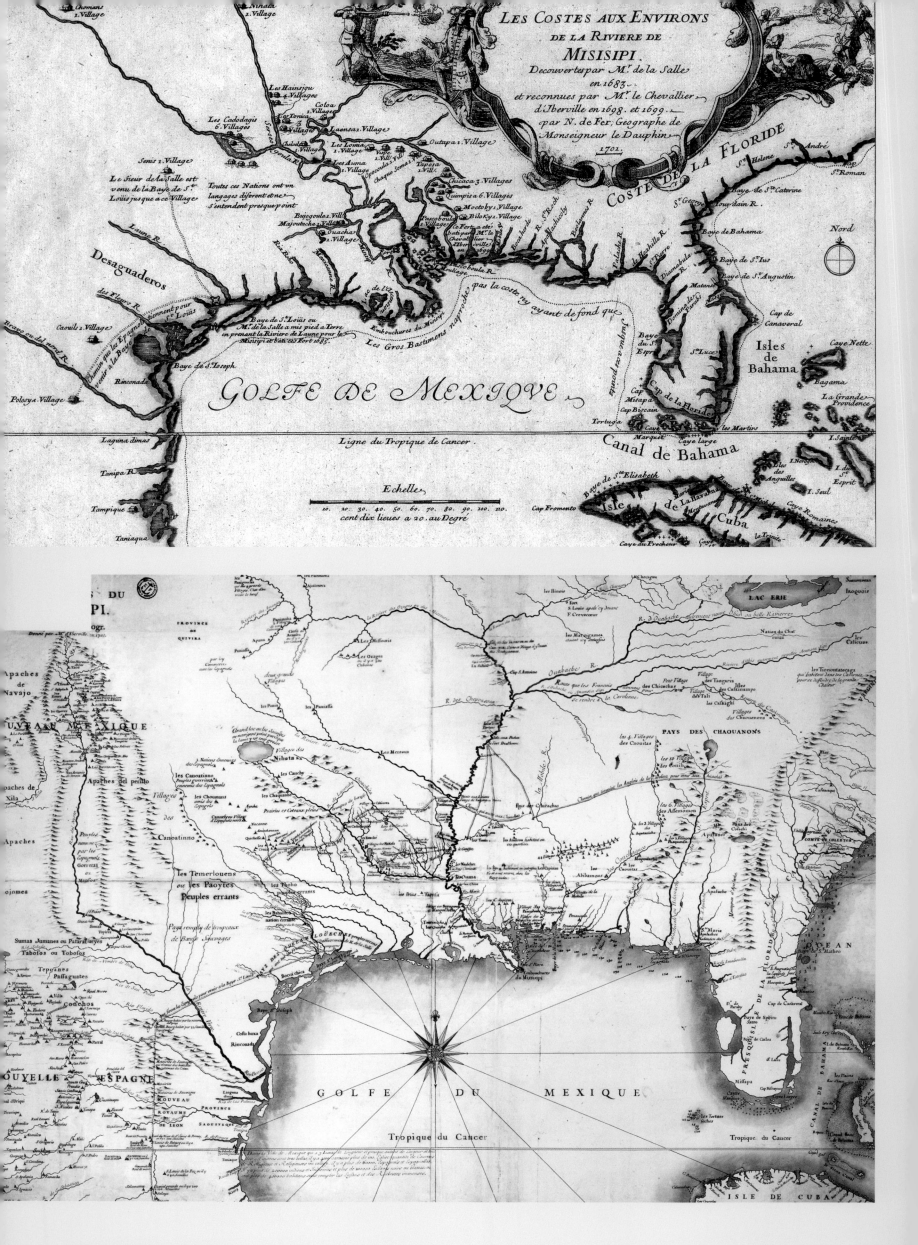

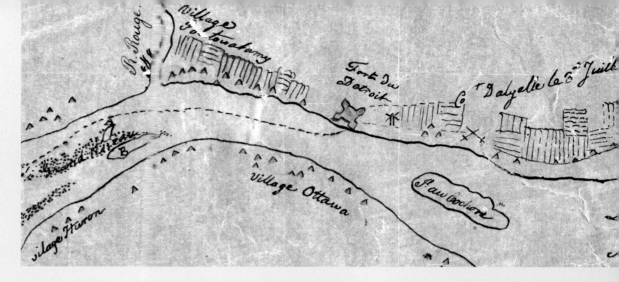

MAP 84 (*left, top*).
French mapmaker Nicholas de Fer drew this map of the Gulf Coast in 1701. The *Chemin que les Espagnols* (route of the Spanish, at far left) is the approximate route of the Spanish overland expedition that located La Salle's Fort Saint Joseph on Matagorda Bay, burning it to the ground. There is considerable detail of Indian villages in the delta area.

MAP 85 (*left, bottom*).
French geographer Guillaume De L'Isle drew this detailed map of what is now the southern part of the United States based on information brought back to France by D'Iberville in 1701. It incorporates the explorations of 1700–1701 by Bienville and Saint-Denis. The *Chemin que tiennént les Anglois* (road taken by the English) is shown from Carolina to the Mississippi. *Ouabache R.* is the Ohio River, *La Riviere des Ozagesou ou des Missouris* is the Missouri, *La Riviere des Akansa* is the Arkansas River, and *Riviere Rouge* is the Red. On the coast, *Bilocchy* is Biloxi, with its fort.

MAP 86 (*right, top*).
At the same time as the founding of Louisiana, Detroit was founded by Antoine Laumet de Lamothe Cadillac. His name would end up as a brand of automobile made in that city. This map shows the strategically located Fort Detroit and surrounding Indian villages, in 1768. Cadillac had sold Louis XIV on the idea of making the Great Lakes region secure for France, but his real motive was to monopolize the fur trade for his own profit.

MAP 87 (*right, bottom*).
During the last fifteen years of the seventeenth century, France and England were frequently at war with one another. As a reprisal for a fearsome Indian raid on Lachine, near Montréal, in 1689, Canadiens and their Indian allies attacked the New York frontier village of Schenectady in early 1690, massacring most of the inhabitants.

In May of that year, a small New England fleet of seven ships led by Sir William Phips captured and plundered Port Royal in Nova Scotia. The English monarchs William and Mary later officially united Port Royal with Massachusetts. When they returned to Boston, the New Englanders found that their plundering had been so profitable that a commercial company was established and stock sold to finance another attack. This time the target was to be Québec, the capital of New France, which promised to yield a good return on investment.

Phips sailed up the St. Lawrence with 2,300 men and 34 ships. The New England fleet appeared before Québec on 16 October 1690. It soon became clear that this was not to be an easy victory. After receiving Phips's demand for the surrender of the city, the French governor Frontenac's famous response was: "I have no reply to make to your general other than from the mouths of my cannon and muskets." Québec was so well located and defended as to be a very difficult target for any attacking force. After two days and nights of ineffective attacks and an outbreak of smallpox, the New Englanders gave up. The season was getting late and Phips realized that he could not risk being trapped by ice. The New Englanders' "investment" turned out to be a dismal failure.

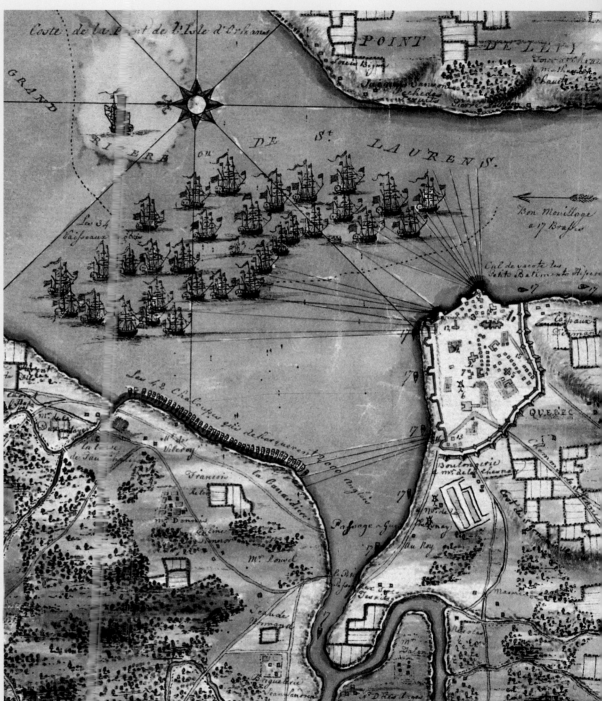

French geographer Guillaume De L'Isle compiled a map (MAP 85, *left, bottom*). It marked the official founding of the new French colony of Louisiana, decreed in 1701. Louis XIV's principal aim in establishing the colony seems to have been simply to forestall the English.

In reality, although on the map the French claim covered a huge swath of land right across the center of America, it was sparsely settled by Europeans. Other than a number of fur trade forts, population remained concentrated in Quebec, with the Mississippi Delta area beginning a slow increase after the founding of New Orleans in 1718.

Forts were built at strategic points to facilitate the French fur trade. These included Fort Detroit, built to control the waterway between Lakes Erie and Huron in 1701. Although properly sanctioned by the French king, Fort Detroit was a private venture designed to attempt to

monopolize the fur trade of the upper lakes (Map 86, *previous page*). An armed fur trade outpost called Fort Conti had been established by La Salle in 1679 where the Niagara River reaches Lake Ontario. It had not lasted long, but other temporary fur trade forts had been built on the site. Then, in 1726, the French decided to create a permanent fort on this highly strategic site guarding the route across the Niagara portage. This was largely a preemptive move to stop the British from New York from doing the same, and in the process grabbing a big slice of the French fur trade.

In the new southern colony of Louisiana, the first significant French settlement was at Biloxi, on the Gulf Coast (now Ocean Springs, Mississippi), but most settlers moved to Mobile Bay in 1701 and then to a better site within the bay in 1710, the present site of Mobile, Alabama. Here considerable fortifications were built to secure the French presence against the British (Map 91, *right*). Mobile was the capital of the colony until 1720, when, after a hurricane blocked the channels into the har-

Map 88 and Map 89 (*above, left*).
The original map showing the location and plans for Fort Niagara, drawn in 1726 and 1727, when the fort was built. The fort was at first a *maison à machicoulis*, a fortified house with overhanging dormers from which to repel attackers. It was designed by the chief engineer of New France, Gaspard-Joseph Chaussegros de Léry, who also chose the site and drew the map (Map 88). The yellow part of the plan (Map 89) is the part that existed when the plan was drawn on 11 October 1726. The photograph shows Fort Niagara as it is today.

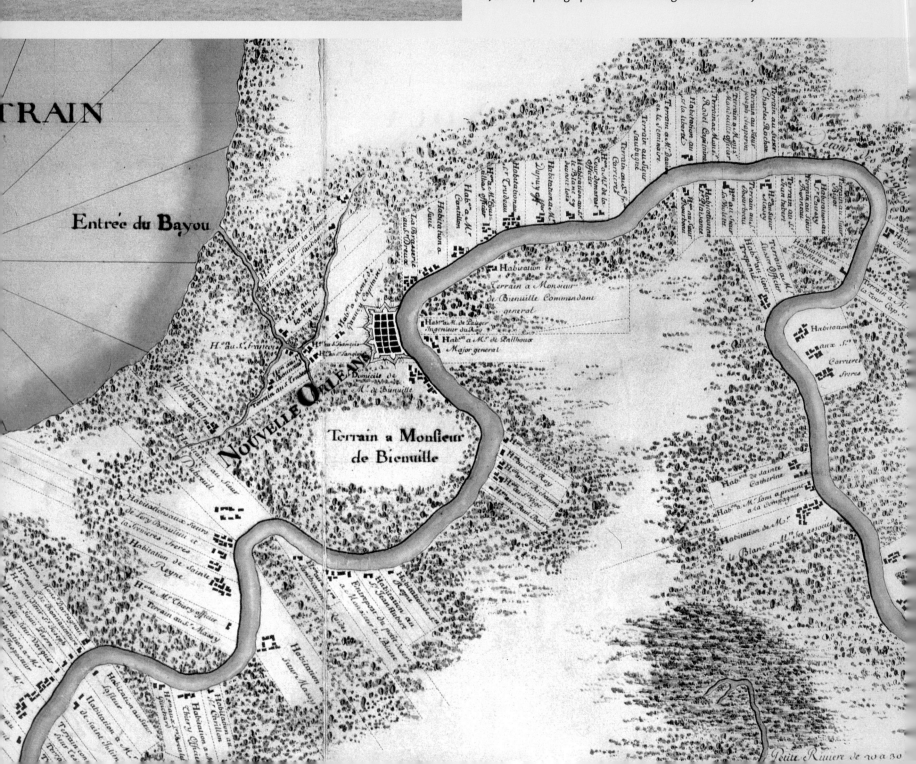

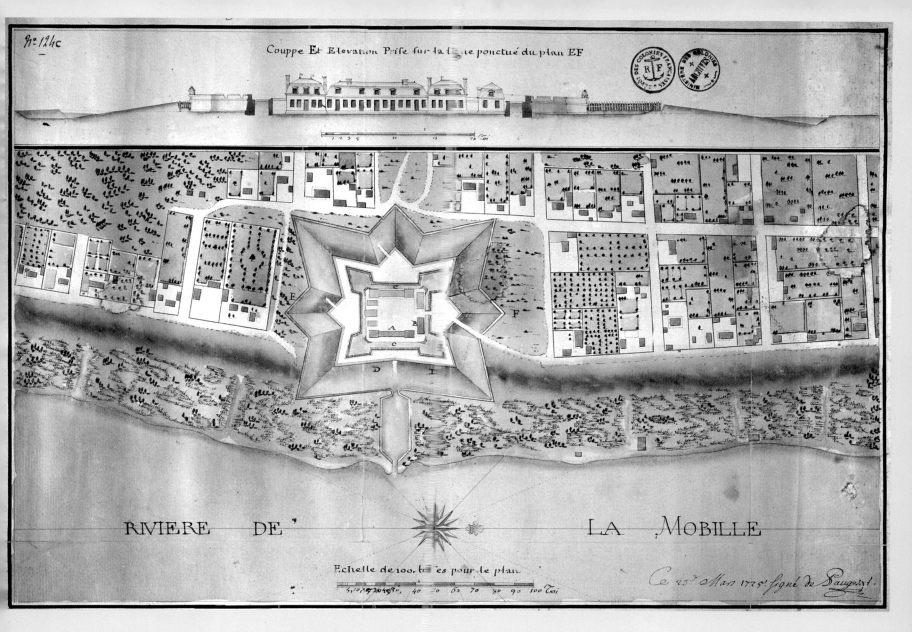

Couppe Et Elevation Prife fur la ligne ponctué du plan EF

RIVIERE DE LA MOBILLE

Echelle de 100. toifes pour le plan

Ce 23.ª Man 1725.ª figné de Pauger.t.

bor, the capital was moved to New Biloxi, and then to New Orleans in 1722.

New Orleans was established in 1718 by Bienville and a Scotsman, John Law. Named after the French regent the Duc d'Orleans, the city is built on the constricted site of a natural levee, a necessity considering that the Mississippi is here ten to fifteen feet *above* sea level. Laid out to be an important city from the beginning, New Orleans was designed by the French military engineer Adrien de Pauger in a classic gridiron pattern surrounded by impressive-looking palisades (Map 92, *right*). It would be almost a hundred years before the city had enough inhabitants to actually fill this grid.

The population of French Louisiana grew very slowly due to careful screening of immigrants, who in general had to be Catholic and conservative. Much later, Acadians—"Cajuns"—deported from Nova Scotia (French Acadia) by the British in 1755–60 settled in the lands surrounding the city, giving a boost to population growth.

One exception to this conservative attitude occurred in a short period between 1717 and 1720. A Scots gambler, John Law, ingratiated himself to the French government by setting up a bank that offered banknotes in exchange for government debt. He then founded a trading

Map 90 (*left, bottom*)
This rather beautiful map shows New Orleans and the surrounding country about 1723. The distinctive pattern of river-frontage lots is immediately obvious. Close to the new city is the *Terrain da Monsieur de Bienville*. This map is a significant historical document, for the names on almost every lot allow a detailed population list to be constructed.

Map 91 (*above*).
Dated March 1725, this maps shows the fortifications of Fort Condé (formerly Fort Louis) at Mobile together with a cross-section elevation above. Mobile had been established in 1702 and moved to its present site in 1710.

Map 92 (*below*).
A plan of New Orleans in 1769, looking much the same as on the 1723 map (Map 90). This is a British copy of a French plan. Although the walls look impressive, they were in reality but a wooden palisade.

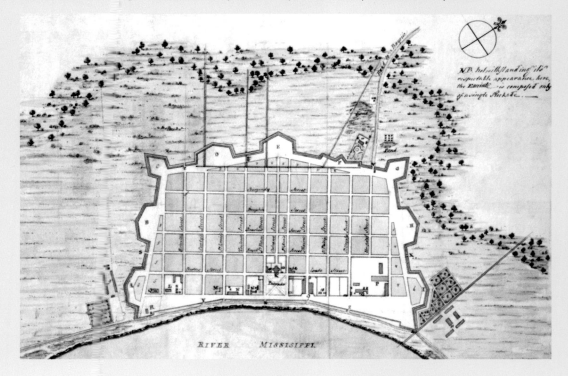

RIVER MISSISIPI

Map 93.

Considered one of the seminal maps of America, this *Carte de la Louisiane* (Map of Louisiana) was published in 1718 by the French mapmaker Guillaume De L'Isle utilizing the best information available at that time. The French claim is clear and large: *La Louisiane* stretches from the Spanish *Nouveau Mexique* on the Rio Grande, at left, to the British colonies of *Virginie* and *Caroline*, at right. No British transcontinental colonies here! The course of the Mississippi is by now quite well defined, and the Lower Missouri, explored by Bourgmont in 1714 and mapped by De L'Isle himself two years later, is shown on this map, though beyond Bourgmont's ascent the map uses only Indian reports. The courses of the west bank tributaries of the Mississippi are almost all incorrect for only their lower reaches had been seen by French explorers by 1718. The routes of La Salle, D'Iberville, Saint-Denis, and others are shown.

company, the Compagnie d'Occident, in 1717, and was given a charter to colonize Louisiana. In 1719, by consolidating this with other companies and (in February 1720) his bank, Law created the Compagnie des Indes, popularly called the Mississippi Company. Law created such a marketing buzz in France that he was able to finance his venture with the sale of stock, which, in classic "bubble" fashion still referred to in business texts, became grossly overvalued. Law painted a picture of Louisiana as a land full of gold, emerald rocks, and fertile lands, but by November 1720, the bubble had burst and Law had to flee from an angry mob. Thousands were ruined and the French currency was destabilized. Thus did Louisiana get off to a rocky start, although there were some benefits. Law had settled several thousand Alsace Germans, which significantly increased

the colony's population, and New Orleans itself was partly the result of the Mississippi Company and its predecessor's potential.

In the years following the establishment of the Louisiana colony, a number of attempts were made to explore rivers westward. The motivation was not imperial but private trade, especially in furs. The Missouri, the extension of the Mississippi to the northwest that would prove to be a major highway in future, was explored as far north as the Platte River in 1714 by Étienne de Véniard, Sieur de Bourgmont. The onetime commandant of Cadillac's Fort Detroit collected detailed information that later allowed the geographer Guillaume De L'Isle to create the first accurate map of the lower Missouri (Map 95, *right, bottom*).

In 1718 the governor of Louisiana, Bienville, having just founded New Orleans, sent out expeditions to attempt to trade with Indians. In 1718 Jean-Baptiste Bénard, Sieur de La Harpe, was sent to the Pawnee country with fifty men and five boats loaded with six tons of trade goods. He ascended the Red River from Natchitoches, a post that had been established by Saint-Denis in 1714 after he was sent to find a trade route to New Spain. Saint-Denis had ascended the Red River and then set out overland through Texas, reaching the Rio Grande before being arrested by Spanish authorities. In 1721 La Harpe also traveled across country, this time to the north, finding the Arkansas River and exploring it both to the east and west before being stopped by unfriendly Indians. The information he collected, however, was substantial, and later allowed construction of a detailed map (Map 94, *right, top*).

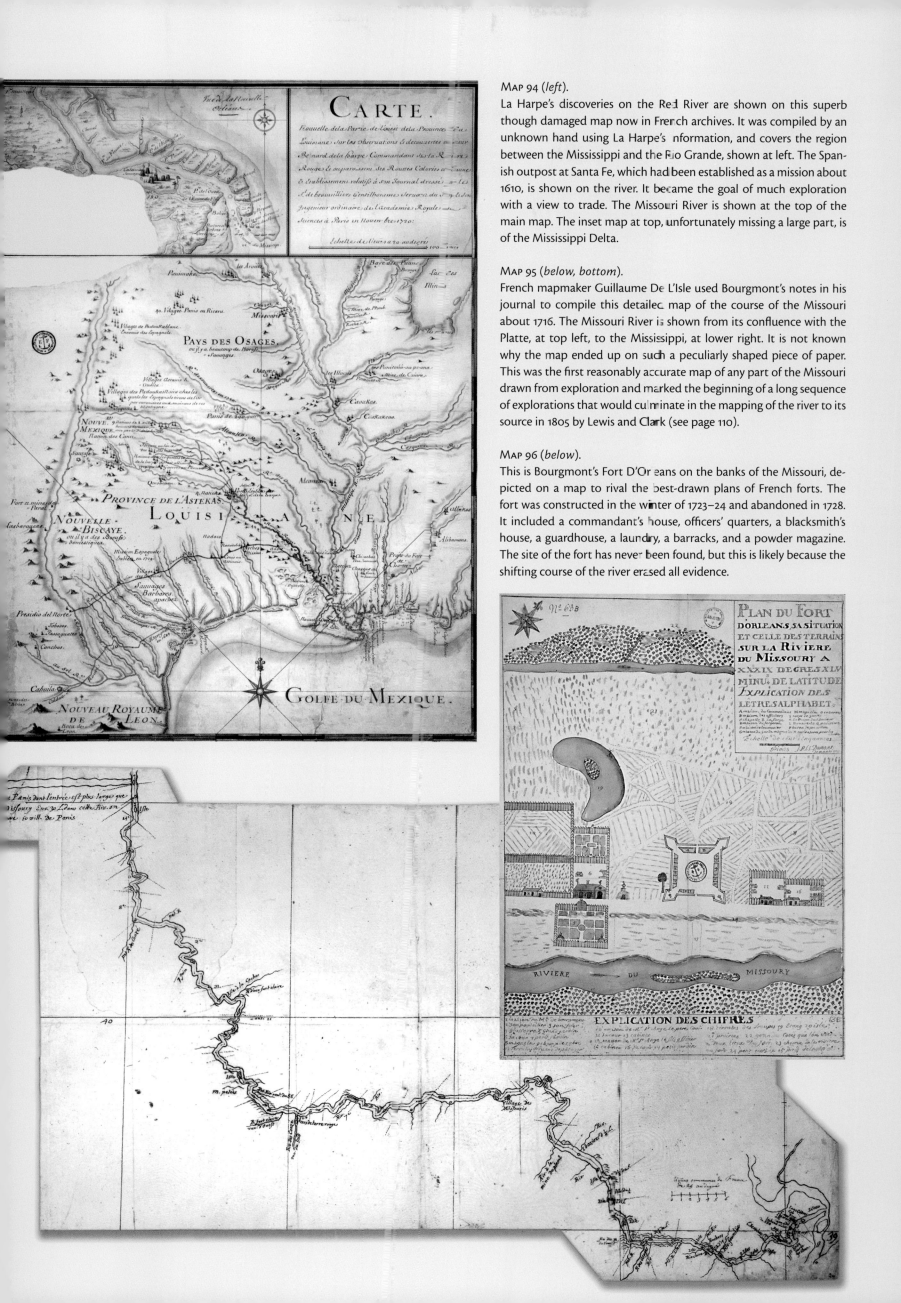

MAP 94 (*left*).

La Harpe's discoveries on the Red River are shown on this superb though damaged map now in French archives. It was compiled by an unknown hand using La Harpe's information, and covers the region between the Mississippi and the Rio Grande, shown at left. The Spanish outpost at Santa Fe, which had been established as a mission about 1610, is shown on the river. It became the goal of much exploration with a view to trade. The Missouri River is shown at the top of the main map. The inset map at top, unfortunately missing a large part, is of the Mississippi Delta.

MAP 95 (*below, bottom*).

French mapmaker Guillaume De L'Isle used Bourgmont's notes in his journal to compile this detailed map of the course of the Missouri about 1716. The Missouri River is shown from its confluence with the Platte, at top left, to the Mississippi, at lower right. It is not known why the map ended up on such a peculiarly shaped piece of paper. This was the first reasonably accurate map of any part of the Missouri drawn from exploration and marked the beginning of a long sequence of explorations that would culminate in the mapping of the river to its source in 1805 by Lewis and Clark (see page 110).

MAP 96 (*below*).

This is Bourgmont's Fort D'Orleans on the banks of the Missouri, depicted on a map to rival the best-drawn plans of French forts. The fort was constructed in the winter of 1723–24 and abandoned in 1728. It included a commandant's house, officers' quarters, a blacksmith's house, a guardhouse, a laundry, a barracks, and a powder magazine. The site of the fort has never been found, but this is likely because the shifting course of the river erased all evidence.

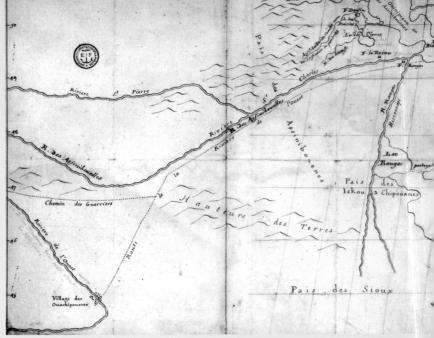

MAP 97 (*above*).

Covering a huge area of the West, this map of rivers and lakes has Hudson Bay at the top edge, Lake Superior at the top right edge, and a River of the West flowing southwest to a Western Sea (*Mer Inconnuë*, unknown sea) at the bottom left corner. The latter may have been the Gulf of California, or it could have been the Great Salt Lake of Utah. This is what the La Vérendryes were looking for, and they sent this map to the governor of New France in 1737. The map is derived as much from their hopes as from reality, but it was used to support a plea to be allowed further exploration. *Lac 8inipigon* is Lake Winnipeg; *Lac Rouge* is Upper and Lower Red Lake in Minnesota.

MAP 98 (*above, right*).

La Vérendrye's journey from Lake Winnipeg to the Mandan villages on the Great Bend of the Missouri is shown on this 1733 map drawn by his nephew, Christophe Dufrost de La Jemerais.

Another trade expedition was sent out by Bienville and led by one of his officers, Claude Charles du Tisné. In 1719 Tisné went up the Missouri and then the Osage River, but was stopped by Pawnee in what is now northeastern Oklahoma.

In 1720 news reached Paris of a Spanish military expedition to stop French incursions into what the Spanish authorities saw as their territory. Both the Spanish and the French at this time thought that the route to Santa Fe lay up the Missouri. This only heightened the French desire to ensure the river was claimed for France. In 1722 Bourgmont, as the reigning expert on the region, was appointed "Commandant of the Missouri River" and dispatched to both make peace with the Indians and establish a trade with Santa Fe.

Delayed by a hurricane, malaria, and Bienville, who wanted to organize his own expedition, Bourgmont set out in February 1723. In the winter of 1723–24 he built a post he called Fort D'Orleans near today's Miami, Missouri, about seventy-five miles east of Kansas City (MAP 96, *previous page*). Bourgmont made a number of forays west, deep into Padouca territory, often accompanied by hundreds of Kansa Indians. He did achieve an alliance with the Padouca, but did not get anywhere near Santa Fe. The alliance ultimately proved unsustainable, and Fort D'Orleans was abandoned in 1728. But French geographical knowledge, if not influence, was extended far to the west.

The Missouri was one possible manifestation of a popular myth that had arisen by this time, that there was a so-called River of the West that flowed to a Western Sea, a supposed embayment of the Pacific Ocean (see page 105). Another French explorer, Pierre Gaultier de Varennes et de La Vérendrye, and his sons and nephew, had been searching westwards farther north, in what is today Canada, finding Lake Winnipeg by 1734. In 1738, on the direct instructions of the governor of New France at Québec, La Vérendrye set off overland to the southwest and found (it is thought) the Missouri, likely at the Mandan villages at the river's "Big Bend" (MAP 98, *above*), well known because of their later association with

MAP 99 (*left*).

Louisiana in 1747. Some of the letters in red are *A* Mobile; *B* Biloxi; *C* New Orleans; and *G* marks the place where the German immigrants were settled.

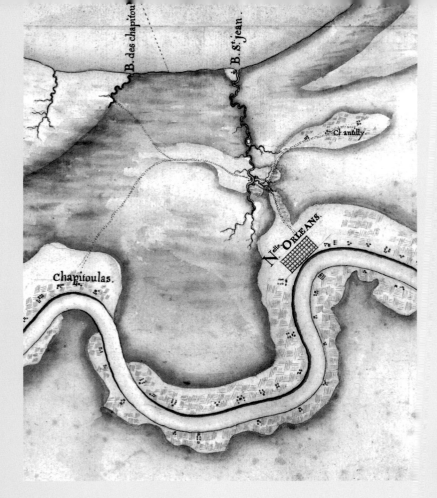

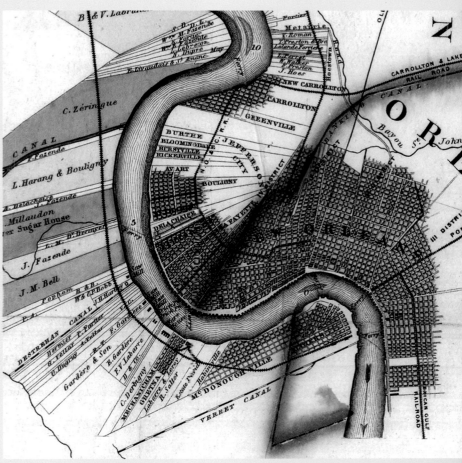

MAP 100 (*left*).
New Orleans and vicinity, shown on a 1749 map. It depicts the distribution of settlement along the levees adjacent to the river, the only dry ground and the only place suitable for building.

MAP 101 (*below*).
The longlot system of land subdivision is shown very clearly on this 1858 map of New Orleans and vicinity.

MAP 102 (*below, bottom*).
Longlots front a bayou, a former meander of the Mississippi now bypassed by the main channel in this colorful map, another part of the same 1858 map as MAP 101. The area shown is just north of Baton Rouge.

Lewis and Clark. In 1743 La Vérendrye dispatched his two sons, Louis-Joseph and François (known as the Chevalier), even farther west, where they made a far-ranging reconnaissance. Unfortunately the pair made no map that has survived, so we do not know exactly where they went, but they did report seeing a range of mountains, which were likely either the Big Horn Mountains in northern Wyoming or the Black Hills of western South Dakota. An apparently genuine lead plate claiming the land for Louis XV was unearthed near Pierre, North Dakota, in 1913. Such was the farthest northwestward staking of the French claim to the territory now the United States.

The elusive Santa Fe was reached in 1739. Two brothers, Pierre and Paul Mallet, reached the Missouri at the northeastern tip of Nebraska, where they were advised by Pawnee Indians to travel overland to the southwest. Following this advice the Mallets reached Santa Fe in July 1739 and were welcomed by its inhabitants, despite the illegality of Spanish trade with the French. The Santa Fe Trail, which would become one of the major routes west, had been found.

Continued evidence of the French period in Louisiana can be found in the layout of lots. The "longlot" system, originally developed in France, was well suited to conditions along the Mississippi. These long and narrow lots fronting onto the river allowed each farmer an equal share of the natural levees, which provided the only well-drained land, as well as the swampier backlot land with its access to fishing and stream transportation. Houses were built on the higher land and thus tended to form a continuous line village (MAP 100, *above*). Modern maps show this system in a number of places where there was French settlement, such as around Cahokia, Illinois; Vincennes, Indiana; Monroe, Michigan; and Detroit, as well as most of lowland Louisiana. MAPS 101 and 102 on this page show examples from the mid-nineteenth century, including New Orleans itself; MAP 90, *page 46*, shows the initial lot layout around New Orleans.

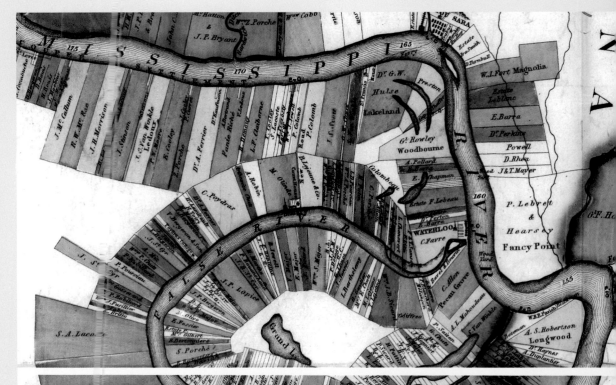

Across the Mountain Barrier

As we have seen, when Europeans first found the North American continent they had been searching for a westward route to China and the riches of the East. It was not until the seventeenth century that explorers set out from eastern coastal settlements to try to find a way to the Southern Sea overland, usually using rivers as their pathways. First they had to overcome the misconception of distance. Early maps, such as Map 104, *below*, and Map 105, *right, top*, still showed their expectations: that the Pacific was just on the other side of the Appalachians. It took news of the French discovery of the Mississippi to disavow them of this idea for good.

One longtime believer that the Pacific was nearby was Abraham Wood, commander of Fort Henry, built at the falls of the Appomattox River in Virginia to counter Indian raids. In 1649 he explored inland with Edward Bland, south to the Roanoke River; although he found no ocean, his belief in the nearby Pacific remained intact. Bland published a book the following year that extolled the glories of Virginia for settlement, and John Farrer, an English merchant, drew a map for the book that incorporated Wood and Bland's geographical ideas (Map 104, *below,* and Map 105, *right, top*).

Another believer in a nearby Western Sea was William Berkeley, the governor of Virginia. He commissioned John Lederer to undertake three explorations in 1669–70, in which he reached the Blue Mountains and the Piedmont of North Carolina. Lederer also wrote a book, in which his friend William Talbot wrote in the foreword: "From this discourse it is clear that the long-looked-for discovery of the Indian Sea does nearly approach." In fact Lederer found no such evidence and conceded that the ocean was more than ten days away. He turned back because of Indian reports of bearded men whom he took to be Spaniards, upon whose territory he did not want to trespass.

After the French discovery of the Mississippi, the English desire to cross the mountains did not lessen, but their motivation changed to Indian trade and discovery of mineral wealth, and later to just the desire for land itself. And here they would clash with the French.

In 1715 a new lieutenant governor of Virginia, Alexander Spotswood, became a promoter of westward expansion both for the gathering of wealth and for containment of the French. He led an improbable expedition of sixty colonial gentlemen, dubbed the Knights of the Golden Horseshoe, through Swift Run Gap across the Blue Ridge Mountains and south along the Shenandoah Valley to where Staunton, Virginia, now stands.

Farther south, the terrain was less daunting, and by the early eighteenth century trade routes had been established deep into the interior (Map 106, *right, bottom*), leading west from the trade center of Charles Town (Charleston, South Carolina). As a result of this trade, the

Map 103 (*above*).
Daunting mountain ranges to be crossed by all those trekking west are shown in a detail of a map drawn in 1765, by which time the rivers on the other side, such as the Ohio, shown here, were well known to Americans.

MAP 104 (*left*).

This engraved version of John Farrer's map (MAP 105) was published in 1651 in a book by Edward Bland called the *Discoverie of New Britaine*. The Pacific Ocean, the *Sea of China and the Indies*, is shown only *ten dayes march . . . from the head of the leames [James] River, over those hills and through the rich adjacent Vallyes*. And there, to establish the English claim to the Pacific coast, is a portrait of Francis Drake, who *was on this sea and landed An° 1577 [sic, 1579] . . . where hee tooke Possession in the name of Q: Eliza: Calling it new Albion*. At far right is the Hudson River, found by Englishman Henry Hudson in 1609 while under contract to the Dutch (see page 31), but it is shown leading almost to the Pacific, from which it is separated by only a small neck of land. An edition of this map published earlier in 1651 had not shown even this impediment to through navigation.

MAP 106 (*right*).

Routes from Charles Town (later Charleston) to the Mississippi are shown in this 1711 map, which promotes an extensive South Carolina at the expense of any French claims. It was drawn by explorer-adventurer Thomas Nairne and incorporates his explorations while slave-hunting in southern Florida in 1702. The Everglades are shown dissecting the tip of the peninsula.

Below. The view west from the summit of the Blue Ridge Mountains in Shenandoah National Park, near Swift Run Gap, Virginia.

MAP 105 (*above*).

Virginia and New England as drawn by John Farrer in 1651, incorporating the explorations—and expectations—of Edward Bland and Abraham Wood the year before. North is at right. Despite its crude outline, the northeastern coast of the United States is quite recognizable. Note *Cape Codd* and *Roanoke*, the site of the first English settlement, now regranted as Carolana. The Roanoke River is at left center and the Hudson River, at right center, leads to the West Sea—the Pacific Ocean.

MAP 107.
John Barnwell's seminal map of 1716, showing all the trails from Charles Town. The map is very detailed and thus difficult to read at this scale. Most of these trails were existing Indian trails found by EuroAmericans; even before they were Indian trails, many parts of them were trails formed by animals. Some trails are marked with the names of their EuroAmerican discoverers. For example, the trail that meets the Mississippi (at left) about halfway up is annotated *The Course Capt Welch took in 1698*. Trader Thomas Welch followed this trail in 1698 and set up a trading post on the Mississippi; this is also shown on the map as *The Captains*. The map also contains notes as to the nature of the country; for instance, the Pine Barrens of Georgia and South Carolina are marked *A vast Pine Country full of Buffalo bear and Venison*. The Ohio River flows into the Mississippi at top left, joining another large unnamed river (the Tennessee) as it does so. Just to the south of the latter river, the crude lines of rocks are marked *A Ridge of high Mountains reaching to the Charokees called by The Spaniards the Aplachlan Mountains*—the Appalachians.

country was relatively well known, and by 1716 Charles Town resident John Barnwell, or "Tuscarora Jack," as he was known, was able to compile a map that depicted the South in considerable detail, far better than the northern interior was known at the time (MAP 107, *above*). Unfortunately not well preserved, the map is what has been called a "mother map," that is, one used as a source for others. Indeed, some of the better known significant maps of colonial America contain information about the South taken from Barnwell's map. These include Henry Popple's multisheet *Map of the British Empire in America* (MAP 69, *page 36*), published in 1733, and John Mitchell's *Map of the British and French Dominions in North America* (MAP 72, *page 37*), published in 1755 and several other editions to 1775.

To the north, where the mountain chains proved a significant barrier to east-west movement, passes needed to be found. One of the widest, the Cumberland Gap, although known since the 1670s, was rediscovered in 1750 by Thomas Walker, a surveyor for the Loyal Land Company, which in 1749 had been granted 800,000 acres of land in the valleys to the west. Between 1775 and 1810 perhaps as many as 300,000 settlers would traverse the Cumberland Gap to reach Kentucky beyond (see page 99).

Traders exploring westward from Virginia found the Ohio Valley. This valuable fur trade region was also claimed by the French as part of the Mississippi system. As such, it was to become a battleground in future years. The Virginia Council granted 10,000 acres of Ohio lands to John Howard in 1737 on condition that he explore west to the Mississippi. Together with a German resident of Virginia, John Peter Salley,

Howard reached the Mississippi in 1742 but was arrested by the French, taken to New Orleans, and thrown in jail. Salley managed to escape and after two years made it back to Virginia, and information from his journal was used by Joshua Fry and Peter Jefferson in their important 1751 map (MAP 111, *right, bottom*), which would guide new settlers to the Ohio Country.

By 1749 the French attempted to definitively claim—in their terms—the Ohio Country for France by sending two hundred soldiers down the Ohio to nail up lead plates proclaiming French ownership. The British took no notice, and that same year granted 200,000 acres of land along the upper Ohio to the Ohio Company of Virginia (also called the First Ohio Company, since there was a later company; see page 98).

The company hired a skilled backwoods surveyor, Christopher Gist, to explore and survey this land. Gist made two explorations of the Ohio, in 1750–51 and 1751–52, reaching as far west as the Scioto River, about a hundred miles east of today's Cincinnati. He found a route west through the mountains along the valley of the Potomac River. In June 1752 he and George Croghan, who had set up a number of trading posts, met with the Indians and negotiated British settlement rights east of the Ohio River itself. But now the French would give the British more trouble; that same year they destroyed Croghan's posts and began building a chain of forts with the intent of keeping the English out. The struggle for the Ohio Country was the main cause of the French and Indian War between France and Britain (see page 56).

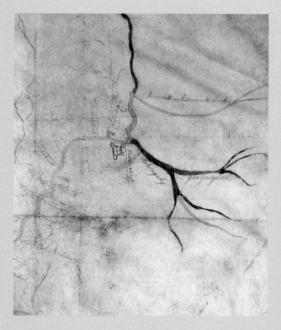

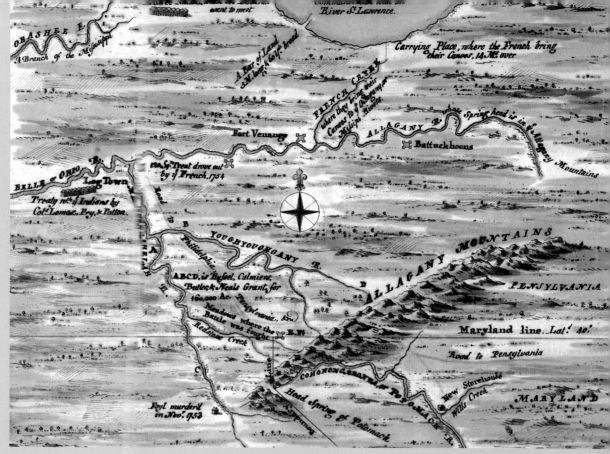

MAP 108 (*above*).
Christopher Gist's map of the Monongahela and Ohio rivers, drawn in 1754 on an animal hide. The new French Fort Duquesne (see page 58) is at the confluence of the two rivers.

MAP 109 (*above, right*).
The goal of many EuroAmericans by the middle of the eighteenth century was the Ohio Valley, shown here rather beautifully on a 1754 map, drawn by one Captain Snow, about which we know nothing, but including "the best accounts he could receive from the Indian traders." French forts at Venango and Duquesne (Pittsburgh) and elsewhere are shown in red. The French attempted to keep other Euro-Americans out of the Ohio Country with a chain of forts at strategic positions.

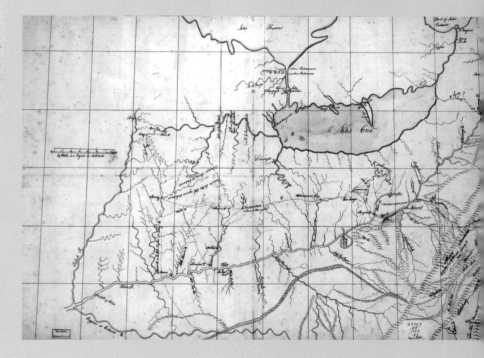

MAP 110 (*right*).
About 1752 a British trader, John Patten, drew this map of the Ohio basin based on a combination of his own knowledge and information from Indians with whom he traded. Essentially accurate, the map reveals that much of the geography was known at least in outline by this time.

MAP 111 (*below*).
This is part of an important map drawn by Joshua Fry and Peter Jefferson (father of Thomas) in 1751. It is their *Map of the most inhabited part of Virginia*, a vast compendium of information from their own surveys and traders and explorers. The representation of the multilinear Allegheny Mountains is particularly striking, emphasizing the need to locate the few places where the rivers breach the mountain chains. This map was used to guide settlers to the Ohio Country.

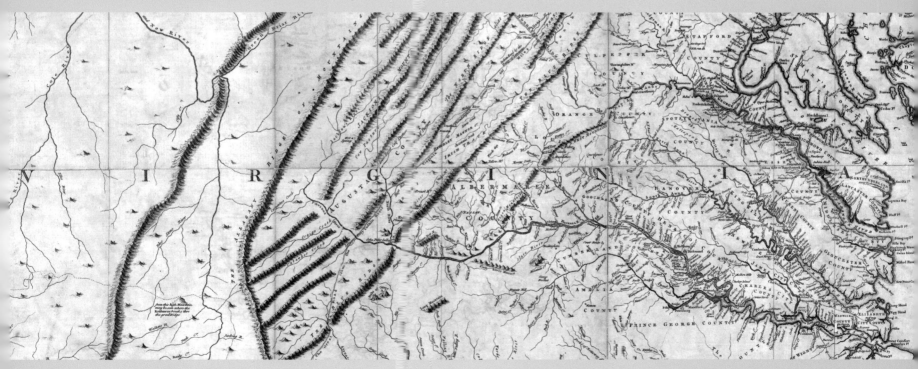

The End of the French Empire

France and Britain had so long been enemies by 1754 that going to war over a clash of territorial ambitions in the Ohio Country seemed inevitable. Britain (before 1707, England)—and by extension its American colonies—was at war with France from 1688 to 1697 (King William's War) and from 1702 to 1713 (Queen Anne's War). In 1711 a huge combined British and New England fleet of more than seventy ships and twelve thousand men under Hovenden Walker had sailed on Québec only to come to grief in the St. Lawrence through incompetent navigation.

An uneasy period of peace after the Treaty of Utrecht of 1713 lasted until 1740, when a European war began over the succession to the Austrian throne, spreading to North America as King George's War in 1744, ending in 1748. In 1745 New England militia captured Louisbourg, a French stronghold that had been built on the coast of Cape Breton Island beginning in 1719. The assault was led by William Pepperrell, a colonel in the Maine militia and a merchant with much to gain from a British victory. He was supported by a British fleet. This was a relatively rare example of cooperation between colonial American forces and British regulars, but it ended in bickering, each claiming the victory for themselves. The Americans were further disgusted when, three years later, the British signed a peace treaty—the Treaty of Aix-la-Chapelle—that gave a hard-won Louisbourg back to the French.

The wars to this time had all been European conflicts that had spread to North America. But in 1754 the long quarrel over the Ohio became a military one, and in 1756 this sequence of events was reversed as the conflict spread to Europe, where it became known as the Seven Years' War. In America, and lasting for nine years, it was called the French and Indian War. To the French in Canada it became known as the War of the Conquest, for it ended in the collapse of the French empire in North America.

In July 1752 a new governor general of New France, Ange Duquesne de Menneville, Marquis Duquesne, arrived at Québec with instructions to secure the Ohio country for France. The following year he ordered forts to be established at strategic points. The first was built on the south shore of Lake Erie at Presqu'isle (now Erie, Pennsylvania) and the second, Fort Le Boeuf, at the other end of a portage to the Ohio system (at today's Waterford, Pennsylvania), on Le Boeuf Creek, which leads to French Creek. The latter was completed in August 1753. News of the building of the two forts reached the British, and in late 1753 the lieutenant governor of Virginia, Robert Dinwiddie, dispatched a young major in the Virginia militia, George Washington, to carry a letter to the French commander in the Ohio region, a letter demanding the removal of the forts.

Washington was very politely rebuffed and in January 1754 returned to Virginia to report. He recommended the construction of a fort at the forks of the Ohio, where the river splits into the Monongahela and the Allegheny. Carpenters were dispatched immediately to begin construction. In April, as the fort, which they named Fort George, was completed, the builders were confronted by a French force and, hopelessly outnumbered, had to abandon the new structure. In turn, the French much enlarged and improved the fort to create Fort Duquesne (MAP 115, *overleaf*).

At the same time Fort George was abandoned, Washington returned with a few hundred men and camped at Great Meadows, about sixty-five miles southwest of the fort. Here he heard of a French force approaching. In fact the French had sent out a party of only thirty-six men, under a junior officer, Ensign Joseph Coulon de Villiers de Jumonville, to ask Washington to leave. Although his orders from Dinwiddie were to "act on the Difensive," Washington was eager to make a name for himself, and with Indian allies attacked the French at their encampment early in the morning of 28 May. The attack turned into a massacre of the wounded, including Jumonville, by the Indians. The war had turned from one of words to one of action.

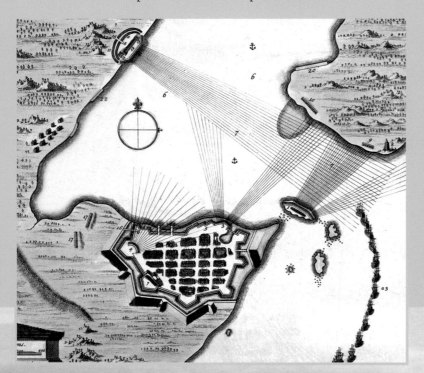

MAP 112 (*left*).
A broadsheet map of the French fortress at Louisbourg, published in 1745 after its first fall, to a New England ground force and a British naval fleet under the command of Commodore Peter Warren, shown here in a semicircle. The harbor was well defended, as the gun ranges and positions show. Indeed, it was probably invincible from a naval attack alone. The town was taken by land, with the New England forces arriving at Gabarus Bay, to the south (not shown on this map) and laying siege. The outlying gun battery, the Grand or Royal Battery on the northwestern shore, was taken first. The British ships blockaded the harbor, then intercepted a large French warship carrying reinforcements and powder. Acting on intelligence that the French were now running out of powder, the New England commander, William Pepperrell, gave his gunners orders to "Fire Smartly at ye Citty," which they did until their cannon "ware So hott they could not fire any more." He was attempting to get the French to use up the rest of their powder. The town surrendered on 28 June 1745.

Below. A view of the fortress of Louisbourg across the harbor as it looks today. The town was completely razed after its second fall in 1758 but has been partially reconstructed and today is a Canadian National Historic Site.

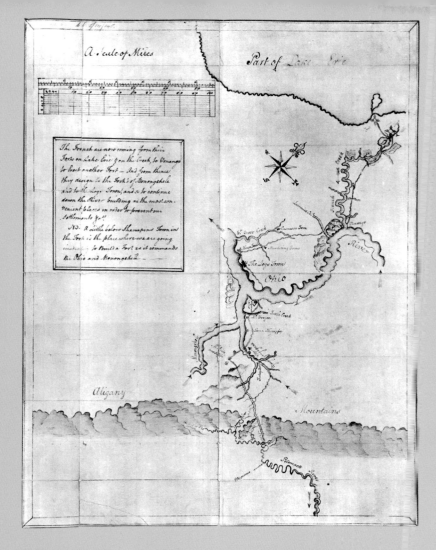

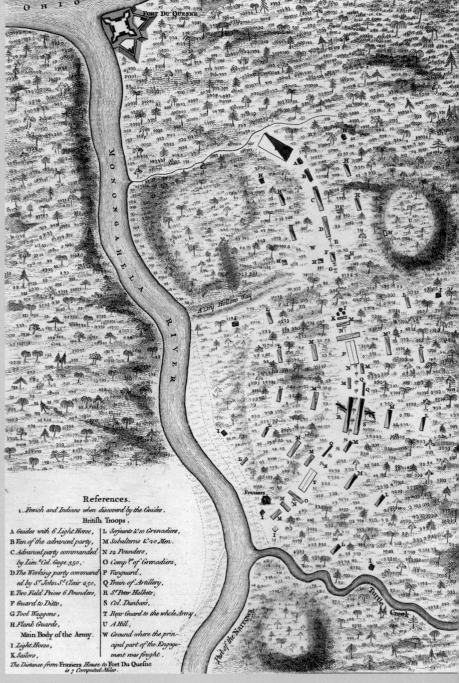

MAP 113 (*above*).
This map of the upper Ohio river system was drawn by George Washington during his first reconnaissance of the region and visit to the French Fort Le Boeuf, November 1753–January 1754. The forts at Presqu'isle and Le Boeuf are shown at top (but not named). Where French Creek enters the Allegheny (Ohio) is Venango, where the French began their third fortification, Fort D'Anjou, late in 1754, which was not finished, and Fort Machault in 1755. This was the site of a later British fort, Fort Venango. At bottom, near the head of the *Potomack River*, is *Wills Creek*, Washington's supply base that became the site of the British Fort Cumberland.

Washington was to regret his impulsiveness, for his small army was no match for the real French strength in the area. Anticipating a reprisal, he retreated to Great Meadows and built a palisade around his encampment, which he called Fort Necessity. When a French force of about six hundred and a hundred Indians attacked, on 3 July, it was pouring with rain. Washington's men, exposed to the wet in shallow trenches, soon could not return fire from the French sheltering in the trees. Facing certain annihilation, Washington accepted surrender terms that allowed him to retreat to his supply base at Wills Creek, at the head of the Potomac River, leaving the Ohio Country in the hands of the French.

This the British could not accept. After political maneuvering, the Duke of Cumberland began to formulate the government policy in North America, a move that was almost bound to escalate the war and extend it to Europe. For Cumberland, favorite son of King George II, was not one for statesmanship. He had earned the moniker "butcher of Culloden" for his vicious suppression of Bonnie Prince Charlie's rebellion in Scotland in 1745 and thought he could do much the same with the French in America. But he had no idea of the differences between operating in Britain and in America, and he appointed as commander-in-chief Edward Braddock, an experienced soldier with no idea either.

The overall plan conceived in London was far too grandiose for the resources available. Braddock was to take Fort Duquesne; colonial troops from Albany were to take Fort Niagara, seen as the key to the Ohio Country; more were to take Fort Frédéric, a French fort on Lake Champlain; and an expedition from Boston was to capture French forts in Nova Scotia.

MAP 114 (*above*).
Originally drawn by one of the few surviving officers of Braddock, this engraved map shows the position of the various elements of Braddock's army at the time it was attacked by the French, repesented by the largest rectangle near the top of the map. *Fort Du Quesne* is shown at top left, but the action was farther away from the fort than this representation would lead one to believe. The British column was led by officers who would take a much larger place in American history later: Lieutenant Colonel Thomas Gage led three hundred men in column C, and Captain Horatio Gates led New York provincials guarding the working party widening the road, at D.

Braddock was insensitive to the Indian cause, telling his own native allies the Ohio Valley was to be British. Hence most disappeared even before he left Fort Cumberland with about 2,200 men on 29 May 1755; this was to make a critical difference. Braddock tried to haul cannon and far too much baggage through the difficult country toward Fort Duquesne, and the road had to be widened as they traveled. Many men fell ill, and horses died. On 9 July, the first part of his by now strung-out army was only ten miles from the fort. Here he was attacked by a much smaller but much fresher French force consisting of fewer than a hundred army regulars and militiamen but supported by over three hundred of their Indian allies (MAP 114, *above*). The area was an Indian hunting ground and had been cleared of much of the underbrush that might have given Braddock's men some cover as they were fired upon from behind the trees. The British tried to fight using their normal battlefield tactics, but these simply did not work under such conditions, and the result was a rout; two-thirds of the men were killed or wounded, and Braddock died from his wounds before reaching Fort Cumberland.

In June and July 1754 colonial government representatives meeting at Albany had reached agreement on a Plan of Union for defense against frontier Indian raids (see Map 145, *page 72*), but the plan had not been ratified by the colonial legislatures. Now the British retreat left a vacuum in the backwoods, and Indians, many now allied to or encouraged by the French, began a murderous rampage that left many remote settlements in flames. It would be several years before the British regained control.

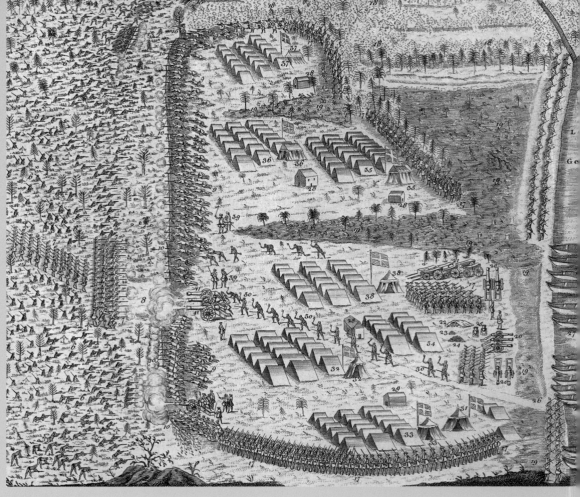

Map 116 (*above*).
This is a detailed British perspective map of the second part of the Battle of Lake George, 8 September 1755. It depicts the battle fairly accurately. Annotated with letters and numbers, the map accompanied an explanatory text. The main French attack was at 8, where the British forces have brought field guns to bear. According to part of the map's long title, 2000 English with 250 Mohawks fought 2500 French and Indians, and the English were victorious, captivating the French Gen[l] with a number of his Men, killing 700 & putting the rest to flight. In fact the French commander, Baron de Dieskau, was captured but later rescued.

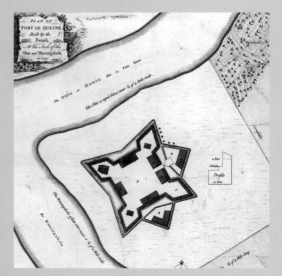

Map 115 (*above*).
The French Fort Duquesne at the forks of the Ohio, engraved from a drawing by Robert Stobo, one of two hostages from Washington's force left behind as part of the agreement to allow him to retreat from Fort Necessity. The plan was smuggled out of the fort by Shingas, a war chief of the Ohio Delawares. Quite elaborate, the structure was built on top of the British Fort George, captured just as it was finished in April 1754. It was, however, quite small, capable of holding only about two hundred men. The fort is now Point State Park in Pittsburgh.

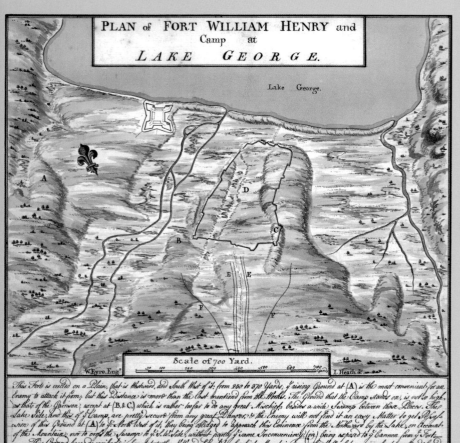

William Shirley, governor of Massachusetts, took over as commander-in-chief, but he was not up to the task. He had been ordered to lead the attack on Fort Niagara, but spent much of his energy fighting his own war with James De Lancey, governor of New York, and William Johnson, who was to lead the British thrust up the Champlain Valley. Neither of these two enterprises succeeded, but the New England attack on the French forts in Nova Scotia was successful, with Fort Beausejour on the isthmus between the Bay of Fundy and the Gulf of St. Lawrence falling in June 1755. This was followed by the British deportation of much of the Acadian population.

Shirley's army never got anywhere near Fort Niagara, but he did rebuild and fortify a trading post on Lake Ontario, Fort Oswego. William Johnson's army of British provincials and Mohawk allies set off to attack Fort Frédéric. They marched north to Lake St. Sacrament—which Johnson renamed Lake George—at the southern end of Lake Champlain. Here, on 8 September 1755, he encountered a French army, now led by Jean-Armand, Baron de Dieskau, who had been sent from France to assume overall direction of the French armies. The first part of the resulting Battle of Lake George (known as the Bloody Morning Scout) was a French ambush of a British advance party, but the second part, with the advance party retreating to a fortified position—barricades of logs, stumps, and wagons—allowed the British to hold off the French attack. This part of the battle is shown in Map 116, *above*. Later that day a company of three

Map 117 (*left*).
Fort William Henry on Lake George is shown on this 1755 map, but the map also shows the location of the fortified encampment (*D*) held by William Johnson's army at the Battle of Lake George on 8 September 1755. *E* is the line of march of the attacking regular French troops while *F* is that of their Indian allies. Fort William Henry was begun in the fall of 1755 to block the French route to Albany.

hundred provincial troops marching to reinforce Johnson's position engaged another band of French and their native allies, overwhelming them, a skirmish known as Bloody Pond, from the bodies thrown in the water.

Having reached what was essentially a military stalemate, the French retreated to the north end of the lake and built Fort Carillon on Lake Champlain, where it would guard the short portage to Lake George. The British, likewise, fortified the southern shore of Lake George with Fort William Henry. This line between the two powers would last until 1758.

Two new commanders appeared on the scene in 1756. John Campbell, Earl of Loudoun, was sent to revitalize British strategy, but spent most of 1756 sorting out provincial rivalries and problems created when the British government unadvisedly decreed that American provincial troops would be of lesser rank that British regulars. The new French commander was Louis-Joseph Montcalm-Gozon, Marquis de Montcalm. He had more initial military success than Loudoun, laying siege to Fort Oswego in August 1756 and forcing it to surrender. With it went any pretense of British control of Lake Ontario.

Loudoun's own priority was the French citadel of Louisbourg. He prepared an invasion fleet and sailed out of New York for Louisbourg in June 1757, meeting a fleet from England in Halifax. But while there he learned from captured letters that the fortress had been resupplied and reinforced. Together with the decimation of his own army by disease, the intelligence caused Loudoun to delay the attack until the following year.

Loudoun's plans elsewhere also went awry that year. In August 1757 a large force of French and Indians led by Montcalm attacked Fort William Henry (Map 117, *left, bottom*), overwhelming it before reinforcements could arrive. Montcalm guaranteed the safety of the surrendering British in the honorable fashion of the time, but to his horror the Indians, out to obtain the booty and scalps that were their only reward, fell on many of the helpless men and a massacre ensued before the French could regain control. This incident did much to explain later apparent cruelties by the British.

In Britain, William Pitt (the Elder) had come to effective power. Sometimes known as the "first imperialist," Pitt was to oversee and support the considerable expansion of the British Empire not only in North America but elsewhere, notably in India, where the conquest of that country was begun by Robert Clive at the Battle of Plassey in June 1757, a defeat of 50,000 Indian troops by only 3,000 British. For the war in 1756 had spread to Europe and was now to be fought in many other colonial or potential colonial venues.

It was Pitt who revitalized British strategy in North America. His idea was to direct enough resources against France in Europe to produce a stalemate while at the same time exploiting French weaknesses abroad,

where profitable gains might be made. He would do this by utilizing the strong British navy to prevent France from resupplying its troops. The principal venue for this strategy was North America. Pitt envisaged a strike at the heart of the French empire designed to remove the French from North America once and for all—a direct assault on Québec itself. The rest of his plans were not unlike those of Shirley and particularly those of Loudoun, but carried an additional thrust on to Québec. The plan was now threefold: capture of French western forts and attack from the west up the St. Lawrence; an attack on Montréal via the Champlain Valley, and an attack on the city of Québec after first capturing Louisbourg.

Pitt dismissed Loudoun, and this immediately made it easier to raise provincial troops, so much had Loudoun been disliked for his aristocratic ways. Pitt also reversed the inferior rank of provincial officers to regular ones and treated the colonies as allies, giving them incentives to send men. The result was that all the troops required were raised from the colonies, some 23,000 in all. And Loudoun's successor, James Abercromby, was to be but a military commander. Although Abercromby would lead the attack up the Champlain Valley, he created a special post of "Major General in America" and gave it to a promising British colonel, Jeffery Amherst, who would lead the assault on Louisbourg.

The initial plan was to take the strongholds of Louisbourg and Québec in a single season, but Louisbourg held out for long enough to foil those plans. Some 14,000 troops on 100 troop transports accompanied by 38 warships anchored in Gabarus Bay, to the south of the fortress, on 2 June 1758. The French had built entrenchments to prevent a landing here but they were overrun, largely due to the decisive actions of one of Amherst's commanders, James Wolfe. A siege was laid (Map 118, *below*) and Louisbourg surrendered, after heavy bombardment, on 26 July.

Fort Oswego, now called Fort Chouaguen, was taken that summer by a British force under John Bradstreet, a provincial officer. He and his men continued across Lake Ontario in over two hundred small boats and on 25 August took Fort Frontenac (now Kingston, Ontario), which had not been anticipating an attack. The loss of Fort Frontenac left the French unable to supply Fort Niagara or Fort Duquesne.

With the massing of British manpower, French America was beginning to look vulnerable, but an expedition against Fort Carillon in July 1758 showed that numbers alone were not enough. Led by the bumbling Abercromby, 16,000 British regular and provincial troops converged on the fort, sailing up Lake George in nearly 900 boats. Abercromby's second-in-command, George Augustus Howe, was a daring acting brigadier who had been expressly attached to Abercromby by Pitt, who was aware of Abercromby's reputation for hesitancy, but he was killed in the opening skirmishes of the battle, leaving Abercromby to make his own decisions. And Abercromby hesitated. Montcalm, at Fort Carillon, had only about 3,500 men, yet he was by far the better strategist. Believing the fort itself to be vulnerable, he took advantage of Abercromby's delays and put his

Map 118 (*below*).
A pictomap of the British attack on Louisbourg. Gabarus Bay, with British troops landing, is at left, while the besieged fortress is at right. The map was drawn by a French officer, Amiral (Admiral) Bockoune.

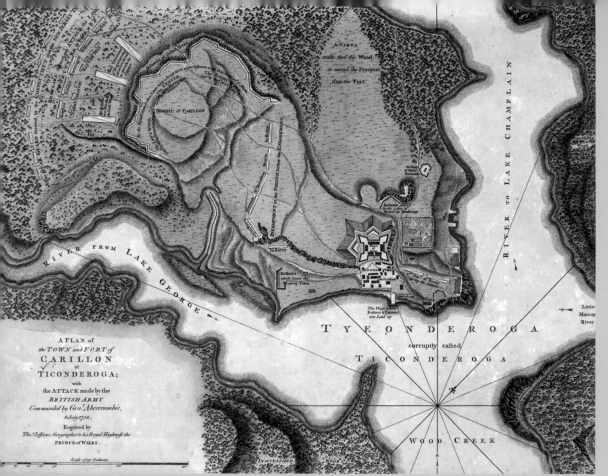

Map 119 (*above*).
The British attack on Fort Carillon (Ticonderoga) on 8 July 1758 is shown on this rather beautiful map. The fort is at center, on a high promontory. An abatis of felled trees (hatching) and breastwork (three solid lines) defends the entrance to the higher ground at left, shown with three columns of British troops attacking frontally. The French encampment is between the fort and the abatis and breastwork.

men to work quickly building an abatis, a defensive barrier of felled trees, and a sandbag breastwork to the west of the fort (Map 119, *above*). Abercromby ordered frontal, virtually suicidal, attacks instead of placing his field guns where they could blast a way through. One Connecticut provincial, the semiliterate Peter Pond (who would go on to become an explorer of the Northwest), wrote in his journal: "The British ware Batteling a Brest work Nine Logs thick in Som plases which was Dun without ye Help of Canan." The result was mayhem, British flight, and a crowning victory for Montcalm, who for two days sent out scouts, hardly believing that the British had gone.

However, despite Abercromby's incompetence, the British military might was being built up so much that they seemed bound to win the overall struggle. The military manpower now arraigned against French Canada was equivalent to about two-thirds of its total population, and in addition, a smallpox epidemic had decimated its Indian allies.

And the British were getting better at negotiation with their Indian allies. Brigadier General John Forbes, after much Indian diplomacy, marched on Fort Duquesne—with a force that included George Washington—and finally succeeded where Braddock had not; the fort was blown up and abandoned by the French on the approach of Forbes's army on 23 November 1758. The French commander, abandoned by France's Indian allies, did not have enough men to resist a British attack. A new British stronghold, Fort Pitt, was built on the French ruins, and a settlement—Pittsburgh—grew up around it.

The British resolved to carry their attack to the heart of the French empire. The French stronghold of Louisbourg was attacked by a large British army and fell in July 1758. In September Pitt relieved Abercromby of his command and appointed Jeffery Amherst in his place. At the same time he gave James Wolfe an independent command to invade Canada. By promising the colonies money, Pitt managed to get them to raise almost 17,000 provincial troops to assist the effort.

Brigadier General John Prideaux led an attack on Fort Niagara (see Map 88, *page 46*) in July 1759, aided by William Johnson, the British superintendent of Indian affairs, and a thousand Iroquois; he also managed to ensure the neutrality of the previously French-allied Seneca. Prideaux was killed early in the fighting when he stepped in front of one of his own cannon; Johnson assumed command. British trenches were nearing the fort (Map 121, *right*) when a French relief force reappeared. This had originally been dispatched from Niagara to the Ohio Country and urgently recalled when the British attack began. But the relief forces were ambushed by the British and destroyed before they could get back to Fort Niagara. At this, the fort surrendered. The siege had lasted nineteen days.

Amherst, meanwhile, had taken an army once more to Lake George, where he built a new fort to replace Fort William Henry, Fort George. Then, on 26 July 1759, he took Fort Carillon. He did

Map 120 (*above*).
The Lake Champlain valley, shown in a 1765 military map. Ville Marie (Montréal) is at the top, and the positions of Fort George (formerly Fort William Henry), Fort Ticonderoga (Fort Carillon), and Crown Point (Fort Frédéric) are indicated, as are other forts defending this strategic corridor.

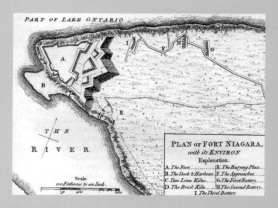

Map 121.
The siege of Fort Niagara, July 1759. The cannon emplacements G, H, and I are connected by a trench dug progressively nearer to the walls of the fort.

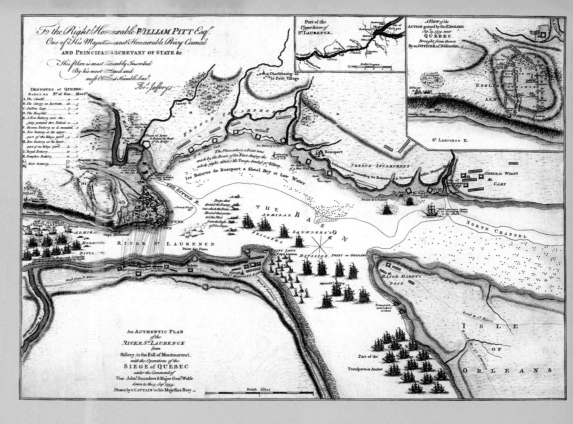

this with only ten thousand men, and it took him only four days and five fatalities. But the circumstances were radically different to Abercromby's attempt the previous year. Most of the defenders had been withdrawn for the defense of Québec. A token force of about four hundred French soldiers remained, and their instructions were merely to delay the British for as long as possible. And Montcalm was not in charge. The garrison soon spiked their guns, blew up the powder magazine, and departed north to Fort Frédéric.

Amherst then sent out his scouts to determine the situation at Fort Frédéric, and they returned on 1 August with the news that the French had also blown up that stronghold and withdrawn northwards once more. Since at this time Amherst did not know whether Wolfe had succeeded with his attack on Québec, and knowing that if he had not, Montcalm could redeploy much more force against him, Amherst decided to complete the season by consolidating his position on Lake Champlain, constructing a new fort at Crown Point (Map 123, below, right) and building armed vessels to counter a French naval presence on the lake.

Indeed, Wolfe had not, by August, taken Québec. With 180 ships and an army of 8,500, he had arrived within sight of the city on 26 June and spent the next two months vacillating, probing the French defenses but finding them so well prepared by his adversary Montcalm that he could do nothing. Québec itself sat atop a virtually impregnable cliff rising from the St. Lawrence, and Montcalm had entrenched troops along the Beauport shore, the lower land just to the east of the city, preventing Wolfe from landing troops and mounting a traditional siege (Map 122, above). Finally, a desperate Wolfe heard from Robert Stobo—the same officer taken hostage at Fort Necessity in 1754 and now recently escaped from Québec—of a chink in the French armor: a narrow pathway up the cliffs just west of the city at a place called L'Anse au Foulon.

With the season becoming short, Wolfe seized on this opportunity. On the night of 12–13 September troops were packed into boats and landed at the cliffs, while sailors rowed up and down the Beauport shore to make Montcalm think the landing was to come there. By the time Montcalm realized he had been fooled, a British army was lined up on the Plains of Abraham immediately west of the city walls. In the ensuing battle both Wolfe and Montcalm were killed, and Québec capitulated five days later. An army hurrying north from Montréal arrived too late to save the city.

The British occupied Québec through the winter of 1759-60, under the command of James Murray, one of Wolfe's officers, only to find another French army in front of them in April. The Chevalier de Lévis, now in command of the French forces, had brought an army from Montréal to try to regain Québec. Another battle followed, the Battle of Sainte-Foy, on 28 April 1760. The French were victorious, but Murray simply withdrew his men within the walls of the city and waited. Lévis's troops were so short of ammunition that they could not lay a proper siege. All would now depend on which nation's ships arrived to resupply its army. Needless to say, it was British ships that arrived. Lévis retreated to Montréal, intending to make his last stand there.

Now the British master plan finally came together: Murray led an army, now resupplied, south from Québec; another army, led by Brigadier General William Haviland, advanced north from Crown Point, and Amherst himself took an army to Oswego and then down the St. Lawrence toward Montréal. This three-pronged vise clamped down on the heart of French America. Murray had about 2,200 men; Haviland 3,500, and Murray 11,000. Lévis had but 4,000, and Montréal was essentially indefensible. Nonetheless, Lévis was ready to fight to the death, but in the end he was overruled by François-Pierre de Rigaud de Vaudreuil, the governor of New France, and a surrender was signed on 8 September 1760. Citing previous atrocities committed by French Indian allies, Amherst denied the French "honors of war" and did not allow them to keep their regimental colors or return to France.

Vaudreuil's surrender at Montréal was confirmed by the Treaty of Paris in 1763, which ended the Seven Years' War. The French lost all their territory in North America to Britain (with the exception of the tiny St. Pierre and Miquelon Islands off the south coast of Newfoundland). They also lost Louisiana, which France ceded to Spain in 1762 in order to prevent it falling into British hands. Now, for what would prove to be only little more than a decade, Britain prevailed in North America.

Map 122 (above).
The battle for a continent: the siege of Québec, June–September 1759. This detailed map was produced by the geographer to the British king, Thomas Jefferys. The inset shows the battle fought before the walls of Québec on 13 September. The main map shows events from several times during the three-month period. The city of Québec is shown at center left, with lines of bombardment across the St. Lawrence. Nearby are the fire rafts with which Montcalm first attacked the British fleet. At bottom right are transport ships at anchor near the Île d'Orleans. Immediately north of them in the North Channel is the failed British attack on the Beauport shore. At far left are the British ships that transported the army to the cliffs at L'Anse au Foulon, marked Landing Place. Finally, the battle is shown just west of the city.

Map 123 (below).
Crown Point, Lake Champlain, occupied by the British in August 1759. The French Fort Frédéric is the smaller fort at K, together with a redoubt built at L when they found the fort's line of sight was not quite right. A is the new British fort. The model is of Fort Frédéric in 1752, displayed at the Crown Point visitor center. The remains of the British fort are shown on the contents page.

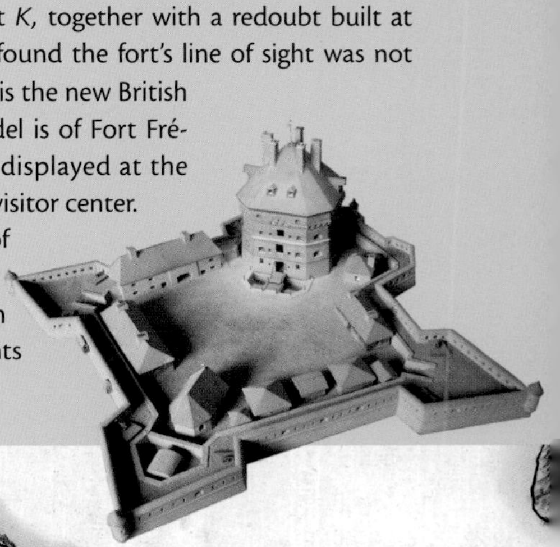

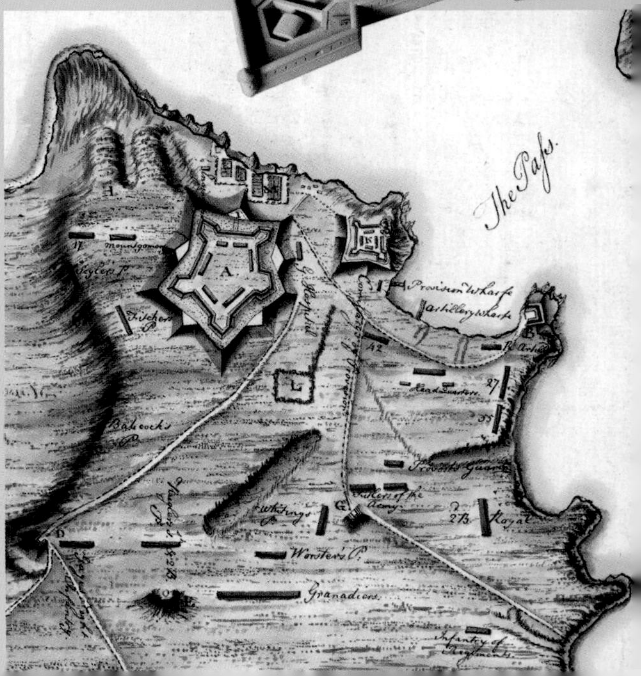

Indians and an Advancing Frontier

The native peoples of America from the beginning of European colonization found the lands they thought of as their own encroached upon, taken without permission, or negotiated away in usually one-sided agreements. Settlement and European-style agriculture were at odds with the hunting and gathering economy of many of the Indians. Various groups made alliances with the French and the English, and international wars were used for native ends, although Indian peoples generally considered their alliances to be nation to nation—and thus, like European alliances, changeable—whereas the Europeans took a change of allegiance as disloyalty. In the eighteenth century, the rapidly changing geopolitical landscape was bound to lead to shifting Indian alliances.

Treaties and agreements for the sale or cession of Indian lands were sometimes coerced and sometimes fraudulent. One of the better-known examples is that of the so-called Walking Purchase, by the Penn family from the Lenape (Delaware) Indians in 1737. The Penns maintained that an agreement from the 1680s had given them all the land west from the junction of the Delaware and the Lehigh rivers as far as a man could walk in a day and a half. This the Lenape accepted, even though it might have been fraudulent, but the Penns hired the best runners in the colony to "walk out" the bounds of the claim. One covered seventy miles in the allotted time, leading to the cession of 1.2 million acres in what is now northeastern Pennsylvania.

With the coming of the French and Indian War, treaties were made to ensure that Indians fought on one side or the other. By the 1758 (second) Treaty of Easton, the Indians in the Ohio Country agreed not to fight on the French side in return for British assurances that settlements would not be established west of the Allegheny Mountains once the war had ended. These assurances would in 1763 be embodied in a Royal Proclamation.

Although the Cherokee were at first British allies, in 1759 various incidents compounded to make them withdraw their support. Local militia often did not distinguish between allied Indians and any others, and murdered them at will. Hunters from along the Savannah River in South Carolina took advantage of the Indian absence when they went north to offer to assist the Forbes expedition (see page 60), taking game illegally from the Cherokee country (the area centered on what is now the western part of North Carolina and Tennessee). Cherokee began raiding frontier settlements, and in response the North Carolina governor, William Henry Lyttelton, led thirteen hundred men to hunt down the culprits. In an attempt to make the Cherokee hand over the persons responsible for murders of settlers, hostages were held at Fort Prince George, a fortification on the Savannah River (now under Lake Keowee). In January 1760 the fort was attacked, but the Cherokee failed to free the hostages and instead laid siege to the fort. Then, with the fort's garrison jittery following repeated Indian attacks, the hostages were killed by their captors. This unleashed a fury of vengeance along the frontier, with perhaps a hundred settlers killed. Apart from those who made it to refuges, such as a stockade called Fort Ninety-six, near today's Greenwood, South Carolina, the bounds of EuroAmerican settlement retreated a hundred miles or more.

The Cherokee tried to enlist the support of the French at Fort Toulouse, on the Alabama River, but no men or supplies could be spared. South Carolina now retaliated, this time with an army that included 1,300 British regulars, 300 provincial troops, and about 50 Catawba Indians. Led by Colonel Archibald Montgomery, they marched into the Cherokee country in June, burning and killing. Despite this force the Cherokee mounted a guerilla-type resistance that resulted in considerable British casualties, and by August Montgomery was back in Charleston.

Meanwhile, to the northwest, Fort Loudoun, a fort built in 1756–57 on the Tennessee River (at Vonore, Tennessee, about thirty-five miles southwest of Knoxville), came under Cherokee attack. By August 1760 the besieged defenders could last no longer and the fort's commander, Captain Paul Demaré, surrendered the fort in return for a promise of safe passage to Fort Prince George. By such was not to be. A day out from the fort the captives were attacked again and many were massacred.

Early the following year, more British regulars arrived from New York under Lieutenant Colonel James Grant, a commander with considerable experience fighting Indians. Joined by provincial troops, an army of 2,600 entered the Cherokee country in May 1760, prepared and supplied for an extended campaign. On 10 June they were attacked by a thousand Cherokee warriors, who inflicted heavy casualties, but used up most of their ammunition doing so. From that point on the Cherokee were powerless to prevent Grant's progression

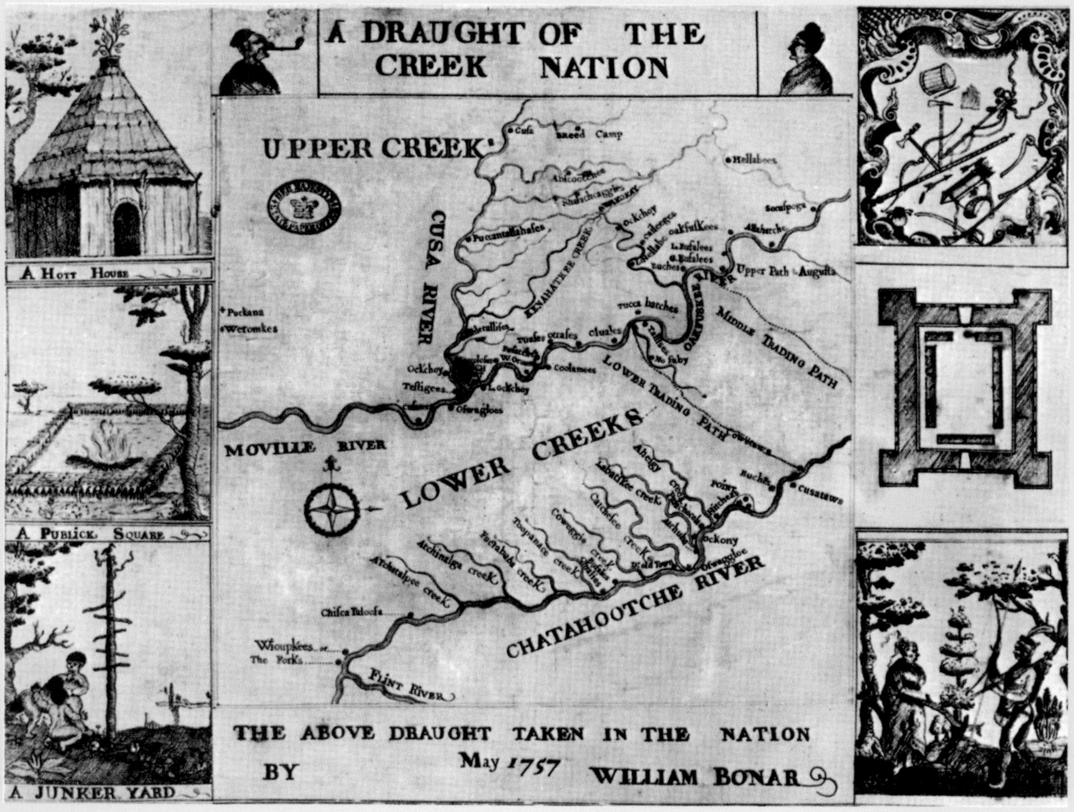

MAP 124 (*left*).
This well-illustrated map shows the country of the Creek Indians, south of that of the Cherokee. It was drawn in 1757 by William Bonar, an aide to the governor of South Carolina, Samuel Pepper. He had smuggled himself into the French Fort Toulouse, on the Alabama River, to determine its strength. He had been captured, but was rescued by Creek Indians on Pepper's instigation. This map was drawn while he was in Creek custody.

through their territory, where he burned fifteen villages and many corn and bean fields. Any Cherokee captured were immediately killed.

The "chastising" of the Cherokee (as Amherst had put it) was thorough and devastating, and by August the Cherokee sued for peace. As part of the settlement, the boundary between EuroAmerican and Cherokee settlements was once again moved west.

The government in London had been appalled at the various conflicts between Indians and British subjects, but certainly realized that most were the result of pressures on Indian lands as the frontier of settlement moved inexorably west. The Earl of Halifax, who had now taken over the responsibilities William Pitt had held, was determined to do something about it, and he drafted the Royal Proclamation, issued on 7 October 1763. This defined Quebec and East and West Florida (the latter two having been acquired from Spain in return for Havana at the end of the Seven Years' War) and expressly forbade all but licensed traders from settling in the area (marked in red on MAP 126, right) outside the limits of any "Proprietary Government." No surveyors were to be allowed to survey, and no colonial government was empowered to grant any lands there, even if within its original charter. It was a valiant effort, but the land was so vast, enforcement so difficult, and pressures so immense, that it was bound to fail. And after the Revolution, a royal proclamation would be but a laughing matter.

In 1761, Neolin, a western Delaware considered by his tribe to be a prophet, stirred up religious fervor among the Indians by predicting a war

MAP 126 (above).
The boundary line between the colonies and the "new governments" of Quebec and East and West Florida (shown in yellow) and the land to be reserved for the Indians (red) according to the Royal Proclamation of 1763. This is a French map, and the new information was clearly added to an earlier base map, for the red area cuts off the names of colonies such as South Carolina, North Carolina, and Virginia originally shown as stretching to the Mississippi—surprisingly perhaps, since the French had never before recognized the British claim to the Mississippi Valley. The Royal Proclamation provided for a fourth "new government," that of the Caribbean island of Grenada, captured from the French during the war.

in the West. He had for some time been preaching that Indians should not be dependent on EuroAmericans and should go back to their precontact customs, revoking even trade. Resentment about encroachment on Indian lands finally boiled over in April 1763, when a great uprising began near Detroit. Ottawa Indian chief Pontiac invoked Neolin's teachings to gather together disaffected tribes to attack Fort Detroit on 7 May. The attack failed, and a siege began. At this signal, Indians throughout the region also attacked other forts. Forts Sandusky, St. Joseph, Miami, Michilimackinac, and several others fell in quick order. Then Indians took all of the forts and blockhouses in the Ohio Country other than the stronger Fort Niagara and Fort Pitt.

A relief expedition of almost 250 men reached Detroit at the end of July and, led by an overenthusiastic Captain James Dalyell, set off to punish the fort's attackers only to suffer an ignominious defeat at a place dubbed Bloody Run; over half of the expedition perished.

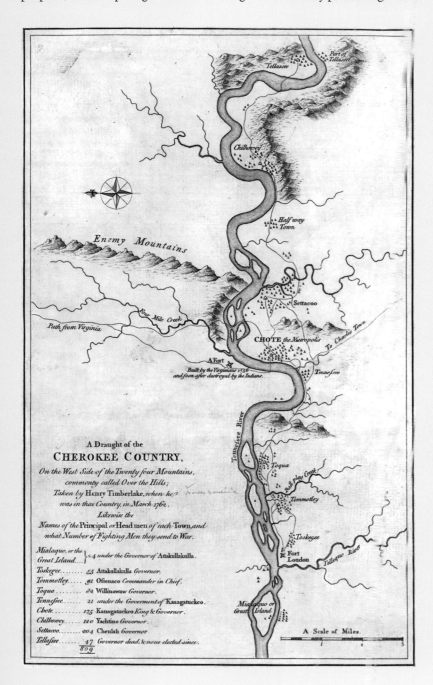

MAP 125 (left).
A map of the Cherokee country made by Lieutenant Henry Timberlake at the end of the Cherokee War. As a mark of the newfound peace, the Cherokee invited him to live among them, and Timberlake stayed for three months, returning to Williamsburg with some of the chiefs, who had expressed a wish to visit King George III. He then accompanied the chiefs to London, where they did meet the king and sat for the painter Joshua Reynolds. The map shows the Overhill region of the Cherokee country; the river is the Little Tennessee, not the Tennessee as marked; Fort Loudoun is shown on the river near the bottom of the map. This map is the first printed map of any part of Tennessee.

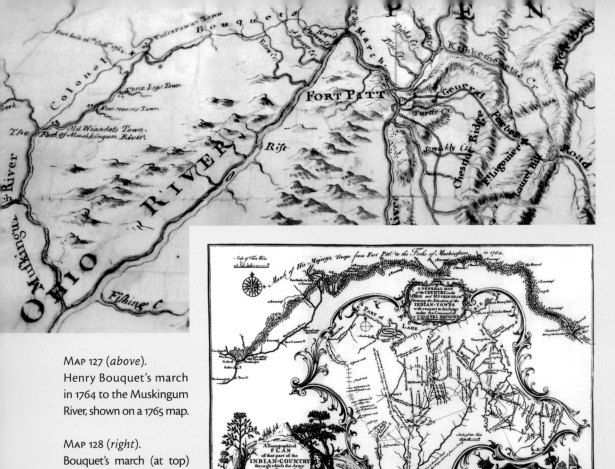

MAP 127 (*above*).
Henry Bouquet's march in 1764 to the Muskingum River, shown on a 1765 map.

MAP 128 (*right*).
Bouquet's march (at top) and an illustrated map of the *Indian-Country* published in 1765 to show his pacification of the Ohio.

At Fort Pitt, some five hundred men were besieged by the Delawares, and at an infamous meeting with the chiefs, the fort's commander, Captain Simon Ecuyer, concluded the meeting by giving them gifts, including blankets from the fort's hospital—infected with smallpox. This seems to be one of the first recorded instances of germ warfare, deemed acceptable even by Amherst because the Indians were regarded as savages. Colonel Henry Bouquet, dispatched in June on a mission to relieve Fort Pitt, was of the same mind: he wrote that he hoped to "extirpate that Vermine from a Country they have forfeited."

Bouquet was approaching Fort Pitt with about four hundred men on 5 August when he was attacked at Bushy Run Creek, about twenty-five miles from the fort. It looked as though what had happened to Braddock was about to happen to Bouquet, but Bouquet by this time was a much more experienced Indian fighter. After being pinned down all night, he arranged an apparent sudden retreat the next day, which caused the attackers to break from their cover in pursuit; instead they were now exposed to carefully positioned infantrymen who mowed them down. The rest of the Indians quickly disappeared. However, so many of Bouquet's pack animals had been killed that he was forced to destroy food in order to have enough animals to carry his wounded to Fort Pitt. Nonetheless, the battle seems to have had a salutary effect, for further convoys of supplies were brought in without harassment.

Farther north, Fort Niagara remained impregnable, but instead, as the winter approached, the Indians attacked the vulnerable portage around the falls, making it for a while impassable and thus cutting off supplies and reinforcements for Fort Detroit and other western posts.

Indian superintendent William Johnson held a council with Six Nations Indians in September in which he gained their cooperation in stopping the violence, arguing that this would allow them to reassert their authority over the Ohio Country.

Amherst was recalled to London in November 1763 to explain how "a few naked savages" could not be controlled by the eight thousand men under his command. He had planned to subdue the Indian uprisings in the Ohio the

MAP 129 (*left*).
The boundaries of the lands assigned to the Indians—and thus the western boundary of the British colonies—after the 1768 Treaty of Fort Stanwix. The map shows the boundaries negotiated in that treaty in red (in the north) and those from other negotiations, in the south, in yellow.

same way he had done in the Cherokee country, and his successor, Thomas Gage, kept more or less to this plan. Three expeditions were organized to "chastise" the Indians.

Major Arthur Loftus was to ascend the Mississippi from the now British West Florida; he never moved, due to Indians blocking his way. Even though they were not allied with the Illinois or Ohio Indians, they remained sympathetic to the French.

Colonel John Bradstreet, meanwhile, was dispatched to Detroit with 1,400 men and 500 Indians. The Indians had been rallied to the British cause by more diplomacy by Johnson at another council at Fort Niagara in July, when perhaps two thousand Indians were given a large number of presents, persuading them that support for the British cause would be profitable. By the end of August 1764 Detroit had been relieved, but Bradstreet had rather more grandiose ideas: he envisaged a new British province—with him as its governor—centered on Detroit. His ambitions proved to be his undoing. Trying to eliminate Pontiac's authority he destroyed a wampum (peace) belt sent by Pontiac, but Indian animosity was again stirred, and he found himself unable to carry out Gage's orders to pacify the country. Then, when he was returning to Niagara in October, a storm sank many of his boats.

Henry Bouquet led another expedition through the Ohio with a great deal more success. Leaving Fort Pitt on 3 October with 1,500 men, he followed the Ohio to Big Beaver Creek and then struck out for the Muskingum River, the center of Ohio Indian resistance to the British forces (MAPS 127 and 128, *left, top*), all the time proceeding cautiously so as to avoid another Bushy Run. Establishing a defensive camp on a hill near today's Coshocton, Ohio, he received promises of peace and had over two hundred captives delivered to him. By the end of November Bouquet was back at Fort Pitt, having achieved a peace for the Ohio Country.

Ultimately, the Indian uprising that has been called Pontiac's War fizzled out because the majority of the Indians came to realize that they were better off cooperating with the British than continuing to ally themselves with the French, whose power was on the wane, and that British trade was required for the supply of guns and ammunition for hunting; a return to the precontact notions of Neolin was unattractive for a people who had tasted an easier way of life. Nonetheless, Indian aggravation would continue because of the constant threat created by the advance of EuroAmerican settlement and its preempting of Indian lands. Pontiac himself died an ignominious death at the hands of another Indian, a Peoria, in April 1769.

A compromise was reached in 1768 that would, at least for a short period, fix a boundary across which no settler was supposed to cross. At Fort Stanwix, established on the Oswego portage at today's Rome, New York, a treaty was negotiated once again by William Johnson in October 1768 between the British and the Iroquois Six Nations. It ceded lands south of the Susquehanna and the Ohio rivers (in which only their dependent Delaware, Shawnee, and Mingo lived) in return for guarantees to preserve Iroquois lands to the north (MAP 129, *left*, and MAP 130, *above, right*). In a pattern that would repeat itself time and time again, the treaty proved of little lasting value, and settlers were soon once again crossing into Indian lands.

The Quebec Act of 1774 extended the boundaries of Quebec south to the Ohio River and west to the Mississippi and extinguished royal charters for any colonies over these lands. The act encouraged Indians along the Ohio to attack frontier settlements. So much did tensions once again build that John Murray, Earl of Dunmore, the governor of Virginia, led a British force of 1,400 into the Ohio much as Braddock and Forbes had before him. Dunmore's second-in-command, General Andrew Lewis, leading a contingent of about 800 farther south, defeated a large Shawnee force led by the Indian chief Cornstalk at the Battle of Point Pleasant (forty miles northeast of what is now Huntington, West Virginia) on 12 October 1774. This battle is considered by some to be the opening battle of the Revolution—the argument being that British royal governor Dunmore *intended* Lewis's provincial force to be annihilated.

British pressure on Indian lands—soon to be *American* pressure on Indian lands—was only temporarily muted by the Revolution and would continue, ever farther westward, for a hundred years (see pages 140 and 200).

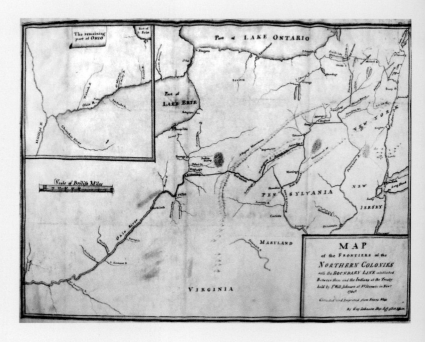

MAP 130 (*above*).
Boundaries negotiated at Fort Stanwix by William Johnson in 1768.

MAP 131 (*below*).
Numerous treaties would be negotiated with the Indians that whittled away at their lands. This map, of land near the Savannah River in Georgia, is the result of one of the more famous treaty negotiations, that held at a congress at Augusta in May and June 1773. Some 2,300 square miles of Creek and Cherokees lands were ceded to "His Majesty." The deal was negotiated by governor James Wright of Georgia together with Indian agent John Stuart. The famous naturalist William Bartram was also in attendance. The map shows *Bufloe Lick*, one of a number of such "licks" previously frequented by wild buffalo that roamed Georgia.

Lines in a Wilderness

In a new land where surveying with primitive equipment was difficult and where numerous individuals and companies had been granted vast tracts, often regranting them in smaller parcels to others, it was almost inevitable that disputes would arise over precise boundaries. And many of the boundaries of the original royal grants to the colonies stretched westward to the Pacific simply because no one realized how far away the western ocean really was.

Land surveying, then, was a prized skill in early America, and all the proprietors of land grants hired surveyors. One of the most famous

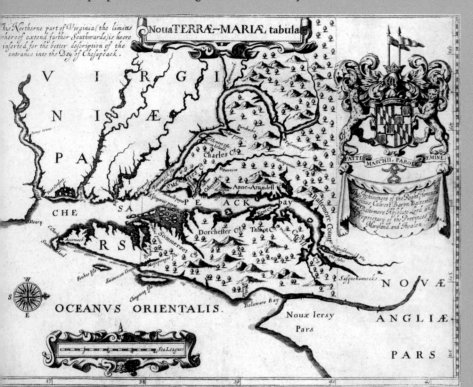

of the disputes between colonies was over the boundary between Maryland and Pennsylvania, a line surveyed in 1763–66 by Charles Mason and Jeremiah Dixon.

In 1635 the first priority had been to allow settlers to survive, and a hastily drawn map (Map 60, *page 32*) was used in England to promote the new colony of Maryland. But this map inaccurately showed the 40°N boundary of the colony as touching the northern end of Chesapeake Bay. Later, when this mistake was discovered, an altered map was produced to correct this (Map 132, *left*). With the establishment in 1682 of William Penn's colony of Pennsylvania immediately to the north and with a charter itself with a confusing legal boundary description, the stage was set for a battle. The Penn family used the 1635 Maryland map as evidence that the boundary between the two colonies was intended to be farther south. An agreement was reached in 1732 whereby the boundary was defined as on a latitude fifteen miles south of Philadelphia; the line was thus to be at 39°43′19″. But Lord Baltimore and the Calvert family had not fathomed the amount of land they were to lose, and the case continued through the British legal system until 1750, when the chief justices finally ruled that Baltimore had to accept the more southerly line.

Thirteen years later, the two families, unable to find local surveyors they thought would do an accurate and unbiased job, hired two astronomers from the Royal Observatory in Greenwich, England, Charles Mason and his surveyor-astronomer assistant, Jeremiah Dixon. They had worked together for some time, most notably on the observation of a transit of Venus from the Cape of Good Hope in southern Africa in 1761. Now they

Map 132 (*above, top*).
The boundary in question. The 1671 edition of Lord Baltimore's map of *Nova Terra Mariæ* shows the northern boundary of Maryland as a dotted line at 40°N (note that this map is oriented with north at right). The boundary has been skillfully moved from its position farther south on an earlier map drawn in 1635 (Map 60, page 32), and trees have been added by the engraver specifically to hide the change.

Map 134 (*below*).
This section of a superbly detailed 1770 map of North Carolina shows the boundary between that colony and Virginia. The line was taken principally from a survey done in 1749 by William Churton, a North Carolina surveyor, to extend the Virginia–North Carolina boundary line westwards. The Virginia representatives on this survey were Joshua Fry and Peter Jefferson (see Map 111, page 55). The map was redrawn in 1770 by John Abraham.

turned from defining the size of the Universe to defining a line between Pennsylvania and Maryland—a much smaller job, but equally perplexing.

First they had to determine the exact position of Philadelphia, and then a latitude exactly fifteen miles south of it, according to the agreement, touching a radius twelve miles from New Castle (just south of Wilmington, Delaware; the northern part of this radius became the northern boundary of the state of Delaware). They then resurveyed the boundary on the Delmarva Peninsula between Maryland and Delaware, extending it up to meet the twelve-mile radius. (However, it did not meet the radius exactly and left a small area of land known as "The Wedge," the jurisdiction of which was not decided until 1921, when it was awarded to Delaware.) From here the survey westward began.

Mason and Dixon picked their way westward with astronomical precision for 224 miles, where, just 36 miles short of the boundary's end, they were stopped by Indians and could go no farther. The survey took almost three years to complete. On its completion in late 1766, following a suggestion from the Royal Society, they stayed to precisely measure a degree of the Earth's meridian on the Delmarva Peninsula, part of a worldwide effort at the time to measure the size of the Earth.

The boundary survey cost the Penns and the Calverts some $75,000, a huge sum. For this they defined the exact limits of their domains—but not for long. Less than a decade later they lost all their land to the Revolution.

The Mason-Dixon Line has entered popular folklore as much more than just the boundary between two states, becoming in popular conception a much longer line separating the North from the South,

MAP 135 (above, top).

This map, part of an earlier survey, shows the boundary line between Virginia and North Carolina. It is dated 7 October 1728. It was likely drawn by or for William Byrd, the commissioner for Virginia. The survey early on presented considerable difficulties in that the boundary passes right through the middle of the Great Dismal Swamp near the coast. On the map there are no distinguishing features other than the name *The Dismal*. The commissioners circumnavigated the swamp altogether, leaving their surveyors to drag themselves through the middle of it. Written on the back of this map is the following: *N.B. The Virginia Commissrs. (being deserted by the Carolina Commissrs.) proceeded much higher into the Country and sent another Plan of the Whole Survey*, a reference to another map that is the westward extension of this one. The Carolina commissioners in fact declared that it would be "an age or two" before settlements reached so far inland (about 241 miles from the ocean). Byrd's surveyors surveyed a further 73 miles to the west. Yet within twenty years encroaching settlements required that the line be extended another 90 miles farther west.

and in particular the line between the free states and the slave states. This dividing line does not extend at the same latitude beyond that surveyed by Mason and Dixon and has little to do with the erstwhile surveyors. It has even been suggested that the name "Dixie" for the South derived from Jeremiah Dixon, although a more likely explanation is that it comes from the old French currency, the dix, or ten. Nevertheless, this popular usage has made two otherwise relatively obscure surveyors, Mason and Dixon, well known to most Americans.

MAP 133 (above and across the page).

Charles Mason and Jeremiah Dixon's map of the boundary line between Pennsylvania and Maryland, surveyed between 1763 and 1766 and published in 1768. At right *The Tangent Line* marks the twelve-mile radius from New Castle, centered on the cupola in the dome of the courthouse. A native *War Path* is at extreme left; this was where Mason and Dixon were prevented from proceeding west and ended their survey. At approximately the middle of the left-hand page is *G. Braddocks Road*, the road cut by Edward Braddock for his ill-fated march to Fort Duquesne (Pittsburgh) in 1755 (see page 57). The large river at right is the Susquehanna, at the head of Chesapeake Bay. Another, separate part of this map (not shown) is the north-south boundary on the Delmarva Peninsula, between Delaware and Maryland.

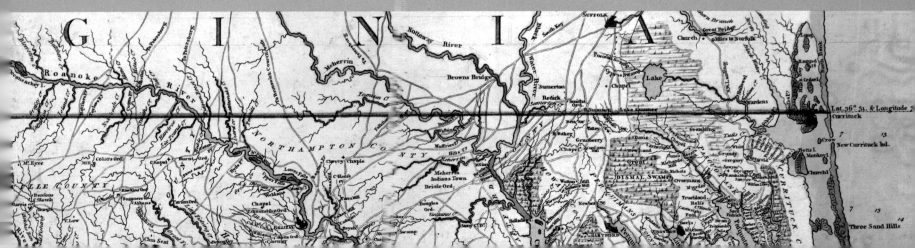

Spanish America

A great deal of what is now the southern half of the United States was for much of its history Spanish territory, early claimed by the conquistadors of Spain peripherally to their conquest of Mexico, the region they called New Spain (see page 14). Spain lost the territories over almost a century: the Floridas in 1763, regained in 1783 and finally lost in 1819; Texas in 1836, to an independent republic, and California in 1846–47.

The effect of Spanish colonization was felt well beyond its frontiers. Horses were introduced into the New World by Spain in 1519, and by the early 1700s Indians along the Rio Grande had acquired them too. From there within a few decades the Indians of the Great Plains also obtained horses, changing forever the balance of power in favor of the warrior Comanche, Sioux, and Apache.

The initial Spanish interest only in raping the land they called New Mexico of gold and any other riches it might contain mellowed somewhat by the beginning of the seventeenth century, when the focus turned to the conversion of the natives to Christianity. New Mexico became a royal province of Spain and missions began to be established, starting with Santa Fe in 1610. Along with the missions were presidios, forts garrisoned by soldiers. By 1630 at least ninety churches had been built by Spain in

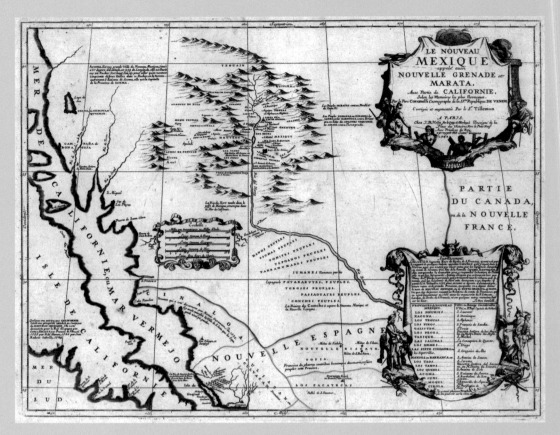

MAP 136 (*above*).
Spanish and native pueblo settlements along the Rio Grande were first revealed to European eyes on this map by Venetian mapmaker Vincenzo Coronelli in 1688 (though this is a later edition). He received the information from a map by Diego Penalosa, briefly governor of New Mexico in 1661–63, who turned against the Spanish and provided a map to the French king in the hopes that France would attack New Mexico from Louisiana. Penalosa is credited by Coronelli in the note in the cartouche at bottom right. *Santa Fé* is shown along with numerous other settlements in the valley of the *Rio del Norte*, the Rio Grande. At the bend in the river farther south is *el Passo*, today the site of El Paso, Texas. The southern part of the Rio Grande is named here the Rio Bravo. Coronelli has extended his map to cover the California coast, but here his information fails him, and a huge *Isle de Californie* is depicted, the island of California shown on most maps at this time.

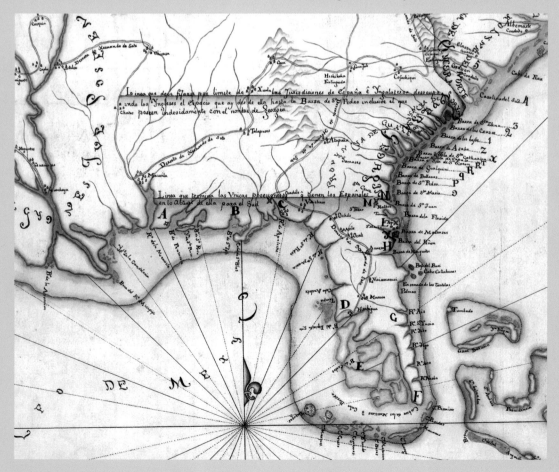

the native pueblos (towns or villages). A thousand Spaniards lived and farmed along the Rio Grande, and another thousand were garrisoned or lived at Santa Fe. The Spanish population grew slowly. Once arrived, a colonist could only leave New Mexico with royal permission.

Yet the Spanish hold was a tenuous one. A crackdown on Indian non-Christian rituals led to an uprising in 1680 led by an Indian

MAP 137 (*left*).
A 1742 Spanish map of the Southeast. The yellow line is the northern limit of lands claimed by Spain, and the green line is the southern limit of lands claimed by the British. The area thus in contention is that of Georgia, the buffer colony established by Britain in 1733 (see page 36). The Florida Everglades is shown as an area of islands. The letters refer to places explored or claimed for Spain. *A* is Pensacola; *L* is St. Augustine; *M* is the location of the French colony destroyed by Menéndez in 1565 (see page 21). The map is an exact hand-drawn facsimile made in 1914 of a 1742 map in the Archivo General des Indias in Seville, Spain.

named Popé. Churches were burned and priests killed, and the Spanish population retreated into Santa Fe and finally, after much savage fighting, evacuated south. The Indians let them go, pleased enough that they were rid of them. About 2,000 of the then 2,800 Spaniards who had lived around Santa Fe made it to El Paso, and there many stayed, beginning a new settlement around a mission.

Popé set himself up as the new ruler of New Mexico until he died in 1688, but during his rule the pueblos had been suffering the depravations of increasingly bold Apache raids. Thus when a bold Spanish military expedition led by Diego de Vargas attempted to retake Santa Fe in 1692 it met with little resistance, and Spanish rule was quickly reinstated.

One of the reasons the Spanish had taken so long to return to New Mexico was that they had been preoccupied elsewhere—along the Texas coast searching for the colony they had heard the Frenchman La Salle had established, in Spanish eyes a clear encroachment on their territory. No less than ten separate expeditions were sent out to find the elusive La Salle (see page 42). Although La Salle was soon found to offer no threat, once the French began to settle in the Mississippi Delta in the colony they now called Louisiana, the danger was once again revived. Spain became increasingly annoyed at the incursions of French traders up the Red River and the founding of Natchitoches on that river by Louis Juchereau de St. Denis in 1713. And so, in 1718, the very year the French founded New Orleans, the Spanish established a presidio and mission at San Antonio to guard the route to New Mexico (MAP 139, below). The mission's chapel was later named after the cottonwood or *álamo* trees that grew nearby; as the Alamo it would pass into history more than a century hence (see page 150).

In 1719 France declared war on Spain, and this led to a Spanish expedition being organized to counter a perceived renewed French threat to Texas. The Marqués de San Miguel de Aguayo, governor of Coahuila, the province adjacent to Texas, led an army into Texas in 1721. He found St. Denis, but St. Denis told him of news that a peace had been signed (in 1720) and hostilities were avoided. St. Denis agreed to withdraw to Natchitoches, the Spanish built more missions and reinforced San Antonio, and an uneasy peace returned. Nonetheless, the Spanish presence in Texas did not grow very much, largely because of the deprivations of the French-allied Comanche Indians. The Spanish finally met their match in 1759 when an army sent to wipe out the Comanche was instead routed by them.

To the west, the Spanish had established a chain of missions in Baja California and, thinking that Baja was an island (see MAP 199, page 1xx), supplied them across the Gulf of California. The Jesuit Eusebio Kino was a tireless explorer for new lands and new souls at this time, and in 1690 he founded a mission near today's Tucson, Arizona. By 1700 he reached the confluence of the Gila and the Colorado rivers and realized that he was north of the Gulf of California. Further explorations in the next two years led him to the head of the gulf, where he could see land continuing to the northwest. Notifying his superiors, he wrote, "California no es isla, sino penisla." Kino had demonstrated that both Baja and Alta California could be reached by land from New Spain (MAP 140, *overleaf*).

MAP 138 (*right, top*).
This 1769 Spanish map shows the profusion of presidios (forts), missions and villas (towns) around *S^{a.} Fée*—Santa Fe. They include the villa of *Alburquerque* (Albuquerque), founded in 1706.

MAP 139 (*right*).
A plan of San Antonio in 1780. Public buildings (2) and the church (1) front a public square at center in this compact and thus defensible Spanish settlement established in 1718 as a counterweight to the French in Louisiana.

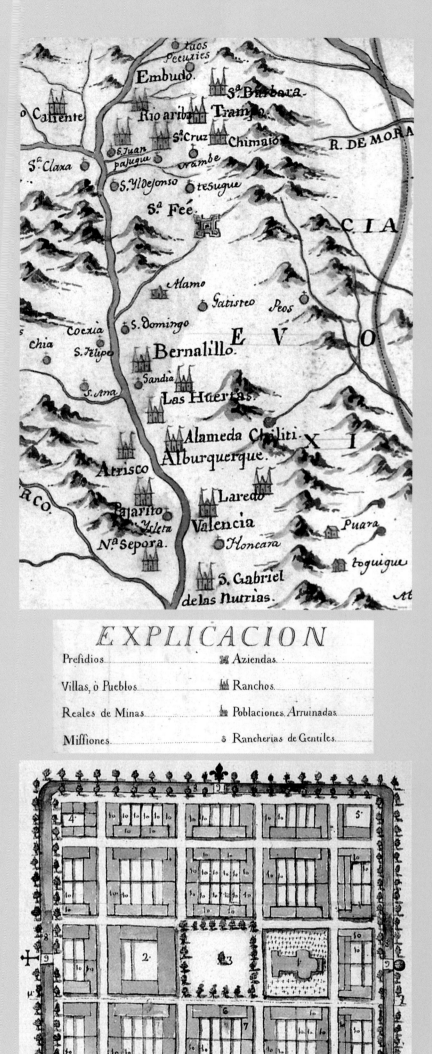

EXPLICACION

Presidios	Aziendas
Villas, ò Pueblos	Ranchos
Reales de Minas	Poblaciones Arruinadas
Missiones	Rancherias de Gentiles

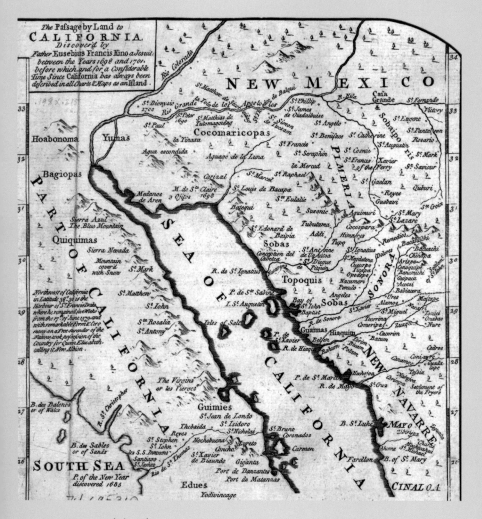

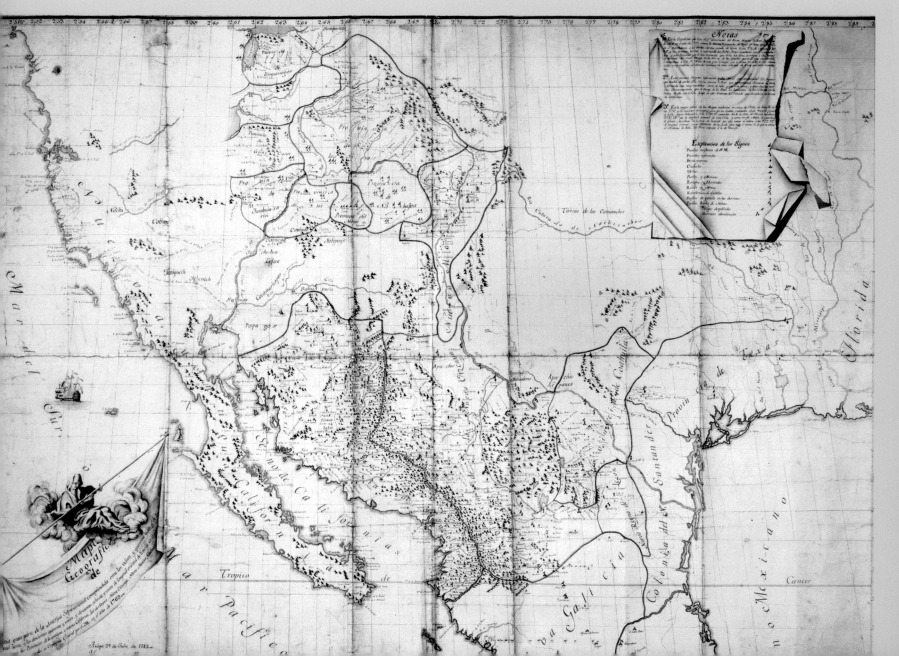

Nonetheless, Kino's discovery did not at the time lead to the establishment of a land route to the Californias. Indeed, mapmakers did not all accept that California was part of the mainland. But after another missionary, Fernando Consag, sailed right around the gulf in 1746, the king of Spain issued a decree officially proclaiming that California was not an island.

The ceding of Louisiana from France to Spain in 1762 led to another interior expedition being dispatched to inspect the new frontiers and recommend locations for new presidios. For almost two years, between 1766 and 1768, the expedition, led by the Marqués de Rubí, ranged over Texas and New Mexico. An engineer and a cartographer who accompanied Rubí, Nicolas de Lafora and José de Urrútia, drew a map, part of which is shown as MAP 138, *previous page*.

Reports of Russian and perhaps British activity to the north finally motivated Spain to begin exploring the coast of Alta California. In 1769 the Spanish fleet was sent to San Diego, meeting an overland expedition led by Gaspar de Portolá up the Baja that arrived shortly afterwards. Here the Franciscan Junipero Serra established the first of the Alta California missions, that of San Diego de Alcalá, in July 1769.

MAP 141 (*below*).
This summary map of Spanish America was drawn in 1782 and shows information from the expeditions of the previous fifteen years (with routes as double red lines) and the missions (black dots on a rectangle) established to that date. The mission at *S. Gabriel* (Los Angeles) is at the convergence of several routes. This is one of the earliest regional maps to show the great coastal indentation of San Francisco Bay. Northwards, beyond the bay, little is named. At center, top is the elongated province of *Nuevo Mexico*, with the *Rio Grande del Norte* and the mission settlements of *Sta Fé*, *Alburqueque*, and, to the south, *El Paso*. Shown at right with much less detail is the *Provincia de Texas*, and beyond that *Florida*.

MAP 140 (*above*).
An English version of Eusebio Kino's map, drawn in 1702, showing his proof that California was not an island. Baja is labeled *Part of California*.

Portolá continued northwards and found Monterey Bay. Here a second mission was founded by Serra, that of San Carlos Borroméo de Carmelo, in June 1770. It was moved to a better site near the Carmel River the following year. Portolá continued northwards, finding San Francisco Bay in October. This was thought to be the mouth of a large river, and it was not until 1775, when Juan de Ayala sailed through the Golden Gate, that it was found to be an extensive bay. In 1773, Juan Bautista de Anza, sometimes called "the last conquistador" for his role in the expansion of the Spanish empire, was instructed to begin the settlement of Alta California. To confirm that there was a viable land link between New Spain and Alta California, he led an expedition in January 1774 north from the presidio at Tubas (near today's Mexico-U.S. border at Nogales), where he was commandant. He took with him thirty men and a Franciscan missionary, Francisco Tomás Garcés, arriving in March at the mission at San Gabriel Arcángel (established in September 1771 at Montebello and moved to San Gabriel in 1776, both within what is today metropolitan Los Angeles; see page 206). Two years later, in 1776, he went north to San Francisco, where, on this strategic bay offering rare shelter on the West Coast, a presidio was to be built. At the same time Garcés journeyed on his own to the San Joaquin Valley and then east to the Colorado River, reaching as far as the Hopi pueblos on the Little Colorado River, near what is today Flagstaff, Arizona.

Two other Franciscans ranged over a wide area in 1776. Francisco Domínguez and Silvestre Vélez de Escalante left Santa Fe intending to find a route to Monterey. Going north along the Rio Grande they discovered a prehistoric Anasazi settlement site near the headwaters of the Colorado. Turning westward they found Utah Lake and learned from the Indians of the larger Great Salt Lake to the north. But they went south, across the dry lands of southwestern Utah today named the Escalante Desert. Here, because of a lack of water and food, they abandoned the search for a route to Monterey. Nonetheless, through them the Spanish had gained knowledge of a vast area of the Southwest.

It was at this time too that several Spanish voyages were made far to the north in search of Russians. One of these voyages, that of Juan Francisco Bodega y Quadra, reached Alaska in 1775 (see page 107).

The Spanish policy of colonization through the founding of missions has been criticized as oppressive and paternalistic, even brutal. A chain of some eighteen missions was established throughout California by the end of the eighteenth century, and three more were added in the following century, the last in 1823. By that time California, always a neglected farthest outpost of Spain, had become part of a new Mexican empire after the independence of Mexico in 1821.

Map 142 (right, top).
San Francisco Bay and the surrounding area, drawn by Pedro Font in 1776. Font accompanied Juan Bautista de Anza in 1776. Anza's route is shown in red, leading to the tip of the peninsula where he was to establish his presidio. Three months later friars from Monterey built a new mission nearby, San Francisco de Asis—San Francisco. Bodega y Quadra's ship *Sonora* is shown off the coast.

Map 143 (right).
Father Silvestre Vélez de Escalante drew this map of his 1776 travels the next year. His route is marked in red. At top left is *Lago de Timpanogos*, a composite of Utah Lake, which he saw, and the Great Salt Lake, about which he heard from the Indians. The lake farther south, *Lago Salado de Teguayo*, is the now dry Sevier Lake. The *Rio de S^an Buenaventura* flows into this lake from the *Sierra de Timpanogos* to the north. This is the river many nineteenth-century maps depict flowing all the way to the Pacific at San Francisco Bay (see page 120). The Buenaventura shown here was in fact the Green River, which in reality flows into the Upper Colorado River, here labeled *Rio Zagucnanas*. The *Rio Colorado* flows off the bottom margin of the map.

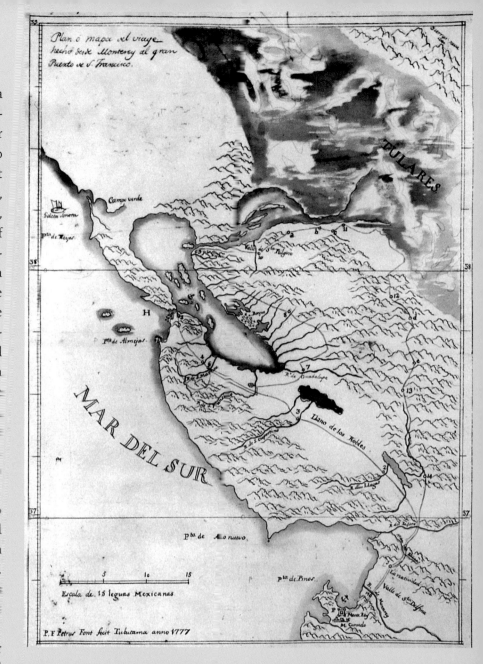

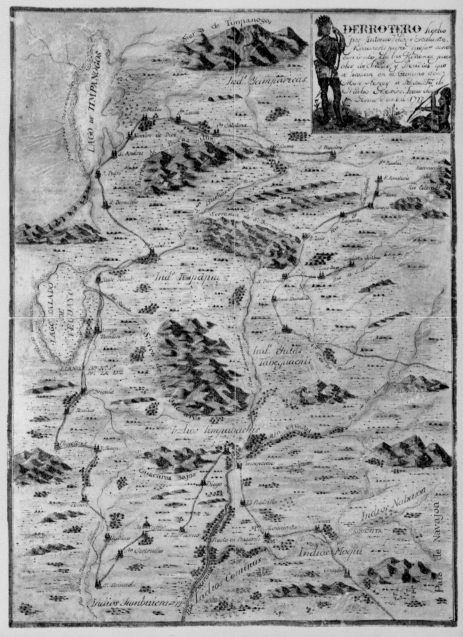

The Last Days of Colonial America

The British colonies in America were a fractious lot. Each was concerned about its own security, its own economic well-being, and did not care much for the others, except perhaps when it came to drawing a boundary line between them. Even efforts to raise troops for the defense of the Indian frontier rarely got much cooperation. Summoned to a congress at Albany in June and July 1754, the delegates seemed more preoccupied with bickering about land claims than with their common defense. Benjamin Franklin's urgings to unite in a common cause (MAP 145, *right*) fell on deaf ears. Yet within two decades, the colonies *were* ready to unite, severing their connection with Britain altogether.

It was the cumulative effect of issues in the period leading up to the Revolution that changed colonial sentiment, rather than any single seminal event, together with a handful of men ready and willing to guide public opinion to a revolutionary path. One of those men was James Otis, a Boston lawyer who in presenting a merchants' petition against searches of private property for smuggled goods in 1761 characterized such searches as endangering both common-law and the natural rights of man. He quickly became an early leader of Massachusetts dissent.

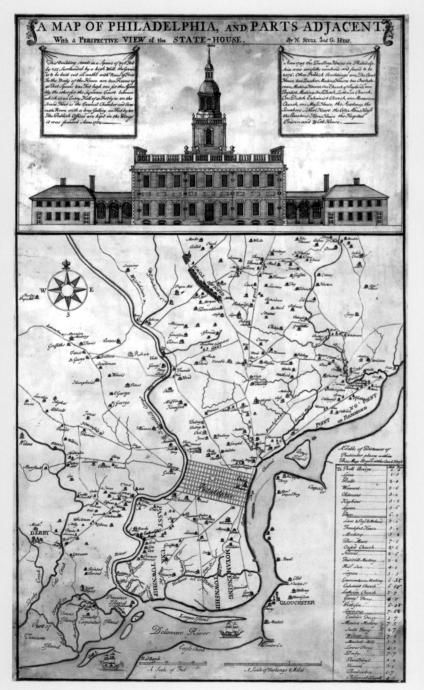

Above. Idyllic scene in the restored colonial capital of Williamsburg, Virginia.

MAP 145 (*below*).
The original version of Benjamin Franklin's famous snake map of the British colonies was published in the *Philadelphia Gazette* on 9 May 1754. Franklin was urging the colonies to unite in a "general government" to deal with Indian raids on frontier settlements, many of which were instigated by the French. Later the snake became associated with colonial union under the banner "Don't Tread on Me."

The Royal Proclamation of 1763, intended to be a "good" measure, was precisely the opposite to the colonists. They expected a British victory in the French and Indian War to lead to an opening up of the "conquered" country beyond the mountains, but instead it led to mandated constriction. And the war had left Britain with a large debt that had to be paid off. Who better to finance it than the very colonies the war supposedly benefited? British first lord of the treasury George Grenville soon introduced several measures designed to raise money from the colonies—but at the cost of increasingly alienating them from the mother country.

The American Duties Act of 1764 (often referred to as the Sugar Act) reduced the existing tax on imported sugar but widened the scope of the tax to include some wines, cloths, silk, and coffee. It also called for much more rigorous collection of the tax than had hitherto been the case. This tax hurt the richer elements of colonial society—and its most articulate—and led to the first cries of "no taxation without representation." Otis published a pamphlet called *The Rights of the Colonies Asserted and Proved.* Later that year the Currency Act disallowed the use of paper money. This mea-

MAP 144 (*left*).
The first edition, published in 1752, of Nicholas Scull and George Heap's famous plan of Philadelphia and vicinity, including a view of the Pennsylvania State House (Independence Hall), where the first and second Continental Congresses would meet in September 1774 and May 1775 and the Declaration of Independence would be signed on 4 July 1776. The drawing was made before the building was completed. Names of landowners dot the countryside. William Penn's plan for the city, stretching between the Delaware and the Schuylkill rivers, gives a false idea of the actual urban area, which is better represented in MAP 146 (*right*).

sure fell hardest on the poorer colonial population. Having alienated both the richest and the poorest elements of society, Grenville then went on to introduce the (first) Quartering Act, by which the colonies had to provide billets and provisions for British troops. But Grenville's pièce de résistance was the Stamp Act of March 1765, which Grenville himself thought—initially—brilliant. Revenue stamps were to be required on all manner of legal documents, from customs papers to contracts. The act's comprehensiveness promised to raise a considerable sum of money for the coffers of the treasury, and prominent men were appointed in the colonies to administer the stamps—with, of course, a commission for themselves. Those who eagerly sought these positions, however, were soon to regret doing so.

Once again, the hostility of the most powerful colonists was assured. An organization calling itself the Sons of Liberty was formed and a boycott of the stamps called for and enforced. Behind this dissent stood Samuel Adams, who was to feature large in the later struggle. In the Virginia House of Burgesses, Patrick Henry promoted a series of "resolves" in May 1765 renouncing the tax—without representation—as an infringement of rights. In May the Massachusetts Assembly invited all colonies to send delegates to a Stamp Act Congress, which, in October, passed a resolution that "no taxes ever have been or can be imposed on them but by their respective legislatures." It was another step on the road to united action. The paralysis of trade affected British merchants, who brought pressure to bear on the British government, from whence Grenville had now departed; amazingly, there were riots in the streets of London as well as Boston. The unenforceable Stamp Act was repealed in 1766, although a Declaratory Act

MAP 146 (below).
This rather artistic map of Philadelphia was drawn in 1777 and is thought to correctly represent the extent of the built-up area at that time.

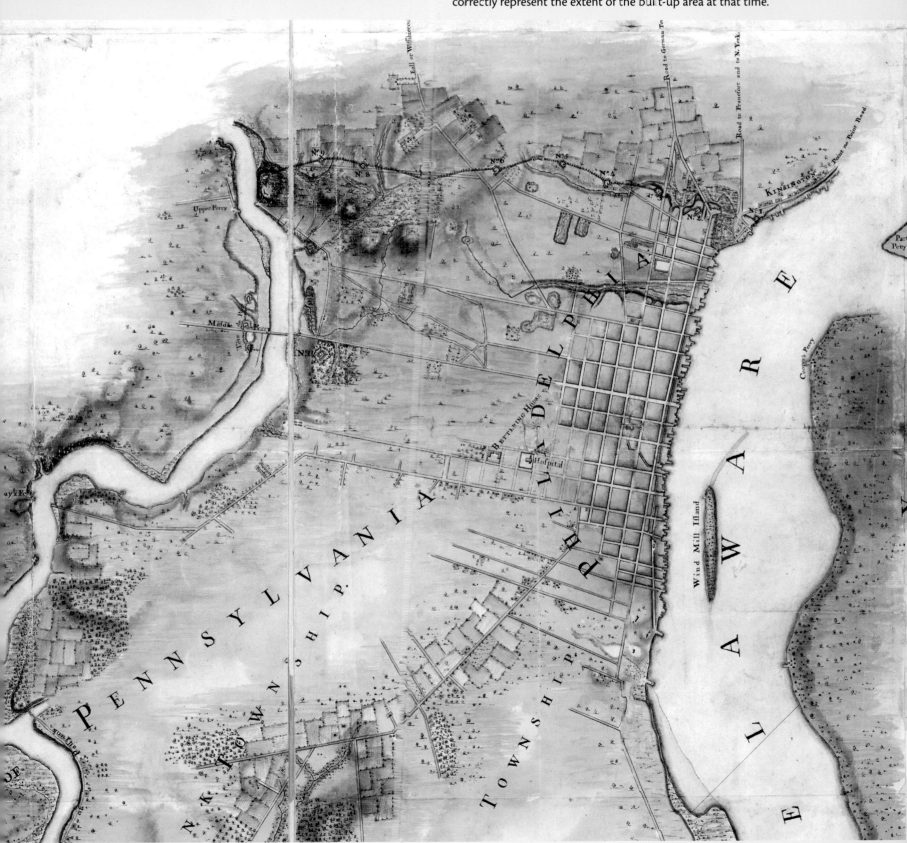

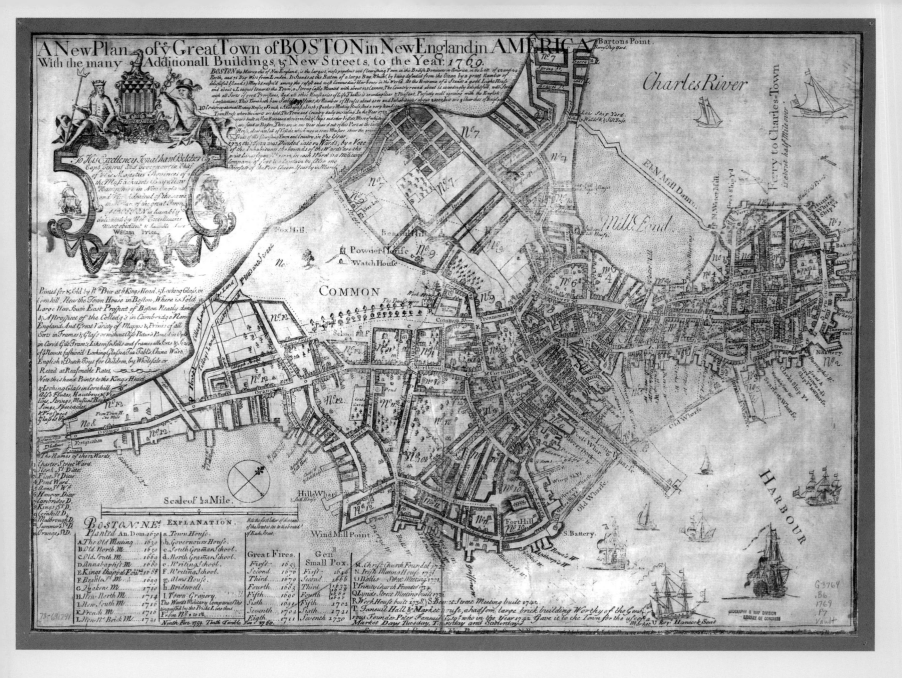

MAP 147 (*above*).

Boston, the hotbed of the Revolution, shown in a 1769 map. This superbly defensible site was only approachable by land by the narrow *Boston Neck*, shown at left, complete with *Gallows*. This detailed map contains much information, including an annotated list of significant buildings with their dates of construction, a list of the fires suffered (eight), and a list of smallpox epidemics (seven).

was passed to continue to maintain the assertion—rapidly becoming the fiction—of Britain's authority to tax the colonists.

The following year a new British chancellor of the exchequer, Charles Townshend, introduced a series of measures designed to raise money from the colonists—he hoped—without protest. Duties on imports were levied rather than charging an internal tax. But this was but a technical difference. These so-called Townshend Acts did not stir up the furor caused by the Stamp Act, but they were still recognized for what they were—taxation by an imperial power. Boycotts of the imports were organized and customs officials assaulted in Boston, which was rapidly becoming a hotbed of discontent.

British troops were sent to Boston to enforce the law, and on 5 March 1770 a small contingent of these "redcoats" fired on an unruly Boston crowd after one of the soldiers was hit by a flying club. Five colonists died. Quickly dubbed the "Boston massacre," the incident was used by Samuel Adams and others as proof of British tyranny, and it fanned rising flames of rebellion. The Townshend Acts were repealed in 1770 as once more unenforceable, and the duties disappeared—except that on tea.

The next three years saw a period of relative calm, although in June 1772 the British revenue schooner HMS *Gaspee* was burned near Providence while stuck on a sandbar. Commanded by a particularly zealous captain, the ship had gone aground while chasing a ship thought to be smuggling, and local colonists decided to get their own back. Reputedly dressed as Narragansett Indians, they boarded the *Gaspee* and destroyed it. So outraged was the British government that a reward of £500, a huge sum in those days, was offered for the conviction of those responsible. The incident has passed almost into popular folklore as the first blow of the Revolution.

In 1773 the East India Company was given a monopoly on the importation of tea, and the company was authorized to sell directly to retailers, thus threatening to put many merchants out of business. At most ports, ships were turned away, but in Boston the company determined to force the issue. On 16 December 1773 a group of men, likely led by Samuel Adams, disguised themselves as Mohawks and boarded three ships and dumped the tea into the harbor. This "Boston Tea Party" escalated the conflict dramatically. Laws had been broken and Parliament, now led by a more hard-line first lord of the treasury, Lord North, felt it had to assert its control, or soon there would be none.

New laws were enacted, in May and June 1774, which as a group were known in Britain as the Coercive Acts and in the colonies as the Intolerable Acts. A Boston Port Act closed the port of Boston until the tea was paid for, which was indeed intolerable for the city, whose very lifeblood was seaborne trade. An Administration of Justice Act allowed royal governor Thomas Gage to send officials accused of capital crimes to England for trial, so as to avoid hostile colonial juries. It was dubbed the "Murder Act" by the colonists. A Massachusetts Government Act effectively abrogated that colony's charter, limiting the power of town meetings and providing for direct control by governor Gage. A new Quartering Act required colonies to provide housing for troops, even in private houses. And then the Quebec Act, which was not

intended as one of North's punitive acts but was widely seen as one of them, extended the province of Quebec south to the Ohio and west to the Mississippi, destroying all charter claims and seemingly handing them over to a principally Catholic government, hemming in the British colonies forever.

The British tightening of the screws led—perhaps inevitably—to the final act. It began with colonial unity. At the First Continental Congress, held in Philadelphia in September 1774, all the colonies save Georgia sent representatives "to consult upon the present unhappy state of the colonies." There British laws were denounced as unconstitutional, parliamentary jurisdiction over the colonies was denied, and colonists were advised to arm and set up militias. A "Continental Association" was established to implement a total boycott of British imports. New York lawyer John Jay composed an eloquent "Address to the People of Great Britain," which memorably began: "When a Nation, led to greatness by the hand of Liberty . . ." It was endorsed, as was a petition sent to the king. Finally, the congress agreed to meet again on 10 May 1775 if matters were not by then resolved

MAP 148 (above).

America on the eve of revolution. This is a 1771 English map derived from French sources as well as English. Most of the colonies are shown more or less according to their claims and thus extend to the Mississippi; Virginia extends northwards, covering much of what is today the Canadian province of Ontario. The colonies of West and East Florida are also shown; these would be lost to the new United States in the 1783 treaty and not regained until 1819. The lands of many of the Indian tribes are indicated.

Of course, they were not. In November 1774, King George III wrote that "the die is now cast, the Colonies must either submit or triumph." By the time the Second Continental Congress met, the first shots of the War for Independence had been fired at Concord and Lexington. Although there were still many in the colonies loyal to the British Crown, events had overtaken them, and the more radical elements were now in charge. Massachusetts was aflame and the rest of the country was soon to follow.

The Shot Heard Round the World

John Adams famously made a distinction between the American Revolution and the War for Independence; the Revolution occurred, he maintained, before the war could take place, a revolution in the hearts and minds of the American colonists that would sustain them through the years of war. Yet we know that even as the war began, perhaps 20 percent of the population remained loyal to Britain and only supported secession as the war went on, indeed, as the war was won. Many did not want independence, and 100,000 Loyalists left at war's end, kick-starting the populating of British Canada. Thus the war was in many senses civil, orchestrated at first by relatively few, notably Samuel Adams and John Hancock. Nonetheless, the countryside around Boston was by early 1775 seething with discontent, a tinderbox requiring only a spark to ignite.

Thomas Gage, military governor of Massachusetts, had learned from spies that there was a cache of military supplies hidden at Concord, including three large cannon that could be used to threaten Boston itself. As a bonus, Samuel Adams and John Hancock were also reported to be at Lexington, on the Concord road. Gage therefore dispatched six hundred men under Lieutenant Colonel Francis Smith in a surprise raid to seize the offending hardware, and with luck the rebel leaders as well. The redcoats were ferried across the harbor instead of marching out of Boston via the

Neck in order to maximize the surprise. But by this time the colonists had set up an elaborate early warning system, one that began with Paul Revere's iconic ride, and just after dawn on 19 April 1775 seventy-seven Massachusetts "minutemen" militia were loosely formed up on the common at Lexington, not expecting more than ill words from their adversaries, Smith's advance guard. Stand firm, they will not fire; we are all Englishmen, are we not? But someone unknown fired, signaling the beginning of the first popular revolution against a crowned head. And from that moment the militiamen were irrevocably no longer Englishmen, but *Americans*.

After the exchange of gunfire, eight militiamen lay dead and ten were wounded, as was one British soldier. The redcoats pressed on to Concord, but news of their deeds preceded them, and more and more minutemen rushed to the scene. Most of the munitions the British had come for were spirited away and, fearing that the British were setting fire to houses in the village, a stand was made at the North Bridge, over the Concord River. "Fire, fellow soldiers—for God's sake fire!" shouted Major John Buttrick of the Concord militia. It was this first deliberate firing on British troops that Ralph Waldo Emerson later poetically characterized as the shot heard round the world. The British retreated in some disarray, saved only by reinforcements in the form of twelve hundred men under Brigadier General Hugh,

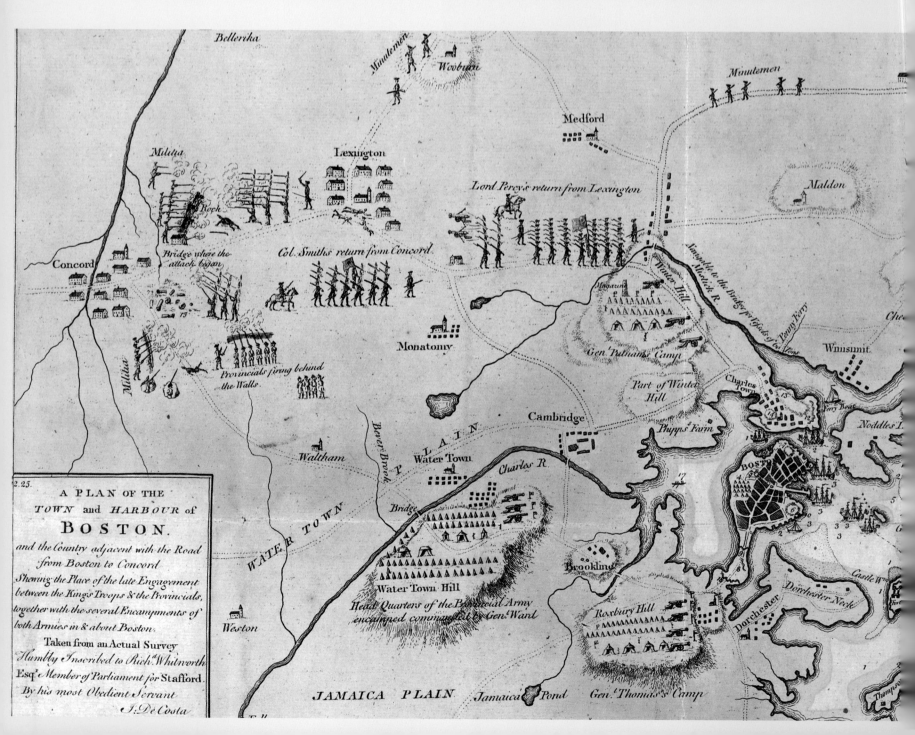

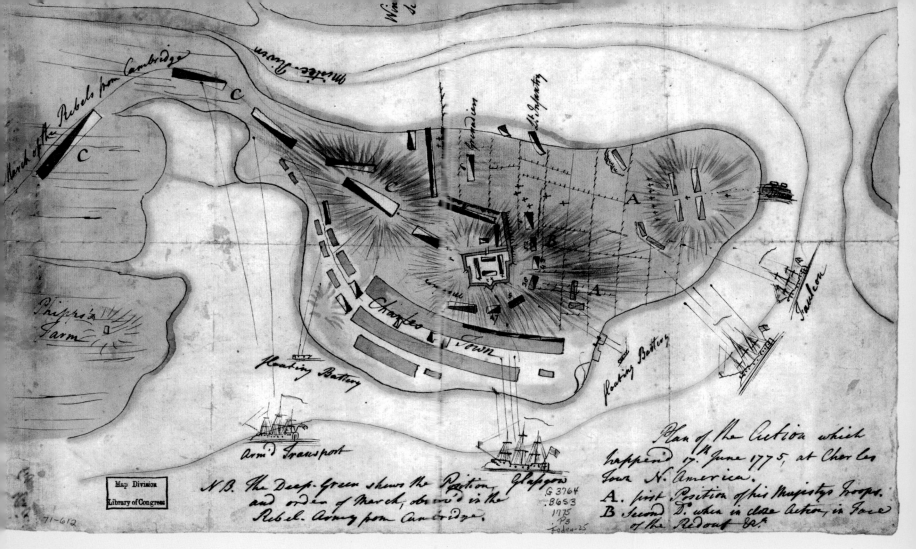

N.B. The Deep-Green shews the Position, Glasgow and order of March, observ'd in the Rebel. Army from Cambridge.

G 3764
.B6S3
1775
.R8
Fedeer 25

Plan of the Action which happen'd 17th June 1775, at Charles Town N. America.
A. first Position of his Majestys Troops.
B. Second D° when in close Action, in Face of the Redoubt &c.

Map 150 (*above*).

The assault on Breed's Hill, always called the Battle of Bunker Hill, 17 June 1775. American militiamen fortified Breed's Hill overnight and in the morning came under fire from British ships in the harbor, followed around noon by a British amphibous landing of about twelve hundred redcoats, with more arriving through the afternoon. The Americans lost the battle but inflicted stunning casualty levels on the British. Lack of coordinated command hurt the American side and pointed to the necessity of an overall command system.

Earl Percy. Even then, constant sniping accompanied the withdrawal, which was to the Charlestown Peninsula rather than Boston Neck, the bridge over the Charles River at Cambridge having been destroyed. Seventy-three British soldiers were killed, 174 wounded, and another 26 were missing. The rebellion had become a war—a war the other colonies would join.

The war had been anticipated; in Virginia a month before, Patrick Henry had given his famous "give me liberty or give me death" speech to a Virginia assembly called to begin preparations for armed combat. "Our chains are forged," Henry proclaimed. "Their clanking may be heard on the plains of Boston."

On 25 May, thousands more redcoats arrived in Boston from England, and with them three major generals who were to play a large part in Britain's war against the Revolution: William Howe, Henry Clinton, and John Burgoyne. The British strength in the city was now about 10,000. Gage made preparations to march out of Boston, and to counter this on the night of 16 June, a number of New England militia units began to fortify Breed's Hill, on the Charlestown Peninsula. Finding as dawn broke

Map 149 (*left*).

This fine explanatory map shows the movements of the British and American troops on 19 April 1775, when the British ventured to seize arms at Concord. The War for Independence began on the green at Lexington that morning. The map shows a sequence of events. Smith's men were ferried across the harbor to *Phipps's Farm*, then marched to *Lexington*, where the first shots were fired. They then continued to *Concord*, where the *Bridge where the attack began* is indicated, surrounded by many more militiamen, who had rushed to defend the town. The return of Smith's men and of Percy's larger contingent is depicted as they march back toward the Charlestown Peninsula. Percy diverted his troops to Charlestown when he found that the bridge at *Cambridge* had been destroyed and the crossing was defended by militia. Later encampments of the provincial army are also shown.

Map 151 (*below*).

The only contemporary map recording the opening shots of the War for Independence is this one, copied by Lieutenant Frederick Mackenzie, a British officer, and pasted into his diary facing the page for 19 April 1775. The map shows the action at Concord; it has been oriented with north at the top and depicts a sequence of events. The North Bridge is at top right; the Concord River winds its way across the top part of the page. Significantly, since the map was drawn by a British officer, the British army units tend to be shown accurately, but the American units, whose size was unknown to the British, are shown larger than they actually were, such as at the third American position at John Buttrick's farm, just north of the North Bridge. The first American position is the divided rectangle at bottom right, the second at the northern end of the high ground, at center right. *Top, opposite*, is the reconstructed North Bridge at Concord as it is today.

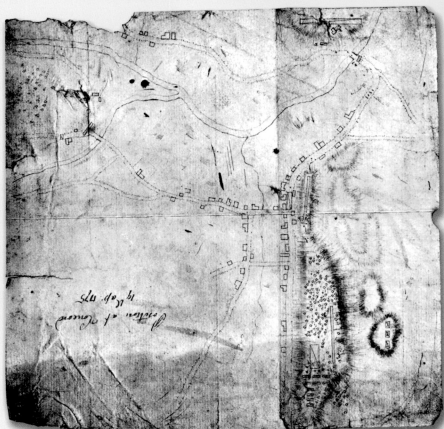

MAP 152 (*above*).
The American attack on Québec, 31 December 1775–1 January 1776, depicted in a British map. The map was published in London in September 1776. The American army is shown in yellow to the west of the city, on the Plains of Abraham where James Wolfe's British army had defeated the French under Montcalm in 1759. *L* is the place Montgomery landed, and *M* is the place Arnold was wounded. Across the river are guns set up in April 1776, hastily removed when the British fleet arrived in May.

rebel fortifications now threatening Boston itself, Gage ordered an attack. Some twelve hundred redcoats under William Howe landed to the east of Charlestown about noon on 17 June and marched to within fifty yards of a position manned by New Hampshire militia under Colonel John Stark, who famously had ordered his men not to fire until they could "see the whites of their eyes." Now, as the redcoats deployed from column to line to charge with bayonets, the whites of their eyes could be seen, and the British were mown down by accurate close-range musket fire. An hour later, Howe regrouped his men for another frontal assault, with similar murderous results. Reinforced by more troops under Clinton, a third charge enabled enough soldiers to get over the American earthworks, face to face with militia whose ammunition was running low.

The Americans fled, and the British had won the day, but at an enormous cost. Out of perhaps 2,500 redcoats engaged, 226 were killed and more than 800 wounded. The Americans lost 140 killed and 301 wounded out of 1,500 actually fighting. There were many others who could have reinforced the American line and were requested to, but too many field commanders—each contingent of militia had its own—led to confusion and defeat. It underlined the absolute necessity for a supreme command and an organized chain of command, especially against a similarly endowed and highly trained British army.

In fact, George Washington had been appointed commander-in-chief on 15 June—but would not take up his duties until 3 July—by the Second Continental Congress, which had convened in Philadelphia beginning 10 May. In July Congress sent the so-called Olive Branch Petition, authored by Pennsylvania delegate John Dickinson, directly to King George III. The king refused to read it and, stating the obvious, instead declared the colonies to be in rebellion.

On the same day the Second Continental Congress first met, Fort Ticonderoga fell into American hands. On 10 May, the fort was taken in a bloodless stealthy early morning raid by a small band of militia under Ethan Allen and Benedict Arnold. Considering the nature of this immense fortification and previous struggles to take it, this was a tremendous coup for the American side. Crown Point was taken two days later; even Fort St-Jean on the Richelieu River north of Lake Champlain was taken and held until a counterattack by British troops from nearby Fort Chambly.

Then in the fall came a more organized American attack on Canada. It was a two-pronged advance reminiscent of the various British plans to attack French Canada during the French and Indian War (see page 56). One army, led initially by Philip Schuyler but when he became ill by Richard Montgomery, this time took both Fort St-Jean and Fort Chambly, and then Montréal on 13 November without a fight. In the meantime, Benedict Arnold led another army up the Kennebec and down the Chaudière rivers—ironically using a route surveyed by the British army—appearing opposite Québec on 13 November. A demand that the city surrender was met the same way New England Admiral Phips's demand had been in 1699—from the mouth of a cannon. Arnold then retreated up the St. Lawrence, where he met up with Montgomery's men moving north.

On the night of 31 December 1775–1 January 1776 a combined assault was launched on the city of Québec. In a blinding snowstorm Montgomery led his troops into an artillery trap and was killed; Arnold had more success penetrating the town but was wounded. Both Montgomery's landing place and the site of Arnold's wounding are shown on MAP 152 (*left*). The American armies continued to besiege Québec, and an attempt was made to persuade the French-Canadian population to join the Revolution, but the delegation, which included Benjamin Franklin and Charles Carroll (who would become the only Roman Catholic signer of the Declaration of Independence), arrived at the same time as a British fleet carrying ten thousand soldiers under the command of John Burgoyne. Outnumbered, the Americans withdrew.

The battle for the hearts and minds of the American colonists was immensely aided in January 1776 by the publication of a pamphlet, *Common Sense*, by Thomas Paine, a Briton who had been in the colonies only a short while. His essay argued powerfully for independence. In June a resolution was introduced to Congress by Virginia delegate Richard Henry Lee that "these United Colonies are, and of right ought to be, free and independent States . . . " The resolution was extensively reworked and added to by another Virginia delegate, Thomas Jefferson, and became the Declaration of Independence. It was approved by Congress and signed by John Hancock as president and Charles Thomson as secretary on 4 July, and by fifty delegates on 2 August. (Five signed later in the year, and one, Thomas McKean of Delaware, did not sign until 1781.)

On 17 March 1776 the British evacuated Boston to Halifax. William Howe had taken over command from Gage in October and now proceeded to plan an assault on New York, which he intended to use as his base of operations. A British army of about thirty thousand, including mercenaries from Brunswick and other German states (collectively known to Americans as Hessians), occupied Staten Island on 2 July, at the very moment Congress was finalizing the Declaration of Independence. Washington's army of about nineteen thousand men held the high ground at Brooklyn Heights and the Brooklyn Peninsula in a heavily fortified position.

But Washington was outmaneuvered by Howe; the British army knew how to engage in large-scale battles, but—as yet—the Americans did not. On 22 to 25 August some twenty-three thousand men were landed on Long Island (MAP 153, *right, top*) and marched at night to outflank and surround the American position on Brooklyn Heights (MAP 154, *below*). American casualties were far greater than those of the British and Hessian troops. Taking advantage of Howe's slow follow-up, on the night of 29–30 August, with the aid of a flotilla of colonial boatmen, Washington managed to evacuate ten thousand of his men across the East River to Manhattan, averting what might otherwise have been a disaster.

Retreating up Manhattan, Washington made a stand at Harlem Heights on 16 September that temporarily held back the British. If nothing else, this had a positive effect on American morale. Howe now planned to outflank Washington and sent troops up the Hudson by boat. Washington left two thousand men at Fort Washington (in northwestern Manhattan) and withdrew to a defensive position near the village of White Plains. The British attacked, were winning the many skirmishes, and would likely have overwhelmed the still inexperienced American army. But a decisive battle never came, for Howe failed to press home his advantage and withdrew.

Howe then turned his attention to Fort Washington, and a British attack was made more effective when an American deserter gave the British a detailed plan of the fort. Fort Washington fell on 16 November, and four days later its sister Fort Lee, across the river in New Jersey, was abandoned. The British were secure in New York City and would remain so for the rest of the war.

Washington retreated into New Jersey and crossed the Delaware River, his prospects grim. Many of his troops would terminate their enlistment contracts at the end of the year, and Washington needed to persuade them to remain. He needed a victory to restore morale. The Americans had initially been pursued by an army under Charles, Earl Cornwallis, but the British had then decided, as was the military norm, to go into winter quarters. A large detachment of Hessian mercenaries commanded by Colonel Johann Rall were encamped in Trenton. Acting on intelligence as to their whereabouts and condition—it was Christmas Day and much drinking was going on—Washington crossed the ice floe–choked Delaware in a fleet of small boats under cover of darkness and a snowstorm and, despite the fact that only a third of his men made it across the river, fell on the town the following morning. The sleepy Hessians were quickly routed, and the Americans took nine hundred prisoners (MAP 155, *overleaf*).

Knowing that Cornwallis's army was not far away, Washington recrossed the Delaware complete with prisoners. Then he regrouped, finding that many of his men whose enlistments were expiring suddenly wanted to remain. With

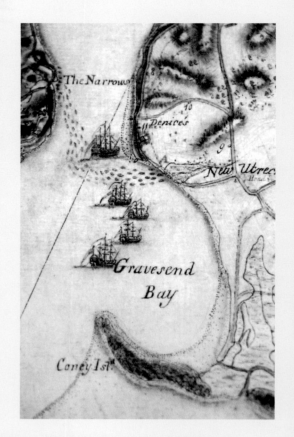

MAP 153 (*right, top*).
The 22 August 1776 landing of British troops on Long Island is depicted in this British military map.

MAP 154 (*right*).
A summary map of the August 1776 Long Island operations of the British army, drawn from the maps of military surveyor Samuel Holland and published in Britain to keep the public up to date with the latest from the American war. Staten Island, the first landing place of the British army, incoming from Halifax, is at bottom left. The landing of the army on the Long Island shores of Verrazano Narrows is shown, and the red lines depict the routes various detachments took thereafter. Most notable is the outflanking movement, which was led by Clinton (not Howe, as stated on the map), around Brooklyn Heights, surrounding part of the American army (in yellow) on the heights. The bulk of Washington's men escaped across the East River to Manhattan during the night of 29–30 August 1776.

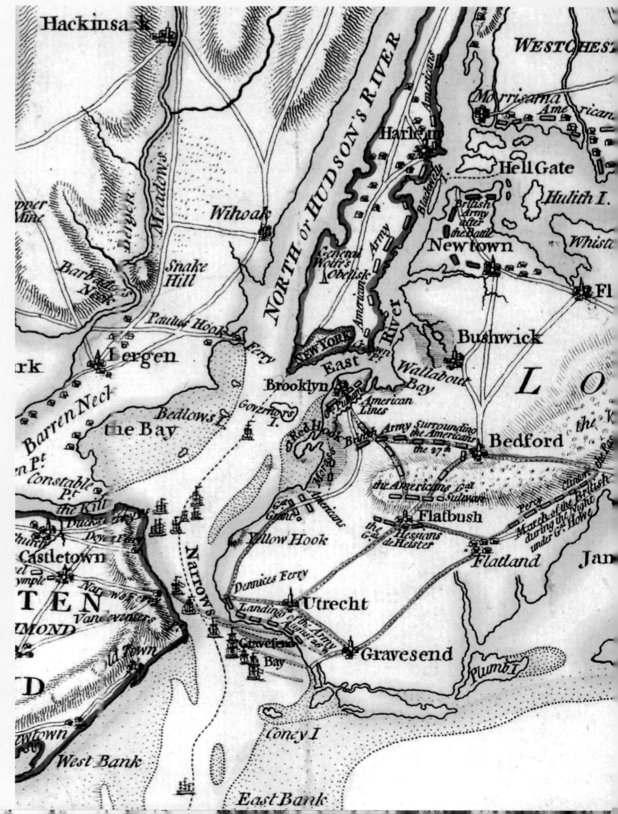

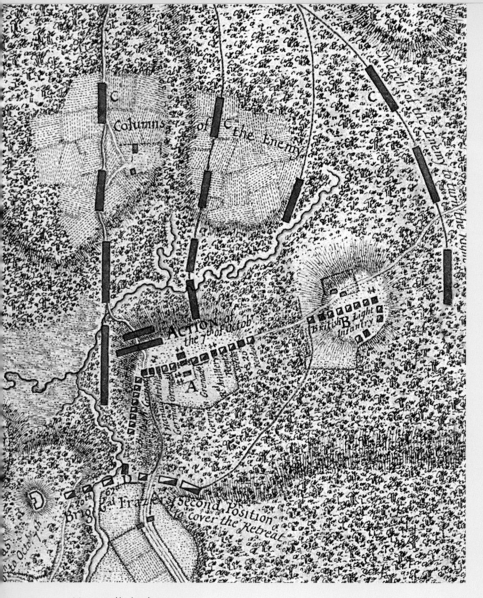

MAP 160 (*left*).
The action at the Second Battle of Saratoga, also called the Battle of Bemis Heights, 7 October 1777. This is a British map, so the American army is labeled *Columns of the Enemy.*

MAP 161 (*below*).
Burgoyne's end. This was the position of the two armies after the British retreated up the Hudson following the Second Battle of Saratoga, while Burgoyne debated whether to surrender. North is to the right, and the Hudson River flows from right to left. The British and Hessian armies occupy the heights surrounded by the American army, shown in yellow. Gates's main force is at left, while the Hessians are outflanked by Daniel Morgan's riflemen at top. Across the river are more American units with two artillery pieces. Burgoyne has nowhere to go. In the end he realized his position was hopeless, and Gates allowed him to sign a generous "convention," which carefully avoided the term "capitulation." The surrender of the whole British army was finalized on 17 October 1777, but only after much dithering by Burgoyne, who had hoped against hope that Clinton's army might still miraculously appear. Gates finally sent him an ultimatum: sign or the American army would attack in ten minutes. Burgoyne quickly signed. This map was part of a set of revolutionary war maps published in 1780 by British mapmaker William Faden, who has the date on the map wrong: *10th of September 1777* should be 10 October 1777.

their casualties, whereas the American army was being augmented every day as men flocked to the cause.

For it was clear that the battle had not yet been decided. Burgoyne fortified his position, encouraged by news that Henry Clinton was ascending the Hudson to meet him, as per the original plan. Deciding on what was essentially a full frontal assault, Burgoyne renewed the attack on the entrenched Americans on 7 October. Gates remained behind the fortifications on Bemis Heights, sending out brigades under Brigadier Generals Enoch Poor and Ebenezer Learned, with Daniel Morgan's riflemen on the left flank. At the height of the battle, Benedict Arnold joined in, against Gates's orders (he had quarreled with Gates and been relieved of his command), directing assaults from the very front and making a critical difference in the ebb and flow of the battle; Arnold was by now undoubtedly the best of the American battlefield commanders. Here, at this battle known as the Battle of Bemis Heights or the Second Battle of Saratoga, Arnold was again wounded in the leg, the same he had wounded at Québec.

As darkness fell, the British had managed to retain their battlefield position, but again only with considerable losses. Leaving campfires burning, Burgoyne's army retreated to the river and the next day withdrew seven miles north before being surrounded by the pursuing Americans. Here, at Saratoga (today's Schuylerville, New York), the British position was clearly untenable: their supply lines were fragile or nonexistent, and they could neither advance nor retreat; further, no help could now be expected from Clinton. After debating for several days, and negotiating generous terms, on 17 October Burgoyne surrendered his army to Gates. This surrender of an entire British army was perhaps the most significant turning point of the war, for it helped convince the French to enter the war on the American side, an alliance that was officially signed on 6 February 1778.

Henry Clinton, in the meantime, had tried to advance up the Hudson to meet Burgoyne but ultimately had retreated, likely saving himself from a similar fate to that which befell Burgoyne. The day before the second Saratoga battle, Clinton had attacked and taken two forts on the Hudson, Fort Montgomery and Fort Clinton, held by his namesakes New York governor George Clinton and his brother, Brigadier General James Clinton. The forts were only about 45 miles upriver from Manhattan. The river at this point was protected by American booms, and so troops were landed downriver and marched north to the forts (MAP 162, *above, right*), where Henry Clinton's superior tactical skills won the day. However, he did not continue north, except to send ships to Kingston, New York, which was burned. Clinton's army never came closer than about 120 miles to Burgoyne's. A privately relieved Clinton turned back because Howe sent him an order to send reinforcements to Philadelphia (see next page), which Howe considered more important than New England. Gates wanted to continue his northward march into Canada; after all, he now had about seventeen thousand men under his command, a formidable army indeed. But he got into disagreements with Washington, who was convinced

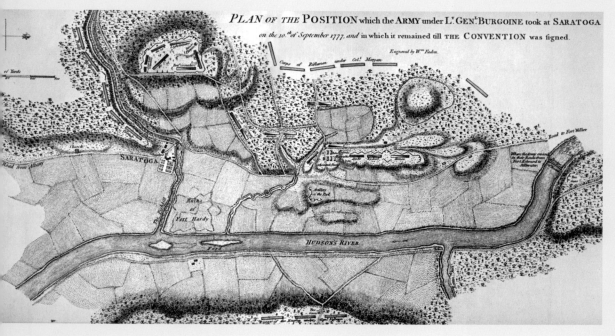

PLAN OF THE POSITION which the ARMY under Lt. Genl. BURGOINE took at SARATOGA on the 10.th of September 1777, and in which it remained till THE CONVENTION was signed.

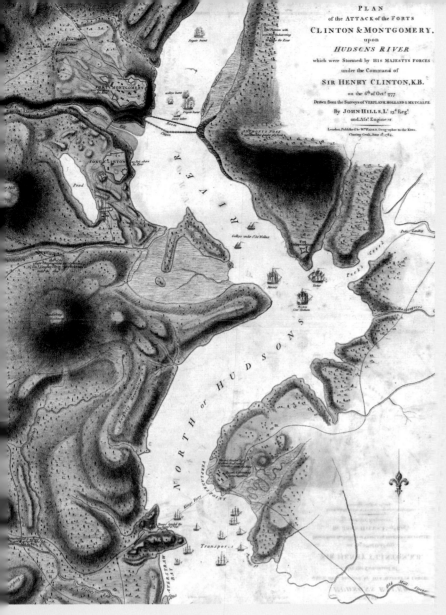

PLAN
of the ATTACK of the FORTS
CLINTON & MONTGOMERY,
upon
HUDSONS RIVER
which were Stormed by HIS MAJESTYS FORCES
under the Command of
SIR HENRY CLINTON, K.B.
on the 6.th of Oct.r 1777.
Drawn from the Surveys of VERPLANK HOLLAND & METCALFE.
By JOHN HILLS, L.t 23.d Reg.t
and Ass.t Engineer.
London, Published by W.m Faden, Geographer to the King,
Charing Cross, June 1.st 1784.

MAP 162 (*above*).
Forts Montgomery and Clinton on the Hudson River just above New York City and the attack by Henry Clinton on 6 October 1777.

that Gates was trying to usurp his position as the overall commander. A chance, perhaps, for a quick end to the war was lost.

British commander William Howe considered that if he could take Philadelphia, Loyalists in the middle colonies would be encouraged to fight the rebels, perhaps splitting the colonies in two. He therefore sailed with an army of about eighteen thousand men from New York to Head of Elk (now Elkton, Maryland), at the northern extremity of Chesapeake Bay, and marched toward Philadelphia. Washington, who after Princeton had managed to rebuild his army, opposed Howe at Brandywine Creek on 11 September 1777. Howe's force included battalions headed by Cornwallis and the Hessian Lieutenant General Wilhem von Knyphausen. The American army, although now numerically comparable to the British, was defeated, largely due to an outflanking movement by Cornwallis. Washington, it is said, badly needed a good map of the area, known for its broken topography (MAP 163, *right*), which Howe seemed to understand better.

There were further skirmishes. One, five days later, did not develop into a real battle due to low cloud and fog; this has been called the Battle of the Clouds. Five days later again, two battalions fell on an American encampment at night, bayoneting about 250 men as they slept. This incident, at Paoli, Pennsylvania, was quickly dubbed the Paoli Massacre and used to encourage recruiting. On 26 September, Howe finally occupied Philadelphia; Congress fled to Lancaster. Fog and cloud played a part once again at Germantown, now within the urban area of Philadelphia, on 4 October. Washington's dawn attack was confused by poor timing, the shooting of Americans by Americans in the fog, and the prolonged resistance of redcoats holed up in a house who would not surrender because they feared a repeat of the Paoli incident.

Howe likely realized that he had made a mistake in his overall strategy for the war when he heard of Burgoyne's surrender at Saratoga. Howe immediately submitted his resignation, although it was not accepted until May 1778, when Henry Clinton took over the British command. In June, Clinton evacuated Philadelphia, reconcentrating British power in New York City. A convoy carrying Loyalists, women, and the sick sailed from Philadelphia at the same time that about fifteen thousand men marched north overland. It is reckoned that about 10 percent of the Hessian mercenaries deserted during this march, melting into the countryside when they saw how comparatively well the American German population lived.

Washington's army was increasingly well trained, benefiting from the drilling of Prussian volunteer Friedrich von Steuben at Valley Forge over the previous winter. And although his army had dwindled in size during the hard winter, Washington now commanded more than fifteen thousand men, most of whom were now his Continentals, a standing army instead of short-term enlisted militia. The strung-out columns and baggage train of Clinton's New York–bound army offered a tempting target to Washington. Nonetheless the attack, which came near Monmouth (Freehold, New Jersey) on 28 June in the middle of a heat wave, nearly proved disastrous.

Washington first sent Charles Lee with about six thousand men to attack the British rear guard, about eight thousand under Cornwallis, but one of his divisions, that of Charles Scott, incorrectly deployed behind that of another, under Anthony Wayne, and was unable to fire on the British lines.

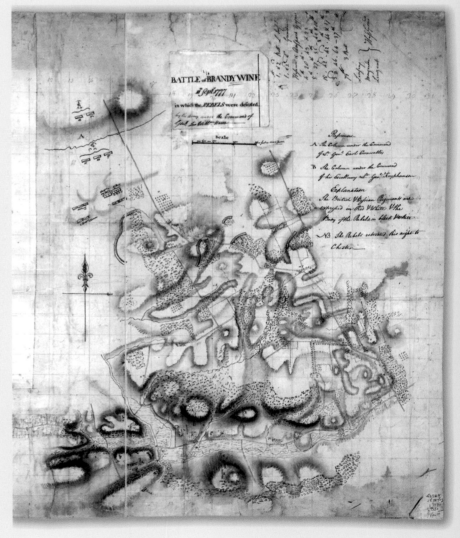

MAP 163.
The Battle of Brandywine, 11 September 1777. After a grand march clockwise around Washington's troops, in the center area of this map, Cornwallis's men appear to the north, at *A*, facing the American rear. Meanwhile an American attack across Brandywine Creek (bottom left) is repulsed as Washington discovers the artillery was left with Knyphausen (to the left of the creek).

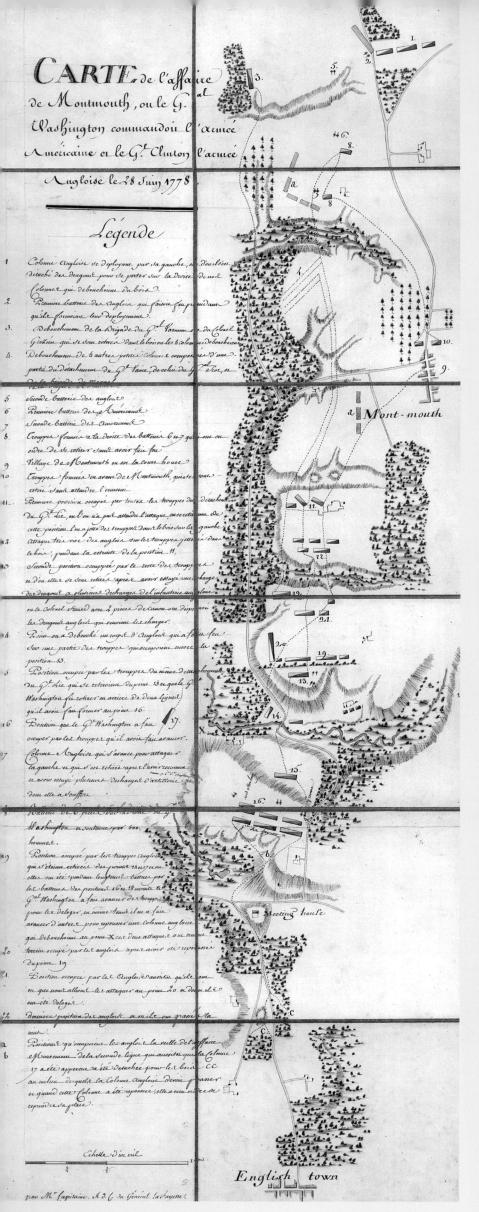

Map 164 (*left*).

The Battle of Monmouth, 28 June 1778, showing sequences of troop positions on a manuscript map made by a French officer. North is to the left. The British positions are in yellow or yellow and black, and American positions are gray and blue. The map is a bit confusing because it depicts multiple positions over the course of the day. The initial attack by Lee was at *11*, on the British troops at *a*. The fallback position behind the ravine, which was successfully held, was at *16*.

Map 165 (*right, top*).

The siege of Newport, shown on a rather beautiful French manuscript map. North is to the right. The besieging American positions are shown in yellow. The ships with blue flags are French, while the British are shown offshore (above). The French landed soldiers on Conanicut Island, opposite Newport, but retrieved them when they sailed off after the British fleet.

The result was a near rout, saved only by Washington himself, who managed to re-form the lines two miles distant. They then retreated to a more defensive position with the other parts of the army, behind a ravine (MAP 164, *left*). It was here that the wife of an artillery gunner, one Mary Hays, made a stand helping with the loading of the cannon after her husband was killed and the loader dropped from the heat, a feat that was transformed in the nineteenth century into the "legend of Molly Pitcher."

At the end of the day men on both sides more or less dropped where they stood, exhausted from the intense heat. The heat is thought to have claimed the lives of nearly a hundred of the combatants. Washington spent the night preparing for a new assault in the morning only to find, as dawn broke, that Clinton's army had slipped away, to meet with the British fleet at the Navesink River, below Sandy Hook. The Battle of Monmouth, which was the last major clash in the north, showed that an American army could stand up to a trained and disciplined British army in full field combat. For this the Continental Army, and Washington, could thank Von Steuben for his drills at Valley Forge.

The Americans pinned great hopes on their new alliance with the French, but the first cooperative effort was a dismal failure. This was an attempt to take Newport, Rhode Island, then held by the British for two years. At that time Newport was as important a port as New York or Boston. A French naval fleet under Rear Admiral Charles Théodat, Comte d'Estaing, was to coordinate an attack with Major General John Sullivan, in command of a Continental army at Providence augmented by militia. Estaing resented Sullivan giving him orders and considered the Americans amateurs. Sullivan resented Estaing's aristocratic behavior. It was a recipe for failure.

The plan was to mount a French amphibious assault while Sullivan crossed to Rhode Island from Tiverton. But Sullivan crossed too early and drove the British behind defensive works that could only be taken by siege. The appearance of a British fleet distracted Estaing, who gave chase, only to see both fleets dispersed in a storm. Sullivan, meanwhile, laid siege to Newport (MAP 165, *right, top*). When Estaing returned he informed an incredulous Sullivan that he had to sail on to Boston for a refit. Sullivan was outraged at what he called this "offence upon the alliance" but could do nothing. Seeing that the battle could not be won, his militia began to abandon him also, and when he retreated up-island he was chased by the defenders of Newport until a counterattack ended this harassment. Clinton arrived by sea a day later with five thousand men as reinforcements, but they were too late to have any effect. Newport remained in British hands until October 1779.

In June 1778, Spain declared war on Britain but, unlike the French, did not ally with the United States. Spain's involvement had little direct effect on

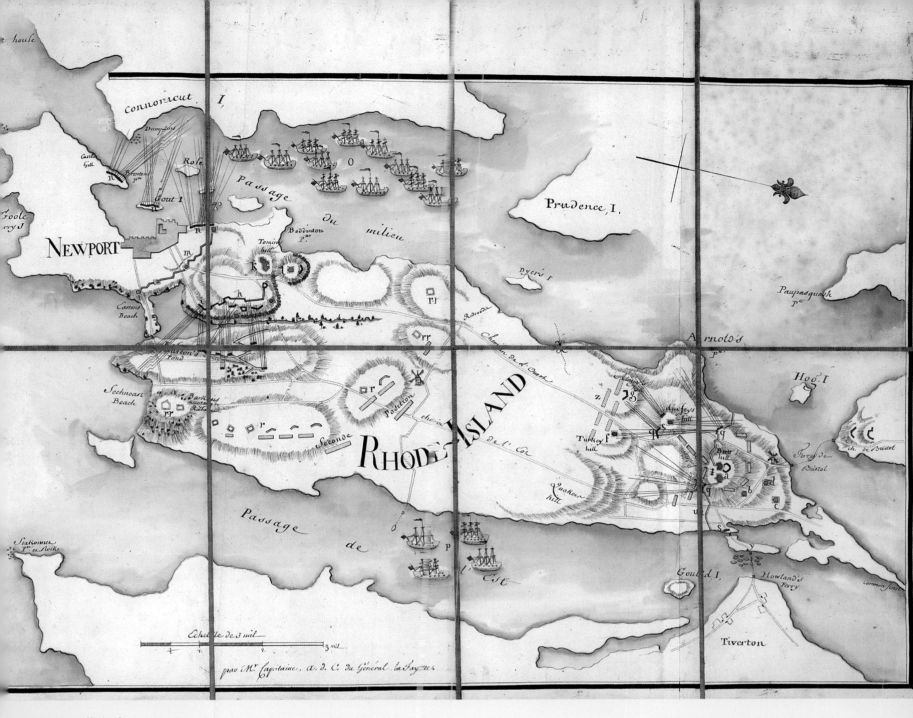

Map 166 (*below*).
The American and French siege of Savannah, December 1778. Benjamin Lincoln's camp is at bottom left and Estaing's at bottom center.

the course of the war, but did mean that at its end, after the machinations of international treaty making, Spain would gain back the Floridas.

To the northwest a young frontiersman, George Rogers Clark, led about 150 Virginia riflemen on a successful expedition to stop Indian raiding of trading posts, raids that had been organized by the British governor of Detroit, Henry Hamilton. On 25 February 1779, Clark took Vincennes (Indiana), and the predominantly French population of the town quickly changed their allegiance to the United States. The war in the Northwest was essentially a sideshow to the War for Independence, but it did establish a firm and significant American claim to the region.

In the south, Savannah was occupied in December 1778 by a British army of 3,500 led by Lieutenant Colonel Archibald Campbell, who discovered a pathway through a swamp that allowed him to attack American positions from the rear. In September the following year the city was besieged by combined American and French forces (MAP 166, *previous page*). The French were commanded by Admiral Estaing, who showed a distinct lack of patience. Despite knowing that the siege would likely succeed in ten days, he ordered a full frontal assault, which was repelled. The Americans, led by Major General Benjamin Lincoln, managed to penetrate the

British defense sufficiently to raise their flag before being forced back. Estaing, as he had done before at Newport, gave up and sailed away.

Washington had learned by this time that the most important thing was to keep his army together as a fighting force rather than defend a particular location. This lesson, however, was lost on the American commander at Charleston in 1780, Benjamin Lincoln. When Clinton shifted his focus to the South that year, a large force was assembled to take Charleston. Nearly nine thousand soldiers, commanded by Clinton, with Cornwallis as second-in-command, were brought to attack the city using ninety transports and ten warships. Lincoln allowed his seven thousand defenders to be outmaneuvered by Clinton and they became trapped inside the city. On 12 May, he surrendered his entire army. Well over five thousand American troops were captured and vast amounts of military supplies were also taken. It was the worst American military defeat of the war, and a counterpoint to the northern victory at Saratoga. It was, in fact, likely only French intervention that prevented an American collapse.

Many smaller battles continued in the South, principally in North Carolina. There were at least thirty, depending on when a skirmish counts as a battle. Of particular note was that at Camden on 16 August 1780, where

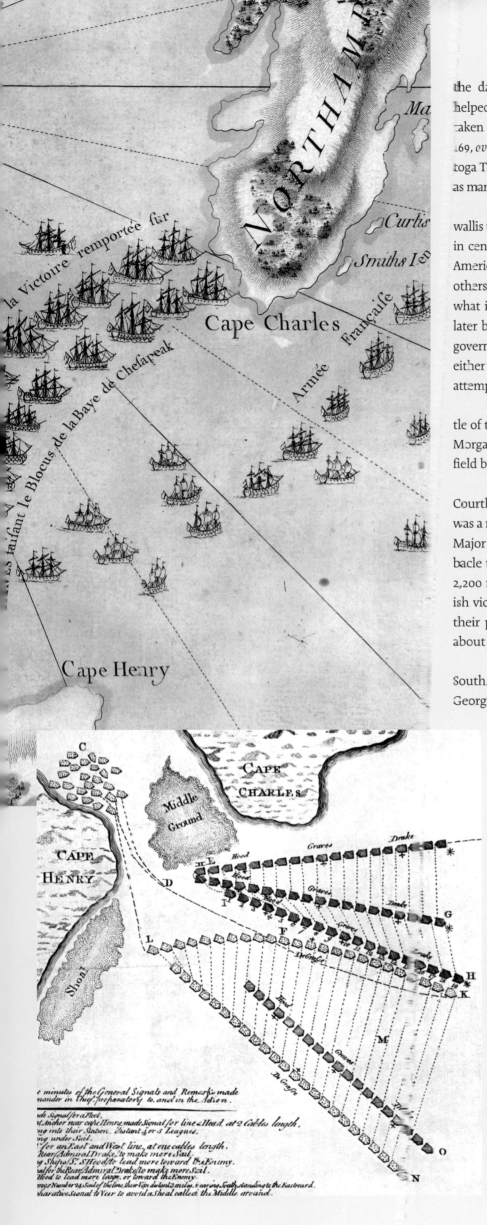

the dashing but vicious British cavalry commander Banastre Tarleton helped Cornwallis defeat an American army led by Horatio Gates, who had taken over command of the South after the surrender of Charleston (MAP 169, *overleaf*). Gates in a few hours lost the reputation he had gained at Saratoga The Battle of Camden was the worst American loss of the war: perhaps as many as nine hundred were killed and nearly a thousand captured.

In October, Major Patrick Ferguson, who had been asked by Cornwallis to rally Loyalist support, was trapped on the top of King's Mountain, in central South Carolina, with about 1,200 Loyalists and his own King's American Rangers riflemen. Surrounding him were about 1,400 militia and others, including the so-called over mountain men, frontier riflemen from what is today Tennessee, led in part by Colonel John Sevier, who would later be involved in the proposal for the "State of Franklin" and become governor of Tennessee (see page 94). Almost the entire Loyalist force was either killed, wounded, or captured. This battle put an end to Cornwallis's attempts to rally Loyalists to the British cause.

In January the following year Tarleton was badly beaten at the Battle of the Cowpens by the mixed riflemen, cavalry, and infantry of Daniel Morgan. Tarleton himself narrowly escaped, being chased off the battlefield by William Washington, George's cousin.

Cornwallis had his last taste of glory at the Battle of Guilford Courthouse, in central North Carolina, on 15 March 1781. Against him was a mixed army of 2,700 militia and 1,600 Continental regulars under Major General Nathanael Greene, who had taken over after Gates's debacle the previous year. With him was Daniel Morgan. Cornwallis had 2,200 men, redcoats and cavalry under Tarleton. The battle was a British victory only in the sense that the Americans were dislodged from their positions, but won at considerable cost. British casualties were about 532, while American losses were 261.

Greene set about destroying the final British positions in the South. In May Lieutenant General Henry Lee laid siege to Augusta, Georgia, which surrendered on 5 June. Of note is the fact that Lee, nicknamed "Light-Horse Harry," later became the father of another general who was to feature prominently in American history, Robert E. Lee.

The final major chapter in the war began in August. After Guilford Courthouse, Cornwallis abandoned his efforts in North Carolina and marched his exhausted army to a place he selected on Chesapeake Bay, where, with his back to the sea, he considered that he could be supplied by the British navy or, at worst, be evacuated. In this strategy he was but following direct orders from Clinton, who had, in turn, been

MAP 167 (*left, top*).
A representation of the events surrounding the Battle of Yorktown, shown on a superb French map. The naval blockade by the French fleet commanded by De Grasse is positioned across the entrance to Chesapeake Bay, while British ships under Graves range along the coast. The Yorktown battlefield, where Cornwallis surrendered to Washington and Rochambeau, is on the York River at *York Town,* left, top.

MAP 168 (*left*).
The naval Battle of the Capes, 5 September 1781. Two positions of the battle are depicted, with the French and British ships of the line arrayed against each other in the classic naval battle pattern of the time. The battle was marked by signaling errors, and seven British ships under Hood never even got within cannon range of the French. The battle was not particularly decisive, but the British ships were driven off, and that was all that was required at this critical moment.

Map 169 (above).
The Battle of Camden, 16 August 1780. Cornwallis's troops approached from the south (bottom of map), engaged with Gates's men at center, and finally drove them off to the north, with Tarleton's *British Dragoons in pursuit*. Gates, who was at the rear of the American lines but at the front of the flight, did not stop for sixty miles.

directed by his government to concentrate on the South. But it was Clinton's idea to establish a base on the Chesapeake from which to raid Virginia. Washington had been in New York, where, with a French army under Jean de Vimeur, Comte de Rochambeau, as well as his own army, he had been contemplating an attack on the well-defended New York City. When he received word of Cornwallis's position, however, he carefully spread rumors that his attack on New York was imminent, but then marched his two armies south to the head of the Elk River at the top of Chesapeake Bay, where Howe had landed British troops on their way to Philadelphia four years before.

At the same time, French admiral François-Joseph, Comte de Grasse, sailing from the West Indies, arrived off Chesapeake Bay with twenty-four ships carrying three thousand troops. On 2 September these troops were landed. British ships under Rear Admiral Samuel Hood could have made this difficult, but Hood thought De Grasse was sailing for New York. De Grasse then went back to sea to engage a British fleet, now nineteen ships under Admiral Thomas Graves, with Hood's ships having returned after the mistake was realized. On 5 September the two fleets fought the naval Battle of the Capes (Map 168, *previous page*), which, while not a decisive French victory, gave the French control of the Chesapeake, a control that was to prove disastrous for Cornwallis, who could now neither supply his army nor evacuate it. More than anything else, it was this temporary lapse in British maritime supremacy that sealed the fate of Cornwallis, and with it, that of British America.

Eight French ships under Vice Admiral Jacques-Melchoir, Comte de Barras, sailed from Newport, picked up Washington and Rochambeau's armies, and transported them to the York Peninsula, together with heavy guns brought from Newport. When De Grasse, having finished with Graves, sailed into Chesapeake Bay, he joined up with Barras's ships; now a formidable French fleet of thirty-two ships guarded the approaches to Yorktown against any further incursions by Graves. Up to this point, Cornwallis could perhaps have escaped up the peninsula, which had been guarded by French volunteer officer Brigadier General Marie-Joseph, Marquis de Lafayette, with only half as many men. But Cornwallis, whose men were sickening from lack of fresh food, did not try, as he expected the British navy to control the waterways for him. By the time he realized that British control of the seas had been lost, it was too late.

And so, on 28 September 1781, the siege of Yorktown began. Arrayed against Cornwallis's 7,500 men were the combined armies of Washington and Rochambeau, now numbering about 16,000 men. Cornwallis's position, hopeless from the beginning, deteriorated daily. By 9 October French artillery was entrenched and began to shell the British positions. On the night of 14 October simultaneous attacks were made on two redoubts held by the British, the first by New York troops led by Lieutenant Colonel Alexander Hamilton and the other by French troops led by Colonel Guillaume Deux-Ponts. Both redoubts were overrun. This then allowed heavy guns to be moved to within almost point-blank range of the British fortifications. With the situation becoming desperate, in the early hours of 16 October Colonel Robert Abercromby led 350 hand-picked men on a sortie to try to silence the guns; they succeeded in spiking four before being driven off. Finally Cornwallis considered evacuating his men to Gloucester, across the river, to a position held by Tarleton, then fighting his way north, but too few ships were available and a storm made it impossible. Cornwallis had no choice but to surrender. Two days later the British and German troops marched out and laid down their arms. Ironically, Cornwallis himself in May had written in a letter to a friend that a successful battle in Virginia "may give us America." Now an unsuccessful one had taken America from him.

When British first minister Lord North heard of the capitulation at Yorktown he is said to have exclaimed: "Oh God! It is all over!" And so it was. His government fell, he resigned, and King George III even prepared an abdication statement, though he thought better of it later. A preliminary peace between the British and the Americans was signed on 30 November 1782, a final one awaiting the end of the war with France and Spain the next year. The British evacuated Savannah on 11 July 1782 and Charleston on 14 December. Finally, New York City was evacuated on 25 November 1783, the British troops leaving with thousands of Loyalists. Over 100,000 Loyalists fled at the end of the war, about half of them to Canada, which was to become the new bastion of British North American power.

Map 170 (left).
This superb manuscript map of Baltimore in 1782 is from a collection of maps depicting the various camps of the French overall commander, the Comte de Rochambeau, drawn by or for him.

ATTAQUE de la
Ville d'York en Virginie
prise le 19 8bre 1781 par les
Armés Combinees de France
et d'Amerique

Troupe Commandé par Mr de Choisy

GLOCHESTER

Regiment de Tourraine

Brigade d'agenois

Redoutes Anglaise
Occupés par
les francais

Simon poay
house

Brigade de
Soissonnois

Brigade de
Bourbonnois

Redoutes
Americaines

Moze house

YORK TOWN

YORK

Camp du gal Siwoins

Camp du gal la fayette

Camp du gal Lincoln

gal Clinton

Camp du

Parc d'Artillerie
Francais

Qier Genel
ces généraux Washington
et Rochambeau

Parc d'Artillerie Americaine

LEGENDE
1 Bourbonnois
2 Deux ponts
3 Soissonnois
4 Saintonge
5 Agenois
6 Gatinois
7 Tourraine
8 Volontaires de St Simon
       Francais
       Americains
       Anglais
A Redoute prise l'epée à la main la nuit du 14 par
       les francais
B Redoute prise l'epée à la main la nuit du 14 par
       les americains
C Vaisseaux francais mouillés au lieu d'york

MAP 171.
The siege of Yorktown, 28 September to 19 October 1781, depicted on a magnificent French map. American positions are those to the south and southwest of Yorktown, while the French positions are to the southeast. Immediately south of Cornwallis's position in Yorktown is shown the system of parallel trenches dug by the French, with the positions of entrenched cannon and their lines of fire. The two hachured features to the southwest of Yorktown are Redoubts 9 and 10, taken by Deux-Ponts and Hamilton early on 16 October. Across the river is Gloucester, held by Tarleton and surrounded by a French division under the Marquis de Choisy.

Defining America

British and American negotiators had been discussing peace since 1780, but no progress was made until after Yorktown. The principal British negotiator was a London merchant, Richard Oswald. An army contractor during the French and Indian War, he had been consulted by the government during the War for Independence because of his knowledge of American conditions. The final treaty was signed, however, by David Hartley, a member of Parliament, on behalf of King George III. On the American side were Benjamin Franklin; John Adams; John Jay, the fifth president of the Continental Congress, and Henry Laurens, who had been its second president.

Early in the negotiations of 1782, Franklin had suggested that Britain "make a voluntary offer of Canada" as a gesture of reconciliation. Oswald was inclined to agree with this, and so did some in the British government. Gibraltar was about to be attacked by the Spanish, and the British wanted peace with the United States at almost any price. Had this "reconciliation" occurred, much of what is today southern Ontario would have been included in the United States. But by the end of September, the situation changed. Gibraltar had withstood the Spanish attack, and now the British wanted a boundary line that would not interfere with their lucrative fur trade centered on Montréal. To ensure Oswald did not give the United States any more land that he had to, secretary of the treasury Henry Strachey was sent to keep an eye on him.

A boundary for the new United States was agreed to during the negotiations in 1782, and a preliminary treaty was signed on 30 November 1782. Because Britain had agreed not to make a separate peace with the United States, the final Treaty of Paris was not signed until 3 September 1783, the same day Britain also signed agreements with France, Spain, and the Netherlands, ending the war in America and in Europe.

There was no map defining the boundary of the United States attached to the Treaty of Paris, but both sides used the best map then available, a map originally published in 1755 by John Mitchell (MAP 72, *page* 37). The British used the latest (fourth) edition, *Map of the British Colonies in North America,* published in 1775, but the Americans used the third edition, published in 1773–74 with the unrevised title *Map of the British and French Dominions in North America.* Both sides marked their own understanding of where the boundary was to be on their own maps but not on a single map where the boundary was mutually agreed. The map now in the collections of the New York Historical Society could be John Jay's copy, but the authenticity of this map has been questioned. Jay marked the boundary between Maine and New Brunswick on the Saint John River, whereas Oswald marked it on the St. Croix (which in any case did not exist where it was shown on the map). This discrepancy was not resolved until 1842 (see page 158).

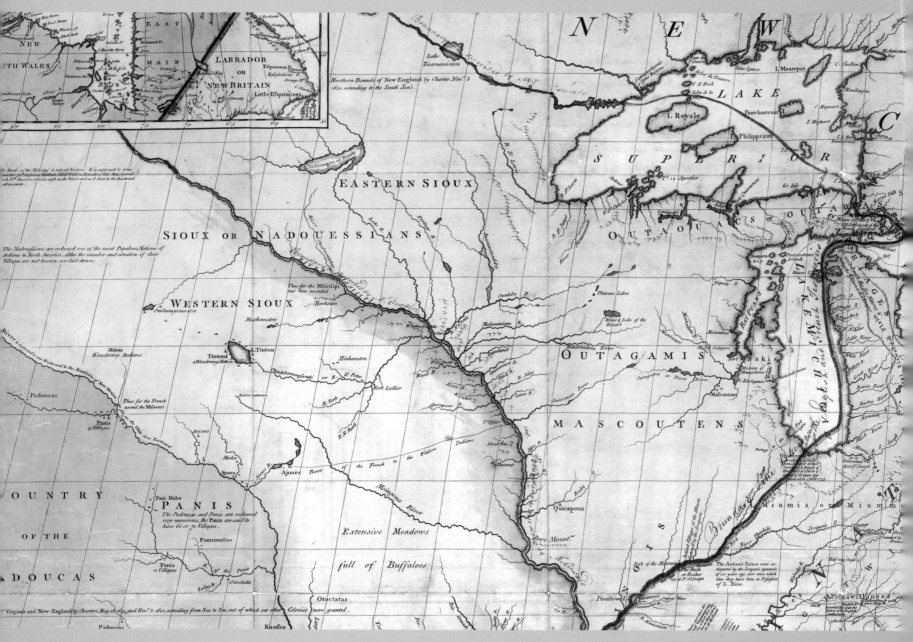

Map 173 (*right, top*).
The boundary line is shown on this 1785 map exactly as specified in the treaty: due west from Lake of the Woods (here Woods Lake) to the Mississippi. That river, however, proved not to be where it was shown on the map.

A yet more serious problem existed with the boundary drawn on both maps. The written treaty description of the boundary stated that the boundary line be drawn from the northwesternmost point of Lake of the Woods (today where the Canadian provinces of Ontario and Manitoba meet with Minnesota) "and from thence on a due west course to the river Mississippi." Entirely possible according to both editions of Mitchell's map, such a boundary was in fact impossible, for a line due west from Lake of the Woods does not intersect the Mississippi. This error would not be resolved until a convention signed in 1818 (see page 136). Nonetheless, the United States was now defined well enough for the requirements of the time. More exact definition could await necessity.

Map 172 (*below*).
Arguably the most important map in American history, this is the fourth edition 1775 John Mitchell map, on which have been drawn the northern boundaries of the United States as understood by Richard Oswald, British negotiator at the Treaty of Paris, which recognized the existence of an independent United States of America. The whole map is huge, four sheets measuring a total of 79 x 56 inches. The annotations were drawn in 1782 for the preliminary treaty of that year, which was identical to the final treaty of 1783. The thinner red line (in ink, not watercolor) is the boundary, and it includes a coastal sea area. After the signing of the Treaty of Paris the map was given to King George III, and along this line in several places the king has written: *Boundary as described by M* Oswald*. Also shown on this map, presumably also drawn by Oswald during the deliberations, are the boundary of Nova Scotia according to the Treaty of Utrecht, 1713, together with the fishing area reserved to Britain under the same treaty (thick red line); the 1763 Proclamation line to separate the British colonies from Indian lands (thin yellow); the 1763 boundaries of British Quebec (wide yellow); the extent of Quebec after the Royal Proclamation of 1774 (the entire area colored yellow, south to the Ohio and west to the Mississippi), and the boundaries of the Hudson's Bay Company lands (thin brown line at top), also interpreted as the red and gray straight line beneath it.

Map 174 (*above*).
When maps showed the course of the Mississippi more accurately, the boundary line no longer intersected with the river. Now the boundary as described in the 1783 treaty does not close. This situation is also shown on **Map 182**, page 95.

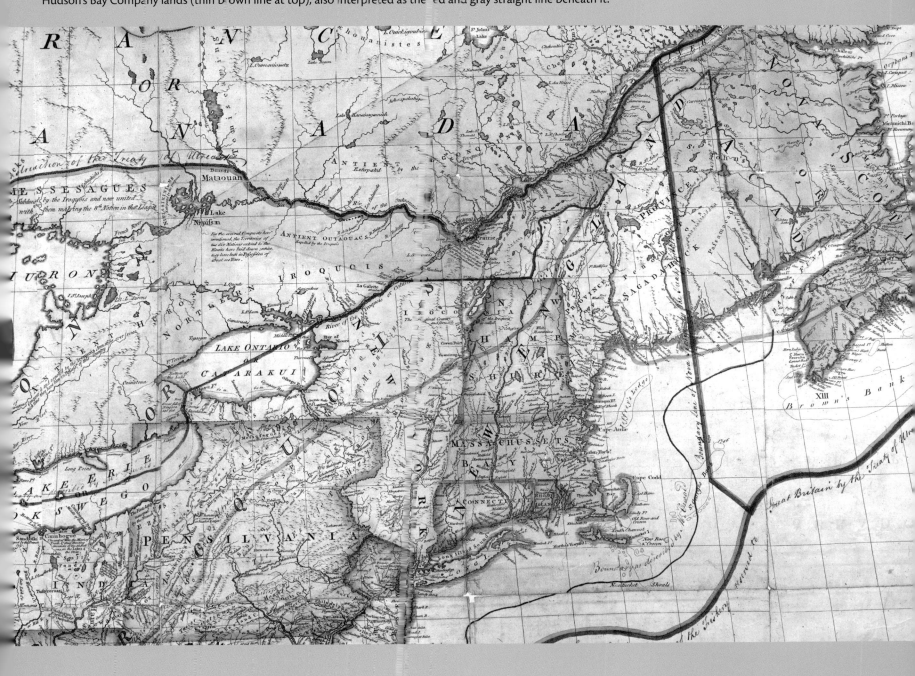

America Independent

Above. Thirteen-starred U.S. flag, from the Massachusetts State House.

Map 175 *(below).*
Mapmakers in 1783 rushed to publish maps showing the new geographical entity of the United States of America. This despite the fact that the final Treaty of Paris would not be signed until November that year. The fourth map to be published was this *United States of America . . . Agreeable to the Peace of 1783,* by British mapmaker John Wallis. It referred to the preliminary peace negotiated in 1782. Note that the northern boundary is conveniently left undefined west of *Lake Minnitigon or Lake Woods* (Lake of the Woods), as is the course of the northern part of the Mississippi, though it is cleverly shown rising off the map, where it might be interpreted as intersecting a northern boundary line.

The formal Declaration of Independence in 1776 had made it necessary for the states to create some form of central government. The Second Continental Congress had appointed John Dickinson to head a committee to consider how this should work, and his committee's Articles of Confederation and Perpetual Union were adopted in November 1777 and sent to the states for approval, where they were ratified by all the states save Maryland, which did not approve them until March 1781.

The loose system of confederation expressed in the Articles had major deficiencies because it did not confer sufficient power on the central government, which was unable to directly raise money through taxation or to regulate trade; it could do very little of substance, in fact, without the states' consent. Nonetheless, the United States was governed under these Articles until a better system could be agreed upon by states suspicious of any higher authority.

Even to get Maryland to ratify the Articles, a major concession was required. The state had no western territories and was afraid of being swamped by those that did as they expanded west and became larger and larger. Others saw the danger as well. Virginia delegates proposed that the states cede their western claims to the central government, which they all did, for most of the land. New York and Connecticut were first, in 1780, followed by Virginia's agreement to do so in 1781—on condition all states ratified the Articles, which meant Maryland, the only state yet to do so. Virginia did not finally cede its claims north of the Ohio until 1784 (and those in Kentucky in 1792), but its willingness

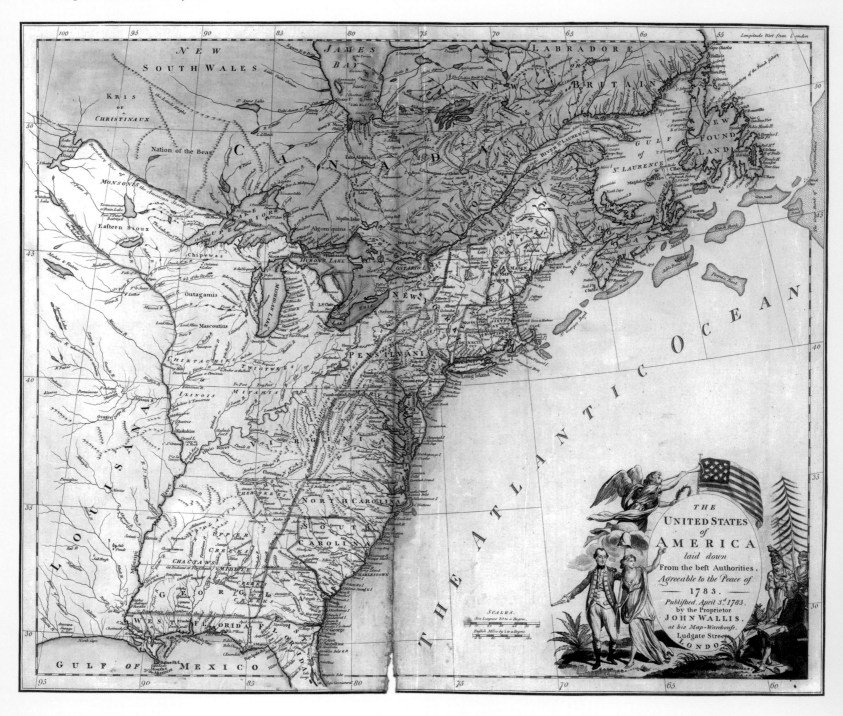

MAP 176 (*above*).
Considered to be the first map of the the new country by an American mapmaker, this *New and correct Map of the United States of North America* was published in March 1784 by Abel Buell. He was not really a professional mapmaker, at least before he published this map, but had turned his hand to cartography after being convicted of counterfeiting money. The map shows very well the claims of the states to western lands at that time. Virginia's claim was the most extensive, but it was Virginia that in 1781 was the first to cede its western lands to the central government. This map is a large wall map, which may account for its rarity. Fewer than six copies are now known.

to do so was influential, because its claims were from the oldest charter of any of the colonies—and therefore more likely to succeed—and they also covered the largest area. The sale of western lands would provide the central government with the source of funds it so desperately needed.

Congress in 1784 agreed on a system for the creation and admission to the Union of new states: that the lands ceded by the states should be divided into territories that, once the population was sufficient, would of right be admitted to statehood on the basis of precise equality with the other states. In this fashion, no single state would be able to grow to dominate the rest. The Land Ordinance of 1784 was largely the work of Thomas Jefferson,

Below. Considered the first cartographic recognition of the United States as an independent republic is a French map, of which this is the cartouche, referring to *les Treize Colonies Unies de l'Amerique Septentrionale* (Thirteen United Colonies of North America). Yet it still talked of "colonies." It was published in 1778.

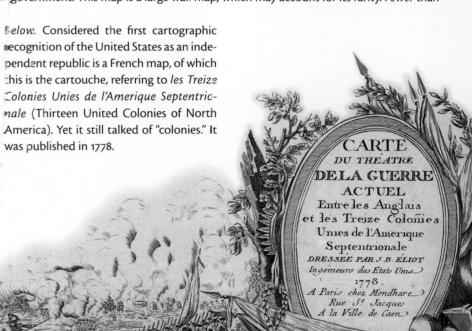

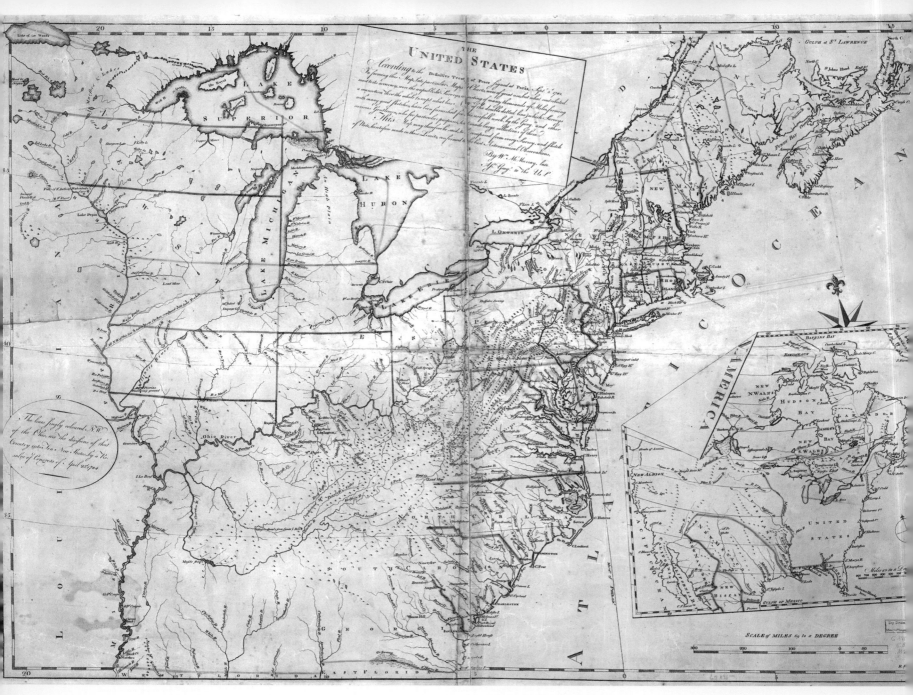

MAP 177 (*above*).
This map shows the states proposed by Thomas Jefferson as agreed to by Congress in April 1784 in the Land Ordinance of that year. There are ten proposed new states north of the Ohio.

MAP 178 (*below*) and MAP 179 (*below, right*).
One proposed state that did not survive—not one of Jefferson's ideas—was the state of Franklin, carved out of the western lands ceded by North Carolina. Both of these maps show the state. Franklin was created in 1784 by delegates from what is now the northeastern part of Tennessee who met at a convention in Jonesborough. By 1785 a constitution had been adopted and a capital—Greeneville—chosen. The state's first—and as it turned out, only—governor was the colorful John Sevier, who had led part of the contingent of "over mountain men" at the battle of King's Mountain in 1780 (see page 87). But Franklin refused to join the United States, and it suffered from Indian attacks that it did not have the resources to repel. By 1790 the region had been incorporated back into North Carolina, whose militias aided the Franklin settlers. In 1796 the area became part of the new state of Tennessee.

whose original idea had been for fourteen new states west of the Appalachians (MAP 180, *right, top*), then for eight or ten states in the Northwest Territory, the lands north and west of the Ohio as far as the Mississippi (MAP 177, *above*, and MAP 181, *right, center*). Although Jefferson's specific state boundaries were not implemented, his principle for the creation of new states from territories was. Two of the names he proposed (MAP 181, *right, center*) actually formed the basis for states: Michigania became Michigan and Illinoia became Illinois.

The Land Ordinance of 1785 built on the 1784 Ordinance by establishing how the government would distribute the land, and thus how the territory would be settled. As the states relinquished land and treaties obtained it from the Indians, government-appointed surveyors were to divide the land into parcels six miles square, or townships. Each thirty-six-

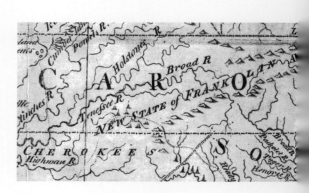

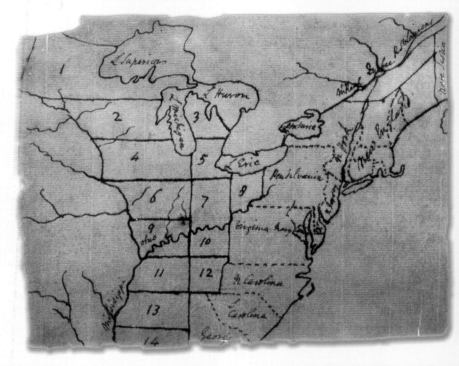

Map 180 (*right, top*).
This sketch map was drawn by David Hartley in 1784 to illustrate Thomas Jefferson's initial proposal for states to be created west of the Appalachians. Hartley, a friend of Benjamin Franklin, had signed the 1783 Treaty of Paris on behalf of King George III.

Map 181 (*right, center*).
An engraved map published in 1785 to show a revised scheme of Jefferson's states, together with their proposed names. Only the proposals north of the Ohio are now shown, and the Southern states are shown still extending to the Mississippi. Jefferson's names are classicized versions of Native American words: *Assenisippia, Metropotamia, Polypotamia, Saratoga, Sylvania,* and the like. Only two survived, in amended form: *Illinoia* and *Michigania.*

Map 182 (*right, bottom*).
The Northwest Territory, here labeled Western Territory, its earlier name, on a 1793 map. Note the improperly defined boundary in the northwest corner. An enlarged portion of part of this map showing the various land claims is shown as Map 184, *page 97*.

square-mile block would in turn be divided into one-square-mile sections, each containing 640 acres. Each section was to be numbered, and sections would be reserved for schools, public buildings, and veterans of the Revolution. Then the rest would be sold by auction at a minimum bid of a dollar per acre, or $640 per section. The first land to be so subdivided was in what is now eastern Ohio, where surveyor Thomas Hutchins, the first geographer of the United States, ran his first line on 30 September 1785 in seven rows, called ranges (Map 183, *overleaf*). This method of subdivision of public lands was followed for over a century as settlement advanced ever farther west, and it affected the shape of future settlement over a vast amount of the land of the United States.

The first implementation of the principles laid out in the 1784 Land Ordinance was in the Northwest Ordinance of 1787, which created the Northwest Territory bounded by the Ohio River, the Mississippi, and the Great Lakes—insofar as it was possible to define it at this time (Map 182, *right*). Formally *An Ordinance for the Government of the United States, North-West of the River Ohio,* it confirmed that the region would be developed as territories that would evolve into states, and in addition banned slavery in the territory, which made the Ohio the effective later division between North and South. The states that would eventually occupy the region were Ohio (1803), Indiana (1816), Illinois (1818), Michigan (1837), Wisconsin (1848), and Minnesota (1858).

The Northwest Ordinance was perhaps the most important piece of legislation passed by the Continental Congress, a body that was proving to be inadequate. Too much power had been left with individual states under the Articles of Confederation, changes could only be made unanimously, and tariffs erected by states against each other were becoming onerous. In September 1786 a convention of five states held at Annapolis recommended that a more inclusive meeting be called to iron out these difficulties. Congress agreed, and a convention was called for Philadelphia in May 1787.

In the interim, events intervened. In August 1786 there occurred an armed uprising in western Massachusetts by small farmers upset by tax burdens and crushing debts following the war. Led by ex–Continental Army

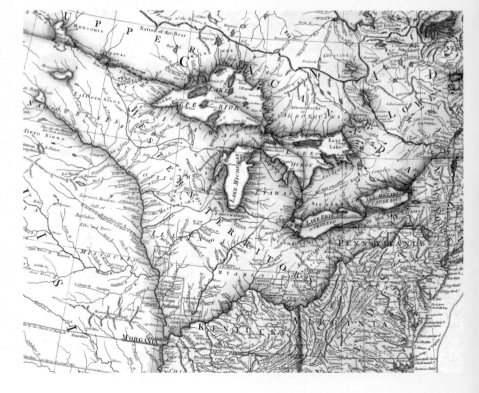

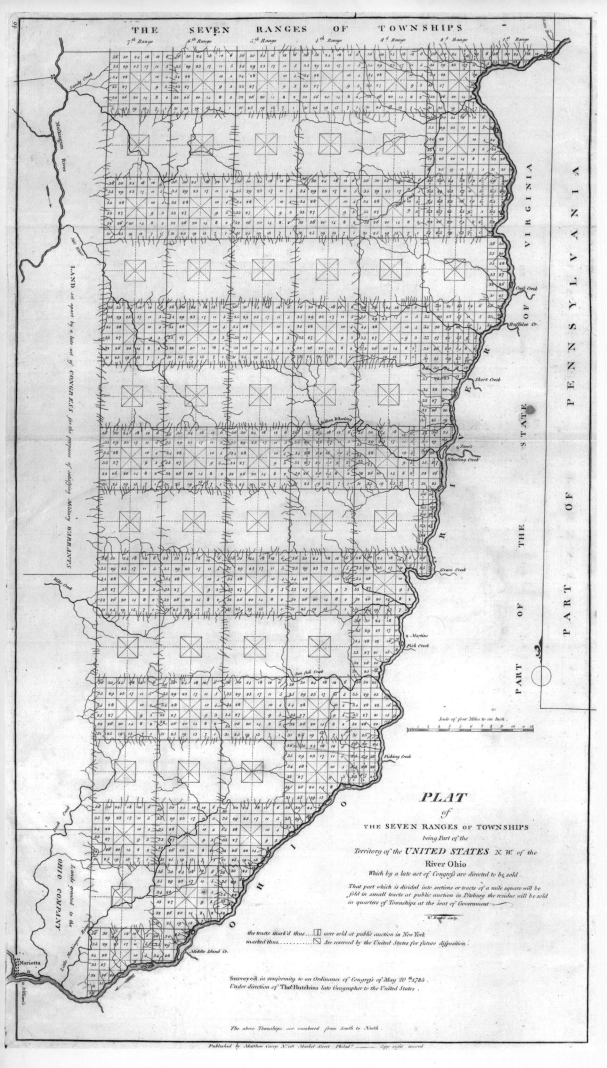

PLAT
of
THE SEVEN RANGES OF TOWNSHIPS
being Part of the
Territory of the UNITED STATES N.W. of the
River Ohio
Which by a late act of Congress are directed to be sold.

That part which is divided into sections or tracts of a mile square will be
sold in small tracts at public auction in Pittsburg the residue will be sold
in quarters of Townships at the Seat of Government

the tracts mark'd thus....⊡ were sold at public auction in New York
marked thus.........⊡ Are reserved by the United States for future disposition.

Surveyed in conformity to an Ordinance of Congress of May 20th 1785.
Under direction of Thos Hutchins late Geographer to the United States.

The above Townships are numbered from South to North.

Published by Matthew Carey No 118 Market Street Philadª.

Map 183 (above).

Thomas Hutchins's map of the seven ranges of townships he began to survey in 1785. The starting point is at the top right of the survey. This method of subdivision, which was built on the one-square-mile (640-acre) townships, was extensively used in the surveying of public lands thereafter. From this place the survey of townships progressed westwards until it reached the Pacific Ocean. Today a nondescript stone marker in East Liverpool, Ohio, marks "The Point of Beginning" for a surveyed grid that reaches across the country. Blocks with diagonal cross-strokes are reserved lands. Note the *Lands granted to the Ohio Company* at bottom left.

captain Daniel Shays, the rebellion required that a mercenary army be raised to quell it, for there was no standing national army—the Articles did not allow it. Shays' followers prevented the debtors' court at Springfield from sitting in September and attacked the federal arsenal in that town the following January, although the assault was repulsed. Militia under General Benjamin Lincoln pursued Shays' men, scattering them at Petersham on 3 February 1787, effectively ending the rebellion. Shays, and all his followers bar two, availed themselves of an amnesty offered by newly elected Massachusetts governor John Hancock, who no doubt harbored a certain fondness for rebels.

Shays' Rebellion proved to be timely and had an effect well beyond its intentions, ensuring that state leaders came to Philadelphia with a sharpened awareness of the need for more federal power. Thus a convention originally charged with considering changes to the Articles of Confederation instead concerned itself with the writing of a completely new constitution.

The Philadelphia Convention, held from May to September 1787, was a tour de force of the decisive over the hesitant. Chaired by none other than George Washington and effectively led by a young Virginia lawyer, James Madison, a constitution for the United States was hammered out, establishing the very principles under which the country would grow and prosper. And future amendments were allowed, permitting the Constitution itself to grow and adapt. Only nine of the thirteen states had to ratify it in order for the new federal constitution to go into effect. As a crowning touch, delegate Gouverneur Morris of Pennsylvania changed the draft wording from "We the People of New Hampshire, Massachusetts," and so on, to the more memorable "We the People of the United States . . ."

Ratification was difficult, and in several states very hard fought, but in the end the new constitution was endorsed by all, though Rhode Island held out until 1791 and even briefly flirted with the idea of separation. The Constitution came into effect on 4 March 1789, and on 30 April, in New York, George Washington was sworn in as the first president of the United States.

But the United States did not yet extend its liberties and equalities to all its people, notably excluding slaves (see page 100) and native peoples. In fact, with the Royal Proclamation well and truly out of the way, dispossession of Indians continued apace—one way or another—in the haste of various land companies to stake their claims (Map 184 and Map 185, *right*).

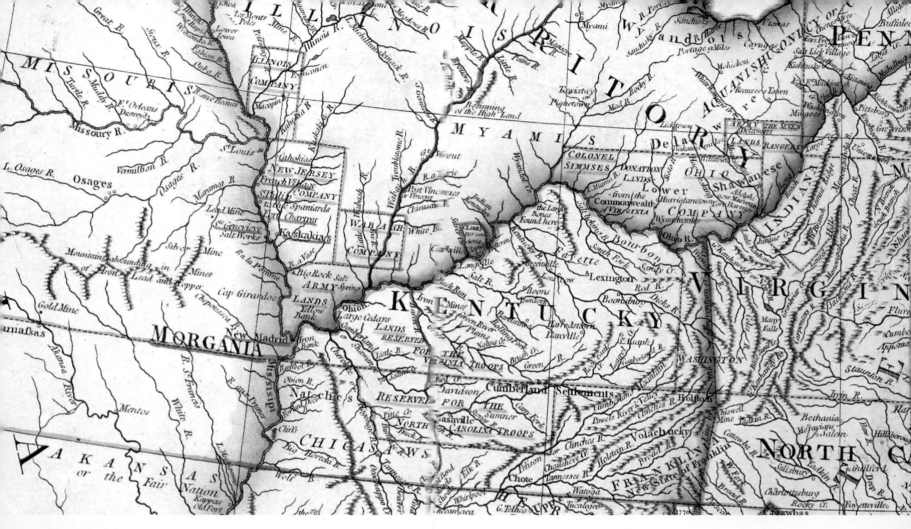

MAP 184 (*above*).

This fine 1793 map, published by the London mapmaker William Faden, shows some of the land claims and grants along the Ohio River. Kentucky, which became the fifteenth state in 1792, is named but not defined as it would be as a state. The Seven Ranges (MAP 183, *left*) are shown at right. Just to their west are the lands of the (second) *Ohio Company*, the Ohio Company of Associates, 5 million acres purchased in 1787. One of the principals of the company, General Rufus Putnam, laid out the townsite of Marietta the following year, and this became the first permanent settlement in what is now the state of Ohio. Next, to the west, are *Donation Lands from the Commonwealth of Virginia*, and then, around the northern bend of the Ohio where the Great Miami River enters is *Colonel Simmses.* This refers to land granted to John Cleves Symmes and includes the site of Cincinnati, founded by Symmes in 1788. Surveyor John Filson (MAP 188, *overleaf*) called it Losantiville but died under mysterious circumstances while surveying the site in 1788. It was Northwest Territory governor Arthur St. Clair who renamed it Cincinnati, in 1790, after the Roman general Cincinnatus, who supposedly resembled George Washington in having been a wartime hero who then retired to farm. Farther west is *Clark's 150,000 Acres*, a December 1786 grant to George Rogers Clark and his Illinois Regiment; Clark received 8,049 acres and privates 108, with the other officers and men receiving grants of a size based on their rank. The grant was for land that Clark had himself accepted from the Shawnees during the war. Straddling the Wabash River are lands of the *Wabash Company*, purchased in 1773 and 1775, in defiance of the Royal Proclamation, by the Illinois-Wabash Company, which was mainly formed of investors from otherwise western landless Maryland and Pennsylvania. After the war the

land was claimed by Virginia and the company had to defend its rights; compromise was reached only after the formation of the Northwest Territory and the ceding of land to the central government. Other land purchases are to the New Jersey Company, another western-landless state, and the Illinois Company. Also shown (at left) is *Morgania.* This was a colony that a friend of Thomas Hutchins, George Morgan, intended to establish in the 1780s within the territory west of the Mississippi belonging to Spain, now the state of Missouri. There was to be a large commercial city called New Madrid strategically located just south of the confluence of the Ohio with the Mississippi. Morgan arrived in 1789 with fifty or sixty settlers, but his proposed commercial center did not prosper due to the interference of the traitorous James Wilkinson (see page 116), who saw Morgan as a rival for Spanish influence. The colony did not materialize but it found its way onto a few maps—such as this one—under Morgan's name. South of the Ohio are *Lands Reserved for the Virginia Troops*, held back from the Virginia grant of western claims to Congress to compensate Virginia militia in the War for Independence, and likewise land *Reserved for the North Carolina Troops. Indiana* in Virginia demotes land purchases of the Indiana Company. Note also *Franklinia*, the *New State of Franklin* (see page 94).

MAP 185 (*below*).

Many of these land grants and purchases are also shown on this map, which dates from 1789. It also shows *Louisville,* across the river from Clark's grant. Louisville had been incorporated in 1780 by the Virginia legislature and named after King Louis XVI of France, which had just entered the war on the American side.

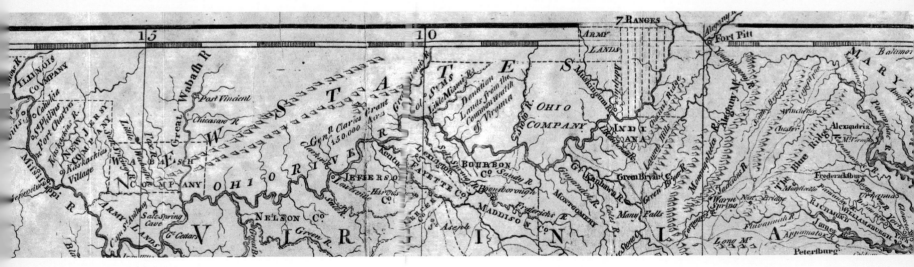

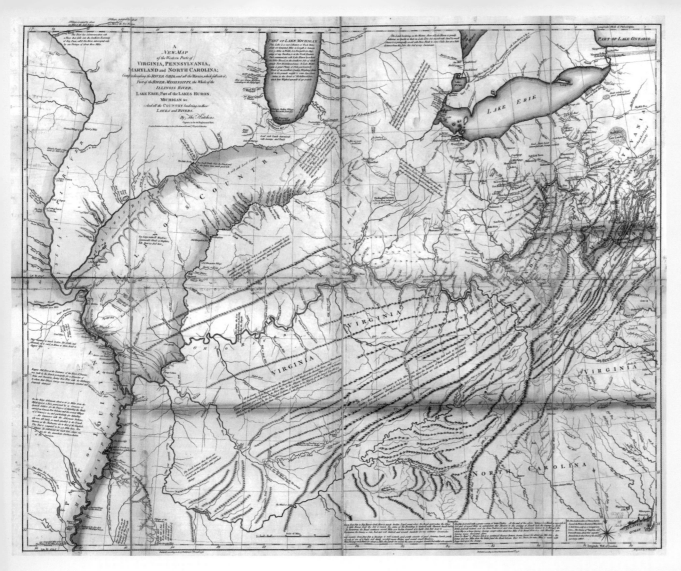

Native peoples had not been signatory to the Treaty of Paris, yet by it the United States had received all lands west to the Mississippi. Naturally enough, when EuroAmericans moved in they were not always welcomed. But the Indians knew they had a better chance of success if they acted together, and so in 1785 they came together as the Wabash Confederacy. Then, and again in 1786, the confederacy insisted on a rollback to the Ohio as the boundary of Indian lands, the boundary agreed to at the 1768 Treaty of Fort Stanwix (see page 65). This the United States could not agree to, and in 1790, tired of continuous Indian harassment, which was aided and abetted by the British (who had still not vacated fur trade forts in the Northwest), the government initiated a major offensive. That year the Americans burned the principal village of the Miamis but were counterattacked by Miamis under their leader Little Turtle. The following year the Northwest Territory governor, Arthur St. Clair, led another military expedition and built a number of forts, but at what is now Fort Recovery, Ohio, several hundred soldiers were killed in an ambush by Shawnee, Delaware, and others.

This proved, however, to be the beginning of the end for the Indians of the Northwest. In 1793 George Washington gave General Anthony Wayne command of an army he called the Legion of the United States. Wayne built a chain of forts, including one at Fort Recovery. Little Turtle again attacked the Americans there, but this time had no success. The Indian confederacy took a final defensive stand along the Maumee River (southwest of Toledo) on 20 August 1794 at a place where trees had been uprooted by a storm. Here Miamis under Little Turtle, Shawnees under their chief Blue Jacket, Delawares under Buckongahela, plus Indians from other tribes and even some Canadian militia were attacked by Wayne's Legion. Quickly routed by superior numbers, military discipline, and outflanking cavalry, the Indians retreated to Fort Miamis, a British fur trade fort. However, its commander, ordered not to directly involve himself in Indian-American conflicts, shut them out. This Battle of Fallen Timbers led to the signing of the Treaty of Greenville (Ohio) the following year, in which the Indian confederacy—seventeen tribes signed or were signed for—in return for $9,500 a year, ceded much of present-day Ohio, establishing a new

Native American–EuroAmerican boundary called the Greenville Treaty Line across the top northwest corner of Ohio. This prepared the way for an influx of settlers and the creation of the state of Ohio in 1803. Specific pieces of land were also ceded, including the sites of present-day Detroit and Chicago. Peace was to be perpetual. But, of course, it was not; Indian resistance would be renewed in earnest at Tippecanoe in 1811 and during the War of 1812 (see page 130) in the face of continued and relentless encroachment by EuroAmerican settlers.

Far away, in London, England, John Jay was trying to negotiate a treaty with the British, which would have redressed some grievances arising from the War for Independence. Much of what the American side wanted was unattainable because of the American refusal to compensate Loyalists for the loss of their property, but Jay did negotiate the removal of British forts from the Northwest, leaving the region now more firmly in American hands. Jay's treaty, signed in 1795, was proclaimed in 1796.

The creation of the first state over and above the original thirteen was not in the Northwest. In 1777 fifty-one towns in the area originally part of the Massachusetts Bay Colony known as the New Hampshire Grants had declared themselves independent, adopting the name New Connecticut or Vermont. Congress had recognized the region's independence in 1790, and on 4 March 1791 Vermont became the fourteenth state (MAP 187, *left, bottom*). The following year Kentucky became the fifteenth. It had originally been proposed as a state named Transylvania in 1775, but neither Virginia nor Congress had recognized it at that time. After the war, however, the stream of settlers crossing the mountains had increased and the 60,000 population level had quickly been reached. In a similar fashion, Tennessee, created from western lands ceded by North Carolina, was declared the sixteenth state in 1796.

MAP 188 (*above, right*).
John Filson's map of *Kentucke,* the first detailed map of the area, published in 1784. Filson's writing did much to create the modern romantic image of the explorer and backwoodsman Daniel Boone, whose house is shown on the map (approximately in the center, south of Lexington) as *Co. Boon's.* The Ohio River runs from top right to bottom left. *Louisville* is depicted, as is *Clarksville,* on the north side of the river, with *Gen¹. Clark's Grant 150,000 Acres. Harrod's Town* (just below center) is Harrodsburg, the first settlement in Kentucky, founded in 1774 in the heart of what is now bluegrass and horse country.

MAP 189 (*below*).
Tennessee in 1795, a year before the territory became the sixteenth state. Knoxville is shown. It was founded in 1791 by territorial governor William Blount and named after Henry Knox, the resourceful artillery officer of the War for Independence who later became George Washington's secretary of war.

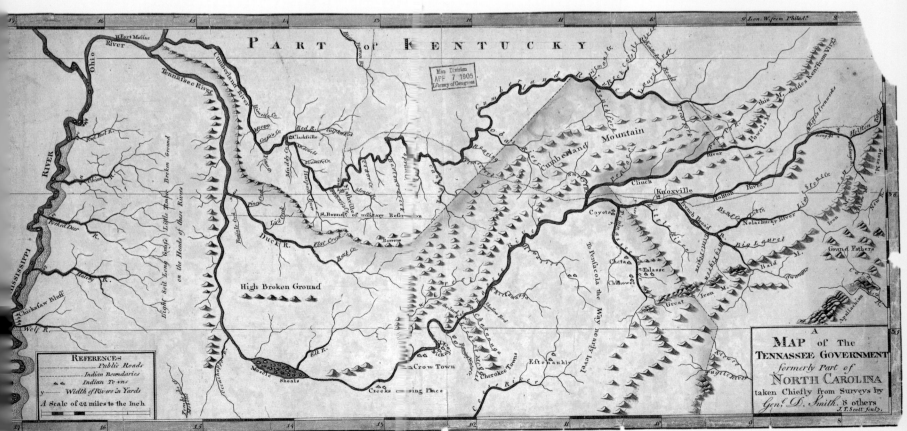

A Man and a Brother

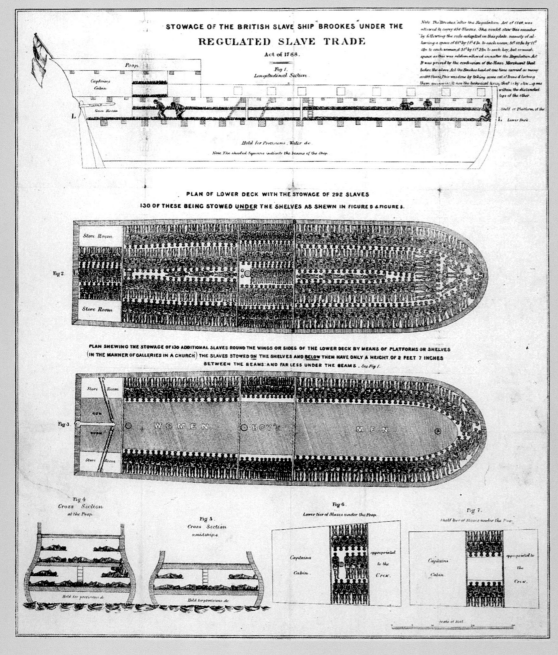

Above. Probably the most common image used by American abolitionists was this "supplicant slave" icon with the caption *Am I Not a Man and a Brother?* Originally devised by Quaker antislavery advocates in Britain, it was adopted in the United States as a powerful aid to the abolitionist cause. This particular version, a woodcut, appeared on a broadside published in New York in 1837.

Slavery—a blot on the histories of many a so-called civilized country—appears to have begun in the United States as a response to the need for cheap labor for the backbreaking cultivation of tobacco. The first slaves to arrive were those brought by the Spanish explorer and colonist Lucas Vásquez de Ayllón in 1526, but their stay in servitude was brief. Later that same year they revolted and fled inland, where they either perished or became assimilated with Native Americans (see page 15). The first recorded instance of the sale of slaves—though in all probability not the first in fact—was in April 1619, when a Dutch and an English privateer captured a Spanish slave ship and brought a hundred slaves to Old Point Comfort, near Jamestown, where they were sold as slaves or as indentured servants. For all their apparent piousness, the colonists were nonetheless willing to force others to do their labor for them. By 1637 we hear the first dissenting voices, however, when Roger Williams in Rhode Island protested against "perpetuall slaverie" of captured Pequots. It was the beginning of a long and nation-breaking struggle of the pro- and antislavery forces in America.

In 1652 Rhode Island became the first colony to at least partially ban slavery; no one was to be enslaved for more than ten years or after the age of twenty-four. But the law had no teeth, for slavery survived in Rhode Island until it was completely prohibited in 1774. There was always more dissent against slavery in the Northern colonies than in the Southern, but this was primarily because the economic system of the North was not conducive to the use of slave labor, whereas the plantation systems of the South, whether they grew tobacco, rice, indigo, or later cotton, were profitable only due to their use of slaves.

By the middle of the seventeenth century, the slave trade was deeply embedded as part of the maritime trading system of many countries, but especially that of the British. The so-called triangular trade involved the sailing to West Africa with goods to trade for slaves, the carrying of slaves across the Atlantic to American ports such as Charleston or the West Indies, and the transporting of sugar, tobacco, or other slave-produced plantation products back to their home ports. It was the westbound leg of this triangle that became known as the Middle Passage, now synonymous with the sense of loss of African peoples as their freedom was replaced with unspeakable agonies.

The United States did not import the majority of African slaves. Estimates of the total number of Africans forcibly removed from their homeland vary, ranging from 10 to 28 million. Of these about 12 million were taken to

MAP 190 (*left*).
This plan of the slave ship *Brookes* was published by a British antislavery organization led by Thomas Clarkson about 1790 to protest an Act to Regulate the British Slave Trade, which permitted ships to pack as many slaves into their holds as they could conceivably carry. The *Brookes* transported 454 slaves in this way, with only 72 x 16 inches for each man, 70 x 11 inches for each woman, and 60 x 14 inches for a boy. Under these incredible, unsanitary, and inhuman conditions millions of Africans were carried to North and South America and the Caribbean, untold thousands dying on the voyage. This plan became one of the most widely distributed antislavery images used by American abolitionists.

the Americas, across the Middle Passage. Of these, about 5 percent, or 600,000, were taken to the Thirteen Colonies or the United States.

In 1808 Congress banned importation of slaves, a year after the British had banned the slave trade within the British Empire. Although Britain prohibited slavery altogether in 1834, the economic ramifications were seen in the American South as just too great. Indeed, just as the political will to ban the international slave trade was gaining ground, the invention of the cotton gin (by Eli Whitney, in 1793) enabled explosive growth in the cotton industry, accompanied by an increase in the demand for slaves, without which no cotton plantation could run.

During the nineteenth century the call for abolition grew stronger. Some wanted to free all black slaves and send them back to Africa. In 1822 the new nation of Liberia was created on the west coast of Africa as a colony of "free men of color" by an organization called the National Colonization Society of America. Some even envisaged an American empire in Africa. The society was even supported by some southerners who feared a black revolt and thought encouragment of emigration the best way to deal with the threat.

The history of the United States in the first part of the nineteenth century is permeated with the struggle between the slavery and abolitionist factions. The Missouri Compromise of 1820 (see page 144) was an attempt to maintain the balance between the two groups in government, as was the later Kansas-Nebraska Act of 1854 (see page 149). Ultimately, the balance could not be maintained, and the result was the Civil War (page 182).

One part of the abolitionist movement helped escaped slaves to get to safety, first to the Northern states, but later to Canada, after the passage of the Fugitive Slave Act in 1850 allowed pursuit and return of slaves who had fled to free soil within the United States. It has been estimated that about forty thousand slaves escaped to Canada; in the 1850s, half of the population of one Canadian town, Chatham (now in Ontario), was escaped slaves. One slave who escaped to Canada was Josiah Henson, Harriet Beecher Stowe's inspiration for Uncle Tom in her famous 1852 abolitionist novel *Uncle Tom's Cabin*. Abraham Lincoln himself is said to have addressed Stowe as "the little lady who started this big war," the Civil War.

MAP 191 (*above*).
The coast of West Africa, the source of the majority of slaves, is shown in this 1688 map produced by Dutch mapmaker Nicolas de Witt. Most slaves were not acquired directly by European slavers but purchased through intermediaries, who were often the most powerful rulers in the region. They would raid their enemies to gather slaves and herd them to the coast, where they would be held in enclosures until their sale was negotiated. The central coast of Guinea was named the Slave Coast on some maps.

Below. A present-day Underground Railroad marker on Roanoke Island, North Carolina. When Union forces took control of the island in 1861 they used part of the island as a camp for the protection of escaped slaves. Almost four thousand former slaves found refuge there.

FIRST LIGHT OF FREEDOM

Former slaves give thanks by the creek's edge at the sight of the island — " If you can cross the creek to Roanoke Island, you will find 'safe haven' ."

NATIONAL UNDERGROUND RAILROAD
NETWORK TO FREEDOM

MAP 192 (*right*).
A map showing the routes used by slaves escaping to Northern states and to Canada between 1830 and 1865, popularly known as the Underground Railroad. The map was published in 1895.

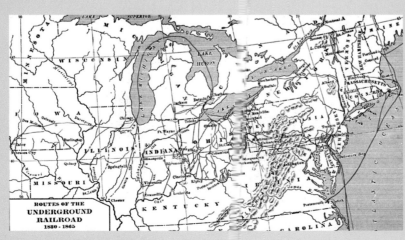

ROUTES OF THE
UNDERGROUND
RAILROAD
1830-1865

A Capital on the Potomac

During the War for Independence, Congress had been forced to move a number of times by an advancing British army, and at war's end, it was established in New York. Congress's decision to move the nation's capital to a new site on the Potomac was made as part of a deal between three men: Alexander Hamilton, then secretary of the treasury and a New Yorker, and James Madison and Thomas Jefferson, both Virginians. Although Hamilton had made remarkable progress in setting up the financial systems required by the new nation, some aspects of his work had attracted considerable enmity. One issue in particular emerged as a thorny one. This was Hamilton's insistence that the federal government should assume the war debts of the states. However, Southern states and especially Virginia had paid off their debts more than those in the North. Thus a deal was made in the summer of 1790: Virginia and the South would support the federal assumption of states' debts if the capital was moved south.

The move was first to Philadelphia, for a ten-year interim period, then to the Potomac, to a site chosen by President George Washington. Rivalry between the states for the capital had resulted in the inclusion in the Constitution of a provision for a ten-mile-square capital territory that was not to be part of any state. Virginia and Maryland ceded land to the federal government, and the towns of Georgetown and Alexandria were included in the new Territory, then District, of Columbia, named after Christopher Columbus. Columbia had been suggested as a name for the country after the War for Independence, and the district took this name rather than the more cumbersome District of the United States. The city, of course, was named after the man who had done so much to create the new nation and set it on its feet, George Washington.

Washington appointed Pierre Charles L'Enfant, a French military engineer who had been on his staff during the War for Independence, to design a plan for the city worthy of its position as the capital. L'Enfant devised a layout based on diagonal boulevards, with the Capitol building at the center, overlain on a more traditional north-south and east-west street grid. His plan was not finished, however, because he could not cooperate with the surveyors hired to lay out the streets, Andrew and Joseph Ellicott, and was fired. L'Enfant took his plans with him, leaving the others to reconstruct them as best they could (MAP 196, *far right, top*).

The federal government moved to Washington in 1800, and the district was formally placed under the jurisdiction of Congress in February 1801. In 1846 the area of the District of Columbia south of the Potomac was returned to Virginia, and in 1871 Georgetown, Washington City, and its suburbs, then Washington County, were unified into Washington, D.C.

MAP 193 (*above*).
Congress's move to Washington from New York, via a decade in Philadelphia, was lampooned in this 1790 cartoon map showing the "Ship *Constitution of America*" being lured onto the rocks by a devil while below the rapids men in a boat plot how to take advantage of the situation, a comment on the profit opportunity for Philadelphia. "Conogocheque" refers to Conococheague Creek, which flows into the Potomac at today's Williamsport, Maryland, eighty miles above Washington.

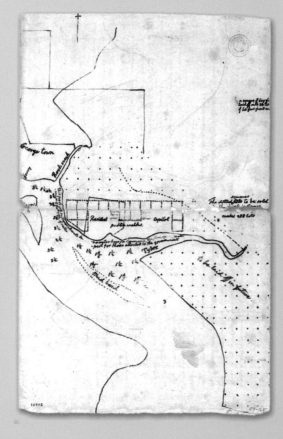

MAP 195 (*below*).
In Pierre L'Enfant's own hand is this survey map of his plan for the new capital, drawn in 1791 (before 19 August). The red dotted lines are survey lines completed up to that time defining what was to become the street pattern.

MAP 194 (*above, center*).
This was Secretary of State Thomas Jefferson's sketched attempt at a plan for the new city, drawn about March 1791. His design was passed over for the more elegant L'Enfant scheme.

MAP 197 (*right, center inset*).
The District of Columbia on an 1850 map, showing the area returned to Virginia in 1846. *Washington City*, *Washington County*, and *Georgetown* are separate; they were united in 1871, becoming Washington, D.C.

MAP 198 (*right*).
Cotemporal with MAP 195, this fine bird's-eye map of Washington was published in 1852. It shows the city before the construction of the National Mall, but with the Washington Monument, which, although begun in 1848, was not completed until 1884. The area between it and the Capitol (again shown complete, though it was not finished until 1863) was a fetid area drained by the canalized Tiber Creek, into which the city's sewage flowed. It was for this area that a commission in 1901 headed by Senator James McMillan recommended the construction of the National Mall. Today, with its collection of public buildings including the Smithsonian Institution museums, the National Art Gallery, and the National Archives, and its extension to the national memorials and monuments, it has created a heart for the national capital, though it is not without its modern critics.

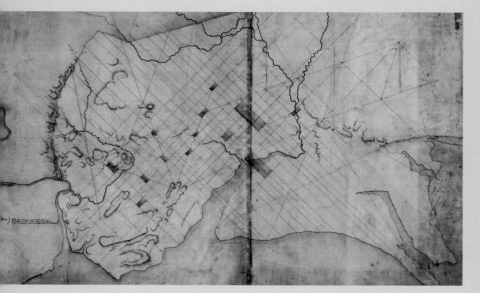

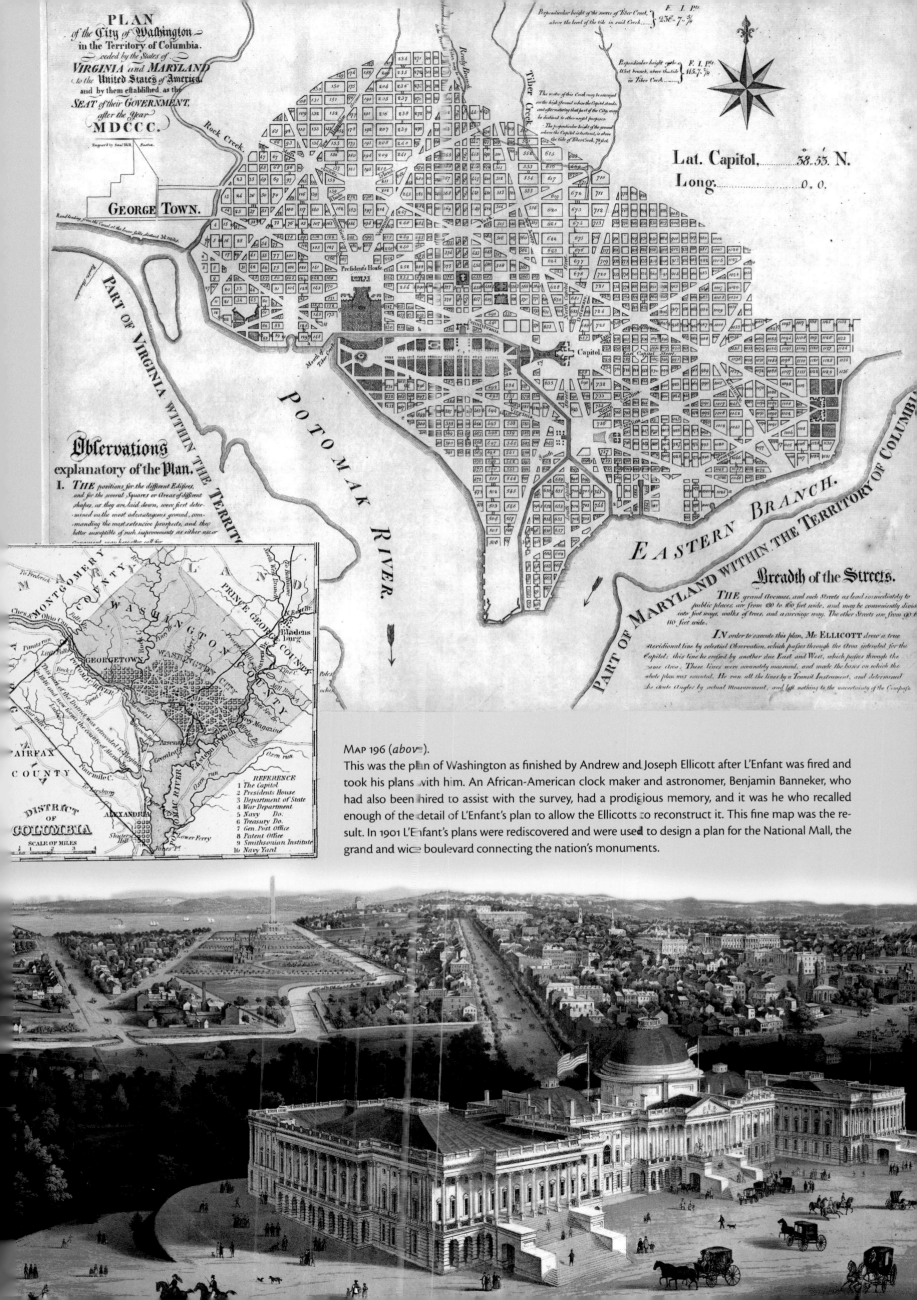

PLAN
of the City of Washington
in the Territory of Columbia.
ceded by the States of
VIRGINIA and MARYLAND
to the United States of America.
and by them established, as the
SEAT of their GOVERNMENT,
after the year
MDCCC.

Engraved by Saml. Hill, Boston.

GEORGE TOWN.

Road leading from the Canal at the Lower falls, distant 3½ miles.

Perpendicular height of the source of Tiber Creek, above the level of the tide in said Creek. } F. I. Pts. 236. 7. ³⁄₁₀

Perpendicular height of the West branch, above that tide in Tiber Creek. } F. I. Pts. 115. 7. ⁷⁄₁₀

Lat. Capitol.............58. 53'. N.
Long:.....................0. 0.

ROCK CREEK

Tiber Creek

Ready Branch

President's House

Capitol

POTOMAK RIVER

Mouth of the Tiber Creek

EASTERN BRANCH.

PART OF VIRGINIA WITHIN THE TERRITORY

PART OF MARYLAND WITHIN THE TERRITORY OF COLUMBIA.

Observations
explanatory of the Plan.

I. THE positions for the different Edifices, and for the several Squares or Areas of different shapes, as they are laid down, were first determined on the most advantageous ground, commanding the most extensive prospects, and the better susceptible of such improvements as either use or convenience may hereafter call for.

Breadth of the Streets.

THE grand Avenues, and such Streets as lead immediately to public places, are from 130 to 160 feet wide, and may be conveniently divided into foot ways, walks of trees, and a carriage way. The other Streets are from 90 to 110 feet wide.

IN order to execute this plan, Mr. ELLICOTT drew a true meridional line by celestial Observation, which passes through the Area intended for the Capitol: this line he crossed by another due East and West, which passes through the same Area. These lines were accurately measured, and made the bases on which the whole plan was executed. He ran all the lines by a Transit Instrument, and determined the acute Angles by actual Measurement, and left nothing to the uncertainty of the Compass.

DISTRICT
OF
COLUMBIA
SCALE OF MILES

REFERENCE
1 The Capitol
2 Presidents House
3 Department of State
4 War Department
5 Navy Do.
6 Treasury Do.
7 Gen. Post Office
8 Patent Office
9 Smithsonian Institute
10 Navy Yard

MAP 196 (above).
This was the plan of Washington as finished by Andrew and Joseph Ellicott after L'Enfant was fired and took his plans with him. An African-American clock maker and astronomer, Benjamin Banneker, who had also been hired to assist with the survey, had a prodigious memory, and it was he who recalled enough of the detail of L'Enfant's plan to allow the Ellicotts to reconstruct it. This fine map was the result. In 1901 L'Enfant's plans were rediscovered and were used to design a plan for the National Mall, the grand and wide boulevard connecting the nation's monuments.

Seas Where They Ought Not to Be

MAP 199 (*left*).
California as an island was a favorite theme on maps of the seventeenth century, and such depictions are avidly sought after by West Coast map collectors today. This is a map by Dutch mapmaker Joan Vingtboons, drawn about 1650.

MAP 200 (*below, bottom*).
This map surely has it all! Produced in 1749 at the request of the Hudson's Bay Company to assist in the defense of its monopoly before a parliamentary inquiry, the map was, not surprisingly, considered inadequate, and all but ten copies were destroyed. The map was engraved by a London mapmaker, Richard Seale, who otherwise produced normal-looking maps, and so it is thought that he merely engraved somebody else's work, a person now mercifully anonymous. The Great Lakes occupy much of the center of North America and almost provide a clear channel through the continent. *Illinois* covers most of the center of America, an oversized *Missisipi River* is placed too far west, *California* is an island, and much of the North Pacific is occupied by a misplaced Alaska, *Compaignes Land* and *De Gama's Land*, reflecting supposed sighting of land and a misplacing of the Kurile Islands north of Japan. To the north is *Barnardo's Coast*, from an account of a fictitious voyage, and North America is attached to Greenland (*Part of Groenland*) and a huge Arctic landmass, making a Northwest Passage impossible. A channel cuts through what is now Maine to connect the St. Lawrence with the Atlantic. The East Coast of the Thirteen Colonies and Florida, and the Caribbean islands, are all that are shown with any degree of accuracy. The area colored red is British territory. This is a regressive map; that is, geographical knowledge was better at the time than the map would suggest.

Throughout history, dreams have often been made to exist—at least on paper. Expectations drove men forward, kept them motivated through hardships, and led to facts being interpreted to fit what was wanted. Without solid information as to what was over the horizon, it was easy to substitute speculation. Much information came from native sources, Indians who were ready to tell their inquirers what they wanted to hear—for were they not the bearer of all manner of desirable trade goods? And European explorers often misinterpreted what they were told, for Indian concepts of geography were sometimes radically different from their own (see page 122).

One of the earliest myths to appear on maps was a passage through the continent—a continent that had originally been discovered by Europeans when it obstructed the way to China (MAP 49 and MAP 50, *pages 28–29*). Another was California shown as an island (MAP 199, *above*). Spanish voyages around the Gulf of California had shown it to be part of the mainland, yet it was shown as an island until well after overland explorer and missionary Father Eusebio Kino demonstrated the land connection in 1700–1701.

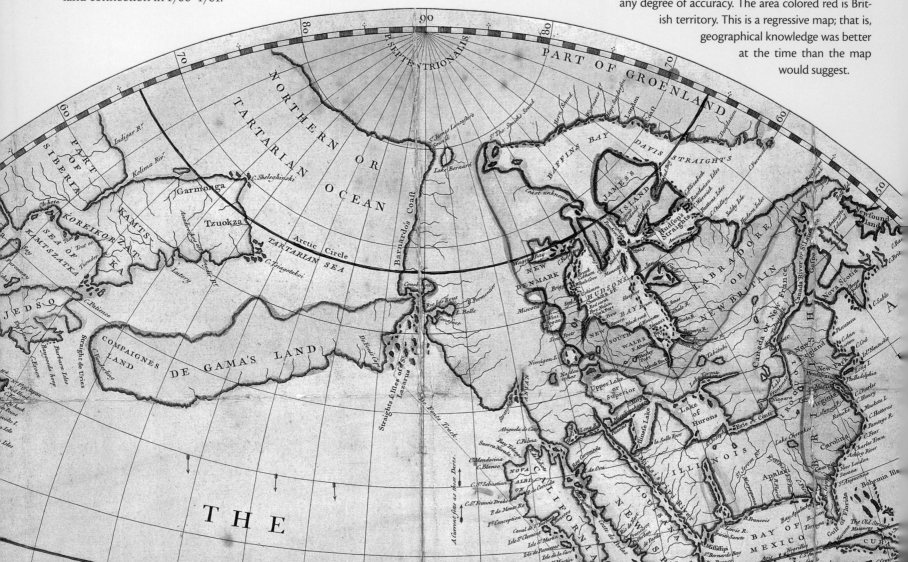

Another long-standing myth was that of the Sea of the West (MAP 201, *right*), an apparition seemingly verified by every large lake found west of the Mississippi. How convenient it would have been to have a bight of the Pacific reaching inland to Kansas!

An even more persistent myth was that of a River of the West. Fulfilling the desire of explorers for an easy route west, native reports of large waterways were frequently interpreted to be this river. One of the earliest, the Long River, found its way into print in 1703 in a book by the French explorer Baron Lahontan (MAP 204, *bottom, right*), which went through many editions over a period of nearly forty years and was immensely popular and influential. Another popular book, the *Travels* of Jonathan Carver, published in 1778, went through thirty editions in several languages, complete with a map that showed a River of the West tentatively flowing to the sea at about the position of the mouth of the Columbia (MAP 202, *below*).

If there was a real River of the West it was the Columbia, found by Robert Gray in 1792 and explored from the Rockies to the sea by Meriwether Lewis and William Clark thirteen years later (see page 110). Yet the river did not flow over or through the mountains, as many mapmakers seemed to portray it.

MAP 201 (*top, right*).
This wonderful map shows a gigantic *Mer ou Baye de L'Ouest* (Sea or Bay of the West) occupying the Northwest north of Cape Mendocino and extending inland to the headwaters of the Mississippi. It was produced by French mapmaker Joseph-Nicolas De L'Isle in 1752.

MAP 202 (*above*).
The *River of the West* as shown on Jonathan Carver's map of America, first published in his 1778 book, which was so popular thirty editions were published. Less spectacularly, the map also shows a river flowing west to San Francisco Bay. This is the mythical Buenaventura River, which was for long thought to flow, like the River of the West, from interior mountains—later considered to be the Rocky Mountains—to the Pacific Ocean (see page 120).

MAP 203 (*above, right*).
Another portrayal of the River of the West, this time by French mapmaker Jacques-Nicolas Bellin, published in 1743. The *fleuve de l'ouest* stretches through a number of lakes toward Alaska and connects with Lake Superior. The direction of the river's flow is unclear from this representation.

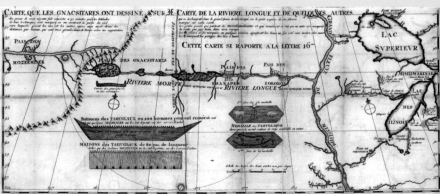

MAP 204 (*above*).
The *Riviere Longue* of Baron Lahontan, first published in 1703, a mixture of fact, fiction, misinterpretation, exaggeration, and lies, nonetheless immensely influential.

Voyages to the Northwest

The west coast of North America north of Cape Mendocino lay unknown to Europeans until the late eighteenth century. So little was known about it that Jonathan Swift used it as the location of his Brobdingnag, or land of giants, in his novel *Gulliver's Travels,* published in 1726. Francis Drake had claimed the west coast of the United States for England in 1579 as his New Albion (see page 23) at a still disputed location likely near San Francisco. In 1602 Sebastian Vizcaíno had mapped as far north as Cape Mendocino (Map 28, *page 17*), but this geographical knowledge was then buried by the secretive Spanish authorities for two centuries. North of this cape, nothing was known, and from the west the Russians would not see any part of Alaska until 1732 (see page 126).

It was the Russians, however, who set off a new interest in the Northwest beginning in 1773. Reports of the voyages of Vitus Bering and Aleksei Chirikov in 1741 led the Spanish to wonder if Russian outposts had been established on the Pacific, which they regarded as their territory. At the same time the Spanish were attempting to expand their influence north into Alta California (see page 68).

An experienced naval captain, Juan Pérez, received instructions in December 1773 to sail north to 60° and return along the coast, "never losing sight of it." He took with him tropical spices to show

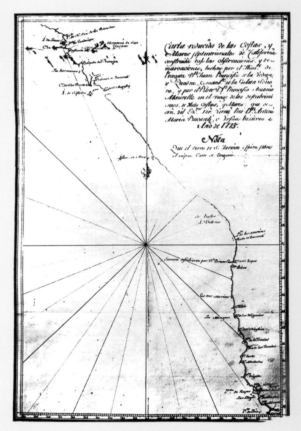

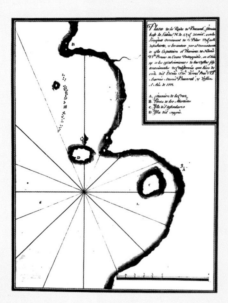

Above. James Cook's ships *Resolution* and *Discovery* on the Northwest Coast in 1778, a painting by Harry Heine.

Map 205 (below).
Juan Pérez's map, the first of the Northwest Coast from exploration, was drawn by his pilot, Josef de Cañizares, in 1774. It shows the coastline from Monterey, at bottom right, to Dixon Entrance, the tip of the Alaska Panhandle, at top. Sketches of prominent coastal features are shown as they would be seen from the sea. At the top is *P^{ta} de Sta Maria Magalena* (Punta de Santa Maria Magalena), now Cape Muzon, the southern tip of Dall Island, Alaska. At center is *Cerra de Sta Rosalia*, now Mount Olympus, Washington.

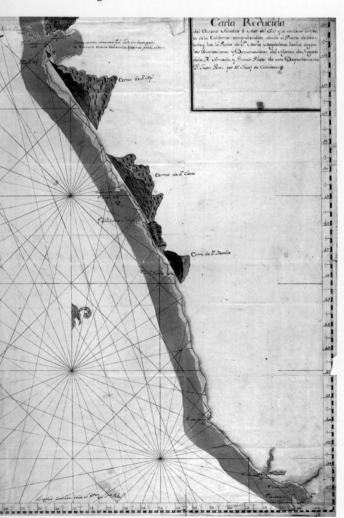

Map 206 (above).
The first map of any part of what is now Washington State, this is Cape Elizabeth, mapped in 1775 by Bruno de Hezeta.

Map 207 (right, top).
Juan Francisco Bodega y Quadra's map of the west coast of North America from his 1775 voyage in the 38-foot *Sonora.* The coast of what is now the continental United States and Alaska is mapped in more detail than the coast between the two because Bodega y Quadra was offshore at these latitudes. A sketchy map perhaps, but a very hard-earned one.

Map 208 (right).
Hezeta's map of the mouth of the Columbia River, which he called *Bahia de la Asunción.*

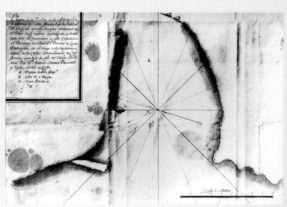

any natives he encountered what he was looking for, a clear indication that the nature of the Northwest Coast was indeed dimly perceived. Pérez sailed from Mexico in his ship *Santiago* and reached Dixon Entrance, between the tip of the Alaska Panhandle and the Queen Charlotte Islands, on 18 July 1774. He traded with natives who approached in canoes but did not go ashore, fearing for his safety, perhaps knowing of Chirikov's earlier attempt in which two boatloads of

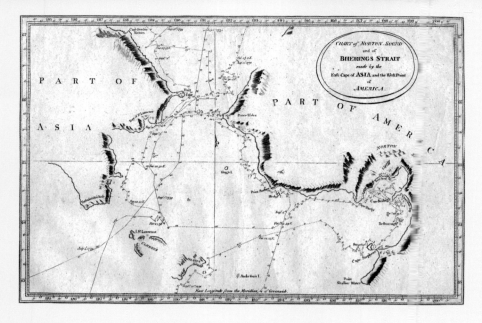

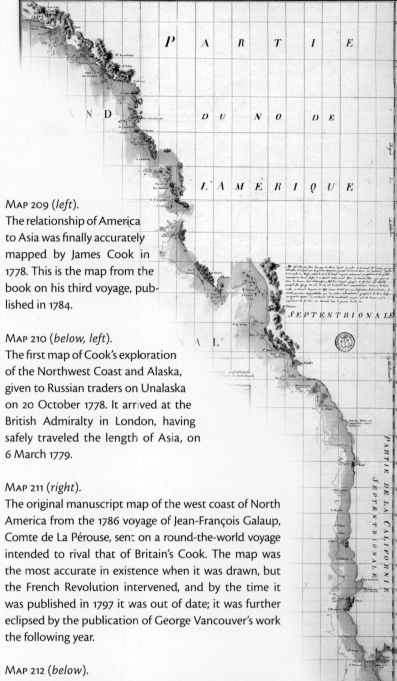

men did not return (see page 126). The location of his landfall, 54°40′N, was significant in that it would later become the rationale for the Alaska boundary. Pérez's voyage produced the first map of the west coast of America north of Cape Mendocino drawn from exploration (Map 205, *far left*).

Pérez had been instructed to sail to 60°N. In this he had failed, and the following year another expedition was mounted, this time with two ships, and the unfortunate Pérez was demoted to first officer on the *Santiago* under Bruno de Hezeta y Dudagoitia. Juan Francisco Bodega y Quadra commanded the other ship, the diminutive 38-foot *Sonora*. A third ship, under Juan de Ayala, sailed with them as far as San Francisco Bay (see page 71 and Map 142). On 13 July 1775 the ships anchored off Cape Elizabeth, where Pérez's fears were substantiated when men were murdered when they went ashore to fill casks with water. Here Hezeta produced the first map of the Washington coast (Map 206, *left, center*). Then, at about 50°N, the ships were separated in a storm, and since Hezeta's men were falling ill—including Pérez, who died at sea—he returned south along the coast, discovering and mapping a large bay that was, unknown to him, the mouth of the Columbia River (Map 208, *left, bottom*).

Bodega y Quadra did not give up, however. Determined to carry out his instructions (and perhaps avoid demotion), he pushed north in heavy seas and on 15 August made a landfall near today's Sitka, Alaska, continuing north to 58°, searching for a supposed strait, a western end of the Northwest Passage said to have been discovered in 1640 by a Spanish admiral, Bartolomew De Fonte, a story later found to be a hoax. Bodega y Quadra's map (Map 207, *left*) shows greater detail in the south and north, reflecting his ordeal offshore trying to sail to Alaska.

Britain was concerned that Spain might find a western end of the Northwest Passage and be able to claim it for itself. So in 1776 the by-now-famous explorer James Cook was dispatched on his third voyage, this time to the Northwest Coast. He made a landfall in heavy seas on 6 March 1778 at a place he named, for good reason, Cape Foulweather, now in Oregon. Sailing north offshore, which the winds and currents of this coast make

Map 209 (*left*).
The relationship of America to Asia was finally accurately mapped by James Cook in 1778. This is the map from the book on his third voyage, published in 1784.

Map 210 (*below, left*).
The first map of Cook's exploration of the Northwest Coast and Alaska, given to Russian traders on Unalaska on 20 October 1778. It arrived at the British Admiralty in London, having safely traveled the length of Asia, on 6 March 1779.

Map 211 (*right*).
The original manuscript map of the west coast of North America from the 1786 voyage of Jean-François Galaup, Comte de La Pérouse, sent on a round-the-world voyage intended to rival that of Britain's Cook. The map was the most accurate in existence when it was drawn, but the French Revolution intervened, and by the time it was published in 1797 it was out of date; it was further eclipsed by the publication of George Vancouver's work the following year.

Map 212 (*below*).
This detailed topographical map from the La Pérouse expedition is of Lituya Bay, Alaska, drawn during an extended stay in July 1786 to collect scientific data.

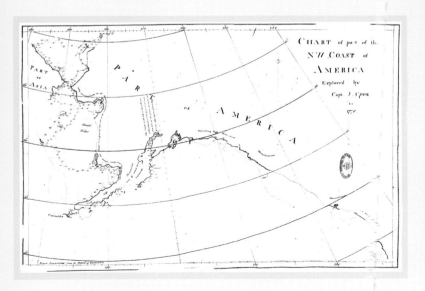

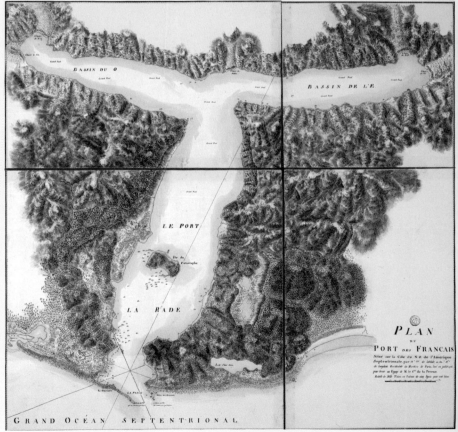

a necessity, he found a harbor at Nootka Sound, on the west coast of Vancouver Island. Here he stayed for nearly a month, repairing his ships, before venturing northwards once more. He began to map the coast at Prince William Sound, Alaska, and explored Cook Inlet, site of today's city of Anchorage. Using a map he had with him (MAP 251, *page 127*), Cook had trouble finding a gap in the Aleutian chain, but he did, and sailed into Bering Strait, accurately mapping the relationship of America to Asia for the first time (MAP 209, *previous page*). Stopped by the ice pack just north of the strait, he returned to Hawaii, which he had discovered on his outbound voyage, for the winter. There he was killed by natives early in 1779.

That year another Spanish expedition got under way after much delay. Ignacio de Arteaga, with Bodega y Quadra second in command, the latter not having reached the 65°N demanded in the instructions for the 1775 voyage, found Prince William Sound and claimed it for Spain, not knowing that Cook had done the same for Britain the year before. Arteaga thus reached 61°N when he had been told to sail to 70°N, and we hear no more from him. Spain itself was by this time beginning to decline as a sea power, and its claims to the Northwest Coast were diminished over the next decade by a flood of British fur traders, searching every inlet for the black gold of the sea otter pelt. Cook's crew had made a tidy profit selling a few otter pelts in Canton, and the lure of profit finally drove men to these shores in numbers greater than at any time before.

Many of these traders tried to profit in another way when they went home—by writing books. In this manner this remote coast became much more familiar to Europeans and Americans. Nathaniel Portlock and George Dixon mapped much detail of the southern Alaska coast; Dixon's name is enshrined in Dixon Entrance, at Alaska's southern extremity. Charles Barkley refound the Strait of Juan de Fuca in 1787, giving it the name he thought it had already acquired from the supposed 1597 voyage of a Spanish ship guided by a Greek pilot of that name, a voyage of which no record has ever been found.

In 1786 the coast was also visited by an explorer in the same grand ilk as James Cook, sent on a voyage of circumnavigation by a French government trying to undermine the glory attached to Britain's James Cook. Jean-François Galaup, Comte de La Pérouse, spent a month at Lituya Bay in Alaska (MAP 212, *previous page*) so a number of scientists with him could examine the region. He then then sailed the entire west coast of North America in two more months, producing a creditable map that was not published until it was out of date, thanks to the French Revolution (MAP 211, *previous page*). La Pérouse, like Cook, never returned from his epic voyage; his ship foundered on a reef in Vanuatu in the South Pacific. Luckily for posterity he had already dropped off copies of his maps and other scientific work at Botany Bay, now Sydney, Australia.

Spanish explorers did not venture north again until 1788. Esteban José Martínez, who had been with Pérez in 1774, and Gonzalo López de Haro sailed north and then west, making maps and claiming possession for Spain. They reached Unalaska Island in the Aleutians and for the first time met Russian fur traders, under Potap Zaikov (see page 127). Martínez and Zaikov, far from fighting each other for possession of Alaska, tried to outdrink each other, thanks to Spanish brandy and Russian vodka.

Spain now determined to find out if there was a western entrance to a Northwest Passage on the Northwest Coast and perhaps establish colonies on the coast to protect it. In 1790, from a base established at Nootka Sound, on Vancouver Island, Francisco de Eliza dispatched Salvador Fidalgo north to Alaska and Manuel Quimper south, both to look for harbors. Fidalgo found Prince William Sound and claimed one of its bays for Spain—Córdova, the name of the modern city. But he retreated after finding Russian fur trade forts firmly ensconced on Cook Inlet and Kodiak Island; despite Spanish probes, the Russians had beaten them to Alaska.

MAP 213.
This map, drawn at the end of 1791 or the beginning of 1792, shows the extent of Spanish knowledge of the west coast of America just before the arrival of Britain's George Vancouver. It was drawn by Juan Francisco Bodega y Quadra. Vancouver's epic survey has tended to overshadow the work of the Spanish explorers who came before him.

MAP 214 (*below*).
Alejandro Malaspina's map of his *Puerto del Desengaño*, or Bay of Disappointment, so named when he found what he was convinced was the western entrance to the Northwest Passage blocked by a massive glacier. It was Yakutat Bay, Alaska, and the Hubbard Glacier, today only a remnant of its size in 1791.

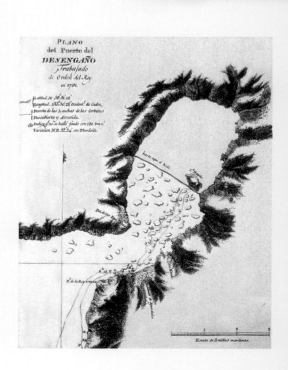

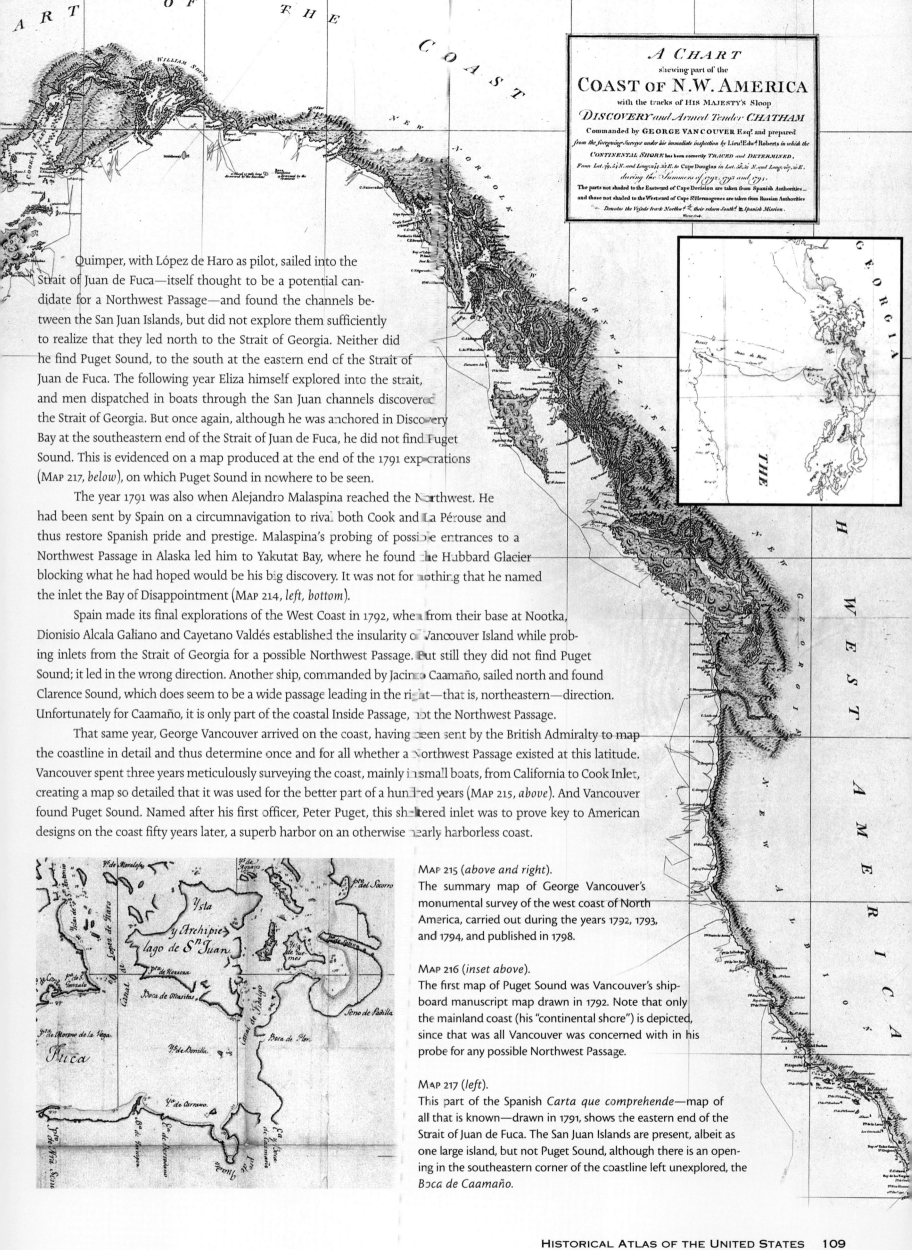

Quimper, with López de Haro as pilot, sailed into the Strait of Juan de Fuca—itself thought to be a potential candidate for a Northwest Passage—and found the channels between the San Juan Islands, but did not explore them sufficiently to realize that they led north to the Strait of Georgia. Neither did he find Puget Sound, to the south at the eastern end of the Strait of Juan de Fuca. The following year Eliza himself explored into the strait, and men dispatched in boats through the San Juan channels discovered the Strait of Georgia. But once again, although he was anchored in Discovery Bay at the southeastern end of the Strait of Juan de Fuca, he did not find Puget Sound. This is evidenced on a map produced at the end of the 1791 explorations (Map 217, *below*), on which Puget Sound in nowhere to be seen.

The year 1791 was also when Alejandro Malaspina reached the Northwest. He had been sent by Spain on a circumnavigation to rival both Cook and La Pérouse and thus restore Spanish pride and prestige. Malaspina's probing of possible entrances to a Northwest Passage in Alaska led him to Yakutat Bay, where he found the Hubbard Glacier blocking what he had hoped would be his big discovery. It was not for nothing that he named the inlet the Bay of Disappointment (Map 214, *left, bottom*).

Spain made its final explorations of the West Coast in 1792, when from their base at Nootka, Dionisio Alcalá Galiano and Cayetano Valdés established the insularity of Vancouver Island while probing inlets from the Strait of Georgia for a possible Northwest Passage. But still they did not find Puget Sound; it led in the wrong direction. Another ship, commanded by Jacinto Caamaño, sailed north and found Clarence Sound, which does seem to be a wide passage leading in the right—that is, northeastern—direction. Unfortunately for Caamaño, it is only part of the coastal Inside Passage, not the Northwest Passage.

That same year, George Vancouver arrived on the coast, having been sent by the British Admiralty to map the coastline in detail and thus determine once and for all whether a Northwest Passage existed at this latitude. Vancouver spent three years meticulously surveying the coast, mainly in small boats, from California to Cook Inlet, creating a map so detailed that it was used for the better part of a hundred years (Map 215, *above*). And Vancouver found Puget Sound. Named after his first officer, Peter Puget, this sheltered inlet was to prove key to American designs on the coast fifty years later, a superb harbor on an otherwise nearly harborless coast.

Map 215 (*above and right*).
The summary map of George Vancouver's monumental survey of the west coast of North America, carried out during the years 1792, 1793, and 1794, and published in 1798.

Map 216 (*inset above*).
The first map of Puget Sound was Vancouver's shipboard manuscript map drawn in 1792. Note that only the mainland coast (his "continental shore") is depicted, since that was all Vancouver was concerned with in his probe for any possible Northwest Passage.

Map 217 (*left*).
This part of the Spanish *Carta que comprehende*—map of all that is known—drawn in 1791, shows the eastern end of the Strait of Juan de Fuca. The San Juan Islands are present, albeit as one large island, but not Puget Sound, although there is an opening in the southeastern corner of the coastline left unexplored, the *Boca de Caamaño*.

Across a New America

Without a doubt the most famous exploration in the history of the United States is the expedition of Meriwether Lewis and William Clark and their Corps of Discovery to the Pacific between 1804 and 1806. This necessary forerunner to Manifest Destiny had tremendous political impact, contributing to the eventual incorporation of Oregon and the Pacific Northwest into the Union. A plan of exploration masterminded for years by Thomas Jefferson, it came to fruition in the wake of the Louisiana Purchase in 1803, which brought with it the need to explore and claim the new territory.

Lewis and Clark were not the first to cross the continent; that honor had gone to Britain's Alexander Mackenzie in 1793. They were not even the first up much of the length of the Missouri. Since French explorers Louis Jolliet and Jacques Marquette had found the confluence of the river with the Mississippi in 1673, various explorers and traders had slowly increased European and then American knowledge up the river. Prior to

Lewis and Clark's great trek, the Missouri was known as far as the Mandan villages at the Great Bend in today's North Dakota, which were likely found by La Vérendrye as early as 1738 (see page 50).

Even when the river was in Spanish Louisiana, St. Louis merchants had obtained a trading monopoly and created the Company of Explorers of the Upper Missouri, usually known as the Missouri Company. A trading venture in 1793 led by Jean Baptiste Truteau had reached the location of the present North and South Dakota boundary, and in 1794 another group led by James Mackay and John Thomas Evans reached the Man-

MAP 218 (*right*).
Many maps before Lewis and Clark simply ran off the paper somewhere in the West, as the mapmaker ran out of knowledge. Here the Missouri wanders from a wilderness, with the notation *Missouri R. its source unknown.* The map was published by British mapmaker William Faden in 1785.

MAP 219 (*below*).
When in 1796–97 John Evans persuaded the Mandan Indians to draw him a map of the land to the west, this is what he received. The Pacific was clearly not just over the horizon, or even just over a single range of mountains, for the native map shows—for the first time—multiple ranges mirroring reality. *River yellow rock* is the Yellowstone River. The westernmost mountain range is the *montagne de roche*—rocky mountain. The Great Falls of the Missouri is marked *the fall.*

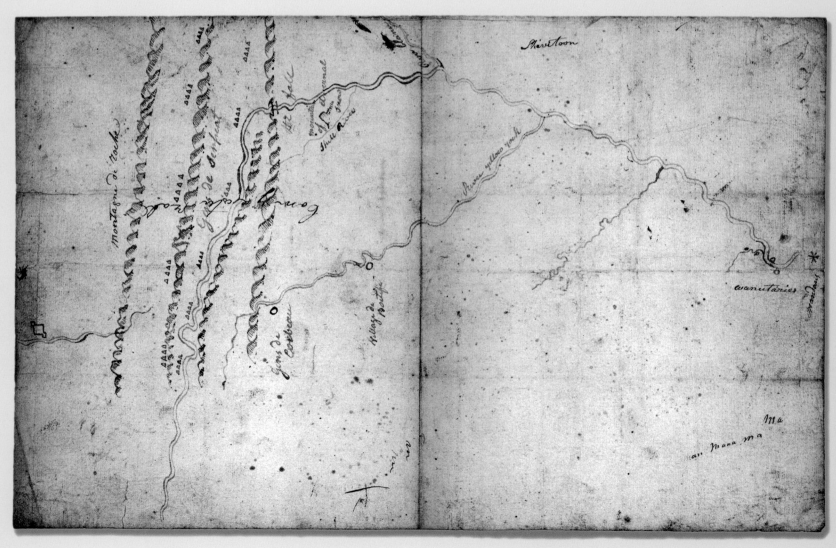

dan villages. Evans was seeking a supposed lost tribe of Welsh Indians he thought might be the Mandans; needless to say, he did not find them. Another effort in 1795–96 planned to cross the mountains, to find the Pacific coast and a passage to India. Contemporary thinking held that the Missouri rose on a "height of land" from which the Columbia also arose to flow west, and thus the portage between the two would be short and easy, as indicated on MAP 221, *below*. Evans was discouraged from this plan when he learned of the multiple mountain ranges and the vast distance involved (MAP 219, *left, bottom*).

Thomas Jefferson had long harbored dreams of a pan-continental United States. In 1793 he had drawn up the instructions for an expedition to the Pacific by French botanist André Michaux, only to see his plans stillborn when Michaux became suspected of spying. Jefferson's instructions were not wasted, however, for ten years later they were given to Lewis and Clark almost unchanged.

Jefferson read Alexander Mackenzie's book in 1802 and was concerned about the advocacy

MAP 220 (above).
A contemporary French copy of a map of the Northwest drawn in 1795 by Antoine Soulard, Spanish surveyor general of Louisiana. It dramatically reflects the popular notion of a Missouri traversing much of the continent and separated from the Pacific slope by only a single range of mountains, looking easy to cross and very near an inviting Pacific. *Possession Anglaise*, English Possessions, the territory of the Hudson's Bay Company, are limited to the area immediately around Hudson Bay, with *Possession Espagnole* covering the rest of the West, a vast extension of Spanish Louisiana from anything commonly accepted elsewhere at the time.

MAP 221 (below).
This is part of a copy of Soulard's map, now in English, made a little later and actually carried by Lewis and Clark on their expecition. The map was likely drawn in 1802, and it now has a few additions, notably the Columbia, marked *Oregan, or R. of the West*, which is shown flowing west from the mountains a scant few miles from the headwaters of the Missouri, reflecting the prevailing hopes that the portage between the two would be short and easy. Although not shown on this portion, the area to the north is now marked *Unknown Country* rather than *Possession Anglaise*. The missing corner is a hole in the map caused by abrasion on a fold while carried in Lewis's pocket.

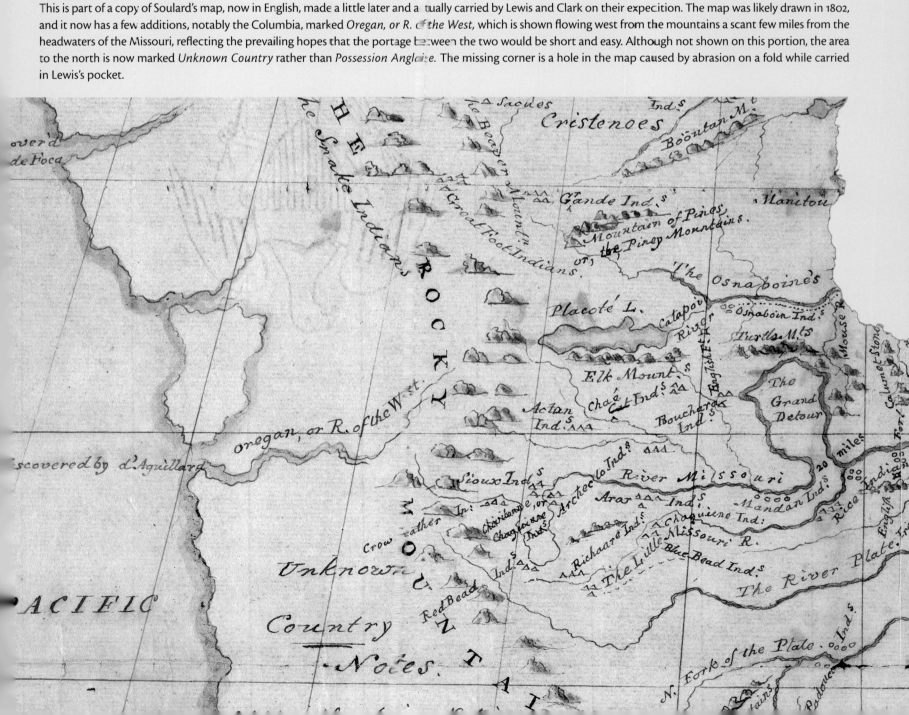

Map 222 (*above*).

This map represented the best information available to Lewis and Clark as they set out on their journey in 1804. The map had been drawn up by commercial mapmaker Nicholas King in 1803 on instructions from Jefferson. He copied much from the latest published map of British mapmaker Aaron Arrowsmith (who was the most knowledgeable at the time because he had an inside track at the Hudson's Bay Company). In particular, Arrowsmith's map included information gained from fur trader and explorer Peter Fidler, who in turn had obtained information on the nature of the Upper Missouri basin from the Blackfoot chief Ac ko mok ki (see **Map 241**, *page 123*). King then added all other information he could find, and Lewis carried the map with him to the Pacific. The Mandan villages (*Pawnee Village*) are at center right. Just to the north the rivers drawn in brown ink were added by Lewis from information gained while at the villages. The headwaters of one branch of the Columbia are shown a short distance from the northernmost branch of the Missouri. In addition, marked *Conjectural*, as indeed it was, one tentative tributary of the Columbia is shown flowing straight around the Rockies, if not actually through them.

of British west coast settlements for the shipping of furs. Mackenzie's book, indeed, can fairly be stated to have been the catalyst for the Lewis and Clark expedition, and it was the unexpected acquisition of Louisiana in 1803 that made such an exploration an urgent necessity. A commercial imperative turned into a national one.

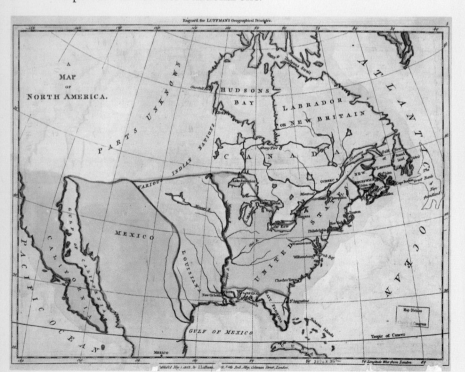

Several expeditions were organized to explore and map the newly acquired territory, of which Lewis and Clark's was the most extensive and successful, and became the most famous, eclipsing the others in the public eye. (The others are described on pages 116–17.)

Lewis and Clark and their expedition, now styled the Corps of Discovery, left St. Louis on 14 May 1804. (Lewis actually caught up with it five days later.) The twenty-seven men started out with a 55-foot keelboat and two pirogues (dugout canoes with sails), filled with five tons of food and other supplies. They overwintered at the Great Bend of the Missouri at the Mandan and Arikara villages. In the spring they continued upstream

Map 223 (*left, bottom*).

The Louisiana Purchase came about almost by accident. The French had regained the territory from Spain by the secret Treaty of San Ildefonso in 1800. Jefferson had sent emissaries James Monroe and Robert Livingston to Paris to negotiate for New Orleans, seen as the key to the Mississippi. Napoleon had just lost control of Hispaniola to a slave uprising led by a freed slave, Toussaint L'Ouverture, and felt little need to retain Louisiana, which had been intended as a source of supplies for the Caribbean island. Thus he offered it to the United States, which, he figured, would keep it out of the hands of his enemy, Britain. For 60 million francs, about $15 million, America acquired about 800,000 square miles, for less than three cents per acre. France received money to fight its wars in Europe.

The lack of knowledge as to precisely what had been purchased in 1803 is graphically illustrated in this map published the same year. John Luffman's *Geographical Principles*, from which this map comes, did not help. Only the wildest approximation of the bounds of *Louisiana* is shown—and the northern bound is at the same latitude as the northern end of the Gulf of California. The most correct part of western North America on this map is perhaps the notation *Parts Unknown*. Although this map may exaggerate the lack of knowledge of the region purchased, the expeditions sent out by Jefferson to explore the new territory were clearly needed.

Map 224 (*right*).

This 1912 map defines what the United States government later officially maintained were the boundaries of Louisiana. But the boundaries were much easier to define in 1912 than they had been in 1803.

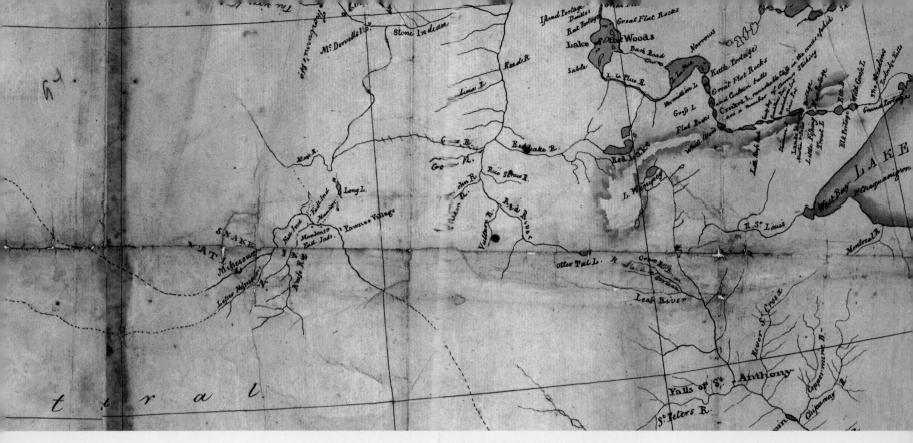

in canoes and the pirogues, and by 26 May were in sight of the "snow-y barrier" of the Rocky Mountains. At one place where the river branched, Lewis ascended one of the tributary streams (which he named the Marias River) for forty miles simply to ascertain that the other was the correct route to take. He had read Mackenzie's book, and Mackenzie had made a similar critical decision that Lewis was well aware of. He knew his decision had been the right one when they arrived at the Great Falls of the Missouri, for it was expected based on their native information; it is marked as *the fall* in John Evans's map (MAP 219, page 110). However, their vindication took them a month to portage around.

By August they were at the Rockies. After considerable delay trying to make contact with wary Shoshone, they purchased horses, thanks to the timely intervention of Sacagawea, the Shoshone wife of one of their guides, Toussaint Charbonneau. Even with horses and a Shoshone guide, their route through the mountains was difficult. Lewis expected to encounter the Columbia flowing away from him to the Pacific, but all he saw were more mountain ranges. They crossed the Bitterroot Range through the Lemhi Pass on the Continental Divide, today the boundary between Montana and Idaho. In the cold and snow they were reduced to eating a horse. But after eleven days the expedition reached a friendly Nez Percé village near the Clearwater—at last a westward-flowing river.

Now in borrowed canoes the going was much easier as they floated down the Clearwater, then the Snake, and then—the Columbia. By 3 November they were in Pacific tidewater, and four days later Clark recorded his famous line: "Ocian in view! O! The joy!" In fact they were still twenty miles from the coast but no matter, they had made it. Near the mouth of the Columbia on 3 December both Lewis and Clark found themselves suitable trees and carved inscriptions on them. Clark's emulated the words Alexander Mackenzie had painted on a tidewater rock farther to the north in 1793 when he carved "Capt. William Clark December 3rd 1805, By Land. U. States in 1804–1805."

From December 1805 to March 1806 the Corps wintered at a log camp they built on a river that would later be named the Lewis and Clark River (MAP 225, *right*). While there, Clark converted his notes of daily courses and distances into a comprehensive map, adding native information for areas beyond the expedition's path. On 14 February 1806 he wrote in his diary: "I compleated a map of the Countrey through which we have been passing . . . We now discover that we have found the most practicable and navigable passage across the Continent of North America." Fine words, but Clark meant them negatively. Clearly the route was *not*

MAP 225 (*below*).
William Clark's sketch map of the mouth of the Columbia River, with the Pacific coast to the south. It was drawn in early 1806 while he was at the expedition's dwelling, Fort Clatsop, indicated by an unnamed rectangle on the *Ne-lul River*, now the Lewis and Clark River, at center. Cape Disappointment is at top left; modern Cannon Beach, Oregon, is at bottom left.

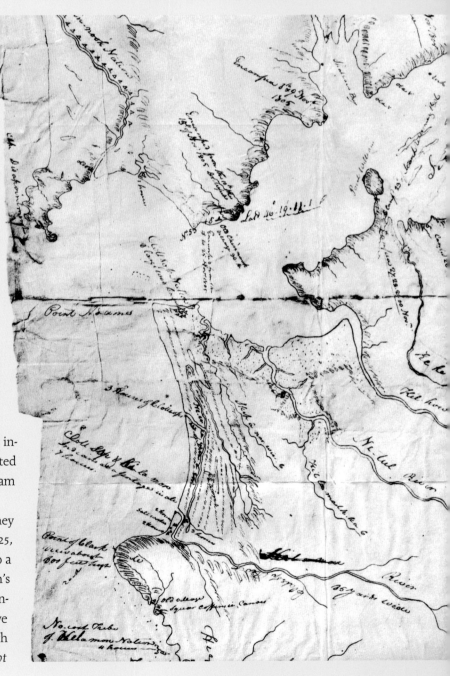

all that practicable, and it certainly did not consist of the navigable rivers and short portage that he had somehow hoped to find, against much of the evidence. On the return journey, begun on 23 March 1806, the Corps did find several easier routes; they split up as they crossed the Rockies so as to cover as much ground and as many potential routes as possible. They met again at the mouth of the Yellowstone River and made a fast, now downstream, passage to St. Louis, where they arrived to much jubilation on 23 September, having been given up for dead by many people.

The dream of an easy overland Northwest Passage was laid to rest by the Lewis and Clark expedition, but it had revealed another dream, that of a transcontinental United States. Although it was to take many more years, it was a dream that would one day become reality.

MAP 226 (*right*).
One of the Corps of Discovery, Private Robert Frazer (or Frazier), kept a journal, and shortly after his return to St. Louis he announced his intention to publish it as a 400-page book. But the book was never published and the journal was lost. The map Frazer drew to illustrate his proposed book, however, did survive. It seems to have been drawn in 1807. Rarely reproduced, perhaps because of its numerous inaccuracies, overall it is a fair representation of the courses of the Missouri and the Columbia, fully depicted for the first time. It also shows the results of the Lewis and Clark expedition unaugmented by later discoveries, un-like Clark's final map and the published map, also shown here.

MAP 227 (*below*) and MAP 228 (*right, inset*).
William Clark's hand-drawn map of the West (MAP 227) and the map published in the account of the expedition in 1814 (MAP 228). Both show for the first time

the entire course of the Missouri River, from the Rocky Mountains to its confluence with the Mississippi. They also show the courses of the Clearwater, the Snake, and the Columbia. In both Lewis and Clark's journals are numerous local maps, many of which were copies of Indian maps drawn for them on the ground

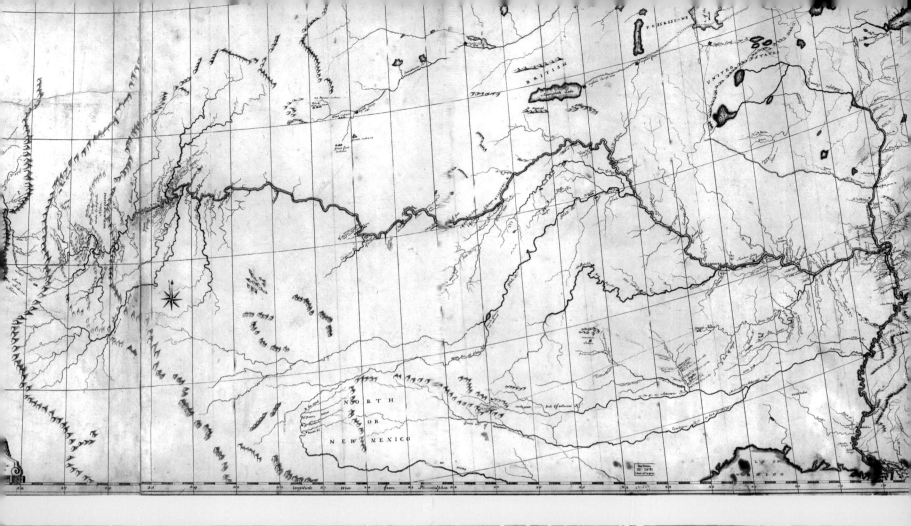

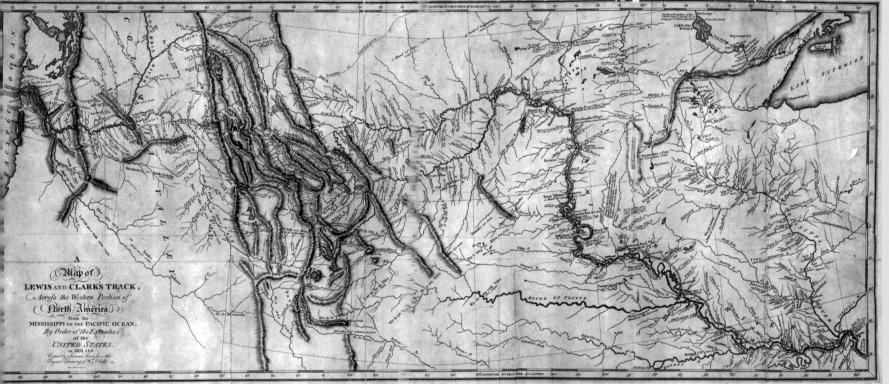

A Map of LEWIS AND CLARKS TRACK, Across the Western Portion of North America from the MISSISSIPPI to the PACIFIC OCEAN; By Order of The Executive of the UNITED STATES. in 1804.5 & 6. Copied by Samuel Lewis from the Original Drawing of Wm. Clark.

A MAP 1751 of part of the Continent of North America

(see page 124). Clark used all these maps to construct a large map of the entire West, and later, as superintendent of Indian affairs in St. Louis, he kept it on his wall, adding information to it as it became known to him. Because not all the additions were accurate, there are some errors in his map, but the information from his own expedition was reasonably correct. Clark's map, completed in 1810, is one of the landmark maps of the United States.

The engraved version of this map (MAP 228) was copied from Clark's hand-drawn map by Philadelphia mapmaker Samuel Lewis (no relation to Meriwether, who had died in 1809, likely, it is thought, by his own hand) and published in 1814 in the "official" account of the Lewis and Clark expedition, the *History of the Expedition under the command of Captains Lewis and Clark, to the sources of the Missouri, thence across the Rocky Mountains and down the River Columbia to the Pacific Ocean*. It is now the most sought-after volume of American exploration literature—and certainly one of the most expensive, because only just over 1,400 good copies were printed. The book was edited by Nicholas Biddle, a Philadelphia lawyer with considerable literary skills whom Clark had found in 1810 when he was searching for an editor soon after the death of Lewis. Ironically, Biddle, who became intimately associated with this most famous tome of exploration literature, had never traveled west of the Susquehanna himself. It is interesting to note that even this experience was less circumscribed than that of Alexander Mackenzie's editor, who languished in a debtors' prison while editing the latter's book, and went nowhere at all.

Finding Routes West

Lewis and Clark may have demonstrated that there was no easy path to the Pacific, but the commercial opportunities along their route did not escape a number of entrepreneurs. A St. Louis merchant, Manuel Lisa, created the Missouri Fur Company and built Fort Raymond at the forks of the Yellowstone and the Bighorn rivers, from which he sent out traders to find furs.

One of Lewis and Clark's men, John Colter, set out in 1807 from the fort and found the geyser region of what is now Yellowstone National Park. Another of the Corps of Discovery, George Drouillard, tried to find a route south to the Rio Grande and Santa Fe but was confused by incorrect ideas of the proximity of that river to the Shoshone River. This supposed proximity is shown on John Melish's map published in 1816 (Map 2, *pages 2–3*). One of Lisa's men, Andrew Henry, briefly established what was the first American trading post west of the Continental Divide, on Henrys Fork, a tributary of the Snake.

Two other expeditions organized by Thomas Jefferson at the same time as that of Lewis and Clark attempted to determine the western boundary of the newly acquired Louisiana. Surveyor William Dunbar and naturalist George Hunter in 1804–05 set out to ascend the Red River (considered a boundary of Louisiana) but after harassment by Osage Indians instead explored the Ouachita River, between the Mississippi and the Red rivers, and the Ozark Plateau. In 1806 another expedition tried again to ascend the Red. Organized by Dunbar, it was led by surveyor Thomas Free-

man. This time it was stopped by Spanish troops 615 miles up the river. These expeditions, together with that of Lewis and Clark, were the first of a long line of government-sponsored explorations of the West.

In 1806 an expedition led by Zebulon Pike was sent out by General James Wilkinson, governor of Louisiana, ostensibly to find the source of the Red River. The dubious Wilkinson was a double agent for the Spanish and for himself, for he was in cahoots with Aaron Burr, from 1801 to 1805 vice-president of the United States. The pair wanted to set up an independent republic between the United States and Spanish territories. Wilkinson sought to create an incident that might lead to war with Spain and thus provide a pretext on which Burr's private troops could take over New Orleans and set up a new republic. Wilkinson thus let the Spanish know that Pike was coming into their territory, hoping that his arrest would spark the incident.

Map 229 (*below*).

Zebulon Pike's map of the *Internal Part of Louisiana*, published in 1810. Pike's route up the Arkansas River (at center right) is indicated. The Rio Grande, which Pike tried to convince Spanish troops he thought was the Red River, is in the hachured valley at left center, labeled *Rio del Norte*. A log structure built by Pike that was discovered by the Spanish troops is marked as *Stockade met by the Spaniards*. The Red River is at bottom right with a trail marked *The Route pursued by the Spanish Cavalry*; the Spanish were searching the Red on information directly from the double agent Wilkinson.

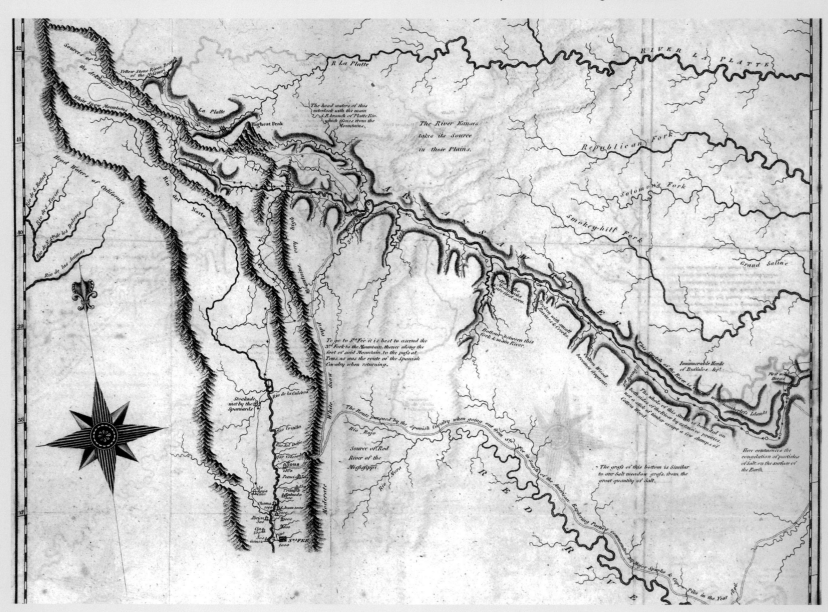

MAP 230.
Stephen Long's important map of the drainage basin of the Mississippi, drawn in 1820 or 1821. The words *Great Desert* mark the southwestern plains; the printed version of this map reads *Great American Desert*. Long's perpetuation of Pike's perception of the region as a desert kept settlers out of the southern plains for many years.

Pike was indeed arrested by Spanish troops, but no incident followed, and Pike returned with much information about the location and strength of Spanish forts, suggesting his mission was that of a spy all along. Pike published an account of his adventures in 1810 in which he stated that the Great Plains were sandy deserts, thus originating the myth of the Great American Desert that persisted for fifty years. Pike thought his observation useful in that it would confine Americans to their own country and make them less inclined to wander west.

The myth was perpetuated in 1819–20 by Stephen Harriman Long, appointed by the government to establish a military post on the Missouri

River at the Yellowstone to counter incursions by British fur traders. His expedition, with a thousand men in six steamboats, reached the Platte in 1819, but most became ill over the winter and the expedition was abandoned. Long, however, with a smaller group, was ordered to explore

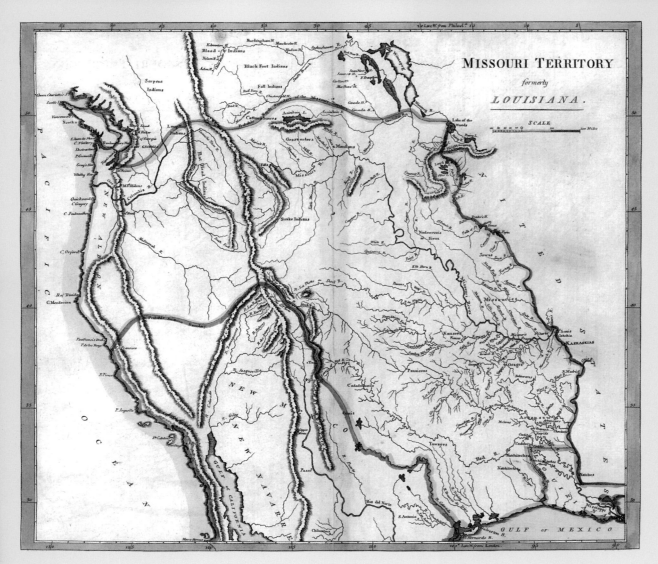

MAP 231 (*left*).
A map of the West created in 1814 by Philadelphia mapmaker Mathew Carey. Louisiana Territory was renamed Missouri Territory on 4 June 1812 to avoid confusion with the newly admitted State of Louisiana, shown separated from the rest of the territory at bottom right. The course of the Missouri River is shown largely from Lewis and Clark information. The boundaries of the territory are both marked *Probable*; the northern boundary would be defined in 1818 as far west as the Rockies (see page 136), while the southern boundary would be better defined in 1819 (see page 139). Both Britain and the United States claimed the Northwest, and this would not be resolved until 1846 (see page 158).

MAP 232 (*below*).
A survey of the route from the Missouri River (top right) to Santa Fe (bottom left), drawn in 1825 by surveyor Joseph Brown. The survey had been commissioned by President James Monroe. The exact location of Santa Fe stills seems to be in doubt, however, judging by this map. At bottom left on the *Rio del Norte* (the Rio Grande) are the words *Santa Fe about here*.

southwest toward Spanish territory, up the Platte to the Arkansas and the Red rivers. All the scientific papers were lost to deserters, but Long's map survives (MAP 230, *previous page*). On it he has marked the Great Desert. Although not really a desert, the southwestern plains were unsuitable for agriculture given 1820 technology, and in addition there was no wood for building or for fuel. For the time being, this would remain a region to pass through on the way to better pastures.

Fearing American takeover, the Spanish had always prevented open trade with their domains. With the Mexican Revolution in 1821, the southwestern plains acquired a new importance; no longer would trade with Santa Fe be circumscribed. The dangers of the route would now lie with attacks from Indians, not Spaniards. In 1825 President James Monroe commissioned a survey of the Santa Fe Trail (MAP 232, *below*).

In 1808 the New York entrepreneur John Jacob Astor founded his American Fur Company and planned to set up a post at the mouth of the Columbia River to facilitate the export of furs. This was exactly what had been suggested by the British explorer and fur trader Alexander Mackenzie (the first to cross North America, in 1793) in the book he had published in 1801, and Astor hoped to implement this plan to the exclusion of rival fur companies such as Mackenzie's. Astor's ship, the *Tonquin,* arrived at the mouth of the Columbia in March 1811 and built Fort Astoria. A land expedition, led by Wilson Price Hunt, left St. Louis that spring. Hunt discovered Union Pass, at the northern end of the Wind River Mountains, and his party, split into two because they were trying to avoid starvation, barely made it to Fort Astoria, arriving in January and February 1812. They were the fifth group to cross the continent (after Mackenzie, Lewis and Clark, and the British explorers Simon Fraser and David Thompson). A return expedition in 1812, led by Robert Stuart, took Indian information about a shorter route and found South Pass, at the southern end of the Wind River Mountains. This route across the Continental Divide was gentle enough to be used by wagons and became, as the century progressed, the critical link in the main route to Oregon—the Oregon Trail (see page 154).

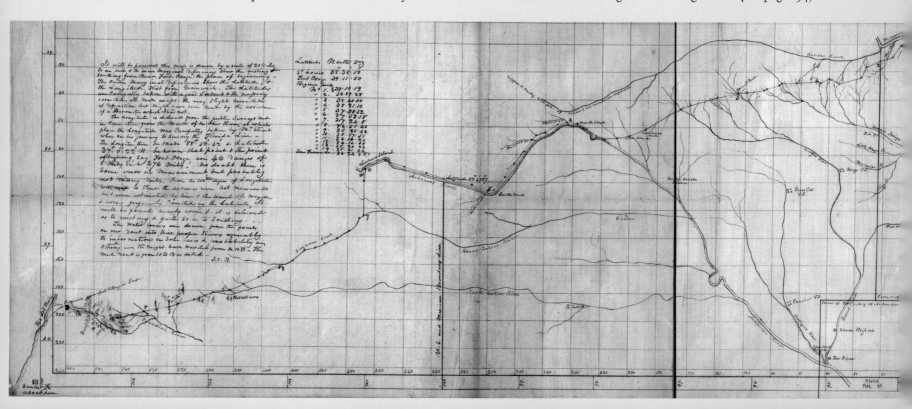

MAP 233 (above).

This is part of a map showing the routes of Wilson Price Hunt going west in 1811–12 and Robert Stuart going east in 1813. The map is from an immensely popular book commisioned by John Jacob Astor: *Astoria*, by Washington Irving. At bottom right (just south of *Wind River Mts.*), is Stuart's route through South Pass, which he found. It is not named on this map, strangely, perhaps, for this was one of the principal legacies of the Astorians, the way across the Continental Divide that would be followed by the Oregon Trail. South Pass as it looks today is shown *below*.

Britain's North West Company had by this time established fur trading posts west of the Rockies, farther to the north. They thought for a time that the Fraser River was a tributary of the Columbia, and only when Simon Fraser reached the Pacific via the Fraser River in 1808 did they realize that it was not. Another Nor'Wester, David Thompson, trying to counter Astor's plans to set up a fort at the mouth of the Columbia, made his way to the mouth of that river, arriving on 15 July 1811 only to find that he had been beaten by the men of the *Tonquin*, who had arrived by sea.

The American flag flew over Fort Astoria. But not for long, for the War of 1812 had begun. In September 1813, John McTavish of the North West Company arrived at the fort with eight canoes full of furs. He brought with him a letter confirming that their supply ship was soon to arrive, accompanied by a British frigate with orders to seize the fort. Expecting the impending arrival of an armed ship, the Astorians made the best of a bad situation and *sold* the fort to the Nor'Westers. When the frigate finally arrived its captain insisted on ceremonially *seizing* the fort, as were his instructions.

Because under the Treaty of Ghent, which ended the War of 1812 (see page 136), all *seized* territory was supposed to be returned to its pre-war owners, a lasting dispute was initiated as to the true ownership of the fort, and it was one of the bargaining points during the negotiations for an international boundary in the Oregon Country in 1846 (see page 158), an argument that all the surrounding territory must belong to the United States. Fort Astoria became Fort George, but the company headquarters was moved to Fort Vancouver (across the river from today's Portland, Oregon) in 1825–26.

By the 1820s the Northwest was covered with the trails of fur brigades, first created by the North West Company and after 1821 (when the companies merged) by the Hudson's Bay Company. The governor of the latter, George Simpson, formulated a plan to keep out encroaching American fur trappers by creating a "fur desert" along the Snake River, a region where it would be uneconomic for competitors to seek furs. In charge of the plan was Peter Skene Ogden, who led six separate expeditions across the West. During his fifth expedition, in 1828–29, Ogden found the Humboldt River, which flows from a point west of the Great Salt Lake west to Humboldt Lake, in the Carson Sink of Nevada (MAP 236, *overleaf*). Significantly, it did not flow to the Pacific, as a river was thought at this time to do (MAP 234 and MAP 235, *overleaf*). The valley Ogden found, however, was a very significant one; in 1866 it would become the route of the first railroad to cross the United States, the Union Pacific and Central Pacific (see page 194).

On his sixth expedition Ogden went even farther, crossing the arid Great Basin of Nevada and reaching the Colorado River, which he followed to the Gulf of California before returning north. Although many of Ogden's maps were lost in 1830 in a whirlpool on the Columbia, much of his information did find its way onto commercial maps, especially those of Arrowsmith in London and Brué in Paris (Map 237 and Map 238, *far right*).

The British supremacy in the western fur trade was ultimately lost to American traders, many of whom arrived in the West after answering a newspaper advertisement in 1822 placed by William Ashley and Andrew Henry. Their recruits became known as mountain men. They included such famous names as James Clyman, William Sublette, Edward Rose, David Jackson, Hugh Glass, Jim Bridger, and Jedediah Strong Smith. "Strong" was an appropriate middle name for Smith; once when his scalp and ear were ripped off by a bear, he made his men sew them back on.

The mountain men covered vast areas of the West in their pursuit of furs. In 1823 South Pass was rediscovered. In late 1824 or early spring of 1825 Jim Bridger floated down the Bear River into the Great Salt Lake, becoming one of the first to find it. He thought it might be an arm of the Pacific because it was salty. Either he or Ogden, or Étienne Provost, a trapper coming north from Taos at the same time, seems to have been the first EuroAmerican to discover the Great Salt Lake.

The wanderings of Jedediah Smith were unequaled. In 1826 he explored west from the Great Salt Lake looking for the Buenaventura River, rumored to flow from the lake to the Pacific. In August he went south to seek out new fur trade sources, heading south along the Sevier River of central Utah to the Virgin River, which flows into the Colorado near today's Las Vegas. After traveling down the Colorado for a while he set out

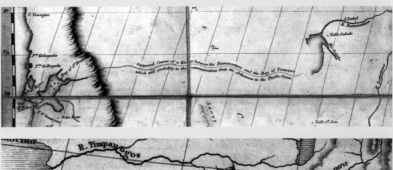

west across the Mojave Desert, then north, once more looking for the elusive Buenaventura, reaching the San Joaquin Valley. In May 1827, after once failing to cross the Sierra Nevada going east due to heavy snow, he tried again, crossing Ebbetts Pass and into the Great Basin. An epic journey followed in which Smith crossed the arid desert lands in thirty-two days and, thirsty and starving, surprised his fellow trappers at their annual rendezvous on the Bear River in Utah. Ten days later the peripatetic Smith set out again, retracing his path to the Colorado, where his party was attacked by Mojave Indians, who killed ten of them.

When Smith reached California once more, the Mexican governor, who was convinced he was a spy, had him arrested. He escaped north to San Francisco by ship, then headed up the Sacramento River and north along the coast to the Umpqua River, learning that the Multnomah River—the Willamette—was just to the north. On the Umpqua on 13 July 1828 Smith and his men were attacked by Indians, who killed fourteen of them. Smith and just three others escaped, making it to the Hudson's Bay Company post at Fort Vancouver in August. At great cost Smith had crisscrossed the West, added many details to the map, and proved that there was no Buenaventura. In the spring of 1829 Smith met the company governor, George Simpson, who did his best to convince him that the Northwest was unsuitable for American settlement. Smith was undeterred, however, and eventually his reports that it *was* suitable reached the United States government. American settlers would begin to pour into the Oregon Country within twenty years (see page 154).

In any case, the boom years of the fur trade were all but over by the mid-1830s. The search for new sources of furs had for a long time provided the motivation for western exploration, but from that time on the impetus would be a search for routes over the Rockies for settlers' wagons.

Map 234 (*above, top*).
A *Supposed Course of a River* connecting an interior lake and the Pacific is shown on this 1819 map. Whether the lake is a representation of Sevier Lake in Utah or Utah Lake, it is shown nearly a hundred miles too far west.

Map 235 (*above*).
On this 1826 map the *R. Buenaventura* connects the now dry Sevier Lake (*L. Salado*) with the Pacific Ocean and an also mythical *R. Timpanogos* does the same from another lake ("Timpanogos"), a combination of the Great Salt Lake and Utah Lake first mapped by Silvestre Vélex de Escalante in 1777 (Map 143, *page 71*).

Map 236 (*left*).
This is Hudson's Bay Company explorer Peter Skene Ogden's map of his fifth expedition, undertaken in 1828–29. Here the map is shown with north approximately at the top. The little flag at top marked *Fort* is Fort Nez Percé, or Walla Walla; the diagonal line at top right is the Snake River; and the lake at bottom left is Humboldt Lake in the Carson Sink, with the Humboldt River flowing from it. The lake at bottom right is the Great Salt Lake, here shown undersized.

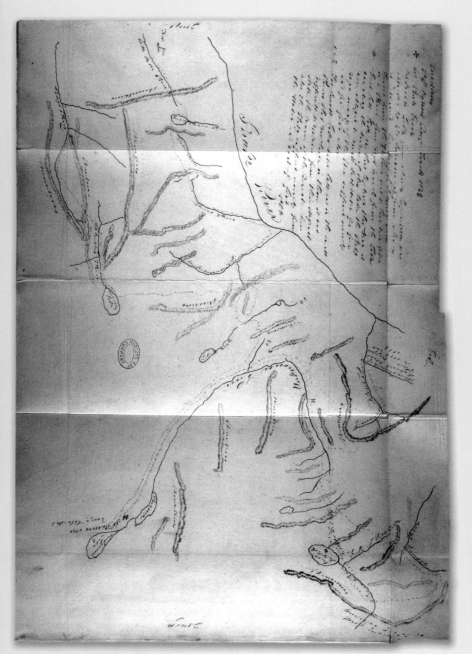

Map 237 (above) and Map 238 (below).
The confusion over the Buenaventura River and the Great Salt Lake is illustrated in these two maps published a year apart by the famous French mapmaker A.H. Brué. Map 237 was published in 1839 and shows most of the routes taken by Jedediah Smith; Brué's information came from both Peter Skene Ogden and Smith.

Map 238, published a year later, more correctly shows a Buenaventura River (actually the Humboldt) flowing into *Lac et Marais Teguayo* (Carson Sink), but this is in turn connected to San Francisco Bay via a tentative *R. Jesus Maria*. The depiction of the Great Salt Lake is more accurate, however.

Indian Maps

Map 239 (left).
Most Indian maps were ephemeral, like this one, which was scratched onto a piece of bark. One of the very few that survived in this form, this one did so only because it was found by a British army surveyor and taken home as a souvenir. More usually, these maps would have disintegrated after a season, although probably after having served their purpose. This map (which is almost impossible to see in a photograph) shows a portage route between the Ottawa and the French rivers to Lake Huron (which allowed the bypassing of Lakes Ontario and Erie) and is the oldest known surviving bark map found in North America. It dates from about 1841 and is on birchbark.

Map 240 (below).
Although cut in the shape of a deerskin, this map is actually a copy made on paper, likewise cut into the same shape. The original skin was given to Francis Nicholson, the governor of the colony of South Carolina, in 1721; he had it copied onto paper. There are two known copies. The map shows the distribution of Indian tribes in the Piedmont region of North and South Carolina and their relationship to one another, imposed on a map of the Southeast. Within thirty or forty years the Siouan-speaking peoples, shown as separate tribes in each of the circles, joined together to become the Catawba Nation. The map is a relational one rather than strictly geographical. The grid system depicted at left is *Charlestown* (Charleston, South Carolina), while *Virginie*, the Virginia colony, is at lower right. Connecting them to the central tribe, the Nasaw, are roads representing trade routes. The one from Charleston is labeled *The English Path to Nasaw.* Another route leads to the Cherokee (*Cherrikies*), which has been interpreted to be the Savannah River and a path to the Appalachians.

Very few maps drawn by native peoples survive today because of the ephemeral nature of the materials used. Yet those that do show that prior to EuroAmerican contact native groups often had extensive knowledge of the geography of the lands in which they lived, knowledge that was often shared with explorers and traders, who incorporated it into their paper maps as their own. Many of the older maps of the United States—including many in this book—show information well beyond the experience of those drafting them, and this is usually derived "from native report." Of course, information was not always interpreted accurately and in some cases was not truthful, being tailored to what the Indian thought the explorer or trader wanted to hear.

Almost all of the native maps that have survived did so because they were copied onto paper. Those etched onto bark (Map 239, *above*) might last a season, while those drawn with a stick in the dust on the ground (such as many of those given to Lewis and Clark) were lucky to last a day. Only those deliberately drawn to last on a skin (Map 240, *below*) might endure by themselves.

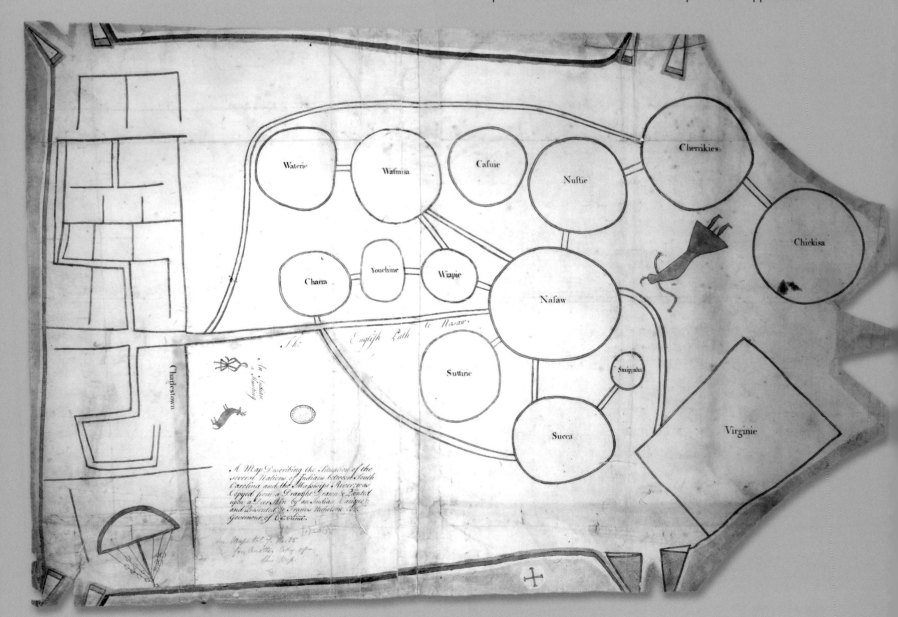

Native maps can be confusing to EuroAmerican eyes, since they do not necessarily have any particular regard for the essentially Western concepts of exact direction, distance, proportion, or scale. However, in this regard they are often not a lot different from the early maps of explorers or traders, who drew similar maps because they lacked the means of accurately fixing their position. Native maps sometimes add another element totally lacking in Western maps, that of the cosmological. Blending the spiritual with the geographical was common practice, and this naturally enough makes maps difficult to comprehend without knowing the native cosmography of the tribe and the period and place where the map was drawn.

Symbolism of one sort or another is used in making all maps. Features cannot be depicted on all maps at an exact scale, and this is the same with native maps, but the symbols used may be different and may have meanings unknown to persons of other cultures. Communication of geographical ideas, like any other, requires that those communicating first understand each other's language.

The entire history of the United States until quite recently involved a progressive encroachment onto previously occupied native lands, and it is thus hardly a surprise that many EuroAmerican maps incorporate native information. The history of America would have been quite different but

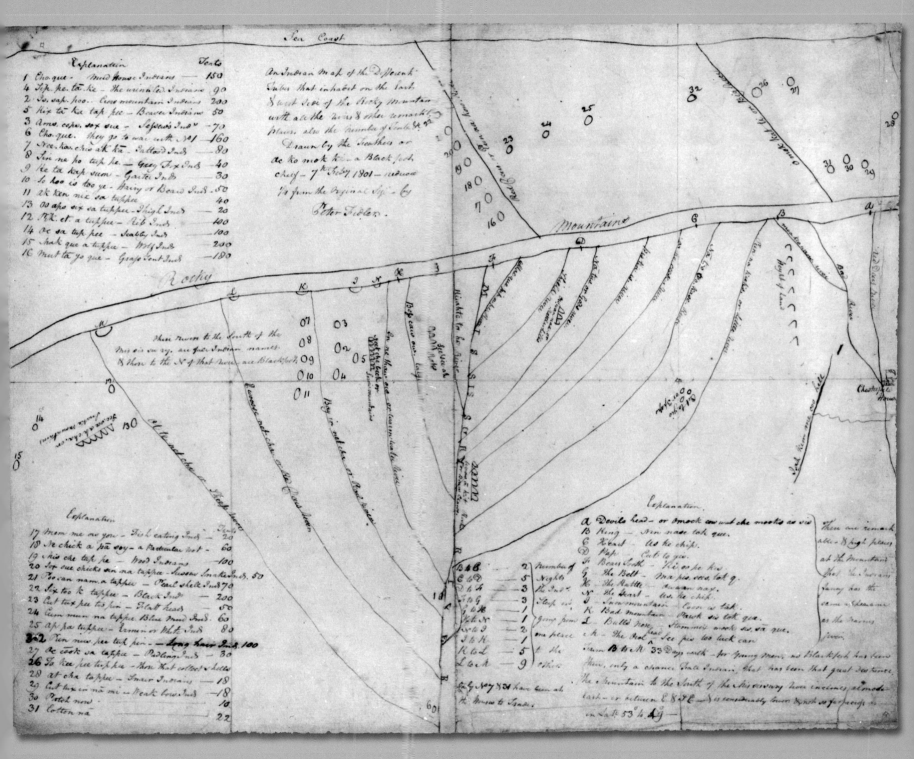

Map 241 (above).

Perhaps the most famous of all the native-derived maps is this one, which shows the entire tributary system of the Upper Missouri and some of what lay beyond the barrier of the Rocky Mountains. It was copied by Hudson's Bay Company explorer and fur trader Peter Fidler from Blackfoot chief Ac ko mok ki, in all likelihood a map scratched on the ground. Its information was incorporated into a map carried by Lewis and Clark (Map 222, page 112). The map was drawn in Fidler's journal in February 1801. North is to the right, and the double line across the page represents the Rocky Mountains. The top edge of the paper is the Pacific coast. On the Pacific slope only two rivers are drawn, indicating a

lesser knowledge of that region by Ac ko mok ki. They have been variously interpreted as the Columbia, the Snake, or the Fraser rivers. The Missouri is the central vertical line, on the eastern (bottom) side of the mountains. Indian populations are represented by circles and numbers, which are the number of tents, for which Fidler has recorded an extensive key. This map is significant not only for its use by Lewis and Clark but also as a record of the extensive and far-ranging geographic knowledge of some native groups. Some information, admittedly, probably comes from other Indians who traded with the Blackfoot rather than Ac ko mok ki's personal experience.

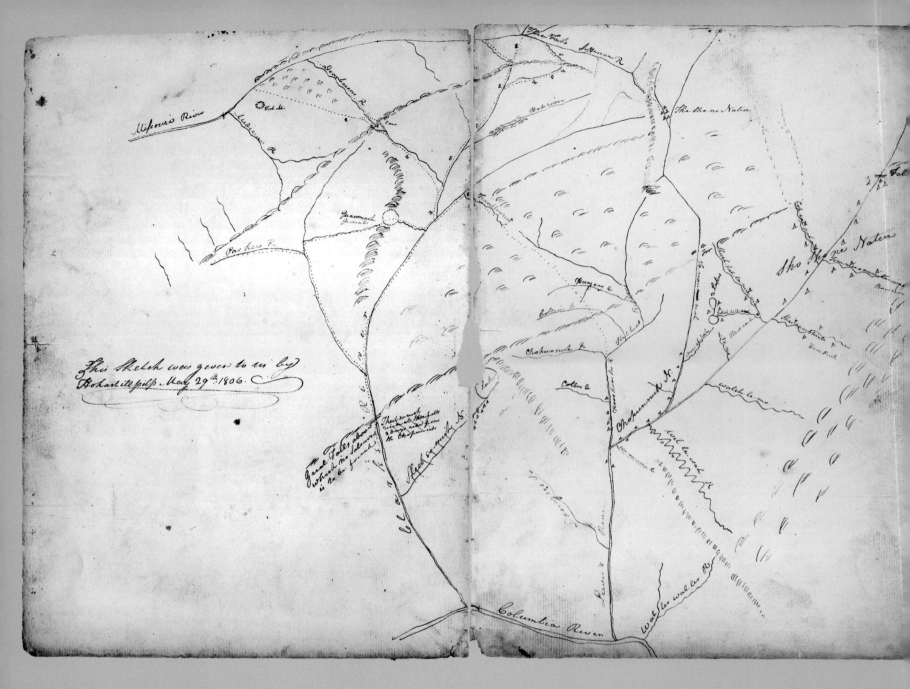

Map 242 (*above*).

One of the many maps provided by native people to Lewis and Clark, this was drawn by the Nez Percé ("Chopunnish") principal chief Hohastilpilp on 29 May 1806, during the return of the expedition eastwards across the mountains. The map shows the main native routes across the divide together with the various rivers. Partly due to this map, Lewis made the decision to split up his men so as to cover as many routes as possible. The *Columbia River* is at bottom and the *Missouri River* is at top left. At right is territory of the *Shoshone Nation,* with villages shown by triangles representing tents. The map reveals a detailed and extensive knowledge of the region.

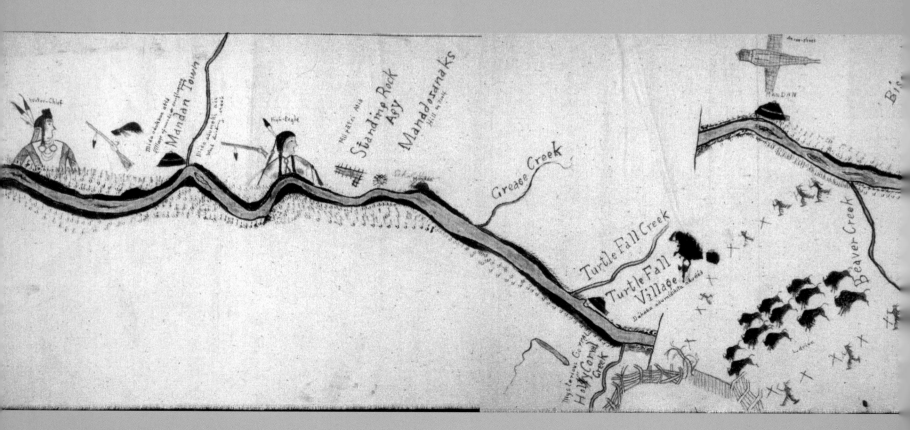

for the intervention and guidance of native peoples on many occasions. Would Lewis and Clark have found their way across the Rockies without native aid? It is possible, of course, but perhaps less likely, and certainly would have meant more delay.

The ephemeral nature of most native maps leads easily to the erroneous conclusion that they were rarely made. Yet there is much evidence that maps were used by Native Americans among themselves to convey information as to a route or the location of a resource, presumably because it was easier to convey this information in a drawn form than in words. Maps were made to record events important to a tribe's history, and they were used on many occasions to present a point of view to a government. Map 243 (*right, top*) was drawn in 1837 to attempt to establish a claim to territory by demonstrating prior use, but the political environment at that time was such that few Indian claims were validated, whether legitimate or not. Ironically, in more modern times, Indian land claims are now often established using evidence of prior native use from EuroAmerican maps rather than Indian maps. Native trails in particular were of great interest to explorers and traders, but villages, watering places, river crossings, and the like were all frequently marked.

Despite the extra effort required to interpret them, old native maps are a vital part of the cartographic historical record. They are an important record of the land in its pre-EuroAmerican state and are often the earliest record, made long before the maps EuroAmericans made on their own.

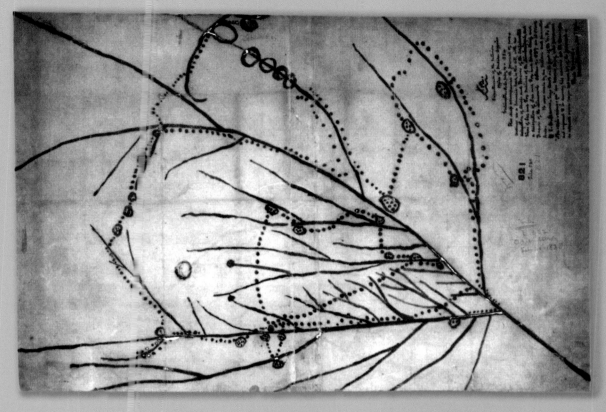

Map 243 (*above*).

This is a map of the drainage system of the upper Mississippi and Missouri rivers created in 1837 by an Iowa Indian chief, Non-Chi-Ning-Ga (or Notchininga). The dotted line represents tribal migrations. The rivers are drawn from memory but are quite accurate in relation to one another, although shown generally as straight lines rather than the more complex actual courses. The map was produced when the Iowas went to Washington to complain to the federal government about land that had been taken from them under the 1825 Treaty of Prairie du Chien, when they had moved from land east of the Mississippi to land between the Mississippi and the Missouri (see page 140).

Map 244 (*below*).

This delightful map is part of one made in 1907 by a Mandan Indian, Sitting Rabbit, at the request of the State Historical Society of North Dakota. It was drawn to record all the locations of old villages, most of which by then had disappeared. The map is executed in Plains pictography style, and notations are in English or transliterated Mandan. In 1954 the Garrison Dam was completed, creating Lake Sakakawea and inundating all physical evidence, thus making this map even more valuable as a historical record.

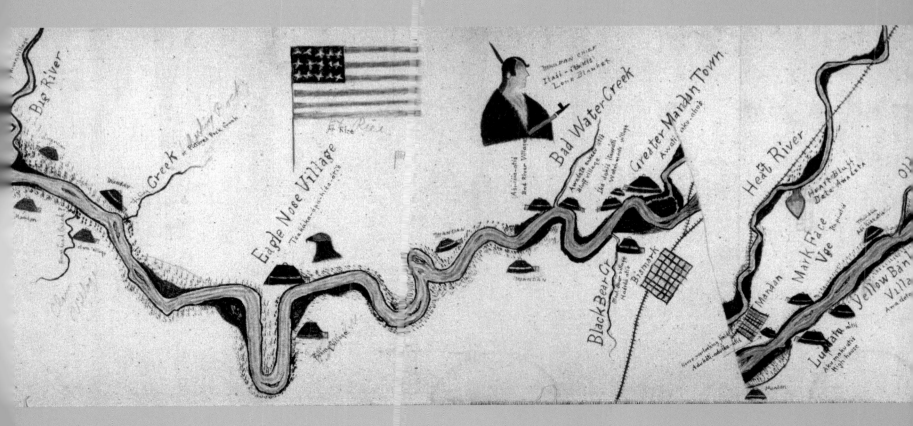

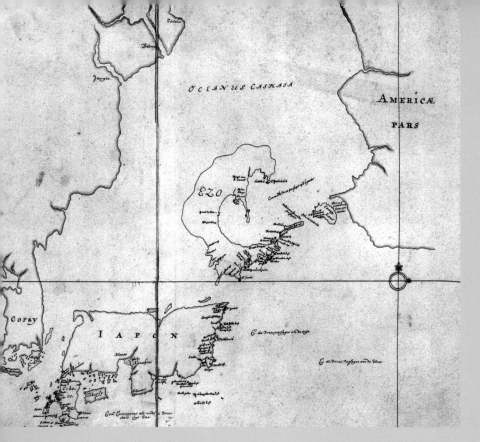

Wherever there was a blank on the map of the world, men imagined continents, and usually lands filled with gold. Alaska was no exception. Some early maps show a vast landmass stretching across the North Pacific.

The very first sightings of land thought to be America came from the west. The Dutch captain Maerten Vries, exploring around Japan in 1643, was searching for islands of gold when he found the west coast of Ostrov Urop, in reality only one of many Kuril Islands, but Vries took it to be the edge of a continent; he named it Compagnies Land, after his employer, the Dutch East India Company. It was soon shown on Dutch maps as part of America (Map 245, *left*).

It would, however, be the Russians, reaching east from Siberia, who would first inherit Alaska. But it took a Dane in Russian employ, Vitus Bering, to first reach America. The Russians had thought that land lay to the east of Kamchatka (Map 251, *below, right*), and reports from natives of a "Great Land" seemed to confirm this. Tsar Peter the Great as early as 1719 had ordered an expedition to determine whether America was joined to Asia, but it was Vitus Bering's 1728 voyage that found the strait now named after him, although he did not then see Alaska. That honor fell to

Map 245 (*above*).
Dutch explorer Maerten Vries's discovery of "Company Land," actually one of the Kuril Islands, in 1643, was transformed by his contemporary Isaak de Graaf into *Americæ Pars*—part of America—on this map drawn in 1644 or 1645.

Map 246 (*above*).
This map was prepared in 1731 by French geographer Joseph-Nicolas De L'Isle as a guide for Bering and was carried by him in 1741. In addition to its vast gaps it also shows the imaginary land of Jean de Gama (south of Kamchatka). Time lost seaching for this misconception contributed to Bering's demise.

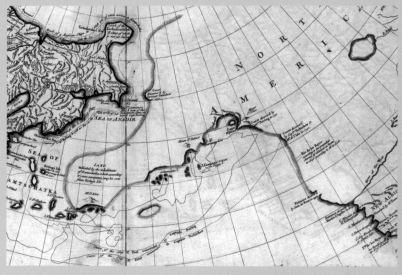

Map 247 (*left*).
A Russian summary map of the voyages of Bering and Chirikov drawn in 1742. The tracks shown are those of Chirikov. Two American coastline positions are plotted due to differences in the calculation of distance (using estimates of speed and elapsed time) going west compared to going east.

Map 248 (*above, top*).
Apparently the first map to name Alaska was this one, drawn by Russian fur traders Pyotr Shiskin and Savin Ponomaryov in 1762 after four years sailing among the islands. It shows the Aleutians, with the North American mainland—and the name "Alaska" (in Russian)—at far right.

Map 249 (*above*).
Published in 1768, this map by British mapmaker Thomas Jefferys shows the Alaska coastline as it was presumed to exist by Gerhard Müller. Sightings of land at many of the Aleutian Islands led to the assumption that the coastline was continuous.

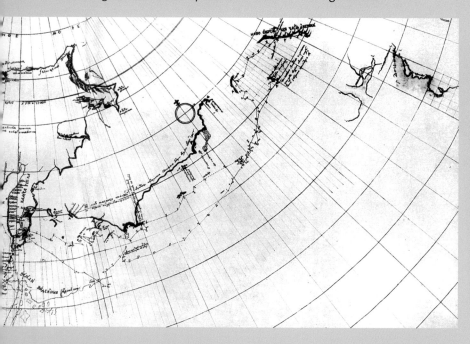

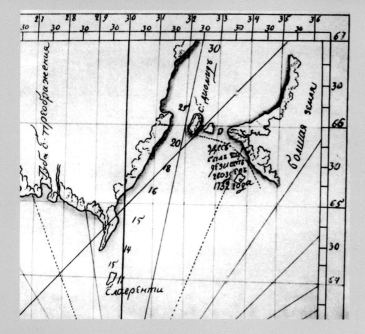

Map 250 (left).
Mikhail Gvozdev's 1732 discovery of Alaska—and the North American continent—is shown in this Russian map drawn two years later. Bering Strait and the Diomedes Islands are at center, with Cape Prince of Wales, the westernmost tip of the North American mainland, at right. This is the first map of any part of Alaska from actual exploration.

Map 252 (right).
The first printed map to name Alaska was this map by German author Jacob von Stählin. It shows Aläschka as a large island. (The "f" is an old-style s.) This map was carried by James Cook in 1778 and made finding a passage through the Aleutians difficult (see page 108). The map represented Stählin's misinterpretation of information from the voyage of Ivan Synd in 1764.

Map 253 (below).
Russian fur trader Potap Zaikov's map, the first accurate map of the Aleutian Islands, drawn in 1779.

Mikhail Gvozdev four years later, although he did not land due to contrary winds. The map showing his discovery (Map 250, above) is the first to show any part of Alaska from exploration.

The tsar ordered a new expedition to locate America, but transportation in Russia was so bad that it was 1741 before Bering with co-commander Aleksei Chirikov, set forth from Kamchatka in two ships. Much time was wasted looking for a supposed landmass to the south called Gama Land (Map 246, left), and Bering's and Chirikov's ships became separated; they continued as essentially individual voyages.

Chirikov reached his landfall in North America first, on 15 July 1741 (Russian dates are old style), at Baker Island, on the coast of the larger Prince of Wales Island, in the Panhandle. Unable to find an anchorage he dispatched men in boats, but they disappeared. A week later he sent more to look for the first, and they also failed to return. Assuming his men must have been killed by natives, he sailed back along the Aleutian chain to Kamchatka.

Bering made a landfall at Kayak Island, under Mount St. Elias, which Bering named, on 20 July. He was able to land, but, fearing for the safety of his ship, spent only ten hours ashore, forcing his scientist, the famed Georg Steller, to work frantically. Bering did not make it back to Kamchatka. His ship was wrecked on an island near the coast, now Bering Is-

land, and he died in December. The survivors managed to construct a new, smaller ship from the wreckage of their original ship, and in it they sailed the short distance to Kamchatka, arriving there in September 1742.

Russian fur traders slowly pushed east using the natural stepping stones provided by the Aleutian Islands. One, G. Pushkarev, reached the Alaskan mainland in 1761. A map produced in 1762 by two traders, Pyotr Shiskin and Savin Ponomaryov, was the first map to use the name "Alaska" (Map 248, left). The first reasonably accurate map of the Aleutians was that drawn by another trader, Potap Zaikov, in 1779 (Map 253, below).

In 1762 Catherine II came to power in Russia, and interest in her eastern domains was renewed because of potential British and Spanish threats. The British dispatched Commodore John Byron into the Pacific in 1764 to seek a Northwest Passage, and later the Spanish sent ships north—to check on supposed Russian incursions into what they saw as their domains (see page 106). Catherine in turn sent Lieutenant Ivan Synd on a voyage into the Bering Sea in 1764. One map produced from his information, though not very accurately, was that by Jacob von Stählin (Map 252, above). There followed a number of British, Spanish, and even French voyages to Alaska, largely motivated by a search for the western entrance to the Northwest Passage. But the Russians had found a lucrative fur trade in Alaska and meant to hang onto it.

The fur trade was consolidated under the umbrella of the Russian-American Company in 1799. Led by Grigorii Shelikov, the group managed to obtain a monopoly from the tsar. First headquartered on Kodiak Island,

Map 251 (left).
This 1723 map uses information from a Russian map drawn by Ivan Lvov in 1710 to portray Incognita, probably Alaska from native report. Siberia is to the west, Kamchatka to the south.

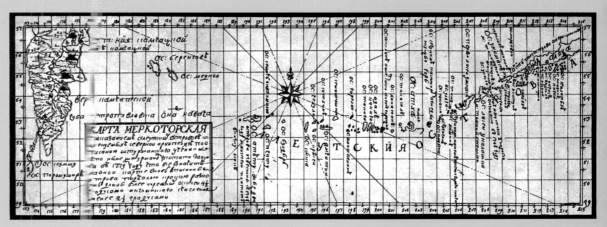

the company moved its operations to Novo Archangel'sk—today's Sitka—in 1804. A fort nearby had been destroyed by the fierce local Tlingit two years before, and a new foothold was only gained with the help of cannon bombardment from a Russian naval ship, the *Neva*, under Captain Urei Lisianskii, which visited Alaska that year as part of a circumnavigation partly intended to assess the feasibility of supplying the company by sea from St. Petersburg instead of via the long and difficult road across Siberia.

The company was run and expanded until 1818 by Alexandr Baranov. Under his aegis in 1812 Fort Ross was established as a supply depot in California, just north of San Francisco. But operations were always expensive, and in 1818 the Russian government took over the company to stave off bankruptcy.

In 1821 the tsar issued a ukase, or edict, claiming Russian sovereignty south to 51°N. He soon came to realize that this territory was too

MAP 254 (*above*).
One of the founders of the Russian-American Company, Grigorii Shelikov, drew this map showing the presumed extent of Russian territory in 1796. The boundary between Russian and British territory is drawn through Great Slave Lake, at about 115°W, about eight hundred miles east of the current Alaska boundary at 141°W. It extends southwards to perhaps 48°N, about the latitude of Seattle. Until 1841, the influence of the Russian-American Company extended as far south as California, where Fort Ross was built in 1812 to provide a source for food and other supplies unobtainable farther north.

MAP 255 (*left*).
Vasili Berkh, who had been an officer with Urei Lisianskii, published an atlas in 1821 that included this map of Russian possessions—as he saw them, at least—extending east to Hudson Bay, which itself is depicted too far west. The coast represents the survey done in 1804 by Lisianskii.

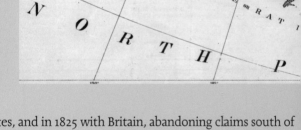

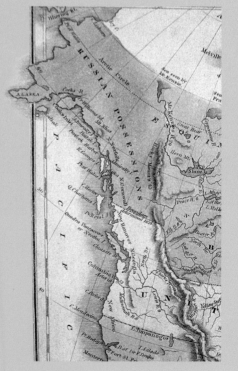

large to hold and in 1824 signed a treaty with the United States, and in 1825 with Britain, abandoning claims south of 54°40´, the southern extent of today's Panhandle. The United States had inherited Spanish claims as far north as this latitude (see pages 106 and 138). The British treaty also established 141°W as the eastern boundary of Alaska.

Much of the exploration of Alaska before 1867 was carried out by Russian naval ships. Lisianskii's expedition was the first; other notable visits include those of Otto Kotzebue in 1816, during which he found Kotzebue Sound, just north of Bering Strait, while searching for a Northwest Passage; and Fedor Lütke in 1827. Lütke carried scientists who accumulated a vast amount of data in many fields. In 1833 Russian-American Company men Andrei Glazunov and Semyon Lukin found the mouth of the Yukon River, and the same year established a post on St. Michael Island, off the coast nearby. In 1838 Petr Malakov ascended the Yukon to the Koyukuk River, where he built Nulato post the following year. Lavrentiy Zagoskin was commissioned to trace the course of the Yukon in 1842 but used a leaky skin-covered boat, an umiak, and only got as far as today's Ruby, Alaska, in 1843, still a thousand miles from the river's elusive source.

Even under government control, the Russian-American Company was still a financial liability. The idea of selling it and its territories was first suggested in 1854. Russia was about to go to war with Britain in the Crimea and

MAP 256 (*left*).
Russian territory depicted on a British map published in 1829. The Russians and the British signed a treaty in 1825 establishing the eastern boundary at 141°W (its current position), much farther west than as shown here. The southern boundary is at 54°40´N, but was by treaty restricted to the coastal zone, not extending to the Rockies as on this map.

NORTH WESTERN AMERICA

SHOWING THE TERRITORY

CEDED BY RUSSIA TO THE UNITED STATES

COMPILED FOR THE DEPARTMENT OF STATE
at the
U.S. COAST SURVEY OFFICE

B. Peirce, Supt.

1867.

The figures denote the depth of water, in fathoms.
The dotted line shows limit of 50 fathoms.

Area of Mainland   549,500   Sq.2.Miles
     " Aleutian Inds.   3630
     " other Islands   22260

Scale 1:000000

Statute Miles
Nautical Miles

G & M Division
3 - MAR 1970
Library of Congress

feared a British attack on Alaska. A temporary sale to an American com-
pany would remove this threat. In the end Russia agreed not to attack the
Hudson's Bay Company in return for assurances Britain would not attack
Alaska. But the seed of an idea had been sown, and negotiations were
proposed after Russia's defeat in 1856. In 1859 Russia offered to sell Alaska,
in the belief that the United States would offset Britain in the Pacific. The
Civil War derailed American interest until 1866, by which time the Russian-
American Company was all but bankrupt.

In December 1866 the Russian government instructed their ambassador in Washington, Edouard de Stoeckl, to once again offer Alaska
to the United States, for a minimum price of $5 million. The arch expan-
sionist secretary of state, William Seward, was so keen to add Alaska to
the United States that he started negotiating without permission from
the president, Andrew Johnson, and at one point in the negotiations increased an offer without first waiting for a counteroffer. In the end Seward
committed the United States to pay $7.2 million. The treaty confirming
the sale was signed on 30 March 1867. Seward then battled opponents of
the sale in Congress, but the Senate ratified the treaty on 9 April.

MAP 257 (*above*).
The United States needed to know what it was purchasing in 1867. This map
was prepared by the United States Coast Survey for the Department of State.
Russian territory is now Alaska. Note the list showing the areas of the mainland
and the islands. Fort Yukon, at the confluence of the Yukon with the Porcupine
River, had been founded in 1847 by Britain's Hudson's Bay Company. In 1869 U.S.
army captain Charles Raymond determined that it was now on American soil
and ordered the British fur traders out. *Inset* is the check for the purchase, dated
1 August 1868.

The actual transfer took place on the cool and misty afternoon of
18 October, with a brief formal ceremony at Novo Archangel'sk, which
henceforth would be known as Sitka. The money for the sale had not even
changed hands at that date. Ratification of a treaty was one thing, but ap-
propriating the money it stipulated was entirely another, and this was delayed over a year. Despite opposition to the purchase of what many dubbed
"Seward's icebox" or "Seward's folly," the United States got a bargain, paying
a little less than two cents per acre. Far from a folly, the purchase of Alaska
ultimately demonstrated Seward's unmatched vision of the future.

The Rockets' Red Glare

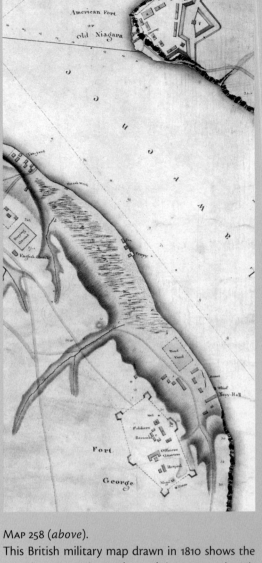

The War of 1812 was brought about by an accumulation of irritants, none big enough to go to war over individually. These thorns included restrictions on trade, seizure of American ships trading with France (at war with Britain since 1793), and impressment into the British navy of Americans who had been born in Britain. In the hands of the so-called war hawks in Congress these issues were escalated into cause for a full-blown war, which some of them saw as an opportunity to seize Canada from Britain while that nation was weakened by having to fight Napoleon in Europe. A land war, this group thought, would meet with more success than challenging the British on the high seas. Thomas Jefferson famously remarked that the taking of Canada would be a "mere matter of marching." He was very wrong; despite an initial numerical advantage, American armies were repulsed many times, especially early in the war when leadership was poor, and the War of 1812 ended as essentially a stalemate, with each country retaining lands it occupied before the conflict.

One early reason for American failures was that the Indians fought mostly alongside the British, whom they considered their only chance to stop the American advance westward. The governor of Indiana Territory, William Henry Harrison, had defeated Shawnee warriors at the Battle of Tippecanoe (near Lafayette, Indiana) in November 1811, and this had the effect of driving the Shawnee leader Tecumseh into an alliance with the British.

War might have been averted had communication across the Atlantic not been so slow, for the British made last-minute concessions. When war was declared, in June 1812, it was not expected to last long; President James Madison almost immediately sent out peace feelers.

The first action of the war was a preemptive one ordered by the canny British commander Major General Isaac Brock. The American fort on Mackinac Island, in the strategic strait between Lakes Huron and Michigan, was taken on 17 July 1812 by British and Indians before the Americans there even knew that war had been declared. The early victory was calculated to drive Indians to the British cause, and this it did.

The American commander in the western theater was Revolutionary War hero General William Hull, the governor of Michigan Territory, who proved not up to the task required of him. He was ordered to Fort Detroit but first had to cut a road from Urbana, Ohio, and did not arrive until 5 July. He took his army across the Detroit River into Canada and issued a proclamation inviting those seeking freedom "from tyranny and oppression" to join him. But the Canadians must not have felt oppressed, for few accepted his invitation, and Hull soon retreated back across the river.

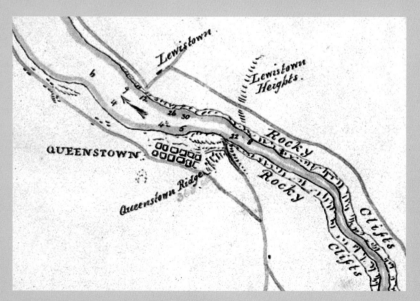

Brock rushed to the scene of the invasion, sailing up the British-controlled Lake Erie. Crossing the river his small British force, accompanied by Indians led by Tecumseh, laid siege to Fort Detroit. Brock carefully led Hull to believe that a native massacre would in all probability follow his taking of the fort, and Hull, who had received news of the fall of Fort Mackinac, surrendered Detroit without a shot being fired. This was a major morale-booster for the outnumbered British. Hull was later court-martialed and convicted of cowardice and desertion of duty.

Hull's concerns about possible Indian depredations were not so far-fetched; he had ordered the evacuation of Fort Dearborn because of the difficulty of supplying it following the fall of Fort Mackinac, but when on 15 August Captain Nathan Heald led his men out, they were set upon and massacred by the Indians (see page 199).

MAP 258 (*above*).
This British military map drawn in 1810 shows the American Fort Niagara (at top), just across the Niagara River from the British Fort George. Lake Ontario is at the top. The town of Newark, burned by the retreating Americans in December 1813, is partly shown at center left. It is now the village of Niagara-on-the-Lake.

Top left. "The rockets' red glare, bombs bursting in air" from an old print of the British attack on Fort McHenry, near Baltimore, in September 1814. The rockets were Congreve rockets, fired on a sixteen-foot guide stick.

MAP 259 (*below, left*).
The battlefield at Queenston Heights and the American crossing place at Lewiston, shown on an 1817 map. The high ground, which continues across the river, is part of the Niagara escarpment, a ridge that curves across the region

A similar event occurred in January 1813, when about 850 Americans who were marching to protect settlers at Frenchtown (now Monroe, Michigan), on the Raisin River, were attacked by about 1,100 British and Indians. Some 300 Americans were killed, including 30 by Indians after the surrender, hence the famous rallying cry—"Remember the Raisin!"

An American army of about 6,000 men under Major General Stephen Van Rensselaer massed on the Niagara Peninsula, seen as an easy invasion route to Canada, in October 1812. They faced only about 2,000 British and Canadians, under Brock. The American attack, which began on 13 October, was marked by mishap. General Alexander Smyth, a regular, was supposed to attack Fort Erie but refused to take orders from the younger Van Rensselaer, a militia officer. A boat loaded with all the other boats' oars was lost down the river. Crossing the river at Lewiston, Captain John Wool led about 600 men who managed to take Queenston Heights (MAP 259, *left, bottom*). But when Van Rensselaer ordered the militia to cross and support them, the militia refused to leave American territory, and Brock then counterattacked the Americans—now under Lieutenant Colonel Winfield Scott—driving them from the high ground and capturing almost all of them. Brock, however, was killed, a considerable loss to the British.

Both sides recognized that control of the lakes was critical. In October 1812 the American commander, Isaac Chauncey, began preparing the small American fleet, based at Sackets Harbor on eastern Lake Ontario for action, and in November a British ship was chased into Kingston, with the American fleet fighting a pitched battle against the shore defense. Naval control of Lake Ontario allowed an attack on the Upper Canada capital of York (now Toronto) the following April. An army of 1,700 men under Brigadier General Zebulon Pike (see page 116) was landed and the British retreated, but not before blowing up a powder magazine, killing many Americans, including Pike. An orgy of burning and looting followed in which the parliament buildings were destroyed. Chauncey then transported the army to the Niagara Peninsula, where Fort George (MAP 258, *left, top*) was captured. Fort Erie was also abandoned by the British.

Events seemed to be going well for the Americans until, on the night of 5–6 June, the fleeing British army turned on its pursuers and although outnumbered, defeated them at the Battle of Stoney Creek. Three weeks later a small Indian force defeated and captured 600 Americans at Beaver Dams, just east of Stoney Creek. The American position continued to deteriorate as British reinforcements arrived, and by December the American army withdrew across the Niagara River. In the process the town of Newark (now Niagara-on-the-Lake) was burned and its inhabitants turned out into the frigid night. The British would not forget.

The British regained much of their strength on Lake Ontario by building more ships at Kingston. In May a squadron had attacked Sackets Harbor while the American ships were away, although little lasting damage was done. On Lake Erie, though, the balance of power turned markedly toward the United States when on 10 September 1813 a little fleet built at Presqu'Ile (now Erie, Pennsylvania) engaged the British at Put-in-Bay, in

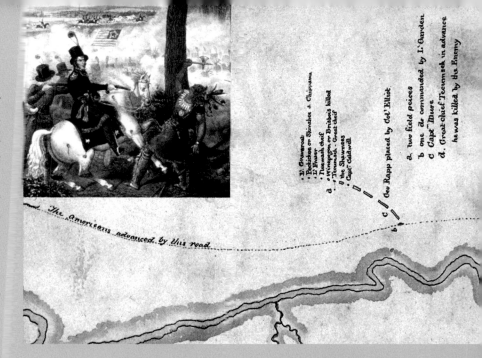

the tiny Bass Islands in the western lake. Captain Oliver Hazard Perry captured American imagination when he transferred his colors in a small boat when his flagship was destroyed under him in the middle of the battle. Despite this loss the entire British fleet was captured or destroyed, and the Americans were left in control of the lake.

The British were then unable to supply their western army. Colonel Henry Proctor, supported by warriors under Tecumseh, began to retreat up the Thames Valley, trying to reach Niagara. The American army, led by Brigadier General William Harrison, the governor of Indiana Territory and the hero of Tippecanoe, gave pursuit. On 5 October he caught up with the British at Moraviantown (MAP 261, *above*), soundly defeating Proctor; Tecumseh was killed in the battle. Although he could have continued east, Harrison did not want to overextend his supply lines and withdrew.

MAP 260 (*below, left*).
The American attack on York (now Toronto) on 27 April 1813 is depicted in this bird's-eye-view map, a view from the southwest.

MAP 261 (*above*).
The Battle of the Thames or Moraviantown (the village is just off the map to the right), 5 October 1813. *Inset*. Shawnee chief and agent of Indian unification Tecumseh is killed during the battle

MAP 262 (*below*).
A contemporary map of Sackets Harbor, at the eastern end on Lake Ontario, showing American ships operational and one under construction: *New ship housed in.*

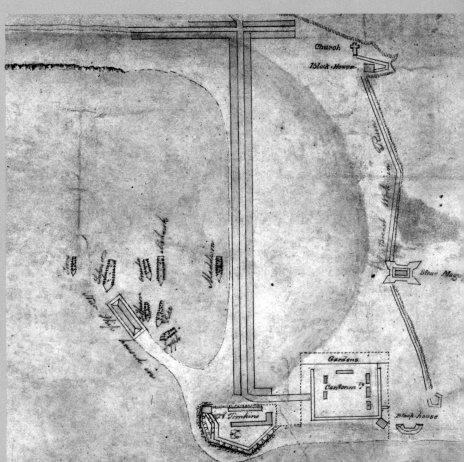

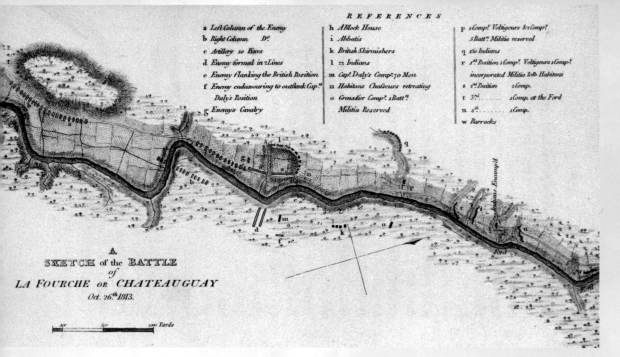

A
SKETCH of the BATTLE
of
LA FOURCHE or CHATEAUGUAY
Oct. 26.th 1813.

MAP 263 (*left*).
The Battle of Châteauguay, 25–26 October 1813. This British map refers to the Americans as the enemy. Wade Hampton was advancing from left to right, descending the river. Montréal is 25 miles to the right.

MAP 264 (*below*).
This American military map shows the site of the Battle of Crysler's Farm, 11 November 1813, on the north bank of the St. Lawrence. *American Troops* advanced across the *Gully* to unsuccessfully attack the *British Army*. American *Boats* are also shown. At left is the British fort at Prescott.

Below. American troops land in the early morning just prior to the Battle of Crysler's Farm. The painting is by Peter Rindlisbacher.

The major American initiative in the east in 1813 was intended to take Montréal. A force led by the shadowy Major General James Wilkinson (see page 116) was to descend the St. Lawrence from Sackets Harbor, while another army, under Major General Wade Hampton, was to march north along the tried-and-true invasion route of the Champlain Valley.

Hampton crossed into Canada on 20 September—minus some of his militia, who again refused to leave American territory. He then turned west to the Châteauguay River, which he began to descend toward Montréal. Twenty-five miles from that city he was met, on 25 October, by a small, near-guerilla force of French Canadians, called Voltigeurs, under Lieutenant Colonel Charles-Michel d'Irumberry de Salaberry, who also had a small number of Indians under his command. This was the Battle of Châteauguay. Despite a still considerable numerical advantage Hampton was forced to retreat; Salaberry passed into Canadian history as the savior of Montréal. Eighteen days later, on 11 November, the other American army, under Wilkinson, was engaged by an again smaller British army under Lieutenant Colonel Joseph Morrison at the Battle of Crysler's Farm, on the north bank of the St. Lawrence. Once more the American army was defeated, and Montréal was safe.

Incredibly, there was a mix-up in American plans for 1814. The government had intended the objective to be Kingston, but somehow the new commander, General Jacob Brown, sent his men to Niagara once more. In July now Brigadier General Winfield Scott took Fort Erie. Brown defeated a British army advancing toward the fort, at Chippewa on 5 July. The American plan was to once again attack York (Toronto), but naval support was delayed and the British regrouped, with General Gordon Drummond taking command of the British army. Then, on 25–26 July, came what was probably the hardest-fought battle of the entire war, at Lundy's Lane, within earshot of Niagara Falls (MAP 265, *right, top*). Beginning in the late afternoon and continuing into the night, the battle caused heavy casualties on both sides, and Scott, Brown, and Drummond were all badly wounded. By midnight the Americans were too exhausted to attack again and fell back; the British, likewise, were too exhausted to pursue them. The American army withdrew to Fort Erie, which the British then tried in vain to capture; the fort was finally blown up when the American army withdrew across the river in November.

During 1814 the offensive initiative had passed to the British. Especially after April, when Napoleon was defeated and exiled to Elba, the

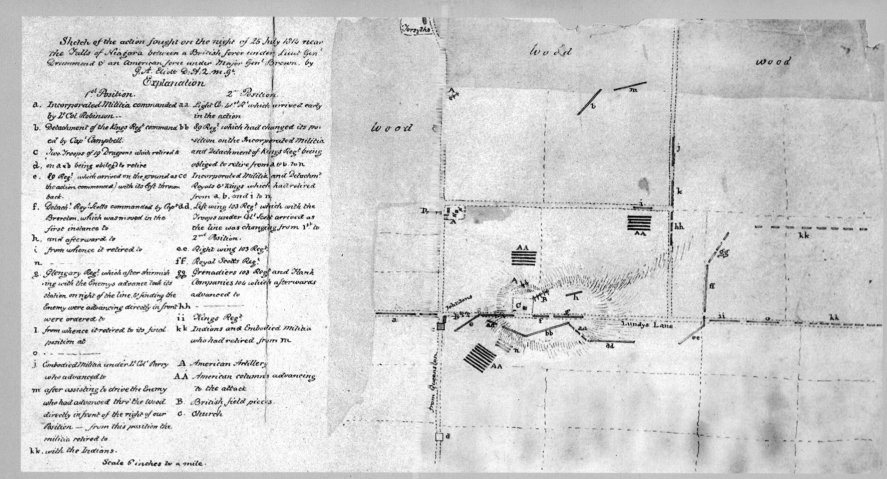

MAP 265 (*above*).
The Battle of Lundy's Lane, fought within in earshot of Niagara Falls on 25–26 Jul 1814.

Left. The Stars and Stripes flies over the British—now Canadian—Fort Erie, across the river from Buffalo, New York, during a reenactment of the American occupation of 1814.

flow of Napoleonic War veterans to Canada increased. By the end of 1814, British troop strength was up to about forty thousand, close to the total American army.

Brigades from the Duke of Wellington's European army under Major General Robert Ross were sent across the Atlantic in the summer with instructions to create a diversion on the east coast of the United States to support Canadian operations. By the time Ross reached Chesapeake Bay he had 4,000 men under his command. He intended to attack Baltimore, but the Royal Navy's inshore squadron commander, Rear Admiral George Cockburn, suggested an attack on Washington. Since it was strategically unimportant, Washington was largely unfortified. Ross landed his troops at Benedict, on the Patuxent River, and marched north, meeting a hastily pulled together American force of about 420 regulars, 1,450 militia, and 400 seamen from gunboats destroyed to prevent their capture. The clash, at the Battle of Bladensburg on 24 August, was, except for the sailors under Commodore Joshua Barney, a rout, soon satirized as "the Bladensburg Races" (MAP 266, *right*). The militia were terrified by the British use of a new weapon, the Congreve rocket. This must be one of the few battles in which there was political interference: Secretary of State James Monroe ordered a rearrangement of the defensive lines in a way that they could not support each other, and President James Madison tried to cross a bridge, preventing it from being blown up to slow the British advance.

The way to Washington was now open. The navy yard was burned as the army approached, but the Capitol and the president's house were burned by the British. The latter would be reconstructed and whitewashed to hide signs of the fire, becoming in the process the "White House."

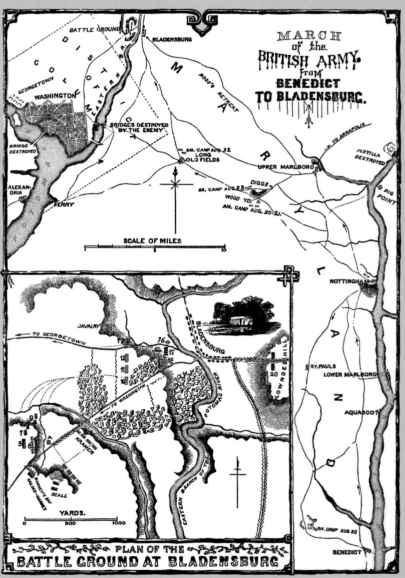

MAP 266 (*above*).
The British landing at Benedict, on the Patuxent River in Maryland, and the route marched to Bladensburg and Washington, with an inset showing the Battle of Bladensburg. It seems that no contemporary maps were made of this battle, perhaps due to the fact that it was one of the least glorious for the United States and one considered only a skirmish by the British, yet one in which its land commander, Major General Robert Ross, was killed. This map was drawn later, in 1868, for a monumental 1,084-page landmark history of the War of 1812.

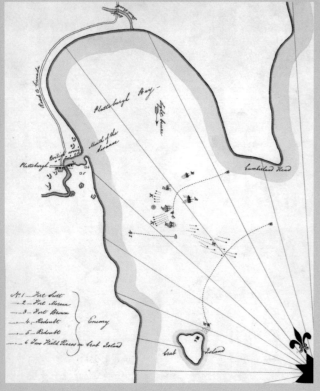

British attention now turned to "make a demonstration upon" Baltimore. The British army was landed twelve miles from the city on 12 September, where they engaged 3,200 militia, defeating them, but not at all with the same ease as at Bladensburg. Baltimore was much better fortified than Washington had been, and in particular Fort McHenry stood as a Southern bastion. The fort endured more than twenty-four hours of pounding from the British fleet but held and returned fire. This overnight battery, on 13–14 September, led to the penning by Francis Scott Key of the lines of what became the national anthem. The flag was indeed still there. The British determined that capture of Baltimore would take too long and withdrew.

Also in September 1814, a British fleet and two thousand regulars captured forts and towns along the coast of Maine. Intended to be a bargaining chip in the peace negotiations by then taking place, the region was held until the signing of a treaty. The British had hoped to gain territory in eastern Maine so as to secure the route between the cities of Québec and Halifax.

George Prevost, the governor general of Canada, planned a major invasion of the United States, once more down the Champlain Valley, to coincide with the British attack on the Chesapeake. He led an army of 17,000 south, pausing at the Saranac River, at Plattsburgh, New York, waiting for naval support before he crossed. A smaller American force of about 6,800 opposed him on the southern bank. A naval battle fought in Plattsburgh Bay on 11 September resulted in a victory for the United States (MAP 267, *left*). At a critical point in the battle, American naval commander Lieutenant Thomas Macdonough managed to swing his flagship *Saratoga* around on its anchor when its starboard guns could not fire, so as to bring its port side guns to bear on the much larger British flagship *Confiance*. The sudden heavy bombardment led to the surrender of the *Confiance*. Prevost, concerned about his supply lines once control of Lake Champlain had been lost, retreated north to Canada.

Another war raged in 1813–14, which brought into prominence a man who would emerge as a war hero and ultimately president, Andrew Jackson. This was the Creek War. The British were not directly involved but certain Creeks, especially a faction known as the Red Sticks, from their painted war clubs, had been incited to violence by a visit from Tecumseh in 1811, who was trying to unify resistance against American incursions onto Indian lands.

The Red Sticks had massacred more than four hundred settlers who had sought refuge at a poorly stockaded farm known as Fort Mims, at the confluence of the Alabama and the Tombigbee rivers, on 30 August 1813. As a result Major General Andrew Jackson was given command of 3,500 Tennessee militia. He defeated the Red Sticks at Tallashatchee, Alabama, on 3 November and then again at Talladega on 9 November, although Jackson then had to retreat because of tenuous supply lines. Further battles at Emuckfau Creek on 22 January 1814 and Enitachopco Creek on 24 January were nearly disastrous for Jackson, because he was outnumbered and his militia were not all that reliable in battle. At the latter confrontation Jackson was only saved by the timely use of a cannon firing grapeshot.

The Red Stick Creeks remained a threat until 27 March, when Jackson attacked them at a fortified village, called Tohopeka, they had created in a loop of the Tallapoosa River. About 1,500 warriors were within, opposed by about 4,500 under Jackson, including 600 regulars. The Battle of Horseshoe Bend, as it is called, is

MAP 267 (*above*).
The situation after about half an hour during the Battle of Plattsburgh is shown on this British map. The British ships are *A* (*Confiance*); *B* (*Linnet*); *C* (*Chubb*, drifting with colors struck), and *E* (gunboats). The U.S. ships are *F* (*Saratoga*); *G* (*Eagle*); *H* (*Ticonderoga*); *I* (*Prebble*, drifting ashore), and *K* (gunboats).

MAP 268 (*below*).
The Battle of Horseshoe Bend, on the Tallapoosa River in Alabama, 27 March 1814, shown on a map prepared soon after the battle by one of Andrew Jackson's officers. The village was on higher ground in the middle of the bend. The canoes, stealthily removed by Cherokee allies, are at the tip of the bend, and a breastwork stockade seals the neck of the peninsula.

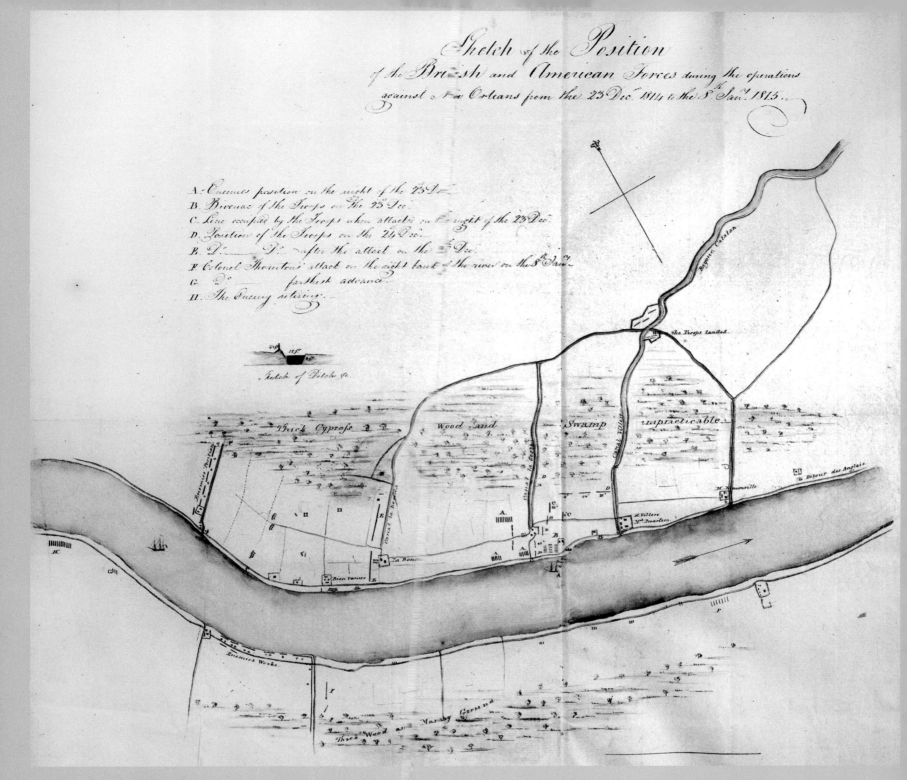

Sketch of the Position
of the British and American Forces during the operations
against New Orleans from the 23 Dec.ʳ 1814 to the 8ᵗʰ Jan.ʸ 1815

A. Enemies position on the night of the 23 Dec.ʳ
B. Bivouac of the Troops on the 23 Dec.ʳ
C. Line occupied by the Troops when attacked on ye night of the 23 Dec.ʳ
D. Position of the Troops on the 24 Dec.ʳ
E. D.º   D.º   after the attack on the ye Dec.ʳ
F. Colonel Thornton's attack on the right bank of the river on the 8ᵗʰ Jan.ʸ
G. D.º   farthest advance.
H. The Enemy retiring.

Sketch of Ditch &c.

depicted in MAP 268 (left). Brigadier General John Coffee crossed the river, giving the Red Sticks concern at their rear. Jackson ordered a full frontal assault on the narrow neck of the river, where the Red Sticks had built a log stockade. The numerical advantage of Jackson's army proved decisive, and they broke through the stockade. An orgy of killing followed. Cherokee allies had stolen Creek canoes to cut off any escape. Some 917 Creek were killed. The battle ended the Creek War, and Jackson later made the Creek sign a confiscatory treaty surrendering 23 million acres to the United States—penalizing Creek allies as well as the Red Sticks. At the same time Jackson used the victory to boost his own reputation.

The next region targeted by the British was the Gulf Coast, which, like the Chesapeake foray, was seen as a means of diverting American strength away from Canada. In August 1814 the British occupied the forts at Pensacola, a Spanish port city, and in September attacked Mobile, unsuccessfully this time. In November Jackson, who with the demise of the Creek now turned his attention to the British, took Pensacola unopposed after the Spanish governor could not decide whether he should fight or surrender; the British blew up the forts and withdrew to the Apalachicola River. Jackson marched to Mobile, where he expected the next British attack to come, but soon realized that they meant to attack New Orleans instead. Jackson hurriedly marched his army west, arriving in New Orleans on 1 December. Here he augmented his army any way he could, with more

MAP 269.

This British map shows the Battle of New Orleans. Several defensive American lines protect New Orleans, which is five miles away to the left. Jackson's defenses, aided by the swamps, which made circumventing them impossible, resulted in a smaller American army being able to defeat a larger and better trained British army. A cross-section of the defensive works is also shown.

militia, and even pirates, flocking to the defense of the city. The pirates, who numbered perhaps a thousand, were led by Jean Laffite and were based at Barataria, in the swamp near New Orleans.

The British army, assembled in Jamaica and about ten thousand strong, was led by Lieutenant General Edward Pakenham, brother-in-law of Wellington himself. The army was to approach the city via Lake Borgne, open to the sea on the east side of the delta. On 14 December they engaged and overwhelmed a small number of gunboats that had been posted to watch rather than fight, but which could not get away quickly due to lack of wind. A British base was established on the Mississippi eight miles downstream from New Orleans. On 23 December Jackson, supported by two ships, the *Carolina* and the *Louisiana*, attacked the British camp before it had reached full strength. The result was inconclusive. The *Carolina* was blown up with red-hot cannon shot on 27 December and the British advanced toward the city, only to be repulsed by intense fire, including

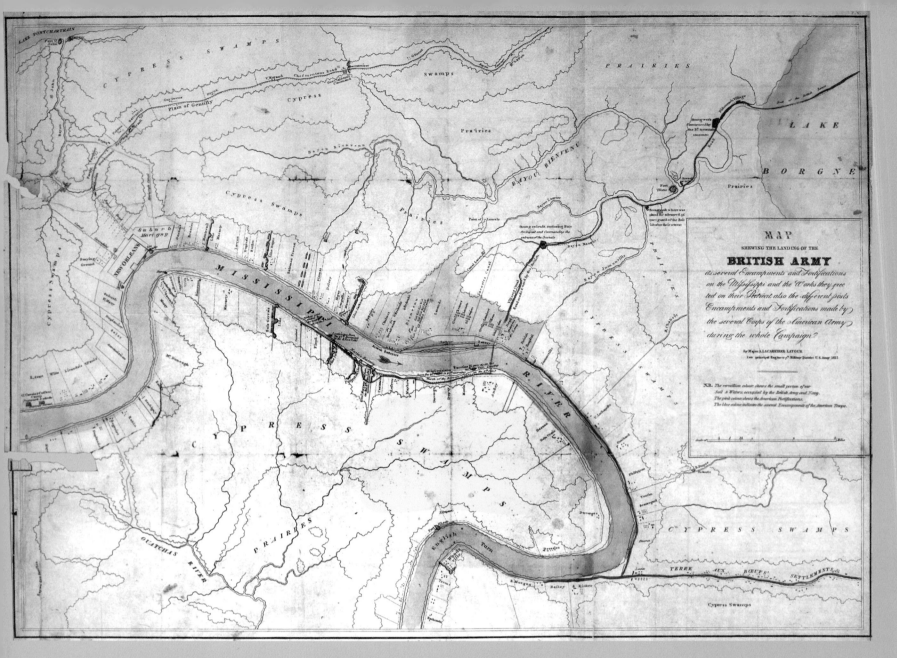

much from the *Louisiana*. Jackson then extended his defensive works, an earth berm fronted by a drainage canal, for a mile into the swamp, completely cutting off any British advance to New Orleans, still five miles away. This structure was to prove critical, for when the main British attack came on 8 January 1815, British soldiers were out in the open and were mown down by intense fire from behind the earthwork that they were unable to counter. Pakenham was killed in the volleys. Laffite's pirates, wearing red shirts, caused much confusion in the British ranks, which, of course, also wore red. Although the attacking British outnumbered the Americans by about 6,000 to 5,300, Jackson's defenses were so good that British casualties from the entire battle totaled 2,450, compared to 350 on the American side.

By the time of the Battle of New Orleans, a peace treaty had already been signed. At the Belgian city of Ghent on 24 December 1814, the two sides had reached an agreement to cease hostilities and return

MAP 270 (*above*).
This American map of the Battle of New Orleans covers a wider area than MAP 269 (*previous page*). New Orleans is shown upriver from the battle scene, and the extent of the British "occupation of our soil" is shown by the red-colored area. The route of the British army from Lake Borgne to the Mississippi is indicated by the red line. The place where the *Carolina* was blown up is marked, and the map also shows the several defensive lines of earthworks thrown up by Jackson's army and progressively barring the way to New Orleans. *Below left* is part of a contemporary engraving of the battle scene.

all occupied territory so that the boundaries of both the United States and British Canada would be the same as they had been before the war. Britain had hoped to retain some of northern Maine and had also hoped to protect the western lands of its Indian allies, but in the end abandoned both demands when the military failures at Baltimore and Plattsburgh became known. Although signed on 24 December, the treaty, unusually, was not to come into effect until both sides had ratified it. Britain did so immediately, but the ship carrying the British-ratified treaty did not arrive in New York until 11 February 1815, and the requisite ratification by the United States was not completed until 17 February. Impressment, perhaps the single most important cause of the war, was not even mentioned. Rarely had a war been fought for so little end.

The Treaty of Ghent established commissions to fix the United States–Canada boundary, which was disputed or ill-defined in numerous places. In 1818 a convention was signed that established an 852-mile boundary as the forty-ninth parallel from Lake of the Woods as far west as the Rocky Mountains. Beyond that, the Oregon Country—the land on both sides of today's border—was disputed and would be left as such until 1846; the Maine-Quebec boundary would also remain in dispute

until 1842 (see page 158). Although the boundary was defined on paper in 1818, it was not surveyed in most part until the 1830s and 1840s. One of its principal surveyors was the famous mapmaker David Thompson. It was he who first surveyed the defined eastern starting point of the forty-ninth parallel, the northwestern point of Lake of the Woods. Difficulties with interpreting precisely where this was led to the creation of Minnesota's Northwest Angle, a peninsula jutting into the lake that is American territory yet isolated from the rest of the state (MAP 271, *below*).

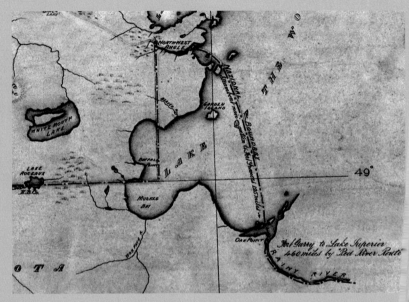

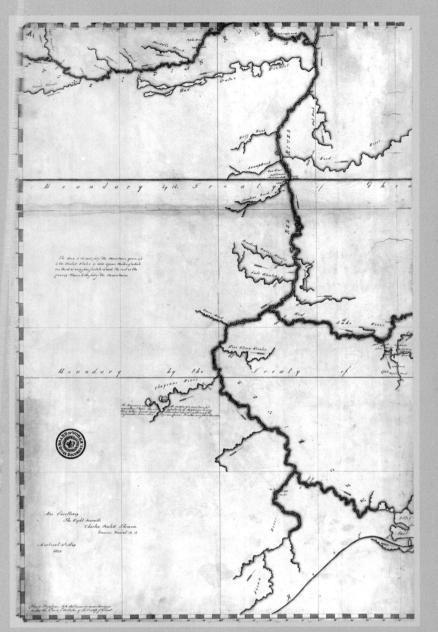

MAP 271 (*above*).
The Northwest Angle of Minnesota, an isolated American peninsula in Lake of the Woods, created by interpretation of the wording of the 1818 convention.

MAP 272 (*right, top*).
Explorer David Thompson fell on hard times in his later years and was contracted to survey some of the 1818 boundary. Such was his reputation that he was trusted by both sides to survey the boundary correctly. In 1840 he produced this map that shows his survey of the forty-ninth parallel across the Red River, between North Dakota and Minnesota, and Manitoba. The boundary line is labeled *Boundary by the Treaty of [Ghent]*.

MAP 273 (*right*).
This map dated 1817 shows a northern boundary for the United States labeled *U.S. division line not yet ascertained.* Note that the boundary touches the Missouri.

MAP 274 (*below*).
Another rendition of the pre-1818 boundary line, copied from John Melish's 1816 map (MAP 2, *pages 2–3*) and used by the boundary commissioners in their negotiations. At right is the area of Lord Selkirk's Grant, a 115,830-square-mile tract granted to Lord Selkirk by the Hudson's Bay Company in 1811 for a settlement along the Red River. After 1818 the grant straddled the new border, and the southern portion reverted to the United States.

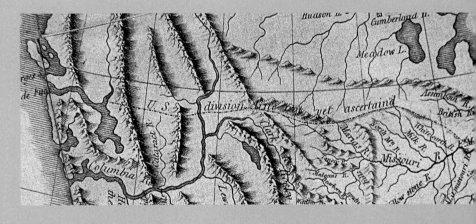

The Decline of Spain

Empires wax and wane, and for none was this more apparent than Spain. A world empire built up in the two centuries after Columbus found America began to collapse as the country suffered wars and revolts at home and could devote fewer resources overseas.

Florida, claimed for Spain by Ponce de León in 1513, had been lost to Britain after the Seven Years' War in 1763, but had been restored to Spanish rule with the end of the American War for Independence in 1783. The 1795 Treaty of San Lorenzo (also known as Pinckney's Treaty) had restricted Spanish territory to that south of 31°N. In 1800 Spain returned Louisiana to France. (It had received this territory from the French in 1762 to prevent it falling into British hands.) Three years later the United States purchased Louisiana from the French, but its boundaries were not well defined, and West Florida (now the southern parts of the states of Mississippi and Alabama), although held by Spain, was claimed by the United States as part of the Louisiana Purchase.

Conflict over Spanish and American claims led to the setting up of the Republic of West Florida in 1810, although this lasted only a month or two before it was annexed by the United States. The Florida peninsula was also lost to Spain. U.S. Army forces led by the perennial Indian fighter Andrew Jackson entered the region in December 1817 to attack the Seminole, who had retaliated against incursions by American settlers and provided a haven for escaped slaves. With the capture of Pensacola in May 1818, all Florida was effectively in American hands.

Beginning in 1810, when Mexico first declared its independence from Spain, and continuing until 1821 when that independence was accepted, Spain was concerned to establish a permanent boundary with the United States so that it could concentrate on the war in Mexico. Negotiations between the American secretary of state, John Quincy Adams, and the Spanish minister in the United States, Luís de Onís, began in 1817 and continued until 1819. Using John Melish's *Map of the United States and Contiguous British and Spanish Possessions* in the 1818 edition (MAP 2, on the title page of this book, is the almost identical 1816 edition), there followed proposals and counterproposals that began with the American offer of the Rio Grande as the boundary and the Spanish of the Mississippi, and progressed from there toward a compromise line between the two.

In a diplomatic coup de grace Adams eventually managed to secure American access to the Pacific Northwest and a compromise boundary at the coast at 42°N, between the Spanish desired 43° and the American 41°, all the time keeping a veiled threat of war over Florida or the Northwest hanging in the air. The western boundaries of the United States were finally

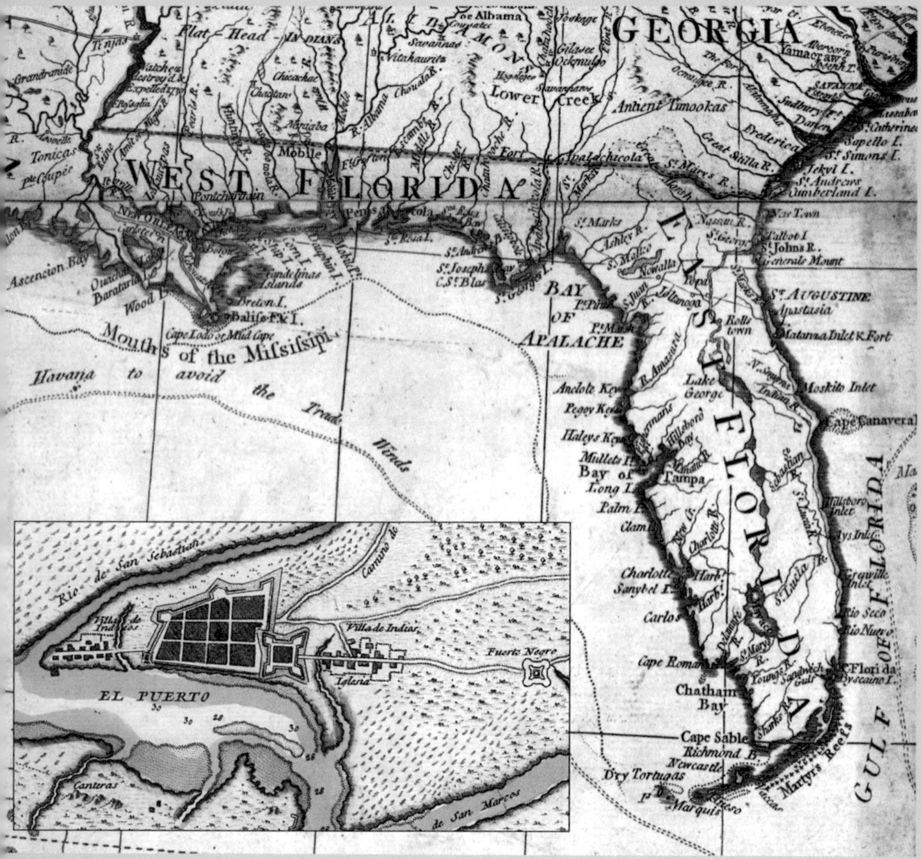

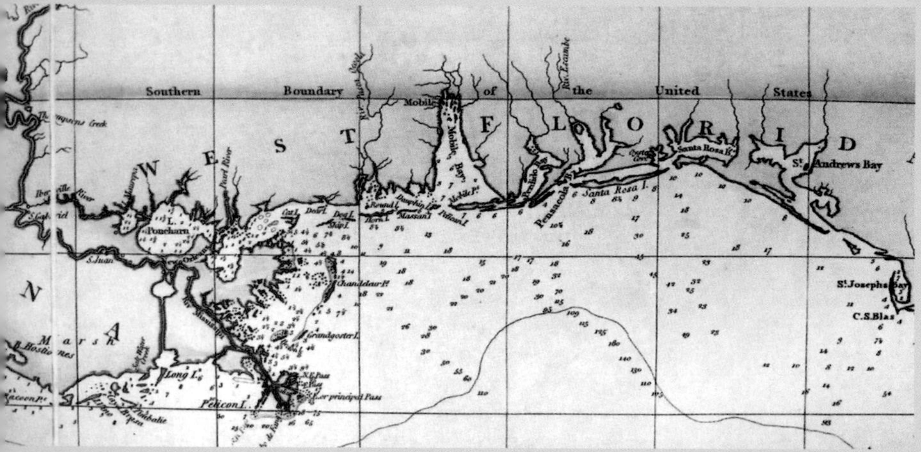

MAP 275 (*above, top*) and MAP 276 (*inset*).
Florida shown on a 1786 map, when the territory had reverted to Spanish rule. Inset (MAP 276) is St. Augustine, the longtime Spanish capital, in 1783.

MAP 277 (*above*).
The disputed territory of East Florida shown on an 1803 map by British mapmaker Aaron Arrowsmith, who has marked 31°N as the *Southern Boundary of the United States*.

MAP 278 (*above*).
This 1814 map of Missouri Territory (the name given to the rest of the Louisiana Territory when Louisiana became a state in 1812) has been updated to 1819. It now shows the forty-ninth parallel boundary with British territory as far west as the Rockies, negotiated in 1818, as well as an early approximation of the Transcontinental Treaty line. This map may be compared with the 1814 edition (MAP 231, *page 118*).

agreed upon in a treaty signed on 22 February 1819, a treaty that included recognition of American ownership of the Floridas. It was a huge diplomatic victory for the United States and for John Quincy Adams. A chastened Onís reported to his government that a better bargain was impossible and that the sacrifices were preferable to war.

Officially known as the Treaty of Amity, Settlement and Limits Between the United States of America and His Catholic Majesty, but also known as the Adams-Onís Treaty or the Transcontinental Treaty, it established the boundaries between many states not at that time part of the United States and those whose territories were: the boundaries between today's Texas and Louisiana; Texas and Oklahoma; Utah and Idaho; Nevada and Idaho, and California and Oregon, the last at 42°N. The boundary agreed upon is shown in MAP 279 (*right, top*), and MAP 280 (*below*).

Spain continued to lose its American territories. It lost Texas in 1836 (see page 150), California and much of the Southwest in 1848 (see page 168), and Cuba, Puerto Rico, the Philippines, and Guam after the 1898 Spanish-American War (see page 226).

MAP 279 (*above*) and MAP 280 (*below*).
These two maps show the western boundary line agreed to by John Quincy Adams and Luís de Onís in 1819 in the Transcontinental Treaty. Today's approximate or exact boundaries between five pairs of states are the result of the line negotiated in 1819. Only the present states of Colorado and Wyoming are bisected by the line. As a result of the failure to agree with the British on a boundary west of the Rockies, MAP 279 shows American territory as far north as 54°40′N, the northern limits of Spanish claims inherited by the United States in this treaty. The Oregon Country, comprising today's states of Oregon and Washington and the Canadian province of British Columbia, formed part of the claims derived from Spain but was still contested by the British. As a result, the 1818 northern boundary convention agree to leave it as a region of "joint occupancy," a situation that was only resolved in 1846 (see page 158).

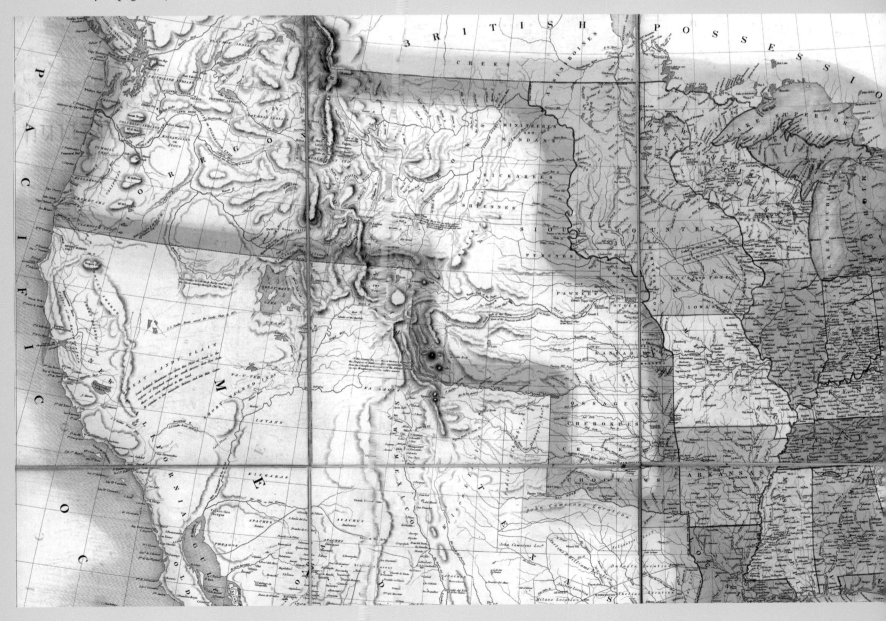

A Trail of Tears

When Andrew Jackson succeeded John Quincy Adams as president in 1829, he brought with him his hard-line ideas about Indians. The victor of many battles with an Indian foe, he was convinced that the security of the United States lay in the separation of Indians from EuroAmericans.

Within a year, Jackson signed the Indian Removal Act of 1830, which authorized the president to negotiate land exchange treaties; tribes within existing states were to be resettled in the Louisiana Purchase territory. In reality, the Indians had no choice and were coerced into signing treaties to vacate the land they had held for centuries and made to travel to land west of the Mississippi that had entirely different characteristics from their homelands. The journey would be onerous, and life in their new environment would also be difficult.

Most eastern Indians realized the futility of resistance, took up the federal government offer of transportation, food, and tools, and moved to new land in the West, much of which was taken from Plains tribes such as the Kansa and the Osage. The land allocations are shown in MAP 284, *right*.

Some tribes defied the federal intention, most notably the Cherokee. They sued the state of Georgia and fought the removal every way they knew short of violence, all to no avail. The Cherokee chief John Ross was essentially circumvented by other factions led by Major Ridge and his son, John Ridge, who signed a treaty with the federal government agreeing to removal in exchange for money and their lands in Georgia and Alabama. This was the Treaty of New Echota, Georgia, signed on 29 December 1835; actual removal was to begin on 23 May 1838. Despite protests from the Cherokee that the treaty had not been signed by anyone authorized to do so, and a 15,000-signature petition, the Senate ratified the treaty. (When the Cherokee eventually arrived in their new land west of the Mississippi they turned on those who had signed the treaty and a civil war raged for

MAP 281 (*left*).
The homelands of many Indian nations are shown on this 1785 map of the Southeast. Prominent at center is the country of the *Creek Indians*, both *Upper Creeks* and *Lower Creeks*. Closer to the Mississippi is the land of the *Chactaws* (the Choctaw), and the *Chicasaws*. To the north, around the *Cherakees* or *Hogoheegee* River, the Tennessee River, is the land of the *Cherakees: Upper, Middle*, and *Lower*.

MAP 282 (*below, left*).
Charles Royce, of the Smithsonian Institution Bureau of Ethnology, compiled a complete register of all Indian land cessions. In 1884 this map was published showing the former territories of the Cherokee Nation, all of which, except a small reservation, were taken from them by a succession of treaties between 1721 (area 1 on this map) and 1835 (area 36). Some of the largest areas were lost under British administration: area 4 in 1770; area 5 in 1772, and area 7 in 1775. The Ohio River is at top, the Tennessee near the bottom, with the Cumberland roughly at the center. Area 36 is the region ceded by the Cherokee at New Echota, Georgia, on 29 December 1835.

MAP 283 (*right*).
In anticipation of its sale to EuroAmerican settlers, this is a survey of part of the Cherokee land ceded at New Echota in 1835. The area depicted is in the northeastern corner of the state of Alabama, just south of the Tennessee River, at top. The map appeared in a government report in 1837. The area depicted is the western part of area 36 on MAP 282.

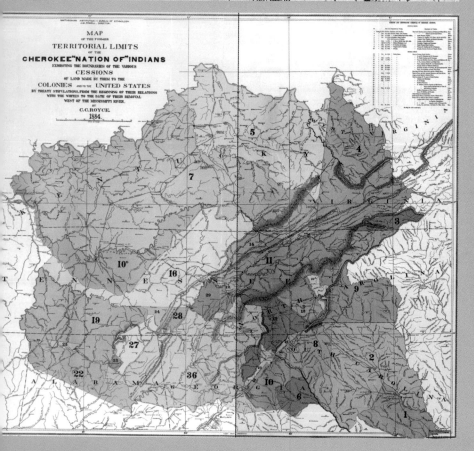

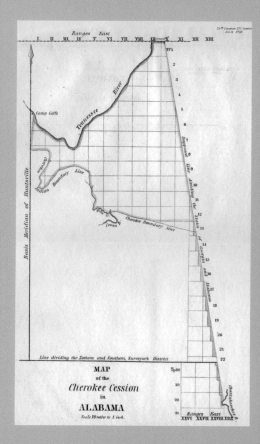

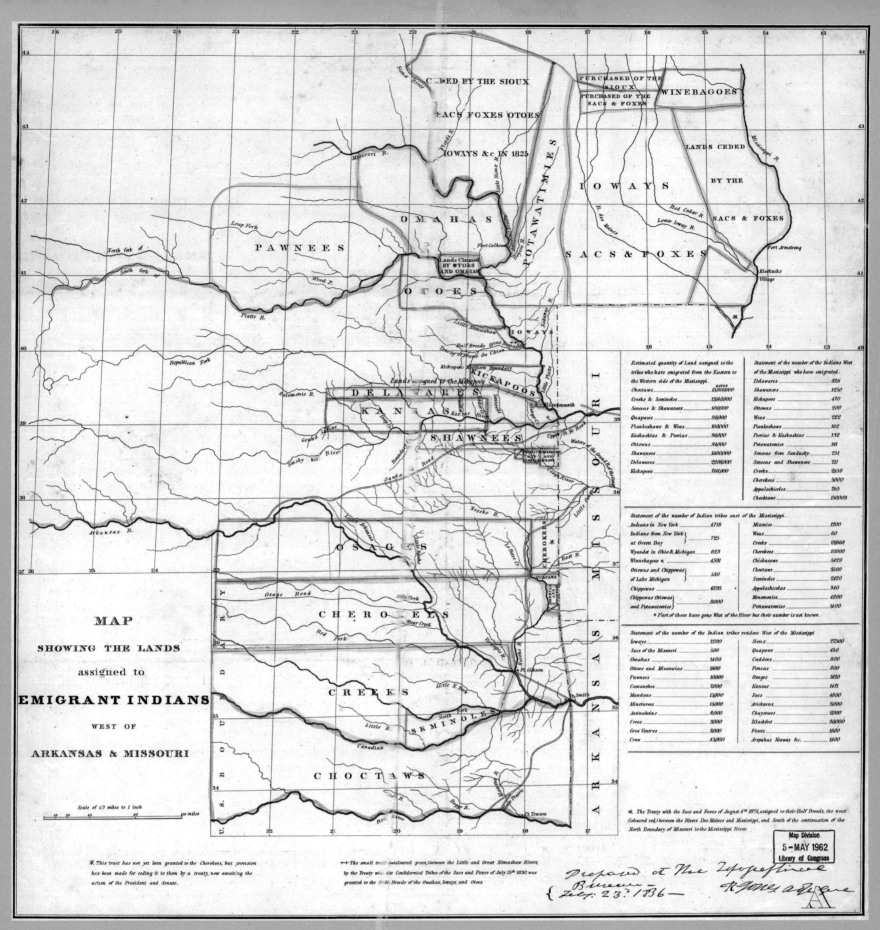

MAP
SHOWING THE LANDS
assigned to
EMIGRANT INDIANS
WEST OF
ARKANSAS & MISSOURI

Estimated quantity of Land assigned to the tribes who have emigrated from the Eastern to the Western side of the Mississippi.	
	acres
Choctaws	15,000,000
Creeks & Seminoles	13,140,000
Senecas & Shawanees	100,000
Quapaws	96,000
Piankeshaws & Weas	160,000
Kaskaskias & Peorias	96,000
Ottowas	34,000
Shawanees	1,600,000
Delawares	2,208,000
Kickapoes	768,000

Statement of the number of the Indians West of the Mississippi who have emigrated.	
Delawares	826
Shawanees	1250
Kickapoes	470
Ottowas	200
Weas	222
Piankeshaws	162
Peorias & Kaskaskias	132
Potawatomies	141
Senecas from Sandusky	251
Senecas and Shawanees	211
Creeks	2459
Cherokees	5000
Appalachicolas	265
Choctaws	15,000

Statement of the number of Indian tribes east of the Mississippi.			
Indians in New York	4716	Miamies	1200
Indians from New York at Green Bay	725	Weas	60
Wyandots in Ohio & Michigan	623	Creeks	22,668
Winnebagoes	4591	Cherokees	10,000
Ottowas and Chippewas of Lake Michigan	550	Chickasaws	5429
Chippewas	6793	Choctaws	5500
Chippewas Ottowas and Potawatomies	8000	Seminoles	2420
		Appalachicolas	340
		Menomonies	4200
		Pottawatomies	1400

* Part of these have gone West of the River but their number is not known.

Statement of the number of the Indian tribes resident West of the Mississippi.			
Ioways	1200	Sioux	27,500
Sacs of the Missouri	500	Quapaws	450
Omahas	1400	Caddoes	800
Ottoes and Missourias	1600	Poncas	800
Pawnees	10,000	Osages	5420
Camanches	7000	Kansas	1471
Mandons	15,000	Sacs	4800
Minetarees	15,000	Aricaras	3000
Assinaboins	8,000	Chayennes	2000
Crees	3000	Blackfeet	30,000
Gros Ventres	3000	Foxes	1600
Crow	45,000	Arapahas Kiowas &c.	1400

Scale of 40 miles to 1 inch

* This tract has not yet been granted to the Cherokees, but provision has been made for ceding it to them by a treaty, now awaiting the action of the President and Senate.

++ The small tract (coloured green) between the Little and Great Nemahaw Rivers, by the Treaty with the Confederated Tribes of the Sacs and Foxes of July 15th 1830 was granted to the Half Breeds of the Omahas, Ioways, and Otoes.

The Treaty with the Sacs and Foxes of August 4th 1824, assigned to their Half Breeds, the tract (coloured red) between the Rivers Des Moines and Mississippi, and South of the continuation of the North Boundary of Missouri to the Mississippi River.

Prepared at the Topographical Bureau, Feby. 23d 1836 —

Map 284 (above).

This federal government map compiled in 1836 shows the lands west of the Mississippi assigned to "Emigrant Indians," those who had been induced to sign treaties and to move from their homelands east of the river. At right are statistical tables by tribe giving the amount of land assigned, numbers who had moved by that time, numbers still east of the Mississippi, and numbers then resident west of the river. Most of the assigned land had been negotiated away from Plains tribes, including most notably the Kansa and the Osage, who lost about 156,000 square miles in 1825 treaties. The map is signed and annotated *Prepared at the Topographical Bureau, Feby. 23d 1836.*

Map 285 (right).

A survey of the lands to be assigned to the Cherokee published in 1837 in a government report. Fort Gibson is shown on the Arkansas River.

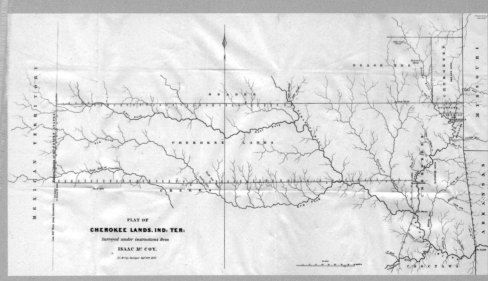

PLAT OF
CHEROKEE LANDS, IND: TER:
Surveyed under instructions from
ISAAC McCOY.

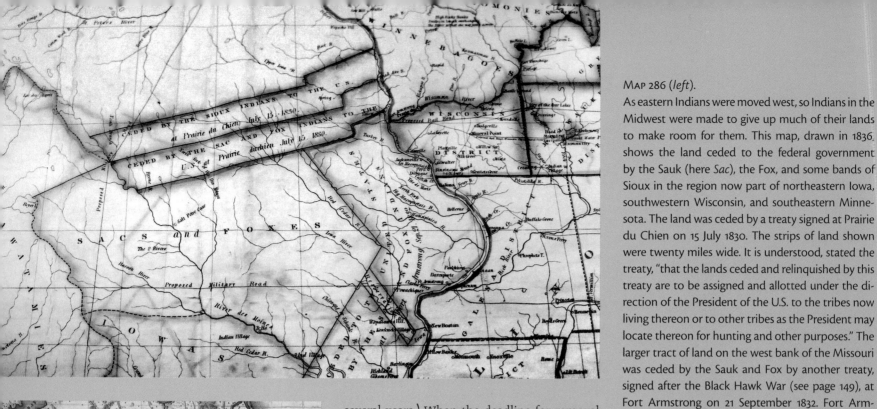

Map 286 (*left*).
As eastern Indians were moved west, so Indians in the Midwest were made to give up much of their lands to make room for them. This map, drawn in 1836, shows the land ceded to the federal government by the Sauk (here *Sac*), the Fox, and some bands of Sioux in the region now part of northeastern Iowa, southwestern Wisconsin, and southeastern Minnesota. The land was ceded by a treaty signed at Prairie du Chien on 15 July 1830. The strips of land shown were twenty miles wide. It is understood, stated the treaty, "that the lands ceded and relinquished by this treaty are to be assigned and allotted under the direction of the President of the U.S. to the tribes now living thereon or to other tribes as the President may locate thereon for hunting and other purposes." The larger tract of land on the west bank of the Missouri was ceded by the Sauk and Fox by another treaty, signed after the Black Hawk War (see page 149), at Fort Armstrong on 21 September 1832. Fort Armstrong (at today's Rock Island, Illinois) is shown on the Mississippi near the river's confluence with the Wisconsin River. Note the infant Wisconsin District; much enlarged this would become the state of Wisconsin in 1848. Just below it is Galena District, the lead mining region of Illinois.

several years.) When the deadline for removal passed, Georgia militia descended on the Cherokee, brutally rounding them up and handing them over to federal troops commanded by General Winfield Scott, who tried to treat them well but was overwhelmed by numbers. Some Cherokee were packed into steamboats and sent down the Tennessee, others dispatched in large groups overland. Hardship, heat, dysentery, and fatigue all took their toll. Estimates of total numbers deported and total deaths vary, but it seems that of 18,000 Cherokee removed, perhaps as many as 4,000 died on what has been dubbed the Trail of Tears. The official government figure was 424.

As many as a thousand Cherokee evaded the roundup and hid in the mountains. Now called the Eastern band of Cherokee, they number about 6,500 on their reservation at Qualla Boundary in North Carolina.

Some Indians resisted, most notably some Seminole in Florida, led by their chief Osceola, who threatened death to any Seminole who tried to leave, and did kill another chief, Charley Emathla, when he attempted to move. The Second Seminole War, a series of battles and skirmishes, was fought against the Seminole between 1835 and 1837 by federal troops led by a number of com-

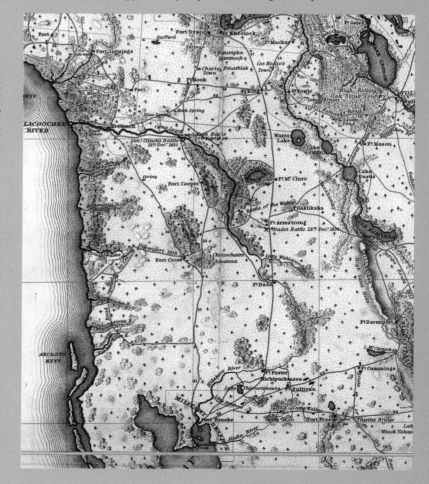

Map 287 (*above, center*).
This 1839 map of southern Florida defines, bounded by the red line, the *District assigned to the Seminoles by the Arrangement of Gen¹. Macomb May 18ᵗʰ 1839.* Alexander Macomb was the commanding officer of the U.S. Army at the time.

Map 288 (*left*).
A 1925 road map of the same area as Map 287 shows the tiny remnant of Seminole Indian Reservation left by that time. The whole map is shown as Map 491, *pages 236–37*.

Map 289 (*right*).
Battles of the Second Seminole War are shown on this map, a northward extension of Map 287. North of Lake Okeechobee is the *Battle of Lake Okeechobee*, where Colonel Zachary Taylor defeated the Seminole in 1837; at map center is *Dade's Battle*, where Indian agent Francis Dade (after whom Dade County is named) was killed in 1835. At top left is *Gen¹. Clinch's Battle*, where General Duncan Clinch narrowly escaped death; other battle sites are scattered through the region. Tampa Bay is at bottom left.

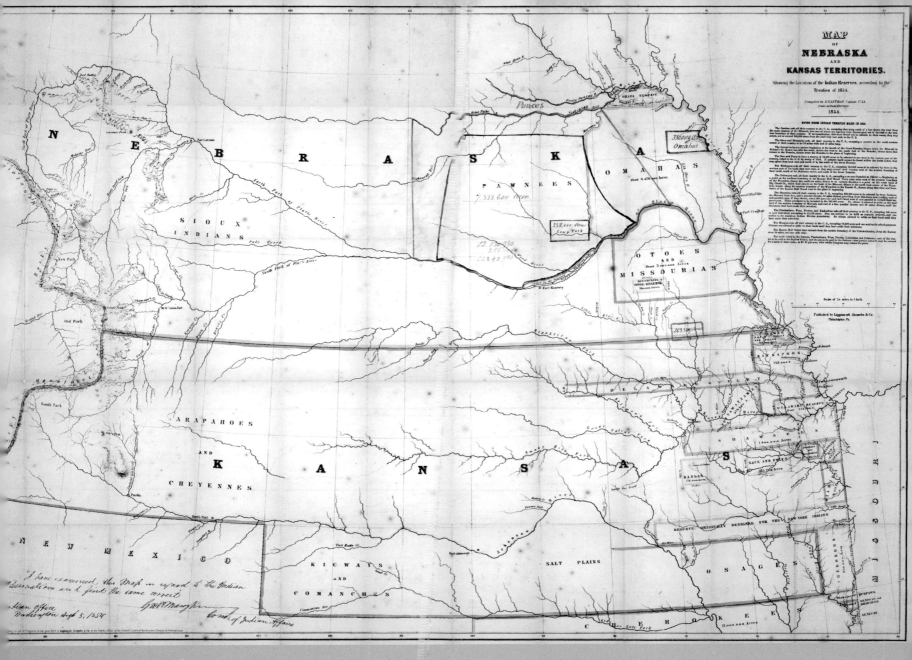

MAP
OF
NEBRASKA
AND
KANSAS TERRITORIES.

Showing the Location of the Indian Reserves, according to the
Treaties of 1854.

Compiled by A.EASTMAN, Captain U.S.A.
from actual surveys.

1854.

manding officers, most notably Colonel Zachary Taylor, who was to later distinguish himself as a leader in the Mexican War (see page 160). On 25 December 1837 he defeated the Seminole at the Battle of Lake Okeechobee (MAP 289, *below, left*). The United States spent $30 million, a massive amount in its day, fighting the guerilla tactics of the Seminole. But for all the effort, the Seminole were not really defeated. Osceola was captured in 1838, and the remnant of the tribe retreated into the Everglades in southern Florida and were left alone. MAP 287 (*left, center*) shows the area "assigned" to them after the army could not flush them out.

Indeed, another war, albeit a more minor affair called the Third Seminole War, erupted in 1855–58 when the Seminole railed against continued incursions into their remaining lands by EuroAmerican settlers. By this time there were only two hundred Seminole left in Florida.

During Andrew Jackson's term of office, which ended in 1837, an official total of 45,690 Indians had been moved west of the Mississippi. With 94 treaties, about 100 million acres of land in the East had been acquired at the cost of about 32 million acres of exchanged western lands and about $68 million. But there was another cost—the untold misery and suffering of a displaced people.

The new lands the Indians had acquired were themselves soon to come under pressure from the tide of EuroAmerican settlement that swept across the continent. Maps such as MAPS 290 and 291 (*this page*) and MAP 295 (*page 149*) document this further confiscation, which continued until the Indians were left with only tiny scattered reservations (see MAP 416, *page 203*).

MAP 290 (*above*).
The ceding of land from the Indians did not stop with the grand emigrations of the 1830s. This War Department map dated 1854 lists lands ceded as the result of treaties that year. It is signed and dated *5 September 1854* by the *Indian Office, Washington*. One entry from the list is typical: *The Miamies cede all their country to the U.S. excepting 70,000 acres and one section for school purposes. Citizens not allowed to settle on their land until they have made their selection.* The Miamis' 325,000-acre reservation is shown outlined in red adjacent to the Missouri boundary at right. They lost almost 80 percent of it in 1854.

MAP 291 (*below*).
From the same report as MAP 282 on page 140 comes this map of the western lands assigned to the Cherokee. Published almost fifty years later, it shows that much of the land supposedly given to the Cherokee in perpetuity was taken from them once again. The fact that most of the Indian tribes aligned themselves with the Confederacy in the Civil War did not help. Areas 38 (the "Neutral Lands") and 39 (the "Cherokee Strip") were ceded to the United States on 19 July 1866, and areas 40–45 sold, or assigned to other tribes dispossessed from lands in the far west. (Area 37 had been taken from western Cherokee in 1828.) Areas 46 and 47 were still Cherokee land in 1884, but that year a U.S. district court in Topeka ruled that EuroAmerican settlement on Indian lands was not a crime. By 1923 (see MAP 416, *page 203*) all these Cherokee lands were gone.

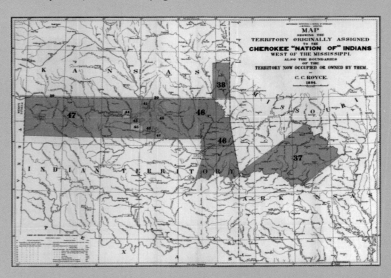

Populating a Heartland

The population of the United States increased from 5.3 million in 1800 to 17.1 million by 1840, and 31.4 million by 1860. Natural increase was aided by a rising tide of immigration. Between 1820 and 1860 over 5 million Europeans landed in the United States, fleeing famine and poverty in their native lands.

The construction of the Erie Canal, connecting the Hudson River with Lake Erie, which opened in 1825, coupled with the development of the steamboat, unlocked the entire Midwest for EuroAmerican settlement. A surge of westward migration began; it would last for nearly a century, not stopping until it had reached the Pacific Ocean. Not only did the canal give settlers easy access to the Midwest, but it gave the Midwest easy access to eastern, and indeed world, markets. The 363-mile-long canal caused freight rates to drop from $100 per ton to $10 per ton, and by 1841 a million bushels of wheat were transported east along the canal. In addition, as well as opening the Midwest, the canal assured the preeminence of New York over its rival, Montréal.

Although the Cumberland Road was completed west to Vandalia, Illinois, by 1838, it was a growing canal network that fueled growth in the Midwest until its role was usurped by railroads (see page 178).

Reaching the required population level, Indiana became a state in 1816, and Illinois two years later. Although at this time 40,000 people was the population level generally required for statehood, Illinois double-counted many to come up with a figure over 40,000; the population in 1818 was more likely only 35,000. Missouri became a state in 1821 only after the Missouri Compromise of 1820, which temporarily resolved a battle between pro-slave and anti-slave factions by balancing the admittance into

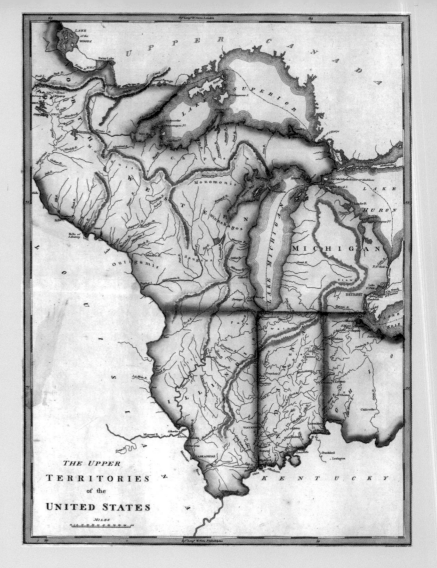

MAP 292 (*above*).
A map of the northern Midwest about 1815, showing the territories of Indiana, Illinois, and Michigan, and the Northwestern Territory, which would become Wisconsin and Minnesota. Illinois successfully petitioned Congress to extend its northern boundary forty-one miles farther north, to its current position, rather than accept it as a westward extension of the Indiana-Michigan line as shown here.

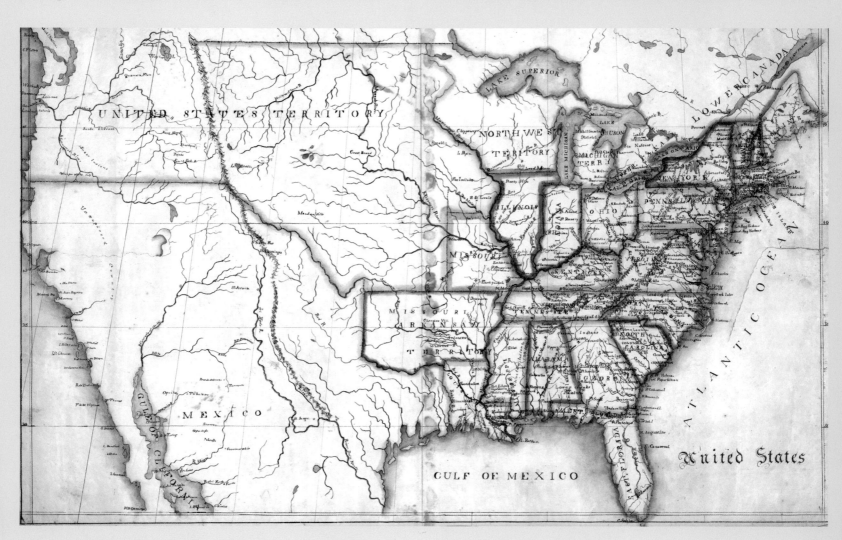

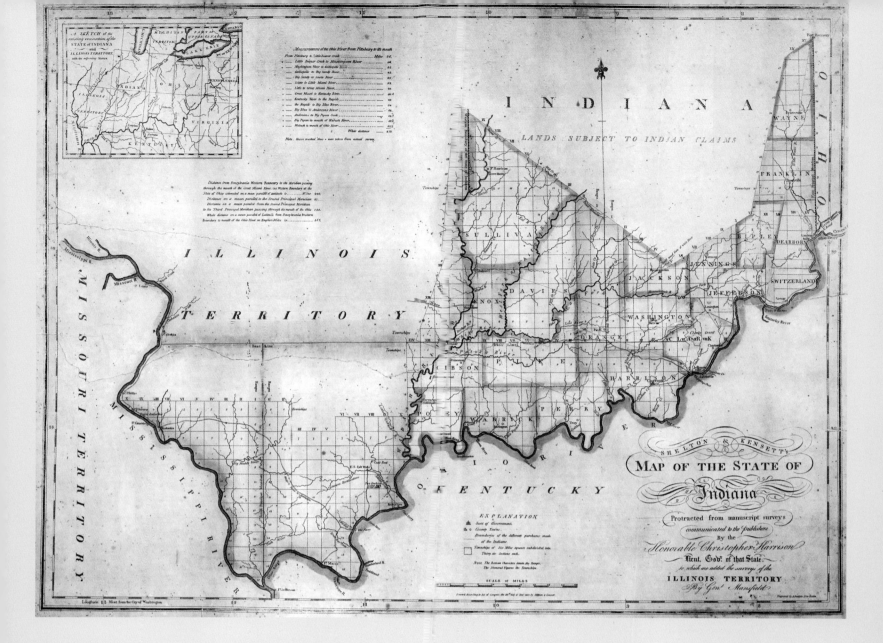

MAP OF THE STATE OF *Indiana*

Protracted from manuscript surveys
communicated to the Publishers
By the
Honorable Christopher Harrison
Lieut. Gov.' of that State.
to which are added the surveys of the
ILLINOIS TERRITORY
By Gen.' Mansfield.

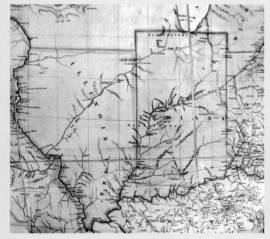

MAP 294 (*above*).
Only the southern part of Indiana, along the Ohio River, was substantially settled by EuroAmericans in 1816, when the territory achieved statehood. This map shows Indiana a year later, together with the settled parts of Illinois Territory, which would become a state in 1818.

MAP 295 (*left*).
This map by Aaron Arrowsmith, dated 1817, shows Indiana as a state and Illinois as a territory, but Indiana is again shown too far west. The northern boundary of Illinois Territory was supposed to be a line continued from the northern boundary of Indiana, but it is shown on this map even farther south. It was renegotiated to its present position (42°30′N) at statehood by the efforts of Illinois delegate Nathaniel Pope. Illinois was given an outlet to Lake Michigan around Fort Dearborn, which would later become Chicago (see page 198). This allowed the Illinois and Michigan Canal—authorized by Congress in 1822 and begun in 1836, but not completed until 1848—to be entirely within the state.

MAP 293 (*left*).
This map of the United States in 1822 shows Indiana, Illinois, and Missouri as states. Arkansas Territory, which was created out of Missouri Territory (itself the Louisiana Purchase less the state of Louisiana; see MAP 278, *page 138*) in 1819. The territory at first included much of what is today Oklahoma. Indiana is too far west, and Illinois, with its northern boundary correctly shown, is pinched by Indiana.

MAP 296 (*below*).
The completion of the Erie Canal in 1825 revolutionized access to the Midwest and ensured a steady flow of settlers from that time on. Begun in 1817, the canal was the brainchild of New York governor DeWitt Clinton. The canal ran from Albany, on the Hudson River, to Buffalo, on Lake Erie, a distance of 363 miles. The canal was 40 feet wide and only 4 feet deep. It was nonetheless able to carry an immense quantity of trade on shallow-bottomed canal barges. Between 1836 and 1862 the canal was enlarged to 70 feet wide and 7 feet deep. It was later enlarged again and route improvements were made several times. This map was published in a memoir written in 1825 for the New York City council to commemorate the opening of the canal; the memoir was presented to the mayor of the city. The Erie Canal is named the *Grand Canal.*

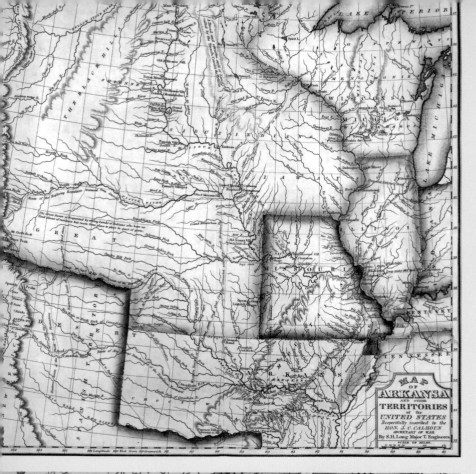

Map 297 (*left, top*).
This map of the area to the west of the Mississippi was published in 1822 and is based on the maps of Stephen H. Long (see page 117). It shows the boundary with Spanish territories from the Transcontinental Treaty of 1819 (see page 138); in 1821 Mexico achieved independence. Missouri is a state, created in 1821. Arkansas, here labeled *Arkansa*, was a larger territory than the state. Created in 1819, its area was reduced twice before statehood in 1836.

Map 298 (*above*).
The Midwest on an 1827 map. *Arkansa* is still enlarged, although by 1824 it had assumed the boundaries that would approximate those of the state.

Map 299 (*left*).
This 1835 map now shows Arkansas much reduced in size, with boundaries similar to those it would have when it became a state the following year. The brown area is Missouri Territory. The region that would become the state of Wisconsin in 1848 is named Huron Territory, one of the proposed names prior to territorial status in 1836.

Map 300 (*below*).
The "settled part" of Wisconsin Territory shown on an 1838 map, with an inset of the whole territory (shown yellow, pink, and green), stretching west to the Missouri. Wisconsin Territory was created in 1836.

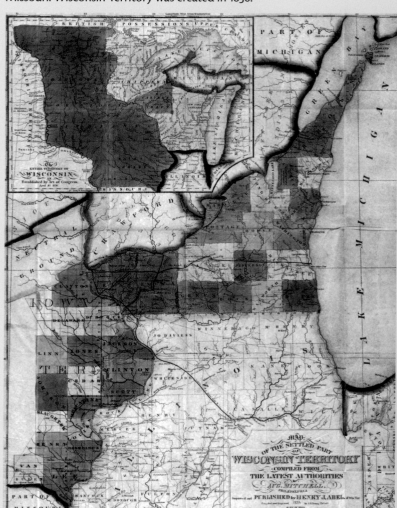

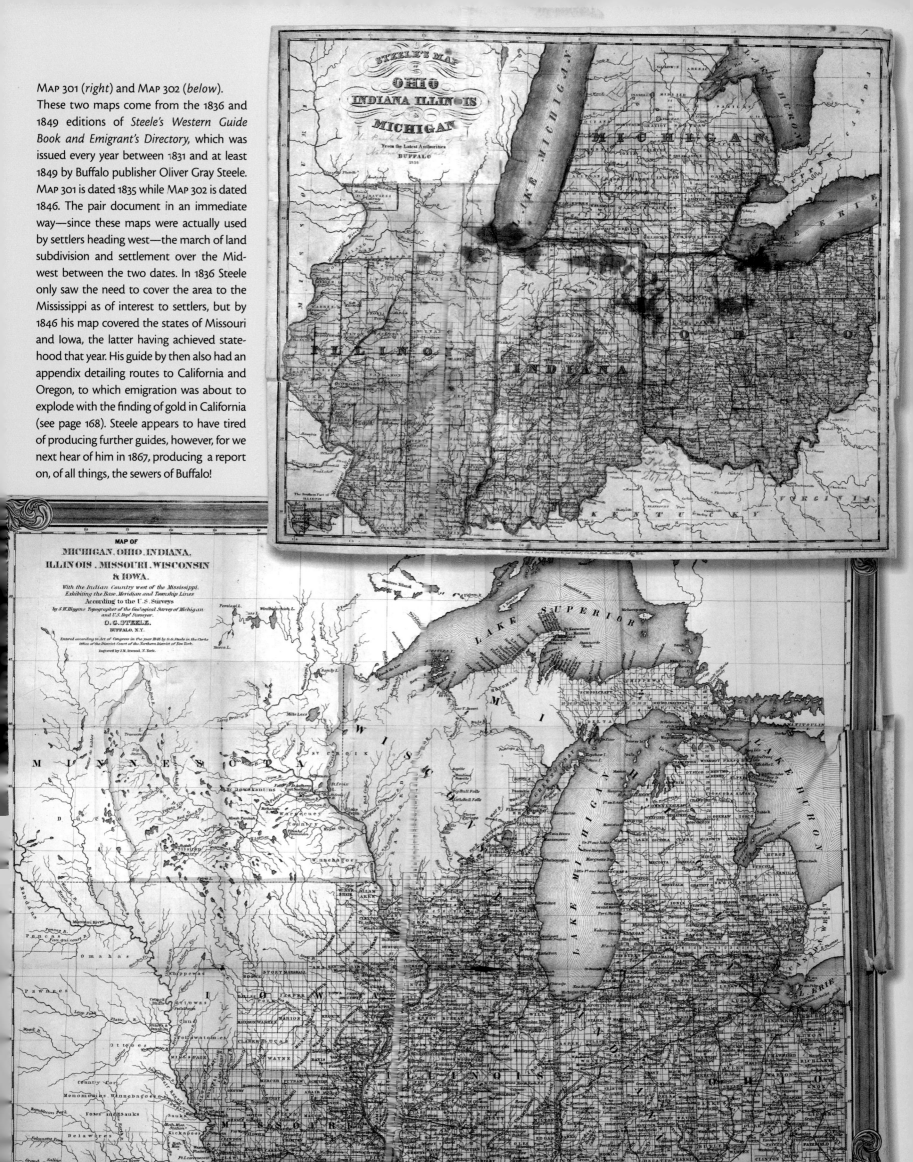

Map 301 (*right*) and Map 302 (*below*). These two maps come from the 1836 and 1849 editions of *Steele's Western Guide Book and Emigrant's Directory,* which was issued every year between 1831 and at least 1849 by Buffalo publisher Oliver Gray Steele. Map 301 is dated 1835 while Map 302 is dated 1846. The pair document in an immediate way—since these maps were actually used by settlers heading west—the march of land subdivision and settlement over the Midwest between the two dates. In 1836 Steele only saw the need to cover the area to the Mississippi as of interest to settlers, but by 1846 his map covered the states of Missouri and Iowa, the latter having achieved statehood that year. His guide by then also had an appendix detailing routes to California and Oregon, to which emigration was about to explode with the finding of gold in California (see page 168). Steele appears to have tired of producing further guides, however, for we next hear of him in 1867, producing a report on, of all things, the sewers of Buffalo!

MAP 303 (*above*).
The Midwest on a map published in 1851. Missouri, Arkansas, Iowa, and Wisconsin are by this date all states. Minnesota Territory was created in 1849, but to the west are *Part of the North-West Territory* and *Indian Territory*, both at this time unorganized. To the south is Texas. This is one of the first maps to show a completed railroad west of the Mississippi, that from St. Louis to Jefferson City, Missouri.

MAP 304 (*below*).
By the 1850s the railroad was creeping west and feeding settlement growth on the Plains. This map shows the network of lines, and proposed lines, by 1855, the date of this map. They connect the East with the Midwest, though interestingly the Central Route advertised here passes through Canada!

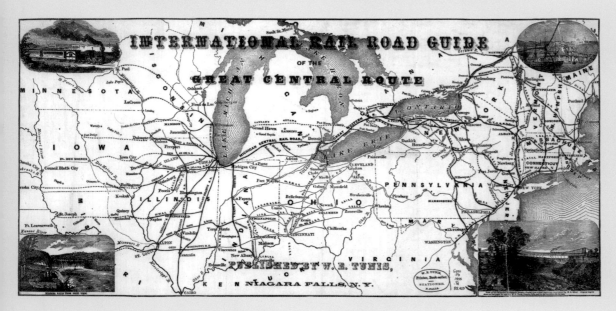

the Union of Maine as a non-slave state with Missouri as a slave state. Slavery was to be banned within the Louisiana Purchase area north of 36°30′. Arkansas was admitted as a state in 1836, Iowa in 1846, and Wisconsin in 1848.

Some of those moving west were searching for greater religious freedom. Mormons, led by founding leader Joseph Smith, trekked from Fayette, New York, to Kirtland, Ohio, in 1831; then to Missouri; and then, after continued non-Mormon persecution (the Missouri Mormon War), to the tiny settlement of Commerce, Illinois—which they renamed Nauvoo—in 1839. From there, in 1847–48, the Mormons would travel to the Great Salt Lake (see page 156).

The Sauk and the Fox of eastern Iowa had lost their Illinois lands in a disputed treaty signed in 1804. In May 1832 Chief Black Hawk led his people back to their homeland on the east bank of the Mississippi, where they found their ancestral villages destroyed. His return sparked near hysteria; the militia was mobilized and the U.S. Army ordered in. A series of battles followed in which Black Hawk's followers were slowly reduced in numbers. Black Hawk realized the futility of his situation and in August he attempted to recross the river, only to be attacked by the army and a steamboat; about four hundred men, women, and children were killed—by U.S. soldiers as well as militia—in what can only be described as an outrage. Black Hawk and the remnant of his men surrendered on 27 August.

Fighting Indians was, it seems, popular in the 1830s. The Black Hawk War advanced the careers of many men, including Zachary Taylor, Winfield Scott, and, most famously, a twenty-three-year-old militia captain named Abraham Lincoln, though he was not directly involved in the fighting. The Indians once again had punitive land cessions forced upon them; Scott and Illinois governor John Reynolds demanded most of eastern Iowa (see MAP 286, *page 142*). Black Hawk and other chiefs were sent in chains first to St. Louis (under the command of Jefferson Davis, later Confederate president) and then to Virginia, although they were eventually released once an impression had been made upon them of the overwhelming power of EuroAmerican society. The chiefs became celebrities in chains, and people flocked to see them wherever they went.

Most settlers in the territories were pleased to receive the autonomy that statehood conferred, although there was often bickering about precise state boundaries. Iowa Territory, however, at first refused statehood on the grounds that the boundaries of the new state would be too restrictive. Northern congressmen, at the time alarmed about the possibility of adding a number of (slave) states instead of a single Texas, tried to allow for the creation of a counterbalancing number of smaller (non-slave) states in the remaining unorganized and territorial areas of the North. Thus they proposed a state of Iowa that would have cut it off from the Missouri with a western boundary about a hundred miles east of the river. A majority of residents voted to reject statehood on the grounds that "mere arbitrary and artificial lines" cut off the "great rivers" deemed essential to the new state's well-being. The issue was resolved once Texas came into the Union as a single state in December 1845, and Iowa joined with larger boundaries a year later.

The vast westward movement of population in the first half of the nineteenth century is illustrated by the position of the nation's center of population (the point of minimum distance to the entire population). In 1800 it lay only eighteen miles west of Baltimore, Maryland, but by 1860, aided by far western as well as western settlement, it was in south central Ohio. The center of population had moved more than three hundred miles west in sixty years.

MAP 305 (below).
The area that would become the state of Iowa in 1846 is shown on this map from six years before. Land subdivision is creeping west from the Mississippi (at right), covering the region taken from the Indians after the Black Hawk War in 1832 (see page 142). The Missouri is at the extreme left edge of this map.

MAP 306 (below, bottom).
The state of Iowa in 1857. Subdivision and county names cover the entire state giving a distinctly more populated look than was the case on the ground.

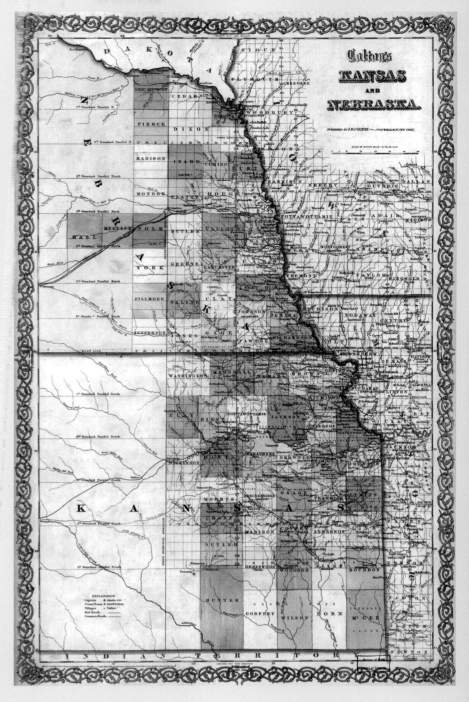

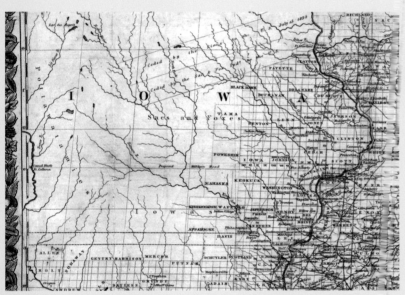

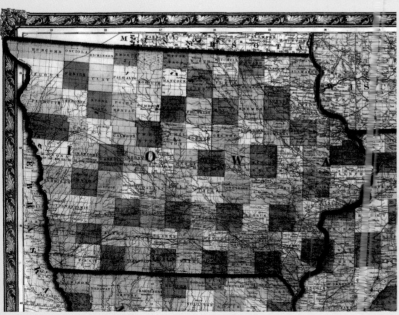

MAP 307 (above).
The advancing settlement frontier, as shown by land subdivision on this 1855 map of Kansas and Nebraska, has now crossed the Missouri on its way west. Both territories were much larger than the parts shown here. Kansas Territory extended west beyond Denver, and Nebraska Territory extended to the Rockies and the border with British North America. These territories were created in 1854 after lobbying by a leading Democrat, Stephen Douglas. This was the region through which a central option for a railroad would pass and was a compromise between the northern route proposed by hard-line antislavery factions and the southern line preferred by those who were pro-slavery. But Douglas's compromise permitted slavery in the two territories. The Kansas-Nebraska Act led to violence in Kansas when the slavery issue was put to a vote, when pro-slavery factions from Missouri tried to influence the vote. The apparently pastoral scene suggested by this map is deceptive; James "Wild Bill" Hickok wrote in 1858 of the lawlessness of Kansas: "Thare has been two awful fights in town this week . . . This is no place for women and children yet."

MAP 308 (right).
Similar evidence of EuroAmerican activity in the form of land subdivision is shown on this 1856 map of part of western Missouri as settlement creeps onto the Plains. The area shown is centered on today's Kansas City, which is not yet in evidence, but the town of Independence, first platted in 1827, is shown.

Remember the Alamo

In 1820 the Mexican government made what in the light of history seems like a huge mistake. At that time there were perhaps only about two thousand settlers in its province of Tejas, and to try to boost the region's growth, extensive land grants were offered to anyone—in particular citizens of the United States—who would bring in settlers to occupy the land.

Moses Austin, a Spanish-speaking merchant from Arkansas, took up the offer and was granted 200,000 acres to settle three hundred American families. He died before he could act on the grant, but his son, Stephen Fuller Austin, not only took up the grant but managed to get it expanded, despite opposition from a new government in Mexico City. Indeed, Austin was appointed *empresario* or administrative authority for Tejas. For a while he believed strongly in working with Mexico.

But the Mexican system proved too rigid for a changing situation. Frictions grew between the Mexican government and the Americans in Tejas, and in 1830 a new law prohibited further immigration, a hurdle Austin was able to circumvent. At a convention at San Felipe in 1833, the

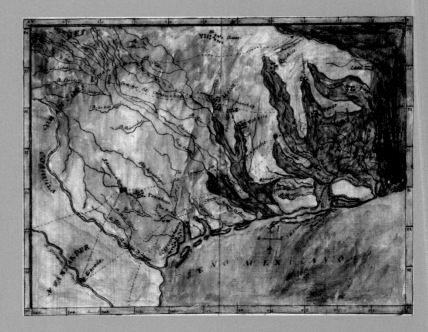

colonists drew up a proposed new constitution for Tejas as a Mexican state and persuaded Austin, against his better judgment, to take it to Mexico City. The Mexican president, the wily Antonio López de Santa Anna, who was to play many roles in Texan, Mexican, and American history, clapped Austin in jail for supposed treason. Released in July 1835, Austin returned to a homeland smouldering with discontent and soon issued a call to arms that ignited the Texas Revolution.

There had been unsuccessful revolts against Santa Anna's rule in other Mexican provinces, but in Tejas, because of the predominance of Americans, the outcome would be different.

The Texian (American Texan) army of which Austin took over loose command was a ragtag lot, ill-disciplined but enthusiastic. More by luck and determination than military strategy, they captured San Antonio de Béxar, the principal city, in December, despite its defense by a recently reinforced Mexican garrison commanded by Santa Anna's brother-in-law, Martín

Map 309 (*above*).
When Stephen Austin visited Texas in 1821–22 to locate the colonization grant to his father, Moses, he drew this map of settlements and the distribution of vegetation. Grasslands are yellow, woodlands blue-green.

Map 310 (*left*).
This map by Stephen Austin was published in 1827. It shows the land *Granted to Stephen F. Austin 1827* and *Austins Colony*. Also shown is *De Witt's Colony*, granted to Missourian Green De Witt in 1825. Note that the Spanish territory of Texas extends south only to the Nueces River. After 1824 Texas was administered with Coahuila, the province south of that river.

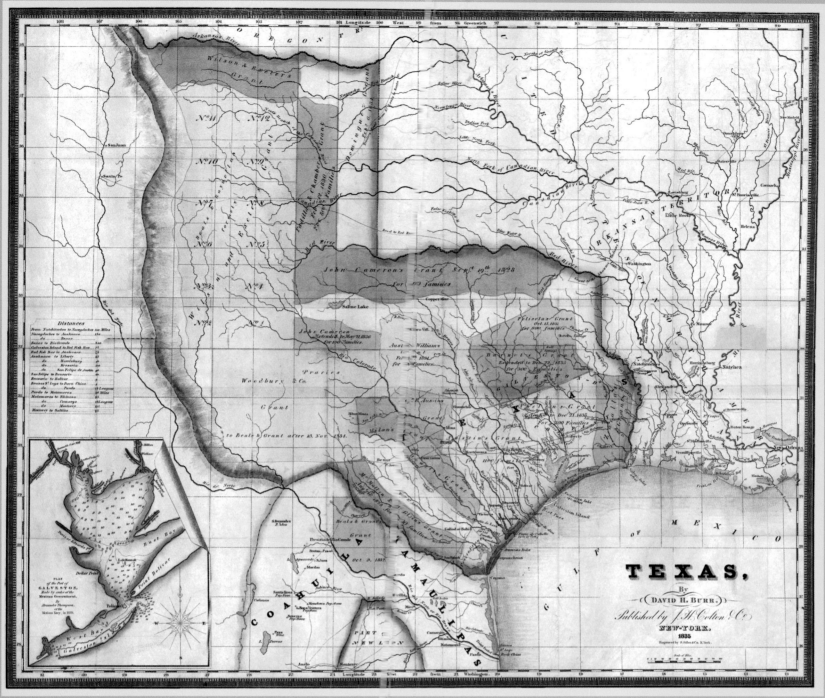

Perfecto de Cos. The fighting in San Antonio featured an innovative method of advance: burrowing through walls of houses to avoid the bullet-strafed streets. With the capture of San Antonio a Texian force took control of the nearby Alamo, a mission established by the Spanish in 1718 and used as a fortress since 1803 (Map 312, *right*). By February 1836 the Alamo had been reinforced by volunteers led by William Barret Travis, who had assumed overall command.

Santa Anna, meanwhile, had assembled an army of more than six thousand men and marched them overland through all weathers to suppress the revolution, arriving in San Antonio on 23 February. Travis knew what was coming and sent out messengers to appeal for assistance. Only thirty-two arrived. The main Texian army led now by Samuel Houston was not yet strong enough to fight its way through the Mexican army surrounding the Alamo.

The attack came at five in the morning on 6 March. It was an episode that has become both a Texan and American legend. The defenders, who included the famous American frontiersman Davy Crockett, fought bravely and to the last man, but all were cut down. Travis died early in the fighting. Only one or two slaves and some women and children were spared. Depending on the account, some 183 to 250 bodies were recovered from the Alamo after its capture. Some 300 to 400 Mexicans were killed and 300 wounded.

An initial declaration of independence had been made on 20 December 1835 after an October battle at Goliad, on the San Antonio River. Four days before the Alamo fell, a convention at Washington-on-the-Brazos (now but a village and a state park some sixty miles northwest of Houston) formally issued the Texan Declaration of Independence. The idea was to declare independence pending an application to join the United States, and indeed Austin had gone to the other Washington, on the Potomac, in December 1835 to present a case for union. He returned in June with the news that an application would not be received, the usual debate about the balance of slave and non-slave states having interfered. Texas statehood would be delayed for another nine years.

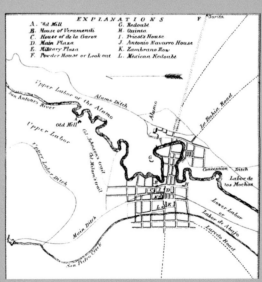

Map 311 (*above, top*).
Land grants in Texas in 1835, together with the number of families that were intended to be settled upon each. Of all the individuals named on the grants, only one, Manuel Lorenzo Justiniano de Zavala (*Zavalla's Grant* on the map), was a signatory to the Texas Declaration of Independence in March 1836. He was briefly the first vice-president of the Republic of Texas.

Map 312 (*above*).
San Antonio, showing the location of the Alamo. The map was drawn in 1855 for a history of Texas.

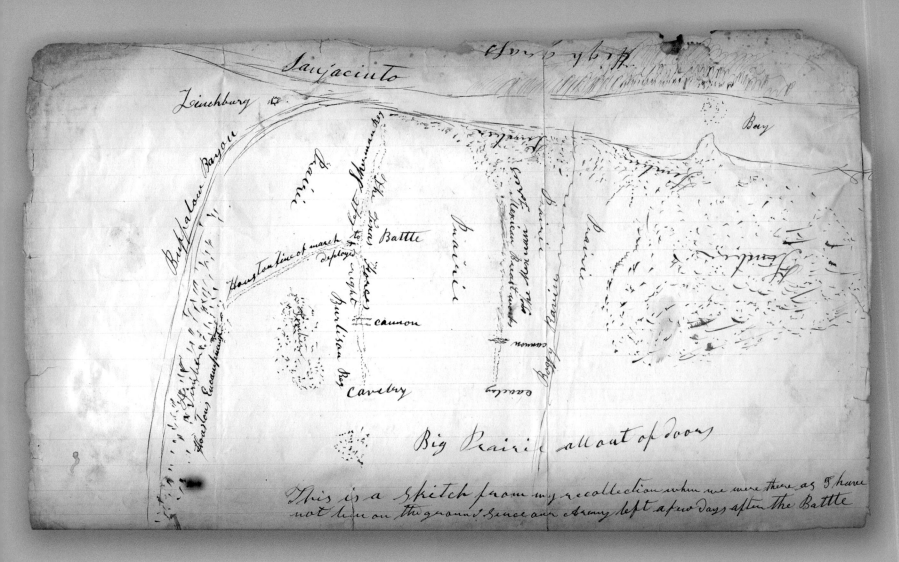

Map 313 (*above*).

This map of the 1836 Battle of San Jacinto, so pivotal to Texas history, was drawn by James Monroe Hill much later, in 1897. Hill in 1836 served in the First Regiment, Texas Volunteers, and fought in the battle. *Houston's Encampment* is at left, backed by Buffalo Bayou; *Houston's line of march* is indicated as is the site of the *Battle*, at center. The San Jacinto River is at top.

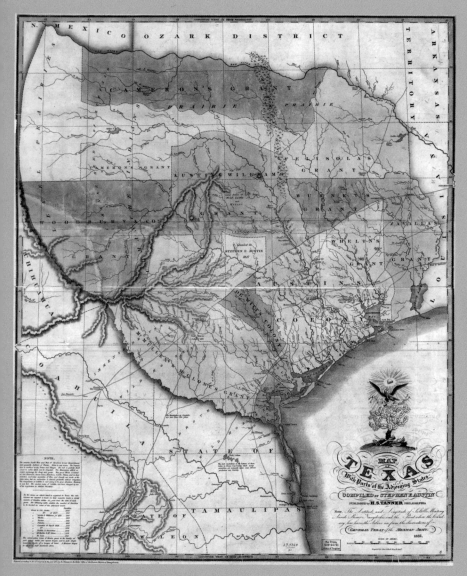

On 19 March 1836 Colonel James Fannin and 500 Texian troops were caught on the open plain by about 1,500 Mexican cavalry under General José Urrea. Surrounded and his position hopeless, Fannin surrendered. The prisoners were marched to Goliad, where orders were received from Santa Anna to execute all prisoners. About 340 defenseless Texians were brutally murdered on his orders. This sorry chapter, called the Goliad Massacre, would come back to haunt Santa Anna.

For the massacre only hardened the resolve of the Texians. On 20 April a 650-strong Mexican army led by Santa Anna himself caught up with the 900-strong Texian army led by General Sam Houston. Thinking that he had the Texians trapped, Santa Anna camped overnight less than 1,200 yards away, waiting for reinforcements led by Cos, who duly arrived the next morning with another 600 men, bringing the Mexican strength up to about 1,250. Still Santa Anna was not in a hurry, thinking he could choose the time for battle. Houston's army was on a sort of peninsula of land bounded at their backs by Buffalo Bayou and the San Jacinto River (Map 313, *above*), and so indeed had no easy way of retreating. But Houston had no intention of retreating; instead, taking advantage of the Mexicans' afternoon siesta, he led a surprise attack on the overconfident Santa Anna. "Remember the Alamo" and "Remember Goliad" was the cry. The whole affair was over in less than twenty minutes. Although brief, the fighting was fierce; Houston had two horses shot out from under him and took a bullet in the ankle. The Texians were in no mood for quarter and a bloodbath ensued, retaliation for the Alamo and Goliad. Houston gave

Map 314 (*left*).

An updated version of one of Stephen Austin's maps, published in 1837, showing the new independent Republic of Texas. The southern boundary is still the Nueces River.

up trying to control his men. "Gentlemen, I applaud your bravery, but damn your manners!" he is reputed to have shouted.

The next day a roundup of stragglers unearthed Santa Anna himself, disguised as a private. Hauled before Houston, he was treated surprisingly well considering all he was responsible for; Houston traded Santa Anna's life for the pullout of the four thousand Mexican troops in Texas and a treaty recognizing Texas independence.

The former happened, the latter did not. After the interim presidency of David Burnet in 1836, Sam Houston was elected president of the Republic of Texas for two years. He was succeeded by his archenemy, Mirabeau Lamar, who opposed annexation with the United States. Lamar emulated Andrew Jackson by conducting a fierce war against the Indians, which drove Texas Cherokee to Arkansas in 1839. Lamar also waged war against the Comanche, who had harassed settlers on the northern borders. In 1840 the Comanche were defeated at Plum Creek, twenty miles south of Austin, and, pursued northwest, at their village in what is now northern New Mexico.

In 1841 the pro-annexation Houston was once more elected president, and Anson Jones, Texas secretary of state from 1841 to 1844 and president from September 1844, worked to achieve either recognition of the Republic of Texas from Mexico or annexation with the United States. In November 1844, James Polk, an ardent expansionist, was elected president of the United States partly on a policy to annex Texas. A few days before he even took up his office the outgoing president, John Tyler, signed the bill authorizing the admission of Texas as a state. Jones, meanwhile, had also sent a final offer to Mexico City, but it was not until June 1845 that Jones's emissary finally returned with a signed treaty recognizing Texas as independent. A vote was then held in Texas to decide between the two options: continue as an independent republic or become a state of the United States. The people voted for annexation, and on 29 December 1845 Texas became the twenty-eighth state of the Union. Another previously Spanish territory, Florida, had been admitted earlier that year, and more once-Spanish domains—California and much of the Southwest—were to follow in the three years ahead, though not without another war, this time with the United States (see page 160).

Map 315 (*right, top*) and
Map 316 (*right, center*).

The plans for a capital city for the Republic of Texas laid out in 1839, creating the city of Austin (Map 315). It was formerly the small settlement of Waterloo, and was renamed in honor of Stephen Austin. Map 316 is a bird's-eye map from an 1840 book published in New York, *Texas in 1840 or the Emigrant's Guide to the New Republic*, by A.B. Lawrence.

Map 317 (*right*).
The 1846 edition of the first map of Texas as a state of the United States. It is an updated version of a series of previous maps of Texas produced by David Burr, who later became geographer to the U.S. Senate. Map 311, *page 151*, is another example. The land grants are still noted, but the most prominent feature is the strip of disputed territory between the River Nueces (here *Nuces*) and the Rio Grande (here *Rio Grande del Norte* or *Rio Bravo*). U.S. ownership of this would not be resolved until 1848, after the war with Mexico (see page 160). Burr was obviously confused by the location of the *Alama 1836*, which he has indicated on the Rio Grande rather than at San Antonio (here *San Antonia De Bexar*), its correct location. As with Map 311, the inset is an 1828 Mexican survey of Galveston Bay.

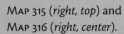

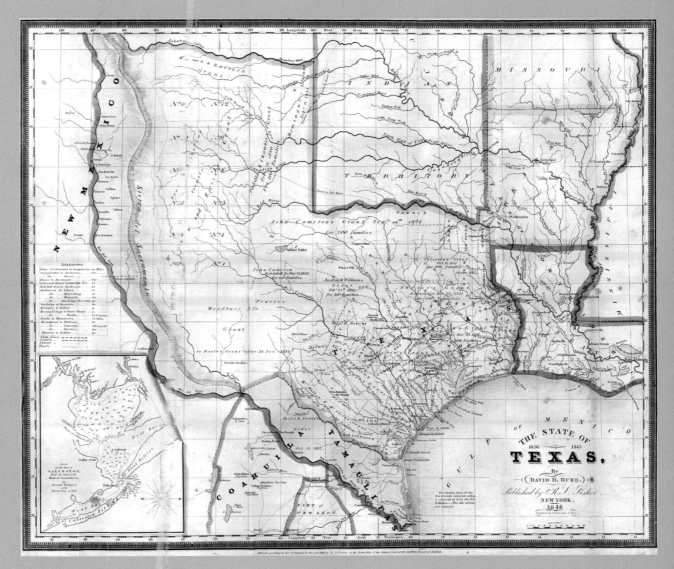

The Trail West

A trickle of westward migration in the 1830s turned into a flood by the end of the next decade. The travelers who had once sought furs were followed by those seeking souls, and then by those looking for land—the good land of Oregon's Willamette Valley or California's San Joaquin—or —as with the Mormons—merely for a place to settle free from religious persecution.

Robert Stuart in 1813 and Jedediah Smith in 1824 had discovered the critical South Pass across the Continental Divide, but the first to take loaded wagons through the pass was Captain Benjamin Louis Eulalie de Bonneville, in 1832. He was either pursuing an official mission to spy on the British fur traders or just having an adventure, we know not which. One of his men, Joseph Reddeford Walker, found Walker Pass in 1833–34: it would become one of the main emigrant routes across the Sierra Nevada into the San Joaquin Valley. While searching for a route through the mountains, it is thought that Walker found the Yosemite Valley with its impressive redwoods, though he realized it was no good as a route for wagons.

In 1829, Hall Jackson Kelley founded an organization called the American Society for Encouraging Settlement in the Oregon Territory. He considered that he had been chosen by God to lead a great migration west, and although he knew nothing of Oregon firsthand, he announced a plan to move three thousand New England farmers to the banks of the Columbia. The next year he published a very influential book, *A Geographical Sketch of that Part of North America, called Oregon*, in which he waxed lyrical about the virtues of the Northwest. Kelley gathered a small group together and set off for Oregon in 1832 via New Orleans, Mexico, and California. All of his followers had second thoughts on the way and dropped out, but traveling north through California he teamed up with a horse trader, Ewing Young, and others reputed to be horse thieves. As a result, when he arrived at Fort Vancouver the chief factor, John McLoughlin,

gave him a chilly reception, and Kelley did not stay; he returned to New England by ship in 1835. The importance of Kelley is not so much in what he did, however, as in his influence on others, for he awakened an interest in Oregon that induced many to travel west to seek his utopia.

Kelley was also responsible for the naming of a mountain. As part of his campaign to promote Oregon he proposed that the Cascades be renamed the Presidents Range, a bold move in light of the fact that Oregon was not yet part of the United States. The Cascades are still the Cascades, but Mount Adams, named after President John Adams, is Kelley's legacy.

Nathaniel Wyeth was influenced by Kelley. In 1831 he formed a company to seek a fortune in Oregon. The following year, guided by fur trader William Sublette, Wyeth's party became the first to negotiate what would come to be known as the Oregon Trail. The company supply ship, which was supposed to meet them at Fort Vancouver, never made it, and the company was disbanded. Three men, John Ball, Solomon Smith, and Calvin Tibbetts, stayed to become the first Americans to settle in Oregon, the latter two joining a small group of Hudson's Bay Company employees already farming in the fertile Willamette Valley.

Wyeth organized a second expedition to Oregon in 1834. This also failed, but with him was a missionary, Jason Lee, who ended up also settling in the Willamette and encouraged others to join him. Some fifty arrived in October 1839. Known as the Great Reinforcement, it set Oregon firmly on the path to annexation by the United States (see page 158).

Below. Kanesville, Iowa (now Council Bluffs), was the major jumping-off place for the Mormon and Oregon Trails in 1849–52. Here a sea of wagons wait to use the Mormon-installed ferry across the Missouri to continue their westward trek. Some waited as long as ten days to make the crossing. The painting is by William Henry Jackson, a photographer and artist who went west in 1866 and later used many of his photographs to document the Mormon migration. In 1870 Jackson became the photographer for the Hayden expedition (see page 204). The painting today is at Scotts Bluff National Monument.

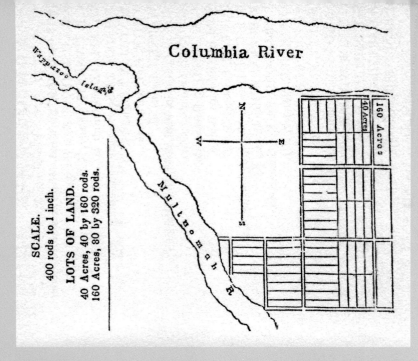

MAP 318 (*above*).
Hall Kelley's plan of a proposed city at the confluence of the Multnomah and the Columbia. Kelley was way ahead of his time, but later the city of Portland arose nearby, and spread to encompass Kelley's proposed site. The tip of the peninsula, on Pearcy Island, is today Kelley Point. It is now the location of Kelley Point Park, acquired by the City of Portland in 1979. The map appeared in Kelley's *General Circular to All Persons of Good Character Who Wish to Emigrate to the Oregon Territory*, published in 1831.

MAP 319 (*above*).
Charles Wilkes's map of Oregon, surveyed by the United States Exploring Expedition in 1841 and published in 1844. Added to Frémont and Preuss's maps, the additional knowledge of Oregon encouraged emigration to the Northwest.

In December 1834 the American Board of Commissioners for Foreign Mission received a petition from a young New England physician, Marcus Whitman, to go to Oregon to determine its suitability for missionary work. After a reconnaissance in 1835 as far as the Rockies, he set out the following year with his new wife, Narcissa, another missionary, Henry Spalding, and others, and they established missions in the interior. Whitman's is shown on MAP 320, *below*, a mission to the Cayuse Indians.

Returning from a trip east in 1843, Whitman guided nearly a thousand emigrants in wagons along the Oregon Trail. The first wagons had arrived at the Pacific only the year before. American migration to Oregon had begun in earnest.

Whitman's mission continued until 1847, when he and Narcissa and twelve others were massacred by the Indians they had labored to convert. The swelling tide of settlers had brought with it measles, to which the Indians were less immune, and Whitman had not succeeded in saving some of the chief's children from the disease. Whitman was killed in retribution. Subsequent punitive expeditions precipitated a minor war and the virtual extinction of the Cayuse as a separate tribe.

The United States Exploring Expedition under Charles Wilkes reached Oregon in 1841. This was a wide-ranging and circumnavigating American government scientific expedition charged in Oregon with assessing its use to the United States. The voluminous reports by both Wilkes and

MAP 320 (*below, left*) and MAP 321 (*below, right*).
John Frémont's topographer Charles Preuss produced a seven-section map of the Oregon Trail in 1846. An amazing ten thousand copies were ordered by Congress specifically to promote emigration to Oregon, the part of which that is now the states of Washington and Oregon, having officially become part of the United States that year (see page 158). MAP 320 is part of the westernmost section, ending at *Fort Wallah-Wallah* (now Walla Walla, Oregon). Nearby is *D*ʳ *Whitman*, the location of the Whitman mission. MAP 321 is the fourth section, showing the Continental Divide and the route through South Pass. Note the *Waters of the Pacific* on the left and the *Waters of the Atlantic* on the right.

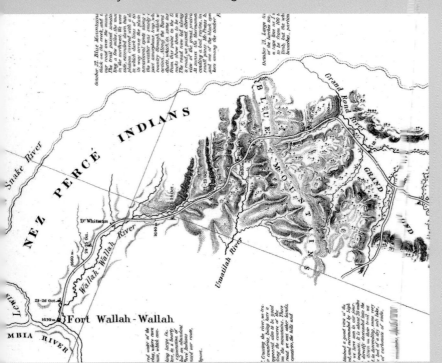

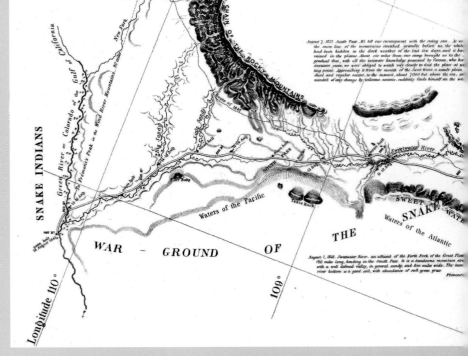

the scientists of the expedition were published in 1844 and added much to American knowledge of the Northwest.

The exact route of the Oregon Trail became much more widely known in 1846 with the publication of a series of sectional maps on a large scale, ordered by Congress to facilitate emigration to Oregon. They were drawn by Charles Preuss, surveyor to one of the more colorful figures in American history, John Charles Frémont, who, as an officer in the U.S. Army Corps of Topographical Engineers, had been ordered in 1842 to survey the trail. He hired mountain man Kit Carson and set off to South Pass, where he dramatically unfurled the flag of the United States on the highest point he could find—and made sure the event was recorded in an engraving in his report the following year. It established his reputation as "The Pathfinder." He later explored the California Trail and ranged extensively over the West, publishing in 1848 what was then the most accurate map of the entire West. MAP 322, *below,* is a section of this map. Frémont was in search of glory any way he could find it, and in 1846 he became involved in the setting up of the California Republic (see page 160). For a while he was the darling of the American public. He made and lost millions investing in railroads and ran, unsuccessfully, for president.

The first emigrant wagon company, led by John Bidwell, traveled west in 1841. Some of the party continued to Oregon; others, including Bidwell, followed the

Persecution of Mormons in Nauvoo, Illinois, which culminated in the killing of church leader Joseph Smith by a mob in 1844, forced Mormons to flee west. Under the guidance of their new leader, Brigham Young, they planned a mass migration to the West, far enough away to escape religious persecution once and for all. Young read about the valley of the Great Salt Lake, which he favored as being more isolated than California or Oregon. In 1846 many Mormons moved to Winter Quarters, on the west bank of the Missouri in what is now Florence, a suburb of Omaha, Nebraska. Then, the following year, with Frémont and Preuss's newly published sectional maps of the Oregon Trail in hand, the exodus west began.

The Mormon Trail, as it became known, was the same route as the Oregon Trail for much of its distance. It follows the Platte all the way from the Missouri and after about 150 miles joins the Oregon Trail, which cuts north

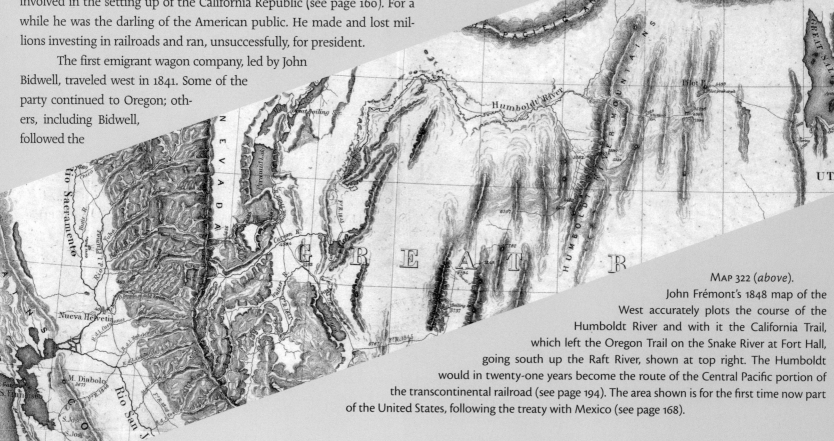

MAP 322 (*above*). John Frémont's 1848 map of the West accurately plots the course of the Humboldt River and with it the California Trail, which left the Oregon Trail on the Snake River at Fort Hall, going south up the Raft River, shown at top right. The Humboldt would in twenty-one years become the route of the Central Pacific portion of the transcontinental railroad (see page 194). The area shown is for the first time now part of the United States, following the treaty with Mexico (see page 168).

Bear River south from what is today Soda Springs, Idaho, round the north end of the Great Salt Lake and on to California. Their wagons did not make it the whole way, but the emigrants did, continuing on horseback.

A book published in 1845, Lansford Hasting's *Emigrant's Guide to Oregon and California,* described a shortcut around the southern end of the Great Salt Lake. In 1846 one emigrant party, the Donners, took the cutoff, but although it was shorter it proved difficult and took longer, and this meant that by the time they reached Truckee Pass—now the Donner Pass—across the Sierras, it was late October. They were trapped by heavy snowfall and forced to dig in for the winter. Supplies dwindled, and a group of fifteen clawed their way west toward Fort Sutter to look for help. When rescuers did finally reach the trapped emigrants in February 1847 they encountered a scene of horror. Those living had survived after they had consumed everything else only by eating their dead. Some forty-five members of the Donner party died in the mountains that winter.

from the Kansas River, via the Blue and the Little Blue rivers and a 25-mile overland trek to the Platte.

A vanguard group, the Mormons' Pioneer Company, with Brigham Young at its head, left Winter Quarters on 5 April 1847, with the main body of Mormons not far behind. On 24 July Young's company came within sight of the Great Salt Lake, and Young confirmed that this was the place his followers would settle. A site for a town was selected, and Young supervised the laying out of a wide north-south and east-west road grid—Salt Lake City (MAP 324, *right*).

Every year after that, until the railroad arrived in 1869, the Mormons organized increasingly sophisticated wagon and then handcart convoys to move new emigrants from the latest railhead to Utah.

The exact number of emigrants who headed west on the emigrant trails is not known, but some estimates suggest that between 1840 and the coming of the railroad in 1869 as many as half a million people crossed the Continental Divide looking for a better life on the other side of the mountains. The migration created the West—and ensured that it became part of the United States.

MAP 323 (*right*).
Commercial mapmaker Samuel Augustus Mitchell's 1846 map of the West marks and names the Oregon route but not the California Trail, which was better defined by Frémont's 1848 map (MAP 322, *left*). At bottom left is a table giving the distances to various places on the Oregon Trail, including the complete distance from the Missouri to Fort Vancouver, 2,024 miles. The map shows the entire Oregon Country north to 54°40′—the forty-ninth parallel boundary was agreed upon in 1846 (see next page), and Mexican territory extends to 42°N, as it would until the end of the Mexican War.

MAP 324 (*below*).
The newly laid out street grid for Great Salt Lake City is shown on this 1850 map. The lake is at top left.

MAP 325 (*below, right*).
In 1849 the Mormons organized the Provisional State of Deseret, with Brigham Young as its governor. Young had intended that Deseret apply as a territory but changed his mind when he heard that California and New Mexico were applying as states. The original proposal for Deseret encompassed not only the area shown on this 1850 map but also most of southern California. In September 1850 Utah Territory was created from the northern portion of the proposed Deseret, part of the Compromise of 1850 (see page 183), which dealt, once again, with the decisive issue of slave versus non-slave states. The idea of a Mormon state lingered until the railroad brought in many non-Mormon settlers.

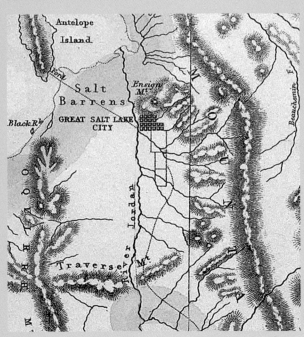

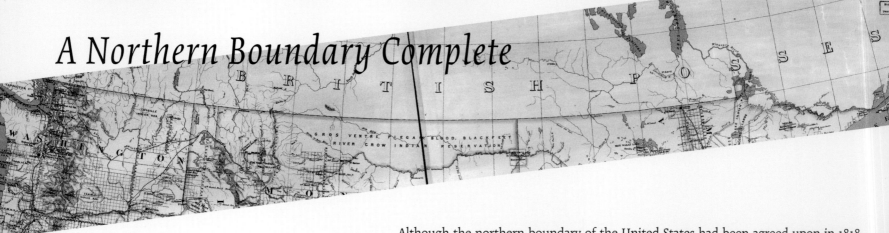

MAP 326 (*above and right, top, center*).
The northern boundary of the continental United States (except for Alaska) is complete for the first time on this 1873 map, the final boundary question, that of the San Juan Islands, having been settled the year before. The forty-ninth parallel extends westward to the mainland shore.

Although the northern boundary of the United States had been agreed upon in 1818, after the War of 1812, the boundaries of Maine in the east and Oregon in the west remained undetermined. In 1830, the Maine–Quebec–New Brunswick boundary dispute was submitted to the king of the Netherlands for arbitration, but he decided on a compromise between the two boundary claims, which was rejected by the United States as being beyond his mandate. The king had in any case lost his job to a revolution in Belgium by the time he handed down his decision.

In 1842 Britain and the United States agreed to negotiate. The American commissioner was Daniel Webster, the secretary of state, and the British commissioner Alexander Baring, Baron Ashburton, a famous banker. The pair hammered out an agreement that accepted the northern boundary that had been the king of the Netherlands' decision eleven years before, but the northwest Maine-Quebec boundary was adjusted in favor of Britain away from the St. Lawrence, as Webster recognized that the security of this vital water route to the interior was of paramount importance to Britain. Even so, Ashburton was ridiculed in Britain for negotiating a poor deal. The claims of each country and the resulting agreed boundary are shown on MAP 327, *left*. The 1842 Webster-Ashburton Treaty also defined for the first time the boundary from Lake Huron to Lake of the Woods, from whence the forty-ninth parallel west had been defined by the 1818 Convention.

The boundary west of the Rockies had been left undefined in 1818 and the Oregon Country, the area that is now Oregon, Washington, and British Columbia, was left as a region of so-called joint occupancy. Until the 1830s, for all practical purposes this had left the Oregon Country to Britain's North West Company and its successor the Hudson's Bay Company, which had set up its headquarters on the Columbia at Fort Vancouver (MAP 329, *below*). American fur traders had generally been few and far between, but once American missionaries and then settlers began to arrive, the situation changed, for the British fur traders rapidly became outnumbered.

As early as 1838, a bill was introduced into the U.S. Senate "authorizing the occupation of the Columbia or Oregon River . . . to be called Oregon Territory," by ardent Oregon

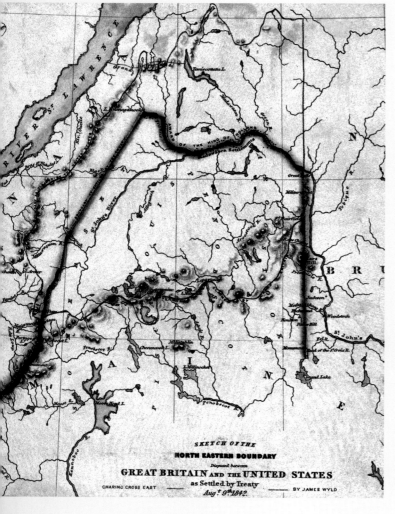

SKETCH OF THE
NORTH EASTERN BOUNDARY
Disputed between
GREAT BRITAIN AND THE UNITED STATES
as Settled by Treaty
CHARING CROSS EAST   Aug.ˢᵗ 9ᵗʰ 1842   BY JAMES WYLD

MAP 327 (*above*).
London mapmaker James Wyld published this map in 1842 to illustrate the settlement reached in the Webster-Ashburton Treaty. The thin red line at the top, close to the St. Lawrence, is the boundary claimed by the United States, while the similar thin red line in the middle of the map is the boundary claimed by Britain. The orange and green line is the final boundary.

MAP 328 (*below, left*).
The plat of Oregon City, surveyed and drawn by Hudson's Bay Company surveyor Adolphus Lee Lewes in 1844, the year it became the first city to incorporate west of the Rockies.

MAP 329 (*below*).
British lieutenant Mervin Vavasour drew this map of Fort Vancouver and its environs in 1845 as part of his survey of the country in preparation for a possible war over the boundary question.

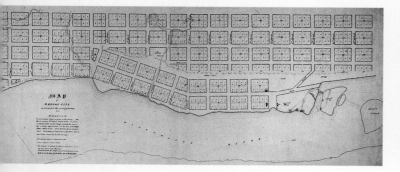

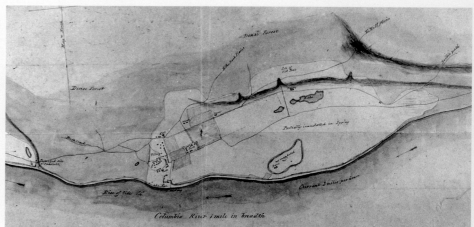

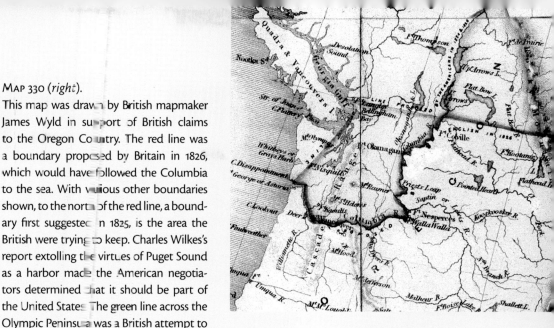

MAP 330 (*right*).
This map was drawn by British mapmaker James Wyld in support of British claims to the Oregon Country. The red line was a boundary proposed by Britain in 1826, which would have followed the Columbia to the sea. With various other boundaries shown, to the north of the red line, a boundary first suggested in 1825, is the area the British were trying to keep. Charles Wilkes's report extolling the virtues of Puget Sound as a harbor made the American negotiators determined that it should be part of the United States. The green line across the Olympic Peninsula was a British attempt to keep the United States away from Vancouver Island, to which the Hudson's Bay Company retreated in 1843, once it became clear that Puget Sound could not be saved.

booster Senator Lewis Linn of Missouri. The map accompanying this bill showed a boundary that continued the forty-ninth parallel west through Vancouver Island. But the time was not yet right, and the bill failed. Linn tried again in 1841, this time with a 54°40´N boundary, but again the bill did not pass.

It was the opening of the western emigration floodgates in 1843 that ultimately led to the annexation of Oregon. That year American settlers at Champoeg, in the Willamette Valley, who had two years before been meeting to determine how to control wolves, met and decided to set up a provisional government. A representative was sent to Washington, D.C., to petition for the region to be made a territory of the United States. The petition was not then acted upon, but the pressure was building. In 1844 Oregon City became the first incorporated city west of the Rockies (MAP 328, *far left, bottom*). Its site had been selected by Fort Vancouver chief factor John McLoughlin for a Hudson's Bay Company lumber mill in 1829. McLoughlin, contrary to his superior's wishes, encouraged the American settlers, earning him the popular moniker of the Father of Oregon.

The British could clearly see that the Americans wanted Oregon, perhaps even to 54°40´, and in preparation for a possible war two army officers from Lower Canada, Mervin Vavasour and Henry Warre, were sent to Oregon to survey and report—spy, really—on strategic positions. Vavasour prepared a map of Fort Vancouver (MAP 329, *left, bottom*) for his report.

But in reality both Britain and the United States wanted to avoid a war over the Oregon Country. Britain thought it too remote, and the United States was about to go to war with Mexico. And so a negotiated settlement became possible. New president James Polk blustered about "54°40´ or fight!" and a mild-mannered British foreign secretary, Lord Aberdeen, was only concerned about protecting the interests of the Hudson's Bay Company. After some proposals and counterproposals, Aberdeen suggested the extension of the forty-ninth parallel, except for Vancouver Island, on which the company had built a new fort and possible headquarters at Fort Victoria. Polk accepted, and Oregon—below 49°—was American.

Except for one hiccup. The boundary line in the resulting 1846 Treaty of Washington was defined between Vancouver Island and the mainland as "the middle of the channel," but this itself was contentious. In 1858 it almost came to a war once more when an American settler on San Juan Island shot a pig belonging to the Hudson's Bay Company. The so-called Pig War turned into a fourteen-year standoff, with a British military camp at the north end of the island and an American one at the south end. In 1871, the boundary question was sent to an arbitrator, this time the German kaiser, Wilhelm I, who established a three-man commission to make the decision. In October 1872 the arbitrator awarded the San Juan Islands completely to the United States.

In 1850 the Donation Land Claim Act was passed to promote settlement in Oregon Territory, which had finally been created in 1848. By granting free land it was a forerunner of the wider Homestead Act of 1862 and was responsible for boosting the growth of the Northwest yet more.

MAP 331 (*below*).
This commercial map published in January 1846 is of the *Disputed Territory of Columbia or Oregon*. The thin red line is the American proposal for a boundary continuing the forty-ninth parallel through Vancouver Island.

MAP 333 (*below*).
The three boundaries through the San Juan Islands from which the arbitrator, Kaiser Wilhelm of Germany, had to decide in 1872. He chose the westernmost line and made all the San Juan Islands American.

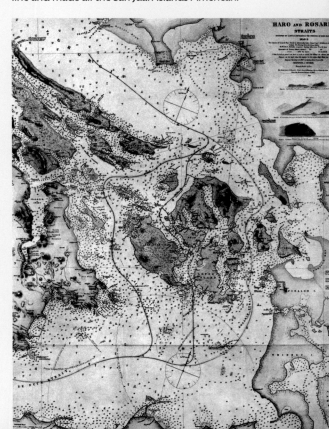

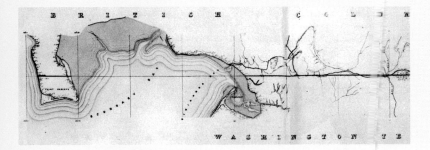

MAP 332 (*left*).
The westernmost extent of the forty-ninth parallel boundary created a cutoff peninsula of United States territory, Point Roberts, today twenty-two miles by road from the rest of Washington.

War with Mexico

The expansionist president James Polk brought Texas into the United States in 1845 and was negotiating the acquisition of Oregon. He also coveted the Mexican province of Upper California. At first he tried to negotiate a purchase, but when in the summer of 1845 the Mexicans looked set to invade the new state of Texas, Polk acted. He ordered General Zachary Taylor and a thirty-five-hundred-strong so-called army of observation into southwest Texas; a formal declaration of war was made on 13 May only after hostilities had commenced.

In mid-1845 Polk sent secret instructions to the U.S. naval squadron in the Pacific ordering the seizure of Californian ports should war be declared against Mexico. He also told the American consul in Monterey, Thomas Larkin, to try to arrange a "revolt" of American settlers. This plan was turned on its head by the arrival in California in January 1846 of the explorer and adventurer John Charles Frémont, determined to find glory. With him were sixty-two men, probably the most efficient military force in California at the time.

1,600 men, taken Santa Fe without a fight on 18 August, and had then declared New Mexico annexed to the United States. Kearny sent the majority of his army south to join up with Taylor's army, by then heavily engaged with the Mexicans. He received the news that California had fallen and so continued west with only about a hundred men.

But the Californian adventure had not gone all the way of Frémont and Stockton, for the *Californios* who had initially backed the Americans had had a change of heart, and Los Angeles and San Diego had been recaptured, although the latter had been taken once more a few days later. As Kearny neared San Diego he bungled an attack on a smaller force of *Californios* at the village of San Pasqual on 6 December, and twenty-two of his men died in the melee. The rest of his beleaguered band was only saved by over two hundred naval men marching out from San Diego.

Stockton and Kearny's forces soon set out north to retake Los Angeles, engaging the Mexicans on 8 January 1847 at the San Gabriel River and again the following day on the plain of La Mesa; the latter is some-

MAP 334 (*above*).
A hybrid view-map of San Francisco, the former settlement of Yerba Buena, in 1846–47. *A* is the uss *Portsmouth*; *B* other American naval vessels; *C* merchantmen. Montgomery Street, named after John B. Montgomery, captain of the *Portsmouth*, is shown here on the shoreline. It is now several blocks inland.

Even today Frémont's motives are not very clear. In February he raised the American flag near Monterey, then had second thoughts and retreated to the Oregon border. There he learned of a revolt by American settlers in Sonoma. They declared independence during what has become known as the Bear Flag Revolt, after the bear on a hastily painted flag of the California Republic. Frémont rushed back to California and became leader of the rebels. The U.S. Pacific squadron, having heard of the declaration of war with Mexico, followed instructions and seized Monterey and San Francisco. Frémont joined forces in an uneasy liaison with the naval forces under Commodore Robert F. Stockton and set off to take Los Angeles and San Diego. On 17 August 1846 Stockton proclaimed the U.S. annexation of California, with himself as governor.

Meanwhile, Polk, having become concerned about the buccaneering of Frémont and Stockton, dispatched an army under Colonel Stephen Watts Kearny. Kearny had left Bent's Fort, on the Arkansas River, on 2 August with

MAP 335 (*above, top*).
Kearny's route near San Diego in late 1846, with the location of the Battle of San Pasqual, shown on a map by William Emory, a topographical engineer with Kearny's command.

MAP 336 (*above*).
Another detail of Emory's map shows the locations of the Battle of San Gabriel and the Battle of Los Angeles (or La Mesa).

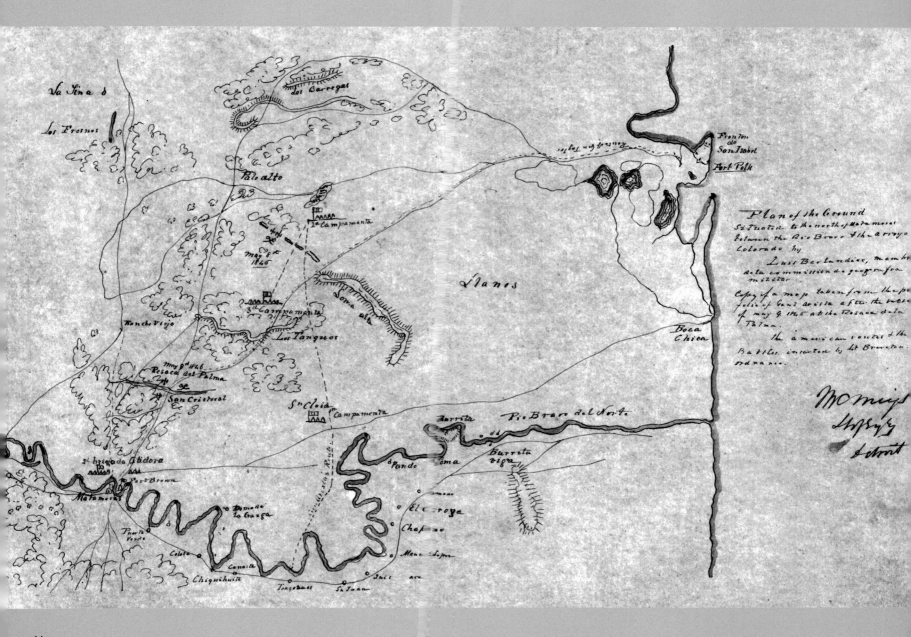

MAP 337.
This map shows the region of the first major engagements of the Mexican War. The river is the Rio Grande, with Matamoros on the southern bank and the American fort opposite. Fort Polk at San Isabel is shown on the coast; this was the American supply point. The locations of the battles at Palo Alto and Resaca de la Palma, both straddling the road between San Isabel and Matamoros, are also shown. The map is an American copy of one captured from the Mexican commander General Arista after the Battle of Resaca de la Palma on 9 May 1846

times called the Battle of Los Angeles. On 10 January Los Angeles was re-occupied. Frémont, coming south with four hundred men, encountered the Mexicans just north of Los Angeles on 13 January and induced their leader, José María Flores, to sign a capitulation, the Treaty of Cahuenga. With this, California was in American hands.

But in whose hands, precisely, was not certain for a while. Kearny had orders from Polk to set up a civil government with himself as governor, but Stockton refused to turn over command and appointed Frémont governor. Frémont in turn refused to accept orders from Kearny. Then Colonel Richard Mason arrived to take over from Stockton, and he immediately accepted Kearny's orders. Poor Frémont was ordered back east with Kearny when he left in June, and was arrested and court-martialed for mutiny. Polk could hardly accept this for a man in large part responsible for the American acquisition of California, and he remanded the sentence of dismissal from the army. An outraged Frémont resigned anyway.

Although highly significant in its consequences, the conflict in California was a minor skirmish in military terms compared to that simultaneously developing along the Rio Grande, or that which would take place in 1847 nearer to the Mexican capital.

General Zachary Taylor and his army were by October 1845 encamped on the coast of Texas and the following spring received orders to advance to the Rio Grande. They arrived at Matamoros and built a fort across the river from a larger Mexican army. But the Mexicans did nothing until the end of April, when a force of elite lancers was sent across the river north of the city and easily defeated an American cavalry patrol. However, when the report of this skirmish reached President Polk fourteen days later, it allowed him to proclaim on 13 May that "by the act of the Republic of Mexico, a state of war exists," resulting in a formal declaration of war.

As was often the case in those days of slow communication, events had already overtaken words. The Mexican cavalry covered a mass crossing of the Rio Grande by 2,500 infantrymen and artillery. Mariano Arista, the Mexican commander, intended to cut off Taylor's supply line to the coast at San Isabel (Fort Polk). Leaving five hundred men in his fort, Taylor hurried to the coast. The fort endured a five-day-long pounding by the Mexicans but did not fall. Taylor, now with 2,228 men to the Mexicans' 4,000, was cut off at a place called Palo Alto by a mile-long line of infantry and artillery. Here, on 8 May, was fought the first major battle of the war. The more modern techniques of warfare practised by the Americans, and the fine leadership of Zachary Taylor, won the day. Particularly decisive were teams of highly mobile artillery that often prevented the Mexicans reloading their cannon. The American army lost only five men killed and

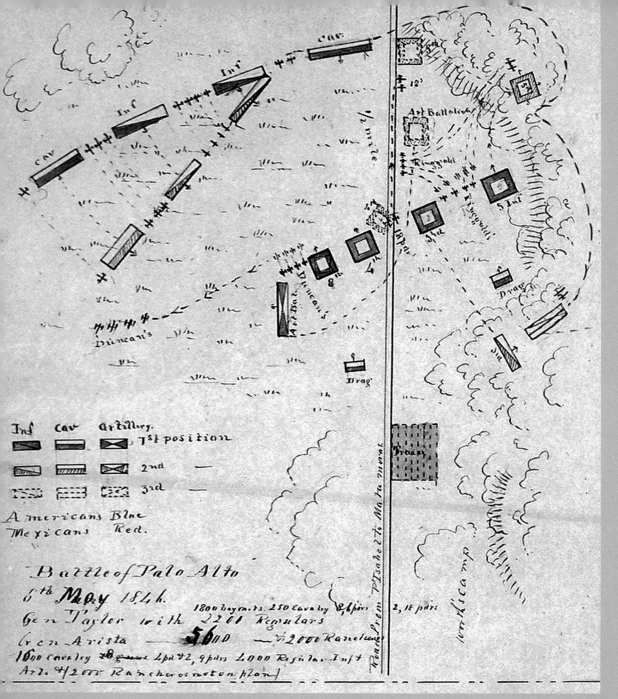

Inf Cav Artillery.
                       7st position
                       2nd ———
                       3rd - - -

Americans Blue
Mexicans Red.

Battle of Palo Alto
6th May 1846.
Gen Taylor with 2201 Regulars
Gen Arista — 5600 — + 2000 Rancheros
1600 Cavalry &c 2pr +2, 9prs, 4000 Regular Inft
Art. + 2000 Rancheros not on plan/

MAP 338 (*above*).
The Battle of Palo Alto, an American victory fought 8 May 1846.

MAP 339 (*below*).
The Battle of Resaca de la Palma, really a continuation of the battle the next day, 9 May 1846. This was also a victory for Zachary Taylor's army.

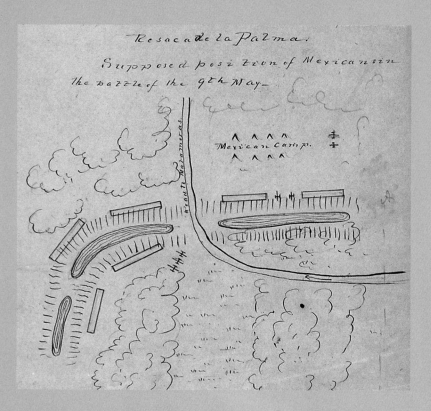

forty-three wounded, whereas Mexican losses were seven times these.

The next day Arista withdrew his army to a new position nearby that he thought impregnable, flanking the road to Matamoros through a narrow ravine called the Resaca de la Palma, cutting off Taylor from his fort on the Rio Grande. Here another battle was fought. But the result was the same. The Mexicans were routed and sent fleeing toward the Rio Grande, fighting among themselves for the two boats that were on the river. Taylor's men reported 33 dead and 89 wounded; the Mexican casualties were reported to be over a thousand. The Americans also captured Arista's silver dinner set.

After a few days of regrouping, resupplying, and tending to the wounded, Taylor sent his army across the Rio Grande. The Mexicans had fled Matamoros, and the Americans occupied the city without a further fight. Here Taylor paused to plan his next step.

A former Mexican president, Antonio López de Santa Anna, was at this time in exile in Cuba. He persuaded the American government that if they allowed him through the naval blockade, he would begin peace talks. When he was permitted through, he instead began to rebuild and retrain the Mexican army.

Taylor's next objective was the fortified city of Monterrey, nearly two hundred miles west of Matamoros. Getting there was more difficult than he had considered, for 1,500 American soldiers died of dysentery and yellow fever before it was reached. And it represented a formidable objective once the American army attacked—indeed, the Mexicans thought it impregnable. The city was guarded by two fortified hills that would also have to be taken if an assault was to be successful.

Monterrey was the scene of the most savage fighting in the war to that date. The attack began on 21 September and was almost immediately repulsed. Three days of determined and bloody fighting from building to building were required to take the city. At one point gunners were reduced to hauling their cannon into the middle of a street with ropes *after* loading and lighting the fuse; to attempt to ready the gun in the street was to invite instant death. In the end it was a strange mixture of luck and pluck that won the day. Monterrey fell on 25 September.

Zachary Taylor became an immediate hero—too much so for Polk, who thought (correctly) that Taylor might run for president. Polk ordered

MAP 340 (*right, top*).
This rather superb Mexican map shows the Battle of Cerro Gordo, west of Veracruz, Mexico, fought on 18 April 1847, when the Mexican army blocked the road from Veracruz to Mexico City in a terrain full of narrow ravines. The result was a stunning victory for the Americans. The Mexican army is at the left, the American at the right. The *Camino de Veracruz* is the road, while the river, unnamed here, is the Rio del Plan. The illustration (*right, bottom*) is an American interpretation of the battle published soon after to feed a voracious public appetite for news of the war.

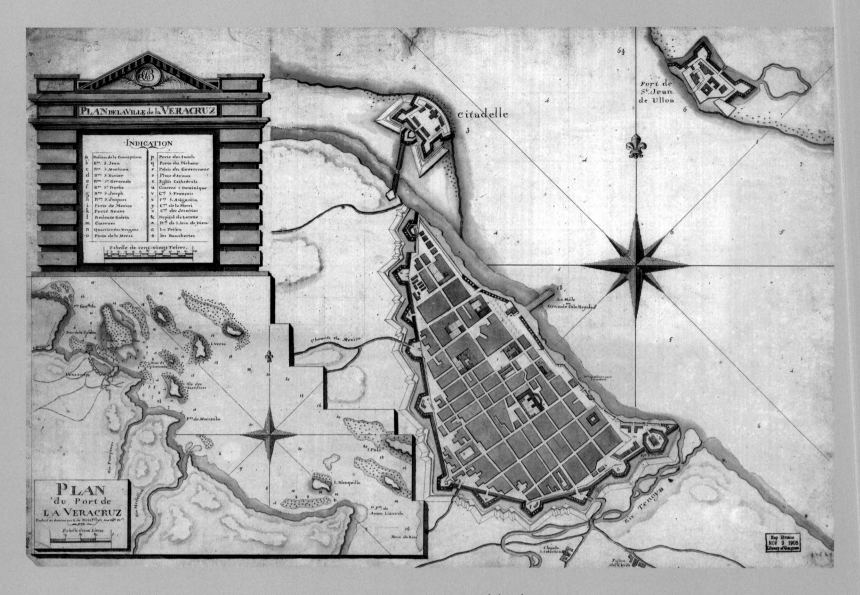

Map 341 (*above*).

This aesthetically pleasing 1798 Spanish map of the fortified city of Veracruz shows very well what the American army was up against. In addition to the city itself, other forts defended critical points outside its walls.

the transfer of many of Taylor's regulars to another army being assembled by General Winfield Scott and ordered Taylor to stay at Monterrey. Taylor, however, by now considered all orders from Polk to be suspect of political motive, and with his army, now consisting mainly of volunteers (except for some critical artillery), he moved west to Saltillo and prepared to meet the new Mexican army raised and led by Santa Anna and now moving north to confront him.

So followed the Battle of Buena Vista, fought on 22–23 February 1847. Taylor had been reinforced by about 2,400 more volunteers led south from San Antonio by General John E. Wool, but Taylor once again showed remarkable leadership, for his army of 6,000 mainly volunteers defeated a much larger Mexican army of about 20,000 men. A major contribution to this triumph was the effectiveness of the remaining regular and fast-firing artillery. Santa Anna had had problems recruiting an army because of a

bankrupt treasury. Nevertheless, Taylor became even more of a popular hero than he had before, no doubt much to the chagrin of Polk.

A final battle of the northern Mexico campaign was fought a few days later at Sacramento, near Chihuahua, by another volunteer force led by Alexander Doniphan, who had been detached from Kearny's army earlier and had been moving to meet up with Taylor. With Doniphan's icing on Taylor's cake, Mexican resistance in the north collapsed.

When the Mexicans refused to negotiate a peace settlement after Monterrey, Polk set in motion a grand plan designed to bring Mexico to its knees. General Winfield Scott was to lead an army to take Mexico City itself.

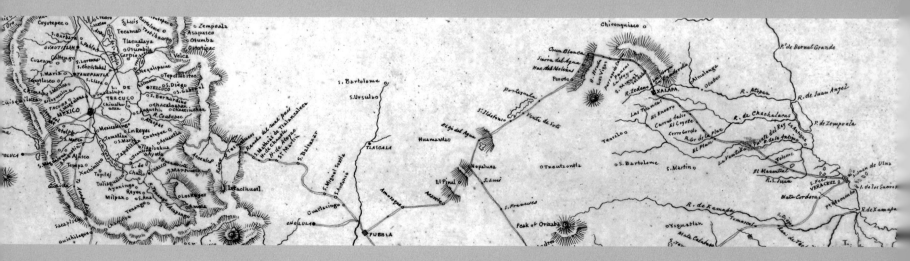

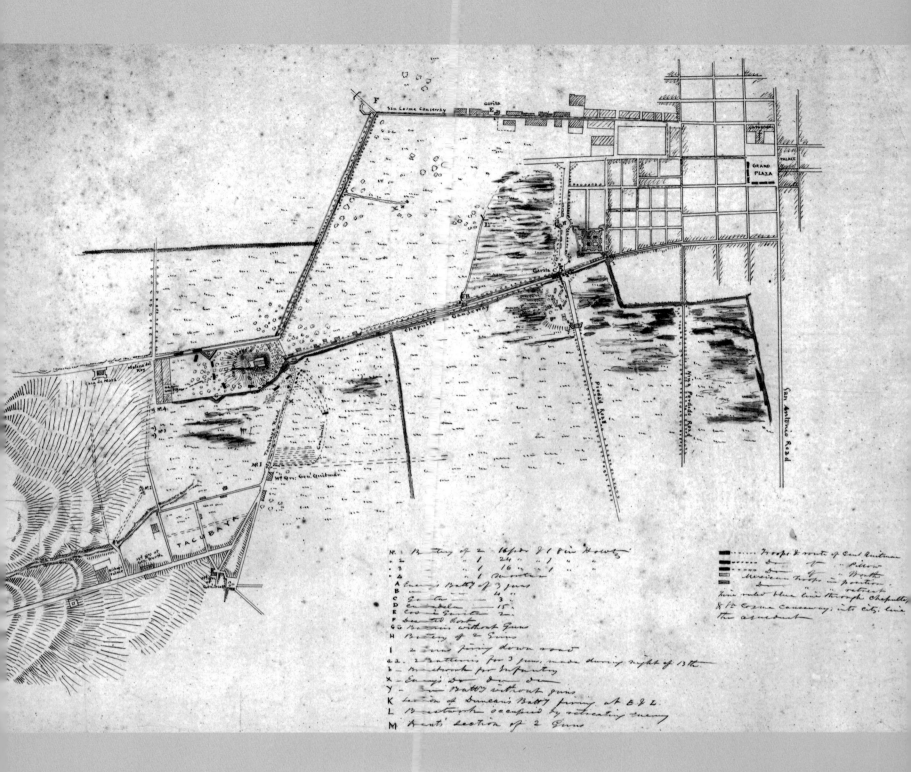

The invasion began on 9 March 1847 with the objective of taking Veracruz, a heavily fortified city on the Gulf Coast. The fortress could not be taken directly, but Scott landed his men nearby and laid siege to the city, bombarding it mercilessly day and night, aided by the navy offshore. The city was full of civilians and the bombardment soon had its effect; morale collapsed and the city fell on 28 March. Only

Map 342 (*left*).
The route from Veracruz to Mexico City taken by General Winfield Scott's army in 1847.

Map 343 (*above*).
A map showing the final assault on Mexico City, across the causeways from the fortress of Chapultepec, on 13 September 1847.

Right. American troops storm the Garita de San Cosmé in this contemporary engraving..

HISTORICAL ATLAS OF THE UNITED STATES 165

faced a severely reduced and considerably demoralized Mexican army. However, 3,700 of Scott's men were volunteers who had signed up for only a year and were now eligible to leave. Despite inducements, most of them departed, leaving Scott with an army of 7,000. The volunteers were soon made up for by the arrival of reinforcements, so that for the final assault Scott had an army of about 11,000 active men. Mexico had 30,000.

On 15 May the city of Puebla was occupied after a token resistance by Santa Anna's dragoons. In June, navy commodore Matthew Perry took a contingent of marines up the Grijalva River to capture Villahermosa (called Tabasco by the Americans), which was considered to be a source of supply for Santa Anna's army. By 10 August Scott's army was within sight of Mexico City, but now faced a series of fortresses that had been built expressly to defend the capital. Scott had to decide on a plan of attack, and he sent out his engineers to reconnoiter the possible routes around the lava fields and across the marshes.

The main road was blocked by Santa Anna with 7,000 troops on El Peñón, a fortified hill, but Scott simply bypassed him by using a minor road. A rough road was quickly cut across a *pedregal,* a lava field, to enable artillery to be dragged across it, so that American guns suddenly appeared where they were not expected.

The Mexicans fell back to Churubusco, a fortified town on the main road into Mexico City from the south. Here the Mexicans began a desperate last-ditch fight to save their capital, and here, on 20 August, astonishing odds were beaten as the American army prevailed through a thunderstorm of fire. The results were sobering: 133 Americans were killed and 865 wounded. But Santa Anna lost a quarter of his army—4,000 killed or wounded and 3,000 taken prisoner.

Still there were more fortifications to be overcome, but at this point Santa Anna, scrambling to save himself, requested a truce. Scott agreed in the hope that the terms of a peace could be arranged without further bloodshed. But Santa Anna's grip on power was waning, and there seemed to be no coherent government with which to negotiate. And the Mexicans continually violated the terms of the truce by strengthening their position. The truce lasted two weeks.

Now the Americans had to deal with reinforced fortifications, though in their favor was the fact that Mexican morale was at a low ebb. In the early morning of 8 September, General William Jenkins Worth (after whom Fort Worth, Texas, is named) led a night assault on a group of buildings called the Molinas del Rey, just west of Chapultepec, the fortress guarding the two western causeways into Mexico City. The field of action from this point on is shown on MAP 343, *previous page.* The attack was a disaster, with massive losses on both sides—787 Americans killed or wounded, and 2,000 Mexicans.

The final attack was through Chapultepec itself. Although a treacherous approach, it was the one least expected by the Mexicans. At the suggestion of General P.T. Beauregard, a feint attack was planned from the south, and men were marched to the southern gates in daylight, and then marched back again at night. Santa Anna took the bait and positioned his army to repel an attack principally from the south.

Chapultepec was bombarded for a whole day and then, in the morning of 13 September, the final assault began. The defenders of Chapultepec included nearly nine hundred military cadets who are today honored in Mexican history. The fortress fell in an hour after vicious hand-to-hand fighting, and the way was cleared to the causeways. Despite gun emplacements on the road and at the *garitas* (gates) of the city and an attack by 1,500 Mexican cavalry, sheer force of numbers drove the Americans through. Santa Anna, too late, realized that, once again, he had been outdone by Scott;

thirteen Americans had been killed and fifty-five wounded, a remarkably small number for such a major battle.

Scott marched his army inland as soon as he could. Wagons had to be assembled, horses procured, and supplies unloaded, but two weeks later the army was on its way west.

The first test came where the road to Mexico City began to climb out of the lowland plain. At Cerro Gordo Santa Anna found an easily defended location between two hills which gave the Americans only a narrow path of advance; here Santa Anna's gunners trained their cannon. The American army was badly outnumbered but thought the Mexicans were 4,000 strong instead of the 12,000 they really were. The Americans had the unenviable task of dislodging the entrenched Mexican force, lugging their guns uphill and firing on the enemy above.

Bravado won the day. Convinced by previous battles that they could defeat the Mexicans, Scott's men overcame the odds and the terrain and routed the Mexicans. Perhaps 3,000 Mexicans were taken prisoner, while another 1,200 were killed or wounded, compared to 431 Americans. Santa Anna escaped, minus his false leg, which became one of the more unusual American spoils of war.

Scott now had almost 10,000 men in the Mexican highlands, safe from tropical diseases that might be expected in the lowlands, and he

ARRANGING THE PRELIMINARIES OF A TREATY BETWEEN THE UNITED STATES AND MEXICO.

Mr. Trist—(*Very firmly*) MY GOVERNMENT, GENTLEMEN, WILL TAKE "NOTHIN' SHORTER."

MAPA
de los
ESTADOS UNIDOS
DE
MÉJICO,

Segun lo organizado y definido por las varias
actas del Congreso de dicha República; y
construido por las mejores autoridades.

LO PUBLICAN J DISTURNELL 102 BROADWAY
(NUEVA YORK.)
1847.

REVISED EDITION

MAP 344 (*left, top*).
A map of the Mexico City region in 1847 drawn by one of Scott's aides, Lieutenant Pierre Gustave Toutant de Beauregard, later a Confederate general.

Left, bottom. In this contemporary cartoon showing the negotiation of the Treaty of Guadalupe Hidalgo, Nicholas Trist is depicted, complete with map, insisting on more territory for the United States.

MAP 345 (*above*).
This is the actual map used by Trist while negotiating the Treaty of Guadalupe Hidalgo, which gave the United States half of Mexico in 1848. The map is of the United States of Mexico and was published in 1847 by American John Disturnell. The positions of El Paso and the Rio Grande are inaccurate, which led to later boundary definition problems. The Gadsden Purchase of 1854 was to some extent designed to clear up the boundary definition.

MAP 346 (*right*).
This commercial map published in 1850 by the J.H. Colton Co. shows the new boundaries of the United States, but before the admission of California as a state that same year. The borders of the United States appear as they are today, with the exception of the adjustment of the southern border by the Gadsden Purchase of 1854 (see overleaf).

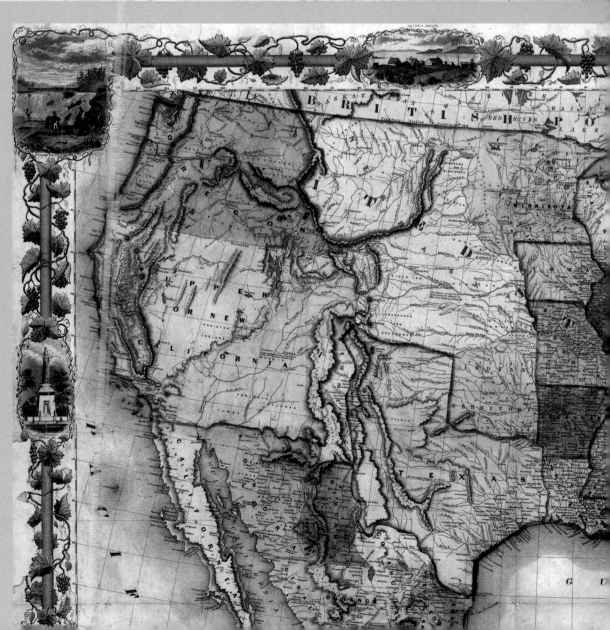

his attempts to reinforce the western gates came too late. By nightfall, the American army was within the city, and by the next day had consolidated their position; Santa Anna and his remaining army fled.

Mopping-up operations continued for the rest of the month, culminating in early October in the handing over of military power by a defeated Santa Anna to a new Mexican government that had emerged under José Manuel de la Peña y Peña. Negotiations began for a peace treaty.

The U.S. negotiator was Nicholas Trist, who had been sent by Polk for the purpose. Unfortunately, by the time Trist could start negotiating, Polk had run out of patience with the process and sent orders withdrawing a proposal for a negotiated peace. Taking advantage of the slow communication between Mexico City and Washington, Trist ignored these new orders and concluded a treaty. This was the Treaty of Guadalupe Hidalgo, named after the village just north of the capital where it was signed on 2 February 1848.

The treaty ceded more than half of Mexico to the United States. The new border was to run along the Rio Grande to New Mexico, then west to a position one marine league south of San Diego. The United States would pay Mexico $15 million and assume $3.25 million in claims of American citizens against Mexico.

When, two weeks later, Polk was confronted with Trist's fait accompli, he was angry at his disregard of instructions, but since Trist had managed to negotiate everything Polk expected anyhow, he sent the treaty to the Senate for ratification. The treaty was ratified on 10 March 1848. With its signing, the United States gained half of Texas and ended the dispute about the rest; it also acquired the area now occupied by California, Nevada, Utah, some of Colorado, and most of New Mexico and Arizona. With the recently acquired Oregon Territory, the country had in only two years suddenly become much larger and had reached the Pacific Ocean.

The Mexican War was the first American conflict on foreign soil, and had been a resounding success. It had also given valuable lessons in military strategy to a whole host of officers who would go on to fight fifteen years later in the Civil War, on both the Union and Confederate sides. Indeed, more than two hundred officers would become Union or Confederate generals. They included Ulysses S. Grant, Robert E. Lee, and Thomas J. ("Stonewall") Jackson, and also Jefferson Davis, later the Confederate president.

Mexico lost California when it considered it of little value, but the territory soon suddenly acquired far greater value with the discovery of gold. In January 1848 gold was found along the American River, northeast of San Francisco, by James Marshall, a carpenter who was building a sawmill. Once the news got out, half the population of California raced to the goldfields. News of the discovery appeared in the New York newspapers

MAP 347 (*above*).
A map of the California gold regions published in 1849 by British commercial mapmaker James Wyld. American River, where gold was first found, flows into the Sacramento northeast of San Francisco. As is often the case with these kinds of maps, even areas with minor finds have been shown in gold.

in August and set off a stampede of gold seekers to California. The first boatload arrived in San Francisco at the end of February 1849, hence their nickname of California '49ers. Between 1846 and 1852, the population of California increased from about 14,000 to 300,000. The discovery of gold and the swelling population added to the demand for statehood for California. But as with all potential states at this time, the thorny question of whether to allow slavery had first to be decided. California itself had no need of slaves, but this mattered not to the Southern states.

James Polk left office in March 1849 and was succeeded by Zachary Taylor, whose presidential contention Polk had tried hard to suppress.

Despite being a slave owner himself, Taylor supported the admission of California, allowing the state to determine if it were to be slave or non-slave. At a convention held in Monterey in

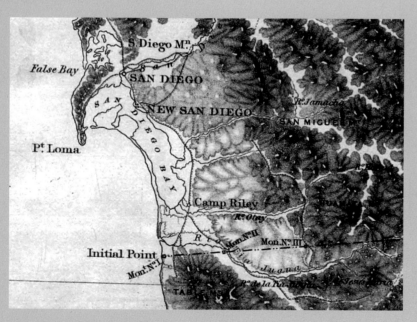

MAP 348 (*left*).
Part of a map of the new boundary with Mexico as surveyed in 1854–55 by William Emory. Here the boundary line reaches the Pacific "one marine league" south of San Diego, as specified in the Treaty of Guadalupe Hidalgo.

MAP 349 (*right*).
The small settlement of San Francisco shown on an 1850 map.

September 1849, delegates voted to exclude slavery, largely because the gold miners did not want slaves working in the mines. The boundaries of the new state were also decided. Elections were held in November, and two senators were elected—one of whom was Frémont. California essentially operated as a state for nearly a year before it officially became one. After a lot of political wrangling over the balance of slave to non-slave states (the Compromise of 1850; see page 183), a new president, Millard Fillmore (Taylor had died in July 1850), signed the bill for the admission of California on 9 September 1850.

The boundary of what would become the lower 49 states was now complete except for one adjustment. James Gadsden was a railroad promoter who dreamed of knitting together southern railroads and creating an all-southern route to the Pacific. When he found that the best route required track to run through Mexico, he got himself appointed U.S. minister to Mexico, and in late 1853 he negotiated the purchase of 45,535 square miles of land south of the Gila River to the current boundary line (Map 352, *below*). This later became the route of the Southern Pacific Railroad. The land cost $10 million, a great deal of money, but the price worked out to only thirty-three cents per acre. Santa Anna, so long a thorn in the American side, agreed to the sale on behalf of Mexico. He became immensely unpopular as a result and was finally banished. When Arizona requested territorial status in 1854, one of the names suggested was Gadsonia, a Latin derivative of Gadsden.

Map 351 (*below*).
The gold workings on the American River in 1850 are shown on this map. The are represented by the little inverted "v"s.

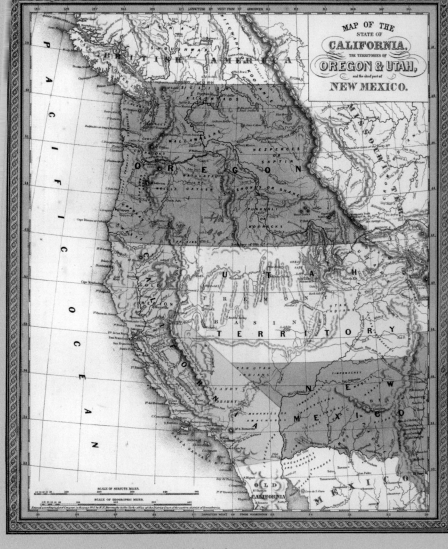

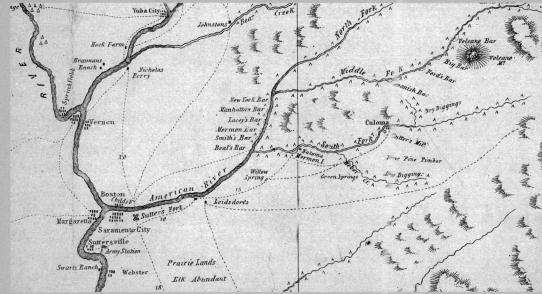

Map 350 (*above*).
One of the earliest maps to show the state of California, rushed into print in 1850 by commercial map-maker Samuel Augustus Mitchell. This was a quick adaptation of an earlier map (Map 323, *page 157*) and did not represent any new survey. The first "official" map of the state of California was published in 1854, the result of work by William Eddy, state surveyor general, and authorized by the California legislature, but due to budgetary constraints even this map utilized much information from other maps.

Map 352 (*below*).
The new southern boundary of the United States as negotiated by James Gadsden. Compare this with the boundary after the Mexican War, as shown in Map 351 (*above*) or Map 346 (*page 167*).

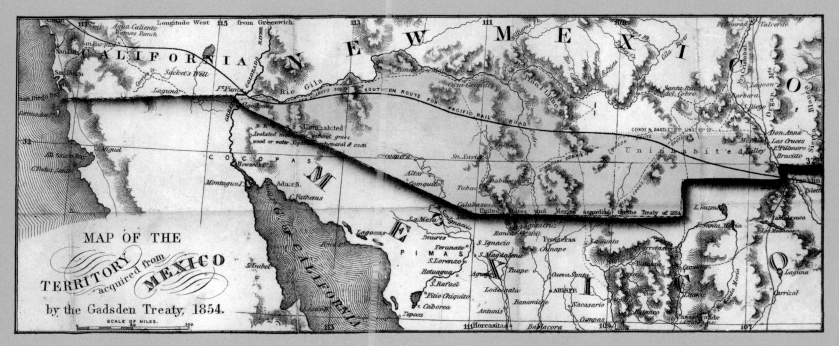

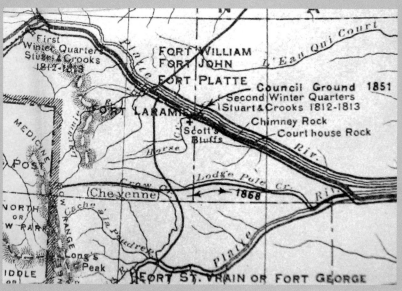

Map 353 (*above*).

Published here for the first time since its restoration is the Library of Congress's map of the West drawn in 1851 by Father Pierre-Jean de Smet to illustrate the areas reserved for each tribe under the terms of the Treaty of Fort Laramie. The map was drawn in St. Louis later in 1851, and has a note that it was presented to *Col. D.D. Mitchell by P.J. de Smet, Soc. Jes.* At the approximate center of the map, just below the *Black Hills* of South Dakota, is *Fort Laramie*. In the top margin is a picture of *Big Robber, Crow Chief*. In the southern part of *Blackfoot Territory* is a *Great Volcanic Reg. about 100 miles in [extent?] now in a state of eruption*, an early reference to the geysers of what is today Yellowstone National Park.

Map 354 (*left*).

This 1905 map indicates the location of *Fort Laramie*, straddling the Oregon Trail where the *Laramie* River meets the North *Platte River*, together with the *Council Ground 1851*, the location of the gathering for the Treaty of Fort Laramie. Northeast of the fort, approximately at the edge of this map detail, is the location of the Wounded Knee Massacre of 1890 (see page 203).

Blackrobe's Treaty

Above. Father Pierre-Jean de Smet, known as Blackrobe. De Smet traveled 200,000 miles between 1843 and 1868 ministering to Indians of all tribes, becoming one of the few truly respected EuroAmericans in the process.

One of the largest gatherings of the Indians of the Northern Plains and the Northwest took place in September 1851. About ten thousand Sioux, Cheyenne, Arapaho, Assinniboine, Mandan, Hidatsa, Arikara, and Shoshone were brought together by Indian agent Thomas Fitzpatrick and superintendent of Indian affairs Colonel David Mitchell, both former mountain men. The pair wanted to try to maintain peace between the Indians and the EuroAmerican settlers who were increasingly intruding on the Indians' hunting and grazing lands, and specifically to prevent Indian attacks on wagon trains traveling the Oregon Trail.

The idea was to define areas for each tribe so as to reduce revenge attacks on each other, and give them presents every year as a reward for a peaceful relationship. Fitzpatrick and Mitchell had concluded that there were only two ways to maintain peace on the Plains: establishment of an overwhelming military presence or the giving of many gifts. They chose the latter.

To assist them in their discussions with the Indians, Mitchell invited Pierre-Jean de Smet, a Jesuit missionary who had gained the respect of Indians wherever he had traveled. The Jesuits, known by the Indians as blackrobes, had had more success in converting the Indians than any other missionaries, perhaps because of the colorful Catholic symbolism. And the charismatic De Smet was perhaps the most respected of all the blackrobes.

In the spring of 1851, aided by fur traders, word of the great pow-wow, to be held at Fort Laramie, was spread all over the West. Notably, Pawnee, Comanche, and Kiowa refused to attend. Indians began to arrive at the fort in August, but Mitchell received word that the wagon train carrying the presents was three weeks late. Doing some quick thinking, he announced that the thousands of horses would eat all the grasslands around the fort and asked the Indians to choose another venue. They chose Horse Creek, thirty-seven miles away, and it took three days for everyone to move there. Then Mitchell further delayed by announcing that no work would be done on the weekend.

Finally the discussions began. Mitchell wanted the tribes to stay within defined areas, and De Smet drew up a map (MAP 353, *left*) to define these. The Indians protested that they were unworkable, and a compromise was reached whereby they could leave their areas only to follow the hunt. A treaty was signed by twenty designated chiefs on 17 September—and the presents, much to Mitchell's relief, arrived three days later. There were so many that it took another three days to distribute them all. According to the Treaty of Fort Laramie, as it is known, an annuity of $50,000 was to be paid to the Indians for fifty years. In ratifying the treaty the Senate reduced this to ten years, assent to which was later procured from all the tribes except the Crow. Eleven chiefs were taken to Washington, D.C., in what had become a tried-and-true method of ensuring compliance: giving the chiefs a sense of the overwhelming power of EuroAmerican peoples.

A brief peace of sorts did ensue, but it was soon broken by a small incident that became a much larger one. A cow was shot by an Indian, and in August 1854 an amateur soldier, a brevet second lieutenant named John Lawrence Gratten who was out to make a name for himself, called for volunteers to punish the offenders. He and twenty-nine others were wiped out when one of the men ill-advisedly opened fire during a tense standoff with four thousand Sioux. The press called it the Gratten Massacre. This, of course, in the military tradition, required revenge, and the following year Brigadier General William Selby Harney led a force that killed eighty-six Brule Sioux, including many women and children. Known to history as the Battle of Bluewater Creek, and by many as the Harney Massacre, it earned Harney the title of "The Butcher" among the Sioux. Unexpectedly, after the Civil War, Harney had a change of heart and began urging the federal government to deal more fairly with the Indians. He was a peace commissioner in negotiations with the Plains Indians in 1867–68. After he died, the Sioux changed his name to "Man-who-always-kept-his-word."

But the government did not often keep its word when it came to agreements with the western Indians. Treaties were broken one after another, being viewed by most EuroAmericans at the time as little more than a means to an end, the domination of the West by EuroAmericans from the East. The Treaty of Fort Laramie was one of the more visible examples where lands reserved for Indians were overrun in a short time by settlers. Indeed, the treaty was only negotiated to make the countryside safe for those moving west. The Civil War would for a while divert government attentions elsewhere, but years of strife lay ahead (see page 200) as the buffalo, a principal native food source, were hunted to near extinction.

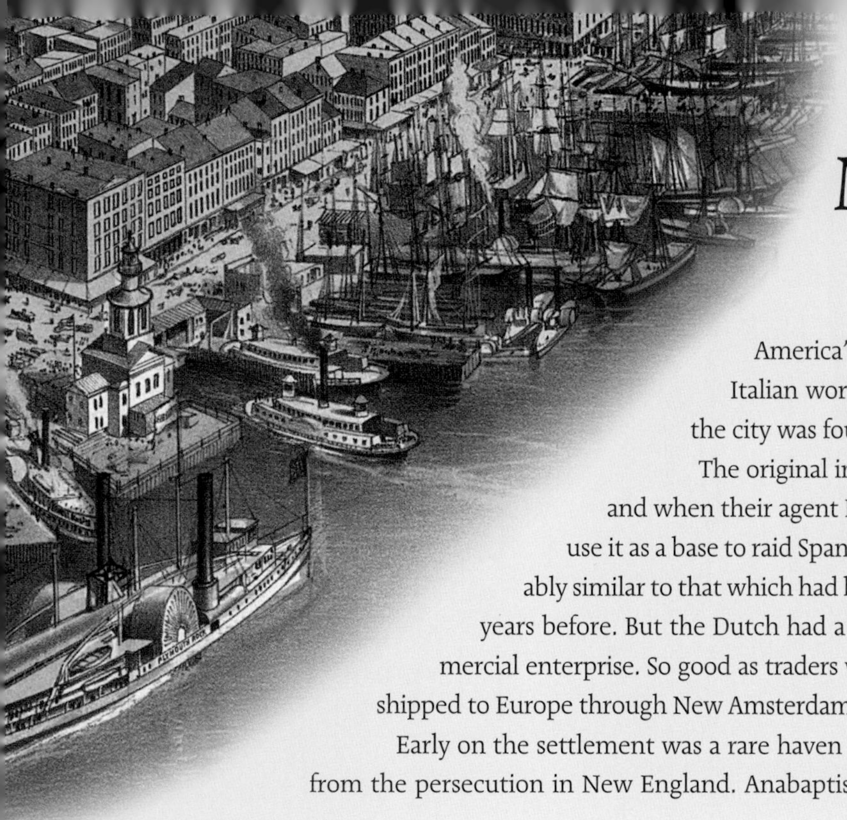

New Amsterdam, New York

America's most populous city has always been a city of many cultures. Its site discovered by an Italian working for a French king, its position noted by an Englishman working for the Dutch, the city was founded by the Dutch as a staging area to attack the Spanish, then lost to the English.

The original intention of the Dutch West India Company when they settled on Manhattan in 1624 and when their agent Peter Minuit purchased Manhattan and Staten Island from the Lenape in 1626 was to use it as a base to raid Spanish shipping, Spain and the Netherlands then being at war. This rationale was remarkably similar to that which had led to the founding of the first English colony on the coast of the Carolinas nearly forty years before. But the Dutch had a far better site and situation, and the wherewithal to turn it into a considerable commercial enterprise. So good as traders were they that by the late 1640s much of the English Virginia tobacco crop was being shipped to Europe through New Amsterdam, and the settlement was already emerging as a significant force on the world stage.

Early on the settlement was a rare haven of religious tolerance, which attracted many a colonist, including a number fleeing from the persecution in New England. Anabaptist Lady Deborah Moody, expelled from the Massachusetts Bay Colony, was granted what is now the southern part of Brooklyn, including Coney Island, for herself and her followers; her little colony was the first American settlement founded by a woman. And the independent thinker Anne Hutchinson and her followers in 1642 fled farther from their persecutors, settling on Pelham Bay in the Bronx, on what is now the Hutchinson River, only to be wiped out by an Indian attack a year later.

The Dutch settlement of New Amsterdam was quite scattered until 1643, when increasing Indian attacks led the company to order a retrenchment to the tip of Manhattan, where the colony would be near the fort and could be properly protected by a wall, as shown on MAP 358, *right*. Today, of course, this is at the hub of the world's finance, Wall Street.

The English never recognized Dutch claims in North America, to their New Netherlands or New Amsterdam, and in March 1664 the restored monarch Charles II granted the entire region to his brother James, Duke of York. He promptly arranged an invasion fleet of four ships, commanded by Colonel Richard Nicolls. Governor Pieter Stuyvesant surrendered the colony on 8 September, without a shot being fired. English possession was confirmed by the 1667 Treaty of Breda, which ended the Second Anglo-Dutch War (1665–67). The English negotiators offered to return New York to the Dutch in exchange for sugar factories in Surinam, which they considered more valuable; the Dutch declined.

New Amsterdam became New York, but many of the Dutch settlers remained, assimilating themselves into what became the center of an English colony and then a royal province.

MAP 355 (*above*).
Detail of a bird's-eye map of Manhattan published about 1856 by lithographer Nathaniel Currier, of the famous print firm Currier and Ives, a partnership formed in 1857. The view shown is of the southeast corner of Manhattan at the entrance to the East River.

MAP 356 (*below*).
This 1639 map of New York and its environs under the Dutch regime is attributed to Dutch cartographer Joan Vingtboons and may be a copy made about twenty-five years later. The title translates as "Manhattan laying on the North River." *Eyland Manatus* is Manhattan Island and *Eylant Staten* is Staten Island. *Fort Amsterdam* is shown at the tip of Manhattan at *A*, and there are three windmills at *B*, *C*, and *D*. The numbers refer to the list of inhabitants' names, making this map a valuable historical record. Number 43 is Jonas Bronck, after whom the Bronx is named.

MAP 357 (*below, right*).
This detail of MAP 53, *page 30*, shows Dutch explorer Adriaen Block's 1614 first depiction of *Manhates*—Manhattan—as an Island. *Hellegatt* marks the constriction in the East River found by Block as he became the first to circumnavigate Long Island; it is also named on MAP 356.

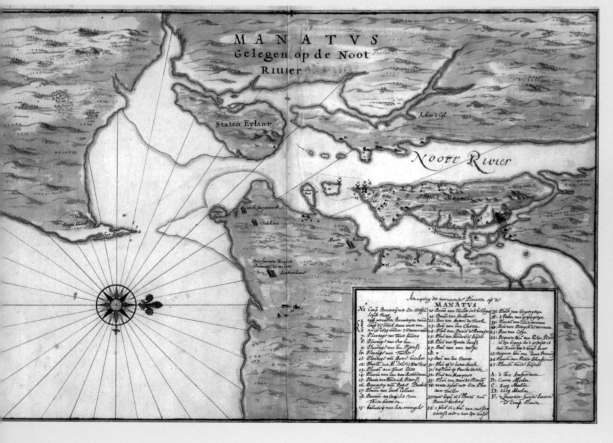

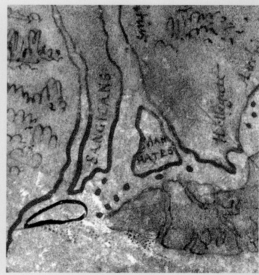

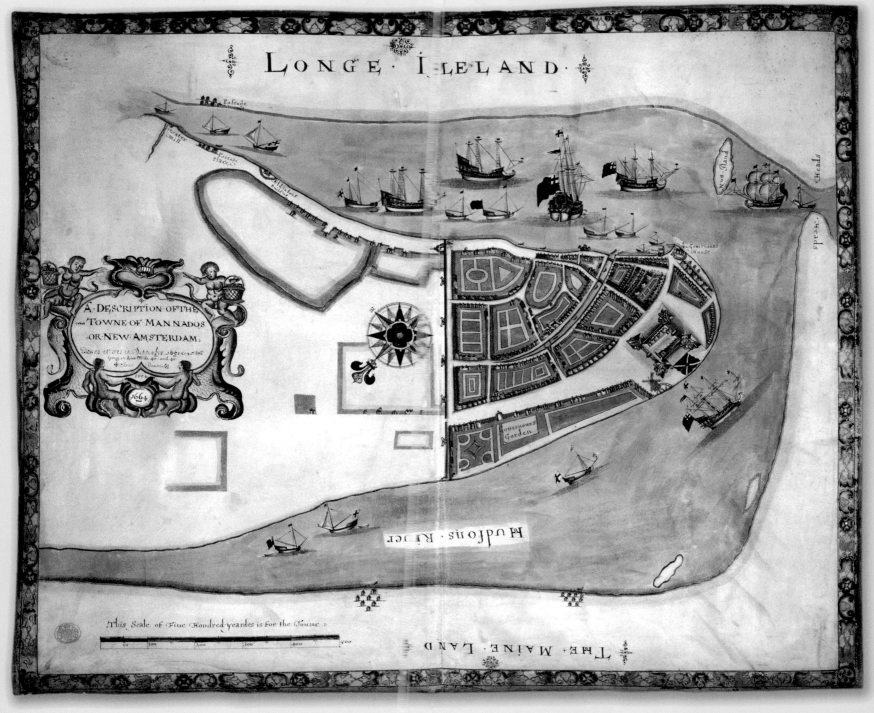

LONGE ILELAND

A DESCRIPTION OF THE
TOWNE OF MANNADOS
OR NEW AMSTERDAM

Hudfons River

THE MAINE LAND

This Scale of Five Hundred yeardes is For the Towne

MAP 358 (*above*).
This famous map, called the Duke's Plan, was drawn in 1664 by an English draftsman, who copied a 1661 Dutch survey. It was likely given to the Duke of York to illustrate his new possession, though it has been suggested that it might have been drawn by an English spy to document the city's defenses before the arrival of the English ships. It would seem rather an artistic map for such a purpose but may be a later copy elaborated for presentation. In any case, it is a fine record of the city of New Amsterdam at the time of the coming of the English.

MAP 359 (*right*).
Manhattan, the focal point of the New Netherlands, shown on a map produced during the Dutch era. This is a later edition, published in 1685.

The key location of the city ensured that it would continue to grow, and by the time of the Revolution, its population was about 30,000. The city was the last to remain occupied by British troops, who finally left on 25 November 1783 (see page 88).

Several events also conspired to make New York grow. Advanced city planning, visionary for its day, helped. In 1811 the New York state legislature adopted the Commissioners' Plan, originally proposed in 1807, which gave city commissioners exclusive rights "to lay out streets, roads, and public squares of such width, extent, and direction, as to them shall seem most conducive to public good." It also allowed the city to expropriate property in the way of the planned development, a right bitterly opposed by some landowners. The result was a street plan for future growth that extended northwards to cover the whole of Manhattan Island. Then in 1825 the Erie Canal was completed. It linked the Hudson River with Lake Erie and opened up the entire Midwest (MAP 296, *page 145*), confirming New York's role as the principal city of North America. When immigration began to build, from about 1827 on, the city was ready. Commerce thrived, and a significant number of immigrants never got any farther than the city, the entry point for most European immigration for a century.

In 1835 and again in 1845, large sections of the tip of Manhattan were burned down by great fires—such fires were almost an accepted hazard of urban life at this time—and they were quickly rebuilt.

In 1853 Central Park was conceived as a lung for the growing city, and some 700 acres was reserved between 59th and 106th Streets. (Another 143 acres north of 106th was added later.) A design competition held in 1857 was won by landscape architects Frederick Law Olmsted and Calvert Vaux, generally regarded as the founding fathers of American landscape architecture. Their innovative "greensward" plan was for a park that would look natural but was in fact highly planned, with separation of pathways for pedestrians and carriages and the incorporation of several water bodies.

By this time the railroad had connected New York to its hinterland. By 1850 lines connected the city to upstate New York, and by 1860 one could travel from New York to the Midwest (see page 178). Within the city, a series of horse-drawn street railroads, beginning with the New York and Harlem Railroad in 1832, were constructed along streets, but these were soon unable to move the volume of people needed by the growing city, and elevated railroads, essentially the first true transit system, began operation in 1871 (MAP 361, right). These in turn began to be superseded in 1904, when the first subway opened. Subways connected Brooklyn, the Bronx, and Queens to Manhattan in an effective and efficient manner; they were immediately heavily used and spurred the growth of the outer boroughs.

Developments in building materials and techniques, and the use of steel and reinforced concrete, allowed the construction of higher and higher structures. The invention of improved water pumps and elevators further facilitated the trend upwards. Elisha Graves Otis invented the elevator, with a safety device to prevent free fall if the main cable broke, in 1853,

and the first elevator was installed in New York in 1857. The first elevators were mainly for freight and were worked by steam or hydraulic power, but the application of electricity to elevators in the 1880s was the factor that made tall buildings truly acceptable.

Manhattan being an island, bridges were needed, and in 1883 the Brooklyn Bridge opened. It was at the time the longest suspension bridge in the world (MAP 363, far right). Many others, as well as tunnels, followed, most in the first decade of the twentieth century.

New York outgrew its boundaries by 1898, growing to encompass the four other boroughs of the city: the Bronx, Queens, Staten Island, and Brooklyn. The latter was enjoined to merge with New York City because it was running out of water, and New York had long before constructed lengthy aqueducts to supply the city. A fall in the water table had made wells no longer possible, and fresh water was an essential component for a growing city to remain a healthy one. By 1900 the expanded New York was a city of 3.3 million; a century later, it held over 8 million people, was at the core of an urban conglomeration of 22 million, and had become the unrivaled commercial center of the United States.

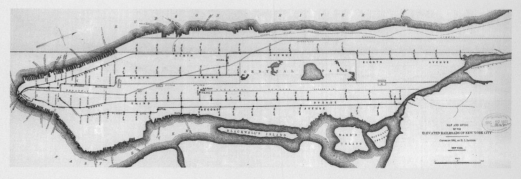

MAP 361 (above).
A map of Manhattan's elevated railroads in 1881. The first line was along Greenwich Street and 9th Avenue to 30th Street, the line here marked *Greenwich St.*

Map 360 (*left, top*).

British army lieutenant Bernard Ratzer carried out the survey for this detailed map of Manhattan in 1767, though it was not published until 1776, one of the many maps hurriedly mass-produced once the Revolution broke out. The urban area by this time well beyond the Dutch bounds of *Wall Street* but still only reaches a mile north. The British fort is at the tip of the island and the wide *Broadway* prominent, leading north to a "y" junction, today Broadway and Park Row, with City Hall and its park between them. A little farther north a water supply system is evident, connected to the large pond labeled *Fresh Water*

Map 362 (*above*).

A superb 1865 bird's-eye map of Manhattan. Bird's-eye maps were a popular nineteenth-century method of advertising the virtues of a city, or of a town that wanted to become one, and it is not surprising that the emerging metropolis of New York led to the production of a fair number of these spectacular maps, given the large potential market for them. For more on bird's-eye maps, see page 208.

Map 363 (*right*).

Tall buildings are just beginning to sprout in this 1905 bird's-eye map of Manhattan. They were built in response to rising land values, in turn due to the limitations of building a great city on a small island. Other than the taller buildings, the most notable change is the two bridges. The bridge on the right is the Brooklyn Bridge, begun in 1869 and completed in 1883. When it was opened it was the longest suspension bridge in the world. It was designed by architect John Roebling, who died in an accident soon after construction began. His son Washington took over direction of the construction, only to be hobbled by decompression sickness from working in a sealed caisson. His wife learned enough technical terms to be able to convey his wishes to the construction managers, but Washington could only watch from a distance through a telescope as the bridge was completed. The bridge on the left is the Manhattan Bridge, which was not completed until 1909, and its presence on this map is to promote New York as a major city. Features that were not yet complete, or worse, projected but never built, often found their way onto these kind of maps—exaggeration for the purpose of advertising.

The Great Coastal Survey

At the beginning of the nineteenth century many nations were undertaking geodetic surveys of their countries. These extremely accurate surveys provided information to scientists about the shape of the Earth, and there were many obvious advantages to having an accurate map for economic or military purposes. Yet the United States had no such accurate surveys, and in particular none of its coast—essential for navigation and commerce.

In 1807 President Thomas Jefferson, a competent scientist himself, persuaded Congress to authorize the Survey of the Coast, and a Swiss scientist recently arrived in Philadelphia was hired to carry it out. He was Ferdinand Rudolph Hassler, a veteran of the geodetic survey of Switzerland and a man obsessed with precision. Hassler drew up a plan for an exact triangulation of the east coast of the United States and in 1811 sailed to Britain to obtain instruments, which had to be hand-made by the finest instrument maker in the country. Unfortunately for Hassler, the War of 1812 intervened, trapping him in Britain. He returned to the United States and finally began his work in 1816, only to have Congress (Jefferson's guiding hand having gone) withdraw its funding after one year due to lack of money.

In 1818 the Survey was made primarily the responsibility of the army, and there was little progress. Not until 1833 was Hassler finally re-hired to get on with the job. Hassler worked on the Survey, which was renamed the United States Coast Survey (uscs) in 1836, for a further ten years before he died in 1843. Although stunningly precise, his work had not progressed south of the southern border of New Jersey.

Nonetheless, he had set the standard, and the need for accurate maps was now better understood. Alexander Dallas Bache, a scientist with a similar appreciation of the need for precision, though not obsessive like Hassler, was appointed superintendent of the Survey in 1843. He oversaw the extension of the Survey south until after the Civil War, but not until almost the turn of the century was the entire coast surveyed. By that time the scope of the work had itself expanded: the West Coast was added in 1846–48 and the lengthy and dangerous coast of Alaska in 1867, both representing additional years of toil to the surveyors.

The additional coastline added greatly to the magnitude of the task. Then, in 1871, the interior of the country was made part of the responsibility of the uscs, and its name was changed once more, to the United States Coast and Geodetic Survey (uscgs), in 1878. This organization lasted until 1970, when the Survey became part of the National Oceanic and Atmospheric Administration (NOAA), as the National Geodetic Survey.

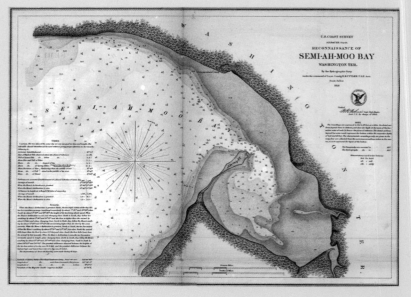

MAP 364 (*above*).
An example of one of the meticulous detailed surveys of the United States Coast Survey. This is Semiahmoo Bay and Drayton Harbor, current site of the city of Blaine, Washington, right on the forty-ninth parallel border between the United States and Canada. Although not marked on this map, the boundary line runs horizontally approximately through the "T" of *Washington*. The map was created in 1858 as part of a survey of the boundary; the Boundary *Commission Camp* is marked. The bay was an important entry point to British territory for American gold seekers trying their luck on the Fraser River during a gold rush that year. Despite the accuracy of the survey, mistakes were made. Here *Washington Territory* is shown extending north across British Columbia. A corrected version was issued later the same year.

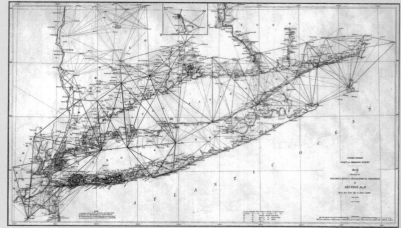

MAP 365 (*above, center*).
A map showing the system of triangulation from New York to Rhode Island, with Long Island, published by the newly renamed United States Coast and Geodetic Survey in 1881.

MAP 366 (*left*).
Surveys of the Pacific coast, part about to be acquired by the United States from Mexico and part (Oregon) acquired in 1846, were carried out by the U.S. Coast Survey in 1848 and 1849. This is part of a three-sheet summary chart showing the result, published in 1854. It shows the coast north of San Francisco (at bottom). As did many such charts, it includes a number of views of the coast as it appeared from the sea; these were an aid to mariners in recognizing where they were. In addition to this small-scale chart, a number of larger-scale charts were also issued, such as MAP 364, *above, top*. Although not shown on this map, it was also surveyed using triangulation.

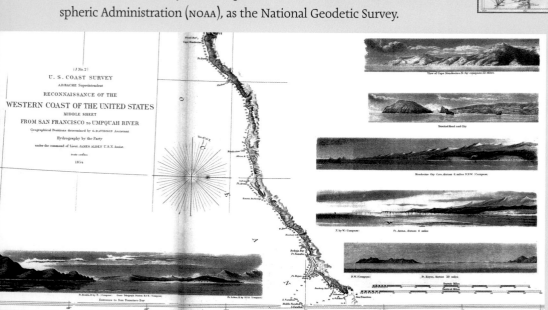

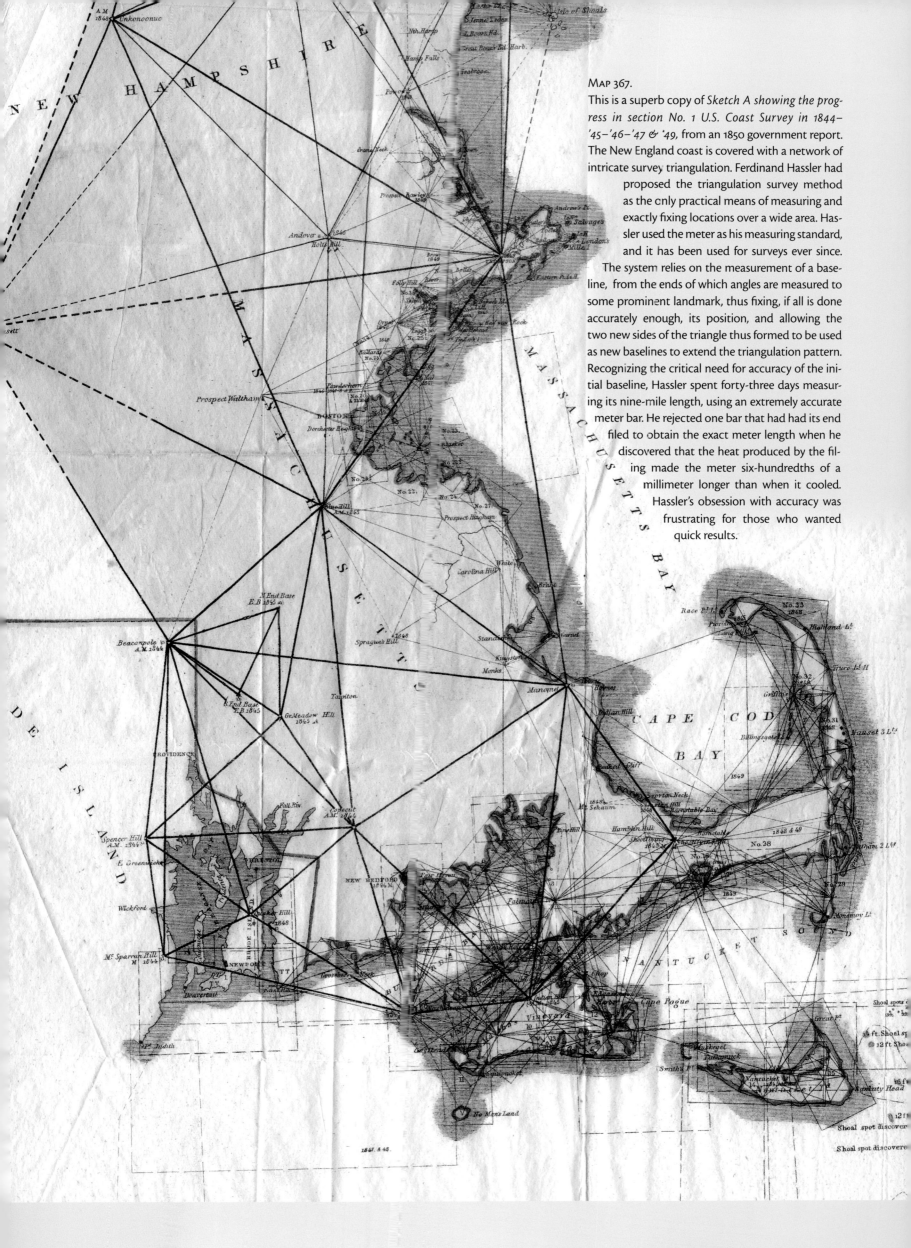

MAP 367.

This is a superb copy of *Sketch A showing the progress in section No. 1 U.S. Coast Survey in 1844–'45–'46–'47 & '49*, from an 1850 government report. The New England coast is covered with a network of intricate survey triangulation. Ferdinand Hassler had proposed the triangulation survey method as the only practical means of measuring and exactly fixing locations over a wide area. Hassler used the meter as his measuring standard, and it has been used for surveys ever since.

The system relies on the measurement of a baseline, from the ends of which angles are measured to some prominent landmark, thus fixing, if all is done accurately enough, its position, and allowing the two new sides of the triangle thus formed to be used as new baselines to extend the triangulation pattern. Recognizing the critical need for accuracy of the initial baseline, Hassler spent forty-three days measuring its nine-mile length, using an extremely accurate meter bar. He rejected one bar that had had its end filed to obtain the exact meter length when he discovered that the heat produced by the filing made the meter six-hundredths of a millimeter longer than when it cooled. Hassler's obsession with accuracy was frustrating for those who wanted quick results.

Steam and Iron Rails

Steam revolutionized life in the United States. First applied to water transportation, and then to railroads and factory mechanization, it was to transform an agricultural nation where life passed at a measured pace into an industrial one with crowded cities of hustle and grime, run by the clock.

Robert Fulton began the first commercially successful regular passenger steamboat service in the United States. His steamboats connected New York and Clermont, 150 miles up the Hudson River, in 1807. In 1817 a steamboat finally made it all the way up the opposing currents of the Mississippi and the Ohio to Cincinnati, and two years later no fewer than sixty steam stern-wheelers plied between New Orleans and St. Louis. When the Erie Canal opened in 1825, steamboats became the principal means of transportation west, and other canals were soon built. Yet relatively easy as this means of transportation was, it was quickly superseded by the coming of the steam railroad, which offered the bonus of speed and a more frequent and reliable timetable.

John Stevens demonstrated the feasibility of steam locomotion on a circular track at Hoboken, New Jersey, in 1826, three years before George Stephenson did the same in Britain. Most of the first commercial railroads provided portage from one watershed to another. The famous *DeWitt Clinton* locomotive (named after the governor of New York) began service on the Mohawk and Hudson Railroad, between Albany and Schenectady, on 2 July 1831; this rail line bypassed extensive

Map 368 (*below*).
One of the earliest railroad surveys was this one, carried out in 1828 for a line connecting Boston with Providence, Rhode Island. Two routes were surveyed, and it was the southernmost one that was approximately followed.

Map 369 (*below, center*).
By the mid-nineteenth century the hinterland of Boston was covered with railroads, almost all the lines shown here having been completed by then. The Boston to Providence line surveyed in Map 368 is shown. It was completed in 1835 and is still in use today, although many of the intermediate stations have closed.

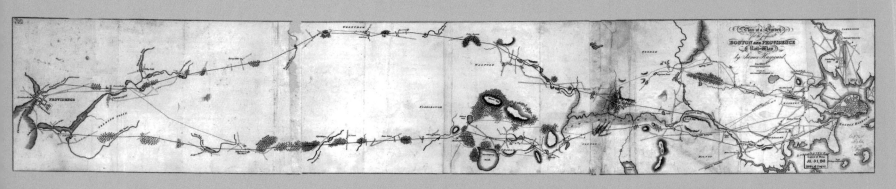

locks on the Erie Canal. Railroads were sometimes hastily constructed to protect or extend a city's trade, and from Boston, Baltimore, and Charleston rails were laid east in the early 1830s. The South Carolina Railroad, west from Charleston, completed in 1833, was briefly the longest railroad in the world. The Baltimore and Ohio, constructed in sections between 1830 and 1853, was notable in that it developed locomotives, rolling stock, and operational procedures that were suited to North American conditions and were followed by most subsequent lines.

By 1840 there were 2,808 miles of railroad track in the United States, almost all in short unconnected segments, and although the length of these segments increased during the 1840s they did not form any sort of coherent network. One could travel from Boston to Buffalo, but not from New York, from Charleston or Savannah to Chattanooga; but lines did not connect northward. Even New York to Washington, D.C., required some stagecoach travel. Yet in the decade between 1850 and 1860, the rail network expanded dramatically, so that by 1859 it was possible to travel by train from New York to St. Joseph, on the Missouri River, more than a thousand miles away. In 1849 Abraham Lincoln traveled from Washington to his home in Springfield, Illinois, a journey that required the use of rail, stagecoach, steamboat, and stagecoach again, and took three weeks.

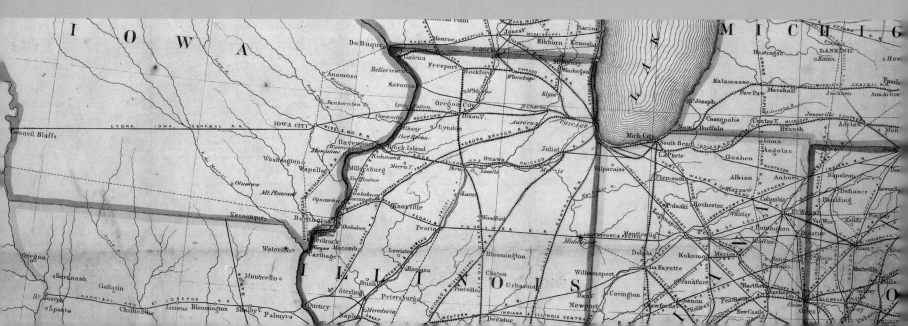

In 1861 he traveled the other way between the two cities, 1,900 miles on a grand tour before his inauguration, taking twelve days, all by rail. And had he wanted to, he could have taken the train directly to Washington and arrived in two days.

The rail network by 1860 had reached 30,000 miles, but it included at least six different gauges, so that although through travel was possible, it quite often required several changes of train. A uniform national gauge was not achieved until the 1880s. The nation's rails, too, were all made of iron, which easily bent or snapped and wore out alarmingly fast under heavy trains. The process for mass production of steel was invented in Britain in 1855 by Henry Bessemer, but the first steel rails were not manufactured in the United States for another ten years. Once available, the changeover was rapid, for steel rails were found to last an astonishing seventeen times as long as iron.

Less than a third of the rails in the United States in 1860 were in the South, and those that were remained disconnected to a much greater extent than those in the more industrialized North. This was to prove a critical factor during the war that would soon consume the nation.

By the end of the 1860s, rails connected Atlantic and Pacific (see page 194). By 1890 there were 164,000 miles of rail, almost all of a standard gauge, 4 feet 8½ inches, a true rail network that would serve until the advent of air travel.

Above. Not everyone was enamored with the new convenience of the railroad. This illustration entitled "The Horrors of Travel" appeared in *Harper's Weekly* in September 1865. Death rides a train plowing over bodies strewn in its path, while at top a collision results in an explosion.

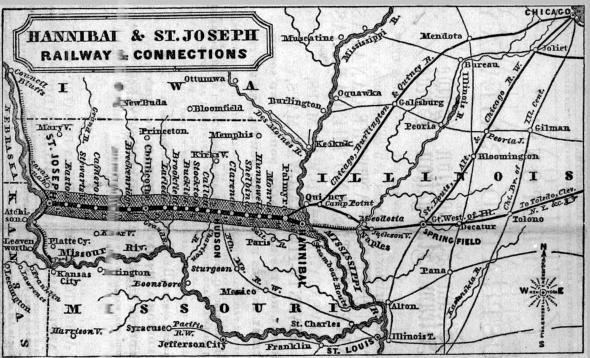

The Hannibal & St. Joseph Railroad Company offer for sale 600,000 ACRES OF THE FINEST FARMING AND TIMBER LANDS IN THE WEST, in lots to suit purchasers, at low prices, on long credits and at low rates of interest—putting a Prosperous Home within the reach of all who seek for a rich soil and a genial climate in the growing West. Read opposite page.

For further information, apply by letter or otherwise to

JOSIAH HUNT,
Land Commissioner, H. & St. J. R. R., Hannibal, Mo.

Map 370 *(below).*
This "slice" of a large map of railroads "in operation and in progress" was published in 1854. Lines in operation are crosshatched, those "in progress" (though not necessarily under construction) are shown as single lines, and those in the proposal stage, many of which would not come to fruition, are dashed lines. There are perhaps as many as yet incomplete lines as those in operation. No lines are complete west of the Mississippi. This map shows the already quite dense network of rail lines in existence prior to the Civil War. The engraving of an early train at *top left* is part of the elaborate cartouche for this map.

Map 371 *(above, right).*
By the time of the Civil War the farthest west it was possible to get by railroad, traveling continuously by rail from the coastal cities of the east, was St. Joseph, on the Missouri River, more than a thousand miles west of New York City. The Hannibal and St. Joseph Railroad was completed in 1859, and as can be seen from this 1863 map, was actively trying to sell land along its route so as to increase its traffic. The railroad when it was chartered in 1852 had managed to procure a land grant of 600,000 acres from Congress. In 1860, mail for the Pony Express to Sacramento, California, was first carried west on trains to St. Joseph. In March the following year, the mail-carrying messenger missed his train from Hannibal and a special train was laid on for him, which covered the 206 miles to St. Joseph in 4 hours 51 minutes, at a record-breaking 40 miles per hour, a railroad speed record that would stand for fifty years. The Hannibal and St. Joseph line is also shown on Map 370, *below*, in the extreme lower left corner.

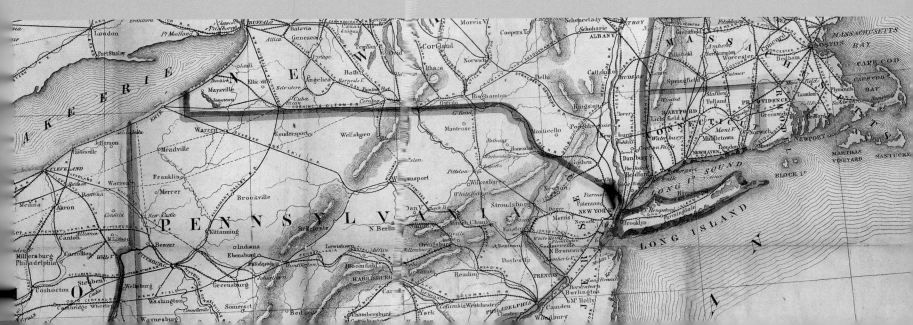

Surveys for a Pacific Railroad

With the acquisition of California and even in anticipation of it, the United States began a series of western surveys that would become more and more detailed over the next forty years. In March 1852 Congress authorized a large-scale survey of potential railroad routes to the Pacific. Reconnaissances rather than true surveys due to the enormous scope of the project, they were under the overall direction of the secretary of war, Jefferson Davis, soon to become the first president of the Confederate States of America.

The routes to be surveyed all resulted in compromises between factions who saw the location of a railroad to the West as an encouragement or otherwise to the spread of slavery. The use of the Corps of Topographical Engineers' military surveyors to survey a number of possible routes was a way of appeasing conflicting political interests.

Three principal routes were mapped. The northern region was surveyed under the new governor of Washington Territory, Isaac I. Stevens. Several passes through the Cascades were surveyed by Captain George B. McClellan, later a general in the Union army. Stevens's possible routes were considered so dubious and perhaps partisan that his own territorial legislature commissioned a civilian engineer, Frederick West Lander, to resurvey them. His work was included in the final report.

Captain John Gunnison began the survey of the middle route only to be killed by Indians at Sevier Lake, Utah. His survey was continued by Lieutenant E.G. Beckwith, who was an artillery officer. Most of his route (MAP 372, *below*) up the Humboldt River was eventually used for the first transcontinental railroad (see page 194), but he was unable to provide cost estimates for the route, and his report was largely ignored because of this.

Lieutenant Amiel Weeks Whipple surveyed a southern route, at the 35th parallel, in 1853, but Congress thought it not far enough south and commissioned another survey. In 1854 Lieutenant John Parke surveyed a route east from San Diego to the Rio Grande, where it connected with another survey by Lieutenant John Pope, surveying west from Fort Washita, on the Red River. Another, separate survey was carried out in 1853 to locate passes over the southern Sierra Nevada. Lieutenant Robert Williamson, with Parke in 1853, concluded that there were no passes suitable for a railroad and recommended a route from Fort Yuma, on the lower Colorado, to Los Angeles rather than San Diego.

The surveys were analyzed in an extensive thirteen-volume report, itself a monumental achievement that included an entire volume of maps, panoramas, paintings, and drawings. Jefferson Davis, being a southerner himself, recommended the southern route, but no consensus could be reached in Congress. Thus although there now was a defined set of feasible routes to the West Coast, none would yet be implemented. The Civil War would divert the energies of the nation to other less productive ends.

Map 372 (left, top).
The initial summary map of the middle route, by John Gunnison along the 38th parallel, and, after his death at the hands of the Paiute Indians in October 1838, by E.G. Beckwith along the 41st parallel. The western end of Gunnison's survey is at Sevier Lake, Utah, which has the notation *Capt. Gunnison killed by the Indians.* The map was published in 1855.

Map 373 (left, bottom).
This 1857 map of the proposed Territory of New Mexico shows a number of potential railroad routes across the Southwest, including some surveyed in 1846 by Lieutenant William Hemsley Emory (the northernmost one in the center) and Philip St. George Cooke (most of the southernmost loop). They had surveyed the routes as part of the movement of troops under General Stephen Watts Kearny to California in 1846, and they were resurveyed as part of the Pacific Railroad Survey by Lieutenant John Parke in 1854. The middle route had been noted by Emory as "a good route if water can be had." This path was used by the Southern Pacific Railroad, completed in 1881 by connection at Deming, New Mexico, to the Atchison, Topeka, and Santa Fe Railroad, and to New Orleans on its own lines in 1883. The realization that this was the only practicable railroad route led to the negotiation of the Gadsden Purchase, which extended the southern boundary of the United States in the Southwest to its current position (see Map 352, page 169). Tucson is marked but not Phoenix, which was founded in 1868 and chartered in 1881. The boundaries shown in red for the proposed New Mexico Territory were at 32° and 34°N, whereas the northern boundary of the states of Arizona and New Mexico is at 37°N.

MAP OF ROUTES
FOR A
PACIFIC RAILROAD
Compiled to accompany the Report of the
HON. JEFFERSON DAVIS, SEC. OF WAR
In Office of P. R. R. Survey
1855.
Statute Miles

Map 374 (above).
One of the most skilled of the Topographical Engineers was Gouverneur K. Warren, who drew this summary map of all the railroad surveys by 1857. In so doing he produced the first reasonably accurate, instrument-based map of the West. This version has had the state and territorial boundaries existing in 1857 added in red, Western culture being imposed on the indigenous. The three main railroad surveys are indicated, with less detail between them.

Map 375 (below).
In 1857 there was a brief clash between the United States government and Mormons in Utah who wished to establish an independent state, the so-called Utah Mormon War. Late that year a Topographical Engineer with the delightful name of Joseph Christmas Ives was sent up the Colorado River to attempt to find a water route that could be used to supply troops in the Great Basin. He used a prefabricated steamboat, the USS *Explorer*, shipped in the hold of a larger ship round Cape Horn to the head of the Gulf of California. Ives was accompanied by a geologist, John Strong Newberry, a cartographer, Frederick von Egloffstein, and an artist, Heinrich Baldwin Möllhausen, who together were responsible for the first popular lithographs of the spectacular Grand Canyon. Von Egloffstein created the innovative map of the Grand Canyon shown here. The method of shadow relief is popular today, but Von Egloffstein seems to have been the first to use the technique. The result, wrote Ives, "is intelligible to every eye."

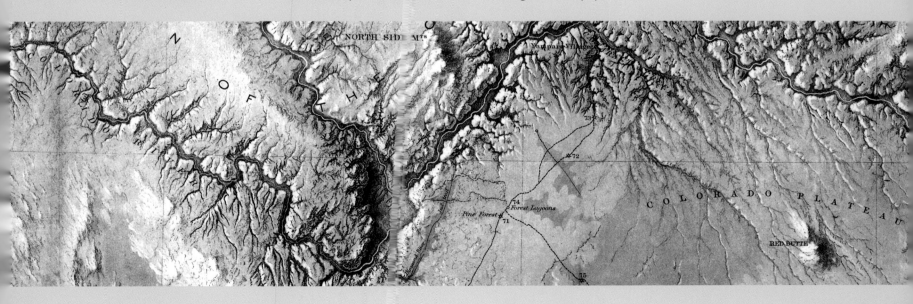

A House Divided

The tumor of slavery was growing inside the United States. The day would come when it would have to be excised, or the patient would die. For many decades before the Civil War, factions had parried with each other, and the occasional statesman had worked out a compromise that kept the issue at bay for a few more years. But ultimately no more compromise was possible.

Yet the Civil War was not simply about slavery, despite the undeniable fact that it was the root cause. States' rights, that infamous issue that had been simmering since the War for Independence, surfaced once more

with the secession of South Carolina and the other states that followed it. Did a state have the unilateral right to secede from the Union? A new Republican president, Abraham Lincoln, decided that the preservation of the Union was paramount and, waiting only until the South fired the first shot in anger, launched what turned out to be a horrific war to maintain it.

Each side had worried for years that the other would gain the upper hand through the admission of new states, changing the balance of power in the Senate, where the South had maintained an effective veto power. One of the accommodations that had kept the slavery issue manageable

was the Missouri Compromise of 1820, which balanced the admission of Missouri with that of Maine and created a line at 36°30´ N, north of which (except for Missouri) slavery was not to be permitted (see pages 144 and 148). The addition of new territory following the war with Mexico raised Southern fears once more, resulting in the complex Compromise of 1850, five bills that admitted California as a free state; banned the slave *trade* (only) in the District of Columbia; created New Mexico and Utah without prohibition of slavery, each to be allowed to decide at statehood; required U.S. citizens to assist in the return of runaway slaves (the Fugitive Slave Act), and compelled Texas to give up claims to western lands (to avoid them becoming part of a slave state).

This particular accommodation lasted but four years. It was destroyed by the passage of the Kansas-Nebraska Act in May 1854, which allowed the decision on slavery in both new territories to be made by a vote, by so-called popular sovereignty. This resulted in a sudden influx of new voters to Kansas from both sides and "Bloody Kansas"—widespread violence as each faction fought to control the outcome. John Brown, a fanatical antislavery advocate, weighed in on this fight, gaining an early reputation for taking the law into his own hands.

Throughout this period a notion was taking root in the South that it could be a viable nation on its own. The concept called for continued expansion, but south rather than west, somehow creating a tropical empire—based on slavery. The Gulf of Mexico was to become the "Ameri-

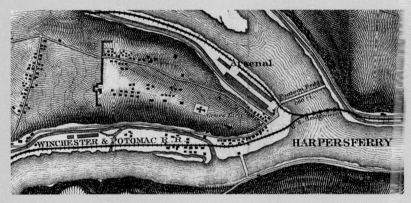

can Mediterranean." In 1854 Southern factions in the federal government hatched a plan to purchase Cuba from Spain, and to take it by force if Spain did not agree to sell. Details of the plan leaked out and caused an outrage in the North, which saw it simply as a plan to extend slavery. The North seemed to many southerners to be foiling the aspirations of the South.

The case of Dred Scott was another aggravation for the North. Scott was a slave who had been taken to unorganized territory north of 36°30´ where slavery was forbidden by the Missouri Compromise. Back in Missouri he sued for his freedom on the grounds that he had been a resident of free soil, but the Southern-dominated Supreme Court saw the case as an opportunity to extend slavery to all unorganized territory and in March 1857 rejected his case, in the process declaring the Missouri Compromise unconstitutional.

In 1854 a new political party, the Republicans, had emerged with the aim of protecting the new territories from slavery. For the 1858 Senate race the party nominated a young Illinois lawyer with a gift for oratory. At Peoria on 16 October 1858, Abraham Lincoln gave his famous speech, which set the tone for the next seven years. "[Agitation] will not cease," he said, "until a crisis shall have been reached, and passed. A house divided against itself cannot stand. I believe this government cannot endure, permanently half slave and half free. I do not expect the Union to be dissolved—I do not expect the house to fall—but I do expect it will cease to be divided."

All this time, the abolitionist movement in the North was growing increasingly vociferous. It was guided and fed by activists such as the tenacious antislavery newspaper editor William Lloyd Garrison and literature such as Harriet Beecher Stowe's *Uncle Tom's Cabin*, serialized in 1851 and published as a book in 1852. One activist, however, took matters into his own hands. John Brown planned nothing less than a massive slave uprising. On the night of 16 October 1859 he led a band of twenty-one in an attack on the federal arsenal at Harpers Ferry, at the junction of the Potomac and the Shenandoah (MAP 377, *left*). He hoped to hold it until he was reinforced by slaves rallying to his cause. He would then lead a grand army of liberation through the South. Unfortunately for Brown, he was soon surrounded by federal soldiers, led by Colonel Robert E. Lee. On the morning

MAP 376 (*left*).
Published in 1856 by the Republican Party, this map shows the free states in red, the slave states in black, and the territories not yet decided in gray. Kansas Territory is emphasized in lighter gray. At top left is John Charles Frémont, the presidential candidate for the new party in 1856 with, at top right, his running mate, William Lewis Dayton. Both ran in the election that year under the slogan "Free Soil, free labor, free speech, free men." They lost to Democrat James Buchanan, but the antislavery Republicans would win the next election—with Abraham Lincoln. Statistical tables at right show slaveholders by number of slaves; census data are at bottom, and at left are the numbers regarding the slavery/non-slavery balance in government.

MAP 377 (*above*).
This 1863 map of Harpers Ferry, West Virginia, shows the *Arsenal* attacked by John Brown and his followers in 1859. The Potomac River is at top and the Shenandoah at bottom.

MAP 378 (*right*).
Fort Sumter and Charleston Harbor in 1861, together with a portrait of Major Robert Anderson, the fort's commander. The position of the supply ship *Star of the West*, fired upon in January, is also shown.

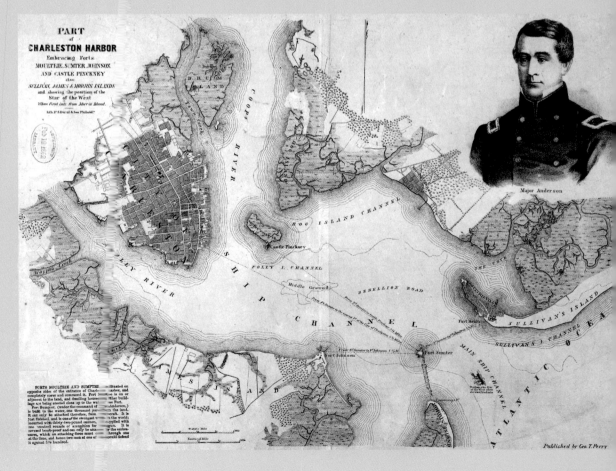

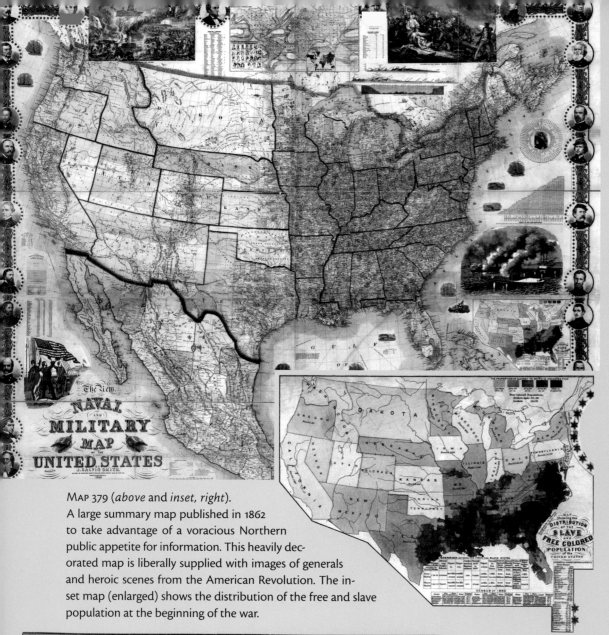

Map 379 (*above* and *inset, right*).
A large summary map published in 1862 to take advantage of a voracious Northern public appetite for information. This heavily decorated map is liberally supplied with images of generals and heroic scenes from the American Revolution. The inset map (enlarged) shows the distribution of the free and slave population at the beginning of the war.

of 18 October they stormed the building where Brown's men were holed up. Brown was captured, though ten of his men were killed. He was tried, found guilty of murder and treason, and in December he was hanged.

Many in the North viewed Brown as a martyr who had died for a just cause and now considered that opposition to slavery could no longer be peaceful. In the South Brown was reviled, and fears of a general slave uprising led by a northerner were magnified.

In November 1860 came the final straw as far as the South was concerned. Abraham Lincoln, widely viewed as an abolitionist, was elected president, despite not even being on the ballot in nine Southern states. It was all too much for the South. South Carolina, already noted for its secessionist tendencies, took the lead. On 20 December 1860 a special convention called by the state legislature voted to secede from the United States. Other states followed; by 1 February 1861, Mississippi, Florida, Alabama, Georgia, Louisiana, and Texas joined South Carolina, and on 4 February the Confederate States of America was created, with Jefferson Davis as president.

Lincoln, though not an ardent abolitionist as such, was an ardent supporter of the Union. The South had demanded the evacuation of all federal forts, but one, Fort Sumter in Charleston Harbor (Map 378, *previous page*), refused. Its commander, Major Robert Anderson, had asked for relief and a supply ship, *Star of the West,* had attempted to resupply the fort on 9 January, only to be warned off by cannon fire from the shore, arguably the first shots of the war. A small Union fleet was near the harbor on 12 April when, at 4:30 in the

Map 380 (*left*).
Another colorful information sheet on the war from the Union side. Here a map is supplementary to biographies of the generals. It was published in 1861.

Map 381 (*above*).
A bird's-eye map of the Mississippi Delta, published in 1861 as one of a set of six maps showing actual and anticipated theaters of war. If the Union navy were to sail up the Mississippi as part of General Winfield Scott's plan to divide and conquer (Map 382, *right, top*), the public would buy this map showing their route. A Union fleet under flag officer Captain David Farragut did sail this route, taking New Orleans in May 1862.

morning, Confederate general Pierre G.T. Beauregard gave the order to open fire. The next day, when he had run out of ammunition, Anderson surrendered. But like MacArthur, he would return.

Lincoln thought a quick war would bring the South back into the fold and called for volunteers for ninety-day enlistments. This had the effect of making four more states secede: Virginia, Arkansas, North Carolina, and Tennessee. It was now clear the conflict would not be short, and it was soon even clearer it would not be easy.

For the first major battle of the Civil War turned into a federal rout. Union forces under Brigadier General Irvin P. McDowell, who had been prodded to attack before he considered his troops ready, advanced into Virginia and were soundly beaten at the First Battle of Bull Run (First Manassas) on 21 July 1861 by a Confederate army under Beauregard. A Union breakthrough was prevented by a brigade of Virginians led by Thomas J. Jackson; Brigadier General Barnard Bee, whose men were retreating, saw Jackson and shouted, "Look, there is Jackson standing like a stone wall! Rally behind the Virginians!" Thus "Stonewall Jackson" became an American legend. The Union army skedaddled (as the press reported it at the time) back to Washington.

Right at this moment Congress passed the Crittenden-Johnson Resolution, which stated that the war was being fought to preserve the Union, and not to end slavery. This was intended to ensure that the slave states still in the Union remained with it.

By the end of the year Brigadier Ulysses S. Grant, who was to rise to command the entire Union army, was advancing up the Tennessee River a part of the strategy of divide and conquer. On 6 February 1862 Fort Henry fell, and ten days later so did Fort Donelson, on the tributary Cumberland River. Surrounded on water by ironclad gunboats and on land by the Union army, some fourteen thousand Confederates surrendered. This was the first major Union victory of the war.

Grant continued south, making for the important railroad center of Corinth, Mississippi, but while camped at a place called Pittsburgh Landing

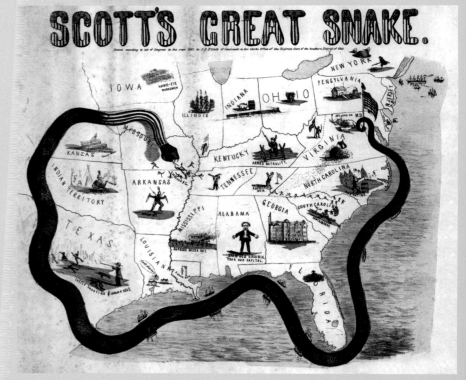

Map 382 (*above*).

General Winfield Scott's so-called Anaconda plan was to encircle and then divide the Confederates using the Mississippi, the Tennessee, and a march through Georgia to the sea, plus the capture of the Confederate capital at Richmond, Virginia. This 1861 simplified cartoon graphic showed the public what he intended to do. Lincoln embraced the plan because he hoped it would lead to a quick end to the war. Much of the plan was implemented, and it was largely successful. However, the initiative was lost after the Union defeat at First Bull Run, and many details in the plan were changed. Scott was thought to be too old for his command and retired in October 1861.

Map 383 (*below*).

The siege of Yorktown, April 5 to 4 May 1862, is superbly illustrated in this bird's-eye-view map. The battle was fought in the same place as the pivotal American Revolution battle of 1781 (see page 88), and the earthworks of both together now confuse the visitor. It is a measure of the severity of the Civil War that this battle is often only rated as a "skirmish," despite the fact that there were nearly five hundred casualties. The outcome was a Union victory in that it allowed the army to continue its advance up the peninsula toward Richmond.

waiting for reinforcements fresh from taking Nashville, Kentucky, he was attacked by Confederate armies under General Albert Sidney Johnston. The Battle of Shiloh, fought on 6–7 April, was the biggest and bloodiest battle to date. Some 110,000 men fought in the battle, and nearly 20,000 were killed or wounded and another 4,000 missing or captured. Grant, despite being outnumbered, prevailed. Johnston was one of the casualties.

In the spring of 1862 there were naval battles on the Mississippi that secured that river for the Union. A major battle at Island No. 10, a fortified island on the Kentucky-Tennessee border, resulted in its capture on 7 April; Memphis fell on 6 June. After an audacious advance up the Mississippi and the capture of New Orleans in May by a Union fleet of warships and mortar bombardment schooners commanded by Captain David Glasgow Farragut (Map 381, page 184), only Vicksburg stood in the way of Union control of the entire river; it would fall in July the following year after a six-week siege, again to an army commanded by Grant.

In Virginia the Union offensive began in 1862 with the Peninsula Campaign, so named because McClellan's army was to land at Fort Monroe, at the tip of the peninsula formed by the York and the James rivers, and push northwards toward Richmond, the Confederate capital. The first part of the operation was successful for the Union. An army of nearly 100,000 began to move up the peninsula. Hampton Roads and Norfolk were occupied. Part of the Confederate army, some 11,000 men, was besieged at Yorktown (Map 383, previous page), the site of the pivotal 1781 battle, but this battle, unlike its predecessor, was inconclusive. After a month of siege the Confederates managed to slip away northwards.

Some 30,000 men, under McDowell, had been retained near Washington, on Lincoln's orders, but were kept from joining with McClellan's forces by the brilliant tactics of a 17,000-strong Confederate army under Stonewall Jackson. His campaign in the Shenandoah Valley alarmed Washington and enhanced Jackson's reputation dramatically.

McClellan's advance up the peninsula was halted by a Confederate army under General Joseph E. Johnston at the Battle of Seven Pines (or Fair Oaks) on 31 May–1 June. Johnston was badly wounded, and his command was taken over by General Robert E. Lee. Another brilliant strategist, Lee brought Jackson's army back from the valley, raising his total strength to about 85,000. With the help of intelligence brought back by his dashing cavalry commander, Brigadier General James Ewell Brown "Jeb" Stuart, who led forays right around the Union army, Lee managed to halt the Union advance. A series of eight battles ensued, usually called the Seven Days Battles, fought around the Chickahominy River immediately south of Richmond. McClellan retreated to the James River, where he was protected by gunboats until August, when the army was evacuated by sea.

McClellan's idea had been to join forces with the rest of the Union army in northern Virginia and attack Richmond once more, this time from the north. But Lee was too quick for him, and the momentum had passed to the Confederates. He marched north himself, hoping to smash the northern Union army, led by Major General John Pope, before it could be joined by McClellan. Lee encountered Pope at Manassas on 29 August and after two days of bloody fighting, assisted by Jackson, forced the Union army to "skedaddle" chaotically northwards once more. This was the Second Battle of Bull Run, or Second Manassas.

The audacious Lee now decided to take advantage of the apparent Union disorder and take the war into the North. On 4 September the first of the Confederate army crossed the Potomac and two days later were camped at Frederick, Maryland. Map 385, right, shows how it was reported in the newspapers. Lee hoped that a victory in the North could bring diplomatic recognition from Europe and perhaps cause northerners to question Lincoln's leadership and force him to sue for peace, or at least lead to demands for peace from Congress. In any case, it would have the effect of drawing Union attention away from Virginia to defend Washington.

Lee drew up a *Proclamation to the People of Maryland* inviting them to embrace the southern cause, and his army was ordered to be polite, not to pillage, and to purchase supplies. Despite this effort, Marylanders ignored him. Lee split his army to cover different objectives, but soon found out he had made a mistake, for as it happened one of McClellan's men discovered Lee's plan (called Special Order 191) in an abandoned campsite, and McClellan—for once—sprang to the attack. Lee reconcentrated most of his forces in a defensive position along Antietam Creek, just east of Sharpsburg. He had about 45,000 men, compared to McClellan's 87,000. The Battle of Antietam, on 17 September 1862 (Map 386, overleaf), was the bloodiest single day in all of North American history. (Gettysburg had even more casualties, but was fought over three days.) Antietam claimed an astonishing 21,000 casualties, nearly 12,000 of which were on the Union side.

One of the turning points of the Civil War, McClellan's victory over Lee at Antietam allowed Lincoln to retain authority over the North's conduct of the war. It induced him to issue the Emancipation Proclamation, which declared slaves anywhere in Confederate territory (only) to be free. This perhaps stopped Britain and France from entering the war on the Confederate side. Certainly Lincoln hoped the proclamation would have this effect.

McClellan reverted to his usual cautious habits after Antietam and did not follow up on the victory, allowing Lee to slip back into Virginia unpursued. Lincoln, furious, replaced him with Major General Ambrose

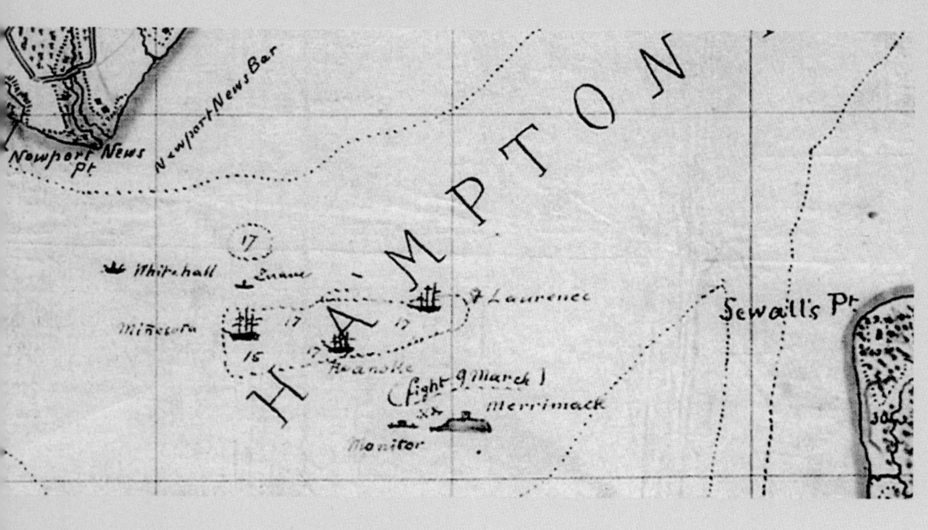

Map 384 (left).
The naval Battle of Hampton Roads, 8–9 March 1862, is depicted on this map detail. This was the first duel between a pair of so-called ironclads, the new metal-sheathed battleships. The Confederate css Virginia had been converted from the Union Merrimac (the name used on this Union map), captured with the Norfolk naval yard at the beginning of the war. The ironclad was used to try to break the Union blockade and caused a great deal of damage to the Union blockade ships in Hampton Roads on 8 March. Overnight, however, the Union ironclad uss Monitor, with a rotating gun turret, entered the fray. The following day the two battled for more than an hour, circling each other and trying to ram each other, but the result was a stalemate, with both appearing impervious to the other's fire. Nonetheless, the duel ended the Confederate attempt to break the Union blockade.

Map 385 (right).
The front page of the New York Herald for 11 September 1862 was full of information—and a map—detailing Lee's invasion of Maryland, which began on 4 September and which would not be halted until the Union victory at the Battle of Antietam on 17 September. On the map, immediately north of Harpers Ferry, and west of Frederick, is Sharpsburg, the location of and the Confederate name for the Battle of Antietam.

THE NEW YORK HERALD.

NEW YORK, THURSDAY, SEPTEMBER 11, 1862.

PRICE TWO CENTS

WHOLE NO. 9494.

THE INVASION OF MARYLAND.

The New Field of Active Operations—All the Important Strategic Points in Pennsylvania, Maryland and on the Line of the Potomac.

THE INVASION OF MARYLAND.

Rebel Pickets Within Four Miles of Ellicott's Mills.

CAPTURE OF TELEGRAPH OPERATORS.

A Noted Secessionist Taken Into Custody as a Spy.

THE ADVANCE OF GEN. M'CLELLAN.

The Town of Barnesville, Near New Market, Occupied by Our Troops.

The Iron Bridge Over the Monocacy Blown Up.

SPIRITED PREPARATIONS IN PENNSYLVANIA.

General McClellan Master of the Situation,

&c., &c., &c.

MAP 386 (*above*).

The Battle of Antietam, known to the Confederates as the Battle of Sharpsburg, fought on 17 September 1862. It produced the most casualties of any North American battle, before or since. The Confederate army (shown in blue) was aligned in defensive positions to the east of Sharpsburg. The Union army (shown in red) was attacking from east to west. McClellan failed to concentrate his forces, fighting three almost separate actions, at top, center, and bottom; this strategy did not let him take advantage of his numerical superiority. The cornfield depicted at the top of the map changed hands, by some reports, fifteen times during the course of the battle. The superb lithograph, *left*, undoubtedly romanticized, illustrates the attack of General Ambrose Burnside's division over a bridge across Antietam Creek, which can be seen at the bottom of the map. It took three or four hours and horrific casualties for Burnside to get across. The bridge was later named Burnside's Bridge.

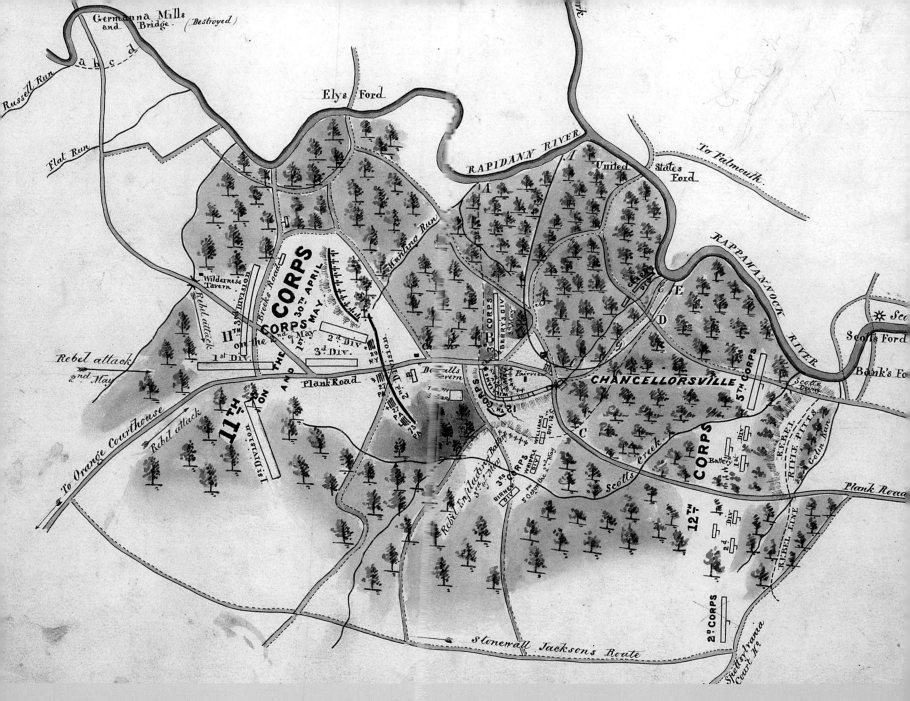

Burnside on 7 November. Burnside was reluctant, being aware of his own military shortcomings; he had been offered the position twice before and had refused. (Burnside had distinctive facial hair, from which comes the word "sideburn.")

With Lincoln prodding him, Burnside planned a late offensive and caught up with Lee's army at Fredericksburg, Virginia, in December. Here more than 100,000 Union soldiers faced about 72,000 Confederate, but Burnside did not have the aptitude to plan such large-scale battles and the result was a Confederate victory. Two months later Burnside resigned and was replaced by Major General Joseph Hooker.

Hooker did not do much better. In May the following year he fought another battle against Lee, which turned into an even more decisive Confederate victory. This was the Battle of Chancellorsville, just west of Fredericksburg (MAP 387, above). The Union had a considerable numerical advantage once again, about 97,000 against 57,000 Confederates, yet Lee's brilliant tactical maneuvering won the day. At a critical moment he divided his army, sending Stonewall Jackson on a flanking movement with most of his men, leaving Lee with only 14,000 facing 70,000 Union troops for several hours. Jackson's attack then surprised Hooker, who retreated. The Union had 20,000 casualties and the Confederates about 17,000, one of whom was Jackson, who passed into Southern myth.

Robert E. Lee, rapidly becoming a legend himself, resolved to capitalize on Confederate momentum at this point and decided to invade the North once more. By so doing he considered that he could threaten Washington, Baltimore, and even Philadelphia, and make the North more likely to sue for peace. Hooker was slow to react to the Confederate movement

MAP 387 (*above*).

The Battle of Chancellorsville, fought 30 April–6 May 1863. Lee's army was on the right on this map, at *Rebel Line* and *Rebel Rifle Pitts*. The route taken by Jackson's men during his outflanking movement is shown with *Stonewall Jackson's Route* at bottom and the *Rebel attack 2nd May* and the red arrows at left. Note that positions are shown over several days.

north, and Lincoln replaced him as overall commander with Major General George G. Meade.

On 1 July 1863 the two armies met at Gettysburg, Pennsylvania, and a battle raged for three days, a battle which has the dubious distinction of having the most casualties of any North American battle ever (MAP 388, *overleaf*). The carnage was stupendous: the Confederates lost a total of 28,000 men and the Union 23,000. Some 7,000 were killed outright on the field of battle, along with 5,000 horses. Considered by many historians to be the most important battle ever fought in the United States, it was without a doubt the major turning point of the war. Gettysburg was a victory for the Union, and it forced Lee to retreat to Virginia, never to return. Once again, however, the Union commander, this time Meade, failed to follow up on the opportunity to pursue and engage Lee while he was at a disadvantage.

Some months later, at the dedication of a soldiers' cemetery at the battlefield, President Lincoln delivered his famous Gettysburg Address. His three-minute speech on 19 November summed up the Civil War as a fight to preserve and advance two fundamental American ideals: constitutional liberty and human equality.

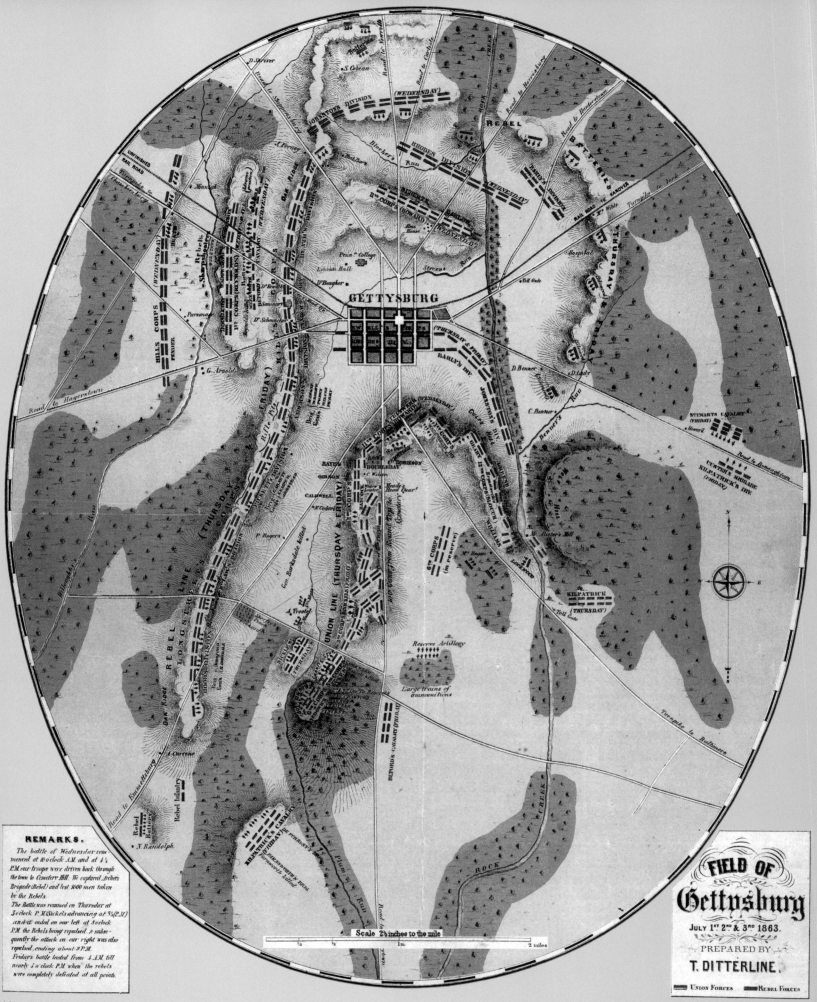

Scale 2⅓ inches to the mile

FIELD OF
Gettysburg
JULY 1ST 2ND & 3RD 1863.
PREPARED BY
T. DITTERLINE.

UNION FORCES   REBEL FORCES

MAP 388.

The Battle of Gettysburg, 1–3 July 1863. This battle was perhaps the most complex of the entire war, involving as it did so many men over three days. Entire books have been written about only one of the three days' fighting alone. At center is the so-called fish-hook line of the Union army, facing on the west and north the line of the Confederate army (in red). This represents the approximate position of the armies on the second and third days of the battle. On the first day the Union army was to the west and north of Gettysburg, then retreated to the position shown in order to occupy higher ground and prevent the Confederates from doing so. More units were arriving on both sides through the second day. At left, on the second and third day, was the command of General James Longstreet, part of which (arriving on the second day) was infantry led by

Major General George E. Pickett and other units. From the center of this line, on the third day, Lee planned a typically audacious move. After a particularly heavy bombardment—likely the biggest artillery exchange of the war—the Union cannon fell silent, and about 12,500 Confederate infantry moved swiftly toward the Union lines. However, the Union guns had been silenced only as a ploy to make the Confederates think they were out of action, and it worked. The federal lines did break but only temporarily, and they were soon filled by reinforcements rushing in from behind. About half of the 12,500 Confederate infantrymen were killed. This is the maneuver known to history as Pickett's Charge, though in fact Pickett was only one of the generals involved and stayed well to the rear, as was the normal practice, and the charge was nearer to a march.

As the Battle of Gettysburg began, Ulysses S. Grant was accepting the surrender of the last impediment to Union navigation on the Mississippi, the fortress at Vicksburg, which fell after a long siege. Union control of the Tennessee was challenged by a Confederate army under General Braxton Bragg, who won a victory over Major General Rosecrans in September in a particularly bloody battle at Chickamauga, Cherokee for "River of Blood," twelve miles south of Chattanooga; Grant in turn defeated Bragg at Chattanooga two months later. Bragg's indecisiveness at critical moments lost the Confederates the interior war and allowed Grant to turn his full attention east.

Grant's aggressiveness and ability to win battles had come to the attention of Lincoln, who made him overall commander of the Union armies in March 1864. Meade retained command of the Union Army of the Potomac but was subordinate to Grant. With Grant, Lincoln finally had a general the match of Lee. Grant developed the concept of total war. For the first time highly coordinated armies would work toward the same end, and they would implement a scorched earth strategy: remove the economic base that supported the Confederates by destroying anything that could be of value. Grant also planned to strike against the Confederacy from several directions at once.

As part of this strategy Grant planned his 1864 Overland Campaign; since the Union army in Virginia was now more than 100,000 strong and Lee's army only about 61,000, it could be a war of attrition. Meade was to follow Lee everywhere he went and destroy his army as soon as he got the chance. Lee went south toward Richmond; Meade, with Grant (who made his headquarters with Meade), followed.

Lee, ever the brilliant tactician, quickly realized what Grant was up to and struck first, and at the Battle of the Wilderness on 5–7 May he managed to get Grant to withdraw, though only temporarily. There was to be no "skedaddling" with Grant. The Wilderness is an area of impenetrable scrub in central Virginia, and Lee had attacked Grant there so that the latter's larger numbers and greater artillery would be of less value to him.

The battles continued, some large, some smaller, but the result was that Lee was pushed farther south. The Battle of Spotsylvania Courthouse, fought from 8 to 21 May, was again inconclusive, which says much for Lee, in that he was now outnumbered by almost two to one. The battles of May

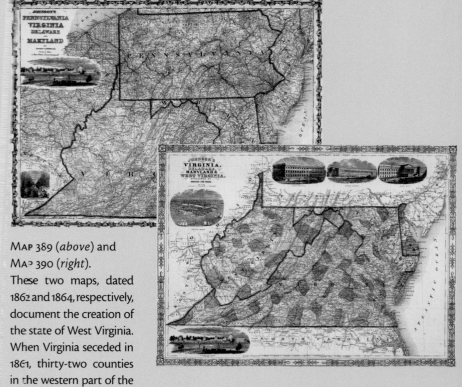

Map 389 (*above*) and
Map 390 (*right*).

These two maps, dated 1862 and 1864, respectively, document the creation of the state of West Virginia. When Virginia seceded in 1861, thirty-two counties in the western part of the state had remained loyal to the Union. Two Wheeling Conventions, under the guidance of John Carlile, created a separate, loyal government of Virginia—not just the western part—so that it could give permission for the creation of a new state. On 31 December 1861 the First Constitutional Convention decided on a name for the new state: West Virginia. Other names in contention had been Kanawha, Western Virginia, Allegheny, and Augusta. On the very eve of Gettysburg, 30 June 1863, West Virginia became the thirty-fifth state. A restored government of Virginia later challenged the creation of the new state, to no avail.

Map 391 (*below*).

Sherman's siege of Atlanta, with troop operations between 19 July and 26 August 1864, is illustrated on this detailed map. Union troop positions have been highlighted in red and Confederate positions in dark blue. Atlanta fell on 2 September.

and June in central Virginia led to what are variously estimated at 39,000 to 66,000 Union casualties and 30,000 to 40,000 Confederate. Finally Grant pinned down Lee's army at Petersburg in June, but the armies dug in for what proved to be nine and a half months of trench warfare, a new kind of mechanized conflict made possible by industrialization and the railroad, which could be used to bring weapons and ammunition up to the front. Petersburg did not fall until 2 April the following year.

Meanwhile, in the Shenandoah Valley, the army of famed cavalry commander Major General Philip Sheridan defeated the aggressive Confederate general Jubal Early at Cedar Creek on 19 October and then, following Grant's strategy, began to destroy the agricultural and industrial base of the region. Also at this time Major General William Tecumseh Sherman, who had taken over as interior commander from Grant when he was promoted to overall Union command, began to march west, and in July laid siege to Atlanta, Georgia. The siege lasted until the beginning of September, at which time Sherman began his well-known "March to the Sea." His army reached Savannah in December, having destroyed crops, livestock, farms, and houses in a wide swath across Georgia. Bales of captured cotton from Savannah were shipped to New York, where they fetched over a million dollars for the Union coffers. From Savannah Sherman turned north, toward Virginia.

The war seemed to be going so well for the Union that Lincoln was reelected in November. His reelection was aided also by the August attack by a Union fleet under Farragut on Mobile Bay, closing one of the few remaining harbors available to the South. Farragut's famous line from this battle "Damn the torpedoes! Full speed ahead!" passed into military folklore. The Union blockade was becoming increasingly more effective. The last significant port still open to the Confederacy was Wilmington, North Carolina. At the entrance to the Cape Fear River stood Fort Fisher, until now impregnable to Union fire. In December renewed attempts to capture the fort were made, to no avail, but on 15 January 1865, after days of bombardment from the sea and an assault from land, Fort Fisher fell (MAP 392, *left*). Within weeks Wilmington was captured, and the last supply line to the Confederate army was broken.

The Union navy had tried to retake Fort Sumter at Charleston for two years without success, but on 17 February, with Sherman's army approaching from Savannah, the fort was evacuated and it was in Union hands again. A little less than two months later a little ceremony was held as Robert Anderson, who had surrendered the fort in 1861, hoisted the same Union flag he had been forced to take down four years before.

The end was near for the Confederates. Petersburg finally fell to the Union army on 2 April after the Confederates were defeated at the battle of Five Forks—the last battle of the many that had taken place around the city—the day before. Grant ordered a grand assault that finally broke the Confederate defenses, and Lee pulled as much of his army as he could save from Petersburg and also abandoned Richmond, which fell the next day. Lee headed west toward Lynchburg, intending to resupply his army and then attempt to join up with General Joseph E. Johnston's army in North Carolina. But it was not to be. Relentlessly pursued by Grant, after a series of running battles he was outflanked by Sheridan's cavalry and cornered at Appomattox. There, on 9 April, Lee surrendered. With the main Confederate army gone, other Confederate forces elsewhere surrendered also, though battles continued in some theaters until May. In North Carolina, Johnston surrendered his army to Sherman on 26 April, despite orders to the contrary from Jefferson Davis. As late as the end of June, Union whaling ships were attacked by Confederate ships in the North Pacific.

President Lincoln savored the Union victory for only a few days. On the evening of 14 April he was shot and killed as he attended a performance at Ford's Theater in Washington; his assassin, John Wilkes Booth, was a Confederate sympathizer.

MAP 392 (*above*).
In early 1865 *Harper's Weekly* published this map of Fort Fisher and the fortifications of Wilmington, North Carolina, the last Confederate supply port. Wilmington was evacuated by the Confederates on the night of 21–22 February.

Below. Confederate officials flee across the James River from Richmond as their city explodes in flame from the Union bombardment, 2 April 1865. The Southern capital fell to the Union the following day.

Above. The scale of the technology of war changed forever during the Civil War. This is a Union mortar nicknamed "Dictator" that was used at the siege of Petersburg. It weighed so much that it had to be transported on a specially strengthened railroad wagon. It could fire a 200-pound shell two and a half miles.

MAP OF
APPOMATTOX COURT HOUSE
AND VICINITY.

Showing the relative positions of the Confederate and Federal Armies at the time of General R. E. Lee's Surrender, April 9th 1865.

Lee's Head-Quarters.

Grant's Head-Quarters.

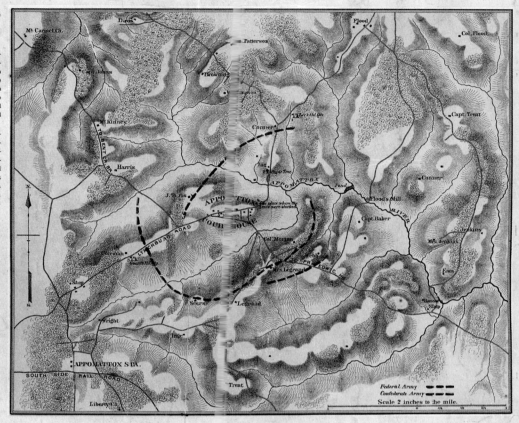

Historical Notes.

On Sunday, the 2d of April 1865, General Lee was holding at Petersburg a semi-circular line south of the Appomattox River, with his left resting on the river, and his right on the South Side Rail Road, fifteen miles from the city. The Federals were pressing his whole line. Sheridan with his cavalry on the right. To save his right flank, General Lee telegraphed to Richmond, that during the night he would fall back to the north side of the river, and ordered that Richmond be evacuated simultaneously.

On the morning of the 3d the retreat commenced in earnest, General Grant hurrying up to get possession of Burkesville—the junction of the South Side and Danville Railroad—in hopes of cutting off General Lee from Danville or Lynchburg. On the 5th a portion of the Federal forces occupied Burkesville, Sheridan with his cavalry being in advance at Jetersville on the Danville Railroad. General Lee at Amelia C. H., 6 miles north of Sheridan's advance. In this situation General Sheridan telegraphed:—"I feel confident of capturing the entire Army of Northern Virginia, if we exert ourselves. I see no escape for Lee." On the evening of the 6th some heavy fighting took place between the Federal advance and Lee's retreating column. Sheridan again telegraphed: "If the thing is pressed I think Lee will surrender." Lee continued to press for Lynchburg—his men probably anticipating the result, daily leaving him by thousands,—until on the morning of the fated 9th of April, 1865, he confronted the overwhelming forces of Gen. Grant with a little less than 8,000 muskets.

The position of the Confederate army was briefly this: occupying the narrow strip of land between the South Side Railroad and the James River; the only road on which it was possible to retreat, was that marked Lynchburg road on the map. Sheridan with his cavalry having struck the railroad at Appomattox Station, obtaining possession of the Lynchburg road, thus effectually cutting off Lee's retreat. Gen. Lee now had the choice of either cutting his way directly through the Federal forces, or immediate surrender. In view of the immense disparity of forces between the ranks of the half starved Confederates and the overwhelming army of General Grant, he chose the latter alternative.

Generals Lee and Grant met at the house of Wilmer McLane, Esq., and after a brief interview, at 3½ o'clock p. m.

on the 9th of April 1865, the Articles of Capitulation were signed by General Lee. While negotiations were being conducted by the two Commanders-in-Chief, the General officers of either army were mingling socially together in the streets of Appomattox C. H., and drinking mutual healths. Gens. Ord, Sheridan, Gibbon, Michie and others of the Federals, Gens. Longstreet, Heath, Gordon and others, of the Confederates.

At 4 o'clock p. m. the announcement of Lee's surrender was made to Grant's army. The wildest enthusiasm immediately broke forth, and all seemed mad with joy.

As the great Confederate General rode past his gallant little band from his interview with Gen. Grant, whole lines of battle rushed to the beloved old chief, and breaking ranks, each struggled with the other to wring him by the hand. With tears rolling down his cheeks, General Lee could only say, "Men, we have fought through the war together. I have done the best that I could for you."

On the morning of the 12th April the Army of Northern Virginia marched by divisions to a point near Appomattox Court House, and stacked arms and accoutrements. Maj. Gen. Gibbon representing the United States authorities.

On the afternoon of the 12th, with an escort of Federal cavalry as a guard of honor, attended by a portion of his staff, General Lee returned to Richmond.

Thus quietly passed from the theater of the most desperate war of modern times the renowned Commander of the Army of Northern Virginia, and the remnants of that once invincible army were quietly wending their way to their long forsaken homes.

LIST OF ENGRAVINGS.

Gen. Lee's Head-Quarters near Conner's House.—Position marked by a flag and No. 1 on the map.

View of Appomattox Court House.

General Grant's Head-Quarters near Coleman's House.—Position marked by a flag and No. 3 on the map.

Place where the arms were stacked. The exact spot is marked No. 4 on the map. In this picture may be seen the famous apple tree, (position marked with a tree and No. 2 on the map,) near Hix's house, where the first meeting between the Commanders was generally, but incorrectly, supposed to have taken place.

McLane's House, in the village of Appomattox Court House, where the articles of capitulation were signed. The signing took place in the front room, on the right of the door, entering from the porch.

McLane's House.

GEN. LEE'S FAREWELL TO HIS ARMY.

HEAD-QUARTERS ARMY NORTHERN VIRGINIA,
APRIL 10TH, 1865.

After four years of arduous service, marked by unsurpassed courage and fortitude, the Army of Northern Virginia has been compelled to yield to overwhelming numbers and resources.

I need not tell the survivors of so many hard-fought battles, who have remained steadfast to the last, that I have consented to this result from no distrust of them; but feeling that valor and devotion could accomplish nothing that could compensate for the loss that would have attended the continuation of the contest, I have determined to avoid the useless

Appomattox Court House.

sacrifice of those whose past services have endeared them to their countrymen.

By the terms of agreement, officers and men can return to their homes and remain there until exchanged.

You will take with you the satisfaction that proceeds from the consciousness of duty faithfully performed; and I earnestly pray that a merciful God will extend to you His blessing and protection.

With an unceasing admiration of your constancy and devotion to your country, and a grateful remembrance of your kind and generous consideration of myself, I bid you an affectionate farewell

R. E. LEE, General.

Place where the Arms were Stacked.

198   Entered according to act of Congress, in the year 1866, by Henderson & Co. in the Clerk's office of the District Court of Maryland.

MAP 393 (above).
This lithograph was published soon after the end of the war to explain Lee's surrender to the public. It shows the position of the Union and Confederate armies at the time of the surrender, and the margins contain details of the event, with, at bottom, Lee's farewell address to his army.

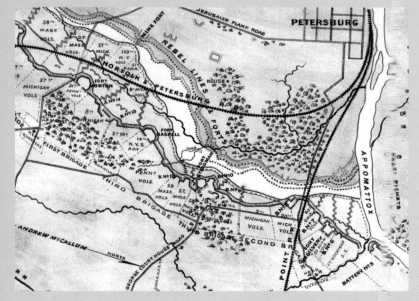

MAP 394 (above).
Part of the fortifications and army positions in front of Petersburg, Virginia, as they were on 1 April 1865, just before Grant ordered the all-out assault the next morning that finally overran the Confederate defenses.

The Civil War had lasted four years. Nearly four hundred battles had been fought (depending on the definition of a battle). Nearly four million men had fought in the war and over 558,000 were killed, 359,500 Union and 198,500 Confederate. Another 412,000 men were left wounded. The Union had been saved, but only at a horrendous cost in human lives.

Reconstruction took many years, and the weak leadership of Andrew Johnson, who followed Lincoln, and later that of others, allowed black people in the South to continue to be cowed by whites for many years. The Thirteenth Amendment, which outlawed slavery, was ratified by the end of 1865. The Fourteenth Amendment of 1868 guaranteed due process and equality under the law, reversing the Dred Scott decision; and the Fifteenth Amendment, passed in 1870, extended the vote to black men, though not to women. Nonetheless, it would be many years before these amendments were fully applied to all in the South.

Ulysses S. Grant was elected president in 1868 and served two terms, 1869–77. William Tecumseh Sherman served as commander-in-chief of the U.S. Army from 1864 to 1884. Robert E. Lee died in 1870. Over 50,000 books have been written about the Civil War, more than on any other topic.

The Transcontinental Link

A transcontinental railroad had been a gleam in many an eye, but Theodore D. Judah was the man whose inspiration made it happen. A young New York railroad engineer, he was recruited by the as yet non-existent Sacramento Valley Railroad in 1854 to survey a line from Sacramento to Marysville, the gateway to the Sierra Nevada.

Investment in an upstart railroad was hard to come by, and the Sacramento Valley ran out of money, so its line, the first in California, reached only to Folsom, a distance of twenty-two miles. But Judah had come to believe that the valleys east of Sacramento could be used for a railroad clear across the Sierra. He surveyed a route using the infamous Donner Pass (see page 156) in October 1860. Then he founded his own railroad to pursue his dream of a transcontinental railroad.

After Judah interested some wealthy Sacramento merchants, the Central Pacific Railroad was formally constituted on 28 June 1861, with Leland Stanford as president, Collis P. Huntington as vice-president, Mark Hopkins as secretary and treasurer, Charles Crocker as a director, and Judah as chief engineer. After much lobbying in Washington—not least by Judah himself, ably assisted by his wife, Anna—many were convinced of the value of a transcontinental link. One in fact existed as of October that year, a single line of metal spanning the country—the telegraph. It in turn had put out of business the Pony Express, which with relays of fast horse riders connected St. Joseph, on the Missouri, with Sacramento in just ten days. The Pony Express lasted but eighteen months.

One of the biggest factors in getting the transcontinental railroad under way was President Lincoln. From his beginnings as a lawyer he had been fascinated by railroads and railroad law, and perhaps more than any other he saw how a transcontinental line would bind the country together. Thus in 1862, despite his distraction with the war, he supported a Pacific Railroad Act that created a Union Pacific Railroad, authorized to build west from the Missouri to connect with the Central Pacific.

Critical to the success of the venture was its financing. The government gave the railroads five alternate sections (square miles) of each side of the track for every mile of track laid and purchased railroad bonds, the money for which was awarded as the work progressed. The act was amended in 1864 to award ten sections on each side of the track. A transcontinental link was now just a matter of time, but Judah did not live to see his dream come to fruition. On one of his frequent trips back to New York he contracted yellow fever while crossing the isthmus of Central America and died just as the first Central Pacific spike was being driven in California.

The first stock in the Union Pacific was sold in September 1862, and its largest paid-up subscriber was Mormon leader Brigham Young, who wanted a railroad to Salt Lake City. The men behind the Union Pacific, particularly its vice-president, Thomas C. ("Doc") Durant, set up a financing and supply business called the Crédit Mobilier, the principal purpose of which seems to have been to ensure, come what may, that the principals would recoup their investment by being paid for the construction. On 2 December 1863, eleven months after the Central Pacific had begun work in California, the Union Pacific began working on the line out of Omaha, but work progressed slowly at first. This was not surprising, for the route itself could be changed if it promised to make more money. The first chief engineer, Peter Dey, resigned in December 1864, after twenty-two miles of track had been graded, when ordered by Durant to abandon his work and

MAP 395 (*below*).
This 1867 map shows the route of the transcontinental railroad, the Union Pacific westward from Omaha and the Central Pacific east from Sacramento. A key is at right. Note that the completed track is shown crosshatched while the route yet to be laid is a plain black line. According to this map, track is complete between Omaha and Cheyenne and between Sacramento and a point a few miles east of the California-Nevada boundary; track remains to be laid south from Sacramento to San Jose, from where the line to San Francisco is complete. With the difficult and slow part of the route, across the Sierra Nevada, behind it, the Central Pacific is by this date about the same distance from the joining place at Promontory, Utah, as the Union Pacific.

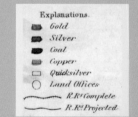

MAP 396 (right).
Theodore Judah's map of the proposed route of the Sacramento Valley Railroad published in an 1854 report. North is to the right. The original line of the Sacramento Railroad from Sacramento to Folsom is indicated, which north to Marysville and beyond is shown as a future extension. The Donner Pass through the Sierra Nevada that Judah eventually found and supported as the most viable route is not named but is in the mountains just to the north of the lake, which, although also not named, is Lake Tahoe. Two other possible routes are indicated. The farthest north gap is shown as *Emigrants Trail,* through Noble Pass, found by William H. Noble in 1851 and first used in 1852. Between it and the Donner is the Beckwourth Pass, found by James B. Beckwourth in 1851. The route down the western slope of the Sierra utilized the difficult Feather River Canyon. The majority of the route had been surveyed for a railroad before, by Lieutenant E.G. Beckwith, conducting the Pacific Railroad Survey of the central route (see page 180).

MAP 397 (below).
The location of *Promontary* (Promontory, Utah), the final meeting place of the Central Pacific and the Union Pacific, is labeled, north of the Great Salt Lake, on this detail of an 1873 map.

build the track on a circuitous route that would add nine miles—but bring in an extra $144,000 and another 115,2000 acres of land grants. Money-making opportunities overrode railroad considerations.

In February 1866 the Casement brothers, John ("Jack") and Dan, were put in charge of the tracklaying operations. The pair of Civil War veteran officers had a reputation for getting things done. The man who would ultimately guide the Union Pacific to completion was Grenville Mullen Dodge, a Union general until 1866 (whose last duties were protecting railroad workers and settlers in the West) and a highly regarded railroad engineer with a string of successes behind him. He had worked before the war for the Chicago & Rock Island Railroad, which was building a line from Chicago to Council Bluffs, across the Missouri from Omaha, and in that capacity Dodge had already surveyed the route taken up the Platte by the Union Pacific. Once Dodge became chief engineer of the Union Pacific he made the tracklaying more efficient by operating on an essentially military footing—not difficult because most of the workers were ex-Union or Confederate soldiers. Durant managed the money end of things, often rather too tightly, for the men were always late being paid.

Dodge was responsible for many details of the route and the precise system used to push the line ever westwards. Surveyors out ahead would place small wooden marker posts in the ground for the graders to follow, who might themselves be several hundred miles ahead of the tracklayers.

On 16 November 1867 the track reached Cheyenne. Financing problems eased as Union Pacific bonds became seen as a sure thing, investors invested, and of course bond money flowed in from the government for every mile of track completed.

Map 398 (*left*) and **Map 399** (*left, center*).
The discovery of gold and silver on the eastern slope of the Sierra Nevada in 1859 gave the directors of the Central Pacific another incentive to build their railroad. **Map 398** is an 1875 bird's-eye-view map. **Map 399** shows land divisions on an 1873 map. In June 1859 prospectors found a high-grade mixed ore with a value of $3,000 per ton of silver and $876 of gold. Virginia City and Gold Hill sprang up almost overnight. The veins of ore, called the Comstock Lode, involved extensive underground mining, which required a lot of capital to finance it. The lure of gold and silver enticed yet more hopefuls to the West. The Comstock Lode eventually yielded nearly $400 million in silver and gold ore. Yet by 1882 it was all gone.

Map 400 (*below*).
Once the Union Pacific had its transcontinental railroad and all the land grants that went with it, land sales began, both to obtain revenue from land sales and to build markets to generate traffic. But the company was not blind to the tourist potential. This rather spectacular 1883 wall map was designed as an advertisement directed at building passenger traffic from the Pacific coast, and it is surrounded by images of scenic beauty along the route. The *Central Short Line* referred to is the Oregon Short Line, completed from the Columbia to join the main transcontinental line in 1882.

The Central Pacific construction was organized and supervised by Charles Crocker, and it began to employ many Chinese workers, recruited principally in San Francisco; the railroad had grand plans to attract more workers to emigrate directly from China, though this plan did not induce many to come. By August 1867 the Central Pacific had crested the summit of the Sierra with the help of many deep cuts, high trestles, and tunnels, and was headed downslope, down the Truckee River valley. The construction turned into a race to see which railroad could lay the most track; after all, laying track, with its attendant government bonds and land grants, was a highly profitable venture, which both companies aimed to make the most of. So much, in fact, that instead of the tracks simply meeting, the railroads laid almost two hundred miles of parallel track after having passed each other, and Congress had to step in, as it did on 10 April 1869, to define a meeting place. The place they chose was Promontory Point, on the north side of the Great Salt Lake.

Ceremonies were planned for 8 May 1869, and the Central Pacific officials duly arrived, but there was a hitch. The train carrying the tight-fisted Durant had been held up by a band of unpaid tie-cutters and graders at Piedmont, on the Wyoming-Utah boundary, and would not be released until they were paid. It might have been a setup to ensure Durant's construction company was paid as well. Nonetheless, two days later the Union Pacific train arrived at Promontory Point, and on 10 May Leland Stanford drove the last spike. "Done" was telegraphed instantly to east and west coasts. The transcontinental railroad was complete.

Of about 1,750 miles from Omaha to Sacramento, the Union Pacific had built about 1,060 miles and the Central Pacific 690, the latter over much more difficult terrain. This first transcontinental railroad was followed in due course by others, and in concert with the Homestead Act of 1862, which gave free land to Plains settlers, the railroads opened the West to EuroAmerican settlement like nothing else could have—and in the process sealed the fate of the way of life of the Indians.

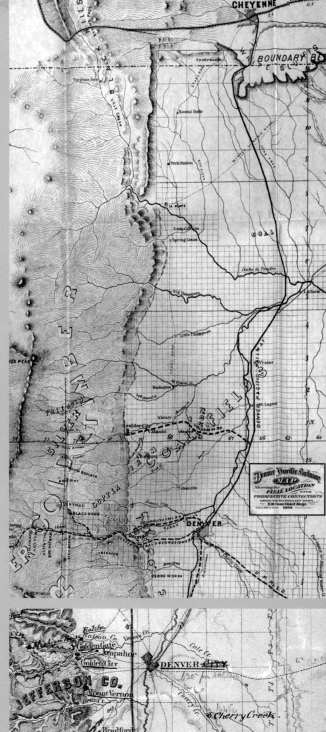

MAP 401 (*below*).
This 1878 Department of the Interior map summarizes the land grants made by the federal government "to aid in the construction of railroads and wagon roads." The amount of land granted is generalized and not to scale, deliberately giving the impression that much more land was granted to the railroads than was actually the case. Bonds, often characterized as a gift, in fact had to be repaid. A final settlement with all the western railroads that had issued bonds to the government was made in 1898–99. Some $167.4 million was repaid on initial loans of $64.6 million, making the Pacific railroads a good deal for the government as well as for the railroads—and for the nation.

MAP 402 (*below, bottom*).
Much more accurate is this 1880 map of the land granted to the Union Pacific in Nebraska, but it still fails to note that it was alternate sections that were granted, not the entire green swath each side of the railroad.

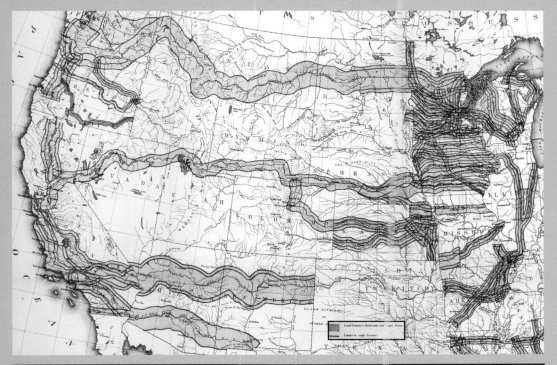

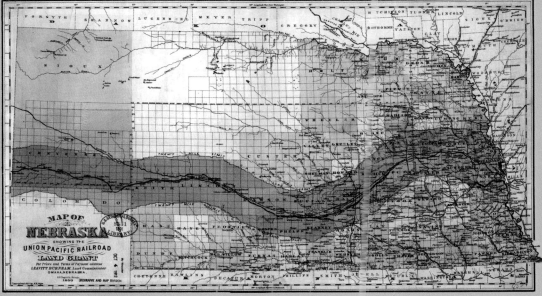

MAP 403 (*above, top*) and MAP 404 (*above*).
The settlement of Denver, founded as St. Charles in 1858, was bypassed by the Union Pacific Railroad, since Cheyenne was expected to grow at its expense. But the Denver region grew after 1859 with the discovery of gold. Colorado Territory governor John Evans gathered together a group of Denver entrepreneurs to invest in a railroad to connect their city with the Union Pacific. The Denver Pacific Railway was built in 1869–70, and the first train pulled into Denver on 24 June 1870. Two months later a competing railroad, aided by investors from nearby Golden, was completed from Kansas to Denver. This was the Kansas Pacific, and its completion and linking with the Denver Pacific was correctly the actual last link in the transcontinental railroad. (When the Union Pacific and Central Pacific lines had joined at Promontory, Utah, the year before, passengers still had to disembark at the Missouri and take a steamboat across the river.) MAP 403 is from an 1868 engineer's report on the feasibility of the Denver Pacific line and includes the word *Gold* prominently shown. The Union Pacific transcontinental line runs through Cheyenne, at top. The *U.P.Ry.* dashed line at bottom was in fact the Kansas Pacific route. MAP 404 shows Denver just four years after its founding; someone has penciled in 630^m *from Atchison*, Kansas.

Chicagou, Chicago

Above. The first Fort Dearborn, shown in 1805, with the Indian Agency house to the right. The scene is from an 1884 history of Chicago.

Europeans first arrived at the site of what is today Chicago in 1673. Louis Jolliet and Jacques Marquette returned from their journey down the Mississippi by traveling up the Illinois River and the Des Plaines River and portaging to the Chicago River, after being told by Indians that this was a quicker way back to Lake Michigan than the way they had come (see page 41). Father Marquette returned the following year to set up a mission on the Illinois River, but not until sometime in the mid-1780s did the first permanent resident of Chicago, Jean Baptiste Point du Sable, build a house near the mouth of the Chicago River.

By the Treaty of Greenville in 1795, land that included Chicago was ceded to the United States by the Indians (see page 98). This prepared the way for the establishment of Fort Dearborn in 1803, founded on orders of secretary of war General Henry Dearborn. In June 1812, the War of 1812

Map 405 (*above*).
This 1718 map by French geographer Guillaume De L'Isle shows both branches of the Chicago River entering Lake Michigan at *Chicagou*. Here the *Chicagou R.* is the Des Plaines River.

Map 406 (*below*).
A copy of James Thompson's first plat of Chicago, laid out in 1830 on the orders of the canal company. The original of this map was lost in the 1871 fire.

Map 407 (*below*).
This map of Chicago as it was in 1812 is taken from a book published in 1844. The *Fort* is Fort Dearborn, and the Chicago River divides into the *S. Branch* and the *N. Branch*. The Indian *Agency House* is below the fort, and the river diversion to create a new harbor mouth is shown; this was constructed between 1833 and 1839 as part of the works for the Illinois and Michigan Canal.

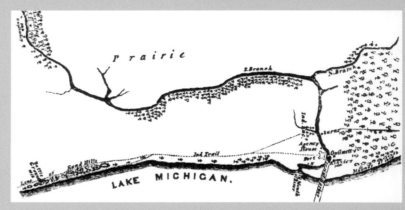

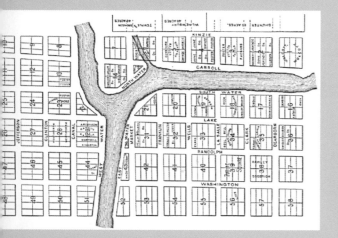

Map 408 (*right*).
Chicago's famous downtown elevated railroad is shown in red on this 1893 bird's-eye-view poster map advertising the Rock Island Railroad (station at center). Although the downtown neighborhood encircled by the elevated track came to be known as the Loop, the name originated in an earlier circle of grade-level streetcar track. The elevated system was begun in 1882 and still runs; the railroad, closed down in 1980, is now the Metra suburban service to Joliet.

Map 409 (*right*) and Map 410 (*below*). Superb bird's-eye maps of Chicago in the booster style of the day, showing ships galore in the river and on the lake and economic activity of all kinds. Map 409 shows Chicago in 1858, three years before the great fire of 9 October 1871, and Map 410 shows the city twenty-two years later, in 1893. The small inset on Map 409 depicts Chicago in 1820.

CHICAGO IN 1868.

from Schiller Street North Side to 12th Street South Side.

began. The fort was considered in-defensible and so was ordered to be abandoned. The retreating garrison and civilians were attacked by Indi-ans incited by the British, and many Americans were killed; the fort was burned. It was rebuilt in 1816, after the war had ended.

Settlement in the vicinity of the fort grew slowly, until in 1829 plans materialized to construct the Illinois and Michigan Canal to con-nect Chicago to the Mississippi, a possibility that had been noted early even by Jolliet and Marquette. The following year James Thompson, a civil engineer employed by the canal commissioners, laid out the first plat of Chicago (Map 406, *far left*), and in September 1830 lots were sold by public auction. Three years later the town was incorporated, with a population of 350. The influx of settlers was such, however, that by 1837 Chicago was able to be incorporated as a city, with by then 4,170 inhabi-tants. The river's mouth was straightened as part of the canal works, but the canal itself was not completed until 1848—just in time to become outmoded by the railroad. That very year the Chicago and Galena Union Railroad began service on the first ten-mile section of its line, as a portage railroad between the Chicago and the Des Plaines rivers. Chicago eventu-ally became the largest railroad center in the world.

Chicago's advantageous position ensured continued growth. With the opening of the Great Plains to EuroAmerican settlement, railroads were built that converged on the city from all directions, and the city grew apace. Industries arose to supply the hinterland, and facilities were created in Chi-cago to handle the produce from the Plains. The huge consolidated stock-yard opened in 1865 and grew to cover a square mile. Beginning with Mont-gomery Ward in 1872, a number of mail order houses opened in Chicago, becoming the main street shopping center for much of the rural West.

A setback occurred in 1871 with the great fire of that year, which started in a west side cow barn, leapt the south branch of the river, and destroyed the downtown. Three hundred were killed, ninety thousand made homeless. Yet the city rebuilt quickly, and three years later little evidence of the fire remained. Growth continued at such a rate that by 1890 the city was the second largest in the United States, with over a million inhabitants.

I Will Fight No More Forever

The arrival of the railroad and the surge of EuroAmerican settlers onto the Plains sealed the fate of the great buffalo herds and with them, the Indians' way of life. Perhaps as many as 75 million buffalo—correctly bison—once roamed the Plains, yet by 1900 there were only about a thousand left. The killing had accelerated after 1871, when a way to create commercial leather from buffalo hides was found. The continued and relentless erosion of the lands available for hunting and the confining of the Indians to ever-smaller reservations created conflict as they tried, ultimately in vain, to turn back the tide. When they did, the government sent in the U.S. Army. The violence reached a peak during the two decades after 1860.

Along the Minnesota River in southern Minnesota in 1862 lived about six thousand Dakota (Santee Sioux), on a reservation created by treaty in 1851. The government had not honored parts of the treaty, and some of the reservation had been lost when Minnesota became a state in 1858. Nonetheless the Dakota Sioux were apparently docilely accepting their lot in return for an annual government annuity. But that year the annuity failed to arrive, merchants refused credit, and bitterness set in. Taking advantage of the fact that many soldiers were away fighting in the Civil War, the Dakota led an uprising to settle scores. Initiated by younger warriors and led by Chief Taoyateduta (Little Crow), it rapidly got out of hand; the army's Fort Ridgely, full of refugees, was besieged, and the town of New Ulm was burnt to the ground. Some 800 settlers were killed, and 30,000 abandoned their farms in panic. Federal help was slow to arrive because of the Civil War, but regiments were eventually assembled. At Mankato a militia of 1,600 was hastily organized and with the federal troops engaged the Dakota at Wood Lake, killing many and taking 2,000 Dakota captive. In Mankato, 303 were sentenced to death, though the sentences of most were commuted by President Lincoln, but thirty-eight were hanged. It was the largest mass execution in U.S. history.

The Minnesota reservation was abolished and about 1,600 Dakota Sioux were removed to a reservation farther west, a move during which perhaps 130 died. But this would not be the last heard from the Sioux.

One of the most infamous incidents of the western Indian wars period was a massacre that took place at Sand Creek, on the Plains of eastern Colorado Territory. A group of about 550 southern Cheyenne and Arapaho, led by Cheyenne chief Black Kettle, had surrendered after signing a treaty ceding their lands and agreeing to move to a reservation in what is now Oklahoma. They were attacked in the early dawn hours of 29 November 1864 by cavalry and other troops under Colonel John Chivington. About 150 men, women, and children—even infants—were shot as they attempted to escape. Chivington was later investigated by Congress, which concluded that he was guilty of a "cowardly and cold-bloodied slaughter." He escaped prosecution only because of the general amnesty after the Civil War.

On the Plains, the massacre led to more years of Indian warfare as revenge was sought. Black Kettle was once more the chief at a village tracked down almost precisely four years later by troops under a man whose name was to become virtually synonymous with Indian wars in the West—Lieutenant Colonel George Armstrong Custer. At dawn on 26 November 1868, on the banks of the Washita River in western Oklahoma, in an action eerily similar to the Sand Creek massacre (though, it must be admitted, there are different versions of events), Black Kettle and forty of his people were cut down as they tried to surrender, again many of them women and children. Eight hundred horses were also killed and much

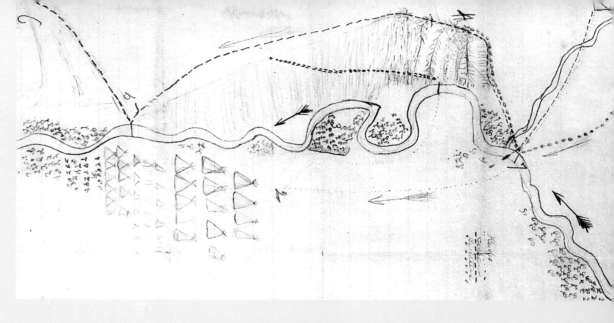

property burned. Custer ordered his men not to kill women and children (and indeed took some as hostages) and thus escaped censure. (His superior officer, General Philip Sheridan, had explicitly ordered that women and children were not to be killed.) Custer was driven off after as many as eight thousand Arapaho, Kiowa, and Cheyenne camped nearby moved to the rescue. The apparent success of this venture—from his point of view—against larger Indian numbers may well have emboldened Custer eight years later.

One notable Indian military success was the war conducted by the Lakota Sioux chief Makhpyia-luta (Red Cloud) in 1866–68. The Lakota waged war on U.S. troops attempting to secure the Bozeman Trail, which led from the Oregon Trail on the North Platte to new goldfields in Montana. On 21 December 1866 Captain William J. Fetterman, who had boasted that he could ride through the entire Sioux Nation with only eighty men, found out that he was wrong. Lured into an ambush by a young warrior named Tasunka Witko—Crazy Horse—he and all eighty of his men were killed. By 1868 the government conceded that Red Cloud had won—for the time being. The second Treaty of Fort Laramie, signed in 1868, established a huge Lakota reservation centered on the Black Hills without any military supervision, an unprecedented concession.

The standoff—for it was little more than that—lasted only a few years. Custer led his cavalry on a reconnaissance into the Black Hills in 1874 and reported that there was gold to be found. His report triggered a gold rush and violation of the 1868 treaty. Sioux and northern Cheyenne joined forces to counter the encroachment onto their hunting grounds. To force Sioux and Cheyenne back to reservations, the U.S. Army planned a three-pronged offensive. Brigadier General George Crook approached from the south, Colonel John Gibbon from the west, and Brigadier General Alfred H. Terry from the east. On 17 June 1876 Crook, with a column of 1,000 U.S. troops and about 300 Indian allies, was attacked by about 1,500 Lakota under Crazy Horse at Rosebud Creek, just east of the Bighorn River in southern Montana. Although the encounter was militarily inconclusive, Crook turned back, a move that would prove fatal to some of Terry's men.

Custer, with about 600 men of his Seventh Cavalry, had separated from Terry's contingent, of which he was part, on 22 June to pursue the Lakota who had attacked Crook, and on the morning of 25 June was nearing a huge Lakota Sioux and Cheyenne village on the Little Bighorn River. Custer, like everyone else, had grossly underestimated Indian strength—which may have approached 2,000 warriors—and, without waiting for Terry or Gibbon, decided to attack. He

MAP 411 (*above*) and MAP 412 (*below*).
Two maps of the Battle of Little Bighorn, fought on 25 June 1876. Both are oriented with north to the top left. MAP 411 was drawn five days later by Lieutenant Robert Patterson Hughes, an aide-de-camp of the expedition commander Alfred Terry. The map was enclosed by Hughes in a letter to his wife, a letter that supports the view that Custer acted rashly by engaging his adversary before help arrived and by splitting his men into three groups despite the odds. The Lakota and Cheyenne encampment is at bottom center, below (west) of the Little Bighorn River, with the arrow to the right of it being the direction of the initial Reno attack. Custer's route is the dashed line above (east of) the river (though this is not known for certain), while the site of the "Last Stand" is at top left. The defense of Reno and Benteen is at right center top. MAP 412 was painted by White Bird, a Northern Cheyenne, on muslin, from memory, about 1895. The emphasis here is on the actual fighting: the Last Stand is at left and the Reno-Benteen defense at right, while Reno's initial attack on the encampment is across the river, to the right of the tents.

Left. A superb photograph of an encampment of Lakota, taken at White Clay Creek, South Dakota, in January 1891, soon after the massacre at Wounded Knee, nearby, and the subsequent surrender of most of the rest of the Indians. The image was taken by John C.H. Grabill, who was responsible for many late frontier photographs of the West.

Map 413 (*above and inset*).

In the spring of 1877 the Nez Percé (Nimi'ipuu), led by Hin-mah-too-yah-lat-kekht, better known to history as Chief Joseph (*photo inset*), were ordered by the government's agent, Brigadier General Oliver O. Howard, to move to a reservation along the Clearwater River in Idaho Territory. Resentment provoked some young Nez Percé warriors to attack and burn ranches in the area southeast of Lewiston, shown as *Ranches burnt* on the map *Scene of the Outbreak* (*inset*). The main Nez Percé camp was attacked by part of Howard's army as a result. The Nez Percé won that day, the Battle of White Bird Canyon, but Chief Joseph knew that his people could not withstand Howard's full army and fled. Over the next four months Joseph led his tribe on a 1,500-mile attempt to escape, first to their allies the Crow, and then, when they learned the Crow would no longer shelter them, to Canada. Joseph was slowed down by women and children and

even livestock, making it a difficult task—and an amazing feat—to evade the more mobile army of Howard and later one led by Nelson Miles. The Nez Percé route is shown on this rare War Department map published late in 1877 as part of Howard's report. The series of skirmishes and battles along the way are also marked. Battlefields are depicted around the edge. That of Clearwater, 11–12 July, is visible at center, bottom. Joseph was finally cornered and defeated only forty miles from the Canadian border at the Battle of Bear Paw Mountains, at top right. Joseph surrendered to Howard and Miles on 5 October. His speech, in translation, of course, was an eloquent farewell to Indian ways: "I am tired; my heart is sick and sad," he said. "From where the sun now stands I will fight no more forever."

MAP 414 (*left, top*).

Indian reservation lands cover Indian Territory, the area that is now all Oklahoma, in this 1872 map.

MAP 415 (*above*).

By the time of this 1903 map Oklahoma Territory, organized in 1890, already covers much of what was once reserved for re-moved Indians. Land was distributed to EuroAmerican settlers by land runs or lotteries. Some 60,000 arrived during the first land run, on 22 April 1889; 100,000 charged onto the so-called Cherokee strip during the largest, on 16 September 1893. Okla-homa would become the forty-sixth state, and cover the rest of the reserved lands, in 1907, entering the Union with a popula-tion of 1.5 million.

MAP 416 (*left*).

By 1923, the date of this government map, Indian reservations have been reduced to a minute portion of the West. Yellow ar-eas are 1923 reservations and black shaded areas are former res-ervations, but many of these have been omitted.

split his men into three. Major Marcus Reno took 140 men to attack the encampment directly, Captain Frederick Benteen, with 125 men, stayed to the south on the other side of the river to catch supposed escapees, and Custer, as was his style, led what was to be a frontal attack.

Reno was surprised to find himself opposed by hundreds of war-riors and was forced to retreat across the river, where he joined Benteen's men, managing to repel attacks into the next day, when the Lakota and Cheyenne slipped quietly away. Custer, however, was surrounded, and he and all his men perished, precisely how is not known, for the battle is still the subject of some controversy. Custer, for all his bluster, passed into myth. Only relatively recently has the Indian view been taken into proper account, and memorials to Lakota and Cheyenne participants have been added to the historic park site.

It was not long before the relentless pursuit of the Indians resumed. The tenuous Indian alliances weakened. Within a year Crazy Horse was defeated at nearby Wolf Mountain, Sitting Bull had fled to Canada and most of the remaining Indians had surrendered.

The Lakota and Cheyenne resistance was only the most well known—and arguably the most successful—of the Indian wars in the West. In southern Oregon and northern California in 1872–73, fewer than sixty Mo-doc warriors engaged close to a thousand U.S. Army soldiers in a series of skirmishes known as the Modoc War, which erupted when a reservation was ordered moved. In the Texas panhandle the so-called Red River War was fought in 1874–75 between Comanche and other tribes and the U.S Army over the continued erosion of reservations and the violation of an ear-lier treaty. The Comanche were led by Chief Quanah Parker, the son of Cyn-

thia Parker, who had been captured by Comanche when she was nine. Quanah gave up the struggle in 1875, accepted a reservation in southern Oklahoma, and went on to become something of a an elder statesman, protecting Comanche in-terests with exceptional skill. He, like Geronimo, made the best of his fate. Both rode in Theodore Roosevelt's inaugural parade in 1905, and Parker even went hunting with the president.

The famous Geronimo (Goyaalé), an Apache, led what was perhaps the longest struggle against government forces and was leader of the last native group to acknowledge government supremacy. Skirmishes occurred from 1862, when the Apache were ordered to reservations, through to 1886, when Geronimo with thirty-eight Apache men and their families evaded 5,000 U.S. troops and the Mexican army for a year, finally surrendering to General Nelson Miles at Skeleton Creek, Arizona, in September 1886.

Finally, there was Wounded Knee. Not a battle but a massacre, this infamous incident took place at the end of 1890 in South Dakota. Sitting Bull had been killed shortly before by Indian police sent to arrest him, but his half-brother, Big Foot, and 153 Lakota were killed by the Seventh Cavalry, and at least 50 more wounded. About 25 cavalrymen were also killed, likely most by their own side's guns. The troops had been sent to arrest practi-tioners of a new Ghost Dance religion, which promised to revive the old ways and was seen as a threat by the U.S. government. In a melee perhaps started by a misunderstanding and the accidental discharge of a rifle, the army, quite aware of their regimental history, took no chances and used their new Hotchkiss guns, an early machine gun, to devastating effect.

Wounded Knee is usually considered the final phase of the Indian wars that had started in the sixteenth century as the native peoples of America first began to feel the exclusionary push of the European inter-loper. It also became the site of a 71-day standoff in 1973 between authori-ties and militant members of the American Indian Movement, an organi-zation set up to protect Indian civil rights.

Surveys for Science

As the railroad opened up the West, many government surveys were carried out to locate the resources of the region so that they could be used to feed the industrial East. The resources, it was thought, were mainly minerals, but attention was also given to defining areas suitable for various forms of agriculture.

A Geological and Geographical Exploration of the Fortieth Parallel was created under the War Department and its scientists headed by Clarence King, a geologist who had been with the first California Geological Survey in 1860–64. The area this survey covered is shown on Map 417, *below*. The map also indicates the area covered by another survey, complementary to King's, which covered much of the Southwest. This survey, that of Lieutenant George M. Wheeler, was an army survey, however, and paid more attention to such things as the "numbers, habitats, and disposition of the Indians." Both King and Wheeler promoted themselves and their surveys to pander to a public appetite for news of the natural wonders of the West. Both took photographers along (see photo, *right*), and Wheeler even took along a newspaper reporter, Frederick Loring, but he was killed by Apache in 1871.

Perhaps the most famous of the western surveyors was John Wesley Powell, who in 1869 traversed the canyons of the Colorado River in small boats. He ended up at the Grand Canyon, surviving Indian attacks and becoming a popular hero in the process. Further surveys followed, and in 1878 Powell published his important *Report on the Arid Regions,* in which he advocated the use of cooperative irrigation and the regulation of grazing and farming.

Another geologist, Ferdinand V. Hayden, undertook an exhaustive survey of the geysers of Yellowstone in 1871 and recommended that the area be preserved as a national park. President Ulysses Grant established it as a "public park or pleasuring ground" a year later, the first of the national parks. Another area destined to become a national park was the Grand Canyon, which featured large in *The Tertiary History of the Grand Cañon District,* a seminal volume on American geology by Clarence Dutton and William Holmes; the latter drew famous and immensely popular panoramas.

There were at times so many surveys that they overlapped and became competitive. This all ended in 1879 with the creation of a coordinating body, the United States Geological Survey. King was its first director; he was succeeded in 1881 by Powell.

Map 417 (*below, left*).
This map by George Wheeler documented the progress of his surveys between 1869 and 1873 as the black and gray areas. The cross-shaded gray area in rectangles east and west of Salt Lake City are the areas covered by Clarence King's fortieth parallel survey. In addition, the routes of numerous other explorers and surveyors that came before him have been mapped as red lines, each annotated with the person's name.

Map 418 (*above*).
The geyser fields of Yellowstone, shown on an 1871 German map. *Old Faithful* is marked. *S.G.* are spouting geysers and *B.G.* are boiling geysers.

Map 419 (*below*).
The development of triangulation allowed the accurate and reasonably fast survey of the West. This is geologist Ferdinand Hayden's 1873 triangulation of Colorado, three years before statehood.

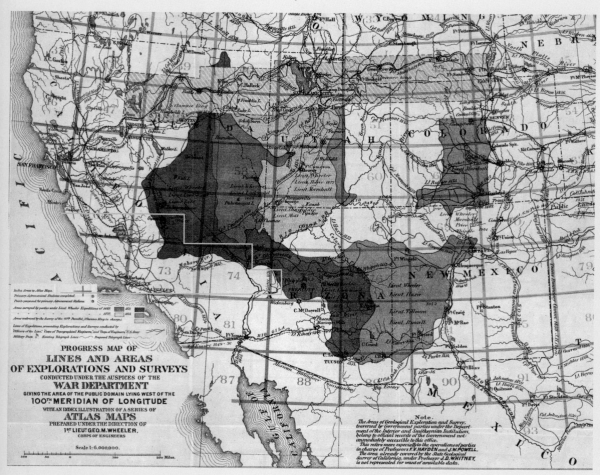

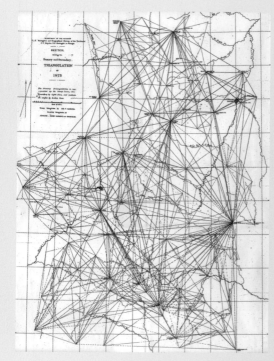

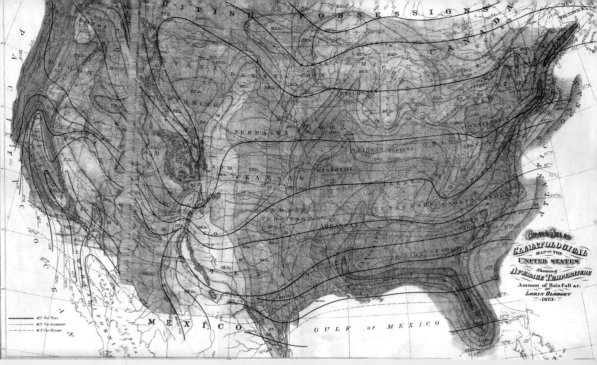

Map 420 (*above*).
Part of a very detailed topographic map of the Grand Canyon, produced in 1882 by geologist and pioneering seismologist Clarence Dutton. The white line is the Colorado River.

Map 421 (*above, right*).
Pioneer climatologist Lorin Blodgett's 1873 climate map of the United States, showing average temperatures (red lines) and rainfall areas (shaded gray to black with increasing rainfall). Blodgett played a role in the establishment of the science of atmospheric physics and in 1857 had published a seminal work on the subject, *Climatology of the United States,* which in the West utilized work he had carried out while engaged on the Pacific Railroad Surveys in 1853–56. This map shows that much of the Great Plains did, at least in theory, have enough rainfall to support agriculture, and was not the "Great American Desert" it had been originally characterized as (see pages 117–18). But agricultural techniques that conserved water would be required, and these were not known until later. The subsequent influx of population overloaded the water resources of the region, leading to the disastrous Dust Bowl of the 1930s, before more ecologically sustainable farming methods were developed.

Map 422 (*right*).
The first comprehensive geological map of the entire continental United States was published in 1874, in the *Statistical Atlas of the United States* of that year. Requested from Congress in 1872 by the American Association for the Advancement of Science, the map was constructed from the accumulation of data from government expeditions to that date, plus individually published state geological surveys, and other sources. Previously all this data had been "published independently . . . without concert or system." The U.S. Geological Survey would be created a few years later, in 1879.

Below. Photographer Timothy H. O'Sullivan accompanied several western surveys. In 1867, while with the Clarence King survey of the fortieth parallel, he took this stunning image of sand dunes in the Carson Desert of Nevada. Horses pulling O'Sullivan's mobile photographic studio wait patiently for him.

LA—From Pueblo to Suburbia

Mission San Gabriel Arcángel was established at Montebello in 1771 and moved because of flooding to San Gabriel in 1776; both locations are within what is today the urban area of Los Angeles. Five years later a small town was founded nearby by *pobladores* and others of mixed ancestry sent in to help secure Spain's control of Alta California. The small town was given a big name: El Pueblo de Nuestra Señora Reina de los Angeles. It became a ranching center, first Spanish, and later Mexican.

After the war with Mexico, Los Angeles became first part of the California Republic and then the United States. The Mexicans were defeated on the plain of La Mesa on 9 January 1847 at what is often called the Battle of Los Angeles (see MAP 336, *page 160,* and pages 160–61).

Los Angeles was platted out in 1849 and incorporated as a city in April 1850. It seems to have acquired a mentality for growth right away, offering thirty-five-acre "donation lots" to anyone who would spend $200 on improvements (MAP 423, *below*).

The city was home to many who saw the potential of the region and wanted to make it grow. The mud flats at San Pedro were excavated in 1871 to create a port, which was connected to the city by a railroad. The port was linked to the city with the annexation in 1909 of a long thin strip of land (shown on the brochure, *above, left*). Oil was discovered in 1892, and the Los Angeles area was by 1923 producing a quarter of the world's supply.

Growth was only inhibited by lack of water. This problem was solved with the opening in 1913 of the Los Angeles Aqueduct, which brought in water from the Owens Valley, 233 miles to the north (MAP 425, *far right, bottom*). The project was the brainchild of water department chief engineer William Mulholland and was the first of several that delivered water to the growing city. Another, the Colorado River Aqueduct, was opened in 1941. Dozens of territorial acquisitions were made by holding out the promise of water, and the city began to sprawl over a vast area.

In the 1930s, Los Angeles had a thousand miles of streetcar track, more than that of the next five major cities combined, an ironic fact considering the extent to which the automobile has shaped the city of today. The streetcars were crowded out by the automobile. To attempt to accommodate these cars a vast network of freeways was built in the second half of the twentieth century; today Los Angeles is a city more than any other dominated by the automobile, by roads, and by freeways.

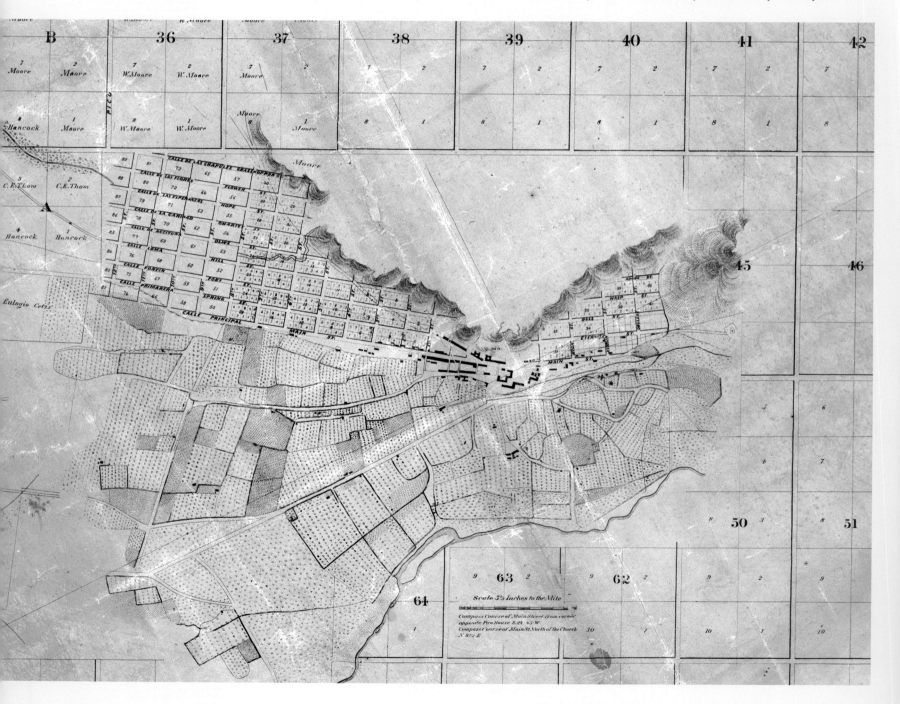

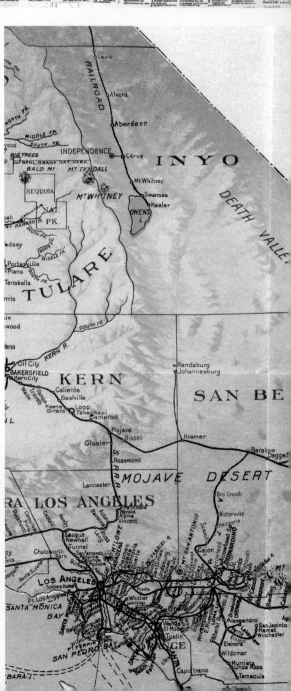

Map 423 (*left*).
The 1849 survey of Los Angeles, by Lieutenant Edward O.C. Ord, is shown in the central part of this map. Around it in a grid pattern are the donation lots offered to anyone who would spend $200 on improvements. The map shows information dating to 1857 but may be a later copy printed about 1875.

Map 424 (*above*).
This superb 1894 double bird's-eye map shows (at top) the core of Los Angeles and its original location between the Los Angeles River and the mountains. The lower map is a view looking south toward the ocean across the Los Angeles Plain, showing the room available for growth; once water was available, there would be no stopping expansion.

Map 425 (*right*).
The relationship of Los Angeles to the Owens Valley to the north is well shown in this 1908 map, published the year construction began on the Los Angeles Aqueduct. Water flowing down the eastern slopes of the Sierra Nevada had been finding its way to Owens Lake, shown on the map, where most of it evaporated. William Mulholland thought that the water could instead be transported 233 miles south to Los Angeles. The Federal Reclamation Service, which had plans for irrigation systems in the Owens Valley, was outwitted by Mulholland and his associates; Owens Lake was reduced to a dust bowl by the aqueduct. Some water is now to be retained to remedy this.

Map 426 (*below*).
Pueblo de Los Angeles is shown on the *Rio de Los Angeles* together with the nearby *Mis. de S. Gabriel* on this 1859 map, drawn from an 1855 survey. Note also the *Los Angeles Plains* and the *San Fernando Plain,* which would much later provide the flat area for urban sprawl. *Inset* is a June 2004 NASA computer-generated satellite view.

Far left, top. A 1915 tourist brochure shows the "key" shape of the city of Los Angeles, with its thin strip of annexed land connecting the body of the city to the harbor at San Pedro. Already automobiles are featured.

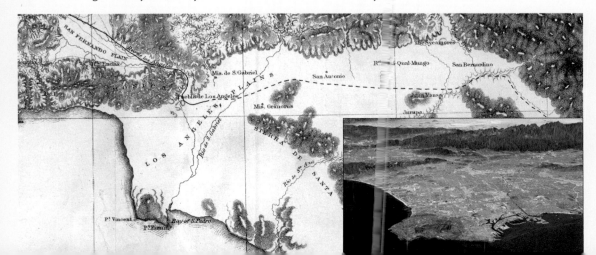

The Art of the Bird's-Eye

THE CITY OF SAN FRANCISCO.
BIRD'S EYE VIEW FROM THE BAY LOOKING SOUTH-WEST.

How do you advertise a city? In nineteenth-century America the answer was easy—publish a bird's-eye map. These often stunning combination map-views, usually published as separate sheets, became a staple of city fathers and real estate salespeople everywhere following the mass commercialization of the lithographic printing process after mid-century.

Deceptively simple, many of these maps were in fact the product of untold hours of labor. Without a plane or even a balloon, an artist had to determine what every building in the city would look like if viewed from a consistent angle above. This involved drawing and measuring every building individually so that the view could be worked out, and then incorporated onto a perspective grid for the streets.

Lithography allowed the artist to draw directly onto the printing plate, thus eliminating engraving as an intermediate step and reducing production costs. However, for the artist this was a dubious advance, for he or she now had to draw the image onto the plate *in reverse*. Bird's-eye maps often were financed in much the same way a television program might be today—from advertising. Businessmen would pay to ensure that their building was prominent in the view, or labeled with the business name, and sometimes individual buildings would frame the map, as in MAP 428, *below*, each space bringing in revenue.

The technique has been much modified with the advent of computers, but the three-dimensional view remains a popular mapping technique because of its unique ability to show complex information in such an easily understood way.

MAP 427 (*above*).
A bird's-eye map of San Francisco, published in 1878 by perhaps the most famous art print company, Currier and Ives.

MAP 428 (*below*).
This large, four-sheet 1908 bird's-eye map of Denver is surrounded by views of individual hotels, retail stores, and factories, and even (at top) an automobile made in the city, all no doubt paid for by the businesses concerned. A business directory is listed at bottom.

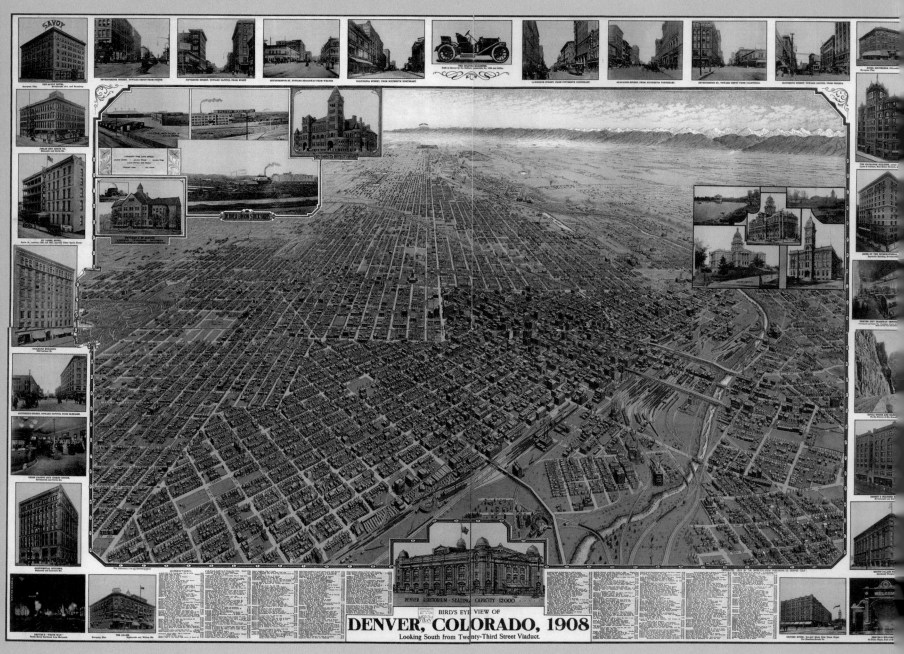

BIRD'S EYE VIEW OF
DENVER, COLORADO, 1908
Looking South from Twenty-Third Street Viaduct.

HOUSTON, TEXAS.
(LOOKING SOUTH.)
1891

Map 429 (*above*).
This detailed bird's-eye map of Houston, published in 1891, is a view southwards over the Buffalo River.

Map 430 (*right*).
Innumerable wannabe western towns had bird's-eye maps published by real estate salesmen to encourage potential purchasers to buy land in the town. This is an archetypical such map, of Frederick, Dakota Territory. It was published in 1883, six years before the settlement became part of the state of South Dakota. Very often these views bent the truth, showing hoped-for development rather than actual development. "Now numbering about 700 population . . . destined to become a prosperous commercial city," says the caption. Frederick still exists, but has a population of about 250.

Map 431 (*below*).
A postcard bird's-eye of the lower San Francisco Bay region published in 1915 by the San Jose Chamber of Commerce, emphasizing the city's easy access from San Francisco and Oakland. This is today's so-called Silicon Valley.

Map 432 (*below, right*).
Another view of Houston, this one of the downtown. It was published in 1912.

BIRD'S EYE VIEW OF
FREDERICK, DAK.
1883.

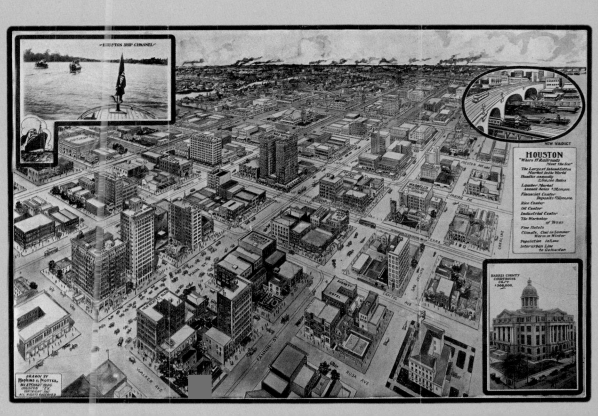

MAP 436 (*right*) and
MAP 437 (*below*).
The popularity of the bird's-eye map outlasted the nineteenth century. This map of the entire state of California (MAP 436), from an unusual viewpoint far to the west, was published in 1936 as part of a tourist brochure. The superb map of the Columbia Gorge and the Willamette Valley (MAP 437) was published in 1923, again as part of a folding tourism information brochure particularly directed at people touring in automobiles. The map depicts an amazing amount of information on one sheet. Multiple views obscure the area across the river in Washington that the publisher, the Portland Chamber of Commerce, did not promote. An illustration from the cover of this map is shown on page 234.

MAP 433 (*above*).
This artistic map promoted Phoenix, Arizona Territory, in 1885. The city had been incorporated four years before. Views illustrating water are prominent.

MAP 434 (*below*).
The archetypical big-city bird's-eye, with the map surrounded by images of business buildings. This is Los Angeles in 1891.

MAP 435 (*below, bottom*).
A magnificent bird's-eye map of Boston published in 1877. The view looks south across the Charles River. The reclaimed lands of Back Bay are visible at right.

A Gilded Age

The era Mark Twain memorably dubbed the Gilded Age was the decade of the 1880s, but the term is often extended to cover the entire period from the Civil War into the early twentieth century. The "gild" was a veneer of respectability covering those who made money, and lots of it, but these were only a relatively lucky few who happened make the right investments, see the opportunities, and have a survival-of-the-fittest attitude to business, cutting down competitors along the way. Fortunes were made in railroads, steel, coal, and oil, the underpinnings of an emerging industrial nation. This was the time of what history has called the robber barons, America's first self-made millionaires, most of whom lived lavishly while their employees labored in poor or dangerous conditions for a pittance. A few, however, redeemed some of their avarice with philanthropy.

The first commercial oil well had gone into production in Canada in 1858, but the next year Edwin L. Drake drilled the first U.S. commercial well just south of Titusville, Pennsylvania, sparking an "oil rush" of sorts. Before long drill sites and towns, refineries and storage facilities sprang up all along Oil Creek between Titusville and the Allegheny River, where the not-very-originally-named Oil City grew up (MAP 438, right). Fortunes were made and lost. Oil was at this time used for lighting: refined as kerosene, it replaced whale oil and likely saved many of the world's whales in the process. It was big business, and as such it attracted ambitious men.

John D. Rockefeller created Standard Oil of Ohio in 1870, and by shrewd if not always totally ethical means—by today's criteria—by 1890 Standard Oil controlled over 90 percent of the refined oil in the United States. The Sherman Antitrust Law of 1890 was used to control some of the company's monopolistic ways, but not until 1911 was the company broken up, leading to the formation of a string of other oil companies—Mobil, Esso, Chevron, Arco, Conoco, and Amoco, to name but a few. (Some of these companies merged with others; today the principal successor to Rockefeller's company is ExxonMobil.)

MAP 438 (right).
Oil wells abound along Oil Creek, in western Pennsylvania, shown here with the names of their individual or company owners. Settlements are shown, some with names unmarketable as residential areas today, but emphasizing their wealth at the time—*Oil City, Petroleum Centre.* The larger river at bottom is the Allegheny River.

Below. A view of oil wells and storage vats at Pit Hole City, Pennsylvania. The engraving appeared in *Harper's Weekly* in 1865. On Pit Hole Creek, southeast of Titusville, Pit Hole City sprang into existence in May 1865 after an oil strike there and by September was home to 15,000 people and no less than 57 hotels. By the end of the next year better strikes had been made elsewhere and the population had dropped to 2,000. Today the town is gone, leaving little more than a few cellar holes in the ground to mark its location.

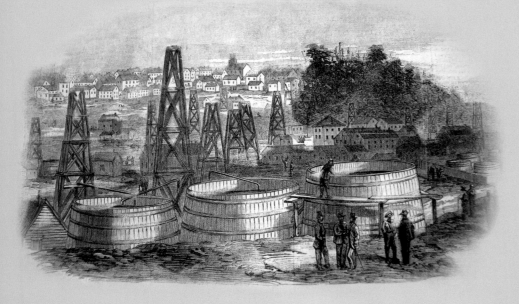

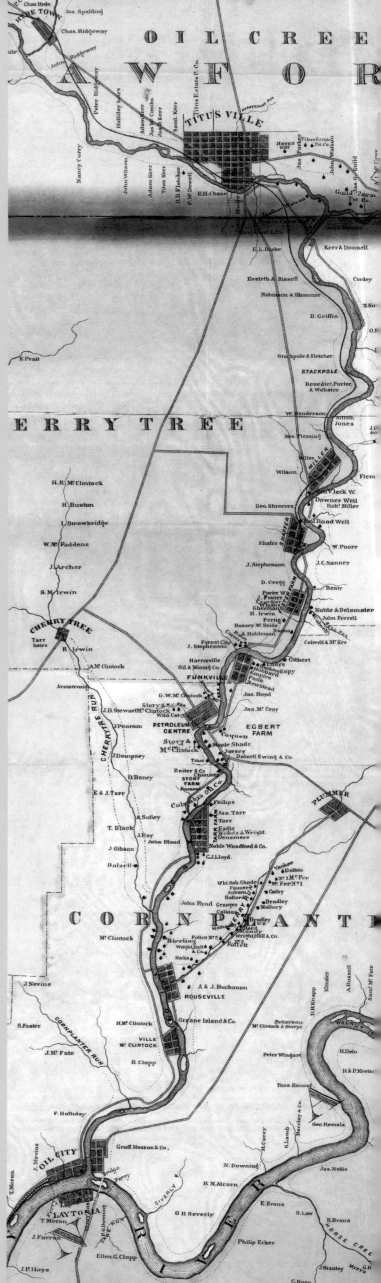

MAP 439 (*above*).
Part of an elegant bird's-eye map of Titusville, on Oil Creek in Pennsylvania, showing oil wells with storage and processing facilities, all made to look so very clean.

MAP 440 (*right*).
This map was produced for the Pittsburgh, Bradford, and Buffalo Railway in 1882 and shows the region from Pittsburgh (at bottom left) to Buffalo (at top center). The gray shaded area indicates the coalfields that were by this time feeding the steel mills of Pittsburgh. The yellow areas are where fire clay could be obtained, and dark brown areas indicate iron ore deposits, both necessary ingredients in the steelmaking process. The numerous black dots are locations of oil wells.

MAP 441 (*below*).
A bird's-eye map of Pittsburgh in 1902, at the height of its industrial glories.

Due to its proximity to major coal deposits, Pittsburgh emerged in the mid-nineteenth century as the principal center of the U.S. steel industry. The prospect of work attracted thousands of immigrants to the steel mills. Industrialization in an atmosphere of unbridled capitalism brought with it sometimes appalling working conditions and resulted in many strikes for better conditions and better pay. During the 1880s alone there were 24,000 strikes involving 6 million workers.

One of the bloodiest of the strikes occurred at the steel mills at Homestead, Pennsylvania, six miles upstream of Pittsburgh, in 1892. Faced with declining prices and wanting to reduce wages, Andrew Carnegie, the

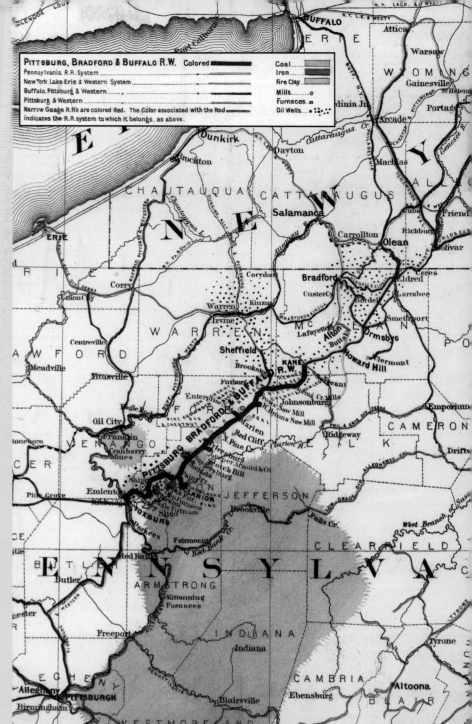

owner, an immigrant from Scotland, decided to break the union and left for a long vacation in a remote region of his native land, leaving matters in the hands of his lieutenant, Henry Clay Frick. Frick prepared for a strike by erecting a twelve-foot-high fence, topped with barbed wire, around the mill, and then, on 2 July, locked out the 3,800 workers, announcing that he would be reopening using replacement, non-union, workers. Frick hired 300 Pinkerton Detective Agency men to guard the plant. However, when they arrived, by barge, in the middle of the night, they were met on the banks of the river by 10,000 strikers and their families, many of whom were armed. In the ensuing fourteen-hour battle, three guards and nine strikers were killed. The Pinkertons surrendered, but then the state militia were sent in, armed to the teeth with the latest Gatling machine guns; 150 union members were arrested and many were charged with murder (though none were convicted). The Homestead strike continued until November, and replacement workers arrived on locked trains. When the union's money ran out, the men reluctantly returned to work, without a union, and had to work longer hours for less pay. Carnegie later regretted what he had done.

Another infamous strike occurred two years later at the Pullman Palace Car Company in Chicago. George Pullman had developed luxurious sleeping and dining railroad cars in the 1870s and in 1880 had purchased 4,000 acres to create a model settlement of company-owned housing around his factories (MAP 444, *right*). Although the company housing was better than most available to workers in Chicago at the time, Pullman completely controlled it, and he deducted rents automatically from wages. When business declined in 1893, workers' wages were reduced by 25 percent, but rents were not adjusted downwards at all.

A new union, the American Railway Union (ARU), founded by Eugene V. Debs in 1893 to create a single union for all railroad workers, fought successfully with James J. Hill and his Great Northern Railway in 1893 after Hill reduced wages. Pullman employees rushed to join the ARU, and in May 1894 they voted to strike.

The railroad owners disliked the ARU immensely and determined to use the Pullman situation to break it. A consortium of railroads called the General Managers' Association coordinated the anti-union activities, and they soon got the federal government involved. Debs had ordered his members to sidetrack all trains with Pullman cars attached—a quarter million complied—and the railroads intentionally made sure Pullmans were attached to mail trains, thus ensuring that sidetracking them was a federal offense.

MAP 442 (*above*).
A 1902 bird's-eye map of part of Homestead, Pennsylvania, a few miles upriver from Pittsburgh. Carnegie's Homestead Steel Works is at center, labeled in several places with the number 9.

MAP 443 (*below*).
Industrial buildings and workers' tenements abound in this 1871 bird's-eye map of Pittsburgh, showing a view up the Monongahela River.

Federal troops were called in, and attempts to get trains running again led to rioting and arson. On 4 July state militia killed four railwaymen. The same day Debs and many others at the ARU were arrested for violating a federal court order. Although Debs was released on bail, he was soon back in jail because the ARU was still sending out telegrams to western locals, which a court interpreted as an unlawful restraint of interstate commerce. Despite a defense by a legal team that included a young Clarence Darrow (later famous for defending the teaching of evolution in the "Scopes monkey trial" of 1925), Debs was sentenced to jail and his appeal disallowed by the federal Supreme Court. This was the first time the federal government had acted to break a strike, and the Supreme Court had ruled that it could.

The Pullman strike collapsed in August 1894, and the company reopened, allowing its employees to work only if they agreed never to join any union.

Throughout the second half of the nineteenth century the United States industrialized rapidly, and growth was augmented by an influx of immigrants from Europe. In 1850 the nation's population was 23 million; by 1900 it had almost tripled, to 76 million. Some settled

MAP 444 (right).
A detailed plan of parts of the Pullman manufacturing complex at Pullman, now a suburb of Chicago. It shows the foundry, the car wheel works, and, as an inset, the company iron and steel works, together with the adjacent company-owned workers' housing, part of Pullman's model town. The streets in Pullman were named after inventors, hence (John) Ericsson (ship propellor), (Henry) Bessemer (steel), (Robert) Fulton (steamship and submarine), and (George) Stephenson (steam locomotive). This is a fire insurance plan drawn in 1886. Red denotes buildings made of brick, while those of wood are colored yellow.

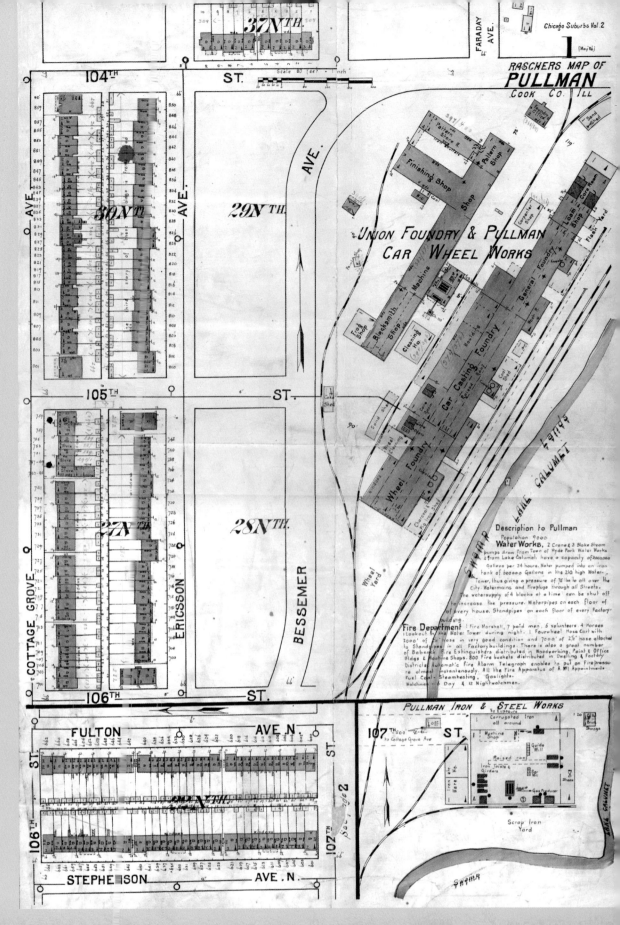

in the West, where six new states were admitted in the nine months between November 1889 and July 1890: North Dakota, South Dakota, Montana, Washington, Idaho, and Wyoming. A single invention was responsible for changing the character of the West: barbed wire. Invented in 1874 by Illinois farmer Joseph Glidden and rapidly varied and copied by others, it allowed easy subdivision of the plains, thus encouraging population growth. On the treeless plains wooden fences were impossible, ordinary wire fences inefficient. There was widespread vandalism of barbed-wire fences by cattle ranchers, who regarded the open plain as their personal rangeland, but the numbers of new settlers tumbling into the West overwhelmed the cattlemen.

Free land disappeared. Some of the last was in Oklahoma, where the final large tracts of Indian lands were taken for EuroAmerican settlement (see page 203). Land was distributed by some strange methods, including lotteries and the famous "land runs," where a virtual stampede of settlers raced to stake claims; whoever got their land staked first—and managed to prevent the stakes being uprooted—took the land.

Facilitating all this growth were the railroads, finally after 1886 a coherent network, using railroad-initiated time zones (though these were not formally adopted by Congress until 1918) and on a standard gauge, a factor which meant that constant changing of trains was no longer necessary and freight cars could be interchanged. Chicago emerged as the hub of western networks, and such centralized functions as stock processing appeared (MAP 447, *right, top*). Mail order companies served a retail function for vast rural areas. Aaron Montgomery Ward sent out the first mail order catalog—a single sheet of paper—in 1872, but it was the company established by Richard W. Sears and Alvah C. Roebuck in Chicago in 1893 that honed the business to a fine art. And all this commerce depended on the railroad.

It took more than ten years following the completion of the first transcontinental line in 1869 (see page 194) for other transcontinental lines to be completed. Most took advantage of generous federal land grants (MAP 401, *page 197*). In 1882 the Atchison, Topeka and Santa Fe joined the Southern Pacific at Deming, New Mexico, which connected to Los Angeles. A year later the Southern Pacific linked New Orleans with Los Angeles. The Southern Pacific, controlled by the "big four" (Collis Huntington, Leland Stanford, Mark Hopkins, and Charles Crocker), had built lines in California south from the Central Pacific, creating a network that had made the four men extremely wealthy.

MAP 445 (*above*).
This detail from a bird's-eye map of Baltimore published in 1912 shows a railroad station and some of the attendant urban concentration, in particular the tenements right beside the track. With steam trains this land was the dirtiest—but cheapest—land.

MAP 446 (*below*).
By 1883, the date of this map, railroads crisscrossed the Midwest, where they played a key role in the development of the region. The Chicago, Burlington & Quincy was popularly known as the Burlington and is now part of the Burlington Northern Santa Fe (BNSF).

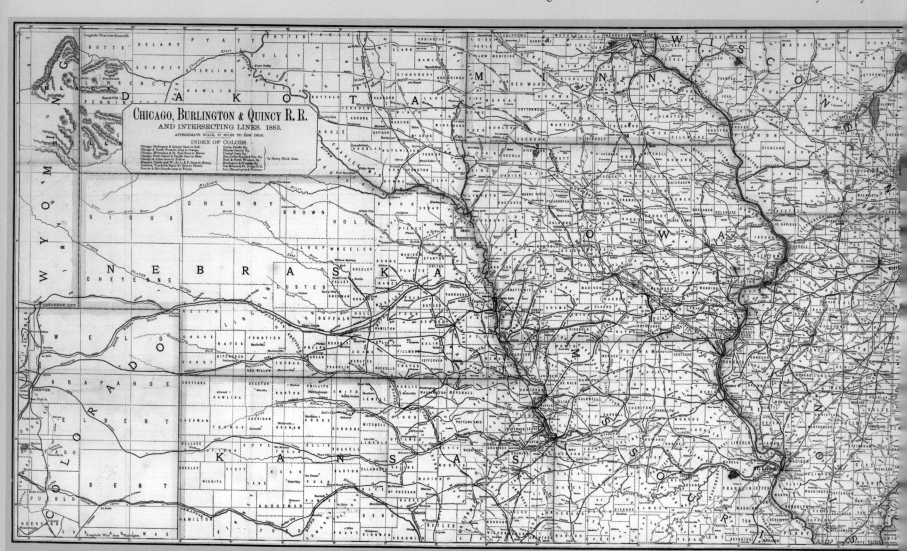

Map 447 (*right, top*).

The railroad made possible the concentration of cattle processing facilities in the hub city of Chicago. This unusual bird's-eye map shows the layout of the Chicago stockyards as they were in 1890. Nine railroad companies purchased swampland in southwest Chicago in 1864 to create the Union Stock Yards, opened the next year. In 1872 meat packers began using ice-cooled railroad cars to enable shipping year-round, and in 1882 the first refrigerated car made its appearance, allowing easy shipment of processed meat to eastern cities. This fueled the growth of the Union Stock Yard, which at its zenith covered an area one mile square and employed 50,000 people, not only meat packers, but workers engaged in the manufacture of a diverse range of items, such as leather, glue, fertilizer, gelatin, racquet and violin strings, and pharmaceuticals. The growth of the federal highway system after the Second World War (see page 234) spelled the end of the huge yard, for now it was possible to decentralize to cheaper rural land. The first business moved out in 1955, and the Union Stock Yard closed its doors for good in 1971.

Map 448 (*right*).

By buying up shares, one of the more famous of the so-called robber barons, Cornelius Vanderbilt, managed to gain control of all direct rail lines into and out of Manhattan. He withheld service between his railroads and the New York Central line, and the result was that in 1867 Vanderbilt gained control of that railroad too. Then he quadrupled the track between Buffalo and Albany passenger and freight trains had their own tracks each way. This 1876 map advertises this fact.

Map 449 (*below*).

This rather innovative 1896 map is an advertisement for the Kansas City, Pittsburgh and Gulf Railroad, then under construction, which was to have as its southern terminus Port Arthur, Texas. The 556-mile railroad from Kansas City to the Gulf of Mexico was completed in 1897 as the renamed Kansas City, Shreveport and Gulf Railway. The line was a project of New York railroad entrepreneur Arthur E. Stilwell, as was Port Arthur itself; the city is named after him. The vast lands available for sale and settlement are touted on this map by the railroad, which notably runs through Indian Territory, soon to be incorporated into the state of Oklahoma. The location of Kansas City as a railroad hub is emphasized.

UNCLE SAM AND HIS SEARCH LIGHT.
LOOKING OVER THE "PORT ARTHUR ROUTE".

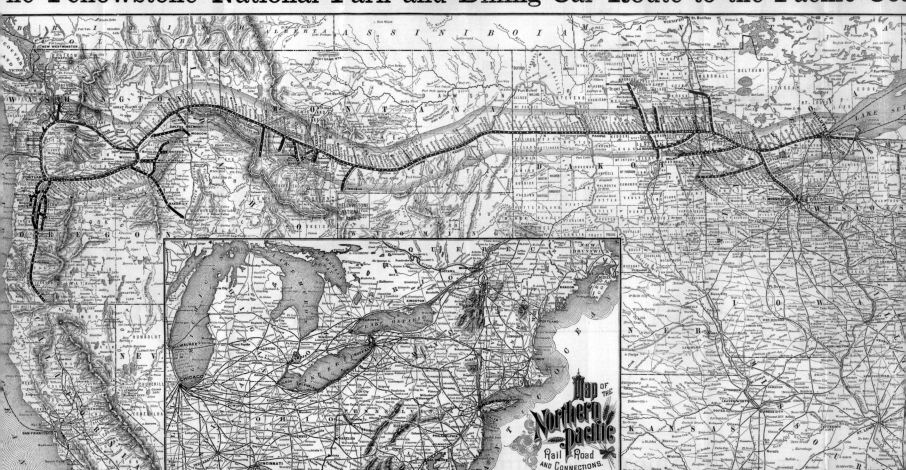

MAP 450 (*above*).

This map of the Northern Pacific Railroad (after 1896 the Northern Pacific Railway) was created in 1887, four years after the transcontinental line was completed. As an additional revenue source, the map promotes tourism to Yellowstone National Park, which had been established in 1872 and to which the railroad built a branch line, shown on this map.

MAP 451 (*below*).

The Atchison, Topeka and Santa Fe—the Santa Fe—completed a line from Atchison, Kansas, to Colorado in 1872, for which it received a 3-million-acre land grant. The second transcontinental line was created in 1883 when the Santa Fe joined the Southern Pacific line at Deming, New Mexico. However, by 1887 the Santa Fe had completed its own line to Los Angeles and San Diego, branching westward from Albuquerque. That route is shown on this detailed map published in 1904. Also shown is a profile of the route from Chicago to California, which involved lesser grades than rival lines.

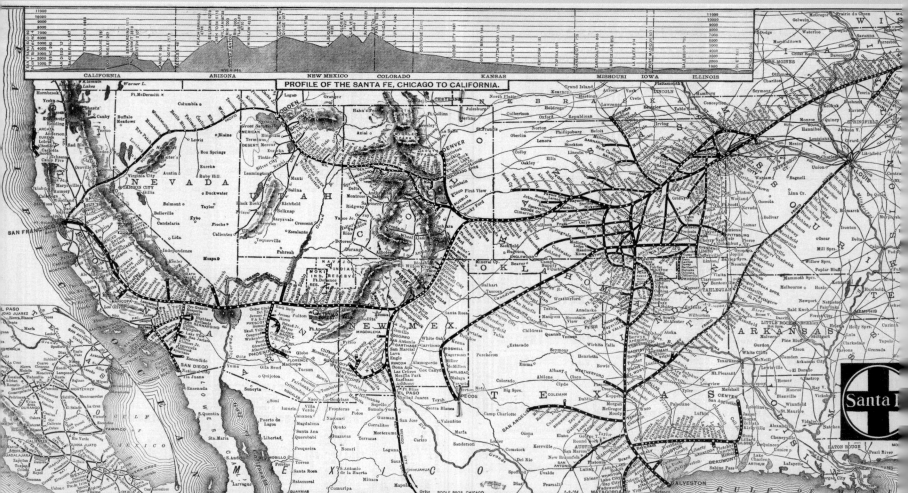

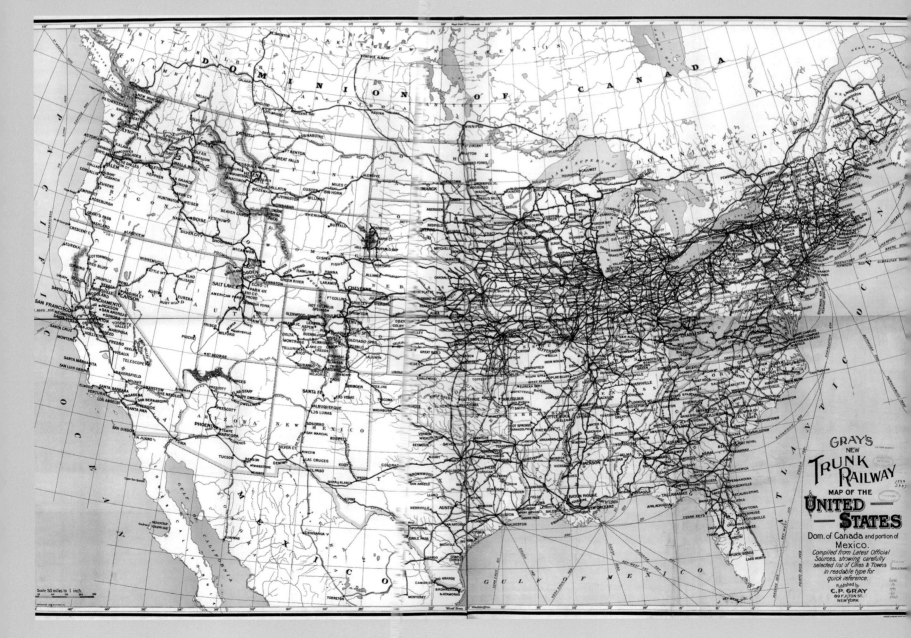

The Northern Pacific Railroad was also completed in 1883, providing a continuous line from Chicago to Seattle. Owned in its early stages by financier Jay Cooke, the railroad collected money from cities anxious to be on the rail route and sought a 500-million loan from Congress in 1873. This was rejected, largely due to the influence of Cooke's rival, J. Pierpont Morgan, and the company collapsed. By 1880 it was under the effective control of Morgan, who sold it to a group of investors under Henry Villard in 1881, and under his auspices the line was completed. Such were the financial and political manipulations of the age.

At this point the central, northern, and southern routes that had been the main contending routes as early as the 1850s (see page 180) were complete. Ten years later, James J. Hill completed his Great Northern Railway from St. Paul to Seattle, without land grants or other federal aid.

Not only had the United States grown dramatically during the Gilded Age and become radically industrialized, but it was connected into a coherent whole like it had never been before. By the end of the century the foundations were in place for the emergence of modern America.

MAP 452 (*right*).
This 1892 brochure from the Southern Pacific advertised its line from New Orleans to California, completed in 1883, the first to link the Gulf of Mexico with the Pacific.

MAP 453 (*far right*).
This unusual 1887 "alligator map" published by the Louisville, New Albany, and Chicago Railroad emphasized its connections to Florida and the South. The line operated under that name from 1859 to 1897 and acquired the Monon moniker from the convergence of its main routes at Monon, Indiana.

MAP 454 (*below*).
The U.S. railroad network in 1898. It would continue to grow until 1916, when there were over a quarter-million miles of track. From that point on, track mileage would decline, due principally to the rise of the automobile.

Above. A Northern Pacific train, a decoration on an 1893 company map.

Facilitators of a Modern Age

The first transcontinental telegraph line predated the railroad by eight years. It was completed in 1861 by the Western Union Telegraph Company and promptly put the still infant Pony Express out of business. The second half of the nineteenth century was to prove an era of innovation at all levels, but two inventions in particular facilitated the transition to the modern era that was then taking place—the telephone and the application of electricity, both to create light and to operate machinery.

The telegraph, the telephone's predecessor, had been introduced in 1837 by Samuel Morse, who the following year demonstrated his famous code and in 1844 completed a line between Washington and Baltimore. By 1857, Cyrus Field was engaged in his first attempt to lay a transatlantic telegraph cable, and the next year, after several failures, he succeeded in

Above.
Alexander Graham Bell and a map of the Americas, on an AT&T share certificate.

making a connection. Much feted (MAP 455, *below, left*), it failed after a month, and not until 1866 was a permanent line laid, using the gigantic steamer the *Great Eastern,* then the largest ship in the world.

Entrepreneur Perry McDonough Collins had the idea that Europe could more easily be connected to the United States by a cable laid through Alaska and Russia, across the treacherous but narrow Bering Strait. He interested Western Union, and a line was completed north from San Francisco to the Skeena River in British Columbia. Crews were working in Alaska when news came that the transatlantic cable had finally been finished. At this Western Union abandoned the Alaska cable, despite original plans to create a continuous round-the-world system (MAP 456, *below, left*).

While it revolutionized communications, the telegraph was no match for the telephone, patented by Alexander Graham Bell on 7 March 1876. Whether he actually invented the device is still debated, but in any case he was the first to patent it. Despite many initial problems with failed connections and noisy lines, his invention was to transform the social fabric of America.

Bell himself did not manage the growth of telephones in the United States, but the companies he created did. His company became American Bell in 1880 and the same year created

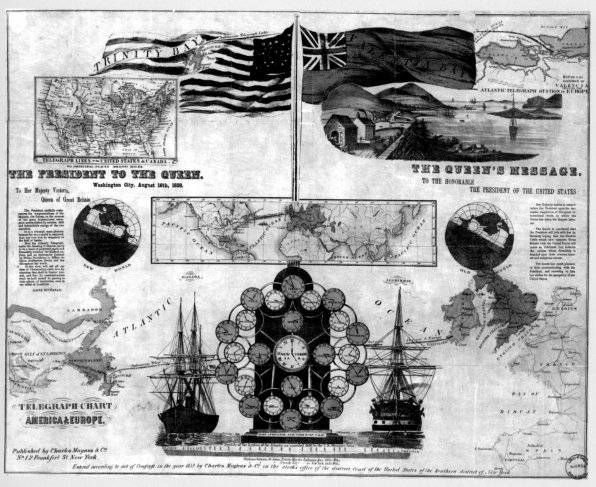

MAP 455 (*left, top*).
A commemorative map published in 1858. It gives the text of telegraph messages passed between President James Buchanan and Queen Victoria. The cable broke within a month and another was not successfully laid until 1866. At top left and shown enlarged below is a map of telegraph lines in the United States and Canada, showing (main) lines only east of the Mississippi. New York was connected—albeit briefly—to London before it was to San Francisco.

MAP 456 (*left*).
Harper's Weekly published this map on 12 August 1865 showing the proposed route of the telegraph through the United States on its way around the world.

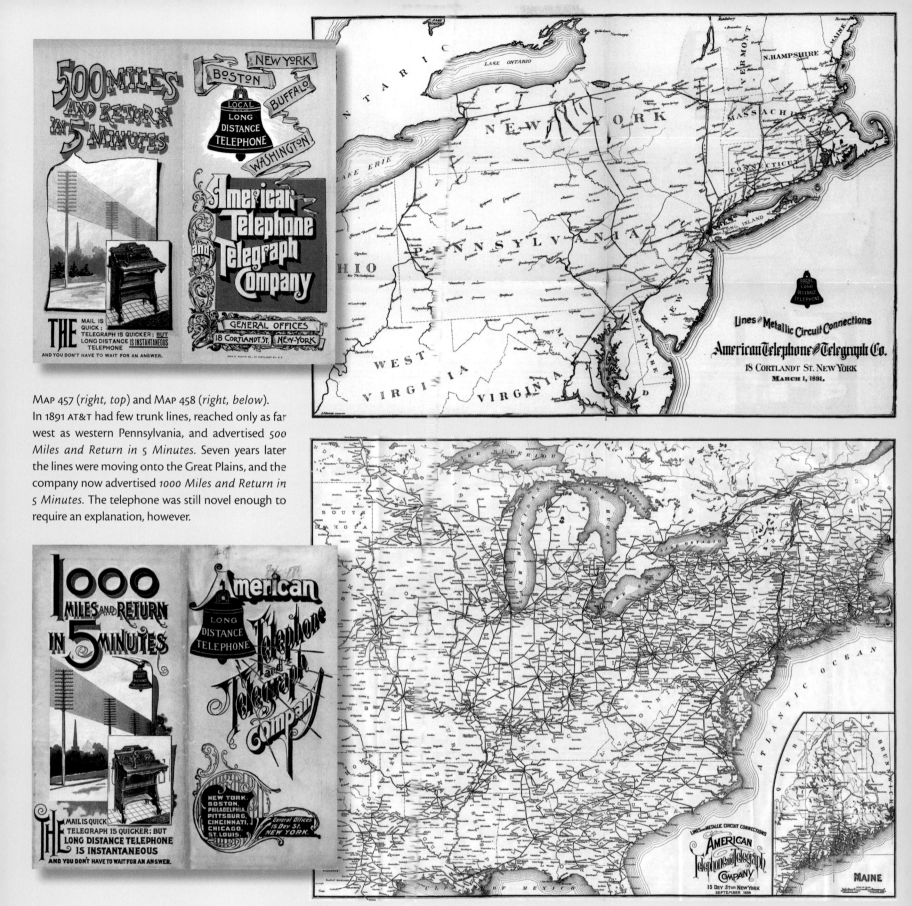

Map 457 (*right, top*) and Map 458 (*right, below*).
In 1891 AT&T had few trunk lines, reached only as far
west as western Pennsylvania, and advertised *500
Miles and Return in 5 Minutes*. Seven years later
the lines were moving onto the Great Plains, and the
company now advertised *1000 Miles and Return in
5 Minutes*. The telephone was still novel enough to
require an explanation, however.

a subsidiary to concentrate on building a long-distance network. This became American Telephone and Telegraph Corporation, AT&T, in 1885. AT&T merged with American Bell in 1899.

Trunk lines began radiating across the country from New York. Map 457 and Map 458, *above,* show the situation in 1891 and 1898, dramatically illustrating the rapid growth in coverage. Chicago was reached in 1892, one year after Map 457 was issued. Telephones finally spanned the continent in 1915, with the completion of a line—for the first time using vacuum tubes for amplification—to San Francisco. This time, transatlantic service came much later. An expensive, radio-based system came into operation in 1927, but the first cable across the ocean had to wait until 1956; less than twenty years later cables were joined, though not superseded, by a satellite-based system.

The invention that revolutionized America, and the world, was the electricity generating and distributing system of Thomas Alva Edison, whose commercialization and mass production of the lightbulb would

free the world from darkness forever. His Edison Electric Light Company, formed in 1878, with the likes of J.P. Morgan and the Vanderbilt family investing in it, was easily able to sell electricity to homes and businesses. In September 1882 Edison switched on the world's first electrical power—direct current (DC)—distribution system, sending electricity to fifty-nine customers in Lower Manhattan. But it was the alternating current (AC) distribution system patented by Nikola Tesla in 1892 and promoted by his friend George Westinghouse that ultimately won the so-called war of the currents (DC versus AC) in the 1890s.

Edison was granted a phenomenal 1,093 patents, covering everything from the long-lasting electric lightbulb to the phonograph. Before long, electricity was being applied to transportation. After first being demonstrated in Richmond, Virginia, in 1888, electric streetcar systems sprang up in major cities everywhere, radically influencing patterns of urban growth until the coming of the automobile.

American Alaska

After the American purchase of Alaska in 1867 (see page 129), only the hardiest of souls ventured to this forbidding northern land. Salmon canneries were opened at various places along the coast beginning in 1878. Whaling continued in the Bering Strait, but on a declining scale as whales became scarcer and kerosene, and later electricity, replaced lighting using whale oil. Sealing, however, grew so much that the Pribilof seal herds, which once numbered 4 million, were reduced to a hundred thousand. Conflict between American and Canadian sealers almost caused a war, with U.S. revenue cutters arresting the intruding sealers and British warships trying to protect them. This situation was resolved by an International Fur Seal Convention in 1911.

Commercial interests, including sealing, were purchased from the Russian-American Company by a group of San Francisco businessmen. Their company soon became the Alaska Commercial Company.

Interest in Alaska suddenly took a markedly upward swing in 1897 with the discovery of gold on the Klondike River, a tributary of the Yukon near the U.S. border. The first gold reached Seattle in July, setting off a frenzied stampede, which for most was already too late. It has been estimated that of the 100,000 gold seekers who set out for the Klondike, only 300 found enough to be considered rich, and of those only 50 managed to keep their new wealth.

The favored route was across the Chilkoot Pass to the Yukon River system, which would allow, in theory at least, a downstream float with the current to the goldfields. The Canadian North West Mounted Police set up a customs point on their side of the Chilkoot Pass to ensure that

MAP 459 (*below*).
After steaming up Lynn Canal, most gold seekers landed at Dyea and then, laded with equipment, trudged up the Chilkoot Trail (photograph, *above*) to the *Chilkoot Pass*, shown here at the head of the *Dyea R.* This is a 1919 map and also shows, in red, the line of the White Pass and Yukon railway through the White Pass from *Skaguay* (Skagway). The rail line was completed to Whitehorse, on the Yukon River, in 1900, and actually took a more circuitous route through White Pass than this map would suggest.

MAP 460 (*below, left*).
Money was to be made in selling maps of the routes to the goldfields, whether accurate or not. This one, rushed into print in 1897, erroneously shows the *Klondyke Gold Fields* stretching into Alaska, with *Dawson City* right on the boundary. The other route to the Klondike, up the Yukon River from Norton Sound, is indicated. Other gold areas abound, notably those labeled *American Gold Fields*.

MAP 461 (*right*).
"Tons of Gold in the Arctic" was the headline in the San Francisco *Weekly Examiner* on 22 July 1897. A map showing the location of the gold and the two main routes to it was sure to sell newspapers. For the price of a newspaper, the map was likely the cheapest available.

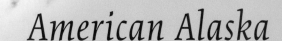

Map 462 (*right*).
Gold was found at Nome, Alaska, the year after the Klondike gold rush, and thousands of prospectors descended on Cape Nome, on the north side of Norton Sound. This 1901 map shows the region at the height of the rush. Two million dollars' worth of gold was taken from the beaches.

Map 463 (*right, bottom*).
The area in dispute between the United States and Canada is shown on this map of the Alaska Panhandle published by the United States for the Alaska Boundary Tribunal in 1903. The red line is the claim of Canada and Britain, the black line the claim of the United States. The boundary today approximates the British claim north of Lynn Canal and is about halfway between these two claims south of it. Drainage of the Pacific littoral is tinted light brown, while drainage to the Arctic Ocean and Bering Strait is tinted darker brown.

each prospector had all the provisions and supplies necessary for survival. In so doing they undoubtedly saved many American lives, but the prospectors had to make backbreaking multiple trips up and down the Chilkoot Trail to transport all their supplies.

The Klondike Gold Rush, like so many, lasted but a year or two. Excitement soon switched to Nome, on the northern coast of Norton Sound in Bering Strait, where in 1899 some Swedish prospectors found gold (Map 462, *above*). Although the initial riverine discovery was small, it turned out that the gold had been carried down the rivers to the coast and could be dug up straight from the beach. For a year or two the beaches of Nome were obscured by diggings and sluices.

Until the discovery of gold in the Klondike, the position of the Alaska-Canada boundary in the Panhandle was not well defined, and no one really cared. But suddenly it was more critical to know where American jurisdiction ended and Canadian began. Canada wanted access to the deep inlets that penetrate the coast, while the United States wanted them for its own harbors. An 1825 treaty had defined the boundary as ten marine leagues from the sea. But where was the sea? At the heads of the inlets, as the United States claimed, or the general line of the coast, as claimed by Canada?

In 1901, President Theodore Roosevelt, who had just become president after the assassination of William McKinley, adopted a hawkish attitude and insisted that the boundary dispute be settled by arbitration. Not only that, if the decision was not in its favor, the United States, fresh from its conquests of the Spanish-American conflict (see page 226), would declare war over the issue. Canada, still a British dominion, reluctantly agreed, and the resulting Alaska Boundary Tribunal, as it was called, had six members, three from each side. The Canadians thought that nothing could be lost due to the lack of a majority by either side.

They had not bargained on a loose cannon in one of their own members, a British judge. He sided with the Americans, and the boundary was established far inland, completely excluding Canada from any access to the ocean along the entire length of the Alaska Panhandle. But at least the United States and Canada did not go to war, and the peace between the two countries has now lasted almost two centuries.

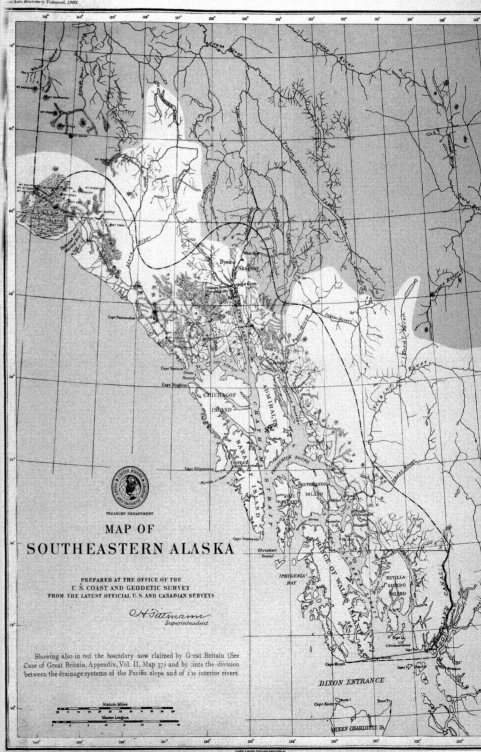

American Aloha

According to recorded history, Britain's Captain James Cook was the first European to discover the Hawaiian Islands, yet some maintain that they were originally found by the Spanish, by a Manila galleon straying off its normal path. Unless some new document turns up in a Spanish archive, we shall never know.

James Cook arrived in January 1778 off the coast of the islands he named the Sandwich Islands, after the fourth earl of Sandwich, at the time acting first lord of the Admiralty. Cook was on his way from Tahiti to survey the northwest coast of North America, searching for any western entrance to the Northwest Passage (see page 107). He returned later that year, intending to overwinter before setting off north once more. The Hawaiians thought he was the god Lono and initially treated him with great respect. On 14 February 1779 Cook went ashore at Kealakekua Bay, Kauai, intending to take hostages to ensure the return of a boat that had been

stolen, but, his godliness having worn off, he was attacked by a group of irate islanders and clubbed to death.

Hawaii proved to be such a well-positioned and tempting winter layover that it was frequented by an increasing number of European vessels from that time on.

Before 1795, interisland warfare was common. After that year, and with the addition of Kauai in 1810, the islands were united under the rule of King Kamehameha I, whose dynasty ruled until 1872, when it passed to King Lunalilo by election following the death of a childless Kamehameha V. Lunalilo lasted only one year before he died, and another monarch, King Kalākaua, was elected. Kalākaua reigned for eighteen years, but in 1887 the rising power of American and European businessmen became apparent when they forced him to sign a new constitution disenfranchising about 75 percent of the native population by imposing property and wealth re-

Above. The Hawaiian flag was created in 1816 under King Kamehameha I and has been maintained into statehood. The design is thought to have been suggested by a British naval officer, who, naturally enough at the time, assumed that the islands would belong to Britain and thus incorporated the British flag. The stripes symbolize the eight major inhabited islands.

MAP 464 (*below*).
More or less exactly reproduced from Cook's own chart, this is the published version of Cook's first map of Hawaii. It followed the publication, in 1784, of the official account of his third voyage, in a volume covering all three of his famous voyages. Near the bottom of the inset map of *Karakakooa* Bay (Kealakekua Bay, Kauai) is the notation *Here Capt. Cook was killed.*

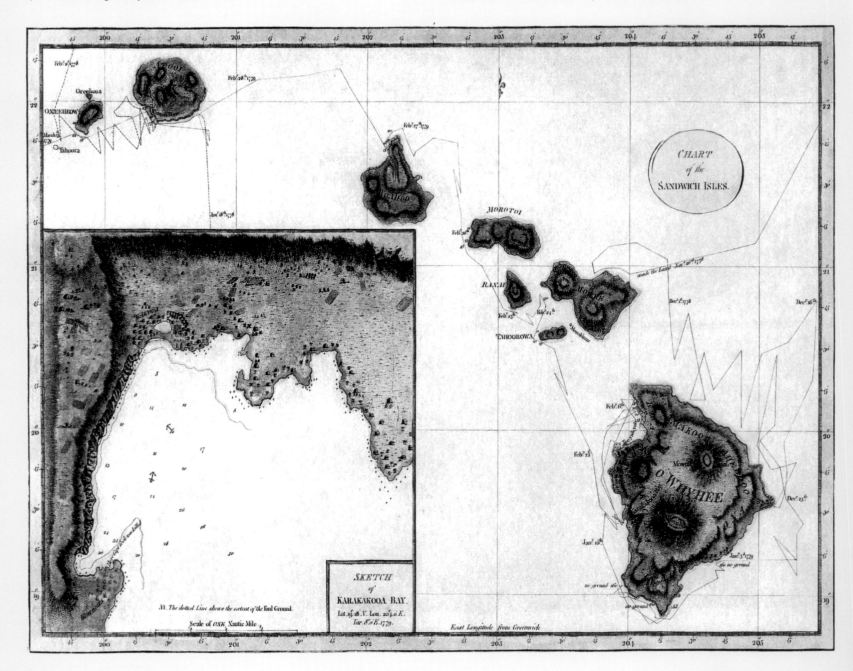

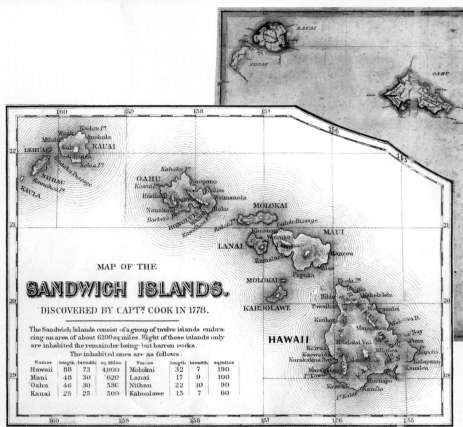

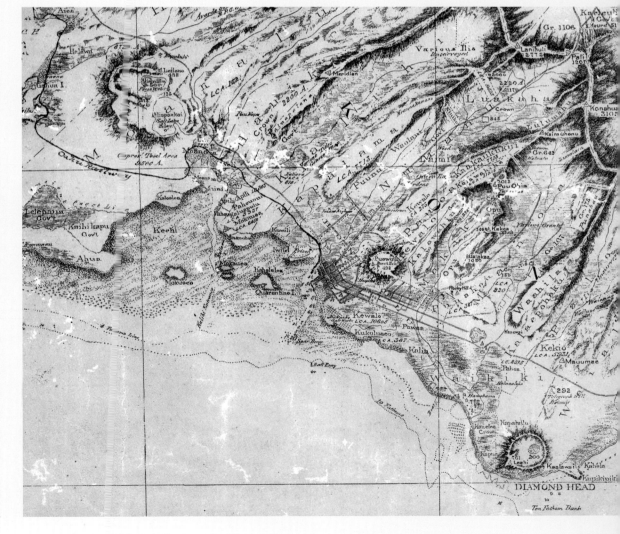

MAP 465 (*left*).
An 1837 map of
Hawaii, drawn in
Lahainaluna Semi-
nary, Maui.

MAP 466 (*far left*).
American com-
mercial mapmaker
Samuel Augustus
Mitchell published
this map of the
islands in 1879.

ties found territorial status convenient, allowing as it did easy importation of immigrant labor for the sugar and pineapple industries. Hawaii became the fifty-ninth state of the Union on 21 August 1959.

The new state expressly excluded Palmyra Atoll, 900 miles south of the main island group, which had been part of both the kingdom and territory of Hawaii. Palmyra now has the unique status of being the only privately owned (by the Nature Conservancy) unincorporated territory of the United States.

MAP 467 (*below*).
Honolulu and environs, shown on an 1881 map. Added later (in red ink) is the line of the Oahu Railway, a narrow-gauge line created in 1888 as the island's only common carrier railroad; all others were sugar-cane railroads. It must have been the only American railroad created by royal charter. The railroad served until 1947, when, worn out from war service, its operations were replaced with trucks.

quirements on voters. The constitution was engineered by a group led by Lorrin Andrews Thurston, the king's interior minister and a Honolulu newspaper publisher. This so-called Bayonet Constitution, because of the way it was forced on the king, gave the wealthy businessmen much more control of the islands' affairs.

Kalākaua was succeeded in 1891 by his sister, Queen Lili'uokalani, who protested the constitution, but this led to her being deposed by the same American business interests that had forced it on the kingdom in 1887.

In 1893 the businessmen in an organization called the Hawaiian League resolved to protect their interests—profits from sugar and the newly introduced pineapple—even further. Sanford B. Dole, of the family whose name was to become synonymous with pineapples, and Thurston, supported by American minister John Stevens, enlisted support from U.S. marines from the uss *Boston* to "protect American interests" and arrest the queen and overthrow the kingdom of Hawaii. A hundred years later an official U.S. apology for the "participation" of its "agents and citizens" was signed by President Bill Clinton. The Republic of Hawaii was proclaimed in 1894, with Dole as its president.

The drama continued toward its final act five years later. The fighting in the Philippines during the Spanish-American War (see next page) made it clear to the expansionist president William McKinley that the acquisition of Pearl Harbor—exclusive use of which had already been granted to the United States by King Kalākaua in 1887—would be strategically advantageous. Congress approved, and a joint resolution of annexation, similar to the one passed annexing the Texas Republic, was introduced by Congressman Francis G. Newlands and signed into law by McKinley on 7 July 1898. The Newlands Resolution created the first United States territory outside of the North American continent. Hawaii was granted self-governance in 1900, and Dole became the first governor of the Territory of Hawaii.

The finale came much later, since the business interests that had fostered American

An American Empire

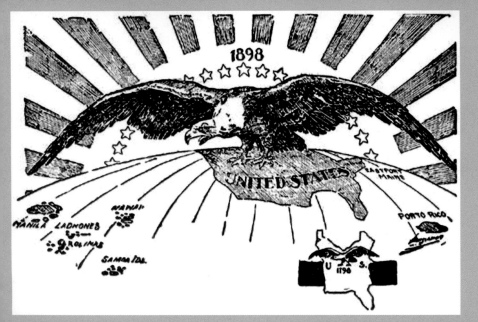

The notion of empire was rampant in the Western world as the nineteenth century drew to a close. Most of the European powers had established, or were busy establishing, colonies in Africa and Asia. There was a good deal of public feeling that a nation could not be a great one without colonies. In addition, there was the new steamship, which while much more reliable than the sailing ship, had a shorter range and required coaling stations all over the world. A book, *The Influence of Sea Power Upon History,* published in 1890 by an American naval captain, Alfred Thayer Mahan, became enormously influential. In it, Mahan argued that possession of a large fleet, overseas bases, a merchant marine—in essence, command of the seas—guaranteed a nation's wealth, progress, and security. It was an irresistible argument to many Americans. Social Darwinism was in vogue—the idea that a "superior" Anglo-Saxon race was destined to spread over the face of the Earth, displacing and "civilizing" so-called "inferior" races. In the United States these concepts translated into a sort of international Manifest Destiny. These ideas may seem outlandish today but they certainly did not in the nineteenth century.

In 1898 a bloody revolution had been under way in Cuba for several years, with rebels battling their Spanish oppressors in a particularly brutal fashion, one that was reciprocated by the Spanish. A revolution, naturally enough, appealed to American sensibilities, and William Randolph Hearst, who had just acquired the New York *Journal* and was determined to boost its circulation by any means he knew, fed the public interest by publishing lurid tales of Spanish atrocities, often wired in by his journalists who in fact never left the comfort of their Havana hotels.

In January 1898, there was rioting in Havana by Spanish loyalists, who feared Cuba might be abandoned by Spain. The American consul, Fitzhugh Lee, requested protection for American citizens, and in response, on 25 January the uss *Maine* arrived in Havana harbor on a "courtesy call." Three weeks later, on the evening of 15 February, the *Maine* exploded and sank, killing 268 of its 374 crew (MAP 470, *right, top*). To this day, no one knows for sure what happened. It could well have been an internal explosion caused by spontaneous combustion in the coal bunker, which was certainly known to happen, but at the time it was widely believed—particularly by readers of the *Journal,* of course—that the destruction of the ship was the responsibility of the Spanish. "An enemy's secret infernal machine," the newspaper called it, whatever that was. The *Journal* went on to demand war with Spain.

Despite Spanish attempts to defuse the situation, even agreeing to an armistice in Cuba on 9 April, events seemed to have taken on a life of their own. The president, William McKinley, who in his inauguration speech had stated "peace is preferable to war in almost every contingency," could have used the Cuban armistice to prevent war, but chose not to. He demanded the Spanish leave Cuba altogether, and when they refused, Congress—on 25 April—voted to go to war. Specifically, however, Cuba was not to be colonized and its independence was guaranteed.

Within a week, the United States had a naval victory to its credit, not in Cuba but half a world away in another Spanish colony, the Philippines. The small American Asiatic fleet under Commodore George Dewey, stationed in Hong Kong, steamed into Manila harbor before dawn on 1 May and opened fire on the Spanish fleet at anchor there. Details are depicted on MAP 473, *overleaf.* When news of Dewey's victory reached the United States, the nation seemed to go war crazy; any opposition there had been to war was overwhelmed.

At Tampa, Florida, the United States amassed a motley force to invade Cuba, under the command of General William Shafter. One volunteer cavalry general, Joseph Wheeler, had been a Confederate general in the Civil War;

MAP 468 (*above*).
This cartoon map, entitled *10,000 Miles Tip to Tip,* appeared in a Philadelphia newspaper in 1898. It compared the new American empire with the original extent of the United States—with a much smaller eagle—in 1776.

MAP 469 (*below*).
Published after Commodore Dewey's victory at Manila but before the invasion of Cuba, this war situation map was supplied with colored pins to represent the ships and troops of the belligerents. The pins were to be stuck into the map to give an ongoing view of the progress of the war. The principal ships of each nation are listed, and some of the Spanish have already been crossed out as a result of Dewey's action only a week after the war began.

MAP 470 (*right, top*).
This map of Havana shows the position of the uss *Maine* when she blew up on the evening of 15 February 1898. This map and MAPS 471 and 472 are from one large American public information map published after the war had ended.

his presence in a Union uniform helped further North-South reconciliation. Another volunteer cavalryman was Lieutenant Colonel Theodore Roosevelt, out to make a name for himself (which he did). Accompanying the 17,000-strong army were 89 newspaper reporters and photographers, in search of a story. Embarkation was a massive scene of confusion, with various corps fighting over ships and most of the cavalry horses being left behind due to lack of space.

It was just as well for the Americans that the Spanish were demoralized and hungry from years of fighting the Cuban rebels. Part of the American army landed at Daiquiri, thirty miles west of Guantanamo Bay, on 22 June, and advanced on Santiago de Cuba, the principal city of southern Cuba (MAP 472, *below*). Between 1 and 3 July Shafter's men took the village of El Caney, well defended by Spanish troops, and San Juan Hill, a crucial defensive position blocking the way to Santiago, where Roosevelt found the action he had been looking for. The American army lost about 10 percent of its men in these two actions, a heavy loss by any standard.

As the battle was being lost, the Spanish fleet left the now untenable Santiago harbor to make a run for it, only to be quickly hunted down by superior American battleships under

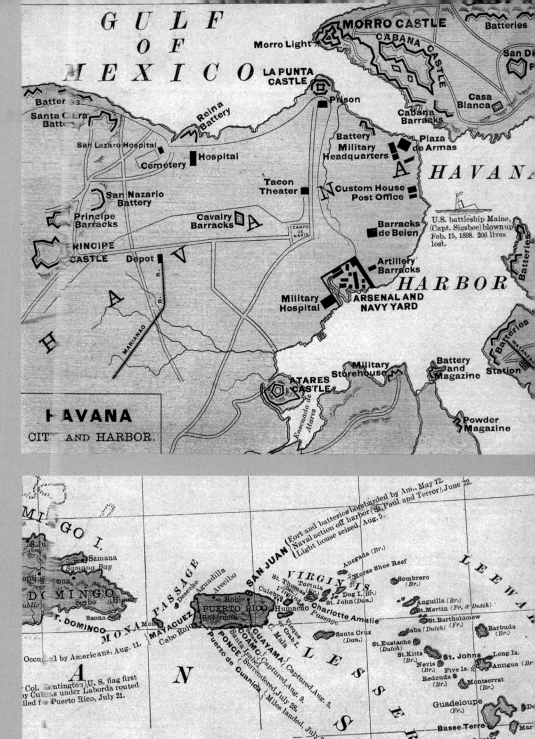

MAP 471 (*right, center*).
The landing place at *Puerto de Guanica* and the operations in Puerto Rico of the American army under General Nelson Miles. The Spanish on Puerto Rico had fallen back after several defeats but were still a threat when a peace treaty was signed on 12 August, ending the war.

MAP 472 (*below*).
The Santiago campaign. Shafter's landing place at Daiquiri (here *Baquiri*) is at right, and the route of his troops toward Santiago is shown by a dashed line. The locations of the battles of San Juan Hill (here *San Juan Heights*) and *El Caney* are marked. The Spanish surrendered the city on 17 July 1898 after the destruction of the Spanish fleet meant that Cuba could not be resupplied.

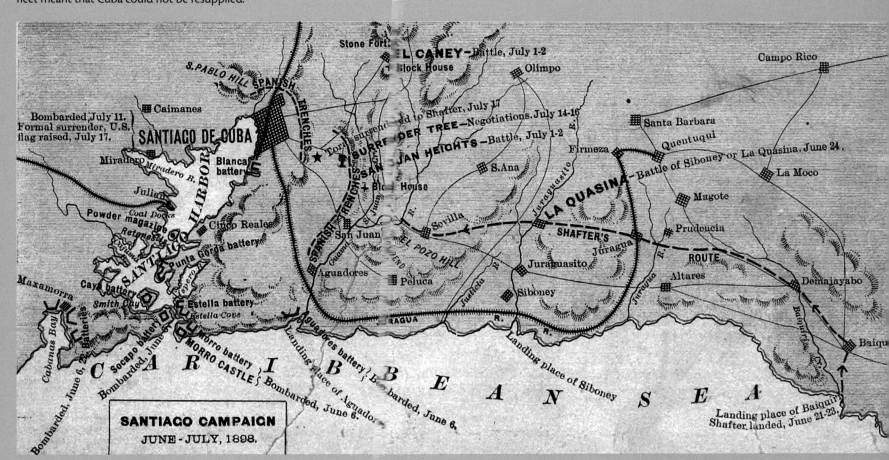

Map 473 (right).
Published in 1907, this map records not only Dewey's attack on Manila but also the Filipino-American conflict that occurred afterwards; this ended only when a peace was concluded on 4 July 1902. The Filipinos, who resented swapping one colonial power for another, were led by Emilio Aguinaldo. His capture in 1901 was the beginning of the end for the Filipinos.

Map 474 (below).
The United States waged another imperial campaign in 1900. This time it was in China, and in conjunction with seven other powers: Britain, Japan, Germany, Austria-Hungary, France, Italy, and Russia. The Boxers, a Chinese rebel faction opposed to foreign influence, staged a major rebellion, attacking the legations of foreign powers and killing any foreigners they could find. A relief expedition was put together by the eight powers, and over fifty thousand troops arrived to put down the rebellion, which the Chinese imperial government itself had been unable to do. The United States played a significant role because of the presence of its troops and ships in the nearby Philippines. A peace agreement known as the Boxer Protocol was signed in 1901. It extracted huge reparations from China and was a factor leading to the fall of the Qing dynasty in 1912, ending two thousand years of imperial rule and establishing the Republic of China.

Commodore Winfield Scott Schley. Cuba could not now be supplied from Spain, and it was only a matter of time before the Spanish would have to capitulate. Santiago surrendered on 17 July.

Another American army, ultimately numbering about 15,000 men, invaded Puerto Rico. The first contingent, under overall commander and Civil and Indian Wars veteran General Nelson Miles, landed at Guánica, on the southern coast of Puerto Rico, on 25 July. The same day Puerto de Ponce, a port city, was captured, allowing easy import of the supplies needed to support the invading force. The American army was generally well received by the population of the island, and the Spanish army surrendered after limited fighting; American casualties here were but thirty-nine, a marked contrast to those in Cuba.

The conflict in Puerto Rico was not over when it was stopped by the signing of an armistice between Spain and the United States, which took effect on 13 August. By that time, American troops had arrived also in the Philippines to secure Manila.

If the United States did not consciously go after an empire in 1898, it certainly acquired one. McKinley, who before the war could not locate the Philippines on a map, suddenly had a revelation that an American presence might "uplift and civilize and Christianize" the Filipinos. The next morning, in his own words, he "sent for the chief engineer of the War Department—our map-maker—and told him to put the Philippines on the map of the United States." With the peace treaty the United States

acquired independence for Cuba, plus the territories of Puerto Rico, the Philippines, and Guam, an island in the Marianas (which had been surrendered to the uss Charleston on 21 June), as colonies.

Awake now to the value of colonies as coaling stations, the United States annexed Wake Island (between Hawaii and Guam) in January 1899, claiming it on the basis of its discovery by the U.S. Exploring Expedition in 1840, and Midway Island (northwest of Hawaii), discovered by the U.S. sealing ship Gambia in 1867. It split Samoa with Germany, establishing a coaling station at Pago Pago. (The eastern part of Samoa is still American Samoa, but the western part that was German is now independent Samoa.) All this occurred in the same few months that Hawaii had also been added to the United States (see page 225). A further expansion of the American empire would come in January 1917, when the Danish West Indies were purchased from Denmark, ostensibly to prevent their invasion by Germany; they are now the American Virgin Islands.

Soon some of the problems that go with an empire became apparent. The Filipinos, who had expected to receive their independence as the Cubans had done, were dismayed at the continued American occupation and turned to guerilla warfare against their erstwhile allies. Led by Emilio Aguinaldo they fought until the capture of their leader in 1901 and the concluding of an uneasy truce in 1902. The many conflicts of this Philippine-American war are documented on MAP 473 (left, top).

Yet another extension of the American empire was the acquisition of the Panama Canal Zone in 1904. If coaling stations were important for colonial power, then the shortcut promised by the Panama Canal was critical. The long-sought passage between the oceans was first a railroad, built by private American interests between 1850 and 1855. Then in 1880 construction of a canal began, a French project under Ferdinand de Lesseps, builder of the Suez Canal, completed in 1869. De Lesseps proposed to construct a canal at sea level, despite the fact that at its lowest point the intervening land rises to 360 feet. He also failed to find a way to deal with the Chagres, a turbulent river that would have crossed the path of the canal. In the end the French company was foiled by the stupendous amount of excavation that this would have required and went bankrupt in 1889. A new company, attempting to salvage the work done to date (about 40 percent of the distance) with a canal built above sea level, also soon ran out of money.

The United States, in both 1897 and 1899, had a Canal Commission investigate the possibility of a canal through the isthmus in Nicaragua. When the French effort failed, Theodore Roosevelt, who had succeeded McKinley as president in 1901, thought that the United States could complete the Panamanian canal. The Nicaraguan proposal was abandoned and negotiations begun with Colombia for permission, but although a treaty was signed, the Colombian senate refused to ratify it. Roosevelt then fomented rebellion in Panama, with American warships standing by to discourage Colombian interference. Panama proclaimed its independence in November 1903 and quickly proceeded to return the favor by granting the United States control of the Panama Canal Zone.

The Panama Canal was built by an Isthmian Canal Commission staffed by American military officers. Yellow fever, which had plagued the French canal builders (twenty thousand had died), was now known to be spread by mosquitoes and was eliminated by improved sanitation and other health measures. The problem of the Chagres River was solved by damming it, creating the large Gatun Lake, which became a major part of the canal system, covering a third of the total distance. The canal was completed on 1 October 1913 when President Woodrow Wilson blew up a final dike. Hailed as a wonder of the world, the 51-mile-long Panama Canal was officially opened on 15 August 1914 with the transit of the cargo ship *Ancon*. In Europe, World War I was just beginning.

The United States now controlled not only a diverse and widespread set of colonial possessions, but the critical pathway between them. It was master of a passage between the oceans prized by all the imperial powers. In a very real sense the nation was now a world power.

MAP 477 (below).
This 1850 map shows the *Proposed line of Panama Rail Road 49 Miles*. Construction began that year, and the first train ran from ocean to ocean in January 1855. At the time, the railroad was the most expensive per mile ever built, a warning that the French canal builders who followed might have heeded.

MAP 476 (right).
This splendid and imaginative map was published to commemorate the opening of the Panama Canal. It was romantically entitled "The Kiss of the Oceans."

MAP 478 (below).
Maps of the complete canal were commonplace in newspapers and magazines long before it was actually completed. This is one from a 1912 West Coast newspaper. Many western ports expected to benefit immensely from the opening of the canal, but the effect was muted for a while because of the First World War, which in Europe lasted from 1914 to 1918.

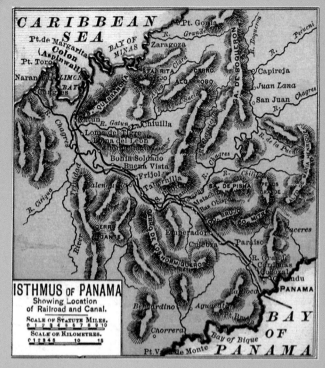

MAP 475 (above).
The Panama Railroad and the location of the proposed French canal, partially completed by De Lesseps, is shown on this 1898 map.

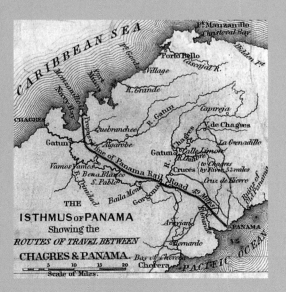

A World Safe for Democracy

Right. American 23rd Infantry in action during the 1918 Meuse-Argonne offensive.

As empires proliferated and grew in the first part of the twentieth century, it was perhaps inevitable that some would eventually come into conflict. It was time for a change in the world order; the day of the absolute monarchy was over, but nothing short of apocalypse would make kings and kaisers go. And the United States was destined to play a role in the destruction of the old world order and the creation of the new.

Domestically, the era of unbridled capitalism and the paternalistic oligarchies of business were being challenged, and signs of unrest were everywhere. The influx of immigrants had created a labor surplus, which allowed exploitation to occur. But some fought back. Working in now high-rise squalid factories in New York City were thousands of garment industry workers, almost all women. In 1910 a widespread strike, called the Uprising of the Twenty Thousand, paralyzed the industry, and in March 1911 came the Triangle Fire, an appalling fire in the overcrowded Triangle Shirtwaist Company factory that killed 146 female workers as they desperately tried to escape the flames. This tragedy focused attention especially on working conditions for females. The women's suffrage movement, gaining strength in the first part of the century, finally achieved its goal of votes for women in 1919, and the 1920 presidential election was the first in which women could participate.

Internationally, the United States, particularly under Woodrow Wilson, who had become president in 1913, meddled in the affairs of South and Central American countries, which were rapidly becoming seen as a zone of American influence; this view culminated with the construction of the Panama Canal (see previous page). A civil war in Mexico led to the occupation of Veracruz by American troops in April 1914 to block delivery of supplies to a regime unfavored by the United States. One rebel, José Doroteo Arango Arámbula, always known as Pancho Villa, killed American engineers and penetrated into the United States, attacking an army unit and burning Columbus, New Mexico. This led to the dispatch of 4,800 troops led by General John J. Pershing to deal with Villa. Although Pershing was not very successful at finding the elusive Mexican, he was nonetheless appointed in 1917 to lead the American Expeditionary Force (AEF), sent that year to Europe after the United States had entered World War I.

Tension between the United States and Germany had been building ever since the war began in 1914. American merchant ships had been sunk by German *Unterseeboots*—U-boats—and the passenger liner *Lusitania* had been torpedoed on 7 May 1915 with the loss of 1,195 persons, some of whom were Americans. In January 1917 a telegram was intercepted from Arthur Zimmerman, the German foreign secretary, to the Mexican government, suggesting that if the United States entered the war, Mexico attack to regain Texas and the Southwest. This was the last straw. On 6 April Congress declared war on Germany.

World War I had been raging for three years when the United States entered. At enormous human cost the Western Front had stalemated across eastern France and become a trench war, a war of attrition.

MAP 479 (*below*).
World War I produced an endless flow of battle reports from places the public had never heard of, and publishers rushed detailed maps into print to inform them. This is part of a large wall map of Europe that shows the position of the front in and around the American sector as it was on 1 May 1918. The St. Mihiel salient, taken by the American army in conjunction with the French between 12 and 16 September 1918, is prominent (center right). The map also shows (dashed blue line) the farthest advance of the German army, when, in March 1918, it broke out and came within seventy miles of Paris before being forced back. The Germans had hoped to win the war with one last all-out thrust before the United States could intervene, which they realized would tip the scales against them. At left top is Compiègne. Here, in a railroad car, the German surrender was signed on 11 November 1918. At the same place, in the same railroad car, Adolf Hitler would in 1940 receive the French surrender.

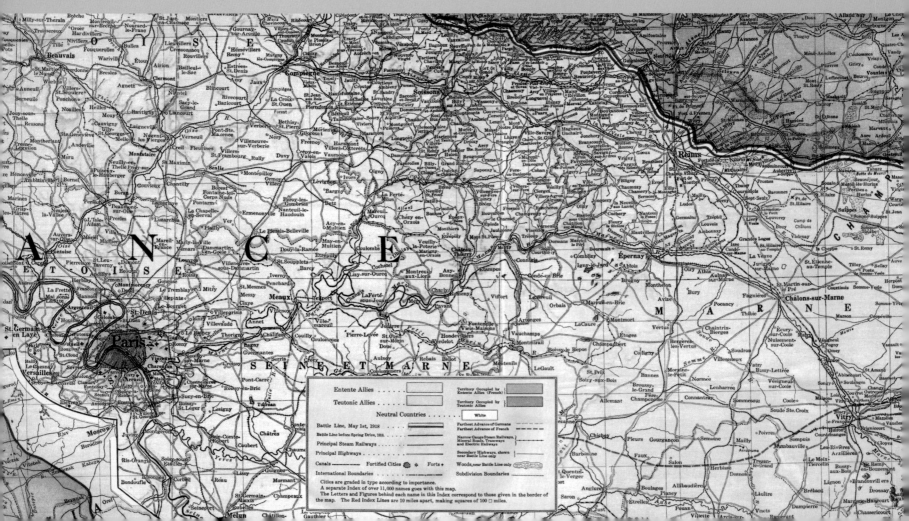

Pershing's AEF, now numbering 300,000 men, first saw action on 12–16 September in the retaking of the St. Mihiel salient (shown on Map 479, *below*), which had been in German hands since 1914. By May 1918 over half a million Americans were in France. The entry of the United States proved to be the factor that tipped the balance in favor of the Allies. On 26 September 1918, 260,000 American troops were sent "over the top" during the final Allied push known as the Meuse-Argonne offensive. By October it was all over for Germany; internal dissent and revolution led to the establishment of the Weimar Republic on 9 November and the surrender of Germany on 11 November. The war had suffered over 31 million casualties, including over 9 million dead. The United States had 360,000 casualties, including 126,000 dead. By war's end there were 2 million Americans in Europe.

Woodrow Wilson was keen to see that a new world order was established in which peace would endure. The United States was now one of the "big three" with Britain and France, and clearly a leader on the world stage. At the peace conference at Versailles in 1919, Wilson proposed his Fourteen Points to "make the world safe for democracy." Not all were incorporated. Germany was made to accept responsibility for the war and pay reparations, discontent over which would become one of the causes of World War II. Wilson's call for "a general association of nations" was included, however, leading to the establishment of the League of Nations. But Wilson could not get agreement at home. The Treaty of Versailles that the United States had initiated was never ratified by Congress, and the country never joined the League of Nations. But the increase in wages brought about during the war, coupled with taxation to pay for it, finally began to reduce what had been until then a vast gap in wealth between rich and poor.

Map 480 (*above*).
The trench warfare of the Western Front called for massive artillery barrages before an attempt was made to advance. The so-called rolling barrage would be directed just ahead of the advancing infantry. This map shows the successive target lines (in green) for the artillery barrage for the Battle of La Selle, an advance of the 27th and 30th American Divisions on 17 October 1918. At bottom left is the *Artillery Start Line* and the *Infantry Start Line*. St. Souplet is about 52 miles northwest of Compiègne, shown on Map 479, *below*, at far left top. The front had advanced that distance in the intervening period between these two maps.

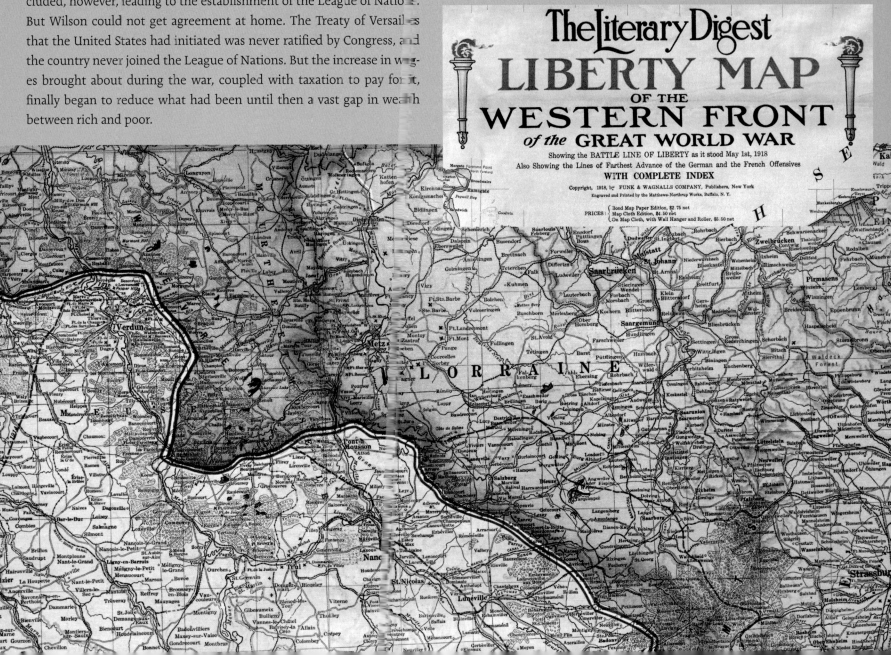

Boom, Bust, and a New Deal

Before the troops were even home, a pandemic of Spanish Flu began its rampage. In 1918–19 it killed 193,000 Americans, more than the number killed in the war. The troops returned also to an era of Prohibition; between 1919 and 1933 alcohol was banned in the United States. This seeming victory for the temperance advocates ushered in a period of crime, corruption, and violence in domestic America. Gangs like those led by Al Capone in Chicago reigned in the large cities, and smuggling, racketeering, and bootlegging were the order of the day. Between 1920 and 1930 over five hundred gangland murders took place, including the infamous and still unsolved St. Valentine's Day Massacre in 1929, likely the work of Capone's men.

Racial inequalities were violently maintained by a growing vigilante organization, the Ku Klux Klan, which boasted more than 4 million members at its strongest. Rural incomes declined dramatically during the 1920s, forcing a veritable exodus to the cities, ironically at the same time communications were making rural life easier. By 1929 more than 26 million automobiles were on the roads of America (see page 234), and radio stations popped up everywhere, relieving the isolation of many—or at least those within range (Map 481, *below*).

Despite successes like Henry Ford's, wealth remained concentrated in relatively few hands. There were not enough consumers for the range of products now being turned out by the factories. Yet the companies' stock kept climbing, fueled not by growth in underlying value but by what in a later day was to be politely termed "irrational exuberance." It was more like greed. Those who had money—and those who did not, borrowed—drove share prices up to unsustainable heights. Then came the reckoning. In September and October 1929 the stock market lost 40 percent, and by July 1932 it had lost an astonishing 89 percent. It would take twenty-five years for stocks to regain their 1929 high. Banks failed everywhere, causing panic; families were evicted from their homes by foreclosures, and 13 million workers lost their jobs. After the war America had become the banker to Europe, and so the financial and then social pain spread internationally. The 1930s was, universally, the decade of the Great Depression.

The president, Herbert Hoover, seemed not to know how to deal with the problems besetting his country, and it took a new president, Franklin Delano Roosevelt, elected in 1933, to initiate a large and diverse program to try to alleviate the effects of the Depression. Roosevelt had promised "a new deal for the American people," and this became the name for his programs.

Many of Roosevelt's policies moderated the worst effects of poverty and unemployment for those lucky enough to be involved in them; still others set the stage for the safety nets Americans expect today. Roosevelt wasted no time; many of his ideas were put into action in what became known as "the first hundred days." He closed the banks until a Federal Reserve System was put in place, which recreated confidence and allowed deposits to flow back, stabilizing the banking system. Then Federal Deposit Insurance was put in place. Federal salaries and pensions were cut to free up money for other uses. An Agricultural Adjustment Act paid farmers subsidies for keeping within quotas, which stabilized prices. Landowners were paid not

Map 481.

By 1924, the date of this "radio map," some parts of the country had a fairly dense network of radio stations, whose names are shown here in red. Some regions, especially in the South, had very few. The power of instant mass communication would soon become apparent. Roosevelt was the first president to use radio to influence public thought, with his famous "fireside chats."

Above, left. The classic Depression image, a photograph by federal photographer Arthur Rothstein. It shows a farmer and his sons in one of the dust bowl storms that added to the misery of the Depression by stripping much of the soil from the Plains. The location is Cimarron County, Oklahoma, in April 1936.

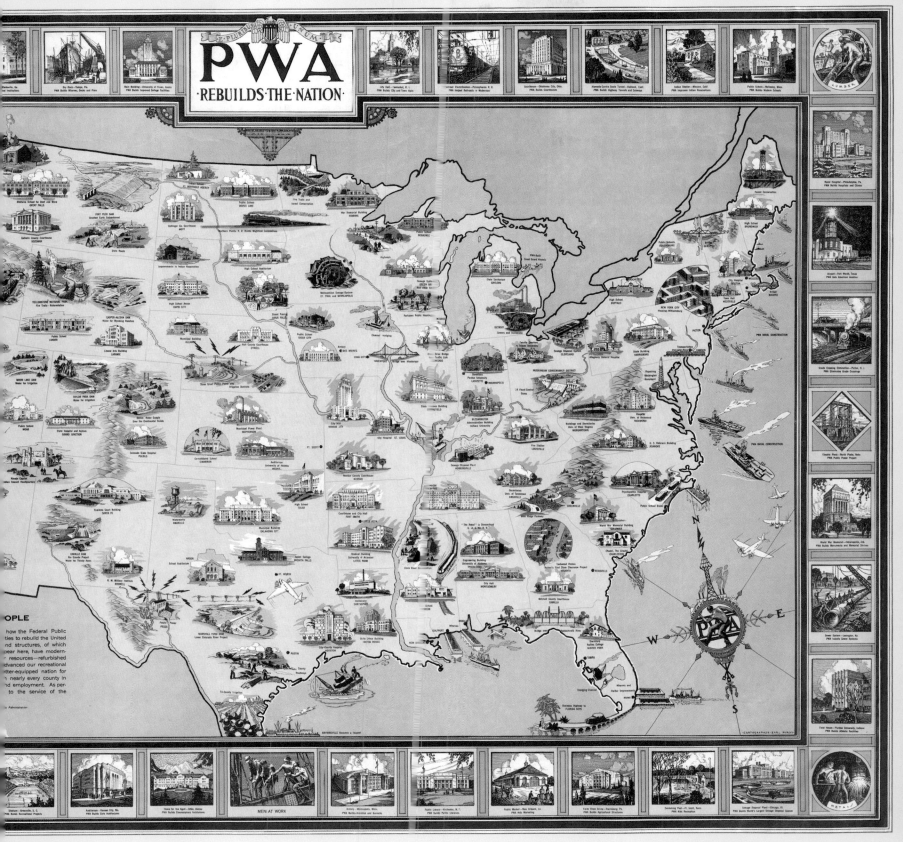

to grow some crops—but there was no provision for their unfortunate sharecroppers. The stock market was regulated by a new U.S. Securities and Exchange Commission (SEC). The National Industrial Recovery Act was passed in June, which, among other features, created the Public Works Administration (PWA), which contracted with private industry to construct over 34,000 diverse projects (MAP 482, above). Also in 1933, the Tennessee Valley Authority (TVA) was created to construct dams and reservoirs to control the Tennessee River (MAP 483, right). The forerunner of today's Social Security, an act passed in 1935 paid pensions to seniors and certain disadvantaged groups. And that year also the Wagner Act granted for the first time the right of existence to labor unions.

In the end, Roosevelt's grand schemes did not end the Depression. For that it took another world war. But he did his ebullient and well-meaning best, and his policies certainly did alleviate for many the worst effects of the economic turmoil. It is a measure of his enduring popularity that he is the only president ever to be elected four times (or ever will be; a two-term limit was initiated in 1951).

MAP 482 (*above*).
This pictorial map was published in 1935 by the Public Works Administration to publicize the myriad of public works it was financing to fight the Depression. Six billion dollars was spent by the PWA. Pictorial views on the map itself are supplemented by vignettes around its edge. Major projects included the Triborough Bridge and Lincoln Tunnel in New York City, the Key West Highway in Florida, and the Grand Coulee Dam in Washington.

MAP 483 (*right*).
This 1930s map from a postcard shows schematically the system of dams and reservoirs that formed the Tennessee Valley Authority Water Control System.

Good Roads Everywhere

From the earliest days there were roads of sorts, but most were little more than trails through the woods, sometimes adequate for the light, horse-drawn traffic they carried, but just as often impassable in wet weather. A notable attempt at creating a set of comprehensive road maps was made in 1789, with the *Survey of the Roads of the United States of America,* published by Christopher Colles. MAP 484 *(below, left)* is a map from this early road atlas.

As America awoke from this slower-paced world, it soon became apparent that the existing road system was woefully inadequate. The growth in automobile ownership was dramatic: in 1895 there were only four cars in the entire country, but by 1917 there were nearly 5 million.

Maps of the early automobile era showed what they called "auto trails" rather than roads as we understand them today. Route maps were complex and required constant alertness to avoid taking a wrong turn. Some companies, such as Rand McNally, developed picture books to guide the intrepid "automobilists" through each turn, and one of the first is said to contain photographs taken by Andrew McNally II as he drove from Chicago to Milwaukee on his honeymoon in 1909.

The road system at this time had no overall coherency and changed from one state to the next. Private automobile owners' organizations made a few attempts to mark major routes across the country, such as the Lincoln Highway, marked in 1912, which ran from New York to San Francisco—if you managed to stay on it. These roads were marked by signs tacked to telephone poles and the like, and motorists required detailed guides like MAP 485 *(right).* By 1925, the date of MAP 491 *(pages 236–37)* there were over 250 named highways, each marked with its own colored signs, which were often positioned haphazardly, leading to considerable confusion. Some highways were even rerouted by local merchants to pass through their otherwise bypassed towns.

By 1916 there were 3 million automobiles registered in the United States. This number climbed to 9 million by 1921 and 23 million in 1929, helped along rather dramatically by the 15 million Model T autos produced by Henry Ford's assembly line between 1908 and 1927, and which sold for just $260 in the latter year.

By this time organizations such as the Good Roads Association (MAP 490, *overleaf,* and MAP 491) had sprung up to pressure politicians for better roads, and it became clear that some coordination was needed to create a truly national road system. In 1925, the Bureau of Roads (then part of the Department of Agriculture), in cooperation with state highway departments, produced a plan for a comprehensive numbered road system, with continuous numbers for a single route, whatever state it was in. The system was implemented by 1927, with 96,626 miles of roads then becoming "US" numbered routes, greatly easing the navigational burden of long-distance driving. The longest of these new routes was US 30, which ran for 3,472 miles from Atlantic City, New Jersey, to Astoria, Oregon.

Although perhaps adequate for the 26.6 million automobiles in America in 1929, the road system eventually became overloaded because of unprecedented growth in the sheer number of automobiles. By 1955, the number of automobiles had reached 62.5 million, and something had to be done to accommodate them. Although attempts at an interstate system had been made after World War II, they had not produced the roads required because of inadequate funding and lack of uniform standards.

The answer was found by a new president, Dwight D. Eisenhower, who had been impressed by the military value of the German autobahns

Above. A good road in 1923. This one, in the Columbia Gorge in Oregon, is part of the cover for a spectacular birds-eye-type map of the Lower Columbia shown as MAP 437, *pages 210-11.*

MAP 484 *(below).*
Part of the route from Philadelphia to Annapolis, Maryland, as mapped by Christopher Colles and published in 1789 in his famous *Survey of the Roads of the United States of America.* His maps are strip maps, showing only the road traveled, features along the route, and roads that intersect. Colles's idea for a road map book was likely born during the War for Independence, when the need for reliable maps was often critical.

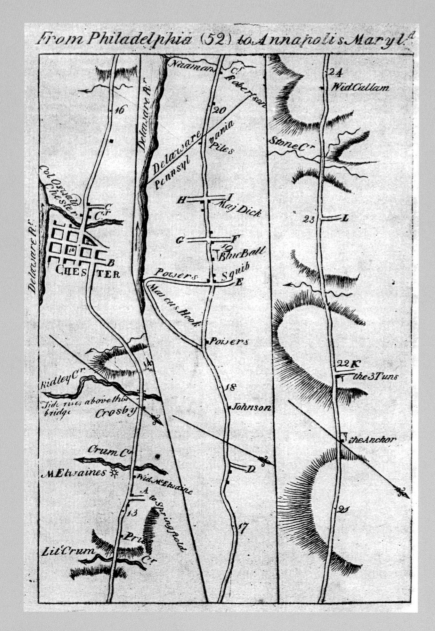

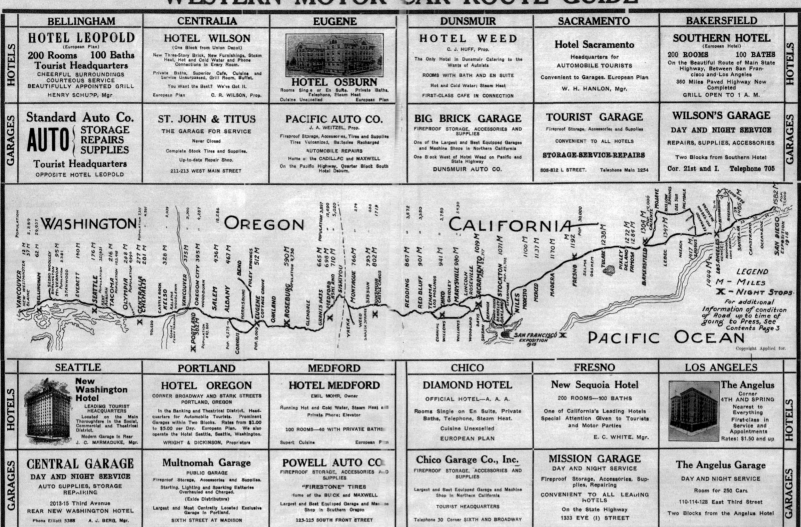

WESTERN MOTOR CAR ROUTE GUIDE

Map 485 (*above*).
Long-distance travel by automobile in 1915 was clearly an adventure. This map showing the automobile route from Vancouver, British Columbia, to San Diego was published that year. The red "X"s are the recommended night stops. There are fifteen stops shown, allowing sixteen days for the entire 1,500-mile trip. The advertisements for hotels and garages carefully tie in with these stops.

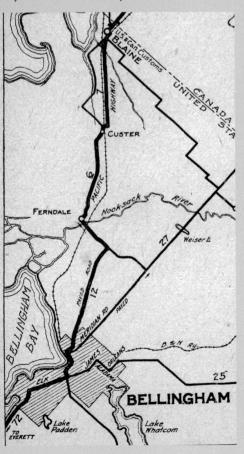

Map 486 (*left*).
Part of a route map from Blaine, Washington, on the Canadian border, to Bellingham, published by the Automobile Club of Western Washington in 1917. The map was printed on card, and there were a series of these covering all the available routes in the state.

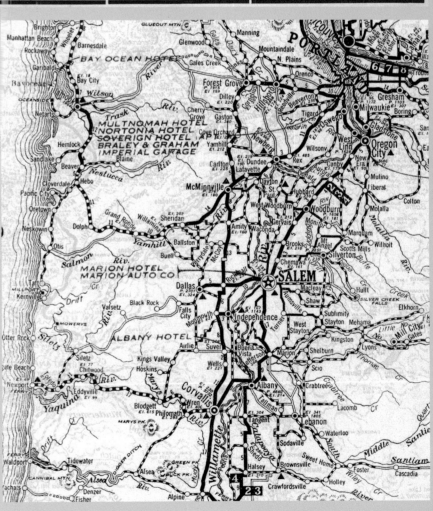

Map 487 (*above*).
The roads of Portland and the Willamette Valley in Oregon are shown on this Rand McNally auto trails map published in 1925. Only the solid-colored roads are paved; the rest are merely graded or, in the parlance of the day, "improved."

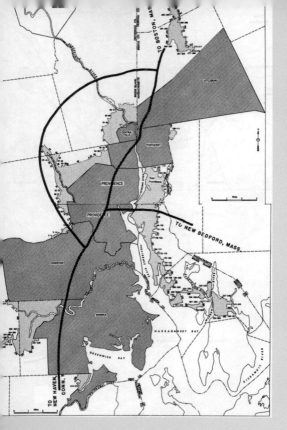

Map 488 (*left*).
In 1955 the Bureau of Public Roads issued a booklet (popularly known as the "Yellow Book" from the color of its cover) showing the "general locations of routes of the National System of Interstate Highways." It contained maps of urban areas like the example of Providence, Rhode Island, and region, shown here.

Map 489 (*below*).
This was the system of interstate highways approved in August 1947, reprinted in the 1955 "Yellow Book."

Right. The Interstate system is named after President Dwight D. Eisenhower, and signs such as this one can be found in numerous locations.

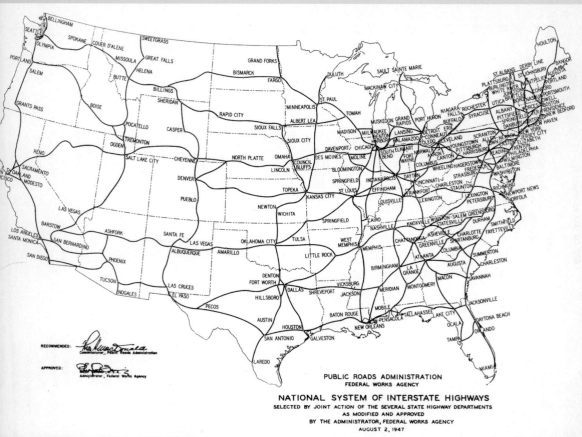

PUBLIC ROADS ADMINISTRATION
FEDERAL WORKS AGENCY

NATIONAL SYSTEM OF INTERSTATE HIGHWAYS
SELECTED BY JOINT ACTION OF THE SEVERAL STATE HIGHWAY DEPARTMENTS
AS MODIFIED AND APPROVED
BY THE ADMINISTRATOR, FEDERAL WORKS AGENCY
AUGUST 2, 1947

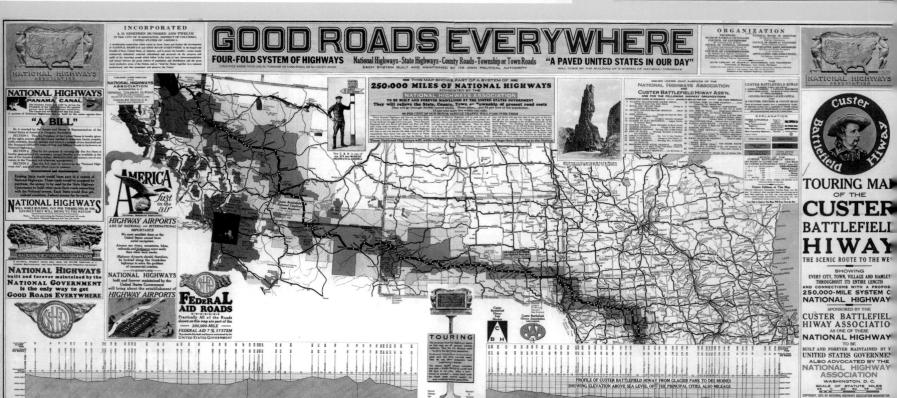

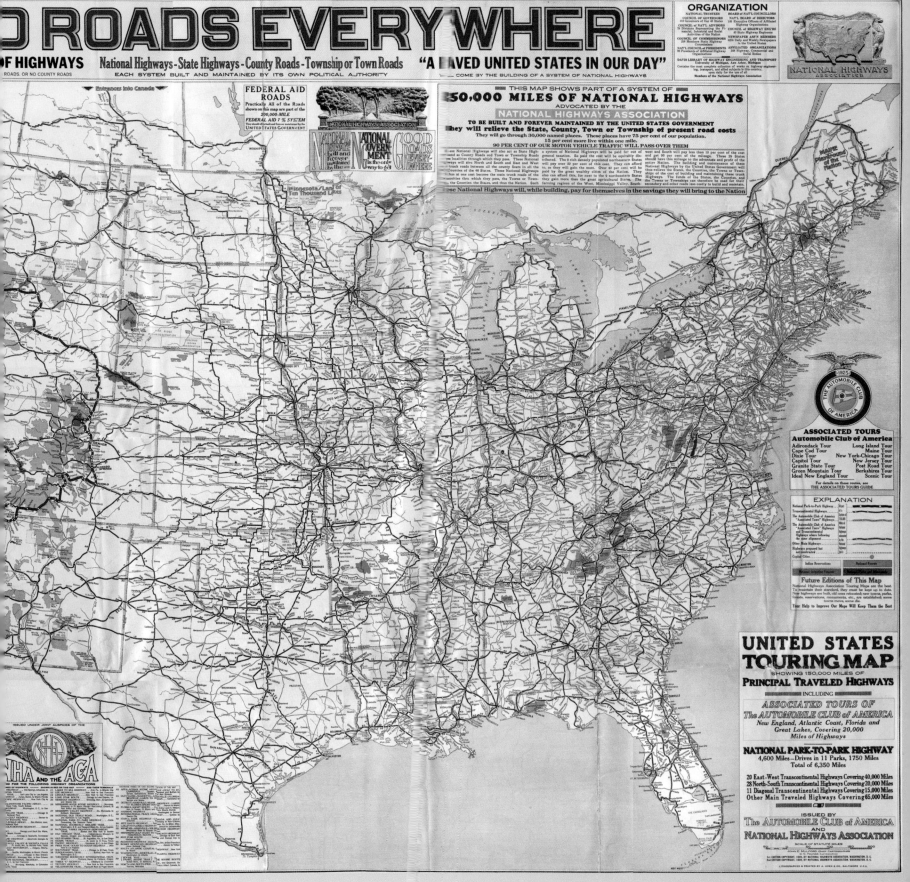

Map 490 (*left, bottom*) and **Map 491** (*above*).

The National Highways Association, created in 1912, lobbied hard for road improvements in the 1920s. These two maps date from 1925 and illustrate the type of map published to promote a particular route (Map 490) and for more general advertising, information, and lobbying purposes (Map 491). Both promote *GOOD ROADS EVERYWHERE*. The maps contain a fascinating panel advancing the idea that a national road network would lead to the creation of highway airports, based on the necessity, in 1925, of air navigation by reference to geographical features on the ground. This might have occurred had instrument flying not been invented. The road system illustrated on Map 491 almost all existed on the ground in 1925, but the map did not necessarily indicate roads of any reasonable standard. It was the federal construction and maintenance of paved highways that the National Highways Association was advocating—*A Paved United States in Our Day*. Beginning in 1925, the date of these maps, the federal agriculture department—then responsible for highways—began to introduce a unified system of road numbering and signs to replace the confusing 250-plus named highways then in existence. These maps do not yet show that unified numbering system.

during the war. He was the motivating force behind the Federal Highways Act, signed on 29 June 1956, which created the "National System of Interstate and Defense Highways." The act authorized $25 billion in funding for 41,000 miles of superhighways of at least four lanes. Part of the logic behind the new road system was that it would allow mass evacuation of cities in the event of a nuclear attack—hence the word "defense" as part of the system's name.

The new interstates were reviled by some as destroyers of neighborhoods, and in more than one instance elevated sections of roads were actually torn down again, notably on the San Francisco waterfront. Yet it is hard to see where America would be today without them. The freeway system has become an almost integral part of the national psyche and unites the states in just the way Eisenhower predicted it would. In 1993 the system was officially renamed the Dwight D. Eisenhower System of Interstate and Defense Highways in recognition of his role in its creation.

America Takes to the Skies

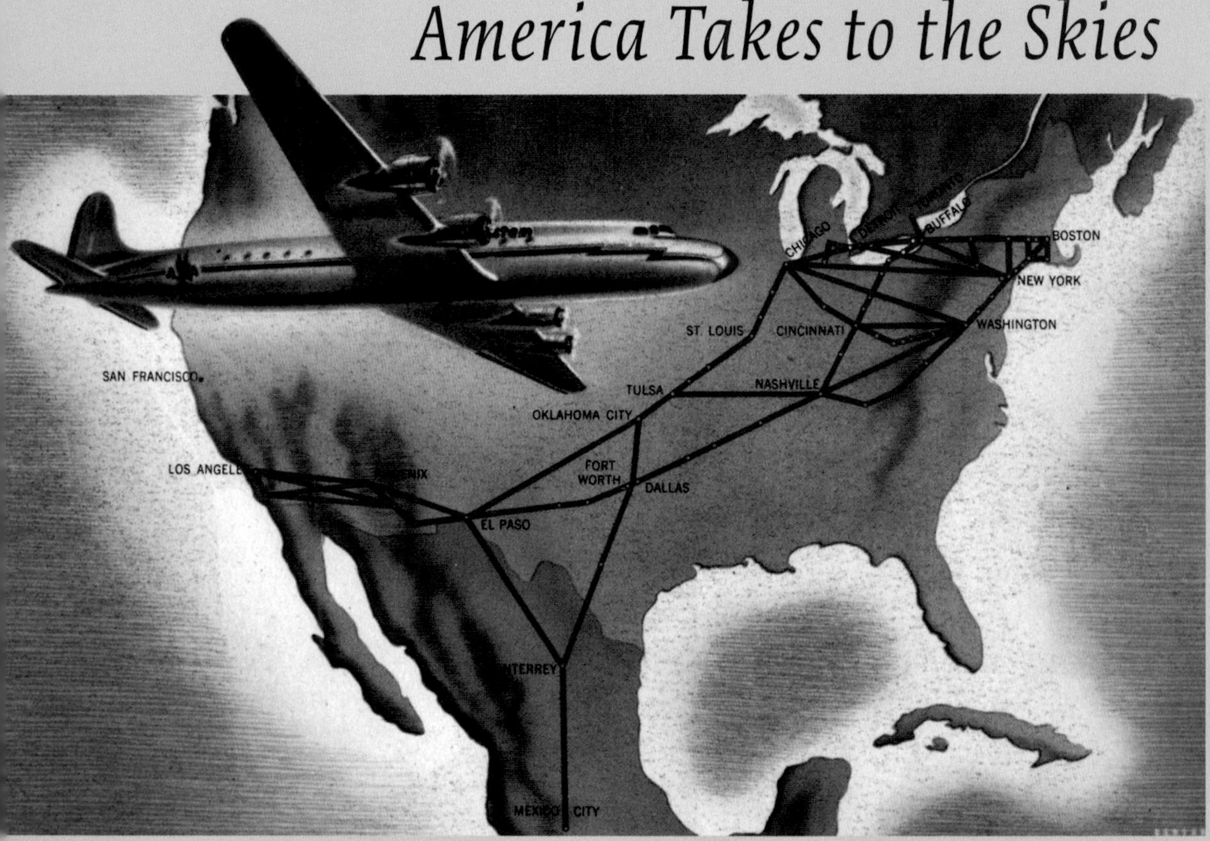

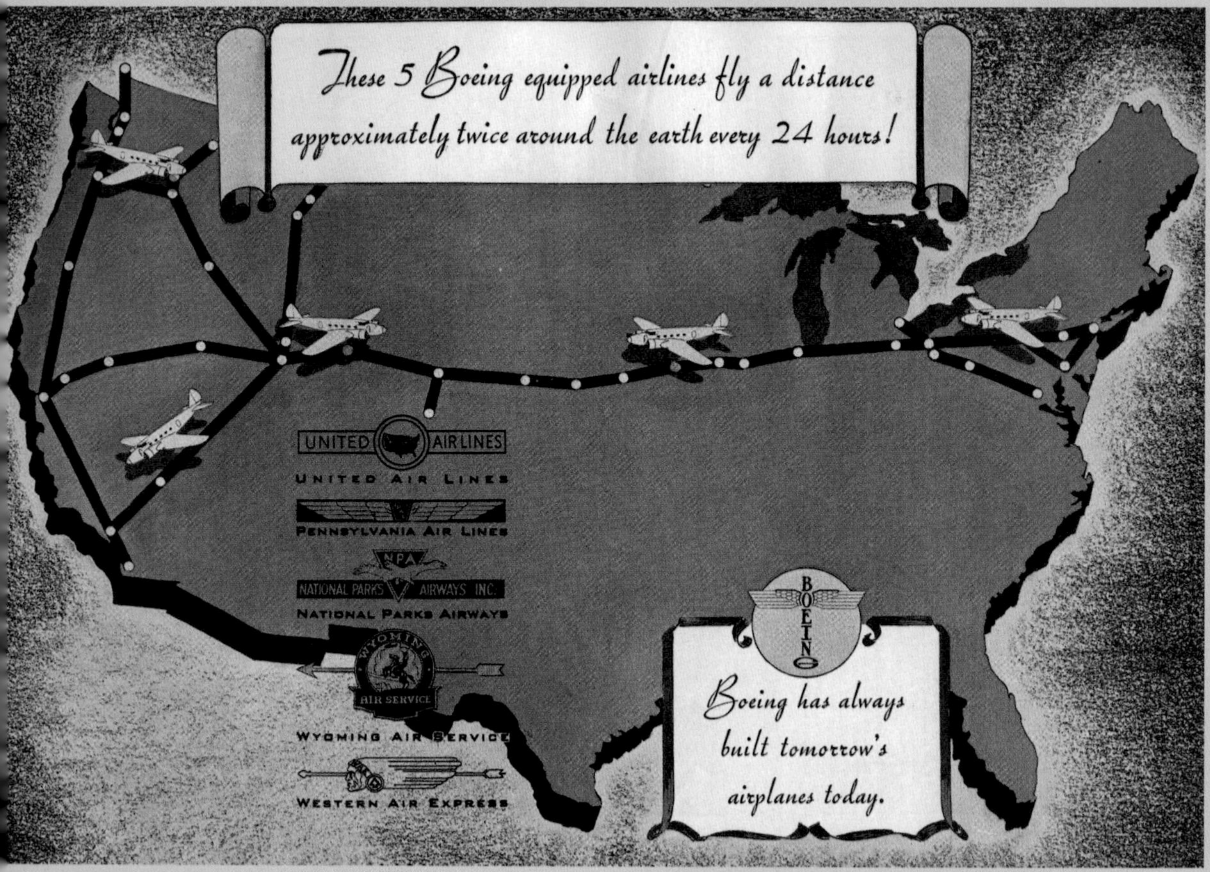

On 17 December 1903 the Wright brothers, Orville and Wilbur, first demonstrated powered, heavier-than-air, controllable flight. But the commercial application of flight did not occur until after the First World War, which itself demonstrated the value of aircraft for military uses.

Europe was initially ahead of the United States; in the early twenties Germany subsidized up to 70 percent of the cost of passenger flights. U.S. commercial flight really began with the carrying of mail, a use for which the government could justify subsidy. Congress had voted funds for a trial as early as 1917, and the first airmail route, between Washington and New York, began operation in 1918.

In 1921, to show what was possible, a team of post office pilots ferried mail from San Francisco to New York in relays. The trip took 33 hours

MAP 492 (*left, top*).
A Douglas DC-6 wings its way across the United States in this route map and advertisement for American Airlines published in 1946. American was an amalgam of over eighty smaller airlines formally incorporated with the AA name in 1934. It is now the largest airline in the world.

MAP 493 (*left, center*).
Routes of United Air Lines and some feeder services are shown in this 1936 pictorial route map. The transcontinental route from San Francisco was through Denver and Chicago, still major hubs for the airline.

MAP 494 (*below*).
The western part of Transcontinental Air Transport's combined air and rail transcontinental passenger route is depicted in this 1929 map from a brochure promoting the service. It lasted only sixteen months, in 1929–30. Passengers were few due to the high ticket cost. The airline merged with others in 1930 to create Transcontinental and Western Air—TWA—which flew the first scheduled coast-to-coast passenger service, in 1933. Compare with MAP 501, *page 242*.

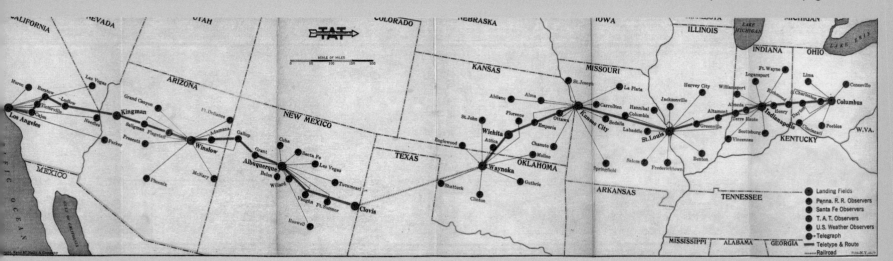

20 minutes and was a great public relations success. In 1924 a system of beacons and emergency airstrips was completed across the country, allowing night flying from coast to coast, a unique American achievement.

A year later came the Kelly Act, which put regional mail flights up for private bid. This induced many pioneers of commercial flight to begin to fly regular air routes, and they started to carry a few passengers too, though doubtless of the more intrepid kind, since flying was still a somewhat hazardous affair. One of the regional operators was a company owned by Henry Ford, who began to build his famous Ford Trimotor in 1926. This was the same year the post office decided to contract out the lucrative transcontinental route.

The San Francisco–Chicago leg was won by William Boeing, who had made a start in commercial aviation in 1919 ferrying mail from ocean liners arriving at Victoria, on Vancouver Island, to Seattle. Boeing Air Transport began carrying transcontinental mail on 1 July 1927. In the next two years Boeing merged with or acquired other companies, including engine maker Pratt and Whitney, to form United Aircraft and Transport Corporation. After a scandal in 1934 involving alleged impropriety in the awarding of mail contracts, the Air Mail Act of that year prohibited the joint ownership of manufacturers and operators. Boeing's company was split into three: Boeing Airplane Company, now the premier American aircraft manufacturer, a parts company (now United Technologies), and United Air Lines. The latter company began scheduled passenger air routes up and down the Pacific coast and across the continent to New York via Denver and Chicago (MAP 493, *left, center*).

The Chicago–New York leg of the transcontinental mail route was won by Clement Keys, who after the war had purchased the famous Curtiss Aeroplane and Motor Company (begun by aviation pioneer Glenn Curtiss). His company, National Air Transport, chose not to carry passengers due to the continued dangers of flying at night, but in 1928 Keys created another company, Transcontinental Air Transport, which, in conjunction with the Pennsylvania and Santa Fe Railroads, carried passengers by day in Ford Trimotors and by night in Pullman sleeping cars. This allowed passengers to travel from coast to coast in 48 hours (MAP 494, *left, bottom*).

Although air travel was gaining in popularity, it was still transportation for the well-off. By 1939, despite the emergence of new, very reliable airliners such as the trusty Douglas DC-3, only 2 percent of travelers flew. The Second World War changed air travel forever. In 1952 the world's first commercial jet aircraft, the Comet, was being flown by BOAC, the British overseas airline, but the design suffered from metal fatigue and led to a number of crashes. Boeing introduced the first successful commercial jet, the Boeing 707, which Pan American Airways flew first, on a flight from New York to Paris on 26 October 1958. American Airlines flew the first transcontinental flight the following January. In September 1959 Donald Douglas's competitive product, the DC-8, began commercial service, flown by United and Delta. The inauguration of the 707 and the DC-8 ushered in the jet age, and passenger traffic climbed rapidly as the competitive advantage of jet speed left the railroads behind. The technology in these aircraft in turn allowed the development of larger models to accommodate the increase in passengers.

MAP 495 (*right*).
The eastern seaboard air routes of American Airlines are shown in this 1945 map from a company brochure. Detailed pictorial maps such as this one helped keep passengers happy as they flew in piston aircraft in short hops at slow speeds and at low elevations. The key for the map is below.

Below. Pan American Airways was created in 1926 as a seaplane service from Key West, Florida, to Cuba. Entrepreneur Juan Trippe expanded to serve South America and in 1935 began flying huge Boeing 314 flying boats, dubbed "clippers," to Honolulu and to China via Wake Island and Guam, principally financed by the mail contract for the route. Pan Am was for many years the principal U.S. international airline. It collapsed financially in 1991, following the bombing of one of its Boeing 747-100s over Lockerbie, Scotland, in December 1988. The brand name has been resurrected several times but has no relationship to the original company.

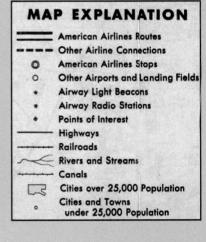

MAP EXPLANATION

▬▬▬	American Airlines Routes
▬ ▬ ▬	Other Airline Connections
◉	American Airlines Stops
○	Other Airports and Landing Fields
★	Airway Light Beacons
✶	Airway Radio Stations
✦	Points of Interest
▬▬▬	Highways
▬▬▬	Railroads
⌇	Rivers and Streams
⌐	Canals
▭	Cities over 25,000 Population
◦	Cities and Towns under 25,000 Population

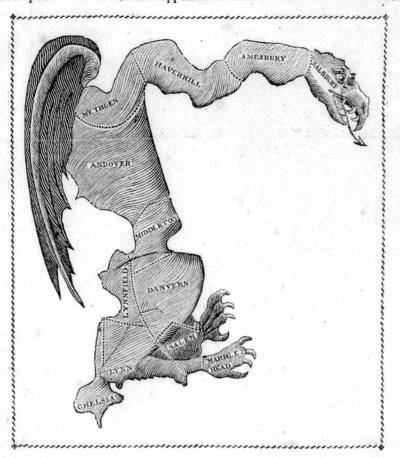

THE GERRY-MANDER.

A new species of *Monster*, which appeared in *Essex South District* in Jan. 1812.

" *O generation of* VIPERS *! who hath warned you of the wrath to come ?*"

THE horrid Monster of which this drawing is a correct representation, appeared in the County of Essex, during the last session of the Legislature. Various and manifold have been the speculations and conjectures, among learned naturalists respecting the *genus* and origin of this astonishing production. Some believe it to be the real *Basilisk*, a creature which had been supposed to exist only in the poet's imagination. Others pronounce it the *Serpens Monocephalus* of Pliny, or single-headed *Hydra*, a terrible animal of pagan extraction. Many are of opinion that it is the *Griffin* or *Hippogriff* of romance, which flourished in the dark ages, and has come hither to assist the knight of the rueful countenance in restoring that gloomy period of ignorance, fiction and imposition. Some think it the great Red Dragon, or Bunyun's *Apollyon* or the *Monstrum Horrendum* of Virgil; and all believe it a creature of infernal origin, both from its aspect, and from the circumstance of its birth.

MAP 496 (*above*).
One of the most famous pictorial maps, and one that introduced a new word to the English language, was this *horrid Monster of which this drawing is a correct representation,* concocted from a map of the electoral districts put together (to pack more voters for the opposition into districts they would win in any case) by the Massachusetts legislature to favor the incumbent governor, Elbridge Gerry. Originally a woodcut by Elkanah Tisdale of Salem, Massachusetts, the figure was supposed to be a *salamander,* but because of Gerry's involvement, became a *gerrymander.* The map appeared in January 1812. Gerry, one of the signers of the Declaration of Independence, was defeated as Massachusetts governor in 1812 over his support for this redistricting. Gerrymandering is still a significant issue in the United States; a number of states have electoral districts of ridiculous proportions, clearly created for political reasons.

Pictorial Maps

The incorporation of pictures into maps or the creation of pictures from map shapes yields a pictorial map. They abound throughout this atlas. On these pages is a selection of a few of the more original or artistic pictorial maps, spanning two centuries, purely for visual enjoyment. A pictorial map is often a work of art at some level, created as a political statement or an advertisement, to persuade or to more eloquently put across a point of view, in a way that demands attention. They are ideal for commercial advertising, of course, and the route maps of the railroads, airlines, buses, and the like particularly lend themselves to the technique. A map may be worth ten thousand words, but it can—for good or for bad—also distort reality more effectively than the written word.

MAP 497 (*above*).
This 1888 map extols the virtues of the state of California and also packs a lot of information into a small space.

MAP 498 (*left*).
It took a bit of ingenuity to visualize the Northern Pacific Railway line as a pointer dog, but this imaginative map is certainly an attention-getter, despite being only in black and white. It was published in 1902.

MAP 499 (*right, top*).
This patriotic map, complete with its depiction of the signing of the Declaration of Independence, was published in 1859, on the eve of the Civil War.

MAP 500 (*right*).
The *Lottery Octopus* map was published in 1890 to protest bribery and corruption in the Louisiana State Lottery, which closed down in 1893 following the exposé.

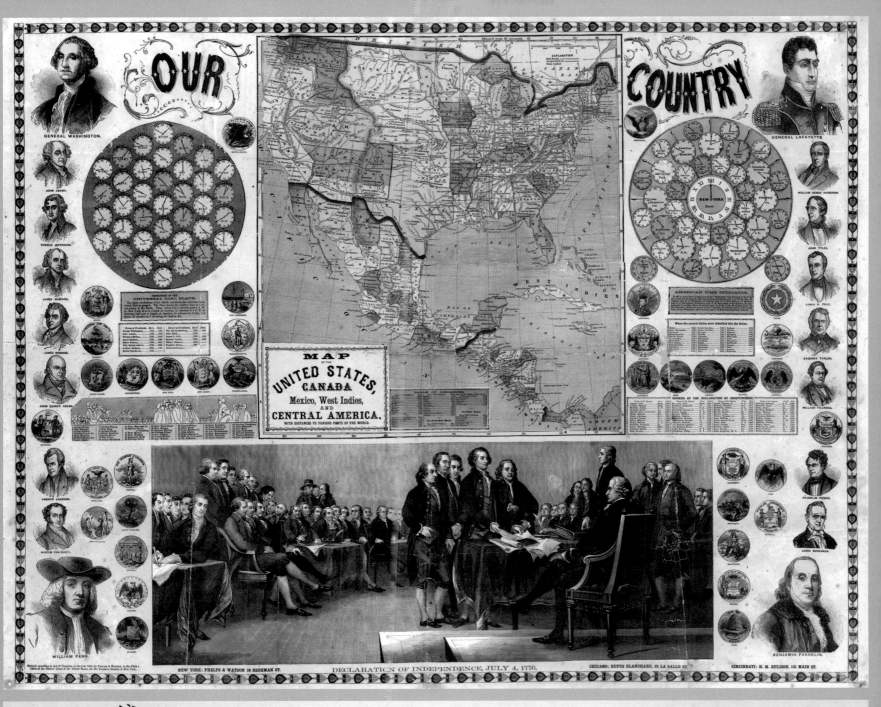

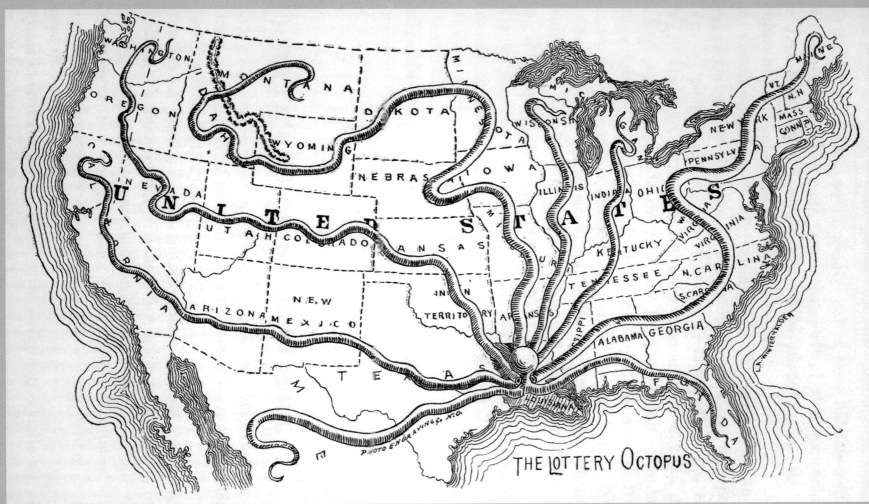

THE LOTTERY OCTOPUS

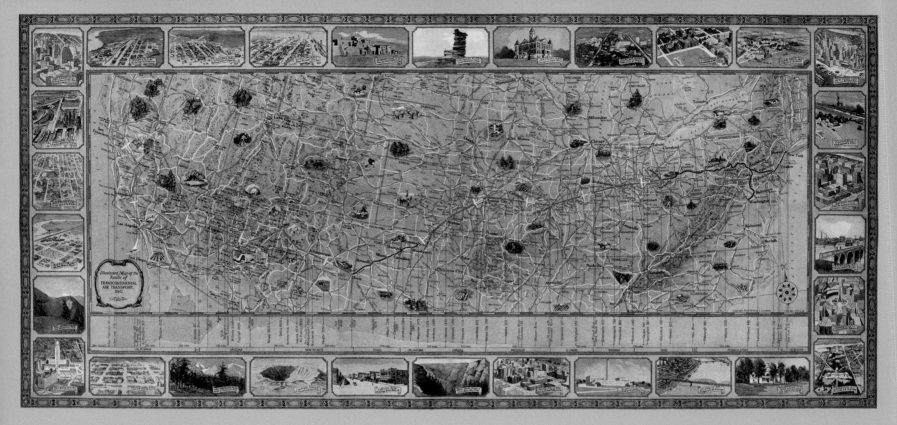

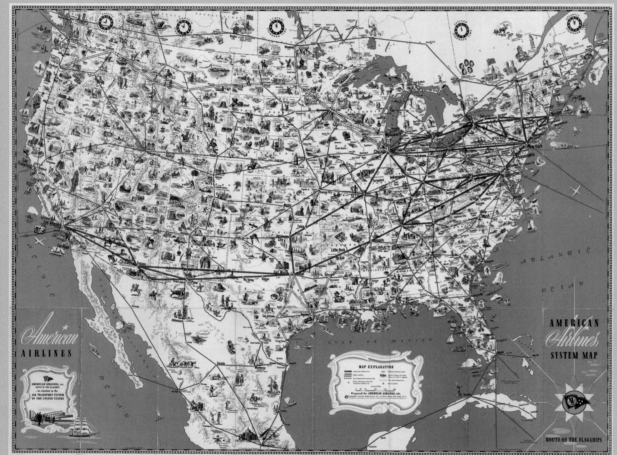

MAP 501 (*above*).
This 1929 map showing the western part of Transcontinental Air Transport's combined air and rail transcontinental passenger route presents an interesting comparison with the much simpler, but much easier to read, MAP 494, *page 238*. A more artistic map is not necessarily a more practical one.

MAP 502 (*left*).
Almost overly pictorial is this 1945 American Airlines route map, a work of art in its own right.

MAP 503 (*below, left*) and MAP 504 (*below*).
Pictorial maps are invaluable in emphasizing your point of view. These two maps, both postcards from the 1950s, show tongue-in-cheek views of the nation from two states.

MAP 505 (*right, top*).
A very detailed "good-natured" Greyhound Lines bus route map from about 1940.

MAP 506 (*right, bottom*).
Another "good-natured" advertising and route map, issued by the Alaska Steamship Company in 1934. It graphically depicts all the reasons to visit the then Territory of Alaska.

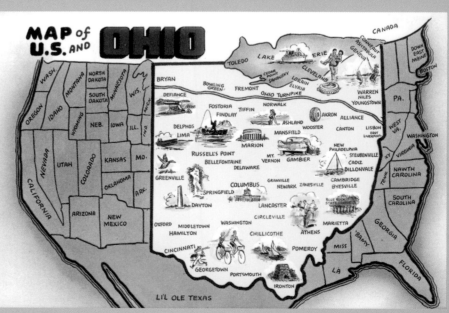

A Day of Infamy

On 11 November 1940 twenty-four British torpedo-bombers, flying from aircraft carriers, badly damaged the Italian fleet at anchor in the harbor at Taranto. The effectiveness of this raid was noted by the commander-in-chief of the Japanese navy, Admiral Isoruku Yamamoto. Eleven months later, having developed a similar plan of attack, which used shallow-running torpedoes, he planned to destroy the American fleet at Pearl Harbor.

In the early morning of Sunday, 7 December 1941, a swarm of Japanese planes descended on the American fleet moored in Pearl Harbor, bombing and torpedoing them and bombing airfields, where the planes had conveniently been grouped together to protect against sabotage. War had not been declared, and at that very moment in Washington Japanese officials were still talking peace. The Japanese attack was launched from six aircraft carriers with over 400 planes, which had approached Hawaii undetected, under radio silence. When the mayhem was over, 2,403 Americans were dead, five battleships sunk and three more damaged; three destroyers and three cruisers were also sunk, and some 188 planes were destroyed and 155 damaged. It was destruction on a scale that the United States was destined to become familiar with over the next four years. Pearl Harbor unleashed a ferocious Pacific War against a vicious and determined enemy.

The Second World War had begun in Europe on 1 September 1939, when the German army smashed into Poland, which invoked guarantees by Britain and France, which declared war on Germany two days later. The war had not gone well. The German *blitzkrieg* drove the British into the sea at Dunkirk, and France capitulated. Britain alone stood against the German onslaught. Adolf Hitler's planned invasion of Britain in 1940 had been narrowly averted by the Battle of Britain, in June, when the Royal Air Force just managed to maintain control of the skies. But Britain is an island, and its shipping was being mercilessly hunted down by German submarines. Winston Churchill appealed to Franklin Roosevelt for help.

Roosevelt gave Britain all the help he could short of declaring war, given the significant isolationist element in the United States. Before the American entry into the war, $37 billion had been appropriated for rearmament and aid to the Allies, 50 destroyers had been given to Britain, and, in September 1940, Congress had passed a conscription law, the first ever peacetime military draft. Roosevelt had met with Churchill in August 1941 aboard a battleship in Argentia Bay, Newfoundland, to agree on the Atlantic Charter, which detailed self-determination and freedoms, and an association of nations, for the postwar period—all agreed before the United States had even entered the war. In October, the first American warship was sunk, while assisting a British convoy.

The declaration of war by the United States on 8 December 1941 following what Roosevelt called the "day that will live in infamy" was, then, hardly a surprise. The country was now committed to fighting a war in two major arenas, the Pacific and Europe. With the entry of Russia into the war on the Allied side earlier in 1941, the war had become global, a true world war.

The attack on Pearl Harbor was quickly followed by other Japanese assaults as Japan sought to carry out its plan of securing a dominating position in the Pacific

Above, top.
This now iconic photograph shows American battleships under attack at Pearl Harbor, 6 December 1941.

MAP 507 (*above*).
The scene of the destruction: Pearl Harbor just three years before it was attacked. "Battleship Row," where the fleet was anchored together, and where the photo was taken, was on the southeast side of *Ford Island*, except for the *Pennsylvania*, which was in dry dock on the mainland just across the channel.

MAP 508 (*left*).
A military map, stamped *Secret*, of the defenses of Oahu, is dated 18 September 1941, just weeks before the attack on Pearl Harbor. Japanese planes approached from the north. The aircraft warning station that first detected them is shown at the top, the *AWS* above *Kawela Bay*.

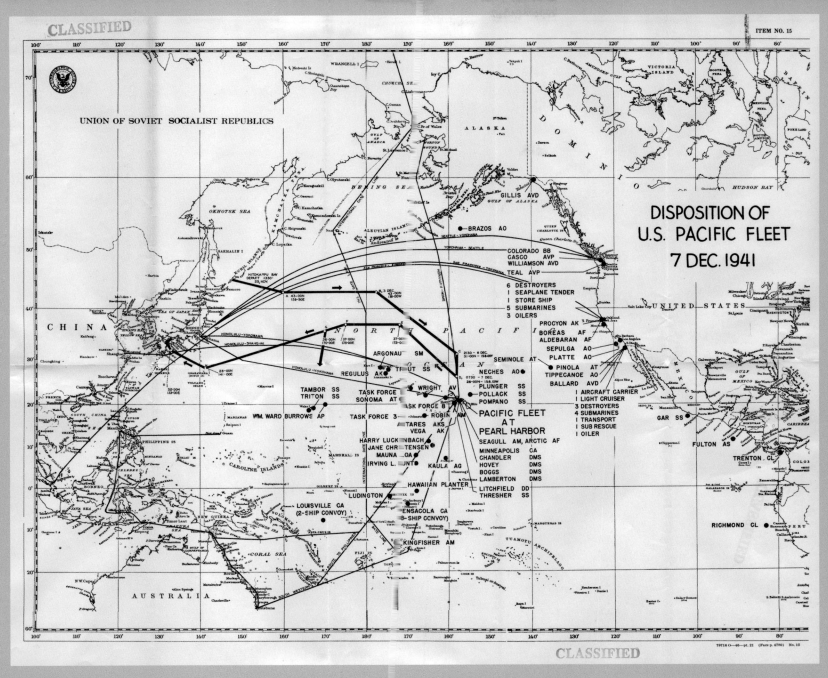

CLASSIFIED

UNION OF SOVIET SOCIALIST REPUBLICS

DISPOSITION OF
U.S. PACIFIC FLEET
7 DEC. 1941

PACIFIC FLEET
AT
PEARL HARBOR

CLASSIFIED

Map 509 (*above*).
This map, stamped *Classified,* is a U.S. naval analysis of the situation on 7 December 1941. The positions of U.S. ships around the Pacific, including the west coast of the United States, are indicated. The route of the Japanese Imperial Fleet from Japan to a position north of Hawaii is shown by the thick black line.

before the U.S. could recover. The Philippines were attacked and Manila fell (after being declared an open city to prevent its destruction) on 2 January 1942. American resistance was first concentrated on the Bataan Peninsula, across Manila Bay from the capital; U.S. forces there surrendered to the Japanese on 10 April, beginning, as it would be for most Allied prisoners, an appalling time in confinement from which they would be lucky to emerge alive. Their commander, General Douglas MacArthur, ordered by Roosevelt, reluctantly left the Philippines, ran the Japanese blockade, and made it to Australia, where on 20 March he gave his memorable statement: "I came through, and I will return." It would take four long years of Allied toil and sacrifice before he could. The last American outpost in the Philippines, the island of Corregidor, at the entrance to Manila Bay, surrendered on 8 May, after heavy fighting.

Map 510 (*right*).
Part of a U.S. government "newsmap" (see MAP 513, *overleaf*), this map shows both the farthest extent of Japanese control, in August 1942, and the area under Japanese control as of 17 December 1944. The arrows show Allied land drives toward Japan and bomber targets.

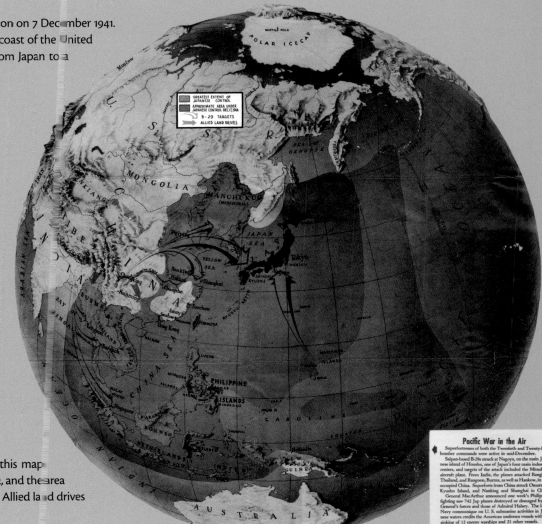

Pacific War in the Air

Superfortresses of both the Twentieth and Twenty-First bomber commands were active in mid-December.

Saipan-based B-29s struck at Nagoya, on the main Japanese island of Honshu, one of Japan's four main industrial centers, and targets of the attack included the Mitsubishi aircraft plant. From India, the planes attacked Bangkok, Thailand, and Rangoon, Burma, as well as Hankow, in Japan-occupied China. Superforts from China struck Omura, on Kyushu Island, and Nanking and Shanghai in China.

General MacArthur announced one week's Philippine fighting saw 542 Jap planes destroyed or damaged by the General's forces and those of Admiral Halsey. The latest Navy communique on U.S. submarine activities in Japanese waters credits the American undersea service with the sinking of 12 enemy warships and 21 other vessels.

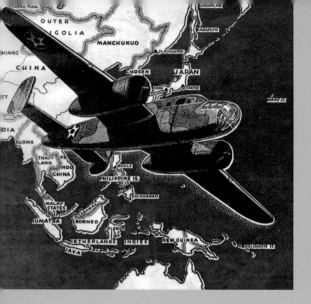

The area under Japanese control grew steadily, until by August 1942 it encompassed all of Southeast Asia as far west as Burma and a huge swath of the western Pacific (MAP 510, *previous page*). In May the Japanese had suffered their first setback when their intention to take by sea Port Moresby, on the south coast of New Guinea, as a springboard to an invasion of Australia, was prevented. This was the Battle of the Coral Sea. The turning point, however, was the Battle of Midway, fought in June off Midway Island in the central Pacific, masterminded—as would be several other major battles—by Admiral Chester Nimitz, commander-in-chief of the U.S. Pacific Fleet. He was helped by the interception of encoded Japanese messages. Three American carriers were involved, under Rear Admirals Jack Fletcher and Raymond Spruance: the uss *Hornet, Enterprise,* and *Yorktown,* the latter damaged, the Japanese thought, beyond quick repair at Coral Sea but turned around in Honolulu in seventy-two hours. Of the four Japanese carriers, three were sunk. The American force lost one—the *Yorktown.* The battle was significant in that it finally brought Japanese expansion to a halt and marked the beginning of the end for Japan, a relentless island-hopping assault by American troops that would eventually lead to Japan itself. The first engagement was a bitter battle for Guadacanal, in the Solomon Islands, which finally fell in February 1943.

MAP 511 (*above*).
The cover of a patriotic booklet-atlas called *America in World War II,* published in 1942, dramatically superimposing a U.S. bomber over a map of Southeast Asia.

MAP 512 (*below*).
Hand drawn on a printed base map, this military map shows the situation in Normandy at midnight on 6 June 1944. It is marked *Secret* (not shown). The U.S. 4th Infantry Division landed at Utah Beach (marked *4*) and the U.S. 1st Infantry Division at Omaha Beach (marked *115, 116,* and *16,* the numbers referring to regimental combat teams). The shaded rectangles are German units, which include the crack 352 Infantry Division (*352* on the River *Vire*).

As a feint, the Japanese had attacked the Aleutians at the same time as Midway, and this caused considerable alarm along the Pacific coast, reinforcing the perceived need for two earlier decisions: the building of the Alaska Highway, completed in October 1942; and the forced relocation, beginning in February 1942, of Japanese Americans living in coastal areas to camps far inland. The government much later apologized for the internment of Japanese Americans, saying it had been prompted by racial prejudices coupled with war hysteria.

Roosevelt had agreed with Churchill that the first priority would be to defeat Germany, partly to ensure that Russia stayed in the war. American forces fought in North Africa against Field Marshal Erwin Rommel's famed Afrika Corps and were beaten badly at the Battle of Kasserine Pass, in the Atlas Mountains of Tunisia, in February 1943, the first major American-German engagement. The Allied commitment to North Africa was such, however, that by May the Germans were finally defeated, and some quarter million Axis soldiers surrendered.

North Africa was then used as a base to launch an attack on Italy. The invasion of Sicily began in July and that of the mainland on 3 September. Italy itself surrendered a week later, and the Italian dictator Benito Mussolini was deposed. But the Germans continued to fight. The Allied armies were stalled at the defensive Gustav Line and the stronghold of Monte Cassino, which controlled the route to Rome. After landings behind the line at Anzio in January, Monte Cassino fell on 4 May 1943, and Rome fell on 5 June.

After keeping Hitler guessing for months, the Allies finally created a beachhead in Normandy on D-Day, 6 June 1944. In the largest amphibious military invasion operation ever, Allied troops that after five days would number

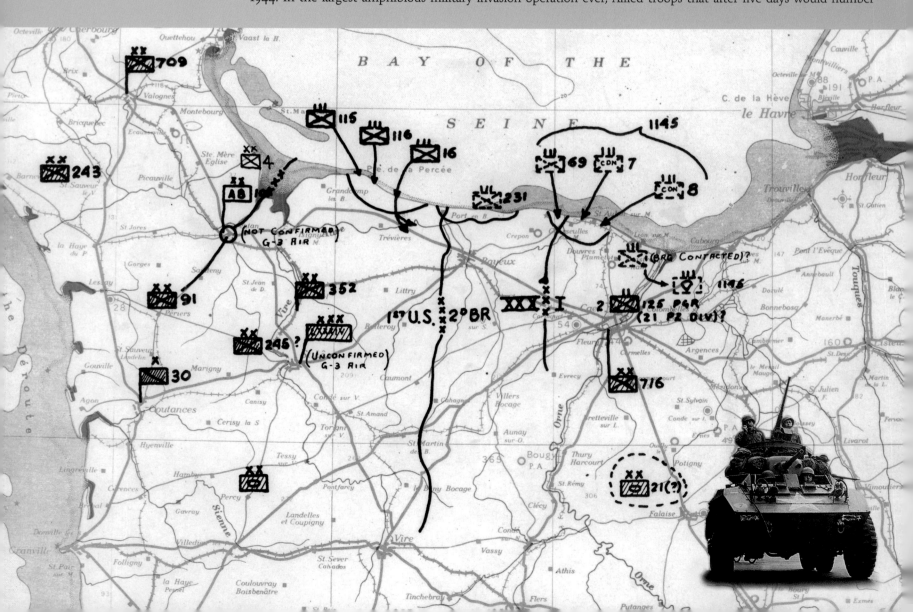

326,000 assaulted the beaches of Normandy beginning in the early hours of 6 June. U.S. troops landed at Omaha Beach and Utah Beach (MAP 512, *left, bottom*). The invasion, code-named Operation Overlord, was to have been the day before but bad weather delayed it. Overall Allied commander General Dwight D. Eisenhower finally gave the go-ahead despite a lingering storm, and this gave the Allies an additional advantage of surprise. Elaborate deceptions had been made as to the landing place. An entirely fictitious U.S. First Army was created, and radio messages built up the illusion that the Pas de Calais was its intended destination. At the critical moment Hitler even ordered Rommel's crack Panzer Division to concentrate there. During the landings, dummy rubber paratroopers were dropped behind the German lines to confuse and divert German resources.

Three days after the initial landings, huge caissons called Mulberry harbors were placed on the beaches to create two places where larger ships could unload supplies. One of them was destroyed in a storm ten days later, but the other remained to land 2.5 million men and supplies over an eight-month period. The critical harbor at Cherbourg surrendered on 26 June, and the city of Caen, originally an objective for capture on D-Day, was taken, only after much hard fighting, in early July. Paris was liberated on 25 August.

Another Allied landing took place on 15 August on the southern coast of France. Operation Dragoon, as it was called, landed 94,000 mainly American troops, who by mid-September had joined up near Dijon with forces from Operation Overlord.

By August there were three U.S. armies, under Generals Omar N. Bradley, Courtney H. Hodges, and the colorful George S. Patton, pushing the Germans eastwards. At the same time the Russians were approaching Germany from the other direction. In September an attempt was made to speed up the advance with an airborne action behind the front lines known as Operation Market Garden. Paratroopers jumped in to take bridges across the Rhine at Nijmegen and Arnhem; the first was taken but not held against a counterattack, and the attempt to take the Arnhem bridge—popularized as "The Bridge Too Far"—failed. In December the Germans attempted a breakout in the Ardennes, with the goal of recapturing the critical port of Antwerp, which the Allies had taken on 4 September. At the beginning of this Ardennes Offensive, or "Battle of the Bulge," bad weather kept Allied planes grounded, and the Germans inflicted heavy casualties before Patton's army arrived to push them back once more.

The end was near for the Third Reich. Confident now of victory, Winston Churchill, Josef Stalin, and Roosevelt met at Yalta in February 1945, agreeing to the postwar division of Europe and the establishment of the United Nations. Berlin was besieged by the Russian army on 16 April, and Hitler committed suicide in his bunker on 30 April. The Germans quickly signed an unconditional surrender on 7 May; the western Allies celebrated Victory in Europe—V-E Day—on 8 May.

Attention could now be turned fully to Japan. Carrier-supported amphibious landings progressed toward the Japanese mainland. The Japanese were ousted from the Solomon Islands in 1943, and in 1944 the Mariana Islands had been captured, including Guam. Japanese naval power was de-

MAP 513.
Part of another U.S. government "newsmap," this one illustrating the bombing of Japan. It is dated 6 August 1945, the very day the first atomic bomb was dropped on Hiroshima. These maps were produced by the War Department to be displayed in factories where war materials were being manufactured, "for the purpose of keeping war workers informed as to the progress of the war and also to graphically associate the production of war materials with victories won on the battle fronts."

stroyed in June 1944 at the Battle of the Philippine Sea by a fleet under Admiral Raymond A. Spruance, when 3 Japanese carriers were sunk. The Battle of Leyte Gulf, off Luzon in the Philippines, in October, was another major American victory. It was the largest naval battle in history; Admiral William Halsey's fleet of 17 carriers, 18 escort carriers (smaller aircraft carriers), 12 battleships, 24 cruisers, 141 destroyers, and many other ships, with about 1,500 planes, defeated a smaller Japanese fleet, sinking 4 carriers and 3 battleships.

The noose around Japan's neck tightened with the stunningly hard-fought capture of Iwo Jima in March 1945. Fighter escorts could now be provided for the bombing of Japan. Tokyo and many other cities suffered conflagration by bombing (MAP 513, *above*), with considerable loss of life due to the dense population. The last major battle of the war was the Battle of Okinawa, in the Ryukyu Islands just south of Japan, fought between April and June. Under General Simon Bolivar Buckner Jr., it was the largest battle in history encompassing sea, air, and land. Buckner himself was killed just four days before the fall of the island, becoming the highest-ranking American to die in the war. By June some 300,000 American troops were engaged on the island; 19,000 were killed, 71,000 wounded. On the Japanese side 76,000 were killed and perhaps another 150,000 civilians. The ferocity of the defense of Okinawa, and the increasing use by Japan of mass kamikaze and other suicidal tactics, has been attributed by most historians as having led to the decision to use the atomic bomb on Japan itself, where it was felt that the American casualty rate using any conventional invasion would be unacceptably high.

In the end, it was a new president, Harry S. Truman, who made the decision to use the atomic bomb. He had succeeded Roosevelt on his death, near his hour of triumph, on 12 April. On 6 August the *Enola Gay* dropped an atomic bomb on Hiroshima, and three days later another was dropped on Nagasaki. It was now clear to the Japanese they could not survive, and they surrendered on 15 August, V-J Day. MacArthur oversaw an official signing of the surrender papers on board the USS *Missouri* in Tokyo Bay on 2 September. Pearl Harbor was finally avenged, and the most widespread conflict in history was over.

Cold and Other Wars

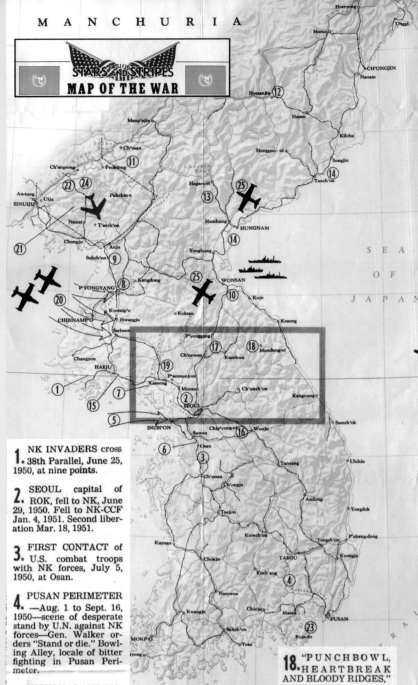

STARS AND STRIPES
MAP OF THE WAR

SEA OF JAPAN

The Second World War resulted in the death of as many as 50 million people—20 million military personnel and 30 million civilian—a number that included such horrors as the Holocaust, the German attempt to exterminate the Jewish people. Franklin D. Roosevelt's proposal for a United Nations was intended to ensure that such slaughter never happened again. The development of nuclear bombs ensured that if a large-scale war did occur, mankind might well be annihilated. The United Nations (UN) was created on 24 October 1945, with 51 member nations; there are now over 190.

Stalin's Soviet Union (USSR) became a problem to the West. In the last months of the war, it had declared war on Japan, as it had been agreed it would, but then invaded and occupied the Kuril Islands, a move not agreed upon. Indeed, Stalin proposed to invade Hokkaido, Japan's main island, to create, as in Europe, a Soviet zone of influence; it was only prevented by the unequivocal opposition of Douglas MacArthur, who had stayed on in Japan to administer that country's transition to a parliamentary democracy.

In Europe, where the USSR now occupied much of the eastern half, the West was unable to prevent the subjugation under Communist puppet regimes of a divided Germany, Poland, the Baltic States, and others. What Winston Churchill so famously called an Iron Curtain descended on Europe. The resistance of the West to Soviet plans for expansion led to a long-term standoff enforced by a counterbalancing force of nuclear arms—the Cold War.

The United States gave Europe $12.4 billion in aid in the period 1947–50 to build up economies and hopefully prevent a recurrence of the misery after World War I that had been the root cause of another war. This European Recovery Program was popularly called the Marshall Plan, after its chief proponent, secretary of state George Marshall.

The first test of the West's resolve to prevent even further Soviet influence came in 1948, when Stalin cut off road and rail access to the now divided and isolated city of Berlin. In a massive operation lasting nearly a year, the Allies flew in everything the city required. The Berlin Airlift transported 2.3 million tons of supplies on 278,228 flights. Much of this was coal, amounting to 1.5 million tons. At the peak of the airlift, an aircraft landed in Berlin every 62 seconds over a 24-hour period. The lesson for the Soviets was significant—and critical for the future.

Above. Harry Schultz, a military photographer, took this dramatic shot of a tank of the 6th Tank Battalion firing on North Korean positions in January 1952.

MAP 514 *(above, right).*
Published in 1953 by the military newspaper *Stars and Stripes,* this informational map enumerates the major actions of the Korean War and shows their locations.

1. NK INVADERS cross 38th Parallel, June 25, 1950, at nine points.

2. SEOUL capital of ROK, fell to NK, June 29, 1950. Fell to NK-CCF Jan. 4, 1951. Second liberation Mar. 18, 1951.

3. FIRST CONTACT of U.S. combat troops with NK forces, July 5, 1950, at Osan.

4. PUSAN PERIMETER —Aug. 1 to Sept. 16, 1950—scene of desperate stand by U.N. against NK forces—Gen. Walker orders "Stand or die." Bowling Alley, locale of bitter fighting in Pusan Perimeter.

5. INCHON LANDING. Sept. 15, 1950—encircling amphibious operation by X Corps.

6. LINK-UP of Eighth Army and X Corps in break-out dash from crumpled Pusan Perimeter; unit of 1st Cavalry meets elements of 7th Division, Sept. 26, 1950.

7. U.S. FORCES cross 38th Parallel near Kaesong, Oct. 9, 1950.

8. PYONGYANG, NK capital, falls to advancing Eighth Army. Oct. 19, 1950.

9. 187TH AIRBORNE RCT dropped on Oct. 20, 1950.

10. WONSAN FALLS to ROK I Corps Oct. 10, 1950. U.S. X Corps lands at Wonsan after Navy clears dense mine fields, Oct. 26, 1950. Wonsan, key communications hub, flattened by over two years of intensive U.N. naval bombardment (1951-53), the longest sustained naval bombardment in naval history.

11. ROK TROOPS reach Yalu at Chosan, Oct. 26, 1950.

12. U.S. 7TH DIVISION elements reach Hyesanjin on Yalu River, Nov. 20, 1950.

13. CCF counteroffensive hits attacking Eighth Army, Nov. 26, 1950; general U.N. withdrawal follows. U.S. Marines and 7th Division break out of encirclement at Choshin Reservoir, Nov. 28-Dec. 11, 1950.

14. X CORPS evacuates Songjin - Hungnam area successfully. Removal of all troops, equipment and 100,000 refugees, Dec. 9-24, 1950. Corps placed under Eighth Army and rushed into line.

15. CCF CROSSES 38th Parallel, Dec. 25, 1950. U.N. ground forces, under Gen. Ridgway, begin new drive north in January, 1951.

16. COMMUNIST offensive stopped cold by U.N. in the winter of 1950-51. Wonju-Chipyondgni area denied enemy by heroic stand of U.N. forces in Jan.-Feb., 1951. Second major CCF offensive crushed by hard fighting, fast moving U.N. troops; Gen. Van Fleet, Eighth Army commander, orders immediate counterattack and pursuit, which routs enemy.

17. "IRON TRIANGLE." enemy build-up area, attacked and neutralized in early June, 1951.

18. "PUNCHBOWL, HEARTBREAK AND BLOODY RIDGES,"

19. KAESONG—site of first cease-fire conferences, July 10—Aug. 2, 1951. Conferences resumed at nearby Panmunjom, Oct. 25, 1951. Charges and counter-charges of neutrality violation caused delay and change of conference site to Panmunjom.

20. BIGGEST AIR STRIKE of the war. Aug. 29, 1952, at Hwanju, Sariwon, and Pyongyang. Planes of the U.S. Air Force, U.S. Marines, U.S. Navy, Australia, ROK, and Royal Navy joined to fly 1,193 sorties, 210 of them by naval planes; 579 tons of bombs, rockets, napalm dropped.

21. GREATEST U.N. aerial victory. July 4, 1952. F-86s shot down 13 MIG 15s, probably destroyed one more, and damaged seven.

22. HUGE AIR STRIKE, June 23, 1952, devastates Suiho dam, cripples Red hydroelectric supply.

23. UN. PW CAMP at Koje Island, scene of large scale PW riots in spring, 1952.

24. MIG ALLEY. Rectangle formed by Antung, mouth of Chongchong River, Suiho Reservoir to Chongchong River.

25. "OPERATION Strangle." Navy and Air Force interdiction has continually attacked these important rail lines; Navy and Marines on coast, Air Force in interior.

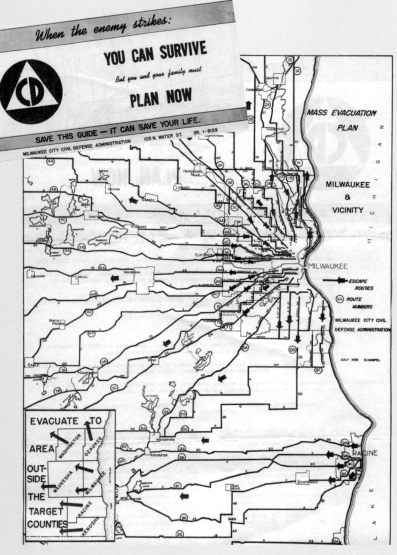

Korea, occupied by Japan from 1910 to 1945, had been under joint administration of the United States and the Soviet Union. While the U.S. had approved a democratic government in the south, set up by UN-supervised elections in 1948, Stalin supported a Communist government, set up in the north. On 25 June 1950 North Korea invaded South Korea with 90,000 troops. The main events of this conflict (to the United States officially a "police action") are shown in Map 514, *left*. Allied forces under the flag of the United Nations were driven back to a pocket in the extreme south until commanding General Douglas MacArthur executed a brilliant but dangerous plan for a large-scale landing behind the enemy lines at Incheaon (Inchon) on 15 September. All was going well for the UN forces until the Chinese intervened massively in October 1950. The war then became increasingly brutal and troubled by the possibility of Soviet intervention and the use of nuclear weapons. A standoff was reached in 1953, when a cease-fire line, the thirty-eighth parallel, was agreed upon. This is, still today, the boundary between North and South Korea.

Concerns about nuclear war continued to grow from the 1950s on. All major cities had evacuation plans, to quickly remove as many people as possible from perceived target zones. The plan for Milwaukee is shown here (Map 515, *left*). Western defense was until the 1960s centered around bombers, a third of them in the air at all times, and early warning stations set up in the North to detect incoming aircraft or missiles. In the late 1950s the Intercontinental Ballistic Missile, or ICBM, was developed, and missile silos covered parts of the country in vast randomly dispersed networks, ready to respond to any attack (Map 516, *below*). This was the principle of mutually assured

Map 515 (*above*).

A mass evacuation plan for Milwaukee in case of a nuclear attack, issued by the Milwaukee City Civil Defense Administration in July 1958. Throughout the United States, city centers and their immediate surroundings were designated as presumed target areas. Evacuation plans involved moving as many people away from these areas in as short a time as possible, often by designating highways as one way only. The emerging interstate highway system would aid fast evacuation (see page 237).

Map 516 (*below*).

A map of the missile silo system around Whiteman Air Force Base (at the large arrow, center) in Missouri. The silos (black dots labeled A-6, B-9, etc.) were carefully dispersed in an essentially random fashion so that their position could not be calculated by an enemy wishing to target them. Once highly secret, the map was specially cleared by the USAF for publication in this book. *Inset* is a photograph of an Atlas Intercontinental Ballistic Missile (ICBM) as it lifts off from Vandenburg Air Force Base in an August 1958 test. This would have been the American response to any nuclear attack.

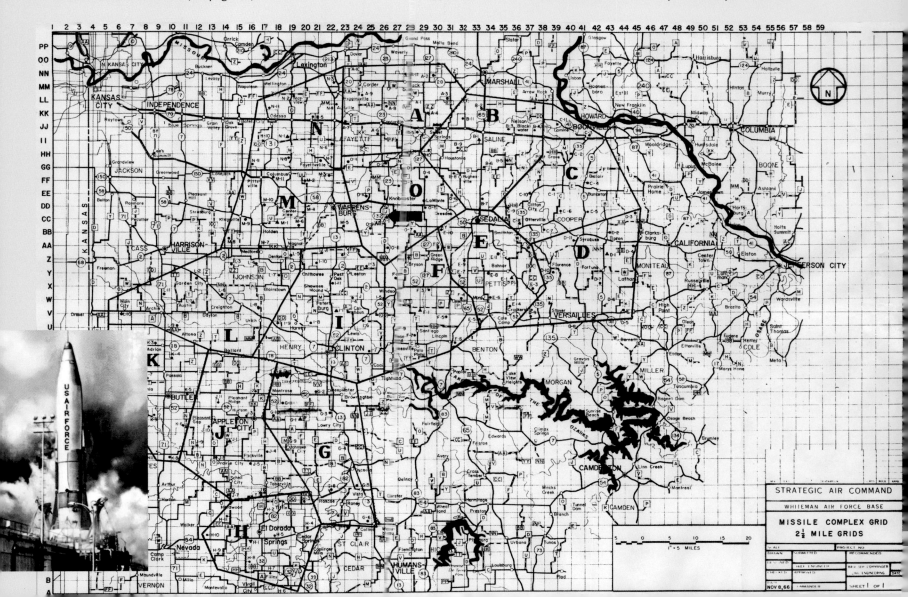

destruction that was supposed to deter any aggressor, a system that, for all its brinkmanship, worked.

One time that it very nearly did not was in 1962, when the United States managed to prevent the continued installation of missiles, and removal of those installed, in nearby Cuba. Tension between the United States and the Soviet Union had been on the increase for some time. In April 1961 the United States supported an invasion of Cuba by Cuban exiles opposed to the dictator Fidel Castro. They landed at the Bay of Pigs, but the venture failed badly. The invasion had originally been planned under Eisenhower, but new president John F. Kennedy had little choice but to accept responsibility. It did, however, have one positive effect in that it gave Kennedy a healthy skepticism of the U.S. military establishment.

Berlin continued to be a focus of concern. The draft had been tripled and reservists called up. In August 1961 the Berlin Wall had been built, first of barbed wire, later of concrete, to keep East Germans—three million since 1945—from escaping to the West.

Then, on 14 October, a u-2 high-altitude spy plane on a regular reconnaissance flight over Cuba came back with photographs showing that medium-range ballistic missiles were being installed in Cuba. With a range of about 630 nautical miles, and presumably armed with nuclear warheads, they posed an immediate danger to the security of the nation. The president set up a special Executive Committee (Ex Comm), headed by his brother Robert. Meanwhile he continued with his schedule of public appearances, so as not to alert the Soviets to the fact their scheme had been discovered.

The United States was at this time far ahead of the USSR in numbers of nuclear warheads and the sophistication of their delivery systems, a fact certainly not appreciated by the American public. Soviet leader Nikita Khrushchev had chosen to take the extraordinarily risky step of setting up missiles in Cuba in a bold attempt to even the balance.

One principle was agreed upon by Ex Comm: the Cuban missiles would have to be eliminated, one way or another, before they could become operational, but even a series of air strikes could not guarantee hitting more than 90 percent of the sites, leaving retaliation as a distinct possibility. Another option, passionately advocated by Robert Kennedy, was that of a blockade. This would at least prevent additional missiles being installed while the situation was resolved. On Monday, 22 October, the blockade was ordered, though the president announced it, on television, as a quarantine, a term intended to avoid the fact that in international law, a blockade was an act of war. At the same time the U.S. military was placed on a war footing. And just to make it crystal clear, Kennedy also announced that any nuclear missile launched from Cuba would result in a full retaliatory response against the Soviet Union.

Tension built throughout the week as Soviet ships, escorted by submarines, approached the Caribbean. Many people throughout the Western world thought that this was likely their last week on Earth. Finally, on Friday, 26 October, Khrushchev's response came, first through a Soviet embassy official to an ABC news correspondent, then in a letter to Kennedy thought to have been written by Khrushchev himself. The USSR would remove the missiles from Cuba in return for a promise not to invade the island. The next day, a publicly released additional letter demanded the U.S. remove missiles from Turkey in return for the removal of missiles from Cuba. The Soviet Politburo seems to have wanted to take a stronger line than Khrushchev had by himself and tried to override his first response. In the end, a secret deal was worked out: the United States would remove the Turkish missiles, which were obsolete anyway, but only after a few months, so that the two actions would not seem connected. Robert Kennedy, who took the proposal to Soviet ambassador Anatoli Dobrynin, convinced him that

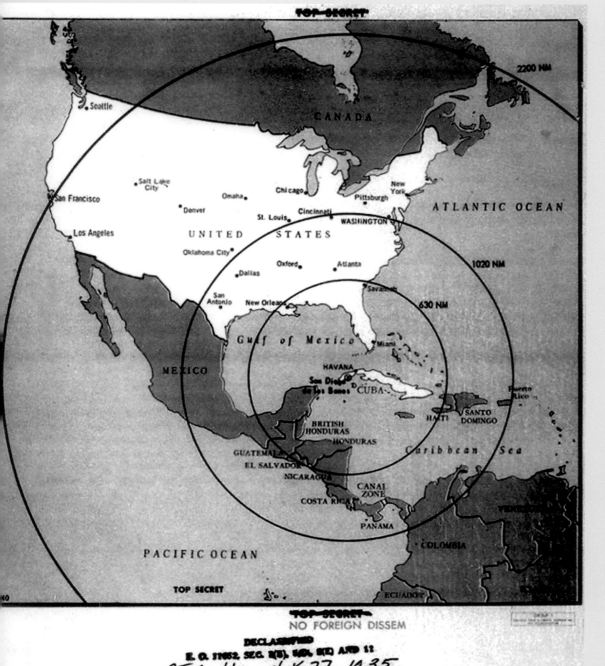

Map 517 (left).
This Top Secret U.S. government map shows the strategic position of the Cuban missile site and what cities could be struck by missiles launched from Cuba or by bombs dropped from Ilyushin-28 jet bombers also being shipped to Cuba. The initial missile range was about the 630 nautical miles of the radius of the inner circle shown on this map, threatening a significant portion of the Southeast. The stamp and writing at the bottom are from the map's declassification by the CIA in 1978.

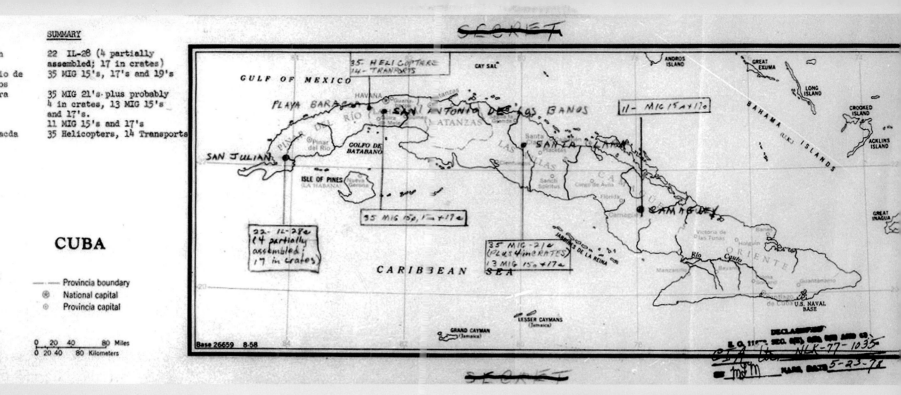

SUMMARY

22 IL-28 (4 partially
assembled; 17 in crates)
35 MIG 15's, 17's and 19's

35 MIG 21's plus probably
4 in crates, 13 MIG 15's
and 17's.

11 MIG 15's and 17's

35 Helicopters, 14 Transports

CUBA

— · — Provincia boundary
⊛ National capital
⊙ Provincia capital

0   20   40   80 Miles
0 20 40   80 Kilometers

Base 26659 8-58

MAP 518 (*above*).
Another secret but now declassified government map, almost certainly originating with the CIA, is this map of Cuba itself. The positions and numbers of Soviet MIG fighter jets are indicated, as are helicopters and transport planes. At San Julian at the western end of the island, is a notation regarding 22 Ilyushin-28 jet bombers—4 partially assembled, 17 in crates. These were being shipped to Cuba along with the missiles. Most of this information was gathered from U-2 spy planes.

Right. The incriminating evidence was shown to the American people so as to leave no doubt of its truth in anyone's mind, though much interpretation was necessary. Even Kennedy, when first shown the U-2 photos, did not know what he was looking at.

the president would not be able to hold off the military's demands for war much longer. It worked. The ships approaching the quarantine zone turned back, and on Sunday, 27 October, Radio Moscow announced that the missiles would be dismantled on the premise that the United States would not attack Cuba.

The world had been taken to the brink of the abyss, and had stepped back. From that point on, leaders on both sides seemed to realize the utter folly of provoking a nuclear conflict. Slowly a series of nuclear arms reduction treaties were agreed upon, beginning in a small but significant way in August 1963 with the prohibition of above-ground nuclear testing. That same month the "hot line" between the White House and the Kremlin became operational, to try to prevent misunderstandings from starting a war. Nuclear weapons were to be used as a deterrent, and hopefully only as that. Kennedy was in the process of extending the nuclear umbrella to India, which had been attacked by China, when he was assassinated in November 1963.

Another war of sorts, a social one, was rocking America at this time. The United States in the mid-1950s was still firmly segregated. African-American people were treated as second-class citizens, especially in the South, where on buses they typically had to sit in the rear. In December 1955, Rosa Parks, a seamstress, going home on the bus after her day's work in Montgomery, Alabama, refused to give up her seat to a white person and was arrested. Her case became the legal challenge to segregation, financed by the National Association for the Advancement of Colored People (NAACP). The legal case was lost, but Parks became a catalyst for black protest. Montgomery's buses were boycotted for over a year, finally producing a legal ruling that bus segregation violated the Fourteenth Amendment. When black people began riding the buses once more, they could sit anywhere. So much anger was generated that some buses were shot at by snipers.

MRBM LAUNCH SITE 2
SAN CRISTOBAL
1 NOVEMBER 1962

MAP 519 (*below*).
More likely for targets than tourism, this Russian map of the Washington-Baltimore area is part of a series of maps of much of North America at this scale (1:500,000) created by the Soviet department of defense and issued by, and apparently restricted to, the General Staff of the Red Army. The maps were obtained, after the end of the Cold War, from an ex-Russian officer. This map is dated 1981.

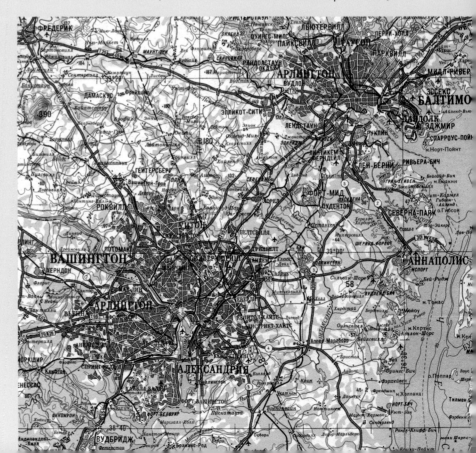

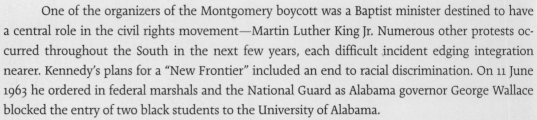

STARS AND STRIPES
MAP OF WAR AREA

One of the organizers of the Montgomery boycott was a Baptist minister destined to have a central role in the civil rights movement—Martin Luther King Jr. Numerous other protests occurred throughout the South in the next few years, each difficult incident edging integration nearer. Kennedy's plans for a "New Frontier" included an end to racial discrimination. On 11 June 1963 he ordered in federal marshals and the National Guard as Alabama governor George Wallace blocked the entry of two black students to the University of Alabama.

On Wednesday, 28 August 1963, one of the largest protest rallies ever was held, organized by King and others. Well over a quarter of a million people—many of them white—joined the March on Washington for Jobs and Freedom. Martin Luther King addressed the assembled throng from the steps of the Lincoln Memorial. About to sit down, he was inspired to make a further impromptu speech, one that became the landmark statement on civil rights in the United States: "I have a dream . . .," a dream of an America of freedom and democracy shared by people of all races, colors, and backgrounds.

The more or less direct result of this great gathering was the passage, in July 1964, of the Civil Rights Act, first proposed by Kennedy in June 1963 but blocked by Southern factions in Congress. The march provided much of the political momentum required to push it through. Not only did it protect black people from discrimination, it also extended such rights to women and thus became, almost unintentionally, a boost to women's rights. The law is widely credited with transforming American society. Kennedy did not live to see its passage, but it is his legacy, along with Lyndon Johnson, his successor as president, who made sure it passed. It is also the legacy of Martin Luther King, gunned down by a racist in Memphis, Tennessee, on 4 April 1968.

Greater equality, however, was a long time coming, and in the interim there were race riots by people dissatisfied with the pace of change and with King's tactics of peaceful civil disobedience. The March 1965 Selma to Montgomery March brought police violence into the homes of all Americans via television images, ultimately helping the civil rights movement. Watts, a suburb of Los Angeles, burst into flame for four days in August 1965, and there were riots in dozens of cities over several more years. In the summer of 1967, nearly a hundred died during rioting in Detroit.

By then, the defining real war for a generation was well under way, that in Vietnam. Indochina had been in conflict after the end of the Second World War as the French sought to reestablish their colonial control. When they were defeated and a peace signed in 1954, the country was partitioned into North Vietnam—a Communist state supported by the Soviets and by China— and South Vietnam, a nominally democratic country but in truth a corrupt and turbulent regime. When the North Vietnamese—under their president, Hò Chí Minh—and their National Liberation Front—the Viet Cong—began to infiltrate the south, the United States, under Kennedy, began sending so-called military advisors to assist the South Vietnamese. But it was President Lyndon Johnson who escalated American involvement into a full-blown war. Johnson was convinced of the then popular "domino theory," whereby the fall of a single small country to Communism would lead in short order to the fall of all those around it. American policy, developed after the Second World War largely by diplomat George Kennan, demanded "containment" of such states.

On 2 August 1964 the uss *Maddox,* which had been monitoring a South Vietnamese attack on North Vietnamese offshore islands in the Gulf of Tonkin, was fired upon by three North Vietnamese torpedo boats. This and a further incident two days later led to congressional approval on 7 August of the Gulf of Tonkin Resolution, which authorized Johnson to "take all necessary measures to repel any armed attack against the forces of the

Left, top. The Texas School Book Depository in Dallas. The photograph was taken from the approximate position of President Kennedy's car at the moment he was shot by Lee Harvey Oswald from the sixth floor of the depository, on 22 November 1963.

Map 520 (*left, center*).
This map, showing the areas in Vietnam assigned to various U.S. army corps, was published about 1967 in the *Stars and Stripes,* a military newspaper.

Map 521 (*left*).
Part of a map produced by Army Map Services of the Corps of Engineers, showing the area around the South Vietnamese capital, Saigon, and including part of the militarily difficult Mekong Delta.

United States and to repel any further aggression." This resolution would be used by Johnson to escalate the war, involving the United States in Vietnam in a combat role.

By November the National Security Council, which included Secretary of Defense Robert McNamara and Secretary of State Dean Rusk, had recommended a strategy to Johnson. The first part was Operation Rolling Thunder, a massive aerial bombardment of North Vietnam intended to destroy the will of the North Vietnamese to fight, destroy its industrial base and air defenses, and stop the flow of men south. Started in January 1965, this onslaught continued for three years but never achieved its goals. The North seemed willing to take the pounding, and because of the American unwillingness to bomb residential areas and civilians, the North Vietnamese set up their anti-aircraft surface-to-air missiles (SAMS) in school playgrounds. It was not a war fought by what had up to then been the norms of war.

MAP 522 (above).
Secretary of Defense Robert McNamara makes a point on a map of Vietnam at a news conference in 1968. He is pointing at Laos, and so is likely discussing the use of Laotian supply lines by the Viet Cong.

The first U.S. ground combat troops landed in March 1965, followed shortly after by Australian troops. After American planes were shot down in July, Johnson escalated the war, sending in more troops, which then numbered 125,000. This he could do on his own authority because there had not been—and never was—a formal declaration of war. The first major ground battle took place in August; 5,500 Marines destroyed a Viet Cong base on the Van Thuong peninsula in Quang Ngai province. After that, the North Vietnamese avoided combat on American terms, fading into the landscape to fight a guerrilla war.

By August 1966 U.S. involvement in the war had reached 429,000. The increase in troop levels allowed General William Westmoreland to order thousands of search-and-destroy missions, by which he hoped to win the war by attrition. To hinder the flow of men and supplies down the Ho Chi Minh Trail, the loosely defined route from north to south, the Battle of Khe Sanh was fought between January and April 1968, and it was an American victory due to the overwhelming use of airpower.

On 30 January that year, the North Vietnamese broke the Tet holiday truce and began a massive and wide-ranging attack on the South. Caught by surprise, the city of Hue was taken—and 2,800 South Vietnamese massacred after they had surrendered—and Viet Cong were fighting in the streets of Saigon before being driven out again. This campaign, called the Tet Offensive, was intended to allow the South Vietnamese people to rise up against their government—and the American forces. In this it failed, but it had considerable propaganda effect in the United States. Television images of Viet Cong fighting at the American embassy demonstrated clearly for the first time that the United States was not in control. It marked a turning point in public opinion about the war, for the public had been constantly told by both McNamara and Westmoreland that victory—and peace—was near. There had been demonstrations against the war since its beginning, particularly among college students subject to the draft, but antiwar feeling was now boiling over. Westmoreland lost his job to General Creighton Abrams, and Johnson ordered a cessation of all bombardment of the North in November. Peace talks in Paris, however, failed.

The morality of U.S. involvement in the war was brought into sharp focus by the revelations of the My Lai massacre of March 1968 and its subsequent cover-up. Lieutenant William Calley was later convicted—though then immediately pardoned by President Nixon—for the killing of several hundred Vietnamese civilians, including women and children.

Richard Milhous Nixon was elected in November 1968 on a promise of "peace with honor," and slowly the United States began to disengage from the war. Nixon's plan was to build up the South Vietnamese forces so that they could take over. Finally, on 15 January 1973, Nixon announced the suspension of U.S. offensive action in Vietnam, and then a unilateral withdrawal that ended U.S. involvement in the war. The Paris Peace Accords were signed on 27 January 1973. South Vietnam fought on, but was doomed without U.S. combat assistance. The Viet Cong renewed their offensive; the city of Da Nang fell on 30 March 1975, and on 29 April the largest helicopter evacuation in history began in Saigon. The next day the capital fell.

Perhaps as many as 2 million people died during the Vietnam War, likely over half of them North Vietnamese military personnel. American forces suffered 58,226 killed and 153,303 wounded. Some South Vietnamese escaped as so-called boat people in the years after the war, many coming to the United States. In 1973 the War Powers Resolution was passed by Congress. The bill limited the power of a president to commit American forces into action without explicit congressional approval.

The decision to pull out of Vietnam in 1973 had been made by President Richard Nixon, who in 1968 had defeated Democrat Hubert Humphrey, who might not have been the Democratic candidate if not for the assassination of the second Kennedy, John's brother Robert, during the California primary in June.

Nixon became the first president to resign from office when he stepped down in August 1974, forced out by the Watergate crisis and the revelation, through tape-recorded evidence of Oval Office conversations, that he had himself interfered in the judicial process and was responsible for a cover-up.

The United States, though chastened by the Vietnam experience, continued in the role of policeman to the world. In an attempt to prevent the rise of another Cuba, the Caribbean island of Grenada was invaded in October 1983 and its Communist government overthrown. Libya was bombed in April 1986, a reprisal for anti-American terrorist activity in the Middle East, but this in turn led to the Libyan terrorist bombing of Pan Am 103, a Boeing 747, over Lockerbie, Scotland, in December 1988, with the loss of 270 lives. A year later, the United States invaded Panama, deposing right-wing dictator Manuel Noriega and flying him to Miami to face charges of drug dealing.

The world slowly began to become a safer place, less liable to utter annihilation, with the negotiation of the Nuclear Non-Proliferation Treaty of 1968, a treaty that was further refined and expanded in 1996. Of great importance were the Strategic Arms Limitations Treaties (SALT). After three years of negotiations with the Soviets, SALT-1, which froze the numbers of nuclear ballistic missiles at then existing levels, was signed in 1971. Continuing discussions resulted in SALT-2 in 1979, which further limited production of all nuclear weapons. Although the treaty was signed by both Leonid Brezhnev for the Soviet Union and President Jimmy Carter for the United States, Congress never ratified it due to a Soviet invasion of Afghanistan. Both sides, however, did abide by its terms.

Of even greater significance for world peace was the virtual collapse of Communism in the last decade of the century, largely through the efforts of Soviet leader Mikhail Gorbachev. After he came to power in 1985 he instituted policies of *glasnost* (political openness) and *perestroika* (restructuring of the economy); Soviet forces were withdrawn from Afghanistan in 1988, and the same year he announced that Eastern bloc nations were to be allowed to control their own affairs. Revolutions followed throughout the previously Soviet-controlled area. The Berlin Wall was opened on 9 November 1989, and Germans were seen happily demolishing the wall for months afterward. At the end of 1991 the Soviet Union itself collapsed and the new Russian Federation was created. Yet by then Gorbachev was not revolutionary enough; he resigned and was replaced by Boris Yeltsin. Gorbachev, who won the Nobel Peace Prize for his efforts, had been almost single-handedly responsible for ending the Cold War.

By 1991 Russians and Americans were cooperating on new ventures to subdue the tyrannies of the world. About twenty-five nations, led ostensibly by the United Nations but in reality by the United States, began an offensive to oust Iraq, led by its dictator Saddam Hussein, from an occupation of neighboring Kuwait. This tiny country was nonetheless rich in what the Western nations prized most highly—oil.

Kuwait had been occupied by Iraq since 2 August the previous year. After a massive military buildup—termed Desert Shield—came the advance into Kuwait, the much anticipated Desert Storm. Resistance, as it

turned out, was minimal, with Hussein's forces no match for the technologically superior American army. Some 60,000 Iraqi soldiers were killed, and 300 American. The conflict was memorable for its legacy of burning oil wells, set alight by retreating Iraqis, creating a hellish landscape and an environmental disaster. But President George Bush made the decision not to press on to Baghdad, and an unrepentant though considerably less powerful Saddam Hussein was left still in charge of Iraq.

Fear that Hussein might be stockpiling weapons of mass destruction (a false intelligence, as it turned out), plus a refusal to allow United Nations weapons inspectors to do their job, led President George W. Bush to avenge his father's lenience. With Operation Iraqi Freedom, in March 2003, the United States invaded Iraq and deposed Hussein. Two years later a long-lost democracy was restored to the country.

In the 1960s and 1970s environmental awareness grew, credited by many as beginning with the publication of Rachel Carson's *Silent Spring* in 1962 (itself credited with leading to the banning of the pesticide DDT). As the postwar baby boom moved into young adulthood various environmental organizations were founded, more activist in nature than the Sierra Club (founded by John Muir in 1892). These included the World Wildlife Fund (WWF, 1961), Friends of the Earth (1969), and Greenpeace (1971). Also influential for a time was a report entitled *Limits to Growth*, published by the Club of Rome in 1972. In 1970 the United States Environmental Protection Agency was created. It has since initiated legislation covering protection of the air, land, and water, and dealing with hazardous waste and endangered species. One of the agency's first major tests was widely publicized. In 1978 it was confirmed that toxic pollutants previously dumped into the disused Love Canal, in Niagara Falls, New York, were making residents ill. The solution involved moving and compensating residents, dumping massive amounts of fill into the canal, and covering it with a special waterproof cover to prevent ongoing leaching.

The biggest test of the national psyche since Pearl Harbor came on 11 September 2001, when four commercial airliners were hijacked by al Qaeda terrorists. Two were flown into the twin towers of the World Trade Center in New York, killing 2,595 people, including 343 firefighters and 60 police officers; all the passengers on the planes were also killed. Images of impact, of the towers on fire, of people jumping to their deaths, of crushed fire trucks, and dust-caked streets will haunt many Americans for the rest of their days. Another hijacked plane was crashed into the Pentagon, in Washington, D.C., killing 125 in the building plus all on the plane. A fourth plane crashed into a Pennsylvania field, killing all aboard. The plane was thought to have been headed for the U.S. Capitol. The acts of heroism aboard that plane can only be imagined. The passenger who led an attempt to overcome the hijackers, Todd Beamer, was heard over a cell phone. His "Let's rumble" became an American byword.

The attacks led to American reprisals as authorities endeavored to find and punish the perpetrators. Troops were dispatched to Afghanistan in 2002 to seek out and destroy terrorist bases, and Iraq was invaded the following year. The fight for liberty has never been an easy one, and the world remains full of threats to enduring freedom. Only with ongoing vigilance, determination, and sacrifice will freedom prevail.

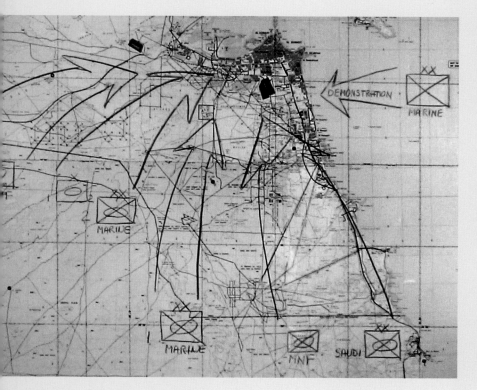

MAP 523 (*left*).
This army field map was used in 1991 to show the troops the plan of attack on Al Kuwayt (Kuwait City) during Desert Storm. The map has two layers: the base topographical map and a Mylar sheet on which the lines of attack have been drawn with a felt-tip pen. The Mylar sheet makes the map very difficult to photograph because it produces reflections.

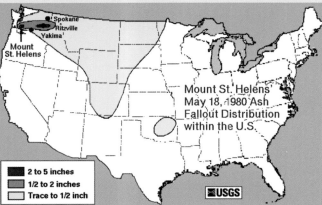

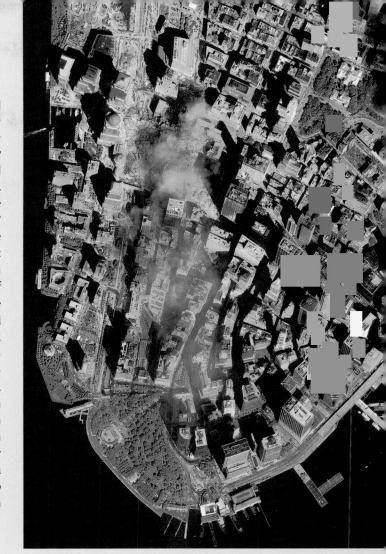

MAP 524 (*above*).

The peace of a quiet Sunday morning was disrupted in the Northwest at 8:32 a.m. on 18 May 1980 as the Mount St. Helens volcano blew 1,300 feet of itself away. The eruption, equivalent to 500 Hiroshima atomic bombs, was heard hundreds of miles away, clear-cut a 200-square-mile area of forest, killed dozens of people and thousands of animals, and distributed ash over a vast area of the West.

MAP 525 (*left, center*).

This planning map of Iraq was produced by the National Imaging and Mapping Agency (NIMA), now the National Geospatial Intelligence Agency, in 2003. No-fly zones are shown. The northern one is north of 36° and was mandated by the United States to protect Kurdish areas, although it in fact covers only about half of that area. The no-drive zone shown was instituted in 1994 but never enforced. The orange-colored boundary with Jordan is an undefined "de facto" boundary. Kuwait's strategic position at the head of the Arabian Gulf is evident. The brown zone inside the Iraq border adjacent to Kuwait was a demilitarized zone set up after Iraq was expelled from Kuwait in 1991.

MAP 526 (*left, bottom*).

Political comment in the form of a map. Within hours of President George W. Bush's electoral victory in 2004, this map appeared on the Internet and was then widely disseminated. It characterizes the areas that voted for Bush as evangelically motivated, hence *Jesusland*, while all the areas that voted for Senator John Kerry are grouped with the supposedly more liberal neighbor to the north as the *United States of Canada*.

Right, top. This satellite photo of the World Trade Center site in Lower Manhattan was taken on 15 September 2001, four days after the attacks. Smoke is still rising from the collapsed buildings.

Right, center and bottom. The Pentagon from space, at 11:16 a.m. 12 September 2001 (center) and two months later (bottom). The yawning gap on the western side is visible. The 12 September image was taken while all planes were still grounded, and this image, which like the others is from the commercial IKONOS satellite of Space Imaging, is thus a unique record.

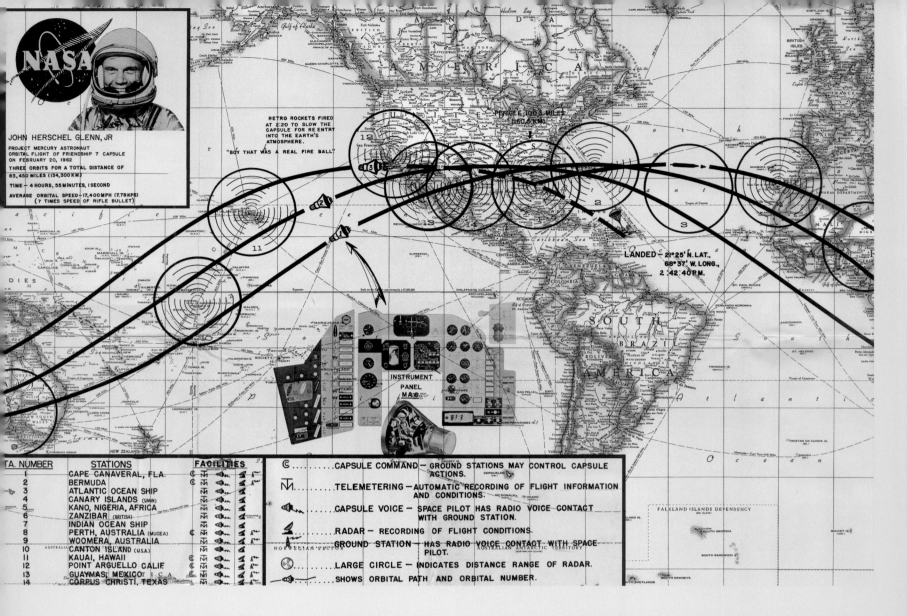

STA. NUMBER	STATIONS	FACILITIES
1	CAPE CANAVERAL, FLA.	
2	BERMUDA	
3	ATLANTIC OCEAN SHIP	
4	CANARY ISLANDS (SMIN)	
5	KANO, NIGERIA, AFRICA	
6	ZANZIBAR (BRITISH)	
7	INDIAN OCEAN SHIP	
8	PERTH, AUSTRALIA (MUCEA)	
9	WOOMERA, AUSTRALIA	
10	CANTON ISLAND (U.S.A.)	
11	KAUAI, HAWAII	
12	POINT ARGUELLO CALIF.	
13	GUAYMAS, MEXICO	
14	CORPUS CHRISTI, TEXAS	

Ⓒ .... CAPSULE COMMAND – GROUND STATIONS MAY CONTROL CAPSULE ACTIONS.

Ⓜ .... TELEMETERING – AUTOMATIC RECORDING OF FLIGHT INFORMATION AND CONDITIONS.

.... CAPSULE VOICE – SPACE PILOT HAS RADIO VOICE CONTACT WITH GROUND STATION.

.... RADAR – RECORDING OF FLIGHT CONDITIONS.

.... GROUND STATION – HAS RADIO VOICE CONTACT WITH SPACE PILOT.

.... LARGE CIRCLE – INDICATES DISTANCE RANGE OF RADAR.

.... SHOWS ORBITAL PATH AND ORBITAL NUMBER.

The United States was, and continues to be, a world leader in space and computer technology. In 1961, President John F. Kennedy promised that the United States would put a man on the Moon, and safely return him to Earth, before the decade was out. On 10 July 1969 Neil Armstrong stepped out of *Apollo 11* and, with his immortal words "That's one small step for Man, one giant leap for mankind," walked on the Moon's surface. The technological achievement this represented was stunning. Only seven years before, John Glenn had made the first manned American venture into space, three orbits of the Earth (MAP 527, *above*).

In the 1980s the emphasis turned to reusable spacecraft, with the development of the space shuttle, which looked as much like a plane as a rocket and landed conventionally. The first flight, of *Columbia*, took place in April 1981. In 1983 Sally Ride became the first American woman in space, aboard the space shuttle *Challenger*. It was this same vehicle that exploded seventy-three seconds after takeoff on 28 January 1986, killing all seven aboard. Further tragedy occurred on the twenty-eighth mission of *Columbia* when the shuttle disintegrated on re-entry on 1 February 2003. Again seven were killed.

MAP 527 (*above*).
Published by the Seattle World's Fair to commemorate the first American orbital space flight by John Glenn on 20 February 1962, this map plots the trajectories of the three-orbit flight. Elements printed on the original full-size world map have been moved. Glenn later became the oldest person to fly into space—in 1998, as part of a NASA experiment to determine the effects of weightlessness on older people. SInce NASA already had the same data for a younger Glenn from 1962, some useful comparisons could be made.

MAP 528 (*left*).
That nature has by no means been tamed was brought home to many Americans in August 2005. The eye of Hurricane Katrina is shown over New Orleans on 29 August in this satellite photograph superimposed on a map of the Gulf Coast. Katrina was a category 5 hurricane as it approached the city, but dropped to a slightly less destructive category 4 once it hit land. The storm still caused extensive damage and flooding. The entire population was evacuated to Houston and many other Southern cities. The death toll from Katrina will likely never be known exactly but is certainly over two thousand. The cost of relief and reconstruction may be as high as $200 billion, making Katrina the most expensive hurricane in history.

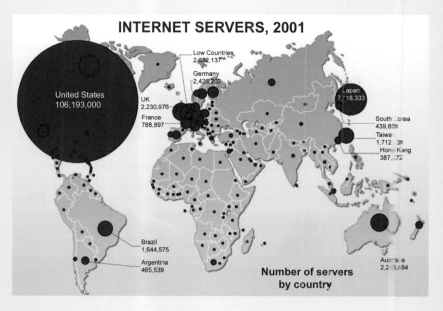

INTERNET SERVERS, 2001

Low Countries
2,632,137

Germany
2,428,202

United States
106,193,000

UK
2,230,976

France
788,897

Japan
7,718,333

South Korea
439,8

Taiwan
1,712 3

Hong Kong
387 72

Brazil
1,644,575

Argentina
465,539

Australia
2,2 3 84

**Number of servers
by country**

MAP 529 (*above*).
American predominance in computer connectivity is seen at a glance in this 2001 world map showing the number of servers, computers that hold information supplied to the Internet.

MAP 530 (*below*).
This NASA photomap shows landing sites on the Moon, all of them American, manned and unmanned, since 1969. At *right* is the iconic NASA photograph of the Earth from the Moon, an image that puts human matters in perspective like nothing else

America has also been a world leader in the field of computing. Herman Hollerith's use of punched cards to handle the data from the 1890 census is well known; his company later formed the nucleus of IBM. The first general purpose electronic computer was the American ENIAC—Electronic Numerical Integrator and Computer—completed in 1946. In modern times American companies lead the world in many different fields of computing technology and software. Microsoft's operating system, Windows, runs the majority of the world's computers. And the technical interlinking of a few university computers in 1969, called ARPANET, evolved into today's Internet. MAP 529 (*above*) shows American predominance in computer interconnectivity in 2001. A new American empire—this time a commercial one—has become a truly global influence.

Luna

Apollo

Surveyor

Map Catalog: Titles and Sources

Uncredited maps are from private collections.

MAP 1 (*half-title page*).
America Septentrionalis
Jan Jansson, 1670

MAP 2 (*title page*).
*Map of the United States of America with the
Contiguous British & Spanish Possessions*
John Melish, 1816
Library of Congress: G3700 1816.M4d mel

MAP 3 (*copyright page*).
The North Part of America
Henry Briggs, 1625
Library and Archives Canada: NMC 6582

MAP 4 (*page 6*).
*Universalis Cosmographia Secundum Ptholomaei
Traditionem et Americi Vespucii Alioru[m]que lustrationes*
Martin Waldseemüller, 1507
Library of Congress: G3200 1507.W3 Vault

MAP 5 (*page 7*).
The United States of North America, with the British Territories
William Faden, 1793
Library of Congress: G3300 1793.F3 Vault

MAP 6 (*page 7*).
The Eagle Map of the United States
Isaac W. Moore, 1832
Library of Congress: G3700 1833.M6 Vault

MAP 7 (*page 8*).
Map of Serpent Mound, 1846

MAP 8 (*page 8*).
Nouvelle France ("The Huron Map")
Anon., c. 1641
Library and Archives Canada: NMC 44351 (photographic copy
of original in the United Kingdom Hydrographic Office)

MAP 9 (*page 9*).
*Map of the Indian Tribes of North America, about 1600 A.D.
along the Atlantic, & about 1800 A.D. westwardly*
Albert Gallatin, 1836
Library of Congress: G3301.E1 1800.G3 Vault

MAP 10 (*page 9*).
Map of the Linguistic Stocks of American Indians
John Wesley Powell, Bureau of Ethnology, 1890
Library of Congress: G3301.E3 1890 .M3 TIL

MAP 11 (*page 10*).
Gronlandia Iona Gudmundi Islandi
Jón Gudmonson, c. 1640
Det Kongelige Bibliotek, Copenhagen, Denmark: gl. kgl. saml.2881 4° (11R)

MAP 12 (*page 10*).
*Geographische Vorstelling eines Globi, welchen Anno 1492.
Herr Martin Behaim*
Copy of Behaim globe by Johan Doppelmayer, 1730
Nordenskiöld, 1889

MAP 13 (*page 11*).
[Unsigned hand-drawn map of the world]
Francesco Rosselli, 1508
National Maritime Museum, Greenwich:
47 MS9928/p.27.f.1; C 4568/B

MAP 14 (*page 11*).
Insula hyspana. Woodcut from Christopher Columbus, *De insulis
nuper in mari Indico repertis*, in Carol Verardi, *Historia baetica*,
1494
Library of Congress

MAP 15 (*page 11*).
*Universalior Cogniti Orbis Tabula Ex Recentibus
Confecta Observationibus*
Johann Ruysch, c. 1507
Library and Archives Canada: NMC 19268

MAP 16 (*page 12*).
[Map known as the Cantino Planisphere]
Anon., c. 1502
Biblioteca Estense, Modena, Italy

MAP 17 (*page 12*).
Tabula Terra Nove
Anon., c. 1513
Nordenskiöld, 1889

MAP 18 (*page 13*).
[Untitled world map]
Juan de la Cosa, c. 1500
Museo Naval, Madrid

MAP 19 (*page 13*).
[Gores for a world globe]
Martin Waldseemüller, 1507
James Ford Bell Library, University of Minnesota

MAP 20 (*page 14*).
Juⁿ Ponce pelea con los de la Florida
Anon., 1728

MAP 21 (*page 14*).
*Præclara Ferdinandi Cortesii de Nova Maris
Oceani Hyspanis Narratio*
Hernán Cortés, 1524
Newberry Library, Chicago: Ayer *f655.51 C8 1524 d, opp. sig. A

MAP 22 (*page 14*).
[Map of the Gulf of Mexico]
Alonzo Alvarez de Pineda, 1519
Archivo General des Indias, Seville

MAP 23 (*page 15*).
[Untitled world map]
Juan Vespucci, 1526
Hispanic Society of America, New York

MAP 24 (*page 15*).
Map del Golfo y Costa de la Nueva España
Alonzo de Santa Cruz, c. 1572
Archivo General des Indias; Library of Congress copy: G3860 1572 .S3 Vault

MAP 25 (*page 16*).
Americae sive qvartae orbis partis nova et exactissima descriptio
Diego Gutiérrez, 1562
Library of Congress: G3290 1562 .G7 Vault

MAP 26 (*page 16*).
[Map of California]
Joan Martines, 1578
British Library: Harley MS 3450, map 10 in atlas

MAP 27 (*page 17*).
[Southern North America, atlas page]
Battista Agnese, 1544
Library of Congress: G1001 .A 1544

MAP 28 (*page 17*).
*Carta de los reconociemientos hechos en 1602
por el Capitan Sebastian Viscayno*
From: *Relación del Viage . . . Atlas*, No. 4, 1802

MAP 29 (*page 17*).
[Map of the Pacific Ocean]
Hessel Gerritz, 1622
Bibliothèque Nationale de France: RCC 1239

MAP 30 (*page 18*).
[Part of a world map]
Girolamo Verrazano, 1529
Bibliotheca Apostolica Vaticana, Vatican City

MAP 31 (*page 19*).
Floridae Americae Provinciae Recens & Exactissima Descriptio
Jacques Le Moyne de Morgues, 1591
Library of Congress: G3930 1591 .L4 Vault

MAP 32 (*page 19*).
[Part of a world map]
Nicolas Desliens, 1541
Sächsische Landesbibliotek, Dresden, Germany

MAP 33 (*page 19*).
[Part of a world map]
Faicte A Arques par Pierres Desceliers PBRE L AN 1550
Pierre Desceliers, 1550
British Library: Add MS 24065

MAP 34 (*page 20*).
[Map of the coast of Georgia and South Carolina]
John White, 1586–87
British Museum, Department of Prints and Drawings

MAP 35 (*page 20*).
Six other rivers discovered by the French
Drawing by Jacques Le Moyne de Morgues, engraved by Theodor De Bry
From: Theodor De Bry, *America*, Part 2, Plate 4, 1591
New York Public Library

MAP 36 (*page 21*).
Le Beau Port (Gloucester, MA)
Samuel de Champlain, 1613
From: *Les Voyages du Sieur de Champlain*

MAP 37 (*page 21*).
[Map of Northeastern United States and part of Maritime Canada]
Samuel de Champlain, 1607
Library of Congress: G3321 .P5 1607 .C4

MAP 38 (*page 22*).
["The Drake-Mellon map"]
Anon., c. 1587
Yale University Center for British Art/Bridgeman Art Gallery

MAP 39 (*page 23*).
[Map of the east coast of America]
John Dee, 1580
British Library: Cotton Roll XIII, 48

MAP 40 (*page 23*).
[Coast of North Carolina]
Thomas Hariot or John White, 1585
National Archives (U.K.): MPG 584

MAP 41 (*page 23*).
The arrival of the Englishmen in Virginia
Drawing by Jacques Le Moyne de Morgues,
engraved by Theodor De Bry
From: Theodor De Bry, *America*, Part 1, Plate 2, 1591

MAP 42 (*page 24*).
[Map of the coast of North Carolina and Virginia]
John White, 1586–87
British Museum, Department of Prints and Drawings

MAP 43 (*page 25*).
The Village of Secota
Theodor De Bry, engraving after John White, 1590
From: Thomas Hariot, *A Briefe and True Report of the
New Found Land of Virginia*, 1590
Library of Congress, Rare Books: F229 .H27 1590 Rosenwald Coll.

MAP 44 (*page 25*).
A Compleat Map of North-Carolina from an Actual Survey
John Collet, 1770
Library of Congress: G3900 1770 .C6 Vault

MAP 45 (*page 25*).
S. Augustini pars est terra Florida
Baptista Boazio, 1589
Library of Congress: G3934.S2 1589.W4

MAP 46 (*page 26*).
[Illustrated map of Virginia]
Robert Vaughan, with engravings based
on those by Theodor De Bry
From: John Smith, *Generall History of Virginia, the Somer Iles,
and New England*, 1624

MAP 47 (*page 27*).
New England
Simon van der Passe, c. 1616
From: John Smith, *Generall History of Virginia,
the Somer Iles, and New England*, 1624

MAP 48 (*page 27*).
Virginia
John Smith, 1624
From: *Generall History of Virginia,
the Somer Iles, and New England*, 1624

MAP 49 (*page 28*).
[Map of the North Atlantic]
Diego Homem, 1558
British Library: Add MS 5415.A, folios 19b and 20a

MAP 50 (*page 29*).
Humfray Gylbert knight his charte
John Dee, 1583
Free Library of Philadelphia

MAP 51 (*page 29*).
*Illustri Viro, Domino Philippo Sidnaes Michael Lok Civis
Londinensis Hanc Chartam Dedicabat: 1582*
Michael Lok, 1582
From: Richard Hakluyt, *Divers Voyages touching
the Discoverie of America*, 1582

MAP 52 (page 29).
Mapa de las Costas
Martin de Echagaray, 1686
Archivo General des Indias, Seville

MAP 53 (page 30).
[Map of the Northeast]
Adriaen Block (?), 1614
Nationaal Archief (Netherlands): 4, VEL520

MAP 54 (page 30).
Pascaert van Nieuw Nederlandt Virginia,
ende Niewe-Engelandt
Joan Vingtboons, 1639 (top part)
Library of Congress: G3291.S12 coll .H3 Vault, Harrisse vol. 2, map 7

MAP 55 (page 30).
The South part of New-England, as it is Planted this yeare, 1634
William Wood, 1634

MAP 56 (page 31).
Novi Belgii Novæ Angliæ nec non partis Virginæ
tabula multis in locis emendata
Nicolas Visscher, 1685
Library of Congress: G3715 169-.V5 TIL Vault

MAP 57 (page 31).
A Map of New England
William Hubbard, 1677
From: John Foster, *A Narrative of the troubles*
with the Indians in New England, 1677

MAP 58 (page 31).
A Map of New England
John Seller, 1675

MAP 59 (page 32).
A New Mapp of East and West Jarsey
From a survey by John Worlidge. John Thornton, 1706
Library of Congress: G3810 1706 .W6 TIL Vault

MAP 60 (page 32).
Nova Terræ Mariæ tabula
For Lord Baltimore, 1635

MAP 61 (page 32).
A Land-Skip of the Province of Mary Land
Or the Lord Baltimors Plantation neere Virginia
George Alsop, 1666 (1869 copy)

MAP 62 (page 32).
Ardenna Nove Sverige
P. Lindström, 1654

MAP 63 (page 33).
A Mapp of Ye Improved Part of Pensilvania in America,
Divided into Countyes, Townships and Lotts
Thomas Holme, c. 1690
Colonial Williamsburg Foundation: Special Collections, John D.
Rockefeller, Jr. Library, Custis Atlas, No.71, image #DS1999-273

MAP 64 (page 34).
A Map of the English Fossessions in North America and
Newfoundland as it was presented and Dedicated
to his most Sacred Majesty King William 1699
Anon., 1699
Library of Congress: G 3300 1699 .M Vault

MAP 65 (page 34).
A New and Exact Map of the Dominions of the King
of Great Britain on ye Continent of North America
Herman Moll, 1731
Library of Congress: C3300 1731 .M6 Am. 1–12

MAP 66 (page 35).
A Compleat Description of the Province of Carolina in 3 Parts: 1st,
the Improved Part from the Surveys of Maurice Mathews & Mr.
John Love: 2ly, the West Part by Capt. Tho. Nairn: 3ly, a Chart of
the Coast from Virginia to Cape Florida; engraved by Johr. Harris
(Reproduction is of part 1).
Edward Crisp, 1711
Library of Congress: G3870 1711 .C6 Vault:Oversize

MAP 67 (page 35).
[1663 Carolina grant]
John Locke, 1671

MAP 68 (page 35).
A New Map of the Country of Carolina
Joel Gascoyne, 1682
Library of Congress: G3870 1682 G3 TIL Vault

MAP 69 (page 36).
A Map of the British Empire in America with the French
and Spanish Settlements adjacent thereto (index sheet)
Henry Popple, 1733

MAP 70 (page 36).
A Map of the County of Savanah
John Oglethorpe, 1735

MAP 71 (page 36).
A View of Savanah as it stood the 29th of March 1734
John Oglethorpe and Peter Gordon, 1734 (1876 copy)

MAP 72 (page 37).
A Map of the British and French Dominions in North America
John Mitchell, 1755
Library of Congress: G3300 755 .M5 Vault

MAP 73 (page 37).
A Map of the New Governments of East & West Florida
Gentleman's Magazine, 1765

MAP 74 (page 38).
Novæ Franciæ Accurata Delineatio 1657
Francesco Giuseppe Bressani 1657
Library and Archives Canada, NMC 6338 (left sheet) and NMC
194824 (right sheet)

MAP 75 (page 38).
Lac Superieur et Autre Lieux ou sont les Missions de Peres de la
Compagnie de Jesus comprises sous le Nom d'Outaovacs
Claude Dablon and Claude Allouez, 1671
From: *Jesuit Relation*, 1671
Library and Archives Canada: NMC 10296

MAP 76 (page 38).
Le Canada ou Nouvelle France
Nicolas Sanson, 1656
Library and Archives Canada: NMC 21100

MAP 77 (page 39).
[Map showing the connection of Lake Michigan to the Mississippi]
Jacques Marquette, 1673
Archives de la Compagnie de Jésus, Saint-Jérôme, Québec

MAP 78 (page 39).
La Floride
Nicolas Sanson, 1657
Library of Congress: G38 1657 .S3 Vault

MAP 79 (page 40).
Carte de la Nouvelle France et del la Louisiane
decouverte dediée Au Roy Au L'An 1683
Louis Hennepin, 1683
From: Louis Hennepin, *Description de la Louisiane*, 1683

MAP 80 (page 40).
Partie Occidentale du Canada ou de la Nouvelle France
Vincenzo Coronelli, 1688
Library and Archives Canada: NMC 6411

MAP 81 (page 41).
Carte de la découverte du Sr Jolliet
Service historique de la Marine, Vincennes, France: Recueil 67, No. 52

MAP 82 (page 42).
Carte Cnlle de la France Septentrionalle,
contenant la découverte du pays de Ilinois
Jean-Baptiste-Louis Franquelin, 1678
Service historique de la Marine, Vincennes, France: Recueil 66, No. 19

MAP 83 (page 43).
[Canada ou Nouvelle France]
Anon., 1699
Service historique de la Marine, Vincennes, France:
Recueil 66, Nos. 12–15

MAP 84 (page 44).
Les Costes aux Environs de la Rivière de Misisipi
decouvertes par Mr. de la Salle en 1683 et reconnues par
Mr. le Chevallier d'Iberville en 1698 et 1699
Nicolas de Fer, 1701
Library of Congress: G42.M5 1701 .F4 Vault

MAP 85 (page 44).
Carte des environs du Missisipi
Guillaume De L'Isle, 1701
Service historique de la Marine, Vincennes, France: Recueil 69, No. 4

MAP 86 (page 45).
Fort Detroit et Environs
Anon., 1768
Library and Archives Canada: NMC 3095

MAP 87 (page 45).
Quebec Ville de L'Amerique Septentroinale [sic]
dans la Nouvelle France
Nicolas de Fer, c. 1693
Library and Archives Canada: NMC 2711

MAP 88 (page 46).
Entree de la rivière de Niagara dans le fond du lac Ontario
où est marqué la maison à machicoulis et le fort proposé
Centre des archives d'outre-mer, Aix-en-Provence, France:
03 DFC 540C

MAP 89 (page 46).
Plans et elevations de la Maison machicoulis Scituee
a la cote de l'ouest du Lac Ontario de la Rivière de Niagara
Centre des archives d'outre-mer, Aix-en-Provence, France:
03 DFC 541C

MAP 90 (page 46).
Carte Particuliere du Fleuve St. Louis dix lieues
et au desous de la Nouvelle Orleans
Anon., 1723
Newberry Library, Chicago: Ayer MS map 30, sheet 80

MAP 91 (page 47).
[Fort Condé, Mobile]
Anon., 1725
Centre des archives d'outre-mer, Aix-en-Provence, France:
04 DFC 124

MAP 92 (page 47).
A Plan of New Orleans
William Brasier, 1769, copied from a survey by P. Pittman, and
enclosed in a dispatch from General Gage, 6 January 1769
National Archives (U.K.): MPG 1/350

MAP 93 (page 48).
Carte de la Louisiane et du Cours du Mississipi
Guillaume De L'Isle, 1718
Library of Congress: G3700 1718 .L5 Vault

MAP 94 (page 49).
Carte Nouvelle de la Partie de l'ouest de la Province de la Louisiane
sur les observations & decouvertes de Sieur Benard de la Harpe
Sieur de Beauvilliers (?) from Benard de la Harpe, 1720
Service historique de la Marine, Vincennes, France: Recueil 69, No. 7

MAP 95 (page 49).
Rivière des Panis jusqu'a l'île aux Cèdres [Missouri]
Guillaume De L'Isle, c. 1716
Service historique de la Marine, Vincennes, France: Recueil 69, No. 20

MAP 96 (page 49).
Plan du Fort D'Orleans
J. P. L. S. Dumont de Montigny
Centre des archives d'outre-mer, Aix-en-Provence, France: DFC
Louisiane, portefeuille VI B, No. 63

MAP 97 (page 50).
Carte contenant les nouvelles découvertes de L'ouest en Canada,
mers, rivieres, lacs et nations qui y habittent en l'année 1737
Service historique de la Marine, Vincennes, France: Recueil 67, No. 42

MAP 98 (page 50).
Carte d'une partie du lac Superieur avec la découverte de la Rivière
depuis le grand portage A jusqu'à la Barrière B
Christophe Dufrost de La Jemerais, 1733
Service historique de la Marine, Vincennes, France: Recueil 67, No. 88

MAP 99 (page 50).
Carte General de Toute La Côte de La Louisianne
Jusqu'c La Baye St. Bernard
Alexandre de Batz, 1747
Library of Congress: G3862.C6 1747 .B2 Vault

MAP 100 (page 51).
Carte Particuliere du cours du fleuve st. louis depuis le village sau-
vage jusqu'au dessous du detour aux angloix, des Lacs Pontchar-
train & Maurepas & de Rivieres & Bayoue qui y aboutissent
F. Saucier, 1749
Library of Congress: G4042.M5 1749 .S3 Vault

MAP 101 (page 51).
Norman's Chart of the Lower Mississippi River
Marie Adrien Persac, 1858
Library of Congress: G4042.M5 G46 1858 .P4

MAP 102 (page 51).
Norman's Chart of the Lower Mississippi River
Marie Adrien Persac, 1858
Library of Congress: G4042.M5 G46 1858 .P4

MAP 103 (page 52).
A Map of the Country from the Western Lakes to the Eastern Part
of the Center Colonies of North America
William Brasier, copied by John Chamberlain, 1765
National Archives (U.K.): MR 519

MAP 104 (page 52).
A mapp of Virginia discovered to ye hills
John Farrer, 1651
From: Edward Bland, *The Discoverie of New Britaine*, 1651

MAP 105 (page 53).
["Ould Virginia, 1584, now Carolana, 1650,
New Virginia, 1606, New England, 1606"]
John Farrer, 1650
From: Edward Williams, *Virgo Triumphans: or, Virginia
richly and truly valued*, 1651
New York Public Library

MAP 106 (page 53).
*A Map of South Carolina Shewing the Settlements
of the English, French, & Indian Nations*
Inset in: *A Compleat Description of the Province of Carolina
in 3 Parts; engraved by John Harris*
Thomas Nairne, 1711; published by Edward Crisp, 1711
Library of Congress: G3870 1711 .C6 Vault:Oversize

MAP 107 (page 54).
[Map of the Southeastern United States]
John Barnwell, 1716
National Archives (U.K.):
CO 700 North American Colonies General 7

MAP 108 (page 55).
Part of Ohio showing the Falls
Christopher Gist, 1752
National Archives (U.K.): CO 700 Virginia 13

MAP 109 (page 55).
*Captain Snow's Scetch of the Country by Himself, and
the best accounts he could receive from the Indian Traders*
[?] Snow, 1754
Library of Congress: G3820 1754 .S6 Faden 4

MAP 110 (page 55).
[Map of the Ohio Country]
John Patten, c. 1752
Library of Congress: G3707.O5 1753 .P3 Vault

MAP 111 (page 55).
*A Map of the most Inhabited part of Virginia containing the whole
province of Maryland with Part of Pensilvania, New Jersey and
North Carolina*
Joshua Fry and Peter Jefferson, 1751
Library of Congress: G3880 1755 .F72 Vault

MAP 112 (page 56).
*A Plan of Louisbourg on the Island of Cape Breton
in North America*
Anon., 1745
Library and Archives Canada: NMC 500

MAP 113 (page 57).
[Map of the Ohio River]
George Washington, with his "journal to the Ohio," 1754 (1927 facsimile)
Library of Congress: G3820 1754 .W3 1927 TIL

MAP 114 (page 57).
*A Plan of the Field of Battle and Disposition of the Troops as they
were on the March at the time of the Attack on the 9th of July 1755*
From: Thomas Jefferys, *A General Topography of North America
and the West Indies*, 1768
Library of Congress: G1105 .J4 1768

MAP 115 (page 58).
*Plan of Fort Le Quesne Built by the French
At the Fork of the Ohio and Monongahela in 1754*
From: Thomas Jefferys, *A General Topography of North America
and the West Indies*, 1768
Library of Congress: G1105 .J4 1768

MAP 116 (page 58).
*A Perspective View of the Battle Faught near Lake George,
on the 8th Sepr 1755, between 2000 English with 250 Mohawks
and 2500 French & Indians*
From: Thomas Jefferys, *A General Topography of North America
and the West Indies*, 1768
Library of Congress: G1105 .J4 1768

MAP 117 (page 58).
Plan of Fort William Henry and Camp at Lake George
Joseph Heath, c. 1755
Library of Congress: G3804.L22:2F6S26 1755 .H4 Faden 22

MAP 118 (page 59).
*Plan de Cap Breton dit Louisbourg avec les environs pries par
L'Amiralle Bockoune Le 26 Juillet 1758*
[?] Bockoune, 1758
Library of Congress: G3424 .L6 S26 1758 .B6 Vault

MAP 119 (page 60).
*A Plan of the Town and Fort of Carillon at Ticonderoga
with the Attack made by the British Army Commanded
by Genl. Abercrombie 8th July 1758*
From: Thomas Jefferys, *A General Topography of North America
and the West Indies*, 1768
Library of Congress: G1105 .J4 1768

MAP 120 (page 60).
*A Map of the Country from the Western Lakes to the Eastern Part
of the Center Colonies of North America* (Lake Champlain part)
William Brasier, copied by John Chamberlain, 1765
National Archives (U.K.): MR 519

MAP 121 (page 60).
Plan of Fort Niagara with its Environ
1759, John Rocque, 1763

MAP 122 (page 61).
*An Authentic Plan of the River St. Laurence from Sillery, to the Fall
of Montmorenci, with the Operations of the Siege of Quebec*
With inset maps:
Part of the Upper River of St. Laurence
and
*A View of the Action gained by the English Sepr 13 1759 near
Quebec Brought from thence By an Officer of Distinction*
Thomas Jefferys, 1759–60
Library and Archives Canada: NMC 97970

MAP 123 (page 61).
*Plan of the Fort and Fortresses at Crown-Point with their Environs
with the Disposition of the English Army under the Command of
Genl. Amherst encamp'd the 1759*
Anon., 1759
Library of Congress: G3804.C92S26 1759 .P5 Vault

MAP 124 (page 62).
A Draught of the Creek Nation
William Bonar, 1757
National Archives (U.K.): CO 700 Carolina 21

MAP 125 (page 63).
A Draught of the Cherokee Country
Henry Timberlake, 1762
From: Thomas Jefferys, *A General Topography of North America
and the West Indies*, 1768
Library of Congress: G1105 .J4 1768

MAP 126 (page 63).
*Carte de Possession Angloises & Françoises
du Continent de L'Amérique Septentrionale*
Jean Palairet, 1763
Library of Congress: G3300 1763 .P3 Vault

MAP 127 (page 64).
*A Map of the Country from the Western Lakes to the Eastern Part
of the Center Colonies of North America* (Ohio Valley part)
William Brasier, copied by John Chamberlain, 1765
National Archives (U.K.): MR 519

MAP 128 (page 64).
*A Topographical Plan of that part of the Indian-Country
through which the Army under the Command of Colonel
Bouquet marched in the year 1764*
and
*A General Map of the Country on the Ohio and Muskingham
Shewing the Situation of the Indian-Towns*
Thomas Hutchins, 1765

MAP 129 (page 64).
["Map showing the boundary lines between the British Colonies and
the country of the Six Nations and the Southern Indians as recommended in the Representation of 7 March 1768 from the Lords Commissioners for Trade and Plantations to the King"]
Anon., 1768
National Archives (U.K.): MPG 1/280

MAP 130 (page 65).
*Map of the Frontiers of the Northern Colonies with the Boundary
Line established Between them and the Indians at the Treaty held
by Sr Will. Johnson at Ft Stanwix in Novr. 1768*
Guy Johnson, 1768
National Archives (U.K.): MPG 1/197

MAP 131 (page 65).
*Map of the Lands Ceded to His Majesty by the Creek and Cherokee
Indians at a Congress held in Augusta 1 June 1773 by His Excellency
Sir James Wright*
National Archives (U.K.): MPG 1/2

MAP 132 (page 66).
Nova Terræ-Mariæ tabula
For Lord Baltimore, 1671 edition

MAP 133 (pages 66–67).
*A Plan of the West Line or Parallel of Latitude, which is the Bound-
ary between the Provinces of Maryland and Pennsylvania*
Charles Mason and Jeremiah Dixon, 1768
Maryland State Archives: SC 1424-1-447

MAP 134 (pages 66–67).
A Compleat Map of North-Carolina From an actual Survey
John Abraham Collett, 1770, after William Churton, 1757–67
Library of Congress: G3900 1770 .C6 Vault, Copy 1.

MAP 135 (pages 66–67).
[Map showing the boundary between Virginia and North Carolina]
W. Byrd et al., 1728
National Archives (U.K.): CO 700 Virginia 3

MAP 136 (page 68).
*Le Nouveau Mexique appele aussi Nouvelle Grenade
et Marata. Avec Partie de Californie*
Vincenzo Coronelli, 1688 (1742 edition)
Library of Congress: G4420 1742 .C6 TIL

MAP 137 (page 68).
*Description Geographica, de la parte que los Españoles
poseen Actualmente en el Continente de la Florida*
Anon., 1742 (1914 copy)
Library of Congress: G3860 1742 .A7 1914 Vault

MAP 138 (page 69).
*Mapa, que comprehende la Frontera, de los Dominios del Rey,
en la America Septentrional*
José de Urrutia, 1769
Library of Congress: G4410 1769 .U7 TIL Vault

MAP 139 (page 69).
[Map of San Antonio, Texas]
[?] Morfi, 1780

MAP 140 (page 70).
The Passage by Land to California
Thomas Pownall, 1786 (after Eusebio Kino)
Inset in: *A New Map of North America, with the West India Islands*
Library of Congress: G3300 1783 .P6 Vault

MAP 141 (page 70).
Mapa geografico de una parte de la America Septentrional
Manuel Agustin Mascaro, 1782
British Library: Add. MS 17,652a

MAP 142 (page 71).
Plan o mapa del viage hecho desde Monterey
Pedro Font, 1777
British Library: Add. MS 17,651, folio 9

MAP 143 (page 71).
*Derrotero hecho por Antonia Vélez y Escalante, misionero
para mejor conocimiento de las misiones, pueblas de indios*
Anon. (?), showing route of Antonio Vélez y Escalante
(Silvestre Vélez de Escalante), 1777
Library of Congress: G4300 1777 .V4 Vault

MAP 144 (page 72).
*A Map of Philadelphia and parts adjacent:
with a prospective view of the State-House*
Nicholas Scull, 1752
Library of Congress: G3824.P5 1752 .S3

MAP 145 (page 72).
Join, or Die ["Snake map" of the British Colonies]
Benjamin Franklin, *Philadelphia Gazette*, 1754

MAP 146 (page 73).
*A Survey of the City of Philadelphia and its Environs shewing the
several works constructed by His Majesty's troops*
Pierre Nicole, 1777
Library of Congress: G3824.P5S3 1777 .N5 Vault

MAP 147 (page 74).
*A New Plan of Ye Great Town of Boston in New England in America
With the many Additionall Buildings & New Streets, to the Year, 1769*
William Price, 1769
Library of Congress: G3764.B6 1769 .P7 Vault

MAP 148 (page 75).
*A New and accurate Map of North America, Drawn from
the famous Mr. D'Anville with Improvements from the Best
English Maps; and Engraved by R.W. Seale*
Peter Bell, 1771
Library of Congress: G3300 1771 .B4 Vault

MAP 149 (page 76).
*A Plan of the Town and Harbour of Boston and the Country
adjacent with the Road from Boston to Concord, Shewing the
Place of the late Engagement between the King's Troops & the
Provincials, together with the several Encampments of both
Armies in & about Boston*
J. de Costa, 1775
Library of Congress: G3764.B6S3 1775 .D4 Vault

MAP 150 (page 77).
*Plan of the Action which happen'd 17th. June 1775,
at Charles Town, N. America*
Thomas Hyde Page, 1775
Library of Congress: G3764.B6S3 1775 .P3 Faden 25

MAP 151 (page 77).
[Map of the events of 19 April 1775 at Concord, Massachusetts]
Page from the journal of Lieutenant Frederick Mackenzie, 1775
From: Allen French (ed.), A British Fusilier in Revolutionary Boston. 1926

MAP 152 (page 78).
Plan of the City and Environs of Quebec
with its Siege and Blockade by the Americans
William Faden, 1776
Library and Archives Canada: NMC 55019

MAP 153 (page 79).
The Landing of the British Army near Utrecht on Long Island
under cover of the Phoenix, Rose, and Greyhound with the
Thunder and Carcass Bombs August 22nd 1776
National Archives (U.K.): MR 1137

MAP 154 (page 79).
The Seat of Action between the British and American Forces
or An Authentic Plan of the Western Part of Long Island
with the engagement of the 27th August, between the
Kings Forces and the Americans
Samuel Holland, 1776
Library of Congress: G3802.L6S3 1776 .H6 Vault

MAP 155 (page 80).
Plan of the Operations of General Washington against the King's Troops
in New Jersey, from the 26th of December 1776 to the 3d of January 1777
Anon., 1777
Library of Congress: G3811.S3 1777 .P6 Faden 61a

MAP 156 (page 80).
A Survey of Lake Champlain including Lake George,
Crown Point, and St. John
William Brasier, 1762, updated to 1776 to include
details of the engagement at Valcour Is and
National Archives and Records Administration:
RG 77, CWMF AMA 66

MAP 157 (page 81).
Plan of Carillon ou Ticonderoga which was quitted by the
Americaines in the night from the 5th to the 6th of July 1777
Michel Capitaine du Chesnoy, 1777
Library of Congress: G3804.T5:2F6S33 1777 .C3 Vault

MAP 158 (page 81).
The Encampment and Position of the Army under
His Excy. Lt. Gl. Burgoyne & Swords and Freeman's Farm
(map overlay: positions 1 and 2)
William Cumberland Wilkinson, 1777
Library of Congress: G3803. S3 1777 .W5 Faden 69a

MAP 159 (page 81).
The Encampment and Position of the Army under
His Excy. Lt. Gl. Burgoyne & Swords's and Freeman's Farm
(map overlay: positions 3 and 4)
William Cumberland Wilkinson, 1777
Library of Congress: G3803. S3 1777 .W5 Faden 69a

MAP 160 (page 82).
The Encampment and Position of the Army under His Excelly.
Lt. General Burgoyne at Braemus Heights on Hudson's River
near Stillwater on the 20th Septr. with the position of the
detachment etc. in the action of the 7th of Octobr. & the
position of the Army on the 8th Octr. 1777
William Cumberland Wilkinson, 1777
Library of Congress: G3803. S3 1777 .W5 Faden 69

MAP 161 (page 82).
Plan of the Position which the Army under Lt. Genl. Burgoyne took
at Saratoga, on the 10th of September [sic; October] 1777, and in
which it remained till the Convention was signed
William Faden, 1777
Library of Congress: G3804 S4S3 1777 .P5 Faden 66

MAP 162 (page 83).
Plan of the Attack of the Forts Clinton & Montgomery, upon
Hudson's River, which were Stormed by His Majesty's Forces under
the Command of Sir Henry Clinton, K.B. on the 6th of Octr. 1777
John Hills, 1777; published by William Faden, 1784
Library of Congress: G3802.H865S3 1784 .H5 Vault

MAP 163 (page 83).
Battle of Brandywine, 11th Septr. 1777, in which the Rebels were
Defeated by the Army under the Command of Genl. Sir Willm. Howe
John Montrésor, 1777
Library of Congress: G3824.C387S3 1777 .B31 Vault

MAP 164 (page 84).
Carte de l'affaire de Montmouth, ou le G'al Washington
commandon l'armée Américaine et le G'l Clinton l'armée
Angloise le 28 Juin 1778
Michel Capitaine du Chesnoy, 1778
Library of Congress: G3812.M64S3 1778 .C3 Vault

MAP 165 (pages 84–85).
Carte des positions occupées par les trouppes Américaines apres
leur retraite de Rhode Island le 30 Aout 1778
Michel Capitaine du Chesnoy, 1778
Library of Congress: G3772.N3S3 1778 .C3 Vault

MAP 166 (page 85).
Siège de Savannah fait par les troupes françoises aux ordres du
général d'Estaing vice-amiral de France, en 7.bre et 8.bre 1779
Pierre Ozanne, 1779
Library of Congress: G3924.S3S3 1779 .O9 Oz 22

MAP 167 (pages 86–87).
Carte de 'a partie de la Virginie ou l'armée de France & États-Unis
de L'Amérique a fait prisonnière l'Armée anglaise commandée par
Lord Cornwallis le 19 octobre. 1781. avec le plan de l'attaque d'York-
town & de Glocester
Esnauts et Rapilly, c. 1781
Library of Congress: G3884.Y6S3 1781 .E8 Vault

MAP 168 (page 87).
[Battle of the Capes, 1781]
Political Magazine, Vol. 6, 1784

MAP 169 (page 88).
[Map of the Battle of Camden]
Anon., 1780

MAP 170 (page 88).
Camp à Baltimore
Jean-Baptiste-Donatien de Vimeur, Comte de Rochambeau, 1782
Library of Congress: G1201.S3 R65 1782 Vault Roch 67, Plate 20

MAP 171 (page 89).
Attaque de la Ville d'York en Virginie prise le 19 8bre 1781
par les Armées Combinees de France et d'Amerique
Anon., 1781
William L. Clements Library, University of Michigan: Clinton 274

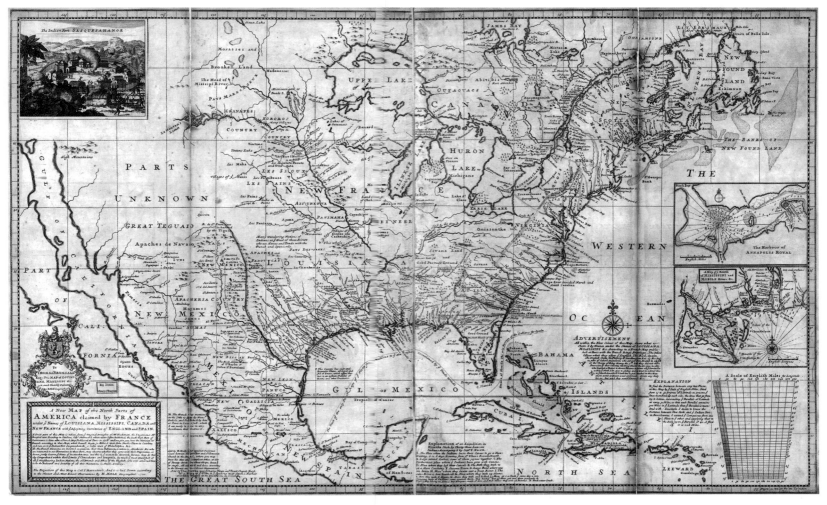

MAP 531.
This 1720 map by British mapmaker Herman Moll shows the extent of EuroAmerican geographical knowledge at the time. Detail on the eastern seaboard of the Thirteen Colonies gives way in the center of the continent to knowledge of the Mississippi Valley gained from Guillaume De L'Isle's French map of 1718 (MAP 93, *page 48*), and the information here is unashamedly copied. Farther west we have *Parts Unknown* and a *Part of California* that still looks suspiciously like an island (see page 104).

MAP 172 (pages 90–91).
A Map of the British Colonies in North America
[known as the "red-lined map"]
John Mitchell, 1755; 1775 edition, with ms additions
by Richard Oswald, 1782
British Library: Maps K. Top. 118.49.b
(northeast and northwest sheets)

MAP 173 (page 91).
British Colonies in North America
Anon., 1785
Library and Archives Canada: NMC 6961

MAP 174 (page 91).
A New Map of the Whole Continent of America
Robert Sayer, 1786

MAP 175 (page 92).
*The United States of America laid down From the
best Authorities, Agreeable to the Peace of 1783*
John Wallis, 1783
Library of Congress: G3700 1783 .W3 Vault

MAP 176 (page 93).
*A New and correct Map of the United States of North America
Layd down from the Latest Observations and best Authorities
agreeable to the Peace of 1783*
Abel Buell, 1784
British Library: Maps *71490.(150)

MAP 177 (page 94).
*The United States According to the Definitive
Treaty of Peace signed at Paris Septʳ 3ᵈ 1783*
William McMurray, c. 1784
Library of Congress: G3700 1784 .M2 Vault

MAP 178 (page 94).
North America Published the 12th of August 1804
R. Wilkinson, 1804
David Rumsey Collection

MAP 179 (page 94).
*A Map of the States of Virginia North Carolina
South Carolina and Georgia Comprehending
the Spanish Provinces of East and West Florida*
Joseph Purcell, c. 1789
From: Jedediah Morse, *The American Geography*, 1789
David Rumsey Collection

MAP 180 (page 95).
["Jefferson-Hartley map" showing
Thomas Jefferson's proposed states]
David Hartley, 1785
From: Hartley Papers, vol. 5, 31–61, letter from Hartley to
Marquis of Carmarthen, 9 January 1785; (presumed) retained copy
William L. Clements Library, University of Michigan

MAP 181 (page 95).
A Map of the United States of N. America
H.D. Pursell, 1785
From: F. Bailey, *Pocket Almanac*, 1785
Library of Congress: Rare Books and Special Collections Division

MAP 182 (page 95).
The United States of North America, with the British Territories
William Faden, 1793
Library of Congress: G3300 1793 .F3 Vault

MAP 183 (page 96).
Plat of the Seven Ranges of Townships
Thomas Hutchins, 1785
From: Mathew Carey, *Carey's General Atlas*, 1814
David Rumsey Collection

MAP 184 (page 97).
The United States of North America, with the British Territories
William Faden, 1793
Library of Congress: G3300 1793 .F3 Vault

MAP 185 (page 97).
*A Map of the States of Virginia North Carolina
South Carolina and Georgia Comprehending
the Spanish Provinces of East and West Florida*
Joseph Purcell, c. 1789
From: Jedediah Morse, *The American Geography*, 1789
David Rumsey Collection

MAP 186 (page 98).
*A New Map of the Western Parts of Virginia,
Pennsylvania, Maryland, and North Carolina*
Thomas Hutchins, 1778
Library of Congress: G3707.O5 1778 .H8 Vault

MAP 187 (page 98).
Vermont, From actual Survey
Amos Doolittle, 1795
Library of Congress: G3750 1795 D61 TIL

MAP 188 (page 99).
This Map of Kentucke Drawn from actual observations
John Filson, 1784
Library of Congress: G3950 1784 .F5 Vault

MAP 189 (page 99).
*A Map of The Tennessee Government,
formerly Part of North Carolina*
John Reid, 1795
From: Mathew Carey, *Carey's American Atlas*, 1795
Library of Congress: G3960 1795 .R4 TIL Vault

MAP 190 (page 100).
*Stowage of the British Slave Ship "Brookes" under
the Regulated Slave Trade Act of 1788*
Broadsheet, c. 1790

MAP 191 (page 101).
Totius Africæ Accuratissima Tabula
Frederik de Wit, 1688
Library of Congress: G8200 1688 W5 TIL Vault

MAP 192 (page 101).
Routes of the Underground Railroad 1830–1865
Anon., 1895

MAP 193 (page 102).
Con-g-ss Embark'd on board the Ship Constitution of America
bound to Conogocheque by way of Philadelphia
Anon. etching, 1790
Library of Congress: Prints and Photographs Division

MAP 194 (page 102).
[Proposed plan for Washington, D.C.]
Thomas Jefferson, 1791
Library of Congress: Manuscript Division

MAP 195 (page 102).
[Dotted line map of Washington, D.C.]
Pierre Charles L'Enfant, 1791
Library of Congress: G3851.B3 1791 L4 Vault

MAP 196 (page 103).
*Plan of the City of Washington in the Territory of Columbia
ceded by the States of Virginia and Maryland to the
United States of America*
Andrew Ellicott, 1792
Library of Congress: G3850 1792 E41 Vault

MAP 197 (page 103).
District of Columbia
Inset in: *Map of the United States of America*
J.H. Young, 1850

MAP 198 (page 103).
View of Washington
E. Sasche, 1852
Library of Congress:
PGA - Sasche (E.) & Company -View of Washington

MAP 199 (page 104).
[Map of California as an island]
Joan Vingtboons, c. 1650
Library of Congress: G3291.S12coll .H3 Harrisse No. 10

MAP 200 (page 104).
North America with Hudson's Bay and Straights Anno 1748
Richard Seale, 1748
Hudson's Bay Company Archives, Winnipeg: G4/20b

MAP 201 (page 105).
Carte des Nouvelles Découvertes Au Nord de la Mer du Sud
Joseph-Nicolas De L'Isle, 1752
Library and Archives Canada: NMC 21056

MAP 202 (page 105).
A New Map of North America From the Latest Discoveries
From: Jonathan Carver, *Travels Through the Interior Parts of North
America in 1766, 1767 and 1768*, 1778

MAP 203 (page 105).
L'Amérique Septentrionale
Jacques-Nicolas Bellin, 1743
Library and Archives Canada: NMC 98179

MAP 204 (page 105).
Carte que les Gnacsitares/Carte de la Riviere Longue
Louis-Armand de Lom d'Arce, Baron Lahontan, 1703
From: *Nouveaux Voyages de Mr. le Baron de Lahontan
dans L'Amérique Septentrionale*, 1703

MAP 205 (page 106).
*Carta Reducida del Oceano Asiatico ō Mar
del Sur que contiene la Costa de la California comprehendida
desde el Puerto de Monterrey. hᵗᵃ la Punta de Sᵗᵃ. Maria Mag-
delena hecha segun las observaciones y Demarcasiones del Aljerez
de Fragata de la Rˡ. Armada y Primer Piloto de este Departamento
Dⁿ. Juan Perez por Dⁿ· Josef de Cañizarez.*
Josef de Cañizarez, 1774
National Archives and Records Administration:
RG 77, "Spanish maps of unknown origin" No. 67

MAP 206 (page 106).
Plano de la Rada de Bucareli
Bruno de Hezeta y Dudagoitia, 1775
Archivo General des Indias, Seville: MP, Mexico 532

MAP 207 (page 106).
*Carta reducida de las costas, y mares septentrionales de California
construida bajo las observaciones, y demarcaciones hechas por . . .
de Fragata Don Juan Francisco de la Vodega y Quadra
commandante de la goleta Sonora y por el piloto
Don Francisco Antonio Maurelle*
Juan Francisco de la Bodega y Quadra, 1775
Archivo General des Indias, Seville: MP, Mexico 581

MAP 208 (page 106).
Plano de la Bahia de la Asunciōn
Bruno de Hezeta y Dudagoitia, 1775
Archivo General des Indias, Seville: MP, Mexico 306

MAP 209 (page 107).
*Chart of Norton Sound and of Bherings Strait made
by the East Coast of Asia and the West Point of America*
From: James Cook, *A Voyage to the Pacific Ocean*, 1784

MAP 210 (page 107).
*Chart of Part of the NW Coast of America
Explored by Capt. J. Cook in 1778*
Map enclosed in letter to Philip Stephens, Secretary
to the Admiralty, sent 20 October 1778 from Unalaska
National Archives (U.K.): MPI 83

MAP 211 (page 107).
*Carte de la Côte Ouest de l'Amérique du Nord, de
Mt. St. Elias à Monterey, avec la trajectoire l'expédition
de La Pérouse et la table des données de longitude
compilées par Bernizet et Dagelet*
Joseph Dagelet and Gérault-Sébastien Bernizet, 1786
Archives nationales, Paris: 6 JJ1: 34B

MAP 212 (page 107).
*Plan du Port des Français Situēe sur la Côte
du N.O. de l'Amerique Septentrionale*
Gérault-Sébastien Bernizet and Paul Mérault de Monneron, 1786
Archives nationales, Paris: 6 JJ1: 30

MAP 213 (page 108).
Carta Reducida de la Costa Septentrional de California
Juan Francisco de la Bodega y Quadra, 1791 or 1792
Library of Congress: G3351.P5 1799 .C Vault, map 1

MAP 214 (page 108).
Num 9 Plano del Puerto del Desengano Trabasdo de Orden del Rey
From: *Relación del Viage Hecho por Las goletas Sutil y Mexicana*,
1802, Atlas

MAP 215 (page 109).
*A Chart shewing part of the Coast of N.W. America with the tracks
of His Majesty's Sloop* Discovery *and Armed Tender* Chatham
Commanded by George Vancouver Esqʳ.
George Vancouver, Vancouver Atlas Plate 14, 1798
Library and Archives Canada: NMC 135034

MAP 216 (page 109).
[Preliminary chart of the west coast from
George Vancouver's landfall to Cape Mudge]
National Archives (U.K.): MPG 557

MAP 217 (page 109).
*Carta que comprehende los interiers y veril de la costa
desde los 48° de Latitud N hasta los 50°. 1791*
José María Nárvaez [?], 1791
Library of Congress: G3351.P5 1799.C Vault, Map 12

MAP 218 (page 110).
*The United States of North America, with the British
& Spanish Territories According to the Treaty of 1784*
William Faden, 1785
Library of Congress: 3700 1784 .F21 Vault

MAP 219 (page 110).
[Sketch map of the Missouri west of the Mandan
villages, derived from Indian sources]
John Evans, 1796–97
Beinecke Library, Yale University

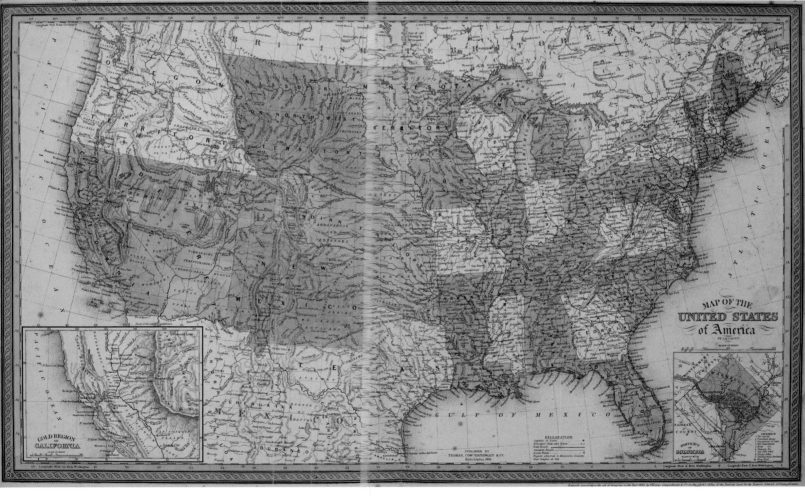

MAP 532.
The United States has spread from ocean to ocean in this 1850 map. The Southwest has recently being acquired from Mexico, and the new state of *California* is shown, together with *Deseret*, the hoped-for Mormon state, and the first, larger *New Mexico*, covering some of what was claimed by *Texas*. In the Northwest is *Oregon Territory*, and east of the Rockies *Missouri or Northwest Territory* and *Minnesota Territory*, while *Indian Territory* still covers a large portion of the central Great Plains.

MAP 346 (*page 167*).
Map of the United States of America
George Woolworth Colton, J.H. Colton & Co., 1850
Library of Congress: G3700 1850 .C6 TIL

MAP 347 (*page 168*).
Map of the Gold Regions of California
Compiled from Original Surveys
James Wyld, 1849
Library of Congress: G4361.H2 1849 .W9 TIL

MAP 348 (*page 168*).
Boundary Between the United States and Mexico
William Hemsley Emory, 1855
Library of Congress: G3701.F2 1855 .E6 TIL

MAP 349 (*page 168*).
Map of the Mining District of California
William A. Jackson, 1850
Library of Congress: G4361.H2 1850 .J3 TIL

MAP 350 (*page 169*).
Map of the State of California, The Territories of Oregon
& Utah and the chief part of New Mexico
Samuel Augustus Mitchell, 1850
David Rumsey Collection

MAP 351 (*page 169*).
Map of the Mining District of California
William A. Jackson, 1850
Library of Congress: G4361.H2 1850 .J3 TIL

MAP 352 (*page 169*).
Map of the Territory acquired from Mexico
by the Gadsden Treaty, 1854
Inset in: *Nebraska and Kansas*
J.H. Colton, 1854
David Rumsey Collection

MAP 353 (*pages 170–71*).
{Map showing areas reserved for each tribe
according to the Treaty of Fort Laramie, 1851]
Pierre-Jean de Smet, 1851
Library of Congress: G4052.S14 1851 .S6

MAP 354 (*page 170*).
Map of the Trans-Mississippi Territory of the United States
During the Period of the American Fur Trade [with] *Father De Smet's*
Travels West of the Mississippi
Anon., 1905
From: *De Smet's Oregon Missions and Travels*
over the Rocky Mountains, 1906

MAP 355 (*page 172*).
City of New York sketched and drawn on stone by C. Parsons
N. Currier, c. 1856
Library of Congress: PGA - Currier & Ives -- City of New York (D size)

MAP 356 (*page 172*).
Manatus Gelegen op de Noot Rivier
Joan Vingtboons, 1639
Library of Congress: G3291.S12 coll .H3 Harrisse No 1, pl. no. 12

MAP 357 (*page 172*).
[Map of the Northeast]
Adriaen Block (?), 1614
Nationaal Archief (Netherlands): 4, VEL520

MAP 358 (*page 173*).
A Description of the Towne of Mannados or New Amsterdam
Jacques Cortelyou [?], 1664
British Library: Maps K.Top.121.35

MAP 359 (*page 173*).
Nova Belgii NovæAngliæ nec non partis Virginæ
tabula multis in locis emendata
Nicolas Visscher, 1685
Library of Congress: G3715 169-.V5 TIL Vault

MAP 360 (*page 174*).
[Plan of the city of New York dedicated] *To His Excellency Sr. Henry*
Moore, Bart., Captain General and Governour in Chief . . .
Bernard Ratzer, 1767, published 1776
Library of Congress: G3804,N4 1767 .R3 Vault

MAP 361 (*page 174*).
Map and Guide of the Elevated Railroads of New York City
H.I. Latimer, c. 1881
Library of Congress: G3804.N4 1881 .L3 RR 454

MAP 362 (*page 175*).
Bird's-eye View of New York and Environs
John Bachmann, 1865
Library of Congress: G3804.N4A3 1865 .B3

MAP 363 (*page 175*).
The City of Greater New York
Charles Hart, 1905; published by Joseph Koehler
Library of Congress: PGA - Hart --City of greater New York

MAP 364 (*page 176*).
U.S. Coast Survey Reconnaissance of
Semi-Ah-Moo Bay Washington Ter. 1858
United States Coast Survey, 1858
White Rock City Archives, British Columbia

MAP 365 (*page 176*).
Sketch Showing the Triangulation & Geographical Position
in Section No. II From New York City to Point Judith
United States Coast and Geodetic Survey, 1881
U.S. Coast and Geodetic Survey Historical Map Collection: 6-6

MAP 366 (*page 176*).
Reconnaissance of the Western Coast of the United States
Middle Sheet From San Francisco to Umpquah River
United States Coast Survey, 1854
University of British Columbia Special Collections

MAP 367 (*page 177*).
Sketch A Showing the progress in Section No. 1.
U.S. Coast Survey in 1844–'45–'46–'47 & '49
United States Coast Survey, c. 1850

MAP 368 (*page 178*).
Plan of a Survey for the Proposed Boston and Providence Rail-Way
James Hayward, 1828
Library of Congress: G3761.P3 1828 .H3 RR 348

MAP 369 (*page 178*).
Map of Rail Road Routes from Rouse's Point to Portsmouth
and Boston; compiled for the Cocheco Railroad Co.
George B. Parrot, 1848
Library of Congress: G3721.P3 1848 .P3 RR 387

MAP 370 (*pages 178–79*).
Map of All the Railroads in the United States
in Operation and Progress
American Railroad Journal, 1848
Library of Congress: G3701.P3 1854 .M3 RR 26

MAP 371 (*page 179*).
Hannibal & St. Joseph Railroad & Connections
G.E. Thomas, 1863
Library of Congress: G4161.P3 1863 .T48 RR 425

MAP 372 (*page 180*).
Skeleton Map Exhibiting the Route Explored by Capt. J.W. Gunnison
U.S.A., 38 parallel of north latitude (1853), also that of the 41 parallel
of latitude explored by Lieutenant E.G.P. Beckwith 3$d·$ Art$^{y·}$, (1854)
F.W. Egloffstein, 1855
Library of Congress: G4051.P3 1855 .E34 RR 164

MAP 373 (*page 180*).
Map of Proposed Arizona Territory
Andrew BeLibrary of Congressher Gray, 1857
Library of Congress: G4301.P3 1857 .G7 RR 172

MAP 374 (*page 181*).
Map of Routes for a Pacific Railroad
Gouverneur Kemble Warren, 1857
Library of Congress: G3701.P3 1857 .W31 Fil 109

MAP 375 (*page 181*).
Rio Colorado of the West Explored by 1$^{st.}$ Lieut. Joseph C. Ives
Joseph Christmas Ives, 1858
Library of Congress: G4302.C6 1858 .I9

MAP 376 (*page 182*).
Reynolds's Political Map of the United States, Designed to
Exhibit the Comparative Area of the Free and Slave States,
and the Territory Open to Slavery or Freedom by the Repeal
of the Missouri Compromise
William C. Reynolds, 1856
Library of Congress: G3701.E9 1856 .R4

MAP 377 (*page 183*).
Military Map showing the topographical features
of the country adjacent to Harpers Ferry, Va.
J.E. Weyss, 1863
Library of Congress: G3894.H25S5 1863 .W4 CW 700

MAP 378 (*page 183*).
Part of Charleston Harbor
George T. Perry, 1861
Library of Congress: G3912.C4 1861 .P4 CW 374

MAP 379 (*page 184*).
The New Naval and Military Map of the United States
John Calvin Smith, 1862
Library of Congress: G3701 .S5 1862 .S6 CW 32.5

MAP 380 (*page 184*).
Military Portraits [with a map of Virginia and Maryland]
H.H. Lloyd, 1861
David Rumsey Collection

MAP 381 (*page 184*).
Bird's Eye View of Louisiana, Mississippi, Alabama
and Part of Florida
John Bachmann, 1861
Library of Congress: G3861.A35 1861 .B3 CW 1.7

MAP 382 (*page 185*).
Scott's Great Snake
J.B. Elliott, 1861
Library of Congress: G3701.S5 1861 .E4 CW 11

MAP 383 (*page 185*).
The Siege of Yorktown, April 1862
C. Worret, 1862
Library of Congress: G3884.Y6S5 1862 .W6 CW 673.7

MAP 384 (*page 186*).
Sheet No. 1 Military Reconnaissance
J.J. Cram and C. Worret, 1862
National Archives and Records Administration

MAP 385 (*page 187*).
The Invasion of Maryland: The New Field of Active Operations
New York Herald, 11 September 1862

MAP 386 (*page 188*).
Map of the Battlefield of Antietam
William H. WiLibrary of Congressox, 1862
Library of Congress: G3844.S43S5 1862 .W5 CW 253

MAP 387 (*page 189*).
Map of the Battlefield of Chancellorsville, Va., 1863
Anon., 1863
Library of Congress: G3884.C36S5 1863 .M3 Vault CW 528

MAP 388 (*page 190*).
Field of Gettysburg, July 1st, 2nd & 3rd, 1863
Theodore Ditterline, 1863
Library of Congress: G3824.G3S5 1863 .D42 CW 331

MAP 389 (*page 191*).
Johnson's Pennsylvania Virginia Delaware & Maryland
Johnson & Browning, 1862

MAP 390 (*page 191*).
Johnson's Virginia Delaware Maryland & West Virginia
Johnson & Browning, 1864

MAP 391 (*page 191*).
Map Illustrating the Siege of Atlanta, Ga., by the
U.S. Forces Under Command of Maj. Gen. W.T. Sherman
O.M. Poe/War Department, 1864
Library of Congress: G3924.A8S5 1864 .P6 Vault: Sher 39

MAP 392 (*page 192*).
[The fortifications of the approaches to
Wilmington, North Carolina]
Harper's Weekly, 1865

MAP 393 (*page 193*).
Map of Appomattox Court House and Vicinity. Showing the
relative positions of the Confederate and Federal Armies at
the time of General R.E. Lee's Surrender, April 9th 1865
Henderson & Co., 1865
Library of Congress: G3884.A6S5 1865 .H3 CW 524

MAP 394 (*page 193*).
Map Shewing the Position of the Lines in Front of Petersburg, Va.
Occupied by the 1st Division 9th Army Corps, April 1st 1865
E. Sachse & Co., 1865

MAP 395 (*pages 194–95*).
Map of the Routes of the Union Pacific Rail Roads
W.J. Keeler, 1867
Library of Congress: G4051.P3 1867 .K4 RR 591

MAP 396 (*page 195*).
Map Showing the Location of Sacramento Valley Railroad
Theodore Dehone Judah, 1854
Library of Congress: G4361.P3 1854 .J8 RR 552

MAP 397 (*page 195*).
Map of the United States and Territories
showing the extent of public surveys
United States General Land Office, 1873
Library of Congress: G3700 1873 .U55 RR 54

MAP 398 (*page 196*).
Birds Eye View of Virginia City, Storey County, Nevada. 1875
Augustus Koch, 1875
Library of Congress: G4354.V4A3 1875 .K6

MAP 451 (page 218).
Santa Fe. The Atchison, Topeka & Santa Fe Railway
and connecting lines. Oct.. 10, 1904
Atchison, Topeka & Santa Fe Railway
Pool Brothers, 1904
David Rumsey Collection

MAP 452 (page 219).
California Texas, Mexico and Arizona Southern Pacific Co.
Poole Brothers, 1892
David Rumsey Collection

MAP 453 (page 219).
Monon Route Louisville, New Albany & Chicago Ry.
Pullman Palace Car Route to Florida
Louisville, New Albany & Chicago Railway, 1887

MAP 454 (page 219).
Gray's New Trunk Railway Map of the United States,
Dom. of Canada and portion of Mexico
Charles P. Gray, 1898
Library of Congress: G3701.P3 1898 .G7 RR 67

MAP 455 (page 220).
Telegraph Chart, America & Europe
Inset (also enlarged at bottom of page): Telegraph Lines in the United
States & Canada to Principal Places 30,000 Miles
Charles Magnus & Co., 1858
Library of Congress: G3201.P93 1858 .M2 TIL

MAP 456 (page 220).
Map of the World, Showing the Telegraphic Systems
for Encircling the Entire Globe
Harper's Weekly, 12 August 1865

MAP 457 (page 221).
Lines and Metallic Circuit Connections
American Telephone and Telegraph Co., 1891
David Rumsey Collection

MAP 458 (page 221).
Lines and Metallic Circuit Connections
American Telephone and Telegraph Co., 1898
David Rumsey Collection

MAP 459 (page 222).
Portions of Alaska, British Columbia and Yukon Territory
Reached by The White Pass & Yukon Route
Poole Brothers, 1919
Library of Congress

MAP 460 (page 222).
Map of the Alaskan Gold Fields
T.S. Lee, 1897
Library of Congress: G4371.H2 1897 .L4 TIL

MAP 461 (page 222).
Map Showing the Two Routes to Dawson City
San Francisco Examiner, 17 July 1897

MAP 462 (page 223).
Map of the New Alaska Gold Fields
J.G. Temple, 1901
David Rumsey Collection

MAP 463 (page 223).
Map of Southeastern Alaska
United States Coast and Geodetic Survey, 1903
From: Alaska Boundary Tribunal, Atlas Accompanying the Counter
Case of the United States before the Tribunal Convened at London
under the Provisions of the Treaty between the United States of
America and Great Britain, Concluded January 24th 1903

MAP 464 (page 224).
[Map of Hawaii] Engraved for Anderson's large folio edition
of the whole of Captn Cook's voyages
T. Conder; Alexander Hogg, n.d. (c. 1784)

MAP 465 (page 225).
Na mokupuni o Hawaii nei / he mau la ka ana,
na Kalama i kakau
Simona P. Kalama, 1837
Library of Congress: G4380 1837 .K3 Vault

MAP 466 (page 225).
Map of the Sandwich Islands Discovered by Captn. Cook in 1778
Samuel Augustus Mitchell, 1879

MAP 467 (page 225).
Oahu, Hawaiian Islands
C.J. Lyons, Hawaiian Government Survey, 1881
With The Line of the Oahu Railway added, 1898
Library of Congress: G4382.O2P3 1898 .L9 RR 199

MAP 468 (page 226).
10,000 Miles From Tip to Tip
Philadelphia Press, 1898

MAP 469 (page 226).
Strategic Map of Our War with Spain
War Map Publishing Company, 1898
Library of Congress: G3701.S57 1898 .W3 TIL

MAP 470 (page 227).
Goff's Historical Map of the Spanish-American War
in the West Indies, 1898
Havana City and Harbor
Eugenia Almira Wheeler Goff, 1899
Library of Congress: G4901.S57 1899 .G61 TIL

MAP 471 (page 227).
Goff's Historical Map of the Spanish-American War
in the West Indies, 1898
[main map, Puerto Rico portion]
Eugenia Almira Wheeler Goff, 1899
Library of Congress: G4901.S57 1899 .G61 TIL

MAP 472 (page 227).
Goff's Historical Map of the Spanish-American War
in the West Indies, 1898
Santiago Campaign June-July 1898
Eugenia Almira Wheeler Goff, 1899
Library of Congress: G4901.S57 1899 .G61 TIL

MAP 473 (page 228).
Goff's Historical Map of the United States
Philippine Islands. Spanish-American War, 1898,
Philippine-American War
Eugenia Almira Wheeler Goff, 1907
Library of Congress: G4901.S57 1899 .G61 TIL

MAP 474 (page 228).
Goff's Historical Map of the United States
Invasion of China 1900
Eugenia Almira Wheeler Goff, 1907
Library of Congress: G4901.S57 1899 .G61 TIL

MAP 475 (page 229).
Isthmus of Panama Showing Location of Railroad and Canal
Inset in: Colombia and Venezuela
Rand McNally, c. 1898
Library of Congress: G5290 1898 .R3 TIL

MAP 476 (page 229).
Meeting of the Atlantic and Pacific "The Kiss of the Oceans"
Postcard, c. 1914

MAP 477 (page 229).
The Isthmus of Panama Showing the Routes
of Travel Between Chagres & Panama
J. Disturnell [?], 1850

MAP 478 (page 229).
[Map of the Panama Canal]
British Columbian, 27 November, 1912

MAP 479 (pages 230-31).
The Literary Digest Liberty Map of the
Western Front of the Great World War
Funk & Wagnalls Company, 1918

MAP 480 (page 231).
[Artillery barrage, Battle of La Selle, 15 October 1918]
National Archives (U.K.): WO 153/1161

MAP 481 (page 232).
Poates Radio Map U.S. and Canada
L.L. Poates Publishing Company, 1924

MAP 482 (pages 232-33).
PWA Rebuilds the Nation
Public Works Administration, 1935
David Rumsey Collection

MAP 483 (page 233).
Diagram of TVA Water Control System
Postcard, c. 1935

MAP 484 (page 234).
From Philadelphia (52) to Annapolis Maryl^d
From: Christopher Colles, Survey of the Roads
of the United States, 1789

MAP 485 (page 235).
Western Motor Car Route Guide
Anon., 1915
Library of Congress: 4231.P2 1915 .W4 TIL

MAP 486 (page 235).
Automobile Road from Bellingham to Vancouver, B.C.
Automobile Club of Western Washington, 1917

MAP 487 (page 235).
Rand McNally Official 1925 Auto Trails Map Washington Oregon
Rand McNally, 1925
David Rumsey Collection

MAP 488 (page 236).
[Proposed location of Interstate Highways,
Providence, Rhode Island]
From: General Location of National System
of Interstate Highways ("The Yellow Book")
United States Bureau of Public Roads, 1955

MAP 489 (page 236).
National System of Interstate Highways
[as approved, 1947]
From: General Location of National System
of Interstate Highways ("The Yellow Book")
United States Bureau of Public Roads, 1955

MAP 490 (page 236).
Touring Map of the Custer Battlefield Hiway
The Scenic Route to the West / Good Roads Everywhere
John C. Mulford, National Highways Association, 1925
Library of Congress: G4126.P2 1925 .N3 TIL

MAP 491 (pages 236-37).
United States Touring Map / Good Roads Everywhere
Automobile Club of America and the
National Highways Association, 1925

MAP 492 (page 238).
[Routes flown by American Airlines]
American Airlines advertisement, 1946

MAP 493 (page 238).
These 5 Boeing equipped airlines fly a distance
approximately twice around the earth every 24 hours!
Boeing advertisement, Aero Digest No. 56, 1936

MAP 494 (page 238).
[Western part of Transcontinental Air Transport's
combined air and rail route]
Transcontinental Air Transport (TAT), 1929
David Rumsey Collection

MAP 495 (page 239).
Boston–New York–Washington Map No 1
[American Airlines route map]
American Airlines, 1945

MAP 496 (page 240).
The Gerry-Mander
Broadside, after Elkanah Tisdale, 1812

MAP 497 (page 240).
The Unique Map of California
E. McD. Johnstone, 1888
Library of Congress: G4360 1888 .J6 TIL

MAP 498 (page 240).
Mark! When You Want a Pointer Regarding Your Western Trip
Northern Pacific Railway advertisement, 1902
From: Olin D. Wheeler, Wonderland 1902
Spokane Public Library

MAP 499 (page 241).
Map of the United States, Canada, Mexico,
West Indies and Central America
Phelps & Watson, 1859
Library of Congress: G3700 1859 .P51 TIL

MAP 500 (page 241).
The Lottery Octopus
From: The Louisiana State Lottery Co.,
Examined and Exposed, 1890
Historic New Orleans Collection: 83-053-RL

MAP 501 (page 242).
Illustrated Map of the Route of Transcontinental Air Transport Inc.
Rand McNally, 1929
David Rumsey Collection

MAP 502 (page 242).
American Airlines Inc. Route of the Flagships—in relation
to the Air Transport System of the United States
American Airlines, 1945
David Rumsey Collection

MAP 503 (page 242).
The True Map of North America
Postcard, Scenic South Card Co., c. 1960–70

MAP 504 (page 242).
Map of U.S. and Ohio
Postcard, Colourpicture, c. 1960–70

Map 505 (*page 243*).
A good-natured map of the United States setting forth the services of the Greyhound Lines and a few principal connecting bus lines
Greyhound Bus Lines, c. 1940

Map 506 (*page 243*).
"The Alaska Line"
Alaska Steamship Co., 1934
Library of Congress: G4371.A5 1934 .A4 TIL

Map 507 (*page 244*).
Topographic Map of the Island of Oahu City and County of Honolulu, Hawaii
United States Geological Survey, 1938
Library of Congress: G4382.O2 1938 .G4

Map 508 (*page 244*).
Island of Oahu / Secret "OPN Map Annex No 1 to Accompany FO 1 Fixed Installations"
Department Engineer Office H.H.D. Ft. Shafter, 1941

Map 509 (*page 245*).
Disposition of U.S. Pacific Fleet 7 Dec. 1941
Classified United States Government map, c. 1941

Map 510 (*page 245*).
[Farthest extent of Japanese control in the Pacific, August 1942]
Newsmap, Industrial Services Division, War Department, December 1944

Map 511 (*page 246*).
[American bomber over Southeast Asia]
America in World War II (atlas cover), 1942

Map 512 (*page 246*).
[Situation in Normandy at midnight, 6 June 1944]
From: *HQ Twelfth Army Group Situation Map*
(first in a series of 412 maps)
Twelfth Army Group, Engineer Section, 1944
Library of Congress: G5701.S7 svar .A4

Map 513 (*page 247*).
In a few months we expect to run out of targets in Japan
Newsmap, Industrial Services Division, War Department, 6 August 1945

Map 514 (*page 248*).
Map of the War
Pacific Stars and Stripes, 1953

Map 515 (*page 249*).
Milwaukee & Vicinity [evacuation plan]
Milwaukee Civil Defense Administration, 1958

Map 516 (*page 249*).
Strategic Air Command Whiteman Air Force Base Missile Complex Grids 2½ Mile Grids
United States Air Force, 1966

Map 517 (*page 250*).
[Map of North America showing ranges of missiles based in Cuba]
United States Government, 1963

Map 518 (*page 251*).
Cuba [showing positions of Soviet armaments]
United States Government, 1963

Map 519 (*page 251*).
[Russian map of Washington, D.C., and vicinity]
USSR Department of Defense, 1981

Map 520 (*page 252*).
Stars and Stripes Map of War Area
Stars and Stripes (U.S. government newspaper), c. 1967

Map 521 (*page 252*).
[Map of Saigon area]
Army Map Services, Corps of Engineers, 1965

Map 522 (*page 253*).
[Secretary of Defense Robert McNamara with map of Vietnam at a news conference]
Marion S. Trikosko (photographer), 1968
Library of Congress: Library of Congress-USZ62-134155.

Map 523 (*page 254*).
[Plan of attack on Kuwait City]
Mylar overlay on topographic map, annotation believed to be by General Charles Horner, 1991
Chris Robarchek Collectio

Map 524 (*page 255*).
[Map of the United States showing the fallout area from the eruption of Mount St. Helens]
U.S. Geological Survey, 198

Map 525 (*page 255*).
Iraq
Central Intelligence Agency Cartography Center, 2003
Library of Congress: G7610 2003 .U55

Map 526 (*page 255*).
["United States of Canada" and "Jesusland"]
Internet map said to be in public domain

Map 527 (*page 256*).
Seattle World's Fair 1962 Souvenir Edition Official Record of the first United States Manned Orbital Flight
Space Travels Inc., 1962, on Rand McNally base map
Cosmopolitan World

Map 528 (*page 256*).
[Hurricane Katrina satellite photo-map, 29 August 2005]
National Oceanic and Atmospheric Administration (NOAA), 2005

Map 529 (*page 257*).
Internet Servers, 2001
Drawn from data supplied by the World Bank

Map 530 (*page 257*).
[Photo-map of the Moon with landing sites]
National Aeronautics and Space Administration (NASA), 2005

Map 531 (*page 261*).
A New Map of the North Parts of America
Hermann Moll, c. 1720
Library of Congress: G33[illegible] 1720 M6 Vault

Map 532 (*page 265*).
Map of the United States of America
J.H. Young, 1850

Map 533 (*page 269*).
Amerique Septentrionale Divisée en Ses Principales Parties
Alexis Hubert Jaillot, 169[illegible]
Library of Congress: G33[illegible] 1694 .[illegible]2 Vault

Map 534 (*page 271*).
The English Empire in America
John Seller, 1679
From: *Atlas Minimus*

Map 535 (*page 272*).
Carte De La Louisiane ou Des Voyages Du Sr. De La Salle
Jean-Baptiste-Louis Franquelin, 1684 (facsimile for Francis Parkman, 1896)
Library of Congress: G3[illegible] 1684 F7 1896 TIL

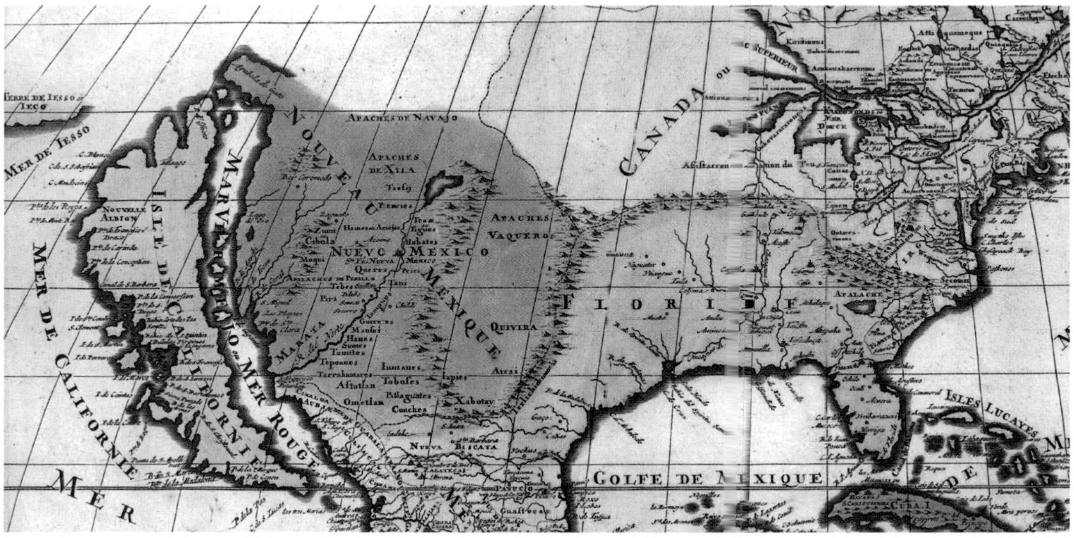

Other Illustration Sources

Sources of images other than maps. Numbers refer to pages. t=top; b=bottom; l=left; r=right; c=center.

5	Author photo
8t	George Caitlin, 1870; Library and Archives Canada
8b	Author photo
9t, 9b	Edward Curtis; Library of Congress
22	Author photo
25	Author photo
26	Author photo
46	Author photo
52–53	Author photo
56	Author photo
61	Author photo
72	Author photo
76	Author photo
92	Massachusetts State House
101	Author photo
106	Harry Heine, 1978
119	National Parks Service
130	Author photo
131	Library and Archives Canada
132	Peter Rindlisbacher
133	Author photo
136	Old engraving, author unknown
150	Robert Runyon, c. 1920
154	Scotts Bluff National Monument, National Park Service
163	Library of Congress
165	Library of Congress
171	Pierre-Jean de Smet, *Life, Letters, and Travels of Father Pierre-Jean de Smet S.J., 1801–1873*. New York: F.P. Harper, 1905
178	Cartouche to Map 370
179	*Harper's Weekly*, 23 September 1865
182	Author photo (frieze on a Washington, D.C., government building)
188	Library of Congress
192 bl, br	Library of Congress
193	Library of Congress
198	Alfred T. Andreas, *History of Chicago*, 1884
200	John C.H. Grabill, 1891; Library of Congress
202	Edward Curtis, Library of Congress
205	Timothy H. O'Sullivan, 1867; Library of Congress
206	Los Angeles City and County, 1915 brochure
207	NASA
212	*Harper's Weekly*, 1865
220	Old AT&T share certificate
222	Library and Archives Canada
230	National Archives and Records Administration
232	Arthur Rothstein, 1936; Library of Congress
234	Cover of Map 437, 1923
239	Pan Am advertisement, 1938
244	Library of Congress
248	National Archives and Records Administration
251	Library of Congress
252	Author photo
255 tl	United States Geological Survey
255 tr	Space Imaging
255 cr	Space Imaging
255 br	Space Imaging
257	NASA

Map 533.
A map of North America published by the French mapmaker Alexis Jaillot in 1694, complete with a prominent and unequivocal island of California.

Bibliography

Adams, Alexander B. *The Disputed Lands: A History of the American West.*
New York: G.P. Putnam's Sons, 1981.

Allen, Oliver E., and the Editors of Time-Life Books. *The Airline Builders.*
Alexandria, VA: Time-Life, 1981.

Ambrose, Stephen E. *Nothing Like It in the World: The Men Who Built the
Transcontinental Railroad, 1863–1869.* New York: Simon & Schuster, 2000.

Anderson, Fred. *Crucible of War: The Seven Years' War and the Fate of
Empire in British North America, 1754–1766.* New York: Knopf, 2000.

———, and Andrew Cayton. *The Dominion of War: Empire and Liberty
in North America, 1500–2000.* New York: Viking, 2005.

Ayers, Edward L. *What Caused the Civil War? Reflections on the South
and Southern History.* New York: W.W. Norton, 2005.

Bass, Patrik Henry. *Like a Mighty Stream: The March on Washington
August 28, 1963.* Philadelphia: Running Press, 2002.

Bicheno, Hugh. *Rebels and Redcoats: The American Revolutionary War.*
London: Harper Collins, 2003.

Boorstin, Daniel J. *The Americans: The Colonial Experience.*
New York: Vintage Books, 1958.

———. *The Americans: The National Experience.*
New York: Vintage Books, 1965.

Carnes, Mark C., John A. Garraty, and Patrick Williams. *Mapping America's
Past: A Historical Atlas.* New York: Henry Holt, 1996.

Catton, Bruce, and William B. Catton. *The Bold and Magnificent Dream:
America's Founding Years, 1492–1815.* New York: Gramercy Books, 1999.
Reprint of 1978 edition.

Chavez, Thomas E. *An Illustrated History of New Mexico.*
Niwot, CO: University Press of Colorado, 1992.

Clark, Judith Freeman. *America's Gilded Age: An Eyewitness History.*
New York: Facts on File, 1992.

Cohen, Paul E. *Mapping the West: America's Westward Movement, 1524–1890.*
New York: Rizzoli, 2002.

———, and Robert T. Augustyn. *Manhattan in Maps, 1527–1995.*
New York: Rizzoli, 1997.

Cumming, W.P., R.A. Skelton, and D.B. Quinn. *The Discovery of North
America.* New York: American Heritage Press, 1972.

———, S.E. Hillier, D.B. Quinn, and G. Williams. *The Exploration of North
America, 1630–1776.* New York: G.P. Putnam's Sons, 1974.

Danckers, Ulrich, and Jane Meredith. *A Compendium of the Early History of
Chicago to the Year 1835 when the Indians Left.*
River Forest, IL: Early Chicago Inc., 2000.

Davies, Philip. *The History Atlas of North America: From First Footfall to New
World Order.* New York: Macmillan, 1998.

DeVoto, Bernard. *The Course of Empire.* New York: Mariner/Houghton Mifflin,
1998 (original edition 1952).

Editors of Time-Life Books. *The American Story: The Revolutionaries.*
Alexandria, VA: Time-Life, 1996.

———. *The American Story: Settling the West.* Alexandria, VA:
Time-Life, 1996.

Ehle, John. *Trail of Tears: The Rise and Fall of the Cherokee Nation.*
New York: Doubleday, 1988.

Elder, Paul. *The Old Spanish Missions of California: A Historical and
Descriptive Sketch by Paul Elder.* San Francisco: Paul Elder, 1913.

Essig, E.O., Adele Ogden, and Clarence John Dufour. *Fort Ross: California
Outpost of Russian Alaska, 1812–1841.* Kingston, ON: Limestone Press, 1991.

Everest, Allan S. *The War of 1812 in the Champlain Valley.* Syracuse, NY:
Syracuse University Press, 1981.

Feher, Joseph (compiler and designer), Edward Joesting, and O.A. Bushnell.
Hawaii: A Pictorial History. Honolulu: Bishop Museum Press, 1969.

Ferguson, Niall. *Empire: The Rise and Demise of the British World Order and
the Lessons for Global Power.* New York: Basic Books, 2002.

French, Alan (ed.). *A British Fusilier in Revolutionary Boston: Being the Diary of
Lieutenant Frederick Mackenzie.* Cambridge: Harvard University Press, 1926.

Gilbert, Martin. *The Routledge Atlas of American History.* New York:
Routledge, 2003.

Goetzmann, William H. *Exploration and Empire: The Explorer and the
Scientist in the Winning of the American West.* Austin, TX:
Texas State Historical Association, 2000 (original edition 1966).

———, and Glyndwr Williams. *The Atlas of North American Exploration:
From the Norse Voyages to the Race to the Pole.* New York: Prentice Hall, 1992.

Going, Chris, and Alun Jones. *Above the Battle. D-Day: The Lost Evidence.*
Manchester, U.K.: Crécy Publishing, 2004.

Grosvenor, Edwin S., and Morgan Wesson. *Alexander Graham Bell: The Life and
Times of the Man Who Invented the Telephone.* New York: Abrams, 1997.

Harlow, Neal. *California Conquered: War and Peace on the Pacific, 1846–1850.*
Berkeley: University of California Press, 1982.

Hayes, Derek. *Historical Atlas of the Pacific Northwest.* Seattle: Sasquatch
Books, 1999.

———. *Historical Atlas of Canada.* Vancouver, BC: Douglas & McIntyre, 2002.

———. *Historical Atlas of the Arctic.* Seattle: University of Washington
Press, 2003.

———. *America Discovered: A Historical Atlas of North American Exploration.*
Vancouver, BC: Douglas & McIntyre, 2004.

Henstell, Bruce. *Los Angeles: An Illustrated History.* New York: Knopf, 1980.

Hickey, Donald R. *The War of 1812: A Forgotten Conflict.* Urbana, IL: University
of Illinois Press, 1989.

———. *The War of 1812: A Short History.* Urbana, IL: University of Illinois
Press, 1995.

Hill, William E. *The Mormon Trail: Yesterday and Today.* Logan, UT: Utah State
University Press, 1996.

Hitsman, J. Mackay. *The Incredible War of 1812: A Military History.*
Toronto: Robin Brass Studio, 1999.

Homberger, Eric. *The Historical Atlas of New York City: A Visual Celebration
of Nearly 400 Years of New York City's History.* New York: Henry Holt, 1994.

———. *The Penguin Historical Atlas of North America.*
London: Viking/Penguin, 1995.

Horton, James Oliver, and Lois E. Horton. *Slavery and the Making of America.*
New York: Oxford University Press, 2004.

Krieger, Alex, and David Cobb with Amy Turner (eds.). *Mapping Boston.*
Cambridge, MA: MIT Press, 1999.

Lavender, David. *Fort Laramie and the Changing Frontier.* National Park
Service Handbook 118. Washington, DC: U.S. Department of the Interior, 1983.

Lewis, Tom. *Divided Highways: Building the Interstate Highways,
Transforming American Life.* New York: Viking Penguin, 1997.

Library of Congress. *Witness and Response: Remembering September 11.*
Washington, DC: The Library of Congress Information Bulletin, Vol. 61,
No. 9, September 2002.

McEvedy, Colin. *The Penguin Atlas of North American History to 1870.*
London: Penguin, 1988.

Maclear, Michael. *Vietnam: The Ten Thousand Day War.* London:
Eyre Methuen, 1981.

McPherson, James M., and Alan Brinkley (general eds.). *Days of Destiny:
Crossroads in American History.* Society of American Historians.
New York: Dorling Kindersley, 2001.

Mariners' Museum, Newport News, VA (various authors). *Captive Passage:
The Transatlantic Slave Trade and the Making of the Americas.*
Washington: Smithsonian Institution Press, 2002.

Meinig, D.W. *The Shaping of America: A Geographical Perspective on 500
Years of History.* Vol. 1, *Atlantic America, 1492–1800;* Vol. 2, *Continental
America, 1800–1867;* Vol. 3, *Transcontinental America, 1850–1915.*
New Haven, CT: Yale University Press, 1986, 1993, and 1998.

National Park Service. *Nez Percé Country.* National Park Service Handbook 21. Washington: U.S. Department of the Interior, 1983.

Nevin, David. *The Mexican War.* The Old West series. Alexandria, VA: Time-Life Books, 1978.

Nofi, Albert A. *The Spanish-American War, 1898.* Conshohocken, PA: Combined Books, 1996.

———. *The Alamo and the Texas War for Independence.* [New York?]: Da Capo Press, 2001.

Nordenskiöld, A.E. *Facsimile-Atlas to the Early History of Cartography.* Stockholm, 1889; New York: Dover reprint, 1973.

Polk, Dora Beale. *The Island of California: A History of the Myth.* Spokane, WA: Arthur H. Clarke, 1991.

Price, Edward T. *Dividing the Land: Early American Beginnings of Our Private Property Mosaic.* Chicago: University of Chicago Press, 1995.

Purcell, L. Edward, and Sarah J. Purcell. *Encyclopedia of Battles in North America, 1517 to 1916.* New York: Checkmark, 2000.

Quaife, Milo M. *Checagou: From Indian Wigwam to Modern City, 1673–18 5.* Chicago: University of Chicago Press, 1933.

Rawls, James J., and Walter Bean. *California: An Interpretive History.* 6th ed. New York: McGraw Hill, 1993.

Reinhartz, Dennis, and Charles C. Colby (eds.). *The Mapping of the American Southwest.* College Station, TX: Texas A & M University Press, 1987.

Remini, Robert V. *Andrew Jackson and the Course of American Democracy.* Vol. 3. New York: Harper & Row, 1984.

———. *The Jacksonian Era.* Arlington Heights, IL: Harlan Davidson, 1989.

———. *The Battle of New Orleans.* New York: Viking, 1999.

Ristow, Walter W. *American Maps and Mapmakers: Commercial Cartography in the Nineteenth Century.* Detroit: Wayne State University Press, 1985.

Schwartz, Seymour I. *The French and Indian War, 1754–1763.* Edison, NJ: Castle Books, 1994.

Shorto, Russell. *The Island at the Center of the World: The Epic Story of Dutch Manhattan and the Forgotten Colony that Shaped America.* New York: Vintage, 2005.

Simmons, R.C. *The American Colonies: From Settlement to Independence.* New York: Norton, 1976.

Smet, Pierre-Jean de. *Life, Letters, and Travels of Father Pierre-Jean de Smet, S.J., 1801–1873.* New York: F.P. Harper, 1905.

Smith, C.R. *"A.A.": American Airlines—Since 1926.* New York: Newcomen Society, 1954.

Stover, John F. *The Routledge Historical Atlas of the American Railroads.* New York: Routledge, 1999.

Sulzberger, C.L. *World War II.* Boston: Houghton Mifflin, 1997.

Summers, Harry G., Jr. *Historical Atlas of the Vietnam War.* Boston: Houghton Mifflin, 1995.

Symonds, Craig L. *The Naval Institute Historical Atlas of the U.S. Navy.* Annapolis, MD: The Naval Institute Press, 1995.

Tutorow, Norman E. *Texas Annexation and the Mexican War: A Political Study of the Old Northwest.* Palo Alto, CA: Chadwick House, 1978.

Utley, Robert M. *Custer Battlefield: A History and Guide to the Battle of the Little Bighorn.* National Park Service Handbook 132. Washington: U.S. Department of the Interior, 1988.

Various authors (essays). *Thomas Jefferson: Genius of Liberty.* New York: Viking Studio, 2000.

Wagner, Henry Raup. *Spanish Voyages to the Northwest Coast of America in the Sixteenth Century.* San Francisco: California Historical Society, 1929.

Ward, Geoffrey C., with Ric Burns and Ken Burns. *The Civil War: An Illustrated History.* New York: Knopf, 1991.

Warhus, Mark. *Another America: Native American Maps and the History of Our Land.* New York: St. Martin's Griffen, 1997.

Weaver, John D. *Los Angeles: The Enormous Village, 1781–1981.* Santa Barbara: Capra Press, 1980.

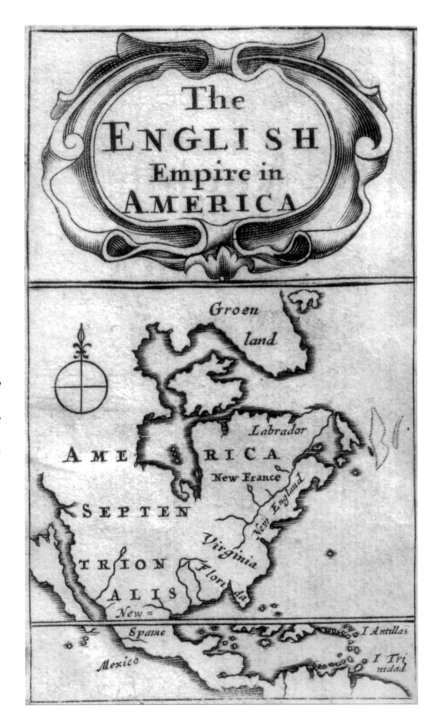

MAP 534.

This map of *The English Empire in America* was published by—naturally enough—an English mapmaker, John Seller, in 1679, in his *Atlas Minimus*—called a small atlas to distinguish it from his larger efforts. Many of Seller's maps are coveted hand-colored works of art, but this map was addressed to a somewhat less wealthy audience than could afford his masterworks. *New England* and *Virginia* are prominent, as is an unnamed California shown as an island.

CARTE
DE LA
LOUISIANE
OU
DES VOYAGES DU S.R DE LA SALLE
& des pays qu'il a découverts depuis la
Nouvelle France jusqu'au Golfe Mexique,
les années 1679, 80, 81 & 82.
Par JEAN BAPTISTE LOUIS FRANQUELIN
l'an 1684.
Paris.

GOLFE
DE HUDSON

NOUVEL
LE

FRANCE

LA LOUISIANE

GOLFE DE MEXIQUE

MAP 535.

The hydrographer of New France, Jean-Baptiste-Louis Franquelin, drew this detailed map in 1684 to record the exploration of the Mississippi to its mouth by René-Robert Cavelier, Sieur de La Salle, two years before. The original map has been lost. The original was in the French archives in 1896, however, when the famous historian Francis Parkman had a copy made, in those days before color photography. This map is that copy, luckily detailed, very well drawn, and almost certainly a close facsimile of the original. Copies are usually avoided by map historians whenever possible, due to the possibility of changes being made during the copying process, but when the original is missing, they are an invaluable substitute. It is apparent from a map like this how the French accessed the Mississippi from Québec, at the narrowing of the *Fleuve St. Laurens* (River St. Lawrence) at top right. The course of the Mississippi is incorrectly shown, perhaps due to La Salle's loss of his compass (see pages 39–41). Note that the title on this map has been repositioned.

Index